INFLUENCE WARFARE

INFLUENCE WARFARE

*How Terrorists and Governments Fight
to Shape Perceptions in a War of Ideas*

Edited by **JAMES J. F. FOREST**

Foreword by **BRUCE HOFFMAN**

Praeger Security International
Westport, Connecticut • London

Library of Congress Cataloging-in-Publication Data

Influence warfare : how terrorists and governments fight to shape perceptions in a war of ideas / edited by James J. F. Forest ; foreword by Bruce Hoffman.
    p. cm.
  Includes bibliographical references and index.
  ISBN 978-0-313-34731-3 (hard copy : alk. paper)
  1. War on Terrorism, 2001—Public opinion. 2. War on Terrorism, 2001—Propaganda.
3. Information warfare. 4. Terrorism and mass media. 5. Mass media and
public opinion. 6. Terrorism—Prevention. I. Forest, James J. F.
  HV6431.I4773 2009
  363.325—dc22   2009012787

British Library Cataloguing in Publication Data is available.

Library of Congress Catalog Card Number: 2009012787
ISBN: 978-0-313-34731-3

First published in 2009

Praeger Security International, 88 Post Road West, Westport, CT 06881
An imprint of Greenwood Publishing Group, Inc.
www.praeger.com

Printed in the United States of America

The paper used in this book complies with the
Permanent Paper Standard issued by the National
Information Standards Organization (Z39.48-1984).

10 9 8 7 6 5 4 3 2 1

Contents

Foreword

SEVEN YEARS INTO THE WAR on terrorism, the United States stands at a crossroads. The sustained successes of the war's early phases now appear to be challenged by al-Qaida's acquisition of a new sanctuary in Pakistan's Federally Administered Tribal Areas (FATA) and surrounding provinces;[1] the rising power of affiliated and associated groups, like al-Qaida in the Maghreb;[2] and, most important by the continued resonance of the movement's message and in turn its ability to ensure a flow of recruits into its ranks, money into its coffers, and support for its aims and objectives.

Although the United States has been tactically successful in killing or capturing key al-Qaida leaders and their foot soldiers, we have been less successful in strategically countering al-Qaida's ideological appeal, its ability to radicalize sympathizers, and its continued capacity to energize supporters and thereby sustain its struggle. *Influence Warfare: How Terrorists and Governments Fight to Shape Perceptions in a War of Ideas* is thus a timely addition to the literature on counterterrorism in general and especially to this often ignored but critical dimension of the war on terrorism.

U.S. strategy to date has largely assumed that America's contemporary enemies—whether al-Qaida or insurgents in Iraq and Afghanistan—have a traditional center of gravity and that they can be defeated primarily by targeting individual bad guys. It assumes that these enemies simply need to be killed or imprisoned and that global terrorism and insurgency will end. Accordingly, the attention of the U.S. military and intelligence community for many years has been directed almost uniformly toward hunting down militant leaders or protecting U.S. forces—not toward understanding the enemy we now face. This is a monumental failing not only because decapitation strategies have rarely worked in countering mass mobilization terrorist or insurgent campaigns, but also because in al-Qaida's case its ability to prosecute this struggle is a direct reflection of its ability to promote and ensure its durability as an ideology and concept.

Secretary of Defense Robert Gates recently explained how "We can expect that asymmetric warfare will be the mainstay of the contemporary battlefield for some time. These conflicts will be fundamentally political in nature, and require the application of all elements of national power. Success will be less a matter of imposing one's will and more a function of shaping behavior—of friends, adversaries, and most importantly, the people in between."[3] Success will also depend on the ability of American strategy to adjust and adapt to changes we see in the nature and character of our adversaries as the contributors to this volume cogently argue. At the foundation of such a dynamic and adaptive policy must be the ineluctable axiom that successfully countering terrorism as well as insurgency is not exclusively a military endeavor but must also involve the fundamental parallel political, social, economic, ideological, and informational activities that Secretary Gates cites. The adversaries and the threats we face today, however, are much more elusive and complicated to be vanquished by mere decapitation. In so fluid an environment, our strategy must embrace influence operations with the same sense of priority and focus that our enemies have.

An effective response is thus one that effectively combines the tactical elements of systematically destroying and weakening enemy capabilities (the "kill or capture" approach) alongside the equally critical, broader strategic imperative of breaking the cycle of terrorist and insurgent recruitment and replenishment that has enabled al-Qaida to survive thus far and continue to marshal its resources and carry on their struggle. It reflects the importance accorded to influence warfare by Field Marshal Sir Gerald Templer in Malaya more than 50 years ago. "The shooting side of the business is only 25% of the trouble and the other 75% lies in getting the people of this country behind us," Templer famously wrote in November 1952, responding to a terrorist directive from the previous year that focused on increasing appreciably the "cajolery" of the population.[4]

"If you know the enemy and know yourself," Sun Tzu famously advised centuries ago, "you need not fear the results of a hundred battles." But if there has been one consistent theme in America's war on terrorism, it is a serial failure to fulfill the timeless admonition. The war on terrorism has now lasted longer than World War II. That we are still equally far from winning cries out for precisely the knowledge that we have instead neglected and which is presented throughout the chapters that comprise this book.

Why is it so important to "know our enemy?" Simply, military tactics are doomed to failure when they are applied without a sophisticated knowledge of whom they are being applied against or an understanding of how the enemy thinks and therefore how he is likely to respond and, moreover, adapt or adjust to those tactics. Without knowing our enemy we cannot successfully penetrate their cells; we cannot knowledgeably sow discord and dissension in their ranks and thus weaken them from within; nor can we think like them in anticipation of how they may act in a variety of situations, aided by different resources; and overall, we cannot fulfill the most basic requirements of either an effective counterterrorist strategy—preempting and preventing terrorist operations and deterring their attacks—or of an effective counterinsurgency strategy—gaining the support of the population and through the dismantling of the insurgent infrastructure.

Until we recognize the importance of this vital prerequisite, America will remain perennially on the defensive: inherently reactive rather than proactive—deprived of the capacity to recognize, much less anticipate, important changes in our enemy's modus operandi, recruitment and targeting. The key to success will ultimately be in harnessing the overwhelming kinetic force of the U.S. military as part of a comprehensive vision to transform capabilities in order to deal with irregular and unconventional threats. A successful strategy will therefore also be one that thinks and plans ahead with a view toward addressing the threats likely to be posed by the terrorist and insurgent generation beyond the current one. These efforts, however, will only succeed when we can credibly claim to know our enemy and thereby to have based our strategy on empirical knowledge and analysis and not conjecture or wishful thinking. The publication of *Influence Warfare* is an important step forward in effecting this process.

Bruce Hoffman
Washington, DC

NOTES

1. Mark Mazzetti and David Rhode, "Amid U.S. Policy Disputes, Qaeda Grows in Pakistan: Bin Laden's Network Successfully Relocates as American Frustration Mounts," *New York Times*, June 30, 2008.

2. Souad Mekhennet, Michael Moss, Eric Schmitt, and Elaine Sciolino, "A Ragtag Insurgency Gains a Qaeda Lifeline," *New York Times*, July 1, 2008.

3. Remarks as delivered by Secretary of Defense Robert M. Gates to the Association of the United States Army, Washington, DC, Wednesday, October 10, 2007 accessed at http://www.defenselink.mil/speeches/speech.aspx?speechid=1181.

4. Quoted in John Cloake, *Templer: Tiger of Malaya—The Life of Field Marshal Sir Gerald Templer* (London: Harrap, 1985), p. 262.

Preface

THOUGHT TRANSCENDS MATTER, IRISH PLAYWRIGHT George Bernard Shaw once wrote. This is particularly true for terrorist and insurgent groups, who seek to mobilize a population toward some vision of the future that they believe cannot be achieved without the use of violence. Because these groups are weaker militarily than nation-states, their ability to recruit and mobilize the masses is a critical part of their asymmetric warfare strategy, and is simultaneously a fundamental vulnerability. Historically, most scholarly discussions of counterterrorism have focused on various strategies for the use of force, intelligence, and law enforcement, with only minor attention given to nonkinetic operations like information warfare or the projection of soft power. Counterinsurgency doctrines, on the other hand, have recognized and emphasized the importance of capturing "hearts and minds" when confronting a violent group seeking to overthrow a government. In both terrorism and insurgencies, states and nonstate actors compete against each other to gain influence among key public audiences—the center of gravity in virtually all contemporary conflicts. Recent events in Afghanistan and Iraq have brought new life to research in this area, and have spawned new studies of conflicts in which the combatants seek to convince a population that their vision of the future is more legitimate than any other.

Victory in this conceptual battlespace requires a sophisticated understanding of strategic communications and an ability to effectively utilize a broad range of technologies. Further, as demonstrated by the chapters in this volume, the global proliferation of information technology has provided new tools for influencing the perceptions of a population, empowering and emboldening terrorists and insurgencies like never before. The key challenge for governments today is thus finding ways to effectively confront its nonstate adversaries in all dimensions of the information domain. The collection of analytic essays and case studies in *Influence Warfare* contributes to this critical goal.

The volume begins with an introductory chapter that identifies and defines key terms used in subsequent chapters and offers a general overview of why and how states and violent nonstate actors engage in strategic communications. The remaining chapters are divided into three sections. The first part of the book provides critical analyses, thematic essays, and examples of how terrorists gain and lose strategic influence. In the next section of the book, authors focus on the counterterrorism aspects of influence warfare, particularly how governments gain and lose strategic influence. The final part of the book offers a diverse collection of strategic influence case studies. Each section and its chapters are briefly summarized here.

PART I: TERRORISM AND STRATEGIC INFLUENCE

In the first selection, Vera Zakem and Aidan Kirby describe how the recent revolution in communications technology driven by the Internet has created a new, more expansive market of ideas. Individuals are now empowered to reach massive audiences with unfiltered messages in increasingly compelling and provocative packaging, rendering the competition for mass influence more complex. The emergence of new means of communication and new styles of virtual social interaction have transformed the context for mass persuasion and have expanded opportunities for extremists to disseminate their message. For example, terrorists have begun using new online tools of social networking in their strategic influence efforts. This new environment makes the ideological battle for hearts and minds more complex. Zakem and Kirby explore the various ways in which this "next generation" of Internet use, and the new forms of social media—as they are sometimes referred to—have shaped the contemporary competition of ideas. Their analysis highlights implications for the ways in which the U.S. government should seek to communicate with the world and recommends strategies that are acutely aware of the significance of both medium and message.

In the next chapter, Gabriel Weimann notes that while there have been several recent studies on how modern terrorists use the Internet for recruitment, support, and operational transactions, less attention has been paid to the use of the Net as a medium for terrorist debates and disputes. He then provides examples of virtual debates among and within terrorist groups, demonstrating how this can tell us a great deal about the mindsets of terrorists, their motivations, and their doubts and fears. Further, he notes, by learning the inner cleavages and debates within a group or movement one can find practical ways to support the voices against terror, to broaden gaps within these dangerous communities and to channel the discourse to nonviolent forms of action. In sum, he illustrates how the Internet serves as a battlefield between and within terrorist organizations that use this platform to conduct ideological debates or even personal disputes, as well as to bridge gaps, unite forces, and resolve disputes. Understanding these activities is fundamental to countering today's most sophisticated terrorist and insurgent groups.

Next, M. Karen Walker examines how the transmission of digital media adds three layers of complexity to our assessment of communicated threats. First, new media can act as an accelerant for communicated threats. Public awareness, interpretation, and reaction to a specific threat can erupt in social networks before intelligence analysts and public officials have an opportunity to evaluate the threat or place it in context. The participatory nature of new media allows individuals to comment on, forward, and replicate messages anew, complicating public officials' efforts to source and authenticate the message. Second, instilling uncertainty and generating fear through the amplification of the threat across Web sites, news channels, and social networks may be the terrorist group's primary objective. Third, benefits and uncertainties of new media accrue to both perpetrators and the public. Taking these factors into account, an understanding of media effects and framing processes can supplement traditional methods of analysis and response to communicated threats. This comprehensive view of new media as a sphere of public discourse suggests that media literacy may be the most effective countermeasure to publicly communicated terrorist threats.

In the final chapter of this section, Cori Dauber examines the measurable amounts of press coverage a terrorist attack can receive and discusses the specific qualities and characteristics of attacks that appear to trip the threshold required by the press in order to be treated as a "spectacular" event. She then explores whether these metrics, which can be applied to terrorist attacks that occur around the world, also apply to those in Iraq, and what might explain any differences that do exist. Finally, some suggestions are offered for more responsible press coverage of terrorist violence. The goal, she argues, should be to balance what the terrorists and the public are both getting out of the story, and ensuring that the terrorists never get more out of a story than the public does.

PART II: IMPLICATIONS FOR COMBATING TERRORISM

In the first chapter of this section, Frank Jones seeks to advance a strategic theory of terrorism as it relates to all types of nonstate actors by using an interdisciplinary approach that integrates social science and the theory of war and strategy. In essence, he proposes a theory that terrorists make choices to attain a future state or condition. Those choices concern how they will use the coercive or persuasive power available to exercise control over circumstances or a population to achieve objectives in accordance with their policy. In posing such a theoretical framework for the study of terrorism, the inevitable question is, "What can a state, particularly a democratic state, offer as a counterstrategy?" The answer is more difficult to construct because of the dilemmas the state confronts in terms of political judgment, institutional response, and policy prescriptions. It must balance policy concerns with a number of other factors, including values, beliefs, the rule of law, and legitimacy, to name a few. Nonetheless, in responding to terrorism, countermeasures have both strategic and operational contexts and rely on the use of strategic appraisal, the relationship of political identity and discourse in a war of perceptions, and the integration of the instruments of power, with some taking precedence. There is no foolproof counterstrategy, however, and because of this, its guiding principles require a realistic understanding of the conditions of security.

Next, Max Abrahms examines how states can exploit the relative ineffectiveness of terrorist groups. Contrary to the prevailing view that terrorism is an effective means of political coercion, his research suggests that, first, contemporary terrorist groups rarely achieve their policy objectives, and second, the poor success rate is inherent to the tactic of terrorism itself. For example, he notes that terrorist groups whose attacks on civilian targets outnumber attacks on military targets do not tend to achieve their policy objectives, regardless of their nature. Terrorism, he argues, is a communication strategy; the attacks on civilians are designed to convey to their government the costs of maintaining the political status quo. The problem for terrorists is that their violence miscommunicates their political objectives to the target country. Ironically, instead of amplifying their policy demands, terrorism marginalizes them for two reasons. First, target governments tend to focus on the terrorist acts themselves rather than their political rationale. Second, terrorism may cause the public to focus on the purely negative aspects of a campaign to the exclusion of the presumably "positive" political message that the terrorists will hope to project. Abrahms then derives policy implications from this research about why countries should be reluctant to make concessions.

In the following chapter, Christopher Paul, Todd Helmus, and Russell Glenn address the challenges and barriers faced by the U.S. government as they engage in the war of ideas—specifically, the challenges faced by Department of Defense efforts to "shape" the perceptions and behaviors of noncombatant populations in areas in which the military conducts operations. Understanding this difficult context helps frame suggestions and solutions and may serve to focus the lines of inquiry of others looking to contribute solutions. Their chapter is drawn from a larger report, published by the Rand Corporation, which offers suggestions in response to these challenges. They assert that U.S. forces can and should attempt to shape more than just an "adversary," or "the battlespace," in pursuit of goals that go beyond "operational objectives." Efforts to influence a much broader range of persons and activities in pursuit of a wider array of objectives and policy goals should be considered part of shaping.

Joshua Geltzer further examines the nexus of strategic influence and the military in his analysis of the nonkinetic aspects of kinetic efforts. In other words, actions themselves convey messages—kinetic (i.e., active, generally violent) counterterrorist measures have crucial nonkinetic (i.e., persuasive, demonstrative) elements and implications. Strategic influence comes through word as well as through deed—and an analytical focus on just how the latter functions as a form of strategic influence toward America's target audiences is a vital contribution to the literature on countering terrorism. Geltzer's chapter aims first to reveal a number of ways in which key American counterterrorist policies are predicated (in significant part) on their potential to exercise strategic influence beyond their direct practical effects; and second, to suggest the difficulty—but also the importance—of assessing what influence those policies have had, are having, and will and can have on their intended audiences, whose members are characterized by rather distinct—and in some respects unusual—worldviews.

Simon O'Rourke then explores the implication of virtual radicalization for law enforcement. He rightly notes how counterterrorism is very much a local challenge—indeed, if all politics are local, then clearly political radicalization (and the context which enables it) is also local. The dissemination of extremist material to a self-selecting audience further complicates the mission for law enforcement, because for the first time extremists across the globe can unite online. After examining the implications of this globally dispersed, Internet-connected terror threat for local law enforcement agencies, O'Rourke identifies some components of a successful counterterrorism response.

Next, Sebastian Gorka and David Kilcullen examine the message that al-Qaida has been broadcasting, what the message from the United States and its allies has been, and the contextual reality behind both. They also explore why al-Qaida has been much more successful in communicating its ideology and the justifications for its actions than the United States and its allies have been. Based on their analysis, they recommend a simple format and preliminary content for a doctrine of strategic communication to undermine al-Qaida and strengthen U.S. national interests.

In the final chapter of this section, Joshua Sinai describes how the widespread use of the Internet by terrorist groups and their supporters offers myriad opportunities for the counterterrorism community to monitor and track their activities, and by doing so uncover insights about their communications, information gathering, training and education, fund-raising, operational planning, command and control, publicity and propaganda, and the radicalization and recruitment of potential operatives. In addition, "official" postings on their Web sites, and discussions in their forums and chat rooms, also provide information about some of the root causes driving their grievances, ambitions, and other factors that motivate them to conduct terrorist activities. He then offers a methodology to enable counterterrorism analysts to hierarchically decompose the underlying factors driving a terrorist insurgency. He recommends examining the content of official terrorist Web sites and their accompanying forums and chat rooms in order to formulate appropriate responses—whether coercive or conciliatory—to contemporary terrorism.

PART III: CASE STUDIES OF STRATEGIC INFLUENCE

Daniel Baracskay begins this portion of this volume by exploring the chronology of American and Soviet communication strategies during the Cold War era, with particular emphasis on their effects on the developing world. In the United States, the Voice of America (VOA) and U.S. Information Agency (USIA) were both created from congressional mandates in the mid-twentieth century to oversee communication strategies and collaborate with private sector media outlets in the transmission of American broadcasts. Conversely, media outlets in communist states were collectively controlled by authoritarian regimes that utilized communications to globally expand Marxist-Leninist doctrines and to counteract the prodemocracy movement. Both Soviets and the Americans competed for influence over the policies of developing states on every continent. However, the information age has affected the ability of government institutions worldwide to conduct public diplomacy. Faced with the threat of terrorism by the transnational al-Qaida network, new strategic communication policies are needed and must be the product of international cooperation and coordination, with presidential direction, bipartisan support from Congress in terms of funding and cooperation, direction and coordination by relevant national security departments and agencies, and support through private–public sector relationships.

In the next chapter, James Dingley provides a case study of how a group's actions can decrease its own strategic influence. In this case, the criminal acts of pro-state terrorists (loyalists) in 1987 were caught on camera in a TV current affairs program (the *Cook Report*) which highlighted the many rackets they ran, and whose proceeds appeared to be going straight into private pockets and not to the organization. Propaganda is a serious weapon for all terrorists; to succeed they need to acquire legitimacy within their own client population and to an outside world. In this sense they need to be able to promote a relatively "pure" image of themselves, both to enhance their own reputation and, by implication, to lessen that of their opponents, usually the state. Above all they must produce an image of themselves as true and incorruptible servants of their cause and the people they claim to be fighting for, which is not always easy since by their nature they are law-breakers. Thus, many believe that the *Cook Report* had a major adverse affect on the loyalists in terms of military and political impact. Dingley examines the true impact of these events, given that the loyalists were relatively easy for police and investigative reporters to penetrate and gather intelligence from.

Next, Sammy Salama and Joe-Ryan Bergoch analyze al-Qaida's strategy for influencing perceptions in the Muslim world. They describe how al-Qaida has learned a great deal from the failures of al-Jihad al-Islami and other domestic Jihadi organizations in the Muslim world—namely, their inability to muster the support of significant segments of Muslim populations for their causes and help them overthrow secular regimes. As a global revolutionary Salafi-Jihadi movement, al-Qaida and its affiliates aim to not only carry out military operations on Western and Muslim soils but also enhance and facilitate their revolutionary activities by instilling their vision, religious ideology, and political doctrine in the minds of the Muslim masses. Unfortunately, recent advances in communication technology have greatly facilitated this endeavor. Unlike the early 1980s, when governments in the Muslim world exercised a virtual monopoly on media outlets that routinely broadcasted their message and orientation, the advent and global expansion of the Internet in recent decades has provided terrorist organizations like al-Qaida with a sophisticated and robust public relations capability, enabling them to influence perceptions in ways previously unheard of. Their case study examines the various aspects of al-Qaida's strategy for influencing perceptions in the Muslim world by (1) using the Internet to export its revolution, (2) borrowing historical terminology to evoke collective memory, (3) demonizing and attacking Westerners to divide the Muslim community, (4) portraying its activities as part of a popular revolution, and (5) redefining the conflict with the West and its allies as a long-term war of attrition in order to minimize the importance of tactical setbacks.

In the next case study, Guermantes Lailari describes how the Lebanese military group Hizballah has been skillful in conducting information operations (IO) since its inception in the early 1980s, while Israel's efforts in the IO realm have been mixed. Most recently, both actors demonstrated their capabilities during the Israeli-Hizballah Summer 2006 War—referred to by the Israelis as the Second Lebanon War and by the Lebanese as the Tammuz War or July War. Lailari's chapter examines the IO war between the two and extrapolates some implications for state policies against violent nonstate actors (and in some cases their state supporters). The main conclusions from this case study are that terrorist groups, much like state actors, continue to improve their technology, fighting doctrine, and IO. Furthermore, a terrorist organization does not have the bureaucratic constraints that state actors have regarding the development and production challenges of new capabilities; their decision cycle is much more flexible and allows for innovation against a Western military. And finally, terrorists have a greater motivation in the fight since to them it is their survival; state actors are not in such dire straits, at least not in the short term. As each capability discussed in this chapter becomes refined and continues to be successful against modern armies, more and more violent groups will be encouraged by these successes. These successes will make the art of fighting against terrorists or insurgents more difficult, and without a clear grand strategy to counter violent nonstate actors and their supporting state actors, coupled with ongoing successes of these actors, current endeavors are likely to fail.

Next, Frank Hairgrove, Douglas McLeod, and Dhavan Shah explore how Hizbut Tahrir-Indonesia (HT-I) has used the Internet to achieve its strategic objectives and mobilization goals. Drawing on data from field research, their study indicates that HT-I uses the Internet mainly for indoctrinating recruits, and that the group is effective at reaching its target audience both online and offline, with members downloading material for distribution among compatriots who are involved with *halaqa* study groups. They also examine the methods used to assess the effectiveness of Internet sites and apply a multimethod approach to exploring Internet content in order to identify the strategic objectives of HT-I and assess the degree to which these objectives have been accomplished. They conclude that the success of the group's efforts can be observed from the organizational growth in terms of numbers as well as the amount of visitors to its Web sites and the impact of its outreach efforts, including the attendance at a recent caliphate conference. Overall, HT-I shows healthy signs in both solidifying its leadership and increasing its influence, and the Internet has played a significant role in this evolution.

Finally, the volume concludes with an integrative analysis that highlights central themes addressed in the thematic essays and case studies, explores various disadvantages faced by governments—and particularly liberal democracies—when competing against terrorists and other violent nonstate actors for strategic influence, and offers some recommendations for policy and further research. In sum, a central dimension of terrorism and counterterrorism involves perceptions of a terrorist group's participants, surrounding communities, government leaders, and other target audiences. A central objective of this volume and the additional research it suggests is thus to help develop a deeper understanding of the ongoing struggle for strategic influence, particularly how states can counter the role that ideologies, the media, and the Internet play in radicalizing new agents of terrorism.

Acknowledgments

AS THIS VOLUME IS PRIMARILY focused on the topic of influence, it is only fitting that I take a moment to thank those who have influenced and supported me throughout this effort. To begin with, I extend my sincere thanks to the faculty and staff of the Combating Terrorism Center (CTC) at West Point, from whom I continue to learn much every day. General (Ret.) John Abizaid, distinguished chair of the CTC, and senior fellow Bruce Hoffman have been significantly positive influences and advocates of my research, and I thank them for their continued support. My CTC colleagues Jarret Brachman, Brian Fishman, Joe Felter, Bill Braniff, Assaf Moghadam, and Scott Taylor were all extremely instrumental in shaping my thoughts about how terrorists pursue strategic influence, and I am sincerely grateful for their commitment to my learning. Also, the staff and faculty in the Department of Social Sciences at West Point—particularly Colonel Mike Meese, head of the Department, and Colonel Cindy Jebb, deputy head—have always provided a great deal of encouragement and guidance, which I sincerely appreciate. And of course, the CTC would not exist without the generous commitment, support, and vision of Vincent Viola, USMA class of 1977. From the very beginning of the CTC in 2003 he has supported all my efforts, and my colleagues and I are forever grateful.

Throughout this project, I have learned a great deal about terrorism and counterterrorism from the authors represented here, and it is an honor for me to showcase their work. Each of these chapters is the product of thoughtful research and analysis, and I offer my sincere thanks to the authors for their hard work and commitment to excellence. The insights and suggestions they have provided in these pages will undoubtedly inform discussions and debate in a variety of policy making and academic settings for the foreseeable future, as well as inspire a new generation of scholars to address complex research questions in the field of terrorism and counterterrorism studies. And finally, I thank my family—Alicia, Chloe, and Jackson—for their patience and support throughout this project.

James J. F. Forest

Introduction

James J. F. Forest and Frank Honkus, III

NATION-STATES AND VIOLENT NONSTATE ACTORS (VNSAs)—including terrorists and insurgents—rely on positive perceptions (or at least acceptance) among key constituencies in order to muster support necessary for achieving their strategic objectives. As illustrated in the chapters of this volume, the information domain requires a sophisticated strategic communications ability in order to influence the policy and behavior of states as well as the hearts and minds of citizens. A core objective of this volume is to help develop a deeper understanding of this ongoing struggle for what some have called strategic influence, and particularly how states can counter the role that ideologies, the media and the Internet play in radicalizing new agents of terrorism.[1] This introductory chapter identifies and defines some key terms used in subsequent chapters and provides a general overview of how strategic influence efforts by states and VNSAs have evolved over the past several decades, with a special focus on the contemporary struggle between al-Qaida and the West.

THE BATTLE FOR STRATEGIC INFLUENCE

As Kim Cragin and Scott Gerwehr explain, when a government seeks to generate favorable perceptions about its policies among foreign audiences, its messages normally justify actions, warn or propose intent to take actions, or provide factual information.[2] According to Brad Ward, a nation's effort to extend its strategic influence requires an "ability to further its national strategic goals and objectives internationally through an integrated, synchronized and interagency-vetted information campaign using the tools of public diplomacy, public affairs and [psychological operations]."[3] Of course, as many scholars have noted, an ineffective strategic communications effort can be counterproductive, in that it may lead a population to distrust (and even grow in animosity toward) the entity conducting the effort.[4]

Similar to nation-states, groups like al-Qaida also seek to influence foreign audiences in support of their strategic objectives. As Thomas Hammes recently noted, "insurgent campaigns have shifted from military campaigns supported by information operations to strategic communications campaigns supported by guerilla and terrorist operations."[5] Managing perceptions is seen by these groups as a vital effort—as al-Qaida strategist Ayman al-Zawahiri explained in a July 2005 letter to Abu Musab al-Zarqawi, "We are in a battle, and more than half of this battle is taking place in the battlefield of the media. We are in a race for hearts and minds of our umma."[6] According to Dell Dailey, the State Department's counterterrorism chief, "Al-Qaeda and other terrorists' center of gravity lies in the information domain, and it is there that we must engage it."[7]

The conceptual battlespace of the twent-first century is a fluid, gray, amorphous, and ill-defined arena in which nation-states and VNSAs attempt to capture hearts and minds. During the latter half of the twentieth century, the strategic influence battle was largely between communism and democracy. Today, the main conflict of ideologies is between Western liberal democracy and a salafi-jihadist interpretation of the Qur'an and Islamist caliphate. Beyond the kinetic forms of this battle (car bombs, suicide bombers, etc.), daily nonkinetic skirmishes take place worldwide in newspapers, on radio and television, and increasingly in the form of videos and Web forum debates on the Internet. Terrorism expert Bruce Hoffman notes that "virtually every terrorist group in the world today has its own Internet website and, in many instances, multiple sites in different languages with different messages tailored to specific audiences."[8]

Further, according to a study by Gabriel Weimann, Web sites are only one of the Internet's services used by modern terrorism: there are other facilities on the Net— e-mail, chat rooms, e-groups, forums, virtual message boards—that are increasingly used by terrorists as virtual training camps, providing an online forum for indoctrination as well as the distribution of terrorist manuals, instructions, and data. He also notes how terrorist organizations capture information about the users who browse their sites, information which can be useful for early stages of recruitment.[9]

To most analysts, a pioneer in this area of online activity is al-Qaida. The *Economist* magazine recently described how al-Qaida uses the Internet as "an ideal vehicle for propaganda, providing access to large audiences free of government censorship or media filters, while carefully preserving their anonymity. Its ability to connect disparate jihadi groups creates a sense of a global Islamic movement fighting to defend the global ummah, or community, from a common enemy."[10] Evan Kohlmann recently observed how radical Web sites "have evolved into a disturbing MySpace–like social-networking hub for [extremists] intent on becoming the next generation of terrorists, hijackers and even suicide bombers."[11] Indeed, Abu Yahya al-Libi, a key leader of al-Qaida in Afghanistan, recently praised the "mujahideen on the information frontline"—the site designers, bloggers, video editors, and others who support the vast online presence of al-Qaida— saying "May Allah bless you lions of the front, for by Allah, the fruits of your combined efforts—sound, video, and text—are more severe for the infidels and their lackeys than the falling of rockets and missiles on their heads."[12]

Within the global conceptual battlespace, nation-states—at least, those viewed by their citizens and the international community as responsibly governed—normally have the advantage of a moral high ground, while VNSAs have a significant challenge of convincing their audiences that the righteousness of their cause justifies their violent attacks. Thus, terrorists and insurgents must constantly articulate and defend an ideology that rationalizes the use of violence toward a set of objectives. The ideology constructed by the leaders of al-Qaida and its affiliates in the global salafi-jihadist movement portrays jihad as perpetual war between Muslims and non-Muslims. As Jarret Brachman recently observed, their use of the term *jihad* (a core Islamic concept of "struggle") in this fashion is unwelcome among many moderate Muslims, who point to particular Qur'an passages that emphasize the use of violence only for self-defense from unsolicited aggressors, but is embraced by other, more radical elements within Islam as a rallying cry for those who see themselves suffering under the draconian policies of governments; for those in a struggle with corrupt imperial overlords for the right to establish a national homeland; for those who see themselves fighting to stave off advanced stages of cultural corruption; and for a host of other reasons.[13]

Indeed, one could argue that the contemporary threat of terrorism is largely fueled by al-Qaida's ability to convince large swaths of Muslims to embrace a particular interpretation of concepts and symbols that have deep historical meaning and context in the Muslim world. For example, Osama bin Laden has now become associated with the historical concept of caliphate; radicalized recruits now think of jihad as killing others, in many places, and war as a way of life. Further, all non-Muslims are considered inherently hostile toward Islam and Muslims, and this justifies the many suicide bombings and other terrorist attacks that have killed thousands of innocent civilians worldwide. As Imam Samudra—the leader of the October 2002 terrorist attacks in Bali, Indonesia—stated in his trial, "As a Muslim I have a conviction that I have to defend oppressed Muslims, as stipulated by the Qur'an."[14] Followers of this ideology thus come to rationalize their violence through what Brachman calls "a pre-defined and coherent body of terms, symbols, and historical parallels, all grounded in the notion of a transcendental authority."[15]

However, al-Qaida and its affiliates must constantly defend this ideology, and are often faced with the challenge of preventing the violence from undermining the legitimacy of their interpretation of Jihad. This has particularly been the case in Iraq. As Mike McConnell, the Director of National Intelligence, noted in his February 2008 congressional testimony:

> The brutal attacks against Muslim civilians unleashed by [al-Qaida in Iraq] and [al-Qaida in the Islamic Maghreb] and the conflicting demands of the various extremist agendas are tarnishing al-Qaida's self-styled image as the extremist vanguard. Over the past year, a number of religious leaders and fellow extremists who once had significant influence with al-Qaida have publicly criticized it and its affiliates for the use of violent tactics.[16]

Within the past few years, the U.S. government has become increasingly committed to identifying and exploiting the challenges and potential vulnerabilities faced by al-Qaida in the information realm. New efforts have sought ways to amplify the voices of respected religious leaders who warn that suicide bombers will not enjoy the heavenly delights promised by terrorist literature, and that their families will be dishonored by such attacks. Saudi Arabia's top cleric, Grand Mufti Sheik Abdul Aziz al-Asheik, gave a speech in October 2007 warning Saudis not to join unauthorized jihadist activities, a statement directed mainly at those considering going to Iraq to fight the American-led forces. Similarly, Abdul-Aziz el-Sherif, a top leader of the armed Egyptian movement Islamic Jihad and a longtime associate of Ayman al-Zawahiri, recently published a book that renounces violent jihad on legal and religious grounds.[17] And governments world-wide praised a recent fatwa issued in the Pashtun Darra Adam Khel region of Pakistan's Northwest Frontier Province that declares the Taliban to be "out of Islam" as a result of their violence, failure to follow Islamic teachings, and takfiri ideology (the latter refer-ring to the salafist-jihadi practice of declaring fellow Muslims "infidels" if they oppose jihadist dogma).[18] The author of the fatwa, Mufti Zainul Abidin, invited other members of the ulama (scholars of Shari'a law) to denounce the "inhuman and immoral" acts of the Taliban, breaking a pattern of reluctance among other Islamic scholars in the region to oppose the Taliban publicly following the still unsolved assassination of Maulana Hassan Jan in 2007 after he declared the practice of suicide bombing "un-Islamic."[19]

These and other criticisms of the tactics used by al-Qaida and its affiliates over the past decade have forced salafi-jihadists to constantly defend their actions. For example, the Jemmah Islamiya field commander Imam Samudra wrote a book in 2004 attempting to justify the October 2002 Bali bombing, which killed over 200 Western tourists. He acknowledges that it is forbidden in Islam to kill women and children, but asserts that this rule only applies when the enemies themselves do not transgress the rule. If the United States and its allies do not attack and kill Muslim civilians, he argues, then the mujahideen should adhere to this basic rule. He then proceeds to list a series of incidents in which U.S. and Western actions have resulted in thousands of innocent Muslim deaths, from embargoes placed on Iraq and Afghanistan to Israeli attacks against Palestinians "with America's military and financial support."[20] His book is also sprinkled with refer-ences to the Qur'an and Hadith about the obligation to wage war against all nonbeliev-ers, and notes that in the case of Bali, the victims of the attack were partygoing Westen-ers, infidels soiling Muslim lands with their nightclubs and revelry. He argues that activities such as the consumption of alcohol are prohibited in Islam, and anyone violat-ing these prohibitions deserves God's punishment.

Meanwhile, Abu Yahya al-Libi—considered by some analysts as the heir-apparent to the head of al-Qaida's central leadership—recently published a book online in which he attempts to justify killing innocent Muslims.[21] His interpretation of the Islamic tenet of *al-Tatarrus*—the exemption to the Islamic prohibition against shedding innocent Muslim blood—is focused on historical instances when a Muslim army is forced to kill other Muslims who are being used as shields by non-Muslim enemies. The non-Muslim enemy, Abu Yahya accurately explains, puts their Muslim captives "in places that make it impossible for the Muslim army to reach them and hit them without killing or injuring the prisoners. This serves as an obstacle in front of the Muslim army to stop them from attempting an attack and as a deterrent to attacking and striking." Abu Yahya even celebrates the fact that previous Islamic scholars have dealt with the topic and conditions of al-Tatarrus, calling their work "a gift from God." As Jarret Brachman and Abdullah Warius point out, he also employs another trick commonly used by al-Qaida thinkers, which is heralding the death of those noncombatant Muslims who have been killed in terrorist attacks by calling them martyrs. Quoting the words of Ibn Taymiyya, Abu Yahya writes, "death is for the sake of jihad and is analogous with the death of

Muslims when fighting [for Islam], in which case they are martyrs."[22] These and other publications by Islamist extremists demonstrate their concern over the need to rationalize and defend their actions against criticism from learned scholars within the Muslim world.

In sum, a battle is raging within the information domain, a battle in which statements from credible authoritative voices within the al-Qaida movement could undermine the acceptance of the narrative constructed and disseminated by its leaders. The Internet provides an increasingly important forum for these voices to be heard. Al-Qaida strategists like Abu Musab al-Suri have consistently encouraged the followers of the movement to use the Internet for mobilizing the umma (the global Muslim community), arguing that communications via open source channels empowers the movement by distributing the ideology and strategically or tactically useful knowledge. However, the ability for virtually anyone to communicate on behalf of the movement introduces a potential struggle for the power to shape the message and direction of the movement, and this has emboldened some individuals from within the community of radical Muslims to voice their disagreements with al-Qaida tactics or strategy.[23] These disagreements, in turn, offer potential opportunities to exploit ideological weaknesses of the movement, as driving wedges in the solidarity of the movement can help undermine and discredit its mobilizing ideology. More on what this analysis suggests for counterterrorism strategies is provided later in this volume.

THE IMPORTANCE OF LOCAL RESONANCE

All politics are local. Thus, the real question of strategic influence is whether governments or VNSAs employ better strategies and skills for effectively influencing local populations. An ideology does not have to be based on fact to be believed; it merely needs to be communicated effectively and persuasively within a favorable cultural, socioeconomic, and political environment which can enable ideological resonance. It is the way in which people react to their environment that enables acts of violence. For example, during the 1930s, a set of prejudices (like anti-Semitism) combined with socioeconomic and political problems throughout Europe enabled a broad acceptance (particularly among Germans) of the need for violence, as articulated by the Nazi ideology. Similarly, counterterrorism analysts have described various preexisting conditions which could enable a potentially violent ideology (including ethno-nationalist separatism, communist insurgency, or apocalyptic visions) to resonate among a particular population. These can be loosely categorized into two types—perceptive enablers and environmental enablers—and help illustrate why the salafi-jihadi ideology has found some resonance in the modern Muslim world.

Perceptive Enablers of Salafi-Jihadi Ideology

On both a global and local level, religious beliefs can serve as a powerful enabler of a terrorist group's ideological resonance, in part by providing an individual with a sense of purpose in life. As British terror expert J. P. Larsson has observed, religious ideologies are often theologically supremacist—meaning that all believers assume superiority over nonbelievers, who are not privy to the truth of the religion.[24] Second, most are exclusivist—believers are a chosen people, or their territory is a holy land. Third, many are absolutist; in other words, it is not possible to be a half-hearted believer, and you are either totally within the system or totally without it. Further, only the true believers are guaranteed salvation and victory, whereas the enemies and the unbelievers—as well as those who have taken no stance whatsoever—are condemned to some sort of eternal punishment or damnation, as well as death. Overall, religious ideologies help foster polarizing values in terms of right and wrong, good and evil, light and dark—values which can be coopted by terrorist organizations to convert a "seeker" into a lethal killer.

The dimension of ideological absolutism (us against the world) is particularly salient for understanding the appeal to some individuals of the salafi-jihadi ideology. If one believes that the world around them is entirely corrupt and evil, it is not difficult to convince them to lash out at the perceived source of this evil—in this case, apostate regimes and the West. In the Muslim world today, there is a longing for retribution against others for perceived injustices, and a desire to address a power imbalance. Jihadis can tap into these sentiments by offering a promise to empower the disenfranchised, and to right the global wrong. Anti-American sentiment—built largely on animosity toward certain U.S. policies and the perceptions of intent behind these policies—do not necessarily lead to an acceptance of violence, but it can lead Muslims to suppress their moral doubts about al-Qaida, in the process giving bin Laden and his leadership cadre more room to maneuver. Thus, according to Steven Kull, majorities of Muslims reject the legitimacy of attacks against civilians, and yet they also perceive al-Qaida as seeking to "stand up to America and affirm the dignity of the Islamic people."[25]

For the United States, the contemporary relationship between foreign policies and strategic influence is particularly important in the areas of the world from which much of the Islamist extremist threat originates. For example, as West Point professor Ruth Margolies Beitler recently illustrated, American policy toward Israel remains a particularly potent source of discontent and reverberates throughout the Arab and Muslim world. Indeed, it is commonplace in the Middle East to hear comments espousing the view that if only the United States would modify or cease its support for Israel, hatred against the United States would end. Her analysis reveals that while the United States has consistently supported Israel's existence, it has not always supported its policies, and yet the overwhelming assessment in the Muslim and Arab world is that the United States retains little objectivity when dealing with the Israeli-Palestinian issue. In reality, whether or not the United States is even-handed when it comes to the Arab world and Israel is almost insignificant, she argues—the key factor fostering resentment in the Middle East is the *perception* that the United States maintains a double standard.[26] Osama bin Laden and others calling for a global jihad refer constantly to these policies and perceptions as supporting rationale for violence and terrorism, although how their argument is received typically depends on local environmental factors.

Environmental Enablers of Salafi-Jihadi Ideology

Within any given political environment, members of a society have expectations, demands, aspirations, and grievances. The degree to which there are opportunities and power to address these without the use of violence is a major determinant of terrorist group formation. Local chaos (for example, in a weak or failing state) can also create an opportunity for an ideology of catastrophic terrorism to resonate. Unemployment, significant ethnic fissures and animosities, sociodemographic pressures (for example, the rising youth bulge in the Arab world), and political regimes that are viewed as overly repressive, authoritarian, corrupt, incompetent, and otherwise illegitimate all contribute to an environment in which a violent ideology can appeal to a broad audience.

Among Arab Muslims in particular, there is a growing sense of crisis and resentment toward their state leaders and Western allies, along with a sense of powerlessness and humiliation that stems from the relative sociopolitical standing of the Muslim world versus the Western, Judeo-Christian world; the Israeli-Palestinian conflict (and current U.S. policy toward it), along with Israel's repeated defeat of Arab armies; and a fear that a creeping globalization or Westernization of cultural values is having a detrimental impact on long-held traditions and belief structures in the Muslim world.

Many of these environmental enablers are certainly found throughout the Middle East, but they are also seen in other parts of the world as well. In Southeast Asia, for example, a host of social and economic inequalities have contributed to the rise of Muslim-led secessionist movements since the 1970s, particularly among the Muslim minorities of the southern Philippines and southern Thailand. In Europe, Muslim communities are filled with comparatively poor, disenfranchised permanent residents, with no hope of naturalization for themselves or their children (as opposed to, say, the more integrated Muslim experience in the United States). In major cities like Copenhagen, London, and Paris, large numbers of Muslims live in so-called ethnic enclaves, neighborhoods with impoverished schools, limited transportation, and few employment opportunities. These and other environmental factors can be described as enablers of ideological resonance, and are cause for concern when confronting the global spread of the salafi-jihadi ideology disseminated by al-Qaida and its affiliates.

TERMINOLOGY AND TOOLS OF STRATEGIC INFLUENCE

A potentially confusing set of common terms—including soft power, political warfare, information operations, psychological warfare, information warfare, public diplomacy, and strategic communications—are often used interchangeably when discussing various forms of strategic influence efforts. While recognizing that there are widely different interpretations of each term (and there is some overlap among them), this chapter offers the following working definitions primarily for the purposes of clarity and consistency for the critical essays and case studies provided throughout the book.

Soft Power

According to Joseph Nye, the former dean of Harvard University's Kennedy School of Government, the term *soft power* encompasses the realm of economics—where the United States, Europe, Japan, and China are major players—and the nuanced world of negotiated relationships among nations and transnational actors (like multinational corporations, nongovernmental organizations, and multinational regimes like NATO, the European Union, and OPEC).[27] In confronting the threat of terrorism, the United States draws on its soft power to convince nation-states and other entities to help counter the threat posed by globally networked terror groups. While economic and financial incentives (or in some cases, sanctions) are important, the most common forms of soft power employed on a daily basis include basic diplomacy, information efforts (including public diplomacy), and intelligence.

Diplomatic efforts are obviously important for dealing with state sponsors and safe havens of terror groups. According to CIA veteran Paul Pillar, "most of the issues underlying terrorism are to be found overseas, as are most things the U.S. can do to combat terrorism." Further, he notes, "most progress in the fight against terrorism ultimately depends on the perspectives and behavior of foreign governments, groups, publics and individuals."[28] Philip Heymann agrees, noting that the United States can most effectively stem the tide of terrorism through a combination of military threats, economic and political incentives, and moral imperatives to pressure such states to act against terrorist groups within their borders.[29] And when diplomatic measures fail to resolve conflicts, as they did when confronting the Taliban in Afghanistan, military force may become necessary. Unfortunately, however, al-Qaida operatives are dispersed throughout the world, and most of those countries are not willing (or perhaps even knowing) providers of safe haven to these terror operatives. While the United States excels at fighting countries with whom we are at war, how do we counter a security threat that stems from within countries we consider friends (e.g., Egypt, Pakistan, and Saudi Arabia)? This is one of the more daunting challenges of countering terrorism today, and involves less state-to-state diplomacy and more "public diplomacy."

Public Diplomacy

Public diplomacy is an activity that involves the promotion of a state's interests, culture, and policies to the general public of foreign nations in the hopes of generating understanding, and perhaps sympathy, toward that state's policy and actions.[30] According to a recent report produced by the Princeton Project on National Security, the goal of American public diplomacy is "to understand, inform, and influence foreign publics in promotion of U.S. national interests and to broaden dialogue between Americans and U.S. institutions and their counterparts abroad."[31] According to most professionals in the field, public diplomacy requires a long-term commitment to building relationships, rooted in trust and consistency. It is very much a human-to-human endeavor.

The Office of the Undersecretary of State for Public Diplomacy—the entity primarily responsible for managing today's U.S. strategic communications efforts—describes its responsibility as helping to "ensure that public diplomacy (engaging, informing, and influencing key international audiences) is practiced in harmony with public affairs (outreach to Americans) and traditional diplomacy to advance U.S. interests and security and to provide the moral basis for U.S. leadership in the world."[32] However, many observers have noted that the broad nature of public diplomacy transcends the purview of any single agency or department, and the public diplomacy landscape remains a patchwork of players with overlapping duties.[33] Several entities share responsibility for waging the "battle of ideas," including the White House, the Department of State, the Broadcasting Board of Governors, USAID, and the Department of Defense (DoD). More on U.S. public diplomacy is provided in other chapters of this volume.

Strategic Communications

Strategic communications has been recently defined by military reports as "focused efforts to understand and engage key audiences in order to create, strengthen, or preserve conditions favorable for the advancement of interests, policies, and objectives through the use of coordinated programs, plans, themes, messages, and products synchronized with the actions of all instruments of national power."[34] The strategic communications battlespace referred to throughout the chapters of this volume can be defined as the contested terrain on which all types of information from competing sources seeks to influence our thoughts and actions for or against a particular set of objectives. According to a 2004 Defense Science Board report:

> Strategic communication requires a sophisticated method that maps perceptions and influence networks, identifies policy priorities, formulates objectives, focuses on "doable tasks," develops themes and messages, employs relevant channels, leverages new strategic and tactical dynamics, and monitors success. This approach will build on in-depth knowledge of other cultures and factors that motivate human behavior. It will adapt techniques of skillful political campaigning, even as it avoids slogans, quick fixes, and mind sets of winners and losers. It will search out credible messengers and create message authority. . . . It will engage in a respectful dialogue of ideas that begins with listening and assumes decades of sustained effort.[35]

Most of the chapters in this volume address the role of strategic communications for influencing terrorist networks as well as their potential recruits and supporters. Of course, both states and terrorist organizations also seek to influence many other audiences, but with different strategic purposes in mind. And strategic communications in the global war on terror must also encourage the support of allies or potential allies, as Frank Jones discusses in his chapter. Also, it is important to remember that strategic communications is merely one element of public diplomacy, albeit one that it is critically important to get right. Joseph Nye uses the phrase "strategic communication" to mean one of three "dimensions" of public diplomacy: "a set of simple themes, much like what occurs in a political or advertising campaign . . . over the course of a year to brand the central themes, or to advance a particular government policy." Nye's other two dimensions are "daily communications," which explain "the context of domestic and foreign policy decisions," and the "development of lasting relationships with key individuals, over many years through scholarships, exchanges, training, seminars, conferences, and access to media channels." His dimensions are distinguished by two central characteristics: time and "different relative proportions of government information and long-term cultural relationships."[36] Overall, communicating effectively is a cornerstone of any public diplomacy and strategic influence effort.

Operational Terms

Other key terms used by various authors in this volume relate to specific activities or operations (often military-related), such as the following.

- *Information operations (IO):* "the integrated employment of electronic warfare, computer network operations, psychological operations, military deception, and operations security, in concert with specified supporting and related capabilities, to influence, disrupt, corrupt or usurp adversarial human and automated decision making while protecting our own."[37] IO can also help enable a commander to interrupt or stop the flow of information to adversaries.[38]
- *Psychological operations (PSYOP):* efforts to convey selected truthful information and indicators to foreign audiences to influence their emotions, motives, objective reasoning, and ultimately, the behavior of their governments, organizations, groups, and individuals. The purpose of PSYOP is to induce or reinforce foreign attitudes and behavior favorable to the originator's objectives.[39] PSYOP employs various media such as magazines, radio, newspapers, television, e-mail, dropping leaflets on adversarial territory, and so forth.[40]
- *Information warfare:* the offensive and defensive use of information and information systems to deny, exploit, corrupt, or destroy an adversary's information, information-based processes, information systems, and computer-based networks while protecting one's own. Such actions are designed to achieve advantages over military, political, or business adversaries.[41]

While the doctrines and practices of information operations, psychological operations, and information warfare are important components of an overall strategic influence campaign, this collection of chapters is focused more on the nature of public discourse and how to effectively use the tools of mass communication to achieve a critical strategic influence objective.

USING THE TOOLS OF MASS PERSUASION

Of course, some countries have more tools of persuasion at their disposal than others. For example, governments that control the primary means of mass communication have a distinct advantage over liberal democracies in terms of regulating and censoring all media within its country. China routinely imprisons journalists and forces newspaper editors to quit over articles that were written and/or printed which it deems critical of the government.[42] It also actively blocks foreign television and radio broadcasts such as the British Broadcasting Corporation, Radio Free Asia, and the Voice of America as well as Web sites that it finds unsuitable. China controls printed and broadcast media through the use of the General Administration of Press and Publication (GAPP). The GAPP holds a monopoly over what is allowed to be published in the country, which enables the government to prevent material that it finds threatening from being printed. The GAPP also controls access to the Internet, and all Web sites that wish to be viewed by Chinese nationals must be licensed or registered with the Ministry of Information. Web sites that are licensed must adhere to Chinese regulations or risk being shut down.[43] As a result of these restrictions, an external strategic influence effort—for example, by the United States or al-Qaida—to muster support and approval among Chinese citizens is likely to have limited impact.

In contrast, governments of liberal democracies can do literally nothing to buffer their citizens from the virulent forms of communications by al-Qaida and other VNSAs. Further, government information operations and strategic communications efforts are often subject to strict legal, political, and ethical standards as well as direct regulations which are meant to ensure a moral high ground. In most liberal democracies, governments must carefully walk a very thin line between public diplomacy and propaganda, the latter being defined as spreading a politicized message—based on truth or otherwise—to a country's own citizens. For example, in the United States the Smith-Mundt Act prohibits the government from distributing propaganda to its citizens. Thus, Secretary of Defense Donald Rumsfeld encountered significant resistance when he attempted to establish an Office of Strategic Information (OSI) during the early years of the Bush administration to support the overall strategic objectives of the global war on terror.

As described in news accounts at the time, one part of the OSI's mission would be to release news items (whether true or not) to foreign media outlets in an attempt to influence foreign audiences' perceptions about the United States.[44] In a press conference, Rumsfeld stated that the program would not use lies in the global campaign, but may engage in "tactical deception,"[45] defining the latter with a hypothetical example: "if U.S. troops were about to launch an attack from the west, they might very well do things that would make the enemy believe an attack was instead coming from the north."[46] Within a few days, a surge of public criticism—citing the potential for these news items coming back to the United States from foreign news outlets, and thus violating the Smith-Mundt Act—led President Bush to express concern about the type of activities in which the OSI would be engaged, and he then ordered that the office be dismantled or reconfigured.[47] The effort lost credibility as a result of the media and public backlash, and when the Bush administration distanced itself from the program, the office was ultimately closed.

Similarly, in 2004 the Lincoln Group—a Washington, DC–based public relations firm—received multimillion-dollar contracts from the United States government in order to conduct public relations in Iraq. However, when it was revealed that military personal were writing stories (typically pro-American and allegedly factual) that were then sent to the Lincoln Group, translated into Arabic, and printed in Iraqi newspapers, the U.S. media screamed foul, portraying the DoD as engaging in propaganda.[48]

The main objection raised was that a democratic government with principles of free speech and press would advocate planting stories in the Iraqi media, and in essence would be seen as disseminating propaganda that in turn would be counterproductive to public diplomacy efforts in the area. The Pentagon ruled that the act of disseminating these stories was part of a broader PSYOP effort in the region to support the broader war effort and was therefore legal, but the effort was eventually abandoned due to domestic political sensibilities.[49]

In both cases, the intentions of these strategic communications efforts were admirable—to spread information in order to gain support for the United States and its efforts to confront the terrorist threats globally and in Iraq.[50] In fact, the historical precedent for Rumsfeld's OSI effort was the U.S. Information Agency (USIA), created in 1953 as a primary conduit for enhancing U.S. strategic influence during the Cold War. The director of USIA reported directly to the president through the National Security Council, and coordinated closely with the Secretary of State on foreign policy matters. The success of USIA varied depending on the location of its public diplomacy efforts and the resources it had available for disseminating information. One of its earliest efforts occurred in 1961 when the Voice of America (VOA) focused its 52 radio broadcast transmitters to nations behind the Iron Curtain to notify the audience of "Communist nuclear testing in the atmosphere."[51] USIA also produced for broadcast "The Wall," which was about the creation of the Berlin Wall in its first year. During this period, USIA was also beginning to expand into Africa and other developing countries throughout the world.[52]

The Soviet Union also had strategic communications efforts similar to those of USIA. Their efforts were coordinated by Radio Moscow, which began broadcasting in 1922 and was initially available only in Moscow and its surrounding areas. However, due to the massive size of Russia, the Soviets soon began to broadcast via shortwave radio signals (shortwave broadcasts could travel significantly farther than AM signals). Soviet leaders continued to refine and add to its broadcasting power, and by 1929, Radio Moscow was able to broadcast into Europe, North and South America, Japan, and the Middle East using a variety of languages.[53] By 1941, the Soviet Union was able to broadcast in 21 languages and, 10 years later, had a year long program schedule of 2,094 hours.[54]

Because most citizens in the Soviet Union had shortwave radios in order to attain news from Moscow, they were also able to receive transmissions from the British Broadcast Corporation (BBC)—perhaps the most well-known and respected global media service today—or the VOA. However, the Soviet Union did not wish to have its citizens hear alternative news from outside sources, so a considerable effort was made to jam them.[55] Even under Soviet jamming, though, VOA broadcasts were still able to get through. In fact, it was believed by the USIA that the Soviet Union spent more money on jamming efforts each year than the USIA had for its annual budget.[56]

Aside from the technological issues, the U.S. strategic communications efforts during the Cold War were considered successful largely because of the information provided through these broadcasts. VOA offered programs that were purposeful, credible, responsible, and relevant to the audience's interests. The overall effort had a clear sense of purpose—mustering support for democracy, while showcasing the failings of communism—and yet the reporters and editors of these broadcasts maintained a perception of journalistic independence, as opposed to the Soviet approach of state-owned media broadcasting official government policy and doctrine. Without credibility, nothing you say or do matters. But most important, the VOA found a receptive audience for its message. All these factors combined to enable the USIA to have a significant influence on the eventual downfall of the Soviet Union and post-Soviet democratic movements.

During the 1990s, due to the end of the Cold War, the USIA was largely abandoned. Professional staff left in droves or retired, and eventually those that remained were transferred to the Department of State when USIA was officially shut down as an independent agency. And yet the need for the United States to engage in soft power/strategic influence activities remained, most pointedly during the military's deployment to the Balkans as part of a NATO mission to quell the violence there. This conflict required that the United States and its allies learn to appreciate the ethnic fault lines that existed between the Albanians and the Serbs. The foundations for these fault lines were built on a victim mentality combined with historical incidents perpetrated by both sides.[57] The first actions of the United States in the multinational brigades they commanded were designed to win over the goodwill of the local population and to legitimize their position. This was done through a combination of air strikes, local communication efforts, and humanitarian aid. Military units were also dispatched to protect Serbian enclaves and cultural sites while also establishing checkpoints and patrolling to show the resolve of the force to establish peace.[58] The goodwill campaign focused on rebuilding destroyed infrastructure, medical assistance, and short-term employment of locals. To attain credibility and legitimacy, face-to-face meetings were held with local political and cultural leaders that would disseminate factual information and hopefully neutralize inflammatory rhetoric before it could cause an outbreak in violence.[59]

Today, in its struggle against terrorists and insurgents in Iraq and Afghanistan, the United States must craft messages that resonate with different types of audiences. The challenge is particularly acute because while most counterinsurgency campaigns seek to reestablish the status quo ante—that is, quell the violence and return to a "normal" way of life, with the government continuing on its predisposed path—in Iraq and Afghanistan, the United States is not seeking to reestablish a status quo ante (i.e., life under Saddam Hussein or the Taliban) but rather is trying to establish new representative governments where they have not existed before. This is a tremendous challenge for influence warfare, because the vision competing against the terrorist and insurgents for legitimacy is hard to explain, and difficult for an oppressed or impoverished society to envision.

In Iraq, the United States communicates to local audiences through various Arabic language radio broadcasts: the VOA offers news and current events, Radio Sawa offers a mix of both music and news and is focused toward young adults,[60] and Radio Free Iraq—broadcast out of Prague since the beginning of hostilities in 2003—seeks to provide fair and objective news to people in Iraq.[61] The United States also sponsors Al Hurra ("The Free One"), an Arabic-language satellite television network that offers objective news coverage while attempting to "broaden its viewers' perspectives."[62] Operated by the Middle East Broadcasting Network, Al Hurra was established primarily to provide an alternative to news reports broadcast by the al-Jazeera satellite network. Its broadcasts reach 22 countries throughout the Middle East with a mixture of discussion programs, news, health, sports, and fashion,[63] and the United States provides its annual budget of $70 million.[64] And of course, the United States is also working with local Arabic TV stations, newspapers, radio, and the Internet in order to communicate American policies and intent in Iraq.

Although these broadcasting initiatives provide opportunities for the United States to explain its policies and intent, there have unfortunately been some less than stellar examples of coercion of the media. One case involved the U.S. military paying television stations in Iraq to portray the American occupation favorably.[65] Military commanders also suggested stories that should be covered that would best portray the United States in a positive light.[66] Worse, coalition-imposed controls placed on the media within Iraq, which limit the freedom of the Iraqi press to cover issues independently, further raise questions of credibility which—as noted earlier—threaten to undermine the effectiveness of any strategic influence campaign. Order no. 14 issued by the Coalition Provisional Authority (CPA) declares that all media within Iraq will be subject to censorship and/or fines if the material

> incites violence against any individual or group, including racial, ethnic or religious groups and women; incites civil disorder, rioting or damage to property; incites violence against Coalition Forces or CPA personnel; advocates alterations to Iraq's borders by violent means; advocates the return to power of the Iraqi Ba'ath Party or makes statements that purport to be on behalf of the Iraqi Ba'ath Party.[67]

Although this would appear necessary for maintaining a peaceful Iraq, censorship of this kind poses a conundrum to the Iraqi people: should a liberal democracy that prominently touts its own freedom of the press impose restrictions on such freedoms in another society? This censorship, coupled with military support for civilian broadcasting in Iraq, can leave many locals with a negative perception of U.S. credibility, which has implications for our ability to effectively achieve the objectives of a strategic influence campaign.

In comparison to the policy and bureaucratic challenges of state-run strategic communications efforts, VNSAs have relatively more freedom to conduct their strategic influence campaign. In Afghanistan, for example, the Taliban use a variety of information products to convey their message, including "night letters" (often handwritten messages, delivered to a specific person with the intent of influencing his or her behavior) and face-to-face confrontations with local leaders and elders to "persuade" them not to support coalition force or the Afghan government.[68] In addition to radio broadcasts, the Taliban also produces tapes, CDs, videos, and DVDs that are available at bazaars and markets throughout the region. They also target the broader world opinion through the international media, including satellite and cable TV and the Internet (although many Web sites are in Arabic, Urdu, and Pashto as opposed to English) and upload their video clips to YouTube. Through these and other means, the Taliban refer to coalition forces as "crusaders" and "infidels" (inspiring memories of the Soviet occupation of Afghanistan) and remind Afghans that these troops will someday leave (largely because of domestic pressures in their home countries), and when they do the Taliban will be sure to settle scores among those who have cooperated with them.[69]

In this context, as with any insurgency, the real battle is over who can win the support of the local population. VNSAs of all types have thus recognized the utility of modern tools of information technology for achieving their strategic objectives. As the *Economist* noted in July 2007, "the hand-held video camera has become as important a tool of insurgency as the AK-47 or the RPG rocket-launcher."[70] Indeed, the widespread advancement of information technologies has enabled VNSAs to conduct new types of communication activities on a global scale. As terrorism expert Bruce Hoffman noted in his May 2006 congressional testimony:

> the weapons of terrorism today . . . include the mini-cam and videotape, editing suite and attendant production facilities; professionally produced and mass-marketed CD-Roms and DVDs; and, most critically, the laptop and desktop computers, CD burners and e-mail accounts, and Internet and worldwide web access that have defined the information revolution today. Indeed, in recent years, the art of terrorist communication has evolved to a point where the terrorists themselves can now control the entire production process: determining the content, context and medium over which their message is projected; and towards precisely the audience (or multiple audiences) they seek to reach.[71]

In March 2008, the Associated Press noted that "al-Qa'ida prizes geek jihadis as much as would-be suicide bombers and gunmen. The terror network is recruiting computer-savvy technicians to produce sophisticated web documentaries and multimedia products aimed at Muslim audiences in the United States, Britain and other western countries."[72] The Taliban, al-Qaida, and insurgents in Iraq have all recognized the value of posting videos to the Internet in support of this hearts and minds mission, according to NATO General Secretary Jaap de Hoop Scheffer. In contrast, he notes, "When it comes to video, we are frankly in the stone age. NATO has no ability to gather video from the field, to show people what is happening. We are also barely on the field when it comes to the Web."[73] In sum, while VNSAs like al-Qaida still invest in the weapons of kinetic warfare, they are also investing heavily in laptops, generators, and video editing software, and making effective use of high-speed Internet connections available at scores of Internet cafés in towns and cities throughout Pakistan and Afghanistan. Their commitment to these kinds of technology is a reflection of how the Internet has become a central battleground in what this volume refers to as "influence warfare."

THE ROLE OF THE INTERNET IN STRATEGIC INFLUENCE EFFORTS

As Steve Coll and Susan Glasser recently observed, "al-Qa'ida has become the first guerrilla movement in history to migrate from physical space to cyberspace. With laptops and DVDs, in secret hideouts and at neighborhood Internet cafes, young code-writing jihadists have sought to replicate the training, communication, planning and preaching facilities they lost in Afghanistan with countless new locations on the Internet."[74] Uses of the Internet include mobilization and radicalization, training, support (fund-raising and friend-raising), financial transactions, logistics arrangements, surveillance, cell-related operational communications, and much more.[75] Thousands of Web sites in all parts of the world reflect a growing virtual community of individuals linked indirectly through association of belief, and who celebrate al-Qaida and its ideas. In this sense of utopian ambition, the Web has become a gathering place for a rainbow coalition of jihadists.[76]

As mentioned earlier in this chapter, conventional military doctrines acknowledge that information is a strategic asset to protect, as well as a weapon to be used against one's adversaries in times of war or struggle. However, this book also takes a broader view of information warfare than found in conventional military doctrine, elevating the Internet and online strategic communications efforts to a central role in a strategic influence campaign—much the way that al-Qaida's media wing as-Sahab has become central to that terrorist organization's campaign against the West.

In the modern global information age, the tools of information warfare have become critical for engaging in the battle for hearts and minds and vital to winning the war of ideas. The United States should no longer think of information warfare as merely focused on attacking an adversary's information systems while defending our own. Instead, we must explore new and creative avenues to influence the kinds of information—particularly pictures, sound and video—that lead directly to how Americans are perceived in the world (i.e., defend and enhance our information stream) while exploiting the vulnerabilities (and especially the internal contradictions) of al-Qaida's information stream. Attacking and closing down Web sites—the typical kinds of activity that comes to mind for conventional information warfare—is not the answer; we must exploit and degrade the integrity of the information which these sites are used to disseminate. Further, governments must sow confusion, dissent, and distrust among militant organizations. And of course, nation-states must find more effective means to harness the power of the Internet to communicate with foreign audiences.

The U.S. State Department, as do all government departments and institutions, provides a variety of information to the public (foreign and domestic) through its Web site.[77] According to the Nielsen Internet rating system, in 2005 this site was the sixth most visited site in the world.[78] The United States has also created several foreign-language Web sites in an attempt to reach out and engage foreign audiences. The State Department has even created "a 'digital outreach team' that engages Arabic blogs and websites with counter-cues and information."[79] These and other efforts seek to create a more positive attitude of the United States in the Arab world.

Great Britain also engages in public diplomacy through the Internet in order to influence perceptions, particularly via its government Web sites and the BBC, which is one of the most recognized Web sites in the world. The British Council has launched several Web sites in various languages with the most popular being their LearnEnglish site with 100,000 hits a month and their FootballCulture site with 70,000.[80] They have also developed the i-UK portal that connects the main public sector Web sites in order to allow for easy access of information, making them more user-friendly.[81]

China is another nation that uses the Internet in order to project soft power and influence foreign perceptions. China has been building its soft power by providing aid, public diplomacy, and investment to Latin American, Asia, and Africa, as well as conducting various strategic communication efforts.[82] Most Chinese government Web sites are offered in several languages, and they all seek to "give an impression of modernity and independence, and even of changing customs and freedom of opinion."[83] State-sponsored media sites such as the Xinhua news agency and the *People's Daily* are offered in seven languages.[84]

But all state-run or state-sponsored efforts to harness the power of the Internet for gaining strategic influence are challenged by one of the most fundamental principles on which the Internet was founded: information should be shared. Governments typically have some sort of information classification system or approval mechanisms which can often inhibit the development of a culture throughout the government of information sharing and effective strategic communications (the old mindset of "need to know" versus "need to share"). Indeed, there is a common bureaucratic instinct to hold on to information; it makes the information bearer uniquely important and valuable to organizations, with possible implications for promotion and power. Further, while the Internet offers an increasingly rich marketplace of ideas where we can ask questions and get solutions, governments typically disseminate carefully crafted official policy messages, hold information closely, restrict access—and then wonder why their target audiences prefer the open discourse available on the Internet.

In contrast, al-Qaida effectively taps into existing models of viral marketing to advance their strategic influence campaigns, using Internet vehicles like YouTube, blogs, Web sites, and so forth to exploit kinetic events, especially spectacular attacks and martyrdom operations, and they offer a relatively simple, clear message to all kinds of "seekers"—join the global jihad. Their propaganda messages also describe the multiple ways in which an individual can participate in the global jihad from the comfort of their own home, such as providing funds, safe havens, or encouragement. The spectrum of participants can thus range from Web site designers to financiers to weapons experts and combat veterans.[85]

It is also important to recognize how al-Qaida's commitment to the Internet extends beyond that of one-way information provider. In December 2007, the as-Sahab media service announced that Ayman al-Zawahiri would take questions from the public posted on a select group of popular Islamic militant Web sites and would respond to them "as soon as possible." More than 900 entries, many with multiple questions, were posted on the site until the cutoff date of January 16, 2008, and on April 2, as-Sahab released the first part of Zawahiri's response in the form of a 1 hour, 43-minute audio statement, which was accompanied by Arabic and English transcripts. A recent analysis of these questions, conducted by the Combating Terrorism Center at West Point, found that Zawahiri is deeply concerned about rising discontent within the jihadist community. Zawahiri's initial decision to hold a virtual press conference demonstrated that he feels the need to resolve concerns among jihadis about the future of the movement. His answers also revealed deep-seated worries about the controversies created by al-Qaida's killing of innocents, and continues to view the Muslim Brotherhood as one of its most dangerous opponents. The Brotherhood offers conservative Sunni Muslims an opportunity to channel their frustrations and grievances in a nonviolent way. Because the Brotherhood draws on many of the same sources of intellectual inspiration and religious justification as the jihadists, it is viewed by al-Qaida as one of the primary threats to its long-term viability.[86]

In essence, al-Qaida has demonstrated the importance of using the Internet to communicate directly with core audiences as well as the general public. In doing so, they can gather feedback, which in turn can help them refine their messages in ways that enhance their resonance among local populations. But as the chapter in this volume by Joshua Sinai describes, the use of the Internet by terrorist groups also provide counterterrorism professionals with unique insights into their concerns and potential vulnerabilities. These vulnerabilities, in turn, offer potential opportunities for us to decrease and undermine their ability to gain strategic influence worldwide.

CONCLUSION

Terrorism is an organized spectacle of violence, driven by a vision of the future—a vision which its adherents believe cannot be achieved without the use of violence. This vision, and the violent ideology which articulates it, is difficult to defend or attract support when the target audiences are relatively satisfied with the status quo. In contrast, when an individual is surrounded by frustration and misery, a utopian vision of the future may be the only source of hope that can be found. Thus, influence warfare can be described as governments and nonstate actors competing against each other to convince target audiences that they offer a more legitimate and credible vision of the future, and that they have a better ability to deliver that vision. This struggle for influence is taking place using various types of strategic communication in which terrorists have shown remarkable proficiency, including the Internet.

However, VNSA activities in the information domain can also offer an important type of transparency, allowing governments a uniquely valuable window into their world that reveals what they consider to be the most important topics of discussion as well as the potential vulnerabilities they worry about. For example, as described earlier in this chapter, al-Qaida and fellow jihadists fear fatwas more than bullets. These insights, in turn, should inform our strategic communication efforts and provide conceptual guidelines and talking points which can undermine and refute the salafi-jihadis ideology.

At the same time, strategic framing (managing expectations at the policy level) is critical for gaining resonance of our strategic communication messages. At the end of the day, the United States has a superior narrative to that put forward by any VNSA. We stand for values of human dignity, freedom, respect, responsibility, tolerance, opportunity—values which al-Qaida and most other VNSAs reject. Our challenge, however, is in communicating our narrative in ways that resonate with the myriad local populations from which the current wave of anti-Americanism and potential threat of violence stems. Pakistani scholar Hassan Abbas recently analyzed U.S. public diplomacy in Pakistan and Iran to illuminate lessons for consideration—for example, he notes, "closing the channels of communication and dialogue has never proved to be a productive measure."[87] His recommendations for U.S. policy makers include acknowledging past mistakes; understanding the limitations of public diplomacy; employing efficient feedback mechanisms to assess the impact of specific policies; establishing and encouraging forums for people-to-people interaction; framing important issues in more constructive ways than "you are either with us or against us"; and supporting reform of the education sector in Muslim countries, especially where madrasa networks are entrenched.[88] Overall, U.S. strategic influence efforts are directly affected by our foreign policies, noncommunicative activities (like foreign aid), and the sincerity and openness with which we listen to others.

Further, while the United States and our allies must improve our strategic communication efforts, the deeper challenge in combating salafi-jihadist ideology involves identifying and enlisting allies within the Muslim world, credible voices who can help us achieve our strategic influence objectives. Among certain communities, we are viewed as a discredited messenger, and thus have limited—if any—chance of persuading those whom we need to persuade. As a result, we must recognize the limitations of the nation-state in the information domain, and embrace the new and innovative ways in which individuals are increasingly empowered to confront hostile ideologies.

Recent efforts of note include the Radical Middle Way, a group of young British Muslims who have rejected the salafi-jihadist interpretation of the Qur'an and are trying to consolidate a mainstream response to fundamentalist Islam. Their public events and Internet activities are funded by the sale of music videos, and are touted by observers in the United Kingdom as an example of how to weaken the resonance of al-Qaida's ideology among the youth in that country.[89] Similarly, in Indonesia, Ahmad Dhani—the leader of the immensely popular rock band Dewa—has used music to influence millions of fans in Indonesia, Singapore, and Malaysia, encouraging them to resist the tide of religious extremism. In 2004, his album *Laskar Cinta* ("Warriors of Love") quickly rose to the top of the charts as millions of young Indonesians embraced its message of love, peace, and tolerance.[90] As Kyai Haji Abdurrahman Wahid, a former president of Indonesia, observed:

> Dhani and his group are on the front lines of a global conflict, defending Islam from its fanatical hijackers. In a world all too often marred by hatred and violence committed in the name of religion, they seek to rescue an entire generation from Wahhabi-financed extremists whose goal is to transform Muslim youth into holy warriors and suicide bombers. For every young Indonesian seduced by the ideology of hatred and fanaticism—including those responsible for the recent, awful attacks in Bali—countless others see through the extremists' web of lies and hatred, in no small part thanks to the visionary courage of people like Ahmad Dhani.[91]

Egyptian Amr Khaled, who runs one of the Arab world's most popular Web sites and hosts a regular show on Iqra (a Saudi-owned religious satellite channel) is a moderate who encourages Muslims to transform their lives and their communities through Islam, while also getting along with the West. He writes, "Osama bin Laden is saying he is talking on behalf of Muslims; Who asked him to talk on behalf of us? Nobody."[92] Efforts like these will do far more to counter the influence of al-Qaida than any U.S. public diplomacy strategy or strategic communications effort.

As Danish security expert Thomas Elkjer Nissen recently observed, "The battle of perceptions is just as important, if not more so, as the physical battle. It is winning the local population, and not the physical destruction of the Taliban, that will win this battle, even though the destruction of pockets of resistance is necessary."[93] The strategic communication efforts of the United States must evolve beyond hierarchically approved boilerplate civics lessons and the rabid promotion of liberal democracy to a more sophisticated approach that embraces competition with the myriad sources of infotainment available on the Internet. The remaining chapters of this volume illustrate the many dimensions that the United States and its allies must appreciate in the current "battle of perceptions" against al-Qaida and its global affiliates.

The views expressed in all chapters of this volume are those of the authors and do not purport to reflect the official policy or position of any agency of the U.S. government.

NOTES

1. Gabriel Weimann, "Virtual Training Camps: Terrorists' Use of the Internet," in *Teaching Terror: Strategic and Tactical Learning in the Terrorist World*, edited by James J. F. Forest (Lanham, MD: Rowman & Littlefield, 2006).

2. Kim Cragin and Scott Gerwehr, *Dissuading Terror: Strategic Influence and the Struggle Against Terrorism* (Santa Monica, CA: RAND Corporation, 2005), http://www.rand.org/pubs/monographs/MG184/index.html.

3. Brad M. Ward, *Strategic Influence Operations: The Information Connection* (Carlisle: U.S. Army War College, April 7, 2003), 1–2, http://fas.org/irp/eprint/ward.pdf.

4. Kim Cragin and Scott Gerwehr, *Dissuading Terror: Strategic Influence and the Struggle Against Terrorism* (Santa Monica, CA: RAND Corporation, 2005), http://www.rand.org/pubs/monographs/MG184/index.html.

5. Thomas X. Hammes, "Fourth Generation Continues to Evolve; Fifth Emerges," *Military Review* (May-June, 2007), p. 2.

6. John Hughes, "Winning the War of Words in the Campaign against Terrorism," *Christian Science Monitor*, May 17, 2006.

7. Eric Schmitt and Thom Shanker, "U.S. Adapts Cold War Idea to Fight Terrorists," by *New York Times*, March 18, 2008.

8. Bruce Hoffman, "The Use of the Internet By Islamic Extremists." Testimony presented to the House Permanent Select Committee on Intelligence (May 4, 2006), p. 18, http://rand.org/pubs/testimonies/CT262-1.

9. Gabriel Weimann, "Terrorist Dot Com: Using the Internet for Terrorist Recruitment and Mobilization," in *The Making of a Terrorist, Vol. 1: Recruitment*, edited by James J. F. Forest (Westport, CT: Praeger Security International, 2005).

10. "A World Wide Web of Terror," *The Economist*, July 14, 2007, p. 28–30.

11. Evan F. Kohlmann, "Al-Qaʻida's 'MySpace': Terrorist Recruitment on the Internet," *Sentinel* 1, no. 1 (January 2008), p. 8, http://ctc.usma.edu/sentinel.

12. Abu Yahya al Libi, "To the Army of Difficulty in Somalia," *al Sahab Media,* http:// 192.31.19.143/sites/uscentcom2/Misc/GMP20070328031003001.pdf.

13. Jarret Brachman, "Jihad Doctrine and Radical Islam," in *The Making of a Terrorist, Vol. 1: Recruitment,* edited by James J. F. Forest (Westport, CT: Praeger Security International, 2005).

14. Taipei Times, AFP, Indonesia, July 17, 2003, http://www.taipeitimes.com/News/world/ archives/2003/07/17/2003059747.

15. Jarret Brachman, "Jihad Doctrine and Radical Islam," in *The Making of a Terrorist, Volume 1: Recruitment,* edited by James J. F. Forest (Westport, CT: Praeger Security International, 2005).

16. Mike McConnell, Director of National Intelligence, Statement for the Record, testimony provided to the Senate Select Committee on Intelligence (February 14, 2008), http://www.dni .gov/testimonies/20080205_testimony.pdf.

17. See Abdul-Aziz el-Sherif, "What Life Gas Taught Me" (Cairo: self-published, August 2007). Cited in Eric Schmitt and Thom Shanker, "U.S. Adapts Cold War Idea to Fight Terrorists," *New York Times*, March 18, 2008.

18. See "Fatwa in Tribal Pakistan Declares Taliban 'Out of Islam,'" *Terrorism Focus* 5, no. 12, March 25, 2008, p. 1.

19. *The News* [Karachi], September 16, 2007, and *PakTribune*, September 15, 2007. Both cited in "Fatwa in Tribal Pakistan Declares Taliban 'Out of Islam,'" *Terrorism Focus* 5, no. 12, March 25, 2008, p. 1.

20. Imam Samudra, *Aku Melawan Teroris* (Solo, Indonesia: Jazera, 2004), p. 109–116. See Muhammad Haniff Hassan, *Unlicensed to Kill: Countering Imam Samudra's Justification for the Bali Bombing* (Singapore: Peace Matters, 2006).

21. Jarret Brachman and Abdullah Warius, "Abu Yahya al-Libi's 'Human Shields in Modern Jihad'," *CTC Sentinel* 1, no. 6 (May 2006), p. 1–3.

22. Ibid.

23. For example, see *Harmony and Disharmony: Exploiting al-Qaida's Organizational Vulnerabilities* (Combating Terrorism Center at West Point, 2006) and *Cracks in the Foundation: Leadership Schisms in Al-Qaida, 1996-2006* (Combating Terrorism Center, March 2008). These and other reports are available online at http://ctc.usma.edu.

24. J. P. Larsson, "The Role of Religious Ideology in Terrorist Recruitment," in *The Making of a Terrorist, Volume 1: Recruitment,* edited by James J. F. Forest (Westport, CT: Praeger Security International, 2005). Also, see James J. F. Forest, "Introduction" in *Teaching Terror: Strategic and Tactical Learning in the Terrorist World* (Lanham, MD: Rowman & Littlefield, 2006).

25. Steven Kull, Testimony to the House Committee on Foreign Affairs, Subcommittee on International Organizations, Human Rights and Oversight (May 17, 2007).

26. Ruth Margolies Beitler, "The Complex Relationship between Global Terrorism and U.S. Support for Israel," in *The Making of a Terrorist, Vol. 3: Root Causes,* edited by James J. F. Forest (Westport, CT: Praeger Security International, 2005).

27. Joseph Nye, *The Paradox of American Power: Why the World's Superpower Can't Go it Alone* (Oxford: Oxford University Press, 2002).

28. Paul R. Pillar, *Terrorism and U.S. Foreign Policy* (Washington, DC: Brookings Institution, 2001).

29. Phillip Heymann, "Dealing with Terrorism: An Overview," *International Security* (Winter 2001–2002), 24–48.

30. Susan B. Epstein, *U.S. Public Diplomacy: Background and the 9/11 Commission Recommendations* (CRS Report for Congress, February 4, 2005), p. 2, http://fpc.state.gov/ documents/organization/43986.pdf; USIA, *United States Information Agency* (February 1999),

http://fpc.state.gov/documents/organization/43986.pdf; and Publicdiplomacy.org, *What is Public Diplomacy?* (September 1, 2002), http://www.publicdiplomacy.org/1.htm.

31. Matthew Moneyhon, "Reinvigorating U.S. Public Diplomacy: A Review of Recent Studies," May 2005, http://www.wws.princeton.edu/ppns/groups/AntiAmericanism, which cites a USIA Informational Brochure, October 1998, available at http://dosfan.lib.uic.edu/usia/usiahome/overview.pdf.

32. Undersecretary of State for Public Diplomacy Web site, http://www.state.gov/r.

33. Moneyhon, 2005.

34. Sharp, *Information*, JP 3-13. See also Air University, *Strategic Communication(s)* (May 1, 2007), http://www.au.af.mil/info-ops/strategic.htm#top.

35. *Report of the Defense Science Board Task Force on Strategic Communication*, 2005, p. 2.

36. Joseph Nye Jr., *Soft Power: The Means to Success in World Politics* (New York: Public Affairs, 2004), pp. 107–110. Cited in Bruce Gregory, "Public Diplomacy and Strategic Communication: Cultures, Firewalls, and Imported Norms," prepared presented at the American Political Science Association, Conference on International Communication and Conflict, Washington, DC, August 31, 2005.

37. Walter L.Sharp, *Information Operations* (Joint Publication 3-13, February 13, 2006), I-2, http://www.dtic.mil/doctrine/jel/new_pubs/jp3_13.pdf.

38. Army, *Manual*, http://fas.org/irp/doddir/army/fm100-6/intro.htm.

39. Sharp, *Information*, II-1.

40. Edward Rouse, *Psychological Operations* (June 5, 2007), http://www.psywarrior.com/psyhist.html.

41. Ivan Goldberg, *Information Warfare* (Institute for the Advanced Study of Information Warfare, December 23, 2006), http://www.psycom.net/iwar.1.html. An excellent example of information warfare would be the alleged Russian DoS attacks on Estonian government Web sites. They effectively flood the Web sites with so many hits that they eventually crash the server. Although it is currently unknown who conducted the attacks, they were successful in shutting down the government servers as well as bringing e-commerce to a halt.

42. Congressional Executive Commission on China, *Freedom of Expression, Speech, and the Press* (December 17, 2006), http://www.cecc.gov/pages/virtualAcad/exp.

43. Congressional Executive Commission on China, *Monitoring Compliance with Human Rights* (2006), http://www.cecc.gov/pages/annualRpt/annualRpt06/Expression.php?PHPSESSID=b9ccfd027b737f95161bbecb17e36557#govlicb.

44. Fairness & Accuracy in Reporting, *Pentagon Propaganda Plan Is Undemocratic, Possibly Illegal* (February 19, 2002), http://www.fair.org/index.php?page=1660.

45. Sally Buzbee, "Rumsfeld: No Lies in Pentagon Plan. Overseas Media Tactics Under Development," Associated Press, February 20, 2002, http://foi.missouri.edu/osi/mediatactics.html.

46. Ibid.

47. Eric Schmitt, "Bush Seals Fate of Office of Influence in Pentagon," *New York Times*, February 26, 2002, http://foi.missouri.edu/osi/osiclosed.html.

48. National Review Online, *Defending Lincoln* (December 5, 2005), http://www.national review.com/editorial/editors200512050918.asp.

49. Editor and Publisher, "Pentagon: Planting Stories in Iraqi Press Was within Law," Associated Press, October 19, 2006, http://www.editorandpublisher.com/eandp/news/article_display.jsp?vnu_content_id=1003285543.

50. Fairness, *Pentagon*, http://www.fair.org/index.php?page=1660.

51. Schoenherr, *Agency*, http://history.sandiego.edu/gen/20th/usia.html.

52. Ibid.

53. James Woods, *History of International Broadcasting* (London: IET, 1992), p. 110.

54. Ibid., p. 110–11.

55. Ibid., p. 110.

56. David L. Stebenne, *Modern Republican: Arthur Larson and the Eisenhower Years* (Bloomington: Indiana University Press, 2006), p. 194.

57. Major Marc J. Romanych, and Lieutenant Colonel Kenneth Krumm, *Tactical Information Operations in Kosovo* (Military Review: September–October 2004), p. 56, http://www.au .af.mil/au/awc/awcgate/milreview/romanych.pdf.

58. Ibid., p. 58.

59. Ibid.

60. Shays, *Middle*, p. 4.

61. ClandestineRadio.com, *Radio Free Iraq* (2005), http://www.clandestineradio.com/intel/ station.php?id=87&stn=76.

62. Al Hurra TV, *Us*, http://translate.google.com/translate?hl=en&sl=ar&u=http://www .alhurra.com/&sa=X&oi=translate&resnum=1&ct=result&prev=/search%3Fq%3DAl-Hurra% 26hl%3Den%26sa%3DG.

63. Al Hurra TV, *About Us* (August 1, 2007), http://translate.google.com/translate? hl=en&sl=ar&u=http://www.alhurra.com/&sa=X&oi=translate&resnum=1&ct=result&prev=/ search%3Fq%3DAl-Hurra%26hl%3Den%26sa%3DG.

64. Khody Akhavi, "Neo-cons Take Spin to U.S.-backed Airwaves," *Asia Times*, June 26, 2007, http://www.atimes.com/atimes/Middle_East/IF26Ak06.html.

65. Jonathan Finer and Doug Struck, "Bloggers, Money Now Weapons in Information War," Washintonpost.com, December 26, 2005, http://www.washingtonpost.com/wp-dyn/content/ article/2005/12/25/AR2005122500659_pf.html.

66. Ibid.

67. L. Paul Bremer, *Prohibited Media Activity*, (October 1, 2007), http://www.al-bab.com/ arab/docs/iraq/media2003.htm.

68. Thomas Elkjer Nissen, "The Taliban's Information Warfare." Copenhagen, Royal Danish Defence College (December, 2007), p.6.

69. Ibid.

70. "A World Wide Web of Terror," *The Economist*, July 14, 2007, p. 28–30.

71. Bruce Hoffman, "The Use of the Internet By Islamic Extremists." Testimony presented to the House Permanent Select Committee on Intelligence (May 4, 2006), p. 3, http://rand.org/ pubs/testimonies/CT262-1.

72. "Al Qaeda Looking for a Few Media-Savvy Geeks," Associated Press, March 5, 2008, http://www.ctv.ca/servlet/ArticleNews/story/CTVNews/20080305/alqaeda_media_080305/2008 0305?hub=SciTech.

73. NATO General Secretary Jaap de Hoop Scheffer, in a seminar on "Public Diplomacy in NATO-led Operations," Copenhagen, October 8, 2007.

74. Steve Coll and Susan B. Glasser, "e-Qaida from Afghanistan to the Internet: Terrorists Turn to the Web as Base of Operations," *Washington Post*, August 7, 2005.

75. See Brachman and Forest, Virtual Sanctuaries, in Innes, *Denial of Sanctuary*.

76. Ibid. Also, for a discussion on the emerging importance of blogs, see James Kinniburgh and Dorothy Denning, *Blogs and Military Information Strategy*, JSOU Report 06-5 (Hurlburt Field, FL: Joint Special Operations University, June 2006).

77. U.S. Department of State, *Understanding*, http://www.state.gov/s/d/rm/rls/dosstrat/2004/ 23506.htm.

78. Lionel Beehner, *Perceptions of U.S. Public Diplomacy* (September 29, 2005), http:// www.cfr.org/publication/8934/perceptions_of_us_public_diplomacy.html?breadcrumb=%2Fissu e%2F50%2Fpublic_diplomacy.

79. James Shanahan and Erik Nisbet, *The Communication of Anti-Americanism: Media Influence and Anti-American Sentiment* (Ithaca: Cornell University Press, May 2007), p. 8, http://www.eriknisbet.com/pdfs/USIP_SG158045_Exec_Summ.pdf.

80. Mark Leonard, Catherine Stead, and Conrad Smewing, *Public Diplomacy* (London: Foreign Policy Centre, 2002), p. 79, http://fpc.org.uk/fsblob/35.pdf.

81. Ibid.

82. Josh Kurlantzick, *China's Charm Offensive* (June 25, 2007), http://www.tpmcafe.com/blog/bookclub/2007/jun/25/chinas_charm_offensive.

83. Jaime Otero Roth, *China Discovers Public Diplomacy* (June 1, 2007), http://www.realinstitutoelcano.org/wps/portal/rielcano_in/Content?WCM_GLOBAL_CONTEXT=/Elcano_in/Zonas_in/DT+24-2007.

84. Roth, *China*, http://www.realinstitutoelcano.org/wps/portal/rielcano_in/Content?WCM_GLOBAL_CONTEXT=/Elcano_in/Zonas_in/DT+24-2007.

85. For more on this, please see the chapter by Sammy Salama and Joe-Ryan Bergoch in this volume.

86. CTC report, May 2008.

87. Hassan Abbas, "A Failure to Communicate: American Public Diplomacy in the Islamic World," in *The Making of a Terrorist, Vol. 3: Root Causes*, edited by James J. F. Forest (Westport, CT: Praeger Security International, 2005).

88. Ibid.

89. See their Web site http://www.radicalmiddleway.co.uk.

90. Kyai Haji Abdurrahman Wahid and C. Holland Taylor, "In Indonesia, Songs Against Terrorism," *Washington Post*, October 7, 2005, p. A23, http://www.washingtonpost.com/wp-dyn/content/article/2005/10/06/AR2005100601559.html.

91. Ibid.

92. Asra Q. Nomani, "Heroes and Pioneers, *Time* (May 14, 2007), p. 99.

93. Thomas Elkjer Nissen, "The Taliban's Information Warfare," Copenhagen, Royal Danish Defence College (December, 2007), p. 9.

PART I

TERRORISM
AND
STRATEGIC INFLUENCE

Jihad.com 2.0

The New Social Media and the Changing Dynamics of Mass Persuasion

Aidan Kirby Winn and Vera L. Zakem

> *We become what we behold. We shape our tools and then our tools shape us.*
> —Marshall McLuhan, 1964

WHEN MARSHALL MCLUHAN—THE RENOWNED thinker on media, communication, and technology, often dubbed the "prophet of the digital age"—introduced his groundbreaking insights into the relationship between medium and content over 40 years ago, he could not have foreseen their relevance for the international security challenges of today. With his famous phrase, "the medium is the message," McLuhan argued that the "message" represents "the change of scale or pace or pattern" that a new invention or innovation "introduces into human affairs."[1] Now, over seven years beyond 9/11 and many years into the ideological battle against Islamic extremism, the concepts he put forth in his seminal work of 1964, *Understanding Media*, have particular prescience. The current era is one of profoundly rapid technological change. It is also an age of broad religious revival and the emergence of nonstate actors and transnational movements as key players on the global stage. Against this backdrop, the spread of radical Islam as a seductive ideology has reached the far corners of the globe, in large part due to the role of the Internet. One of the most pressing challenges the United States currently faces is the urgent need to construct a more successful strategy for waging the "war of ideas." This war is playing itself out in diverse spaces: from the streets of Baghdad to the chat rooms of cyberspace. But the complexity of this challenge has been steadily accelerating over recent years, as the platforms for idea dissemination have diversified. The emergence of new means of communication and new styles of virtual social interaction have transformed the context for mass persuasion and have expanded opportunities for extremists to disseminate their message. This new environment makes the ideological battle for hearts and minds more complex. And while it offers new mediums through which a counterstrategy can be employed to confront the challenge of online radicalization, it also demands new ways of conceiving of strategic communication. The focus of this chapter is to explore the various ways in which this next generation of Internet use, and the new forms of social media as they are sometimes referred to, have shaped the contemporary competition of ideas.

TERRORISM, THE INTERNET, AND WEB 2.0

The introduction of the Internet fundamentally transformed how terrorist organizations operate. Innovations powered by the World Wide Web have been seized on by these radical groups with astounding efficiency. The Internet has facilitated the creation of a unique environment that "enables groups and relationships to form that otherwise would not be able to, thereby increasing and enhancing social connectivity."[2] It has proven to be a transformative tool for spreading radical messages because it attracts individuals of all demographics. It also lends itself to the promotion of broad, utopian goals as its nature tends to downplay local differences and build consensus around overarching grievances. Terrorist groups have capitalized on these qualities by using the Internet to spread propaganda and extremist messages and incite hatred. While many organizations and movements rely on strong leadership to sustain themselves, the Internet has helped diminish the need for a single leader in today's terrorist movements. To a large extent, the goal espoused by the theoretician Abu Mus'ab Al-Suri of a "leaderless jihad" has been realized.[3] By replacing a physical base with a virtual sanctuary, counterterrorism and law enforcement authorities face a more difficult task in dismantling terrorist organizations and capturing individual terrorists. Counterterrorism officials and policy makers continue to be perplexed at the challenges stemming from the global war on terror's rapid migration to the Internet. New York Police Commissioner Raymond Kelly recently described the Internet as the "new Afghanistan," while U.S. Secretary for Homeland Security Michael Chertoff has expressed deep concerns over the unique challenges emanating from a global Web-based radical movement: "The hardest thing to determine is the purely domestic, self-motivated, self-initiating threat from the guy who never talks to anybody, just gets himself wound up over the Internet."[4]

While terrorists' exploitation of the Internet has been a subject of study for a number of years now, it is a dynamic and constantly changing problem. The Internet itself has changed significantly in recent years, thus, the opportunities it offers have also developed. The term *Web 2.0* has been used in marketing and advertising circles to refer to distinct developments that now characterize the way the Internet is being used.[5] There are many qualities that distinguish the Web 2.0 from earlier manifestations of the Internet; one of the most central and unifying characteristics being that it is dominated by the end user to a much greater degree. The ease with which individuals can create and disseminate content, for any purpose—benign or sinister—has been radically enhanced through a variety of technological developments. Some of the technological developments that have given rise to Web 2.0 applications include increased bandwidth (speed of Internet connection), improved tools for posting content, digitization of technology (using high-quality, user-friendly cameras and video editing tools), Internet penetration (more people have access to the Web and the cost has been reduced), advances in social networking, and capitalization of the Internet (people are making money by posting content and generating traffic). These developments have a created a new cyberenvironment which has placed power in the hands of individuals and created incentives for them to shape what exists on the Internet, to circulate ideas and messages, all free from interference by governments or major corporations. A key defining characteristic of Web 2.0 is actually the separation of *form* and *content.* Users are now able to "mash" content (through what are known as "mash-ups") with little effort. For instance, users or organizations can create a site and pull data from multiple third-party sources (photos, videos, etc.) to create compelling content with ease. The earlier version of the Web possessed far less flexibility, which meant Web development lay in the hands of a few. By using the new language of XML, as opposed to HTML, Web 2.0 enables automated data exchange free of formatting constraints. This allows users to both upload and export data with ease, facilitating collaboration, information sharing, and network formation. Digital text is no longer just linking information; in Web 2.0 it is linking people.[6]

One of the effects of these technological advances has been that the Internet has become more than just a tool or a medium to pursue activities, communicate, and conduct business; it has become a distinct social space. It is a place where virtual communities reside, where movements are born and develop, and an incredibly vast amount of information is shared by regular people from all over the world. These changes, which have emerged gradually over the past few years, but whose impact has recently accelerated dramatically, have been of greater interest to corporations, online advertising firms, and students of social media and computer-mediated communication to date than they have been to political scientists, security analysts, or governments.[7] The analysis that has accompanied these changes has mainly consisted of a focus by the private sector on the question of how best to leverage the new phase of Internet use to generate profit. Companies are asking how Web 2.0 shapes the opportunities for brand management and how the recent explosion of these virtual communities can be harnessed to create wealth. For anyone who is concerned with the ways in which radical Islamist movements are currently exploiting the Internet, Web 2.0 is a topic of crucial relevance. At the core of Web 2.0 is a significant shift in the way messages and images are shared and, as a result, the way perceptions are formed. When it comes to the war of ideas against militant Islamist ideology, these developments have fundamentally changed the battlefield.

In discussing the emergence of Web 2.0, one of the central concepts to acknowledge is that of "user-generated content." User-generated content refers to the material created and posted by the end user, whether it is a consumer of a brand-named product, who posts a review of her new blender, newlyweds posting their wedding photos on Flickr to share with family and friends, or an aspiring jihadist posting his ruminations on his personal blog or uploading a graphic video to YouTube. The phenomenon represents a broad change in the way in which the Internet is being used by individuals, a change that cuts across diverse societal groups and demographics. The concept of viral marketing is also important to recognize. In the advertising world, viral marketing refers to "any strategy that encourages individuals to pass on a marketing message to others, creating the potential for exponential growth in the message's exposure and influence."[8] The term *viral* is used to emphasize the fact that the dynamics of the message spread are rapidly multiplying. Some of the characteristics often used to describe viral marketing include effortless transfers between individuals, scaling easily from small to large, exploiting common behaviors and motivations, and utilizing existing communication networks.[9] Although the term originated to describe an explicit strategy adopted by companies seeking to exploit the cyberenvironment to increase awareness of their brands, many of the aspects of this strategy have significant parallels with the ways in which militant Islamists have sought to disseminate their messages and use this the new environment to their strategic advantage.

Another distinguishing characteristic of Web 2.0 is that the activities and Web sites that define this new era of connectivity are inherently *social*. As opposed to some of the conveniences that were first introduced with widespread Internet use, like online shopping or online banking, the fastest growing Web sites today are sites that are built around social interaction. Video and photo sharing, as well as networking sites like MySpace and Facebook, derive their purpose from a social basis—from people inputting information about themselves and their beliefs, tastes, and activities with the goal of broadcasting this content to a wide audience and creating a social connection. As the technologies leveraging user-generated content began to demonstrate their appeal, these different social media began borrowing from each other to incorporate the power of all mediums. Although we treat video sharing, blogs, social networks, and games separately for the purpose of this discussion, it is important to realize that at this stage in the Web 2.0 environment, much of this technology has been fused and integrated. For instance, once you begin uploading videos to YouTube, you can create a profile much like that appearing on a social network site, and the comment forums on YouTube function similarly as the space for feedback available on blogs.[10]

Given what is already known about the power of virtual communication in creating social bonds and in promoting group cohesion and identity formation, clearly these changes promise to greatly impact the future direction of radical Islam as a global social and ideological movement.[11] Some of the cornerstones of Web 2.0 have already been used extensively by radical groups and individuals, while others are still beginning to be explored. Another important function included in many Web 2.0 applications is language translation. With the integration of this capability, the audiences for particular messages are dramatically expanded instantly, though the click of one button. The Web 2.0 promises to be a great enabler of the global growth of many diverse ideologies, including radical ones. The remainder of this chapter explores the ways in which specific innovations including YouTube, MySpace, and virtual online games like Second Life present opportunities for radical movements to expand their influence.

THE RISE OF USER-GENERATED CONTENT: YOUTUBE AND THE BLOGOSPHERE

The use of videos by radical Islamist groups for the purpose of incitement and radicalization is not a new tactic in itself. Videos depicting the horrors of war—whether it be footage of Afghanistan, Chechnya, or Bosnia, aimed at capturing the plight of Muslims and portraying their experience as victims of Western aggression—have long been traded among like-minded groups, and they have found a place on the Internet for many years.[12] But the recent emergence of various video-swapping Web sites, which facilitate easy upload, enjoy a vast viewership and provide an accompanying forum for commentary have enhanced the strategic value of such images and helped guarantee their ubiquity. The most popular of such sites, YouTube, has proven to be an extremely useful tool for those intent on posting videos depicting insurgent attacks on American soldiers in Iraq. Often these videos are posted initially on more obscure al-Qaida–affiliated Web sites, sometimes with Arabic subtitles, but they are easily transferred to YouTube, even by Western users, where their exposure is then exponentially enhanced and they are accessed by a much broader audience.[13] One of the disturbing dimensions of this trend is that their migrations from the far corners of cyberspace to popular sites like YouTube is often facilitated by users in the United States who are inspired by the videos and seek to promote a view that is sympathetic to the various radical groups operating there. The most popular videos, many of which receive thousands of views daily, depict roadside bombings and sniper attacks and generally glorify the "courageous resistance" of the mujahideen engaged in the jihad in Iraq.[14] The vastness and openness of the YouTube platform defies efforts to control content, and from this attribute it derives its strategic significance in the competition for influence. Although some videos are ultimately removed from the site once complaints are registered, the structure of these open, user-dominated formats make regulation highly challenging. For the most part, the content is both user-generated *and* user-regulated. One video may be removed one day for its offensive content, only to appear with a new name, posted by a different user days later. Improvements in digital video technology have allowed these productions to be easily paired with music and captions with the end products attaining a level of slick professionalism next to which the grainy videos of a few years ago pale in comparison. Some of the most popular videos have had soundtracks integrated and are edited so well that their visual quality rivals some of the music videos on MTV.[15]

The central strategy promoted by Abu Musab al-Zarqawi, the leader of "al-Qaida in Iraq" until his death in June 2006, was to capture as much of the carnage as possible on video, and then disseminate it broadly. The implementation of this strategy in Iraq emerged concurrently with many of the Web 2.0 developments that now greatly facilitate the creation and dispersion of content. The adoption of the video camera as a weapon of war, aided by the accompanying technological changes which define the Web 2.0 era, have made the conflict in Iraq what some have referred to as the first "YouTube war."[16] While the first Gulf War changed the nature of war coverage thanks to recent developments in the style of reporting and the birth of the 24-hour news cycle as well as other technological improvements, the graphic and unedited manner in which the current Iraq war is being broadcast reaches an entirely new threshold. These technological developments have allowed troops to convey their experiences in a new medium as well. Al-Qaida insurgents have no monopoly on the production of violent videos; there have been cases of U.S. soldiers using these mediums to similar ends. But what is of greatest concern in the broader struggle against Islamic extremism is the way insurgents in Iraq have been able to reach an unprecedented array of audiences with radical messages and intensely anti-U.S. propaganda. The effect has been a discernible radicalization effect in pockets of youth populations from areas all over the globe.[17] And as many scholars of terrorism have noted, these youth have shared a vivid, vicarious battle experience largely thanks to these new platforms.[18]

Iraq is not the only conflict zone in which YouTube is impacting events on the ground as well as the hearts and minds battle in a direct way. NATO commanders in Afghanistan have had to revisit their strategies regarding public information in light of the Taliban's successful exploitation of YouTube as a means of shaping people's perceptions. The Taliban has benefited from Web 2.0 platforms in carrying out its propaganda campaign through the quick upload of battlefield images and their resultant broad visibility. Taliban fighters deploy with video cameras and the images are broadcast often only hours later. NATO commanders feel that this content has significantly shaped public opinion regarding the direction of the war and has helped create the perception that the Taliban are strong and are in control of events, while the NATO commanders are "on the run."[19] As a response to this aggressive propaganda campaign, NATO has begun declassifying some of their own videos and making them publicly available in attempts to compete with the Taliban's influence and present an alternative image of the war. This decision followed an admission that YouTube and many similar sites have assumed key roles in shaping public attitudes, and it is becoming increasingly clear that these Web sites comprise a crucial dimension of the information war. The use of Web 2.0 applications extends beyond the theaters of Iraq and Afghanistan. In Chechnya, mujahideen have created videos and posted them on the Internet to disseminate their messages, raise much-needed funds, and demoralize Russian citizens.[20] Operational and propaganda videos are widespread not only on Chechen jihadi Web sites but also on YouTube and Google Video. Many of the videos feature prominent Saudi mujahideen, including Amir al-Khattab, a veteran of the Afghan-Soviet conflict of the 1980s who ambushed Russian troops repeatedly during the 1994–1996 Chechen-Russian war.[21]

The style of video sharing to which YouTube has given rise is still a relatively new phenomenon. Some of its significance has manifested itself clearly, but its future role as a weapon in the ideological battle against Islamic extremism remains unclear. There are many possible applications of YouTube to the jihadist cause. For instance, in April 2007 the use of YouTube by a number of Mexican drug gangs gained attention in the U.S. media.[22] In this case the platform was being used by a number of groups involved in organized crime to disseminate threats, post violent content, recruit members, and generally glorify the narco-trafficking lifestyle. Over time, grisly images including torture and beheadings eventually appeared on YouTube. While they only remained there briefly before viewer complaints led to their removal, it was long enough to deliver a powerful message. This exploitation of YouTube by the Mexican drug trade illustrates the risk of its visibility being harnessed to carry out domestic acts of terror in the United States. It offers unregulated access to mass media, it provides a forum in which any image can be broadcast and instantly be viewed by thousands, possibly even millions of viewers before any regulatory action could be triggered.

In January 2007, a U.K. plot by indigenous militants to kidnap and behead a British Muslim soldier while broadcasting the execution live over the Internet, was disrupted at an imminent stage.[23] The nature of the plot represented a significant departure from previous plots originating in the West which, to date, have consisted of coordinated explosions aimed at mass casualties. But a single beheading—such a dark and macabre act being carried out inside a liberal Western democracy and then broadcast to thousands of viewers—it would have had a unique and unprecedented psychological impact on the population. One of the most powerful aspects of YouTube is that it threatens to elevate low-tech and low-death-toll terrorist acts to the realm of spectacular by virtue of their broad dissemination. As enhanced security measures and intelligence efforts make the staging of large-scale attacks more difficult, there is a strong likelihood that homegrown cells may turn to smaller scale plots and seek to enhance their impact through new publicity strategies. The attributes of YouTube and similar user-controlled sites with massive viewership clearly open up innumerable new avenues for radical groups to project influence on a mass scale.

Another realm of user-generated content that has been harnessed effectively to propagate radical Islamic ideologies is the world of blogs. Blogs (or Web logs, as they were originally named) are a specific type of Web site that in many ways lend themselves well to the purposes of jihadist propagandists. In general, blogs tend to be written in the format of personal journals or diaries that use Web publishing technology which facilitates quick and easy updates and displays postings in reverse chronological order. The culture of blogging involves a stream-of-consciousness style of writing that is often spontaneous and emotionally charged. Blogs have a distinct composition and format unique from other Web sites in that they usually contain lots of links to other related Web-based content: articles, Web sites, videos, or anything of interest to the blog writer. One of the key distinguishing features of a blog is the forum it provides for reader's comments. These forums, which instantly publish feedback, can help facilitate the formation of virtual communities united by shared interests, but they can also be a fertile field for debate. The popularity of blogs has increased dramatically in recent years, and now their sheer number as well as scope and diversity is astounding. While some are basically online diaries chronicling the rather mundane events of people's lives, some are politically motivated, while others are dedicated to various hobbies, interests, religious issues, and subcultures.

Blogging has become a popular form of political expression throughout the Muslim world.[24] In some contexts it offers an outlet for criticisms of the current government or for espousing liberal and progressive ideals, while in other environments the content takes a more militant tone. These platforms offer opportunities for pontificating on various questions related to Islam, discussing jihad, and the countless other divisive theological issues that spark debate between Muslims. While most of the blogs focused on Islam are not radical or militant in nature, some clearly have an explicitly pro–al-Qaida agenda. Bloggers like Samir Khan, a 21-year-old based in North Carolina who publishes his pro–al-Qaida site, "Inshallahshaheed" out of his parent's basement, can use these forums to broadcast views to broad audiences and to generate support for the jihadist cause at the grassroots level.[25] Born in Saudi Arabia and raised in the United States, Khan was drawn to a radical interpretation of Islam in his teens (despite his secular household), and now enjoys publishing insurgent videos via his blog and broadcasting an American interpretation of al-Qaida's message for English-speaking audiences. Further, despite many registered complaints, there are no existing U.S. laws to constrain him in his efforts to publish this content. His is just one example of an increasing number of similar blogs, many of which are specifically tailored to attract potential sympathizers among Western audiences.

The power (and potential danger) of the blog in this context, is that it offers aspiring citizen-journalists an opportunity to bypass traditional media outlets to publish their views and frame current affairs according to their own particular ideologies. The extensive constellation of blogs on the Web, and their authors' tendencies to cross-reference each other and therefore reinforce prevailing attitudes (not to mention the many new search engines designed exclusively for navigating their content), offers the opportunity for average people to become highly visible within in certain communities and emerge as a key influencers or thought leaders on a given issue, despite having no real credentials or deserved authority.[26] This is a significant departure from publication in the pre-Internet age, where book and news editors had a more powerful gate-keeping role in rigorously fact-checking information to ensure that it was accurate and appropriate to be disseminated to broad audiences. In the current era, where the transmission of ideas and the ability to frame complex issues for impressionable audiences are such a profound elements of the broader war against radical Islam, bloggers possess a valuable weapon.[27]

FRIENDSHIP, RADICALIZATION, AND ONLINE BELONGING

In the 1990s, rapid developments in Internet technology helped give rise to new forms of online social interaction. These new web applications, including features like instant messaging and chatrooms, were most enthusiastically and immediately embraced by teenagers. The new forums and communications platforms enabled youth to have instant interactivity in a relatively unregulated environment. A new social reality for these demographics emerged, whereby social interaction moved rapidly from the physical world, supported by the occasional phone call or e-mail, to the virtual world. During that time, instant messaging and chat rooms were the cutting edge of cyber-based social communication, but in recent years they have been replaced by a host of new mediums. The technological advances in the twenty-first century have created many new ways for young people to not only communicate directly with one another but manage their social existence on the Internet, including the birth of online social networks.

Since 2002, many social networks have exploded onto on the Web. In the last few years, Friendster, MySpace, Facebook, and Orkut (Google's social network site) all burst onto the online social scene. Most began by catering to specific subcultures, then subsequently attracting more mainstream use. For example, Friendster was launched primarily as a dating social network site,[28] but later evolved into a general social network site. Then MySpace followed in 2003 as a major social network experiment; however, its popularity was quickly enhanced when musicians started to join to advertise their music, concerts, and appearances.[29] It proceeded to take off as a major social phenomenon that has transcended from 20- and 30-something music aficionados and spread to teenagers looking to socialize with their friends online, because it's "cool." As one teenager wrote regarding its social significance, "If you're not on MySpace, you don't exist."[30] Then in 2004, a Harvard University student created Facebook to give college students their own online social network space. In the last several years, Facebook has taken American colleges by storm and has even become the hip virtual social community for a much broader demographic. Statistical data provides solid proof of the increasing prominence of social networks:

> MySpace traffic accounted for almost 5% of all U.S. cyber traffic, with Facebook accounting for almost 1% of all cyber traffic during the week of October 13, 2007. And all social networks in the U.S. combined accounted for almost 7% of all online traffic during the same time, up about 20% from last year.[31]

Like all technological revolutions, the power of the social network Web sites have had major both positive and negative impacts. On the positive front, young people can socialize and interact freely with their peers in their communities and all over the world; they can rekindle lost friendships and expand their social circles in a way that pre-Internet generations could never have done. Moreover, they've been able to educate themselves on contemporary social and political issues and become engaged in these important questions through social network Web sites.[32] When one decides to share content, it reaches everyone in the network simultaneously; this type of networked social existence has empowered young people to share their ideas and convey beliefs and opinions to a vast virtual community.

The darker side of online social networks includes the dangers of exposure to sexual predators, pornography, and cyberharassment. These problems have received increasing attention in recent years and are being met with new legal approaches.[33] The post-9/11 era has also witnessed the emergence of Islamic extremism and radicalization within the social network communities. Militant Islamists and terrorists have become extremely Web-savvy and have recognized the value of social network sites in reaching out to prospective followers. They have exploited online social network communities, establishing a jihadi "community within a community," recruiting potential members, spreading their radical message, and attempting to garner additional support.

It is easy to create extremist communities within an existing social network because the nature of these sites is highly decentralized and the massive membership makes surveillance nearly impossible. Therefore, members who also belong to an al-Qaida community can take advantage of this open environment.[34] Militant Islamists have not only been able to proselytize and spread propaganda, they have also been able to use these social databases for operational purposes. One group of radicals used Facebook and other similar social networks to obtain personal information on Western troops in hopes of carrying out terrorist attacks against them. Britain's MI5 has warned troops returning from service in Iraq and Afghanistan not to publicly post their personal information and details about their military tours due to the risk of possible terrorist activities being carried out against them. The soldier's identity was uncovered by the militants after he posted information about his tour on a social network site.[35]

By creating their own communities within mainstream social networks such as MySpace, Orkut, Facebook, and others, Islamist extremists are able to seek out and recruit vulnerable or alienated individuals who might be predisposed to radical ideologies and thus willing to join their cause. According to terrorism experts, al-Qaida sympathizers are using Orkut, a popular, worldwide Internet service owned by Google, to rally support for Osama bin Laden, share videos and Web links promoting terrorism, and recruit.[36] It is suspected that Orkut has at least 10 communities that openly sympathize with al-Qaida and support jihad.[37] To find these communities all one needs to do is to create a username, password, and profile, and then one can easily search for other individuals and groups that share his/her interests. The U.K. case of Samina Malik, who was known as the "lyrical terrorist," offers a good example of the potential dangers. Malik was recently arrested under the newly enacted British antiterrorism laws for making a posting regarding her interests of "helping the mujahideen in any way which [she] can" on HI-5, a popular British social networking site.[38]

Militant Islamists cast their nets wide: they look for support from the traditional Islamic circles and, more and more, from the Western world. According to Michael Moss and Souad Mekhennet, extremists are "seeking to appeal to young American and European Muslims by playing on their anger over the war in Iraq and the image of Islam under attack."[39] In particular, online social network communities provide a great platform to recruit individuals from the West. As Rita Katz, director of the SITE Institute points out, "We know for sure that al-Qaeda is trying to recruit as many people as possible from Western societies. This is a good place to be if you want to recruit people."[40] It is also particularly easy for militant Islamists to find young recruits inside the online social networks while exploiting the power of preexisting social bonds.[41] Young people tend to be idealistic, are often drawn to charismatic leaders, and many are seeking a cause to believe in, even if that cause promotes violence, hatred, and destruction. They often do not see the fine line between indulging curiosity about a particular group and being recruited by that group.[42] As Jonathan Evans, the head of MI5, points out, al-Qaida is trying to reach to children in Europe who are as young as 15 years old.[43]

Online social network communities are a great way for militant Islamists to garner support and create a community of believers, as they constitute an interactive venue where, as Perry Aftab observes, "aberrant attitudes and beliefs may be exchanged, reinforced, hardened, and validated. This mutual affirmation in turn gives rise to a sense of community and belonging—a virtual *ummah*."[44] All one has to do is post a jihadi message on Facebook's wall or MySpace's comments section, and with one click of a button, every member who belongs to that particular jihadi community can see the message, respond to it, and even start a blog on the topic of the message. Therefore, the ability to easily create jihadi online communities within social networks, communicate with other jihadis, and recruit more individuals furthers the radicals' goals of creating a leaderless, virtual network of jihadists. While the roles of traditional leaders like Hasan Nasrallah and Osama bin Laden remain significant in terms of operational leadership and to some extent, the direction of grand strategy for their movements, the nature of their leadership has changed. These new social networks that help constitute the leaderless jihad do not replace the traditional networks on which the organizations were founded. But they may help inspire and cultivate the autonomous "self-starter cells" that carry out acts of jihad in the name of al-Qaida, without the operational linkages. They add a new, more amorphous dimension to these movements' anatomy.

NEW GAMING EXPERIENCES AND THE VIRTUAL WORLD

Video games are valuable tools for shaping perceptions and for portraying a particular world view. They are powerful mediums, because while they typically cast the user in the role of the hero, the opponent is often effectively demonized through its visual depiction and through other elements of the game's context. Embedded messages and images can have an insidious impact on the user, as he or she is directly focused on the immediate challenges of the game, earning points or acceding to the next level while the exposure to these subtle elements may ultimately shape ideas, values, and attitudes. Video games are generally consumed primarily by children and teens, thus they present a valuable vehicle for the transmission of messages to an impressionable audience. The users may be largely unaware of the ideological, political, or cultural significance that is contained within the game. Many modern video games serve as reflections of the prevalent values and attitudes of the broader culture in which they are created.[45] They comprise one element among many diverse forms of entertainment consumed regularly by today's media-saturated generation.[46] Although the role of video games in inciting violence or even desensitizing people to it remains a contested issue, it is not hard to see how the technologically sophisticated games of today could help cultivate radical sentiments and help glorify violent acts as heroic.[47]

The Lebanese Hizballah has been using video games as a central aspect of their information campaign for many years, in an effort to influence youth perceptions. Hizballah carries out its public relations, propaganda, and communication campaign primarily in the southern suburbs of Beirut. In these suburbs, one finds posters of Sheikh Hassan Nasrallah, the leader of Hizballah and Iran's Ayotollah Khomeini, the spiritual inspiration of the group. In this suburb called Harek Hreik, it is not difficult to find computer arcades packed with kids who are playing the latest Hizballah video games. The ultimate goal for Hizballah's video game propaganda campaign is to ensure that the group's messages of resistance, courage, and hatred toward Israel resonate with the young Lebanese population, so that these youngsters will aspire to become Hizballah fighters.

At the beginning of the second Palestinian Intifada, the Hizballah Internet Bureau created a video game called *Special Force*. During this game, the user tries to kill former Prime Minister of Israel Ariel Sharon and other Israeli dignitaries. The user can also engage in simulated low-intensity conflict by throwing grenades at Israeli soldiers in an effort to kill them.[48] The success of the first version of *Special Force* prompted Hizballah to create *Special Force 2* in the aftermath of the Israeli-Hizballah war. Immediately after the war, Hizballah declared victory based on its ability to weaken Israel, capture Israeli soldiers, and retain a good portion of its weapons to carry out future terrorist operations. It created *Special Force 2* to give Lebanese children a chance to virtually experience attacking Israeli soldiers, launching Katusha rockets at Israeli towns, and ultimately claiming victory against Israel. In both versions of the game, role-playing is interspersed with real video footage of Hizballah militants engaging in combat with Israeli Defense Forces. As Sheikh Ali Dahir, the head of Hizballah media activities explains, "the Lebanese child has the right to know what happened in the south so as to imitate the jihadist action and the act of liberating the land."[49]

Hizballah supporters proclaim that these games are not only fun for the kids but also have a message and a purpose to educate them about the importance of resistance, jihad, patriotism, and why it is legitimate to hate Israel and the United States. During the *Special Force* games, the users get a sense that the Arabs and the Muslims are strong and can take on anyone, even the military superiority of Israel. In addition, the *Special Force* games share with the young Hizballah supporter the Palestinian struggle, and portray Israelis as horrible aggressors who seek to kill the Palestinians and take their land. Thus, through these games the young player builds a natural sympathy with the Palestinians and their cause. One player of *Special Force* explains why this game is his favorite: "I don't like Israelis and I want to shoot them because they're bombing us and they're bombing the Palestinians. I want to shoot them in real life as well. In this game the Israelis don't win—the resistance always wins."[50] Furthermore, through these overarching themes, *Special Force 2* conveys the resistance techniques that were successful during the 2006 Hizballah-Lebanon war. Hizballah's Sheikh Dahir explains that "the features which are the secrets of the resistance's victory in the south have moved to [*Special Force 2*] so that the child can understand that fighting the enemy does not only require the gun . . . It requires readiness, supplies, armament, attentiveness, and tactics."[51]

The key attribute to recognize in virtual or simulated experiences is the way in which the imaginary becomes blended with the real, in the mind of the player. While the *Special Force* games represent the cutting edge of conventional video games, packed with propaganda value and available for purchase and download on several Web sites, the Web 2.0 era has helped usher in a new and different generation of games. They are not only more technologically sophisticated, they incorporate a dimension of social interactivity that serves to blur the line between virtual and real in new and more dramatic ways. These massive multiplayer online role playing games" (MMORPGs), as they are sometimes called, are fundamentally different from conventional video games as they dynamically connect real users, from geographically disparate physical locations in real time through the virtual game environment. *Second Life*, a game created by Linden Labs of California, is one of the most popular MMORPGs as it appeals to a broad cross-section of the population.[52] It has drawn such wide participation that major corporations have begun investing in the virtual world for the purposes of advertising as it provides a distinct audience and potential market. *Second Life* players create avatars (characters to represent them in the virtual environment) and players then go about real-life type activities like shopping, buying real estate, and socially interacting with the eight million other "residents."

But the online world of *Second Life* is not a utopia; violence and crime take place there as well. In July 2007 the virtual world drew real-world media attention when a string of terrorist attacks was carried out by a virtual group known as the Second Life Liberation Army.[53] A helicopter was flown into the Nissan building, and then in a separate virtual incident a group of *Second Life* militants forced their way into an American Apparel clothing store and shot several other shoppers.

What is one to make of such actions carried out by virtual characters in a world which only exists in cyberspace? Many dismissed these incidents as most likely the activities of angry or alienated teenagers, seeking to cause some destruction and using the *Second Life* environment as a platform to express their angst. It is certainly possible that this is the case. However, this expression of a violent and destructive agenda raises questions about how the virtual world is perceived by some users and how it might be exploited to serve extremist goals. In discussing these virtual terrorist attacks, Australian security services expressed concerns that these acts could have been carried out by home-grown militants.[54]

The vast social network of *Second Life* and its many counterpart games clearly offer unique opportunities for like-minded players from all over the world to connect, interact, and communicate. It is this varied social landscape that draws people to the game. At the same time, the sophistication and realism of the virtual medium offers a forum for propaganda and recruitment, as well as offering tactical opportunities such as experimenting with various weapons and plotting mass-casualty scenarios. These attributes of the game could be easily exploited by a group, lacking a physical sanctuary, yet motivated to plan and ultimately carry out sophisticated terrorist acts. Because *Second Life* is a dynamic environment driven by decisions and behavior of real-world players, even virtual acts of terror have social impact distinct from conventional games where the user's experience is socially isolated.

RECOMMENDATIONS

Clearly, given the complex environment in which ideas are now being shared, a more nuanced and forward-looking strategy to counter radical messages is desperately needed. This must begin with an understanding of the current context for message creation and dissemination. Militant Islamist movements have been quick to effectively weaponize the current media environment, while the United States and its allies have been slow to recognize its strategic importance. Public diplomacy and strategic communications efforts remain sluggish and reactive and are still largely disseminated via traditional media. As a result, this new powerful tool in the battle of ideas, the world of Web 2.0, has been relinquished to our enemies. But the very nature of the Web 2.0 is that the Internet, as a medium, is now infused with many more voices. To suggest that the U.S. government could harness its power in a direct way so as to *control it* would be misleading. The challenge that we have sought to describe here is, in many respects, a civilizational challenge. The ideas that will constrain and ultimately dissolve bin Laden's appeal will emanate from many varied sources, and it will be the sustained and cumulative impact of their authenticity that will erode the power of the violent and hopeless vision of al-Qaida.

Counternarratives

Given the current context, the United States is still faced with the task of advancing ideas and framing events in a way that enhance our influence in the world. Developing a counternarrative—or probably more accurately, an array of counternarratives—to compete with and help expose the weaknesses of these militant views is a challenging task which will require sustained effort, resources, and incredibly innovative thinking. This challenge has begun to receive increasing levels of attention by scholars and researchers in recent years, but implementation is a daunting task. David Kilcullen has recognized the magnitude of the challenge and has offered a number of valuable insights, helping highlight the difference between tactical and strategic initiatives in this ideological battle and the need for a new paradigm to define the nature of the problem.[55] But Kilcullen goes further than just framing the challenge; he offers concrete suggestions on how the U.S. government needs to begin approaching it. He argues for "disaggregating" the conflict that has, to date, been painted as "monolithic" and for finding ways to address local grievances.[56] This is extremely difficult in the current era, because the Internet helps facilitate the illusion of a global, deterritorialized religious ideology built on shared grievances, when in fact local circumstances and agendas are often very diverse and particular.[57] But effective disaggregation is essential to winning the information warfare, and our efforts in that respect may also require improving the quality of our lexicon used to denounce acts of terror and those that support violent means.[58]

It is important to recognize that there will always be those who are beyond reach, whose beliefs won't be shaken. But these individuals are the overwhelming minority. While creative efforts should still be made to challenge the messages that hardened radicals share and trade with other "true believers," the thrust of our strategies must be directed at the much larger group, those who are forming new opinions and attitudes everyday based on a wide variety of inputs, including both words and deeds. One of the most disastrous and largely unforeseen consequences resulting from the war in Iraq (and now to some degree from the conflict in Afghanistan as well) is the profound and far-reaching radicalizing impact these ventures had on the global audience of Muslim youth. These conflicts played perfectly into the existing narrative of bin Laden and appeared to confirm his assertions: the United States seeks to destroy Islam, steal oil wealth, and occupy Muslim lands. Then, "evidence" of the truth of the global jihadist narrative was supported by the successful harnessing of the current media environment.

While actions often do speak louder than words, greater efforts to frame our policies early on—through a greater variety of media—could have impacted what followed. As insurgents were flooding video swapping Web sites with images of IEDs, beheadings, and sniper attacks, where was our information counteroffensive? One of the lessons from these conflicts is the overwhelming importance of the information dimension. If we don't offer a compelling narrative to frame our actions up front, and then find innovative and diverse mediums to deliver that narrative, others will seize that opportunity and fill the void with another story. Furthermore, this new information environment demands that the perception dimension be more explicitly factored into the foreign policy decision-making process. If the ultimate outcome of a given policy actually worsens the problem it is meant to address, even if this occurs as a result of propaganda and distortion, it stands to reason that the given policy may not be the best course. At the very least, the potential consequences of how that action will be framed must be anticipated and weighed carefully into whether it will ultimately threaten our strategic interests.

Incorporating New Insights

The challenge of advancing counternarratives and messages that cast doubt over militant Islamist ideologies is often better carried out by voices that already carry authority among the populations we are trying to reach. A lot has been written in recent years about the need to find and amplify "moderate voices," yet so far our efforts in this area seem to have met with little success. To do this we need to understand the communities we are speaking to, including the virtual ones. Doing this successfully requires more than just translators; it demands that we appreciate the character of the cultures and demographics we are addressing and gain insight into how ideas travel and which personalities and symbols carry currency among those groups. This is an area where the new forms of social media can be leveraged and insights from the private sector should be welcomed.

Consider the following excerpt taken from an online marketing blog addressing message creation:

> It is essential to define the goals of the mission, including scope, desired results, and expectations. Online conversation needs to *flow*. It is responsive and organic . . . talking points are more flexible than preparing a script. The model message you prepare should be flexible and define the outside boundaries of your marketing conversation. Engaging in online conversation as a member of an online community requires your language, delivery, humor, and tone to mirror that of the community The model message should be flexible enough to allow for interpretation but strict enough to prevent the brand from being misrepresented online.[59]

Replace the phrase "marketing conversation" with "public diplomacy agenda" and you have a useful perspective for this discussion. While U.S. foreign policy goals are not a "brand," these are valuable principles that have relevance for our endeavors in shaping perceptions about our role in the world. The private sector, especially the world of online marketing which lives and dies by these new social medias, has invested heavily in understanding the nature of online message creation and dynamics of the competition for influence. Of course, their wars of ideas tend to focus on who's leading the pack in running shoes, MP3 players, and cars—but the competition dynamic is not entirely divorced from the challenge with which we are concerned. Insights can be gleaned from this field. Above all, participation and engagement is key, as Web strategist Chris Abraham observes:

> You'll never be able to control the blogosphere conversation. Don't even try. You'll never be able to manage your blog coverage like you manage the press. Don't even try.

But what you can do is participate, earn respect, and tell your story. Jump in, join the conversation, and be a part of it.[60]

These industries have begun to come to terms with the fact that the media environment is no longer dominated by large corporations. The same is true for governments. U.S. strategic communications and public diplomacy efforts often fall short by addressing a self-selecting audience in environments where it retains ultimate control over message delivery. Strategy papers, press releases, and public addresses by government envoys are, of course, much easier to control than this new communications environment, but they are unlikely to compete successfully for the hearts and minds of a younger generation against the dynamic online world. To truly shape hearts and minds in the real world and on the Internet, the United States needs to start thinking outside of the box.

Organizing for the Challenge Ahead

Under the direction of former Undersecretary of State for Public Diplomacy Karen Hughes, the United States has undertaken some important and steps in counterterrorism public diplomacy and strategic communication. One noteworthy effort was the establishment of the Counterterrorism Communication Center (CTCC). Drawing on expertise from strategic communication professionals across the U.S. governmenet, the purpose of the center is to produce counterterrorist messages, public diplomacy, and strategic communication plans that affect key countries and regions such as Europe and the Middle East. To better coordinate counterterrorism public diplomacy and strategic communication strategies, Hughes created the interagency strategic communication fusion team at the National Security Council and has published the first ever *National Strategy for Public Diplomacy and Strategic Communication*. Aside from the creation of the CTCC, the strategy calls for the creation of Arabic and Persian Web sites that showcase the positive side of U.S. foreign policy; the creation of the Digital Outreach Team that uses mainstream online newspapers, podcasts, and blogs as platforms to challenge extremist ideologies; and the active engagement of U.S. embassies all over the world to reinforce antiextremist messages in their posts.[61] While our success in future strategic communications efforts will not primarily be a product of bureaucratic reshuffling, there are some organizational changes which may help support the mission.

NEW ROLES AND DOMESTIC PARTNERS.   Presently, the CTCC is housed within the State Department's Bureau for Public Affairs and Public Diplomacy. The State Department is only one arm of the community executing the counterterrorism strategic communication agenda. To better address the future challenges in this field, the CTCC should be placed in an interagency environment, which can successfully fuse the intelligence and homeland security dimension of its task with the public diplomacy aspect. Counterterrorism messaging is in fact a hybrid field which requires intelligence capabilities as well as broader knowledge of strategic communication. The task of challenging the jihadist ideology head-on will require a unique combination of skills from varied parts of the government. An agency with this mission does not currently exist.

CTCC STRUCTURE.   The CTCC should be divided into three distinct departments: public diplomacy, digital outreach team, and international cooperation. The public diplomacy department should focus on major issues outlined in the *National Strategy* such as "diplomacy of deeds" and many others. The department of international cooperation should focus on sharing best practices and lessons learned with key allies in the area of counter-terrorism strategic communication. The United States can learn a great deal in this arena from its allies in Europe and other regions who have been dealing with these issues on a larger scale in recent years.[62] Finally, given the role the Internet has played in terrorism and radicalization, the digital outreach team needs to be given a major priority within CTCC. We propose that this team be divided into two groups. As the *National Strategy* advises, one group should focus on monitoring mainstream online news, Web sites, and blogs. Another group should focus on new media: jihadi and user-generated content sites such as YouTube, jihadist communities on MySpace and Facebook, blogs, and even radical elements within online games. The CTCC must invest in researching and establishing a presence in these forums. As such it will be better able to gather sound intelligence and help support the formulation of appropriate countermessages for the targeted audience.

CAPACITY BUILDING.   According to Duncan MacInnes, principal deputy coordinator for the Bureau of International Information Programs at the State Department, the current digital outreach team only has two Arabic linguists who monitor mainstream blogs and online media.[63] In a recent congressional testimony, MacIness pointed out that he hopes to hire four more Arabic bloggers for this effort.[64] Unfortunately, having only six Arabic linguists is far from sufficient to execute the current agenda and future goals of the digital outreach team. While the desperate need for greater linguistic skills seems to becoming an ongoing theme in discussions about improving intelligence capability, it is relevant here as well. A more robust effort would require a significantly larger core group of Arabic, Farsi, and Pashto linguists and analysts who can examine both the mainstream and the jihadi online news outlets and postings. While recruiting and retaining such a staff will be extremely difficult given the widespread shortages of such skills, it should be made top priority. Efforts to expedite the screening and the granting of security clearances should accompany this capacity building program.

INTERNATIONAL COOPERATION.   The challenge of persuasion and counterterrorism messaging in the Web 2.0 world is not exclusive to the United States. America's allies all over the world face similar challenges in fighting radicalization and confronting the jihadi messages that circulate on the Internet with the help of Web 2.0 applications. Thus, it is important that CTCC and the U.S. interagency engage in a strategic dialogue with allied countries such as France, the United Kingdom and others, as well as with international organizations such as NATO who share this challenge. Through collaboration, the United States and its international partners can only benefit from an exchange of ideas and practices on how to best address counterterrorism strategic communication and public diplomacy, an issue that is a critical component of the global war on terrorism.

Having offered these modest suggestions with respect to specific organizational change, it should be noted that this challange cannot be confronted by simply moving boxes on organizational charts or even through creating new agencies. Bureaucratic reorganization is likely to be only a small part of the answer to this complex and dynamic problem.

The Power of Many Voices

Given the nature of the Web 2.0 environment and the fact that governments will only be one voice among many in its market of ideas, it important for everyone to consider creative, unconventional approaches to harnessing its power to discredit violent ideologies and offer credible and inspiring alternatives. Without question, the most powerful messages denouncing radical interpretations of Islam will come from Muslims themselves. Their voices are more likely to carry weight with other Muslims and their efforts to expose the manipulation of their faith are likely to be most persuasive. The very same tools that have been used so effectively to circulate militant agendas can be adopted to counter them. Blogs offer opportunities for those who oppose violence to broadcast their messages widely. They can be powerful vehicles for expression, enabling ordinary citizens to project their voices globally and become thought leaders.[65] In recent years, profiles have aired on major news networks showcasing stories of "former terrorists" who have renounced jihad and adopted a more moderate approach to pursuing their political goals.[66] Individuals who have personally undergone such transformations should seek out a greater variety of mediums to effectively reach youth audiences. YouTube and other video sharing sites can be used to circulate images that deplore the use of terrorist violence. Public demonstrations have taken place in all corners of the globe denouncing terrorism and uniting moderate majorities; those who take part in such public demonstrations should consider ways to amplify their own political voices by uploading videos of the events to YouTube, sharing them with global audiences, and helping compete with the many videos seeking to incite hatred and rage. People should also continue to use comment forums and feedback loops offered on many video, blog, and social networks sites to condemn material that is hateful and inaccurate. In aggregate, these small actions taken by individuals will help challenge the messages of extremists and build an authentic counternarrative to compete for influence.

CONCLUSION

The recent revolution in communications technology driven by the Internet has created a new, more expansive market of ideas. Individuals are now empowered to reach massive audiences with unfiltered messages in increasingly compelling and provocative packaging, rendering the competition for mass influence more complex. All of this has profound implications for the way in which the U.S. government should seek to communicate with the world, as well as for its approaches in denouncing dangerous ideologies that threaten our interests. This environment clearly demands new strategies that are acutely aware of the significance of both medium and message. We need to determine how we want to frame our policies and ideals and then deliver these messages via the platforms that engage the most strategically valuable audiences. We must also find better, more inventive ways of exploiting this environment to our own ends—in the wise words of Marshall McLuhan, "our age of anxiety is, in great part, the result of trying to do today's jobs with yesterday's tools."[67] But ultimately we must recognize that the job that lies ahead is not the exclusive domain of the U.S. government. The Web 2.0 era dramatically eroded the monopoly of large organizations over the formation of ideas and their transmission on the Web. So merely adopting these new platforms to communicate official agendas is one small step that on its own fails to exploit the full potential of this tool. The voices to which Web 2.0 has given the power to be heard are essentially everyone's. It is in exploring how to best harness the power of this overwhelmingly moderate, peaceful, and tolerant "everyone" to more effectively stifle messages of hate that the enduring insights will be found.

ACKNOWLEDGMENTS

The authors benefited from insights shared by Shawn Brimley, Jeffrey Heisman, Burgess Laird, and Cornelius O'Leary.

NOTES

1. Marshall McLuhan, *Understanding Media: The Extensions of Man*, McGraw-Hill, 1964.

2. "NETworked Radicalization: A Counter Strategy." George Washington University Homeland Security Policy Institute and University of Virginia Critical Incident Analysis Group, 2007.

3. Marc Sageman, "Leaderless Jihad, Terror Networks in the Twenty-First Century," University of Pennsylvania Press, January 2008; and Brynjar Lia,"Architect of Global Jihad: The Life of Al Qaeda Strategist Abu Mus'ab Al-Suri," Columbia University Press, January 2, 2008. Note: The doctrine of leaderless resistance was developed by Louis Beam, the self-described "ambassador at large, staff propagandist and 'Computer Terrorist to the Chosen' of the Aryan Nations"—see Jessice Stern, *Terror in the Name of God*, Harper-Collins, 2003, p. 151.

4. Dan Eggen, "Secretary Chertoff: Officials Tout U.S. Anti-Terrorism Record," *Washington Post*, May 25, 2006, A08.

5. Tim O'Reilly, "What Is Web 2.0: Design Patterns and Business Models for the Next Generation of Software," September 30, 2005, http://www.oreilly.com/pub/a/oreilly/tim/news/2005/09/30/what-is-web-20.html.

6. The authors benefited from discussions with Jeffrey Heisman regarding the novelty of Web 2.0 and his perspective helped generate a more accurate description of its characteristics.

7. For a discussion of Web 2.0 from a business perspective see, "Serious Business: Web 2.0 Goes Corporate," *Economist Intelligence Unit*, 2007.

8. Dr. Ralph F. Wilson, E-Commerce Consultant, "The Six Simple Principles of Viral Marketing," *Web Marketing Today*, http://www.wilsonweb.com/wmt5/viral-principles.htm.

9. Ibid.

10. See http://www.youtube.com/fightglobalists for a U.S.-based user who posts many propagandistic videos and has a following of subscribers to his frequent video posts. He also posts a link to his blog in his profile.

11. Mark Sageman, *Understanding Terror Networks*, University of Pennsylvania, Philadelphia, 2004.

12. Gathering to watch war videos from Chechnya and other conflicts was a significant group radicalizing activity for the London cell, and the cell disrupted in Toronto in June 2006 had traveled to a makeshift training camp to view such footage and even film their own videos of themselves imitating warfare, in the style of al-Qaida's pre-9/11 training videos. See Michael Frisolanti, Jonathon Gatehouse, and Charlie Gillis, "Homegrown Terror: It's not Over," *Macleans*, June 19, 2006; Michelle Shepard and Isabel Teotonio, "School Kinds to Terror Suspects," *Toronto Star*, June 5, 2006 on the Toronto cell; Olga Craig, "Bowling for Paradise," *Sunday Telegraph*, July 17, 2005; and Jason Burke, Antony Barnett, Mark Townsend, Tariq Panja, Martin Bright, and Tony Thompson, "The London Bombs: Three Cities, Four Killers," *Observer* (London), July 17, 2005, on the London plot.

13. Edward Watt, "Anti-US Attack Videos Spread on the Web," *New York Times*, October 6, 2006, http://www.nytimes.com/2006/10/06/technology/06tube.html.

14. Tariq Panja, "Militant Islamic Groups Turn to YouTube," Associated Press, February. 11, 2007, http://www.msnbc.msn.com/id/17107489.

15. The most notorious video to date remains "Dirty Kuffar," the 2004 jihad-style rap video produced by Islamic British rappers Sheikh Terra and the Soul Salah Crew, which was downloaded millions of times and was eventually available through all the major video sharing sites. Since that time, others have been made in the same tradition.

16. For discussion on the impact of YouTube on chronicling soldiers experiences in Iraq, see Ana Marie Cox, "The You Tube War," *Time,* July 19, 2006, http://www.time.com/time/nation/article/0,8599,1216501,00.html.

17. The cells that carried out the 2004 Madrid train bombings, the 2005 London bombings, and the cell that was disrupted in Toronto in 2006 all cited the Iraq war as the grievance that drove their actions.

18. For more discussion of the radicalizing impact of videos, see Daniel Benjamin and Steven Simon, *The Next Attack: The Failure of the War on Terror and a Strategy for Getting it Right,* Times Books, 2005.

19. Paula Newton, "NATO's new Afghan battleground: YouTube," CNN, Nov. 28, 2007, http://edition.cnn.com/2007/WORLD/asiapcf/11/28/nato.youtube.

20. Andrew Gregor, "You Tube: The New Video Front for Chechnya's Mujahideen," *Chechnya Weekly,* 8, no. 12, March. 22, 2007, http://www.jamestown.org/terrorism/news/article.php?articleid=2372734.

21. Ibid.

22. See Manuel Roig-Franzia, "Mexican Drug Cartels Leave a Bloody Trail on YouTube," *Washington Post*, April 9, 2007.

23. Nick Britten and Duncan Hooper, "Nine arrested over alleged kidnap and beheading plot," *Telegraph,* Jan. 2, 2007, http://www.telegraph.co.uk/news/main.jhtml?xml=/news/2007/01/31/nterror131.xml.

24. See Mark Lynch's discussion of blogging among the younger generation of the Muslim Brotherhood in "Brotherhood of the Blog," *Guardian Unlimited: Comment is Free*, March 5, 2007, http://commentisfree.guardian.co.uk/marc_lynch/2007/03/brotherhood_of_the_blog.html.

25. Michael Moss and Souad Mekhennet, "An Internet Jihad Aims at U.S. Viewers," *New York Times*, October 15, 2007, http://www.nytimes.com/2007/10/15/us/15net.html.

26. *U.S. National Strategy for Public Diplomacy and Strategic Communication*, White House, May 31, 2007.

27. The case of "Irhabi (Terrorist) 007" is instructive here. While Younis Tsouli was not a blogger per se, he exploited various Web-based discussion forums under this pseudonym to earn himself status and authority. The sheer volume of Tsouli's postings began to earn him the trust of

other participants; as a result he began to wield a strong influence within the online community. See "A World Wide Web of Terror," *The Economist*, July 12, 2007; and Rita Katz, and Michael Kern, "Terrorist 007, Exposed," *Washington Post*, March 26, 2006.

28. Boyd Danah, "Why Youth (Heart) Social Network Sites: The Role of Networked Publics in Teenage Social Life," *MacArthur Foundation Series on Digital Learning—Youth, Identity, and Digital Media Volume,* (ed. David Buckingham), MIT Press, 2007, p. 1.

29. Ibid.

30. Ibid.

31. Perry Aftab, "Using the Web as a Weapon: the Internet as a Tool for Violent Radicalization and Homegrown Terrorism," U.S. House Committee on Homeland Security, Nov. 6, 2007, http://homeland.house.gov/hearings/index.asp?ID=102.

32. Ibid.

33. Ibid.

34. Kasie Hunt, "Osama bin Laden fan clubs build online communities," *USA Today*, March 8, 2006.

35. Sean Rayment, "Troops warned off Facebook over terror fears," *Telegraph Daily*, November 12, 2007, www.telegraph.co.uk.

36. Ibid.

37. Ibid.

38. Duncan Gardham, "Lyrical Terrorist Samina Malik Guilty," *Telegraph Daily*, November 12, 2007, www.telegraph.co.uk.

39. Moss and Mekhennet, "An Internet Jihad Aims at U.S. Viewers."

40. Hunt, "Osama bin Lade fan clubs build online communities."

41. This is a valuable aspect of online social networks; research on radicalization dynamics highlights the value of pre-existing social bonds in formation of terrorist cells.

42. Aftab, "Using the Web as a Weapon."

43. Rayment, "Troops warned off Facebook over terror fears."

44. Aftab, "Using the Web as a Weapon."

45. Some of the most notorious games in Western culture which glorify violence and crime and include *Grand Theft Auto*, *Thrill Kill*, *Mortal Kombat*, and *Manhunt*.

46. Bruce Hoffman, , "Using the Web as a Weapon: The Internet as a Tool for Violent Radicalization and Homegrown Terrorism," U.S. House Committee on Homeland Security, November 6, 2007, http://homeland.house.gov/hearings/index.asp?ID=102.

47. There has been an ongoing debate regarding the impact of violence in video games on children's behavior and it continues to remain controversial.

48. Toby Harden, , "Video Games Attract Young to Hizballah," *Telegraph Daily*, February 21, 2004, www.telegraph.co.uk.

49. "Inside the New Hizballah Video Game: Special Forces 2," *Asharq Al-Awsat*, August 8, 2007, www.aawsat.com.

50. Harden, "Video Games Attract Young to Hizballah."

51. "Hizballah Game Celebrates 2006 Clash with Israel," *Game Politics*, August 17, 2007, www.gamepolitics.com.

52. *World of Warcraft* actually has a larger number of active users than *Second Life*, but the nature of its content tends to draw from a distinct subculture, whereas *Second Life* enjoys a more broad and varied participation.

53. Chris Gourlay and Abul Taher, "Virtual Jihad Hits Second Life Website," *Times Online*, August 5, 2007, http://www.timesonline.co.uk/tol/news/world/middle_east/article219 9193.ece.

54. Natalie O'Brien, "Virtual Terrorists," *Australian*, July 31, 2007, http://www.theaustralian.news.com.au/story/0,25197,22161037-28737,00.html.

55. David Kilcullen, "Countering Global Insurgency: A Strategy for the Global War on Terrorism," *Small Wars Journa* 2.2, Nov. 30, 2004, http://smallwarsjournal.com/documents/kilcullen.pdf.

56. George Packer, "Knowing the Enemy," *New Yorker*, December 18, 2006, www.newyorker.com/printables.

57. Roy, Oliver, *Globalized Islam: The Search for a New Ummah*, Columbia University Press, 2004.

58. Amy Zalman, , "Strategic Communications and the Battle of Ideas: Winning the Hearts and Minds in the Global War Against Terrorists," U.S. House Armed Service Committee, Subcommittee on Terrorism and Unconventional Threats and Capabilities, July 11, 2007, http://armedservices.house.gov.

59. Chris Abrahams, "Blog Messaging and Counter Messaging," January 21, 2007, http://www.cabraham.com/blog-messaging-and-counter-messaging.

60. Ibid.

61. "U.S. National Strategy for Public Diplomacy and Strategic Communication," White House, May 31, 2007.

62. The United Kingdom has struggled with domestic radicalization on a much larger scale than the United States in recent years. They have begun devoting resources to better understanding the phenomena of Web-based radicalization. Key insights and best practices in this area should be leveraged as much as possible.

63. Duncan MacInnes, "Strategic Communication and Countering Ideological Support for Terrorism," U.S. House Armed Services Committee, Subcomittee on Terrorism and Unconventional Threats, November 15, 2007, http://armedservices.house.gov.

64. Ibid.

65. See the discussion of Egyptian bloggers demonstrating against terrorism on Global Voices Online, www.globalvoicesonline.org/2005/07/24/egyptian-bloggers-against-terrorism.

66. "The Network: Hassan Butt Tells Bob Simon Killing In The Name Of Islam Is A 'Cancer,'" March 25, 2007, http://www.cbsnews.com/stories/2007/03/23/60minutes/main2602308.shtml.

67. McLuhan, *Understanding Media*.

When Fatwas Clash Online

Terrorist Debates on the Internet

Gabriel Weimann

TERRORISTS ARE USING THE INTERNET, as several studies have revealed, for various purposes.[1] Modern terrorists are using the Internet to launch psychological campaigns, recruit, raise funds, incite violence, and provide training. They also use it to plan, network, and coordinate attacks. Thus, not only has the number of terrorist Web sites increased, but the uses to which terrorists put the Internet have also diversified. However, most of the attempts to monitor and study terrorist presence on the Internet have focused on the practical and communicative uses of this channel, while less attention has been paid to the use of the Internet as a medium of terrorist debates and disputes. Computer-mediated communication is ideal for terrorists: it is decentralized, cannot be subjected to control or restriction, is not censored, and allows free access to anyone who wants it. The typical, loosely knit network of cells, divisions, and subgroups of modern terrorist organizations finds the Internet both ideal and vital for inter- and intragroup networking. These advantages have not gone unnoticed by terrorist organizations and they have moved their communications, propaganda, instruction, and training to cyberspace. Web sites, however, are only one of the Internet's services to be used by terrorists; there are many other facilities such as e-mail, chat rooms, e-groups, forums, and virtual message boards.

This chapter is based on a 10-year-long project of monitoring thousands of terrorist Web sites.[2] When this research began in the late 1990s, there were merely a dozen terrorist Web sites; by 2000, virtually all terrorist groups had established their presence on the Internet and in 2003 there were over 2,600 terrorist Web sites.[3] The number rose dramatically and by the end of 2007, our archive contained over 5,800 Web sites serving terrorists and their supporters. But the Internet also serves as a battlefield between and within terrorist organizations that use this platform to conduct ideological debates or even personal disputes. Recent years have seen a growing frequency of disputes and debates online. Indeed, a previous study documented this emerging trend (of online disputes) using several illustrative cases.[4] This chapter reviews several different types of virtual debates among terrorists: debates between terrorist organizations, debates within terrorist organizations, personal debates, debates over actions, and debates among supporters. The chapter also examines how the Internet is used by terrorists to bridge the gaps, to unite their forces, and to resolve disputes.

DEBATES BETWEEN TERRORIST ORGANIZATIONS

Disputes and arguments between different terrorist groups have found their way to cyberspace. These debates may reflect religious differences (e.g., Shiites against Sunnis), clashes of political agendas (e.g., various insurgent groups in Iraq), disagreement over actions and operations (e.g., the Chechen rebels' criticism of Hamas for accepting Russian President Vladimir Putin's invitation to visit Moscow in 2006) and conflicting visions (e.g., al-Qaida's criticism of Hamas). The following section illustrates these online intergroup debates.

Al-Qaida versus Hamas

A harsh dispute between Hamas and al-Qaida has emerged on these organizations' Web sites.[5] The Palestinian Hamas movement and al-Qaida have a very complex relationship. According to Reuven Paz, al-Qaida and the affiliated salafi-jihadi or tawhidi-jihadi groups around the world are trying to manipulate the Palestinian problem and the Israeli-Palestinian conflict while the Hamas uses the same issues for its own propaganda, recruitment, and fund-raising. According to Reuven Paz, al-Qaida and its affiliates

> also adopted from Hamas the *modus operandi* of suicide attacks and much of the Islamic justification for them. On the other hand, Hamas has so far tended to reject attempts to create organizational links with the global jihad, or to expand its terrorist activities beyond Israel and the Palestinian territories . . . Hamas leaders did their best not to link their struggle in Palestine to the global Jihad of al-Qaida.[6]

On March 11, 2007, Ayman al-Zawahiri—bin Laden's second-in-command— lashed out at the Hamas movement, accusing it of abandoning jihad and "selling Palestine" for seats in the Palestinian unity government. In an audio message posted on jihadi Web sites, al-Zawahiri accused the Hamas government of falling into the "swamp of surrender" by agreeing to abide by the international agreements signed by the Palestinians when the Hamas movement joined the Palestinian unity government. Thus, he claimed, Hamas joined the humiliation and surrender of Egyptian president Anwar Sadat. The Hamas movement reacted in an official announcement, published on its Web site on March 12, 2007. Titled "You have misunderstood, Dr. Al-Zawahiri, and you failed in your statement," the announcement stresses that Hamas considers Palestine to be a land of Islamic religious endowment (*waqf*) and therefore even the smallest part of it may not be relinquished. According to the announcement, Hamas still adheres to the path of jihad and resistance (i.e., violence and terrorism) and will continue to do so, sacrificing shahids "until not a single trace of occupation remains in Palestine." The announcement ends with the following: "Rest assured, Dr. Ayman . . . Hamas is still the same movement it has been since its foundation."[7]

This was not the first time that Ayman al-Zawahiri strongly criticized the Hamas movement. Immediately after the establishment of the Hamas government (March 2006), an audio message was distributed online with a message from Ayman al-Zawahiri calling on Muslims to embark on jihad (holy war) against the corrupted Arab regimes and against Western countries. The message also included a direct appeal from al-Zawahiri to the Hamas movement, in which he pointed out several fundamental principles in the worldview of al-Qaida (not too different from the Hamas worldview). He warned Hamas that no one has the right to relinquish even one grain of Palestine, since it is an Islamic land occupied by infidels. Moreover, he stated that cooperating with secular representatives, who "sold" Palestine, goes against the values of Islam; the agreements between the Palestinian Authority and Israel ("the agreements of surrender") are opposed to Islamic religious laws.

The roots of the fierce debate between Ayman al-Zawahiri and the Hamas movement lie in the results of Hamas's victory in the Palestinian elections of January 25, 2006. That victory was a political earthquake not only on the internal Palestinian scene but across the entire Middle East. For the first time in its history, the Middle East saw the rise to power through democratic elections of a radical Sunni Islamic terrorist organization. Al-Qaida's criticism reflects this shock: "The Hamas leadership has sold out Palestine, and earlier it had sold out referring to Shari'ah as the source of jurisdiction. It has sold all that to be allowed to maintain one-third of the government" claimed the posting (March 11, 2006) on the as-Sahab Web site. The accusations from al-Zawahiri and the response from Hamas have both lent to furor in the jihadist Internet community, with members divided between their support for one group or the other. For example, the general manager of paldf.net, a popular Hamas-affiliated forum, published a message on March 11, 2007, regarding al-Zawahiri's comments. The message was subsequently posted to password-protected al-Qaida–affiliated forums, such as al-Hesbah, where members were critical of the posting and of Hamas. In the message, the manager charges that al-Zawahiri was "never with Palestine even for one day," and has allegedly long held prejudice against Palestinians. As he provides examples of this bias, he states that al-Zawahiri has "great hatred" for Hamas because it is an expansion of the Muslim Brotherhood, and regards them as losers. Pointing to al-Zawahiri's hard-line ideology and his failure to recognize the political term of "respect," the manager adds that the al-Qaida leader does not understand Hamas.

On April 29, as-Sahab—al-Qaida's media production company—posted a 36-minute video message by Abu Yahya Al-Libi, the al-Qaida leader in Afghanistan, titled "Palestine: A Warning Call." In his message Al-Libi focuses on Hamas's strategic choice to prefer a political course over jihad. Al-Libi describes Hamas's choice as a dangerous "slippery slope," which causes deception and "fata morgana" (illusion or mirage), dangers that can only be neutralized by an unequivocal return to jihad. In referring to Hamas's recent political dialogue with Russia, Al-Libi mockingly asks:

> Have the tyrant Putin and his . . . political party become more protective . . . of Palestine and the Palestinians' interests than the *mujahid* Sheikh Ayman Al-Zawahiri? Has this criminal . . . who destroyed an Islamic country, annihilated an entire nation in

Chechnya, and drove it to the valleys and deserts . . . become closer to you than the people who proved their . . . loyalty to Allah, His Messenger and to the believers?[8]

Jihadi Criticism of Hizballah

When Israel and Hizballah exchanged prisoners on January 29, 2004, Hizballah and its leader, Hasan Nasrallah, enjoyed a glorious image. According to Reuven Paz, this created criticism and resentment among several Arab groups and in particular among jihadi-salafi groups that support Qa'idat al-Jihad:

> The Lebanese Shiite group has never been popular among the Salafi adherents of Global Jihad, given their fundamental hatred towards the Shi'ah. The collapse of the Ba'athist regime of Saddam Hussein and the conflict between the Shiite majority and the Sunni minority in Iraq, added additional fuel to the fire of traditional Salafi enmity towards the Shi'ah. Since the start of the attempts at establishing a new government in Iraq, Salafi web sites and forums on the Internet have stepped up their attacks against the Shi'is, Iran, and Shi'i doctrines with every possible arsenal of verbal arms. Accompanying the growing phenomenon of severe verbal attacks against the Iraqi Shiites and the Lebanese Hizballah are condemnations of Iran prevalent on several web sites, and initiated primarily by Saudi supporters of Global Jihad. Furthermore, in the past year there was a growing attempt by Saudi Salafi scholars and laymen to link the Shiites to Jews, both in history, and in present times.[9]

The most significant verbal attack, according to Paz, was the labeling of Hizballah with the salafi term "Hizb al-Shaytan" (the Party of the Devil). One of the primary salafi online forums against the non-Sunnis, primarily the Shiites—Al-Difa an al-Sunnah (Defense of the Sunnah)—led the attacks with numerous writings, several of them citing important Islamic writers (e.g., Khomeini, Khamenei, Khoei, and Sistani).

Their Web site presented articles such as "The actions of the murderer so-called Shiite Mahdi," "The crimes and betrayals of the Shi'is throughout history," "Meetings between Shiite clerics and Jews and Christians," and "The scandals of Shiite clerics and religious authorities," referring to Shiite leaders including Khomeini, Khamenei, Khoei, and Sistani—as well as Hizballah. The "Hezbollah File" in this Web site indicates why the salafis criticize Hizballah and Hasan Nasrallah: "The secretary general of Hezbollah portrays himself and is portrayed by others as the 'New Salah al-Din al-Ayubi,' and a superior commander at the forefront of the struggle against Israel." Thus, the younger Islamists use the jihadi forums to attack Nasrallah, and one of them posted in the jihadi forum of Al-Erhap his criticism titled "Hasan Nasrallah, leader of Hezbollah—the most famous and corrupt traitor in the history of the nation."

The 2006 war between Israel and Hizballah in Lebanon ignited a robust debate on jihadist Web sites over backing for Hizballah, which set off the crisis when it seized two Israeli soldiers on July 12. This conflict is one more reflection of the widening divide between Shiite and Sunni Arabs in parts of the Middle East. The Al Hesbah Web site, associated with al-Qaida, posted messages like "Lebanon today is exposed to a Zionist war not only against Hezbollah, but against all Lebanon. This is what Hezbollah wanted."

Mr. Kanani, the Sunni jihadist, wrote on the site that Hizballah earlier conspired with Israel to secure Israel's northern border, thus allowing Israel to direct its wrath toward the Palestinians. "The Shiite party has no ideological problem with making peace with Jews, collaborating with them and being friendly with them," he wrote. Another author, "an Egyptian holy warrior" who recommended that al-Qaida not aid Lebanon, wrote, "It is known that most of the inhabitants of Lebanon are Shiites and cross worshipers." Accusing Palestinians of being anti-Shiite, one Iraqi Shiite militant bitterly wrote, "It is better to concentrate one's efforts on helping the Shiite kinfolk rather than the Sunnis."

Shiite-Sunni Split in Iraqi Insurgency

It was in the deserts of Iraq that the Sunni-Shiite fault line originated in the seventh century, following the death of the Prophet Muhammad, and the split centered on the question of who was to take over the leadership of the Muslim nation. Sunni Muslims agree with the position taken by many of the prophet's companions, that the new leader should be elected from among those capable of the job. This is what was done, and the Prophet Muhammad's close friend and advisor, Abu Bakr, became the first caliph of the Islamic nation. The word *Sunni* in Arabic comes from a word meaning "one who follows the traditions of the Prophet." However, the Shia Muslims share the belief that leadership should have stayed within the prophet's own family, among those specifically appointed by him, or among imams appointed by God himself. Thus, the Shia Muslims believed that leadership should have passed directly from the Prophet Muhammad to his cousin/son-in-law, Ali. Throughout history, Shia Muslims have not recognized the authority of elected Muslim leaders, choosing instead to follow a line of imams which they believe have been appointed by Muhammad or God himself. The word *Shia* in Arabic means a group or supportive party of people. The commonly known term is shortened from the historical "Shia-t-Ali," or "the Party of Ali." From this initial question of political leadership, some aspects of spiritual life have been affected and now differ between the two groups of Muslims. Today, Sunni Muslims make up the majority (85 percent) of Muslims all over the world. Significant populations of Shia Muslims can be found in Iran and Iraq, and large minority communities in Yemen, Bahrain, Syria, and Lebanon.

Sunni Arab and Shiite militant groups battle one another daily across Iraq. Sunni groups form the largest of the terrorist organisations operating in Iraq, including Ansar al-Islam, as well as radical groups like Al-Tawhid Wal-Jihad, Jeish al-Taiifa al-Mansoura, Jeish Muhammad, and Black Banner Organization. After the bombing of the Shia Al-Askari Mosque, relations between the Sunnis and the Shia severely declined, sparking off a wave of revenge killings against Sunnis. This conflict is evident on the Internet, too. On January 18, 2007, members of the password-protected jihadist forum Mohajroon provided military advice, some technical and some crude, to the Sunni people in Iraq to confront the alleged Shiite aggression against their people and mosques. Included were manuals for explosives, suggestions for placement of bombs and positions of soldiers, and nontraditional methods such as training guard dogs and placing booby-traps. Some members suggested that every Sunni should take up weapons, regardless of sex or age, and organize into groups for dispersal in strategic locations to fight the Shiite militias.

Others, however, believed that women and children should be protected as the men contribute to the fighting. Snipers have been stressed as mandatory for the confrontations. Another member provided instructions for engaging in hand-to-hand combat with the enemy, even using a newspaper as a weapon, arguing that the Shiites are weak in this realm: "Our enemies neglected the physical training and depended on the power of the modern weapons."[10]

In January 2007 on the password-protected al-Qaida–affiliated forum al-Hesbah, several postings sought to defend Ayman al-Zawahiri against an accusation that he is an "agent" of the Shiites. The charge was made by a writer from the al-Salat Web site who challenged readers that if anyone could provide one word of evidence from al-Zawahiri that he is against the Shiites, he would abandon his position. Al-Hesbah members posted portions of transcripts from al-Zawahiri's recent speeches, "The Correct Equation" and "Realities of the Conflict Between Islam and Unbelief," in addition to a portion of an interview with al-Ansar Publication in 1995 in which he heavily criticizes Iran.

In October 2006, Sheikh Abu Usama al-Iraqi, a man alleging to be a jihad leader in Iraq from the "Word of Truth" (Kalimat al-Haq) organization, spoke in a 17-minute video message issued to jihadist forums. His message to bin Laden concerned allegations of aggression perpetrated by mujahideen in Iraq against other Muslims and Sunni insurgents, specifically by al-Qaida in Iraq against the Twentieth Revolution Brigade and the Islamic army in Iraq. Abu Usama al-Iraqi claims that at first Abu Musab al-Zarqawi's group of Tawhid Wal Jihad, and then al-Qaida in Iraq, did nothing wrong, but then became corrupted as other insurgency groups fell silent. Al-Qaida in Iraq allegedly dismissed the advice of al-Zawahiri and Sheikh Abu Muhammad al-Maqdisi and attacked Muslims: "They also terrorized and fought the worshippers in the mosques, they killed tens of Imams and speakers, and they threatened hundreds, until the mosques are now empty of worshippers. Some of the mosques were even shut down because of transporting weapons in and out of them." He also argues that those mujahideen who heeded the fatwas of scholars to rebel were also subject to killings and beatings. This video appeared on several jihadist forums, including al-Hesbah, and was immediately repudiated by members as propaganda and was subsequently deleted.

On January 31, 2007, the Kalimat al-Haq Foundation distributed a second video, 18 minutes in length, from Sheikh Usama al-Iraqi. His statements were directed to Abu Omar al-Baghdadi, the emir of the Islamic State of Iraq. He described the crimes committed against the Sunni people in Iraq and the fabrication-laden statements from the Islamic State that cover these actions. In particular, he focused on the audio speech from Abu Omar al-Baghdadi, "Truth has Come and Falsehood has Vanished," published in December 2006, and denounces claims made within concerning Sunni tribes and Iraq insurgency groups uniting under its banner. Throughout the speech Abu Usama al-Iraqi refers to the Islamic State as deniers of both the Sunni and Shia Muslim doctrines, and claims that this position allows them to call all Muslims apostates for the purpose of justified murder. He adds that the Islamic State steals money from Muslims, destroys their houses atop their heads, and that the shouts of what they consider approval from the people are actually cries of protest. For all these charges, Iraqi addressed Ayman al-Zawahiri and questioned his open support for the Islamic State of Iraq.

On June 4, 2007, a 9-minute, 43-second audio statement was posted online, containing a statement by Ali al-Nu'aymi, the media spokesman of the Islamic Army in Iraq, in which he accused al-Qaida and the "other names under which it operates" of attacking and killing the men of the Islamic Army in Iraq and Iraqi Sunnis. Al-Nu'aymi described the recent clashes between the insurgents in Al-Amiriyyah and its surrounding areas. He said that the Islamic Army in Iraq "holds Abu-Hamzah al-Masri and Abu-Umar al-Baghdadi responsible for the actions of their followers against the Sunnis in general and the mujahidin in particular."[11] Describing the Shiites' actions, the posting argued that

> they attacked the Sunnis and went too deep in killing them and accusing them of being infidels. They targeted their areas and gatherings, which had a very serious outcome, since these actions and transgressions turned the cities of the Sunnis into ghost cities. . . . We are moving forward on the path of jihad in the cause of the Almighty until we realize the goals for which jihad was mandated by the power and strength of God, including the driving out of the American and the Magi-Iranian occupation. Second, we will stand firm in the face of the sectarian militia and in defending the blood, the honor, and the possessions of the Sunnis.[12]

DEBATES WITHIN TERRORIST ORGANIZATIONS

Postmodern terrorism is not formed in the organizational structures of the twentieth-century terrorism. Al-Qaida, for example, is a notably and deliberately decentralized, compartmentalized, flexible, and loosely knit network. According to Zanini and Edwards,

> What has been emerging in the business world is now becoming apparent in the organizational structures of the newer and more active terrorist groups, which appear to be adopting decentralized, flexible network structures. The rise of networked arrangements in terrorist organizations is part of a wider move away from formally organized, state-sponsored groups to privately financed, loose networks of individuals and subgroups that may have strategic guidance but that, nonetheless, enjoy tactical independence.[13]

Within such loosely knit networks, disagreements and arguments may appear, exposing the cleavages and splits.

Debates within al-Qaida

Al-Qaida, a nonstructured and loosely organized web of groups' movements and cells, is often challenged by inner conflicts between groups associated with al-Qaida. One example, as studied and reported by Reuven Paz, is the case of such a rivalry within al-Qaida.[14] It appears that from within this organization emerged a group of young Saudi Islamists who wanted to play a more important role. Many of them were students and disciples of the older groups of Wahhabi clerics and scholars who could not come to terms with the

American presence on Saudi soil. In recent years they radicalized their positions and began calling for political violence against the United States, Western culture, and, in recent years, the Saudi royal regime, while providing Islamic legitimacy for these actions. In 2002 they began to issue new electronic pamphlets via the Web sites of their supporters, under a new name: Qa'idat al Jihad (the Jihad base). The severe conflict between the groups within the Saudi jihadist movement led to an online publication of a 460-page book titled *Osama bin Laden: Mujaddid al-Zaman Wa-Qahir al-Amrikan* (*Osama bin Laden: The Reformer of Our Times and Defeater of the Americans*) by Saudi scholar Abu Jandal al-Azdi. This book was circulated on several Web sites but mainly on one of the most important sites of the jihadi Salafiyyah. The book attempts to raise bin Laden to a new level of a major reformer or reviver, a status bestowed on only a very few scholars.

Another example of using the Internet for internal disputes is found in the ninth issue of al-Qaida's *Sawt al-Jihad* (*Voice of Jihad*) online magazine, published in January 2004. Most of this issue is devoted to a dispute within al-Qaida circles in Saudi Arabia regarding the al-Qaida bombings in Saudi Arabia. The text, by an anonymous author, seeks to justify the jihad in Saudi Arabia:

> My Muslim mujahid brother, can you not see Muslims killed in Afghanistan, and then in Iraq. . . . Can you not see the corpse of the children completely torn, their skulls and brains scattered all over the [television] screens? Can you not see the Muslims in this worst condition of shame, humiliation, pain, harm, and injury? Can you not see that the headquarters of the war was from the [Arabian] Peninsula and that the center of all kinds of logistical support was this land, which the Prophet, may peace be upon hHim, commanded be purified from the polytheist?
>
> You have seen the war on Iraq, and you have seen how all the military powers in the land of the two holy mosques were in the hands of the Christians, including military bases, and even more—the civilian Arar airport has been changed to a military base because of its strategic location, which was indispensable in attacking Iraq.[15]

Recently, the insurgent groups in Iraq have been conducting an online debate. This debate is among the Sunni jihadist groups following the establishment of the al-Qaida–sanctioned Mujahideen Shura Council and the announcement of the establishment of the Islamic State of Iraq. This was an attempt by the leading insurgent groups to restore the caliphate in Baghdad and to set up a skeleton infrastructure of a nation-state. Six months later they announced the establishment of the Cabinet, making a wide range of ministerial appointments. According to Laura Mansfield, this process provoked criticism from other insurgent groups.[16] Kuwaiti cleric Hamid al Ali, who seems to wield a considerable amount of influence among the jihadis, posted a fatwa suggesting that the Islamic State of Iraq (ISI) should undo its creation. He went so far as to question the motives of the founders of the state, saying that the mujahideen are only human and have faults of which they are not cognizant, including a love of power and control. Al Ali questioned the legitimacy of ISI Emir Abu-Umar al-Baghdadi, pointing out that under Islamic law, people cannot swear allegiance to a "hidden, weak, anonymous ruler, who is lacking in empowerment."[17] He went on to say that the establishment of the state under illegitimate leadership and forcing it on the citizens "with the sword" will backfire. In April 2007, the Sharia Commission of the Ansar al Sunnah group posted a notice in a jihadist forum that they were resigning from the group. In their statement, the members of the commission criticized the emir of the group for ignoring the religious advice provided by the commission. In their online statement, they alleged that "deviations in the concepts and practices that contradict the teachings of the prophet spread, and corruption grew" within the group.[18] Ansar al Sunnah responded with a statement that any postings not released by their official media arm, Al Fajr, should not be considered legitimate. At the same time they acknowledged that two of their leaders had left the group.

In 2007 members of the password-protected al-Qaida–affiliated forum al-Boraq began discussing why al-Qaida does not strike Iran, believing that doing so would fit within the conflict between Sunnis and Shiites. One of the postings asked why suicide bombings and car bombings have not taken place in the street of Qom, Iran, as the "Iranian hand is dripping the Sunnis' blood in Iraq,"[19] and al-Qaida in Iraq has already hit the Shiites in that state. Answering the question, one posting argues that al-Qaida would not hit Iran due to not wanting to open additional jihad fronts, while another posting argues that even suggesting that al-Qaida should do this is a "sin." The writer believed that the Sunni-Shiite divide is already being exacerbated by the United States in order to drive a wedge between Muslims.

PERSONAL DEBATES

Online debates may also take the form of personal attacks on other terror groups' leaders, on terrorist spiritual or religious figures or on competing personalities within the same group or network. This section illustrates this with several examples.

Criticizing al-Zarqawi

Abu Mus'ab al-Zarqawi, the first leader of al-Qaida in Iraq, was often criticized on jihadi Web sites as well as in the Arab media. The first criticism came from one of the most important and influential clerics of the jihadi-salafi part of the global jihad movement: Abu Muhammad al-Maqdisi, the Jordanian-Palestinian Islamist scholar and spiritual guide of Al-Tawhid wal-Jihad in Jordan and Iraq. In a July 2004 online interview, he criticized the Islamist insurgents in Iraq, led by Abu Mus'ab al-Zarqawi, for the mass killing of Muslims in Iraq. On July 5, 2005, he repeated his criticism, noting that "the indiscriminate attacks might distort the true Jihad." This criticism generated a wave of responses by jihadi scholars, clerics, and youngsters.

Later, a religious dispute emerged between al-Zarqawi and his spiritual mentor, al-Maqdisi.[20] The dispute between the two took the form of statements and counterstatements, primarily on Islamist Web sites and message forums, and from there it spread to Arab media. The debate focused on the question of the legitimacy of certain jihad operations in Iraq, and in particular on the issue of the legitimacy of attacking Muslims, particularly Shiites, as well as noncombatants. It began in July 2004 when al-Maqdisi criticized certain operations in Iraq and argued that harming Muslim civilians in Iraq was not justified by Shari'a law. Later, al-Maqdisi published his criticism of "the extensive use of suicide operations" in which many Muslims were being killed, and stated that suicide operations were not at all a traditional Islamic means of warfare, but rather an exceptional means, for use only in specific circumstances. Al-Zarqawi responded by posting an online audio message in May 2005 in which he tried to justify the victimization of Muslim civilians within the context of jihad. According to al-Zarqawi, Allah had ordered the killing of infidels by all means, even if this caused the killing of infidels who did not constitute targets such as women and children, or the killing of Muslims. With regard to attacks on Shiites, al-Zarqawi said in a later message (July 2005) that it was a duty to wage jihad against the Shiites because they were apostates (murtadoon) and had formed an alliance with the crusaders against the jihad fighters.[21]

In July 2005, al-Zarqawi published a third statement discarding al-Maqdisi's accusations. In this statement al-Zarqawi attacked al-Maqdisi personally, arguing that although al-Maqdisi had been his mentor, he (al-Zarqawi) no longer follows al-Maqdisi's teachings but rather follows the advice of other ulama whom he trusted more. Moreover, he argued that al-Maqdisi had no right to criticize the fighters in Iraq since he had not taken part in the jihad in Iraq. Al-Zarqawi also mentions that during the time they both were fighting in Afghanistan, he and al-Maqdisi had agreed that suicide operations were prohibited, but that afterward he had changed his mind regarding Iraq and considered such operations permissible and even desirable.

Al-Zarqawi was criticized also by other insurgent organizations, including the Army of Muhammad, Al-Qa'qa' Brigades, the Islamic Army in Iraq, the Army of Jihad Fighters in Iraq, and the Salah Al-Din Brigades. The latter posted messages and announcements stating that "the call to kill all Shiites is like a fire consuming the Iraqi people, Sunnis and Shiites alike. . . . The resistance and its military attacks target [only] the occupation and those who assist it. The resistance does not target any Iraqi, whatever his sectarian or ethnic affiliation, unless he is connected to the occupation."[22]

Debate Between Salafi Sheikhs

An interesting clash among leaders of Salafi Islam erupted online over jihad against "heretical" Arab regimes. On July 16, 2007, Sheikh Abu Basir Al-Tartusi responded on his Web site[23] to a claim made by Sheikh Hamed Al-Ali on his own Web site[24] that jihad against the Arab regimes is doomed to failure while jihad against foreign forces occupying Muslim lands is destined to succeed. Tartusi wrote:

> I [recently] had the opportunity to read an enjoyable article by Sheikh Hamed bin Adballah Al-'Ali from May 27, 2007, titled "The Status of the Emblems of Jihad . . . " I found it to be a very useful article in terms of its topic and purpose, but one paragraph caught my attention. [This paragraph] said that "the jihad program is a program of transformation for a nation that needs to awaken, and if it is not [carried out] in a supportive environment, it will fail." Consequently, plans to confront the [Arab] regimes will not meet with success, while plans to resist occupation will be successful.

Tartusi warned that this claim could be exploited by various elements to discourage the Muslims from launching jihad against the regimes that oppress them. He added that Islam commands the Muslims to wage jihad against any Muslim leader who has "become completely heretical," and that disobeying this command can only bring greater oppression and suffering to the Muslims:

> Therefore, to those who shed crocodile tears over the losses and the civil wars that may result from waging [jihad against tyrannical and heretical regimes], we say: The greatest civil war breaks out when peoples accept [the rule] of heretical, oppressive and apostate tyrants. . . . All this is legitimate and is not regarded as sinful by the religion—[on the contrary,] it is one of the most honorable [forms] of jihad. You will find that, when carried out in this manner . . . it is easier than you thought and feared, and the price of fighting the oppressive tyrants is smaller than the price of suffering [their oppression].[25]

Personal Disputes Among Iraqi Insurgents

After al-Zarqawi's death, his successor, Abu-Hamzah al-Muhajir, became a target for online criticism by other insurgent groups. On December 7, 2006, a jihadist Web site posted a letter addressed to the "Al-Qaeda Organization in the Land of the Two Rivers" titled "The Solid Structure." The author, "Abu-Hamzah al-Ansari," introduced his message as a response to the call of Abu-Hamzah al-Muhajir on jihadist groups in Iraq to pledge allegiance to the Islamic State in Iraq, and urged al-Qaida members in Iraq to "show courage by listening to the other views." "Jihad al-Ansari" even proposed that mujahideen emulate "the courage of the West led by America in its practice of self-criticism." He said that while it is true that the Americans practice "hypocrisy and denial of justice in their dealings with the rest of the world," they are "quick to point out problems, criticize, and acknowledge mistakes among themselves." "Jihad al-Ansari" used Qur'anic text and Hadith to support his argument that "the leader (in Islam) cannot impose himself on the subjects without their deliberation and consent." He wrote that he accepted al-Qaida's appointment of "Umar al-Baghdadi" as the "Commander of the Faithful" but added that he viewed the appointment as "the election of Umar al-Baghdadi as a candidate for the Caliphate . . . but not as a sovereign," adding that that the latter required consultation with other Muslims. "Jihad al-Ansari" added that "it is not possible (for the rest of Muslims) to evaluate whether or not (Umar al-Baghdadi) is fit to lead them toward repelling occupation and establishing an Islamic state, despite the virtues cited in Abu-Hamzah al-Ansari's letter about Al-Baghdadi's character and noble family."

On December 8, 2006, jihadist Web sites posted reactions from the Al-Buraq Web site and forum participants criticizing Jihad al-Ansari's letter to Abu-Hamzah al-Muhajir. In the first message titled "Al-Buraq Website Exposes Jihad al-Ansari and the So-Called Ali (Ibn-Abu-Talib) Brigade," there are claims that al-Ansari and his group, "if it ever existed" had evil intentions and that his statement clearly reveals his "evil Ba'thist inclinations." It calls his statement "a joke" and compares him with "the crook Abu-Usamah al-Iraqi" (who had issued a statement to Osama bin Ladin in October 2006, urging him to disown al-Qaida in Iraq). The Web site says that after seeing him for what he is, they feel obliged to "expose him in support of the legitimate mujahidin, whom he is trying to hurt with his twisted crafty ways." The statement closes by warning everyone to beware of people such as al-Ansari. In another posting on the Ana al-Muslim Web site titled "What Does Jihad al-Ansari Mean?" participant "Khayal Najd" criticizes Jihad al-Ansari, whom he refers to as "a claimant of jihad" and starts by saying that al-Ansari's writings reveal his poor knowledge of the Arabic language, concluding that he is either Iranian or Western. Al-Ansari is presented as aiming to undermine al-Qaida and creating strife among various jihad groups. "Khayal Najd" ends his message by advising his readers: "We must reveal to the people the danger he poses and explain to them that all he wants is to divide the mujahidin."

Personal Criticism of Nasrallah

On January 26, 2007, a message attributed to al-Qaida strategist Abu Musab al-Suri, titled "Nasr-Ellat [*sic*] is Setting Lebanon on Fire," was circulated among jihadist forums, including al-Hesbah. The misspelling of the name was intended: calling Hizballah leader Hassan Nasrallah as "Nasr-Ellat" is a reference to a pre-Islamic pagan goddess. The text explains that jihad is an incumbent duty on Sunni Muslims, exacerbated by the Shiites and Hizballah asserting influence in the region over the people. The text includes personal statements such as: "Here he is, the fake Nasr-Ellat declaring his failure, and the failure of his satanic party. And here they are, his followers, the Cross-worshipers who have a history in slaughtering the Lebanese people, went out to the streets, set the green trees and the cars on fire, destroyed the storefronts, and threatened to kill the people."[26]

Another posting about Nasrallah on the al-Hesba Web site claimed: "Let us explain that the party of Hassan Nasrallah, for us, is a party which has a Shia ideology. Thus, he is considered our enemy like our enemies the Jews, the Christians." Suspicions among Sunnis over growing Shiite power have come to the fore during the Iraq war and fighting in Lebanon. Animosity is especially powerful among Sunni militants who adhere to a conservative strain of Islam that views Shiites as infidels. And like many of the region's Sunni leaders, they see Hizballah as a puppet of Iran, whose Shiite Persian majority has traditionally been seen by Arabs as a mortal enemy. A prominent cleric in Saudi Arabia, Sheik Abdullah bin Jabreen, issued an announcement online that said of Hizballah: "The support of that Shiite party is not allowed, and to supplicate for their victory and their establishment is not allowed. We advise the Sunni people to disown them, desert whoever joined them and to reveal the Shiite enmity to Islam and the Muslims." The sheik, like many Sunni militants, belongs to the fundamentalist Salafiya branch of Islam, which regards Shiites as little better than non-Muslims. Osama bin Laden is a Salafist, as was Abu Musab al-Zarqawi. This criticism has provoked some bitter responses on radical Shiite forums. One writer on www.yahosein.com questioned Palestinian loyalty to Hizballah, asking, "For all the assistance the Shiites provide the Palestinians, why don't the Palestinians wave pictures of the Mujahid Hassan Nasrallah or banners of his victorious party?" In the same thread, an Iraqi Shiite named Abu Zeer al-Ghafari said, "Hezbollah should only support the Shiites, because only the Shiites support them."

DEBATES OVER ACTIONS

Terrorist activities are a subject for bitter criticism, not only from outside but also from within. Terrorists and their supporters are often involved in online debates over the legitimacy, rationality, or effectiveness of various actions. These may include, as the next examples illustrate, past activities or future activities.

Debating a Mother's Suicide Action

Reem Raiyshi, a mother of two infants, was sent by Hamas to blow herself up in the Gaza Strip. On January 15, 2004, she killed four Israelis by blowing herself up at a border crossing. This act touched a nerve inside a society that normally celebrates the bombers as heroes. This time many Palestinians expressed shock that Hamas and the Al Aqsa Martyrs' Brigade, which took joint responsibility for the attack, would send a mother to her death, leaving two toddlers behind. Hamas's spiritual leader, Sheik Ahmad Yassin, condoned the use of female suicide bombers from the beginning, although at the time of the first operation, conducted by Al Aqsa Martyrs Brigades, he said that Hamas had enough male volunteers and therefore did not need to deploy women. But after his group sent Raiyshi, he issued a fatwa stating that "jihad is an imperative for Muslim men and women." The Internet was also used by Hamas to respond to its critics. In January 2004 Hamas posted photos on its Internet site of Reem Raiyshi, posing with her two young children. The terror group's posting was an attempt to answer the critics. In the pictures Raiyshi is posing in camouflage dress and the Hamas headband, holding an assault rifle and her three-year-old son, who holds a mortar shell. Sheik Saed Seyam, a Hamas leader, claimed, "This picture shows the outrage the Palestinians have reached. This scene should urge people to ask themselves what motivates women, who are known for their attachment to their children and families, to leave them forever."[27] When the sheikh was asked why Hamas had sent a mother to her death, he answered that there are many volunteers who want to carry out attacks: "Some of them cry [to be chosen], which makes the military leadership submissive to their pressure for this honor."[28]

Debating the Attack on Hotels in Jordan

The Internet also facilitated a critical debate over the November 9, 2005, bombings of Jordanian hotels in Amman by members of al-Zarqawi's network. Three suicide attackers detonated nearly simultaneous explosions at hotels in downtown Amman, killing 67 people and wounding more than 150 others. Following the bombings, al-Qaida in Iraq posted several communiqués on Islamist forums in an attempt to explain the killing of innocent Muslims. The first of these communiqués, posted November 10, was a mere claim of responsibility for the bombings. The second communiqué, also posted on November 10, explained the reasons for choosing the particular locations that were targeted. The third, posted November 11, gave details on the operation and on the individuals who carried it out. And on November 18, a new message referred to the bombings: al-Zarqawi issued an online audio recording in which he reiterated the reasons for the attacks. Addressing the Muslims directly, he explained that that the killing of the celebrants at the wedding feast (in one of the bombed hotels) was totally accidental, and that his organization would never even consider harming innocent Muslims.

In the first communiqué the action is described as meant against the Jordanian king, the "crusaders," and the Jews:

> In spite of the security measures taken by the traitor [King Abdallah] son of the traitor [King Hussein] in order to protect these dens, Al-Qaeda soldiers managed to reach their targets and carry out [their task]. . . . The leaders of infidels in Amman should know that the protective wall that was built for the Jews to the east of the Jordan [River], and the rear base [that was established] for the armies of the Crusaders and of the government of the descendents of Ibn Al-Alqami [i.e., the Iraqi government] are within the range of the jihad fighters and their operations.[29]

In the second communiqué al-Zarqawi explained the reasons for selecting the targets in Jordan: "We saw fit to clarify—primarily for the monotheists—the reasons which motivated the jihad fighters to target these dens, so that everyone will know that we selected these targets only after verifying that they serve as centers for the war on Islam, and as [centers] of support for the Crusader presence in Iraq and Saudi Arabia, and for the Jewish presence in Palestine." In the third communiqué al-Zarqawi was desperate to answer his critics (in the Arab media and even in Jihadi Web sites) and tried to find excuses for choosing Jordan as a target: "They [the suicide bombers] shook these dens of malignancy, heresy and debauchery, which have long served as centers from which the Jews and their followers launch their conspiracies to harm the Muslims under the protection of the leader of the infidels in Amman."

Debating the London 2005 Bombings

A harsh online debate erupted after the London bombings on July 7, 2005. The criticism came from Syrian Mustafa Abd al-Mun'im Abu Halimah, better known as Abu Basir al-Tartusi, a Syrian jihadi scholar residing in London. On July 9, 2005, Abu Basir published a fatwa on his Web site that protested the London bombings and the killing of innocent British civilians.[30] Abu Basir described the London bombings as a "disgraceful and shameful act, with no manhood, bravery, or morality. We cannot approve it nor accept it, and it is denied Islamically and politically." He refused labeling the British citizens as "attackers" (Harbiyyun), emphasizing instead the social alliance (Ahd) of Muslims in the United Kingdom with the British government and society, among which they live. He added, "if this act was done by British Muslims it does not mean that Islam or the Muslim community in the UK approve of this act."

Abu Basir's criticism and fatwa drew many angry responses in jihadi forums.[31] These harsh responses led Abu Basir to publish yet another online declaration on July 11, 2005, under the title "The Love of Revenge or the Legal ruling." In this second announcement he explained that his criticism of the London attacks was not a retreat from his former support of jihad. But, he argued, there should not be any symmetry of revenge between the Muslims and their oppressors. Abu Basir's fatwa and his criticism of the London bombings led to an online response in the form of a long and unsigned long fatwa titled "The Base of Legitimacy for the London Bombings and Response to the disgraceful Statement by Abu Basir al-Tartusi." This response to Abu Basir is similar in form and arguments to the Islamist justifications for the September 11, 2001, attacks. One critic of Abu Basir argued that Muslims need no fatwa or other form of writing, each time an attack takes place on enemy soil since "This is an integral part of the Muslim Sunnah." The Muslims should be glad and show their joy for every tragedy that happens to the infidel oppressors and aggressors, he argues, and stop being sympathetic with them. Moreover, he criticizes the condemnations of the London bombings, claiming that they are contradicting Islam: "I warn my believing brothers to stop criticizing their brothers, the Mujahidin, especially these days."[32]

Debating a Kidnapping

The Army of Islam (Jeish al-Islam), a jihadist group operating in the Gaza Strip which kidnapped BBC reporter Alan Johnston, issued a statement through the Global Islamic Media Front to jihadist forums on June 26, 2007. The posting questioned Hamas and its military wing, the Ezzedeen al-Qassam Brigades, over the kidnapping. Hamas had demanded the release of Johnston, going as far as threatening a military response against the Army of Islam. The group claimed that the Ezzedeen al-Qassam Brigades had "dared" to kidnap two of its members, a field commander and a mujahid, when they were returning from dawn prayer, and believed this action and their siding with Britain was tantamount to abandonment of Islam and denial of Shari'a. They announced to Hamas: "you were not the first to be deceived by the mirage. Do not follow he who sold his religion cheaply to get the satisfaction of Britain. In the Name of Allah, Britain will not be pleased with you unless you follow its religion. So are you going to follow it?!!"[33] On June 27, 2007, a communiqué was issued in the name of Jaysh Al-Islam, reiterating that if its demands are not met, "[Johnston] will remain in captivity for 1,000 years, or will be slaughtered like a lamb." It warned Hamas that if the latter continued in its aggression, Jaysh Al-Islam would respond in kind by declaring an all-out war on Hamas. The Army of Islam also threatened those scholars whom they accused of issuing "misleading fatwas," and reiterated its refusal to negotiate for the release of those they captured, stating: "No haggling and no discussion, even if they remain in captivity for a thousand years or are slaughtered like sheep."

Debating the Use of WMDs

Within jihadi circles there has been a lingering debate as to what role weapons of mass destruction (WMDs) would play in future strategy. Since al-Qaida has taken the role of the ideological and strategic leader for the global jihad, it is noteworthy to monitor al-Qaida's reaction to the debate.[34] Al-Qaida has opened the door for its supporters to use chemical, biological, radiological, and nuclear (CBRN) weapons to further the goals of the global jihad. To this end, al-Qaida has provided the religious, practical, and strategic justifications to engage in CBRN activities. These steps have served to strengthen the acceptance of such weapons among sympathetic audiences, dispelled objections to unconventional attacks and prepared the ground for jihadi leaders to operationalize CBRN weapons into their repertoire of tactics. Moreover, the group has attempted to frame the acquisition and use of CBRN weapons as the religious duty of Muslims.

For example, in 2001 Osama bin Laden stated that "if America used chemical and nuclear weapons against us, then we may retort with chemical and nuclear weapons. We have the weapons as a deterrent." In 2002, al-Qaida spokesman Suleiman Abu Gheith claimed that "we have the right to kill 4 million Americans, two million of them children . . . and cripple them in the hundreds of thousands. Furthermore, it is our obligation to fight them with chemical and biological weapons, to afflict them with the fatal woes that have afflicted Muslims because of their chemical and biological weapons."[35] But al-Qaida needed more than that to overcome the doubts and critics. Until May 2003, al-Qaida did not have sufficient Islamic grounding on which to convincingly justify a WMD attack. In that month, however, a young Saudi cleric named Shaykh Nasir bin Hamid al-Fahd published "A Treatise on the Legal Status of Using Weapons of Mass Destruction Against Infidels." This was an important and detailed fatwa on the permissibility of WMDs in jihad. He stated that since America had destroyed countless lands and killed about 10 million Muslims, it would obviously be permitted to respond in kind.

Shaykh al-Fahd's fatwa was posted online and cited in numerous jihadi sites. It is often quoted in debates on the legitimacy of using WMDs. Why is using WMDs permissible? First, he cites three examples from the Qur'an in which God says that Muslims may respond reciprocally for attacks made on them. "Anyone who considers America's aggressions against Muslims and their lands during the past decades," al-Fahd wrote, "will conclude that striking her is permissible merely on the rule of treating as one has been treated. Some brothers have totaled the number of Muslims killed directly or indirectly by their weapons and come up with a figure of nearly 10 million." Then al-Fahd argues that large civilian casualties are acceptable if they result from an attack meant to defeat an enemy and not an attack aimed only at killing the innocent. "The messenger of God [the Prophet Muhammad]," al-Fahd wrote,

> commanded an attack on the enemy. In many traditions, he attacked others. . . . He was not prevented from this by what we know, namely that he knew that women and children would not be safe from harm. He allowed the attack because the intent of the attackers was not to harm them. . . . Thus the situation in this regard is that if those engaged in jihad establish that the evil of the infidels can be repelled only by attacking them at night with weapons of mass destruction, they may be used even if they annihilate the infidels.

Shaykh al-Fahd concludes by addressing the issue of whether Muslims can kill other Muslims in pursuing jihad in God's name. He says that indeed, the lives of Muslims are considered sacred and there is no permission from God to wantonly kill another Muslim. But, al-Fahd maintains, "If we accept the argument unrestrictedly, we should entirely suspend jihad, for no infidel land is devoid of Muslims. As long as jihad has been commanded . . . and it can be carried out only in this way [i.e., with Muslims being killed in attacks by Muslims], it is permitted." God allows this, al-Fahd explains, "so that the enemy cannot force us to abandon jihad by imprisoning a Muslim among them."

Later that year, purported al-Qaida trainer Abu Muhammad al-Ablaj continued the preparatory justification for eventual WMD use when he stated, "as to the use of Sarin gas and nuclear [weapons], we will talk about them then, and the infidels will know what harms them. They spared no effort in their war on us in Afghanistan and left no weapon but used it. They should not therefore rule out the possibility that we will present them with our capabilities." Al-Ablaj again emphasized the thematic justification of reciprocity concerning WMDs. Although the core of al-Qaida has been primarily concerned with justifying WMD attacks based on reciprocity, Mustafa Setmariam Nasar (a.k.a. Abu Mus'ab al-Suri), a highly experienced jihadi, veteran of the Afghan conflicts, and associate of al-Qaida and the Taliban, has taken another line of justification. Al-Suri's position is similar to the legal judgment of al-Fahd, as indicated when he wrote that "if those engaged in jihad establish that the evil of the infidels can be repelled only by attacking them with weapons of mass destruction, they may be used even if they annihilate all the infidels."

The debate is not over yet: in April 2007 the Islamist Web site Al-Firdaws posted an article by Abu Zabadi titled "Religious Grounds for [Launching] a Nuclear Attack."[36] The article, presented as a response to "recent rumors about Al-Qaeda's plan to attack the U.S. with WMDs such as a nuclear bomb," unequivocally opposes the use of WMDs by Muslims against the West, and attempts to counter the legal justifications for their use recently put forward by some prominent religious scholars affiliated with al-Qaida and other jihad movements. The author's main concern is not the legitimacy of obtaining WMDs for purposes of deterrence, but whether Islam sanctions a first-strike nuclear attack by al-Qaida against the United States or Europe. The author states that such an attack is forbidden, and presents several arguments in support of his position: (1) using WMDs may provoke U.S. WMD counterattack; (2) "If God Wishes to Wipe America Off the Face of the Earth . . . The Matter Is In His Hands"; and (3) "If Bin Laden and His Followers Wish to Respond [to U.S. Attacks] in Kind, They Should [Confront] the Evil Troops on the Battlefield."

The posting of this article sparked a fierce debate among participants on the forum, with some participants supporting the author's reasoning and conclusions, and others forcefully rejecting them. Most of the forum participants who criticized the article took up religious arguments made in the past by prominent contemporary Islamist sheikhs.[37]

Another aspect of the debate focused on the issue of "strike the Infidels when their women and children are with them." The supporters of using WMDs, like one writer named Abdal Al-Sham argued:

> The principle of retribution in kind applies, for example, when the infidels do something that is completely forbidden to Muslims, such as mutilating corpses. It is prohibited for Muslims [to do such a thing] unless the infidels commit [this crime] against Muslims!!! . . . However, striking the infidels when their women and children are with them is permitted independently [of] the principle of retribution in kind.

Moreover, another argument was that "legally, Americans Are Considered a Single Individual":

> It is clear that the elected American government, . . . the military and civil organizations associated with it, and [the American] nation [as a whole] legally constitute "a single individual" when it comes to [responsibility for] the killing of women, children and the elderly . . . by U.S. troops in Muslim lands. This aggression is committed by every American who is [a citizen of] the United States and does not wash his hands of it or keep away from it. . . . Legally, all of them are considered "one individual."

Debating Attacks in Arab Countries

On May 16, 2007, Dr. Naser bin Sulayman al-Omar, a leading Saudi salafi scholar, published on his Web site an article about recent terrorist attacks in Algeria. The article, in a style of a fatwa, was titled "The Position regarding Explosions in Muslim Countries." The article criticizes the killing of innocent Muslims or foreigners on Muslim soil. A response to al-Omar came from one of the new jihadi "Internet scholars," Abu Yahya al-Libi. On July 11, 2007, the Al-Fajr Information Center (run by supporters of global jihad) posted in jihadi forums his response, titled "The Disperse of the Diamonds in Discussing the Denier of the Explosions in Algeria." According to al-Libi, most of the Muslims, in Algeria or elsewhere, are weakened by oppression and only a small group of mujahideen can defend them: "We should fight all the infidels, whether apostates or Crusaders, nationals or foreigners, Arabs or non-Arabs." Al-Libi also opposed the differentiation made by Abu Omar and others between Iraq, Palestine, or Chechnya, where the fight is against the foreign infidel occupation and hence, jihad is legitimate and blessed; and the Arab lands, where it is prohibited since these lands are not occupied. According to al-Libi, "the apostate Arab governments are those that enable the occupation of the foreign infidels in Muslim lands." Therefore, there is no difference at all between the jihad in those occupied lands and in lands occupied by Arab apostates. As Reuven Paz observes, al-Libi's response is therefore not just a reply to al-Omar's opinion but also a fundamental element in the growing debate over terrorist attacks against Muslim civilians or in Muslim lands.[38]

DEBATES BETWEEN SUPPORTERS' WEB SITES

The last form of online debates involves the often harsh exchanges within the communities of sympathizers and supporters of terrorist groups. They often use their Web sites, semiofficially or fully activated by the terrorists, to present their criticism and differences, either within the same community or, more often, challenging other supporters' communities.

Al-Tajdeed Against Al-Hesbah

A major struggle was launched by the al-Tajdeed Web site,[39] operated by the Saudi Islamist opposition located in London, against the al-Hesbah Web site,[40] a leading Islamist site often used for postings of messages from al-Qaida.[41] Al-Tajdeed accused al-Hesbah of serving Arab and Western intelligence agencies. Al-Hesbah was accused of exposing the founders of the famous al-Ansar Web site,[42] including the operator known as "Irhabi 007." On March 5, 2006, al-Tajdeed published an article signed by "Omar bin Hanif," titled "A Series of Exposures of Spies—[Who Is] the Traitor who Sold Irhabi 007?" He stated that the arrest of "Irhabi 007" by the British authorities, and the arrest of GIMF (Global Islamic Media Front) members were caused by al-Hesbah:

> Now the aspects of the plot [that led] to the capture of brother 'Irhabi 007' by the worshippers of the cross have become clear: After the suspicious entrance of [Muhammad] Al-Zuheiri and his aides as supervisors of the jihad websites, Al-Zuheiri gave the IP numbers [i.e., addresses, of the computers from which material was being posted] to the Jordanian intelligence, and these infidels monitored brother ["Irhabi 007"] until they caught him.[43]

Later, on March 26, 2006, a posting by "Abu Al-Dardaa" on the al-Tajdeed site argued: "Since it became known to me that most of the supervisors of the Al-Hesbah site were from Jordan, I have been suspicious . . . because Jordanian intelligence is the most powerful Arab intelligence [apparatus]." For almost a month al-Hesbah stopped operating and al-Tajdeed took advantage of al-Hesbah's temporary silence to launch additional verbal attacks. When al-Hesbah returned to the Internet, al-Tajdeed warned visitors to this rival Web site that their identities may be revealed. During al-Hesbah's absence, al-Tajdeed had also attempted to attract jihadists who had used al-Hesbah forums by promoting alternative Web sites such as al-Akhbar, al-Alamiyya, and al-Ghuraba. However, on April 4, 2006, al-Qaida operatives posted a communiqué rejecting the accusations against al-Hesbah, stating: "we stress that these allegations are false. Everything we know about our brothers in al-Hesbah is good—and even if we assume, for the sake of argument, that [the Web site] had been infiltrated, [we assure you that] every [necessary] precaution was taken in this regard, and that the fall of the brothers had nothing to do with the Internet." Al-Tajdeed responded immediately, arguing that the communiqué was inauthentic and even an attempt by Arab-Zionist intelligence apparatuses to keep up the activity of "the al-Hesbah espionage site." When al-Hesbah reappeared on April 14, 2006, it contained a statement explaining its month-long absence due to numerous attacks and that its activity had been restored after the necessary precautions had been taken.[44]

According to Hazan,

> the sharp rivalry between Al-Tajdeed and Al-Hesbah reflects the struggle between the two rival political forces behind them, . . . conflicts between the Islamist and Jihad websites. These multi-faceted conflicts, which involve an array of individual postings, should not be looked at as a phenomenon of individual Islamist participants battling on the Internet (as has been done thus far by various media and research outlets). Rather they should be seen in a larger context, as a phenomenon reflecting the conflicts between rival Arab and Muslim political forces in whose service these websites operate.[45]

Hamas Supporters versus Fatah Supporters

The battle between the two Palestinian groups, Hamas and Fatah, is in fact a war between Islamism and nationalism. It is also a struggle between two groups each wanting the benefits of leadership—namely, power, prestige, and money. With the demise of the Palestinian leader Yasir Arafat and the corruption and internal splits within Fatah, the way was open for the Hamas landslide victory in the January 25, 2006, election. Since then, power has been divided between Mahmud Abbas (Abu Mazin), the Palestinian Authority's leader and self-styled president, and a Hamas-dominated Parliament and Cabinet. Abbas has unilaterally given himself control over borders, the media, and some security agencies. The Hamas-Fatah conflict is also reflected in online debates between their supporters' Web sites. In December 2006, members of the al-Hesbah forum discussed the Fatah movement and Palestine and its alleged lack of Islamic faith. The debate was triggered by a posting asking: "Why don't the Mujahedeen in Fatah Movement behead Abu Mazen [or Mahmoud Abbas, the Palestinian President and leader of Fatah]?" Members scoff that there are mujahideen in Fatah, and one states that only people similar to Abu Musab al-Zarqawi can do that act, and another claims that Fatah is a "Mafia" organization full of criminals. This derision aimed at Hamas is prevalent throughout the discussion. One member responds in a moderate voice and explains that Hamas and Fatah are the only parties to chose from for the Palestinians, and this is dovetailed by another individual who believes that the Palestinians must be imbued with the "correct path" of Islam and reject sectarianism and factionalism.

An article posted on May 16, 2007, by Sheikh Shaker Al-Hiran on a Palestinian Web site[46] was titled "Oh People and Officers of the Security Forces, Blessed Be He Who Was Killed by Their Hands, They Are the Neo-Khawarij." (*Khawarij*, in Arabic: "those who go out," is the group that during the reign of the third caliph, 'Uthman, accused the caliph of nepotism and misrule, and the resulting discontent led to his assassination. The rebels then recognized the prophet's cousin and son-in-law, Ali, as ruler but later deserted him too and fought against him.) The text is mainly a series of legal arguments aimed at proving that Hamas should be categorized as Khawarij and as such must be fought against. The article responded to the recent cycle of bloodshed between Hamas and Fatah in the Gaza Strip, placing the blame on Hamas and accusing Hamas of acting against a legitimate ruler. After listing their "Khawariji" characteristics, the article recommends that the following measures be taken against Hamas:

> We [should call] upon the media to [invite] their scholars to appear on TV or on the Internet to [be asked] about those criminal murderers. If they say that what they [i.e., Hamas members] do is prohibited, then you should kill them cold-bloodedly, [and you will] be rewarded by Allah for ridding Muslims of their influence and evil. Jews have more mercy towards our nation than [Hamas]. If they [i.e., the scholars] say that their conduct is permitted, then kill their scholars . . . they are all the same.[47]

In a later posting (May 18, 2007) on the Fatah Web site, al-Hiran went even farther, comparing Hamas to the Jews (the posting was titled "The Common Characteristics of Hamas and the Jews"). This article triggered harsh reactions and prompted online messages from readers questioning al-Hiran's existence.

USING THE INTERNET TO DISSOLVE DISPUTES AND DEBATES

As demonstrated in this chapter, online communication used by terrorists and their supporters reveal their inner disputes and campaigns. However, the same arena is also used for bridging gaps, overcoming splits and debates, and dissolving inner conflicts. Let us illustrate some of these bridging functions.

Online Denial of Split

The first measure to dissolve a split is by denying its existence. For example, the salafist Group for Call and Combat (GSPC), an Algerian terrorist group affiliated with al-Qaida, issued a statement on December 21, 2006, denying reports by Algerian press, particularly L'Expression, that the emirs of the group had engaged in conflict over the sharing of wealth garnered from various operations. Claiming that this was a "smear campaign," allegedly for the purpose of tarnishing the image of the mujahideen and jihad, GSPC also argued that the allegations against Yahya Abu al-Haitham, a leader within the GSPC, were all false. According to the posting, al-Haitham was reported as having been removed for his involvement in financial corruption. But GSPC denied all those allegations, stating that al-Haitham was innocent and the fortunes reported was a lie and "myth"; they added that the self-funding of jihad activities barely covered the cost of mujahideen supplies and weapons. GSPC claimed that no inner conflicts ever existed:

> all of them stated that there are conflicts between the leaders of the Salafist Group for Call and Combat over the sharing of the wealth of spoils. . . . And if it is not in our interest to keep the issue of jihad clean and clear . . . and if we were not eager to keep the minds of our Muslim Ummah from being spoiled by the mean media devils, we would not take the trouble to respond to these lies known by everybody who mingled with the Mujahideen, tested their truthfulness, and knew of their giving and abandonment of the greed of life.[48]

Online Attempts to Unite the Insurgents in Iraq

The insurgency in Iraq is comprised of different groups. The Internet is used by them not only to express their autonomous positions but also to bridge gaps and hostilities among them. In February 8, 2006, the Information Department of the Mujahideen Shura Council in Iraq posted an audio online message calling for other insurgency groups to join its ranks.[49] By mid-2006 the Mujahideen Shura Council was composed of seven insurgency groups in Iraq: al-Qaida in Iraq, the Victorious Army Group, the Army of al-Sunnah Wal Jama'a, Ansar al-Tawhid Brigades, Islamic Jihad Brigades, the Strangers Brigades, and the Horrors Brigades. The purpose of the Mujahideen Shura is stated by the posting: "They vowed by Allah that they will not abandon the weapons until the chosen religion prevails or they will die trying to achieve this goal. . . . This council will be, God willing, the center that will gather all the groups working in the same area, around it. Also, it will be a provoking point to other groups which have the proper methods." The posting called upon other insurgency groups in Iraq to align with the council, asking them to join the group whose "hands are stretched and the hearts are open." A day earlier, on February 7, 2006, the Islamic Army in Iraq issued a communiqué stating that a joint operation with mujahideen of the Mujahideen Shura Council and Ansar al-Sunnah was executed in al-A'azamiya, in which several mortar shells and improvised explosive devices were used against "crusaders" and Iraqi forces. According to the message, due to the collaboration of the insurgency groups in the attack, the operation was dubbed "sticking together."

On January 23, 2007, the Global Islamic Media Front (al-Qaida's online mouth-piece) published a document that was distributed among jihadist forums, including the al-Qaida–affiliated al-Boraq network, inviting insurgency groups in Iraq to join the Islamic State of Iraq, as well as offering advice to the State. Emphasizing unity in the ranks of the mujahideen according to the Qur'an and the Sunnah of the Prophet Muham-mad, the author, Abdul Aziz bin Muhammad, argued that fighting in one line and under one flag would enable the Muslims to not appear weak to the enemy nor allow the "cru-saders" and apostates to concentrate attacks on dispersed people or groups. He writes: "You have to know that the separation and turning your back to the group are the reasons for defeat, disappointment and failure, and the reason for losing power."[50]

The issue of Saddam Hussein's execution and the question of him being an infidel or Muslim at the time of his demise caused disputes among members of some jihadist forums. The dispute caused the Global Islamic Media Front (GIMF) and al-Hesbah administrators to react by publishing online statements in January 2007 advising that such discussion to cease for the benefit of more important subjects. Al-Hesbah even threatened to delete any message questioning Hussein being Muslim, stating that their sheikhs had spoken on the issue. The GIMF message chastised forum members for focus-ing so heavily on Saddam Hussein, stating: "is the issue of Saddam's Islamic faith worthy of our neglect of the case of our brothers in Somalia, which is considered to be the case of Islam in Somalia?" and "How can we say that the topic of Saddam is not one of the most preferred, when it kept us busy from the developments of the situations in Iraq? . . . This span of time is not only the most important stage of Jihad in Iraq, but probably one of the most important stages of the struggle between Islam and infidelity in history."[51]

However, postings on the Internet have also denied unity between groups. The lead-ership of Ansar al-Sunnah issued an online statement on March 29, 2007, denying news of rumors that it had agreed to unite with the Islamic Army in Iraq, Salah al-Din al-Ayoubi Brigades of the Islamic Iraqi Resistance Front, and the 1920 Revolution Bri-gades. According to the message, they claim to be "astonished" by this news, and abso-lutely deny any such union: "For our part, as the Ansar al-Sunnah Group, we say: we are very astonished by this news. We have no idea about this subject and there is no such thing. We completely deny the union between the mentioned brigades."

Even within the Islamic State of Iraq, attempts to dissolve inner disputes failed. According to a SITE report,[52] the Islamic Army in Iraq and al-Qaida in Iraq, a constitu-ent group within the Islamic State of Iraq, have been embroiled for some time in con-flict. The conflict was both physical and rhetorical in terms of an information war. It spilled over to the Internet on April 5, 2007, when the Islamic Army brought the dispute public. Accusing al-Qaida in Iraq of murdering mujahideen from other brigades, such as the Mujahideen Army and 1920 Revolution Brigades, and wantonly killing Sunnis whom al-Qaida charged with apostasy—words which were repeated by its spokesmen, Dr. Ibrahim al-Shemari and Dr. Ali al-Na'ami—the Islamic Army in Iraq has since felt the brunt of a jihadist backlash, as the group has been marginalized from the jihadist Internet community. The Islamic Army ultimately announced on June 6, 2007, that a truce was brokered between the two parties involving a ceasefire and forming of a judicial commission to adjudicate all outstanding issues between the two sides.

The Role of Fatwas in Resolving Disputes

Very often, the best way to overcome splits and disagreements is through the publications of religious rules or fatwas. As Moss and Mehkhennet argue:

> The jihad etiquette is not written down, and for good reason. It varies as much in interpretation and practice as extremist groups vary in their goals. But the rules have some general themes that underlie actions ranging from the recent rash of suicide bombings in Algeria and Somalia, to the surge in beheadings and bombings by separatist Muslims in Thailand.[53]

Some of these rules or fatwas are issued by prestigious religious leaders (e.g., the Egyptian Islamic scholar Yusuf al-Qaradawi) and appear in online versions. These fatwas can bridge gaps and solve disagreements since they are often issued to do so and solve lingering dilemmas among terrorist communities. Recent research by Moss and Mehkhennet described six of these basic Jihadi rules. (1) You can kill bystanders without feeling a lot of guilt; (2) you can kill children, too, without needing to feel distress; (3) sometimes, you can single out civilians for killing; bankers are an example; (4) you cannot kill in the country where you reside unless you were born there; (5) you can lie or hide your religion if you do this for Jihad; and (6) you may need to ask your parents for their consent.[54]

Finally, bin Laden himself published an online call to resolve the inner conflict. On October 23, 2007, al-Hesbah posted a 34-minute video featuring a new address by bin Laden titled "To Our People in Iraq." In the video, produced by al-Qaida's media company as-Sahab, bin Laden praises the jihad fighters in Iraq for their steadfast struggle against the "crusader" occupation, which, he says, has brought honor to the Islamic nation. Then he urges them to unite their ranks and to resolve all differences based on Islamic Shari'a. Those who err or sow division among the Muslims, he adds, should be tried according to Islamic law. Last, bin Laden criticizes the phenomenon of jihad fighters who blindly follow the orders of their organizations and commanders, forgetting that infallibility is a virtue that only Allah and the prophet possess.

CONCLUSION

The Internet has become a popular instrument for postmodern terrorists. They use the Internet to spread their propaganda, to coordinate actions, to collect information, to instruct and train their operatives, to find potential recruits, and to launch psychological campaigns.[55] As noted in previous studies, the Internet also became a major channel for terrorist communications and networking. Several reasons explain why modern communication technologies, especially computer-mediated communications, are so useful for modern terrorists in establishing and maintaining their communication networks. Michele Zanini and Sean Edwards suggested several factors:

> First, new technologies have greatly reduced transmission time, enabling dispersed organizational actors to communicate and coordinate their tasks. . . . Second, new technologies have significantly reduced the cost of communication, allowing information-intensive organizational designs such as networks to become viable. . . . Third, new technologies have substantially increased the scope and complexity of the information that can be shared, through the integration of computing with communications.[56]

Also, the Internet connects not only members of the same terrorist organizations but also members of different groups. For instance, dozens of sites exist that express support for terrorism conducted in the name of jihad. These sites and related forums permit terrorists in places such as Chechnya, Palestine, Indonesia, Afghanistan, Turkey, Iraq, Malaysia, the Philippines, and Lebanon to exchange not only ideas and suggestions but also practical information, or, as this chapter illustrates, to conduct their arguments and debates.

Terrorists use the Internet as a channel of communication among groups, within groups, from leaders to operatives, among followers and sympathizers, and among different currents within the same movement. Yet the communication is not always harmonious: it also includes harsh disputes and disagreements. The analysis of the online controversies, disputes, and debates may tell us a lot about the mindsets of terrorists, their motivations, and their doubts and fears. In many ways, it allows us to open a window to a world we know little about. It may also serve those who intend to fight terrorism or to minimize its damages. The war on terrorism is becoming more and more a psychological war fought over hearts and minds . In such wars, learning the cracks within the enemy's forces, leaders, and public is a valuable tool for counterterror propaganda campaigns. Wedge driving, in the case of counterterrorism, is intended to distance followers from their leaders, to widen preexisting splits between terrorist factions, and to promote doubt and distrust within the terrorist community. By learning the inner cleavages and debates one can find practical ways to support the voices against terror, to broaden gaps within these dangerous communities, and to channel the discourse to nonviolent forms of action. The phrase "divide and conquer" (derived from the Latin saying *divide et impera*) may become a more vital component of future forms of counterterrorism campaigns, and for this strategy the Internet should be regarded as a gold mine for learning about terrorists' inner debates and conflicts.

NOTES

1. Conway, 2006; Thomas, 2003; Tsfati and Weimann, 1999, 2002; Weimann, 2004, 2006a.
2. Weimann, 2006a, 2006b.

3. Weimann, 2004. Our monitoring of terrorist Web sites involves tracking them, downloading their contents, translating the messages (texts and graphics), and archiving them according to a preset coding system. This allows for various content analyses focusing on the attributes of the contents, the intended receivers, the technologies used and more.

4. Weimann, 2006b.

5. Paz, 2004a.

6. Ibid.

7. Cited in a special report by the Intelligence and Terrorism Information Center at the Israel Intelligence Heritage & Commemoration Center (IICC), March 22, 2007, http://www.terrorism-info .org.il/malam_multimedia/English/eng_n/html/al_zawahiri_e.htm.

8. Cited in MEMRI's Islamist Websites Monitor no. 9, May 4, 2007, http://memri.org/bin/ articles.cgi?Page=archives&Area=sd&ID=SP157207.

9. Paz 2004b.

10. See www.al-mohajroon.com, January 18, 2007.

11. The full text and translation was provided by Laura Mansfield through http://www.laura mansfield.com.

12. The full text and translation was provided by Laura Mansfield through http://www.laura mansfield.com.

13. Michele Zanini and Sean J.A. Edwards 2001. pp. 43–44.

14. Paz 2003. See also, "Cracks in the Foundation: Leadership Schisms in al-Qaida 1989– 2006," Combating Terrorism Center at West Point (2007), http://www.ctc.usma.edu.

15. Translated by SITE Institute, http://siteinstitute.org/bin/articles.cgi?ID=publications250 4&Category=publications&Subcategory=0.

16. Mansfield 2007.

17. Cited by Mansfeld 2007.

18. Cited by Mansfeld 2007.

19. www.al-boraq.com, January 8, 2007.

20. Yehoshua 2005.

21. Cited by Yehoshua 2005.

22. See http://www.islamonline.net/Arabic/news/2005-09/18/article10.shtml.

23. See http://www.abubaseer.bizland.com.

24. See http://www.h-alali.info/index.php.

25. Cited in MEMRI's Special Dispatch Series no. 1668, July 27, 2007, http://www.memri .org/bin/articles.cgi?Page=archives&Area=sd&ID=SP166807.

26. See www.alhesbah.org, January 26, 2007.

27. Cited in "Happy Snaps of a Suicide Bomber," published in the South African *Star*, January 27, 2004, http://www.thestar.co.za/index.php?fSectionId=129&fArticleId=334925.

28. Ibid.

29. Text were translated and published by MEMRI, see MEMRI Special Dispatch nNo. 1043, December 5, 2005, "Al-Qaeda Explains Amman Bombings Threatens: 'In a Few Days, the Infidel Leaders Will Witness an Event that Will Make [the Amman Bombings] Seem Insignificant," http://memri.org/bin/articles.cgi?Page=subjects&Area=jihad&ID=SP104305.

30. See http://www.abubaseer.bizland.com/hadath/Read/hadath17.doc.

31. The main responses appeared on the salafi forum al-Hesbah. See for example http://www .alhesbah.org/v/showthread.php?t=26865, http://www.alhesbah.org/v/showthread.php?t=26751.

32. Cited by Reuven Paz 2005.

33. From a SITE special report, http://siteinstitute.org/bin/articles.cgi?ID=publications2980 07&Category=publications&Subcategory=0.

34. Wesley, 2005.

35. On al-Qaida's Web site, http://www.alneda.com, then still active.

36. See http://alfirdaws.org/vb/showthread.php?t=28142.

37. See MEMRI's Special Report no. 34, "Contemporary Islamist Ideology Authorizing Genocidal Murder," September 15, 2004, http://memri.org/bin/articles.cgi?.

38. Cited by Reuven Paz 2007.

39. See http://www.tajdeed.org.uk.

40. See http://www.alhesbah.org.

41. Hazan 2006. D. Hazan is director of MEMRI's Islamist-Jihadi Website Initiative.

42. See http://www.al-ansar.org.

43. Quoted in Hazan 2006.

44. Hazan 2006.

45. Ibid.

46. See http://www.palpress.ps.

47. Translated by MEMRI, see Special Dispatch Series no. 1595, May 23, 2007, http://www.memri.org/bin/opener_latest.cgi?ID=SD159507.

48. From SITE special report, http://siteinstitute.org/bin/articles.cgi?ID=publications237506&Category=publications&Subcategory=0.

49. "An Audio Message from the Information Department of the Mujahideen Shura Council Calls for All Insurgency Groups in Iraq to Join their Ranks," SITE report, February 8, 2006, http://siteinstitute.org/bin/articles.cgi?ID=publications146306&Category=publications&Subcategory=0.

50. See http://www.al-boraq.com.

51. See http://www.alhesbah.org, January 7, 2007.

52. Site Institute's Special Report: Islamic State of Iraq Clarifies Recent Developments with Islamic Army in Iraq, June 18, 2007, http://siteinstitute.org/index.html.

53. Moss and Mehkhennet 2007.

54. Ibid.

55. Weimann, 2004; 2006a; see also, Brachman and Forest 2007, "Terrorist Sanctuaries in the Age of Information: Exploring the Role of Virtual Training Camps," *Denial of Sanctuary: Understanding Terrorist Safe Havens*, edited by Michael Innes. London: Praeger Security International.

56. Zanini and Edwards 2001.

4

New Media's Influence on the Assessment of Publicly Communicated Terrorist Threats

M. Karen Walker

THE WIDESPREAD AVAILABILITY AND INFLUENCE of new media has affected our perceptions of the global terrorist threat, the adequacy and reach of counterterrorism measures, and the nature of national and personal resilience. A terrorist group's intent and capability, two factors in threat assessment generally, also bear on our assessment of the group's publicly communicated messages threatening harm. Regarding intent, one may ask whether the communicated threat fits a known pattern of behavior and whether the level of consequence is consistent with the group's ideology and proclivity toward violence. Regarding capability, one may ask whether the group has carried out similar threats in the past. If the threat suggests a progression in violence over past behavior, or if the group or individual is previously unknown, the next step is to determine whether the group has the requisite knowledge, financing, and operational skill to act on the threat.

New media—defined as "electronic technologies that enable the creation, storage, and transmission of digital media content from point to point or point to multipoint"[1]— add three layers of complexity to our assessment of communicated threats. First, new media can act as an accelerant for communicated threats. Public awareness, interpretation, and reaction to a specific threat can erupt in social networks before intelligence analysts and public officials have an opportunity to evaluate the threat or place it in context. The participatory nature of new media allows individuals to comment on, forward and replicate messages anew, complicating public officials' efforts to source and authenticate the message. Second, instilling uncertainty and generating fear through the amplification of the threat across Web sites, news channels, and social networks may be the terrorist group's primary objective. In this case, determining the message's authenticity and sincerity becomes a secondary concern to tracing the diffusion of the threat to multiple audiences and the degree of active information seeking (i.e., information pull) about the threat. Third, benefits and uncertainties of new media accrue to both perpetrators and the public. Taking these factors into account, an understanding of media effects and framing processes can supplement traditional methods of analysis and response to communicated threats.

THE NATURE AND PURPOSE OF COMMUNICATED THREATS

Charting new media's influence on publicly communicated terrorist threats requires parsing of individual terms. This discussion is limited to terrorist threats, distinguished from criminal threats such as extortion. Likewise, this chapter concerns communicated threats that target a group of individuals or a population segment, and may be considered in tandem with or separately from communication surrounding terrorist acts such as hostage-taking. Moreover, a terrorist group's use of new media to issue threats is distinct from the use of new media for recruitment and indoctrination or the operational planning and financing of terrorist attacks. These knowledge areas have been explored comprehensively by authors Jarret Brachman, Michael Dartnell, and Gabriel Weimann, among many others.[2] New media such as satellite television can be used for mass communication, understood as a message from a single source to a large audience. The influence of new media is strongest, however, in public communication—the diffusion and replication of opinion and message content by many with many. The discussion of publicly communicated threats assumes that a given terrorist group purposefully communicates its intent in advance of an attack.

Preliminary Questions about the Group's Intent

A preliminary question is whether the terrorist group's *modus operandi* is to keep its activities secret, either to elude disruption and capture or to maximize surprise. Alternatively, one might ask why a terrorist group would choose to communicate a threat. Situating motives and associated attacks within the theater of terror,[3] or what Brigitte Nacos describes as the post-9/11 "spectacle of terror,"[4] the group's primary (if not single) purpose is to instill uncertainty and fear and otherwise interfere with the quality of life of a community. The January 2008 cancellation of the Dakar Rally, which handed al-Qaida's North African affiliate a propaganda coup, is but one example.[5] If members of the public perceive a communicated threat to be possible—if it fits in with their understanding of terrorist threats generally and "rings true" with what they already know—the specific message can reduce the individual's sense of control, defined as a belief in one's ability to influence outcomes through personal or social action or in dialogue with government officials.[6] An individual's processing of the threat may involve the recognition of constraints—that is, the extent to which factors beyond the individual's control limit protective actions.[7] Put simply, a perceived lack of control and low self-efficacy can increase the potency of a communicated threat.

Beyond the desire to bring previously unsuspecting individuals into the theater or spectacle of terror, a terrorist group may communicate a threat for the purpose of testing the countermeasures of its targeted opponent. In such an instance, the terrorist group's purpose in communicating a threat is to gain comparative advantage by exploiting weaknesses in operational response, protective measures, and the management of public reaction and official communication. The information learned can also aid the terrorist group in reducing risks associated with carrying out a similar threat in the future. A terrorist group may communicate a threat in an attempt to disrupt domestic political processes and foreign policies of enemy governments. For example, al-Qaida's production company, Al-Sahab, released a bin Laden statement prior to the 2004 U.S. presidential election, in which bin Laden implied that states voting against President Bush would be spared from al-Qaida's target sites.[8] A more recent example is the Global Islamic Media Front's (GIMF) explicit ultimatum to the peoples of Germany and Austria, issued on March 11, 2007, that their governments' failure to withdraw troops from Afghanistan would invite terrorist attacks. A subsequent opinion poll conducted by Spiegel Online reported that 57 percent of those surveyed favored the withdrawal of German troops. Whereas one cannot make a definitive correlation between the public's views and the GIMF ultimatum, the poll results as well as government officials' responses and media reaction were incorporated in GIMF's propaganda.[9]

In the exceptional case of a threat to carry out an attack with weapons of mass destruction (WMDs), the group may seek to gain competitive advantage over other terrorist groups and achieve a sense of legitimacy in the eyes of its goal-sharing constituencies and in the group's bargaining with foreign governments.[10] An open question is whether the threat alone would be sufficient to achieve the level of respect the group desires absent the demonstration effect of an improvised nuclear device or radioactive dispersal device or the detectable release of a biological or chemical agent. More certain, the immediacy and specificity of a communicated threat of a WMD attack, and the surrounding information context, guides the public's degree of alarm. The November 14, 2006, media announcement by British counterterrorism officials, forewarning of al-Qaida's efforts to recruit scientists and wage a nuclear attack in the United Kingdom, appears to have been duly but calmly received by the public. As reported by the *Guardian*, "UK officials detected 'an awful lot of chatter' on jihadi websites expressing their desire to acquire chemical, biological, radiological or nuclear weapons."[11] In response to press questions, officials said that they harbored "no doubt at all" that al-Qaida's acquisition efforts were preparatory to an attack against the West, including the United Kingdom, with a nuclear weapon; the officials spoke of al-Qaida's "aspiration," "attempt to get material," and "attempt to get technology."[12]

The media announcement came a day before the unveiling of additional counterterrorism measures and a week after MI5's public warning of at least 30 active plots to attack Britain. Previous news coverage of Abu Ayyab al-Masri's appeal for nuclear scientists, along with experts in other scientific and technological fields, would have conditioned the communication environment and contributed to public awareness. Acknowledging that some members of the public could have discounted counterterrorism officials' warning as an excuse to impose additional security measures, one may infer that the parameters of the counterterrorism officials' briefings gave the British public a manageable spectrum of risk that both reduced uncertainty and bolstered self-efficacy and control. Because the realization of this particular threat depends on the future development al-Qaida's capability, the seriousness with which the public attended to the officials' briefings may have been tempered also by its hypothetical rather than immediate realization.

Preliminary Questions about the Group's Mode of Communication

Having addressed the question of whether and how a publicly communicated threat is consistent with a terrorist group's mode of operation and general intent, a second question concerns how the group introduces its intent to the public. In answer to this question, the terrorist group's Web site content, especially published manifestos and communiqués, may provide sufficient detail for the public to engage in preparedness behaviors. The assessment of Web site content, however, is not as straightforward as one might assume. In a seminal study of content on terrorist groups' sites, Yariv Tsfati and Gabriel Weimann found that almost all the sites surveyed, with the notable exceptions of Hizballah and Hamas, avoided presenting and detailing violent activities.[13] The authors surmise that by refraining from any reference to violent actions and fatalities resulting from attacks, the propaganda and image-building motives of the sites may be preserved.[14] The authors also observed that at the time of the analysis, the Internet sites tended to recycle materials such as books and audio messages that had been previously distributed through mass media and other communication means.[15] The level of specialization achieved by terrorist networks such as al-Qaida suggests that mastery of new media is part of the terrorist organization's learning curve.[16]

In comparison to Web sites known to be affiliated with or sympathetic to terrorist groups and their ideology, hate speech disseminated through online communication is more problematic. Groups that use Web sites to promulgate hate speech—defined as an "expression which is abusive, insulting, intimidating, harassing and/or which incites to violence, hatred or discrimination"[17]—operate in a regulatory and policy environment that strives to balance censoring such speech with freedom of speech. In the United States, hate speech cannot be officially silenced unless it meets the "fighting words" exception,[18] defined as "words that by their very utterance inflict injury or tend to incite an immediate breach of the peace."[19] By this measure, "fighting words" would be a precise and immediately identifiable marker of targeted violence. New media tools that enable individuals' ability to capture, edit, and share videos present additional challenges to owners of sites such as YouTube that rely on community guidelines to manage content. For example, a January 2008 analysis published by the Middle East Media Research Institute found that Islamophobic videos were uploaded to YouTube, despite guidelines prohibiting videos featuring "hate speech which contains slurs or the malicious use of stereotypes intended to attack or demean a particular gender, sexual orientation, race, religion, or nationality."[20] The videos analyzed were produced by residents of Germany, Norway, Spain, Sweden, and the United States; the videos depicted the burning of the Qur'an, incitement to nuke Mecca and the Ka'ba during the Haj, and the slander of Islam and the Prophet Muhammad.[21]

Recent history has signaled the potential danger of diffuse and pervasive ideologies of exclusion and hatred. A notable example is the commingling of white supremacist and American Nazi beliefs with the extreme fringes of the Christian Identity movement as expressed in the *Turner Diaries*, which in turn inspired Timothy McVeigh.[22] Jessica Stern relays a more vivid example in her conversation with members of the "save the babies" movement, a term of reference for pro-life movement members who support murdering doctors and attacking abortion clinics.[23] Quoting member Bob Lokey: "Everything I found on the Internet looked wimpish to me. I wanted to establish my own site that makes the evil of baby murder more clear. I indicted the Supreme Court for its support of baby murder. I explain it all on my website."[24] Not irrelevant to the discussion, Lokey freely admits to Stern that he spent 20 years in San Quentin State Prison for first-degree murder. Movement leader Paul Hill has called for the assassination of Supreme Court justices and also for the use of chemical and biological weapons to thwart the "abortion industry."[25] Reacting to these comments, Stern expresses the view that the most frightening aspect of virtual terrorist networks (and their messaging) is the potential for mass-casualty attacks by small groups with minimal coordination and cross-talk.[26]

The proactive monitoring of terrorist Web sites relies on content analysis tools and techniques. Through content analysis, broadly considered, patterns of communicative behavior and resultant warning norms can be developed over time. Explicit threats registered in traditional media are but one data point.[27] Implicit threats are much more difficult to discern except in hindsight, a lesson learned from the March 11, 2004, bombings of commuter trains in Madrid. In the aftermath, analysts at the Forsvarets Forskningsinstitutt, a Norwegian think tank, recalled a document titled "Jihadi Iraq: Hopes and Dangers," that was published in December 2003 on an Islamist Web site under the banner of the Media Committee for Victory of the Iraqi People, also known as the Mujahideen Services Center.[28] The document did not break through the noise when it first appeared. Working backward, the document reads like a terrorist attack road map, notable for its calculus vis-à-vis the Spanish electoral calendar and rationale for the attacks.[29]

CHARACTERISTICS OF NEW MEDIA

With some insight into the considerations a terrorist group may take into account in deciding whether to issue a public threat, and with what degree of explicitness or subtlety, the selection of traditional or new media becomes a second-order decision. Traditional mass media and new media share the capacity to aid terrorist groups in achieving their communication objectives, including attention-getting and awareness-building for the group's cause, public recognition of the group's motives, accrual of respect and sympathy, and public attribution of a quasi-legitimate status to the group.[30] Distinguishing characteristics of new media are well rehearsed. Conway lists nine key properties that separate the Internet from traditional media and generate its influence: volume of information or data, speed, multimedia format, two-way interactive direction of content, individual control, anonymity, evasion of government control, reduced transaction costs, and global scope.[31] To this list, Weimann adds the ability to shape coverage in traditional mass media that rely on the Internet as a source for stories.[32]

New media, and the Internet in particular, offer the added advantage of meeting the public's requirements for information-seeking and information sufficiency in responding to threats. New media also offer journalists, public officials, and experts a higher degree of flexibility in anticipating the public's questions; for example, within 24 hours of the World Trade Center attacks *Slate* published a detailed civil engineering explanation of why the Towers fell and a full biographical profile of Osama bin Laden.[33] To further illustrate the point, newspaper coverage of bioterrorism threats following the 2001 anthrax attacks failed to provide complete definitions of bioterrorism, bioterror agents that could be used in an attack, or high-efficacy recommendations for citizens' protective action,[34] knowledge gaps that individuals could address through access to official, academic, medical, and social knowledge Web sites.

Reliance on traditional media such as newspapers and television news treats the communicative process as a means to impart information. Speaker–audience interaction is sequential, with the audience placed in a passive receiver role. Expert opinion dominates, and in the case of science-based issues, which come to the fore in discussions of WMDs and emerging threats, the process assumes that scientific knowledge is fixed and certain. By contrast, new media support the generation, sharing, and validation of social knowledge. Social knowledge cannot be discovered or verified through observation of material fact, but rather depends on one's acquaintance with or personal relationship to other people in a social world.[35] New media allow the traversal of social worlds in both physical and virtual space. In the virtual space, communicative relationships—through which claims to knowledge are constructed, tested, and negotiated—are diffuse and non-hierarchical. The language used is colloquial, situated, and immediate.[36]

In sum, new media invite and create incentives for dialogue, initiated by audience members who are active seekers of information and who interpret expert opinion with subjectivity.[37] Whereas individuals use traditional or broadcast media for general information and context, judgments more frequently come from interpersonal relationships and channels based in family, colleagues, and community. Whereas mediated channels predominate as sources of information for issues that pose a perceived risk to society, interpersonal channels predominate for perceived risks to personal welfare.[38] Mental and emotional aspects of decision making converge in computer-mediated communication. Links to official and other expert sources meet cognitive requirements, whereas blogs and social networking sites respond to the affective dimension of information-seeking and use.

Both traditional and new media can aid a terrorist group in waging what many terrorism analysts have called "propaganda of the deed" (with due credit given to various French and Bolshevik revolutionaries and anarchists of the early twentieth century) requiring terrorist groups to calculate how the risk or daringness of an attack and its consequences will play out in subsequent media coverage.[39] Propaganda of the deed disrupts and imbalances the relationship between an elected government and the citizenry within whom its legitimacy rests. The distinguishing characteristics of new media change the risk calculus and increase probabilities that the public's interpretation may differ from the terrorist group's intent. Consider the example of the terrorist cell responsible for the March 2004 Madrid attacks, in which the group selected a traditional media channel to communicate its threat. The cell sent a communiqué to the Spanish daily *Abc* threatening additional attacks unless the Spanish government were to withdraw its soldiers from Afghanistan and Iraq by April 4.[40] The cell also made a video reiterating the threats, which authorities recovered following cell members' near capture and collective suicide. The group's reliance on *Abc* as a communication channel extended two benefits. First, it limited the number of interpretative frames available to the public, and second, the frame selected—the humiliation of the Muslim community—offered substance to select Arab media dedicated to "strengthening of solidarity bonds between Muslims throughout the world by the portrayal of a globally victimized and humiliated Muslim community."[41]

New Media and Diffusion Processes

To summarize and simplify the characteristics that give new media its influence, three watch-words—amplification, coproduction, and diffusion—characterize new media as a communication system or process. Commonly defined in the context of innovation, diffusion theory explains how ideas spread via certain communication channels, over time, among the members of a social system.[42] Diffusion theory incorporates concepts that adapt it well to computer-mediated communication: critical mass, the point at which enough individuals pick up, reinterpret, and resend a message to make further diffusion self-sustaining; reliance on social networks; and reinvention, the process through which an idea or narrative is changed by message recipients.[43] In other words, new media create an organic multiplier effect that is culturally and socially customized to those who participate in the diffusion process.[44] Diffusion through traditional media and word of mouth occurs through a reciprocal relationship of opinion-seekers and opinion leaders. New media and computer-mediated communication in particular have blurred the lines between leader and seeker, with multiple sources of authority beyond expertise, and shared responsibility for generating new knowledge and building communities.[45] This change suggests that online opinion leaders can serve a positive role in responding to communicated threats, alternatively engaging their online networks in taking precautionary and protective measures and acting as a circuit breaker on threats (and hoaxes) that officials deem improbable.

Owing to its characteristics of openness and participation, new media can overtake traditional media in "breaking" a story. The typical cycle through which a story becomes distinct, relevant, and accepted starts in special interest news media with a limited but attentive audience. If the special interest news media make the story sufficiently compelling, it can then migrate to media outlets that are widely accessible to the general public. To offer an example, a story about an impending international crisis that begins in the pages of *Foreign Affairs* may be summarized for the lay public by foreign affairs reporters for major daily newspapers and then further distilled by national news networks. New media short-circuit this process. Attentive consumers of foreign affairs news for whom a particular region or issue has direct and personal significance can obtain information through personal networks over e-mail, or from indigenous news sources available through Web publishing, satellite TV, or satellite radio, and then blog about their interpretation of the situation and offer their own remedies, bypassing altogether traditional media and "official" news framing.

New Media and Media Effects

The foregoing section perhaps overstates the separateness of traditional and new media that in practice interplay and reinforce content. Gabriel Weimann alludes to this symbiotic relationship in his mention of traditional media's sourcing Web sites for information; as previously noted, coverage in traditional media can set the context in which Web-based information is sought, used, and internalized. From a media effects perspective, terrorist groups can use new media tools to prime future coverage in a variety of news and social networking groups. Priming, a theory usually associated with political campaign communication, explains how exposure to a message triggers a specific idea or emotion, increasing the probability that the resulting thought, memory, or emotion will weigh more heavily in interpreting future messages.[46] Adapting the priming process to the counterterrorism context, an example was the November 26, 2007 announcement by al-Qaida's as-Sahab media production wing, posted on an Islamic Web site and subsequently reported by the Associated Press, to expect a message from bin Laden to the "European nations."[47] The release did not specify the format or content of the message, promising only that the statement would come within 72 hours; one could reasonably posit that it raised expectations of a forthcoming threat. On November 29, the Islamist Web site Al-Ekhlaas posted the promised audio message, in which bin Laden portrays European leaders as vassals of the United States and calls on Europeans to pressure their governments to withdraw their forces from Afghanistan.[48]

Priming effects diminish as the number of nodes crossed to reach the public increases, typically following a linear and multistep path. The January 19, 2006, audio message of bin Laden, in which he threatened future attacks on the United States, moved from its originating point on Al Jazeera, to monitoring sites such as the Middle East Media Research Institute, to wire services such as AP, Knight Ridder and UPI, to news outlets as diverse as the *Guardian* of London, the *Statesman* of India, and the *Japan Economic Newswire*. By the time the story reached the American public, the dominant news themes concerned authentication of the message, comparisons to previous ones, and official assurances that the security level would not be raised. A caveat to understanding priming effects in this context is the role of monitoring organizations as gatekeepers who translate and sometimes also help authenticate message content prior to its release to news media. The increasing presence of English-language pages on Arabic-language forums and jihadist blogs in English[49] may shift public surveillance functions from intermediary organizations to the media. Surveillance of the larger environment is a role historically embraced by the media, as a precursor to achieving consensus among segments of society and the transmission of culture, including validation of civil society values. The wider availability of English language sites will also challenge media representatives' service in conferring legitimacy to advocacy groups and leaders of social movements, whose success depends on gaining wider, mainstream attention.

Framing explains how the presentation of issues or causes affects judgment about those issues. In the study of media effects, framing explains how news media construct views and storylines, through headlines and news leads, for example. Frames become shorthand labels for the ideas used to organize both news presentations and personal thoughts about an issue or event, including pertinent definitions, causes, judgments, and remedies. An example of framing regarding Osama bin Laden is presented in Samuel P. Winch's analysis of news coverage in major newspapers worldwide between 1999 and 2002.[50] Winch found that bin Laden was constructed as an evil genius archetype with near mythic abilities, knowledge, and power, a characterization buttressed by attributions of bin Laden's media savvy. This archetype served several functions: giving the United States a worthy adversary, making bin Laden understandable to audiences based on the archetype and familiar narrative of a crusade of good versus evil, and inflating the enemy to help audiences understand the failure to apprehend him. In a similar vein, Jack Lule's analysis of *New York Times* editorials reveals that the *Times* framed the September 11 attacks with a vocabulary that the reading public would find familiar, including "the end of innocence," "victims and heroes," and "the foreboding future."[51] In addition, the news frame selected sacrifice and suffering, as a precursor to healing and recovery, over more martial themes in the nation's response.[52]

Internet-based journalism adds an additional layer of framing and interpretation. Quoting AlterNet.org senior editor Tamara Straus:

> Never before have so many people ostensibly had access to so much news and opinion from so many sources. Never before has it been possible to gauge so many viewers— not only in the United States—but from Europe and the Middle East. Public opinion is now vulnerable to what is reported outside the [American] news borders.[53]

Individuals employ frames to locate, perceive, identify, and label occurrences or life experience,[54] making them active participants in coproducing a narrative. Consequently, frames do not appear constructed whole; rather, they gain in complexity and coherence over time as new data points are incorporated. To participate effectively, individuals exercise some level of deliberate, heuristic, or paradigmatic choice in adopting or supplanting a dominant frame. The element of choice implies that individuals assign meaning to events independently and heterogeneously. To highlight the point, an experimental study on the interpretation of a news story about a Ku Klux Klan rally found significant variance in tolerance for the event, depending on whether the right to free speech or the preservation of public order framed the story.[55] Choices are aided (or conversely constrained) by individuals' capacity to access cultural and rhetorical resources, elevating framing to an ideological contest over who is responsible for and who is affected by the issue at stake.[56]

TERRORIST GROUPS' NEW COMMUNICATIVE ENVIRONMENT

The coproduction and competition among interpretive frames presents benefits and detriments to the terrorist organization interested in taking a threat public. If a terrorist organization seeks a high degree of control over how its message is interpreted, a low-profile communication strategy—relying on traditional media, paired with a relatively static Web site—may be preferred to reduce the risk of unintended diffusion or misinterpretation of the group's message. Alternatively, some terrorist groups and networks, including al-Qaida and its affiliates as the most prominent, may seed public discourse to achieve the purposeful amplification of the threat. Because speculation creates uncertainty in the amplification process, the effect may be especially dynamic and virulent if the threat is outside the public's experience.

Through diffusion and amplification, new media offer the potential for nearly instantaneous and wide audience reach. New media also offer terrorist groups the capacity to implement demonstration strategies, such as simulations of attacks, training videos, and suicide bombers' declarations of intent, with relatively little risk of disruption or capture. Further, new media support indirect messaging, in which the intended audience is different from the audience directly addressed. These advantages are balanced with potential negatives. The group loses the ability to test the public's reaction and to self-correct or save face. If the terrorist group benefits from state sponsorship, the underestimation of the reach and intensity of the threat's amplification can make the group appear unreliable, jeopardizing continued support or safe harbor. Because diffusion processes are unpredictable, the terrorist group cannot easily segment its constituencies and could generate schisms among its base of supporters. Extensive diffusion and amplification also exposes the threat to enhanced scrutiny from multiple knowledgeable parties in addition to officials directly charged with analysis and authentication tasks.

Leaderless Resistance

Functioning as an open communication system, new media are especially advantageous to terrorist groups that form and operate through leaderless resistance. The doctrine of leaderless resistance was developed by Louis Beam, the self-described "ambassador at large, staff propagandist and 'Computer Terrorist to the Chosen' of the Aryan Nations."[57] Individuals and groups operate independently of each other, and never report to a central headquarters or single leader for direction or instruction. Ideological content on the group's Web sites and news coverage of group actions serve group cohesiveness. Elaborating on previous research on leaderless resistance as a strategy that terrorist groups adopt to avoid detection, infiltration, and prosecution, Paul Joosse argues that leaderless resistance has allowed the Earth Liberation Front (ELF) to avoid ideological disunion in its calls for direct action to halt the degradation of nature.[58] ELF began as a splinter group of Earth First!, itself conceived as the radical arm of the environmental movement. After Earth First! evolved its strategy from wilderness protection to systemic change, ELF not only adopted but intensified the rhetoric of agitation, adding arson to its ecodefense arsenal. New media, and Web sites in particular, continue to play a major role in ELF's direct action strategy. The group uses Web sites to disseminate guidelines, provide instructions on how carry out direct actions successfully, and report on direct actions committed in its name.[59] Therefore, new media allow ELF to recenter its energy on direct action that individual activists can justify on multiple ideological grounds.

NEW MEDIA'S INFLUENCE ON RESILIENCE IN PUBLIC RESPONSE

Whereas diffusion and amplification generate both positive and negative considerations for terrorist groups' use of new media to communicate threats, the participatory and interactive nature of new media entail both positive and negative implications for public response. From a preparedness perspective, the public may experience difficulty maintaining vigilance throughout a nearly constant stream of threat and intelligence assessments and scenarios that fill up a 24/7 news cycle. Members of the public for whom terrorism and homeland security issues are especially salient may project their individual anxieties into the public domain. Nevertheless, the interactive capacity of new media provides a more robust remedy to public concern about terrorism. New media create space for dialogue, conflict resolution, consensus building, and relationship development, strengthened by social roles and cultural ties that inform individuals' perceptions of risk. When a communicated threat has been officially discounted, government officials' participation in constructing the narrative gives people the cues they need to go about their business and follow individual pursuits in relative stability while maintaining appropriate vigilance.

As a mechanism for coproduction and public participation, new media reduce the potential for a rhetorical crisis, defined as a situation "in which rhetors lack adequate language to define, explain and assimilate urgent events, and audiences struggle to understand information or set criteria for evaluating policy and locating viable options for action."[60] The participatory nature of new media can speed corrective information when the threat is misattributed or misdiagnosed and can aid the evaluation of a threat, should technical and social reasonings become confused. The learning and perspective-taking that occurs through Web-based communication may compensate for situations in which costs and benefits are unequally distributed across a society, or when information alone cannot resolve the collision of self-interested opinions. Additional benefits of reliance on the Internet include the ability to quickly deliver information to a wide range of people with a depth that is not achievable in broadcast formats, and to allow simultaneous access to customized content. Innovative tools such as interactive tutorials are promising, and the convenience, detail, and currency are attractors in information-seeking behavior. These benefits must be balanced, however, with ongoing concerns about quality assurance of information and equitable access.

Beyond messaging, new media aid in the activation of social networks in response to a communicated terrorist threat or actual attack. In *Terror in the Name of God*, Jessica Stern describes the phenomenon of swarming, which involves widely dispersed but networked units converging on their targets from multiple directions. A swarm is able to coalesce rapidly and with stealth against a target, with equally rapid and stealthy dispersal.[61] Stern's examples include the Chechen resistance, the Zapatista movement, and the "Battle of Seattle" against the World Trade Organization. Whereas these examples match Stern's context of leaderless resistance movements, swarming can also be a phenomenon to aid the public good. In response to a threat or attack, "smart swarms"—empowered individuals aided by technologies designed to ensure situational awareness and mobile communication—can act quickly and with flexibility to provide aid and bridge gaps in official responses.

Another response that is unique to new media involves the use of humor in recovery and resilience. Russell Frank's analysis of digital images created through Photoshop and shared via the Internet charts a barometer of emotional response that is inaccessible through conventional media. The images express emotions too raw to be covered in the news media and thus function as both an emotional outlet and a protest against the decorousness of the press.[62] Frank incorporated in his analysis 41 images that he personally received through his own online networks and discussion groups between September 11 and November 1, 2001, supplemented by a Web search, which surfaced an additional 26 images.[63] The images expressed both victimhood and revenge.[64]

In the revenge motif, the images sometimes used an ironic frame. Bombing Afghanistan back to the Stone Age didn't make sense, given it was "already stuck there"; cyber-cartoon magazines instead showed the country transformed into either a lake or a parking lot. Parodying humorous commercials was also a popular tactic, such as a take-off of MasterCard's "Priceless" ad campaign. Concerning victimization, the graphic artists took a darker view at the precariousness of life, exemplified in the image of "tourist guy," sometimes called "Ground Zero Geek," which became its own saga.[65] In the original image, a blissfully unaware tourist stands on the observation deck of the World Trade Center as one of the planes approaches from behind. Contradictions in the visual details (e.g., the tourist's winter coat, the clarity of the image of the plane) readily revealed the photo as a hoax, which led to parodies of the hoax itself. Using Photoshop, graphic artists replaced the plane with a subway car, a hot air balloon, and even the Ghostbusters Marshmallow Man. Ground Zero Geek also made appearances in images of other disasters, including the easily recognized limousine view of the Kennedy assassination. When images of the initial hoax replaced the Tourist Guy with Osama bin Laden, the emotional cycle of victimization and vengeance became complete.[66]

Frank's exploration of the use of Photoshop and other digital imaging tools is a clear example of how individuals use their innate creativity to aid in recovery and build resilience. Such creativity, with a greater emotional range, is on full display in the We're Not Afraid Web site, a series of galleries of photographs and visual artworks. The site describes itself as

> an outlet for the global community to speak out against the acts of terror that have struck London, Madrid, New York, Baghdad, Basra, Tikrit, Gaza, Tel-Aviv, Afghanistan, Bali, and against the atrocities occurring in cities around the world each and every day. It is a worldwide action for people not willing to be cowed by terrorism and fear mongering.[67]

Regrettably, the small team of individuals who generated the We're Not Afraid site (as a nonprofit) did not have the wherewithal to maintain a dynamic site. The galleries, team blogs, and hotlinks are preserved online, a permanent reminder of the 2005 terrorist attacks in London.

These examples of individuals' interaction through the Internet and with digital media sublimate the more imperative issue of individuals' capacity for deliberation and critical evaluation within the public sphere, which Gerard Hauser defines as "a discursive space in which individuals and groups associate to discuss matters of mutual interest and, where possible, to reach a common judgment about them."[68] Critical norms associated with authority, appropriateness, correctness, and convincingness reside in and are regulated by the discursive practices that people use to explain material facts of a world that is socially constructed.[69] Officials can better appreciate and understand the influence of new media by expanding its definition from a mere information source to a medium of public discourse, with its users engaged in the communal framing and construction of meaning.

Recent developments within the public diplomacy arena exemplify this change of perspective. America.gov, the redesigned Web site for overseas audiences, aims to present information about America and its policies in ways that are interesting and engaging. Interactive fora, spot polls, blogs, and chats are among the features that encourage mutual ownership of the site's content and promote empowerment through information-seeking and dialogue.[70] Advancing the mission of information programs are the State Department's rapid response teams, who respond to the daily agenda of the foreign press with sound bites that meet journalists' expectations for simple, memorable, and quotable remarks. Complementing the rapid response teams are the department's media hubs located in Brussels, London, and Dubai that offer media availabilities with U.S. officials (often traveling to or transiting through these locales) to Arab and other news outlets. The London hub, for example, is able to draw on the talents of more than 15,000 official visitors to brief the British, European, and Arab media on key issues. The Arabic-speaking spokesperson in the Dubai hub appears daily on Arab satellite television, providing an American perspective in the most influential Middle East media outlets.

The Internet and associated new forms of mediated dialogue and exchange have posed a unique challenge to the State Department's Bureau of International Information Programs. Adhering to the provisions of the Smith-Mundt Act, the Department's international broadcasting and information programs are separated from public affairs and domestic outreach. With the advent of Internet-based communication, the Department can no longer compartmentalize receivers of information content by foreign and domestic consumption.[71] This new dimensionality of international information programs requires careful attention to framing of official responses. Message framing is a particular area of expertise of the Counterterrorism Communication Center, whose staff members understand which vocabularies have resonance within the foreign audiences for whom messages are intended and help craft messages accordingly.

New media have also allowed the State Department to blend its cultural, intellectual, and professional interactions of people-to-people diplomacy with information exchange. Following the conventional wisdom that public diplomacy is most effective in face-to-face interaction, new media allow "a three foot conversation with a whole lot of people."[72] Guiding this transition from official policy to the blogosphere is the department's digital outreach team, organized under the auspices of the Bureau of International Information Programs. As explained by Duncan MacInnes, a senior public diplomacy official with the U.S. Department of State,[73] the team members, who are fluent in Arabic, Urdu, and Persian, join in conversations that are taking place in mainstream Web sites within the Arab and Muslim public spheres. Rather than address policy issues with prepackaged press releases and guidance, the team relays the American perspective as a conversation introduced through a shared lens, such as poetry, and in discussion of shared interests, such as global sporting events. The members generate their postings

and replies without official guidance or clearance. They do identify themselves as affiliated with the U.S. Department of State. The majority of Web site hosts and fellow bloggers have been surprisingly welcoming to their presence as a way to avoid insularity in
discussions, providing a counterpoint for their usually critical views of the United States
and widening the diversity of opinions that give the Arab and Muslim public spheres
their robust and multilayered character. In addition, the digital outreach team takes the
long-term perspective on encouraging alternative and new ideas, nurtured in conversations that play out over many exchanges and across multiple online forums. Based on
the positive reaction to the digital outreach teams, MacInnes foresees opportunities for
the expansion of the effort to other regions, involving individuals conversant in Russian
and the languages spoken by the larger population segments in Malaysia, Indonesia, and
Somalia.

This comprehensive perspective of new media as a sphere of public discourse suggests that media literacy may be the most effective countermeasure to publicly communicated terrorist threats. Media literacy includes individuals' familiarity and comfort
level with the use of new media. Media literacy also involves competence to participate
in online debate; the recognition and critical evaluation of motivational terms such as
<liberty,> <freedom,> and <security>; the ability to discuss public issues in their full
complexity; the ability to draw on and speak to cultural and historical memory; and the
willingness to uphold civility in public discourse. The achievement of a higher degree of
media literacy potentially may replace adversity in the public sphere—the competitive
practice of individuals and collectivist groups claiming their rhetorical space by wrest-
ing it from others and maintaining its defense—with a more hopeful, unitary, and organic
expression.

NOTES

1. Bruce Klopfenstein, "Terrorism and the Exploitation of New Media," in *Media, Terrorism
and Theory: A Reader*, ed. Anandam P. Kavoori and Todd Fraley (New York: Rowman & Littlefield, 2006), 109.

2. See Jarret M. Brachman, "High-Tech Terror: Al-Qaeda's Use of New Technology," *Fletcher
Forum of World Affairs* 30, no. 2 (Summer 2006): 149–164; Michael Y. Dartnell, *Insurgency
Online: Web Activism and Global Conflict* (Buffalo, NY: University of Toronto Press, 2006); and
Gabriel Weimann, *Terror on the Internet: The New Arena, the New Challenges* (Washington, DC:
U.S. Institute of Peace, 2006).

3. Gabriel Weimann, "The Theater of Terror: Effects of Press Coverage," *Journal of Communication* 33, no. 1 (Winter 1983): 38.

4. Brigitte L. Nacos, *Mass-Mediated Terrorism: The Central Role of the Media in Terrorism
and Counterterrorism* (New York: Rowman & Littlefield, 2002), 37.

5. Jamey Keaten, "Terror Threats Cancel Dakar Rally," AP Online, January 4, 2008, accessed
through NewsEdge. Information about the race is available on the Dakar Rally's official Web site,
http://www.dakar.com/indexus.html.

6. Michael Palenchar and Robert Heath, "Strategic Risk Communication Campaigns: Some
Insights from the culmination of a Decade of Research," paper, International Communication

Association (Dresden, Germany, June 19–23, 2006), 8. Controllability is among the central factors in risk communication identified by Vincent T. Covello. Additional factors that could be triggered by a communicated threat depend more precisely on the message content, and involve dimensions of catastrophic potential, uncertainty, familiarity (e.g., conventional explosives versus WMDs), dread, and how consequences would affect children and future generations.

7. Linda Aldoory and Mark A. Van Dyke, "Roles of Perceived 'Shared' Involvement and Information Overload in Understanding How Audiences Make Meaning of News About Bioterrorism," *Journalism & Mass Communication Quarterly* 83, no. 2 (Summer 2006): 348.

8. "Islamist Websites as an Integral Part of Jihad: An Overview" (Washington, DC: Middle East Media Research Institute, February 21, 2007).

9. "How Islamist Internet Forums Are Used to Inform Mujahideen of News from Western Media" (Washington, DC: Middle East Media Research Institute, June 8, 2007).

10. Bruce Hoffman, *Terrorism and Weapons of Mass Destruction: An Analysis of Trends and Motivations* (Santa Monica, CA: RAND, 1999), 13.

11. Vilcram Dodd, "Al-Qaida Plotting Nuclear Attack," *Guardian,* November 16, 2006, 6.

12. Ibid.

13. Yariv Tsfati and Gabriel Weimann, "www.terrorism.com: Terror on the Internet," *Studies in Conflict and Terrorism* 25 (2005): 321.

14. Ibid., 322.

15. Ibid., 323.

16. See Horacio R. Trujillo and Brian A. Jackson, "Organizational Learning and Terrorist Groups," in *Teaching Terror: Strategic and Tactical Learning in the Terrorist World,* ed. James J. F. Forest (New York: Rowman & Littlefield, 2006), 52–68.

17. Irene Nemes, "Regulating Hate Speech in Cyberspace: Issues of Desirability and Efficacy," *Information & Communication Technology Law* 11, no. 3 (2002): 196.

18. Ibid., 195.

19. Michael J. Mannheimer, "The Fighting Words Doctrine," *Columbia Law Review* 93, no. 6 (October 1993): 1527.

20. R. Barducci, "Burning the Koran on YouTube: Islamophobia on Video-Sharing Websites (II)," *Inquiry & Analysis,* no. 417 (Washington, DC: Middle East Media Research Institute, January 30, 2008).

21. Ibid.

22. Mark Juergensmeyer, *Terror in the Mind of God: The Global Rise of Religious Violence,* 3rd ed. (Berkeley: University of California Press, 2003), 33–35.

23. Jessica Stern, *Terror in the Name of God: Why Religious Militants Kill* (New York: HarperCollins, 2003), 147.

24. Ibid., 153.

25. Ibid., 152.

26. Ibid.

27. Robert M. Clark, *Intelligence Analysis: A Target-Centric Approach* (Washington, DC: CQ Press, 2004), 161.

28. Lawrence Wright, "The Terror Web," *New Yorker,* accessed December 8, 2007 http://www.newyorker.com/archive/2004/08/02/040802fa_fact.

29. Ibid.

30. Brigitte L. Nacos, *Mass-Mediated Terrorism: The Central Role of the Media in Terrorism and Counterterrorism* (New York: Rowman & Littlefield, 2002), 20.

31. Maura Conway, "Terrorism and New Media: The Cyber-Battlespace," in *Countering Terrorism and Insurgency in the 21st Century: International Perspectives,* vol. 2, *Combating the*

Sources and Facilitators, ed. James J. F. Forest (Westport, CT: Praeger Security International, 2007), 364–365.

32. Gabriel Weimann, "www.terror.net: How Modern Terrorism Uses the Internet" (Washington, DC: U.S. Institute of Peace, March 2004), 3.

33. Andrew J. Glass, "The War on Terrorism Goes Online," in *Terrorism, War, and the Press*, ed. Nancy Palmer (Hollis, NH: Hollis Publishing, 2003), 53–54.

34. Sun Mi Chun, "U.S. Newspaper Coverage of Bioterrorism After the September 11 Attacks," PhD diss., Iowa State University, 2005, 59.

35. Thomas B. Farrell, "Knowledge, Consensus, and Rhetorical Theory," *Quarterly Journal of Speech* 62, no. 1 (February 1976): 5.

36. Maurice Charland, "Searching for the Rhetorical Sphere," *Review of Communication* 3, no. 2 (April 2003): 106.

37. Michael Palenchar and Robert Heath, "Strategic Risk Communication Campaigns: Some Insights from the Culmination of a Decade of Research," paper, International Communication Association annual meeting (Dresden, Germany, June 19–23, 2006), 5.

38. Sharon Dunwoody and Kurt Neuwirth, "Coming to Terms with the Impact of Communication on Scientific and Technological Risk Judgments," in *Risky Business: Communicating Issues of Science, Risk, and Public Policy*, ed. Lee Wilkins and Philip Patterson (Westport, CT: Greenwood , 1991), 20.

39. Brigitte L. Nacos, *Mass-Mediated Terrorism: The Central Role of the Media in Terrorism and Counterterrorism* (New York: Rowman & Littlefield, 2002), 13.

40. Rogelio Alonso, "The Madrid Attacks on March 11: An Analysis of the Jihadist Threat in Spain and Main Counterterrorist Measures," in *Countering Terrorism and Insurgency in the 21st Century: International Perspectives*, vol. 2, *Lessons from the Fight Against Terrorism*, ed. James J. F. Forest (Westport, CT: Praeger Security International, 2007), 205–206.

41. Ibid., 217.

42. Everett M. Rogers, "A Prospective and Retrospective Look at the Diffusion Model," *Journal of Health Communication* 9 (2004): 13.

43. Ibid., 19.

44. Tao Sun and others, "Online Word-of-Mouth (or Mouse): An Exploration of Its Antecedents and Consequences," *Journal of Computer-Mediated Communication* 11 (2006): 1105.

45. Ibid., 1111.

46. Douglas M. McLeod, Gerald M. Kosicki, and Jack M. McLeod, "Resurveying the Boundaries of Political Communications Effects," in *Media Effects: Advances in Theory and Research*, ed. Jennings Bryant and Dolf Zillmann (Mahwah, NJ: Lawrence Erlbaum, 2002), 215.

47. "Al-Qaida Wing: Bin Laden Message Coming." AP Online via NewsEdge, November 27, 2007.

48. "Bin Laden's Message to the Europeans," Special Dispatch of the Jihad and Terrorism Studies Project, no. 1776 (Washington, DC: Middle East Media Research Institute, November 30, 2007).

49. "Jihadists Broaden Reach by Launching English-Language Forums, Blogs," Special Dispatch of the Jihad & Terrorism Studies Project, no. 1777 (Washington, DC: Middle East Media Research Institute, December 4, 2007).

50. Samuel P. Winch, "Constructing an 'Evil Genius': New Uses of Mythic Archetypes to Make Sense of bin Laden," *Journalism Studies* 6, no. 3 (2005).

51. Jack Lule, "Myth and Terror on the Editorial Page: The *New York Times* Responds to September 11, 2001," *Journalism & Mass Communication Quarterly* 79, no. 2 (Summer 2002): 280.

52. Ibid.

53. Andrew J. Glass, "The War on Terrorism Goes Online," in *Terrorism, War, and the Press*, ed. Nancy Palmer (Hollis, NH: Hollis Publishing, 2003), 61.

54. Erving Goffman, *Frame Analysis: Essays on the Organization of Experience* (New York: Harper and Row, 1974), 21.

55. Baldwin Van Gorp, "The Constructionist Approach to Framing: Bringing Culture Back In," *Journal of Communication* 57 (2007): 69.

56. Zhongdang Pan and Gerald M. Kosicki, "Framing as a Strategic Action in Public Deliberation," in *Framing Public Life: Perspectives on Media and Our Understanding of the Social World*, ed. Stephen D. Reese and others (Mahwah, NJ: Lawrence Erlbaum, 2001), 40.

57. Jessica Stern, *Terror in the Name of God: Why Religious Militants Kill* (New York: HarperCollins, 2003), 151.

58. Paul Joosse, "Leaderless Resistance and Ideological Inclusion: The Case of the Earth Liberation Front," *Terrorism and Political Violence* 19, no. 3 (Fall 2007): 352.

59. Ibid., 354.

60. Thomas B. Farrell and G. Thomas Goodnight, "Accidental Rhetoric: The Root Metaphors of Three Mile Island," reprinted in *Landmark Essays on Rhetoric and the Environment*, ed. Craig Waddell (Mahwah, NJ: Lawrence Erlbaum, 1998), 76.

61. Jessica Stern, *Terror in the Mind of God: Why Religious Militants Kill* (New York: HarperCollins, 2003), 151.

62. Russell Frank, "When the Going Gets Tough, the Tough Go Photoshopping: September 11 and the Newslore of Vengeance and Victimization," *New Media & Society* 6, no. 5 (2004): 633.

63. Ibid., 637–638.

64. Ibid., 635.

65. Ibid., 646–648.

66. Ibid., 651.

67. We're Not Afraid!, http://www.werenotafraid.com/about.html, accessed December 6, 2007.

68. Gerald A. Hauser, *Vernacular Voices: The Rhetoric of Publics and Public Spheres* (Columbia: University of South Carolina Press, 1999), 61.

69. Ibid.

70. Duncan MacInnes (senior public diplomacy official, U.S. Department of State), in discussion with the author, January 18, 2008.

71. Allen W. Palmer and Edward L. Carter, "The Smith-Mundt Act's Ban on Domestic Propaganda: An Analysis of the Cold War Statute Limiting Access to Public Diplomacy," *Communication, Law & Policy* 11, no. 1 (Winter 2006): 2.

72. Duncan MacInnes (senior public diplomacy official, U.S. Department of State), in discussion with the author, January 18, 2008.

73. Ibid. See also Neil MacFarquhar, "At State Dept., Blog Team Joins Muslim Debate," *New York Times*, September 22, 2007, A1.

5

The Terrorist Spectacular and the Ladder of Terrorist Success

Cori E. Dauber

IT HAS BEEN WIDELY ACCEPTED for some time in the literature on terrorism that the metric that has the most meaning for terrorists is not necessarily people killed or property destroyed, but rather the amount of attention their attacks receive—which in a media age means the amount of press coverage. The role played by press coverage is equally important to modern insurgencies, which now frequently borrow from the terrorist playbook. Colonel Kenneth Tovo, commander of the U.S. Army Special Forces 10th Group and commander of the Combined Joint Special Operations Forces Task Force, Arabian Peninsula in Iraq during 2006 made this historical comparison:

> I would say that at least for Iraq it's almost always been a media fight . . . When you look at insurgent movements in history, clearly there are some [insurgencies] that thought they could win militarily. But in the end, really the center of gravity is always the people. You're always fighting a battle for the hearts and minds of the people, so I don't think it has changed with the rise . . . of the internet and cameras everywhere, it's just easier for insurgents to reach the people . . . I think the insurgents in Iraq clearly don't think they have any hope of beating us militarily. It's purely a fight for influencing the population [and] the U.S. population, to lose heart and will, [and] influence[ing] the other international actors to drop support for the U.S. effort. So I'd say the information component has grown in importance over time.[1]

Yet despite the fact that the importance of coverage to terrorists has been acknowledged in the literature for years—with analysts going so far as to suggest that the amount of coverage received serves as a metric for terrorist groups—no one has developed a systematic view of what such a metric might look like. Can the way the press differentiates between attacks be used as a metric?

Yes, because there is an order of progression, from minor attack to Terrorist Spectacular, that moves up not in terms of the degree of damage done or how many are killed (the measures which may be most important to *us*). The degree of media attention given a particular event does not always run parallel to the amount of violence done and can be used to assess how successful a particular terrorist attack might have been from the perspective of the perpetrators.

The amount of coverage an attack receives can be charted on what might be called a "Ladder of Terrorist Success." This also gives us a way to produce measurements that are not purely subjective. What makes one act of terrorism, as opposed to another, a "Terrorist Spectacular?" The Terrorist Spectacular is the attack that reaches the final rungs on the Ladder of Terrorist Success. And those rungs are met by specific, measurable levels of coverage.

This chapter describes the various rungs of the ladder in terms of the measurable amounts of press coverage a terrorist attack can receive and discusses the specific qualities and characteristics of attacks that appear to trip the threshold required by the press in order to be treated as a Terrorist Spectacular. Additionally, the discussion explores whether these metrics, which can be applied to terrorist attacks which occur around the world, also apply to those in Iraq and what might explain any differences that do exist. Finally, some suggestions are offered based on this research for more responsible press coverage of terrorist violence.

THE LADDER OF TERRORIST SUCCESS AND THE TERRORIST SPECTACULAR

Trees That Didn't Fall: The Attack That Isn't Reported at All

Some terrorist attacks (perhaps the majority) are complete failures in that they are never reported in the press. To be clear, many terrorist attacks will never be reported in the *American* press because they are a part of conflicts that Americans are not interested in, and this will not be considered a failure from the perspective of those terrorist groups because shaping the attitudes of the American population was not their goal. For example, up until recently, the majority of suicide attacks were committed by the Tamil Tigers fighting against the Sri Lankan government,[2] a conflict which has received substantial press coverage in Canada and Australia, countries with large Tamil diaspora populations,[3] but almost no attention from American outlets. That is different from an attack flying completely below the media radar.

Why would an attack escape the attention of the press? It might simply be too small, although, as will be discussed below, in the context of Iraq, the size that will attract the media's attention is relative, with the bar shifting over time in that conflict. It might be a function of where the attack took place, with some conflicts being simply too remote to matter to anyone not involved or for word to reach the outside world. (Most attacks against the oil industry in Nigeria may simply be too remote to be reported except through official channels.) It might be a function of what else has happened that day, what other events the attack has to compete against for the media's attention. In the immediate aftermath of Hurricane Katrina, for example, essentially no other news broke through American television for a period of days.[4]

Other attacks go unreported because the American press categorizes them as not relevant to any conflict the United States is participating in, because it is standard practice to delink attacks against Western European or Canadian targets from those in the

United States, rather than categorizing them as part of the same overall global insurgency.[5] Thus, for example, while there was some coverage in the United States of the riots around the world in response to the publication in Denmark of cartoons believed by some to insult Islam, there was almost no reportage of the subsequent rioting in Denmark the following year after Danish papers republished the cartoons or of arrests of several men plotting to kill one of the cartoonists.

Under the Spotlight: The Stand-Alone Story

At the next highest rung of the ladder, the first that could be considered a success by those launching an attack, the attack would be treated as so serious that a story should be devoted to that attack and that attack alone. If you consider the regular daily coverage coming out of Iraq (during the periods when Iraq is in the news), the typical story functions as a "round-up" of events, heavily focusing on acts of violence. Thus during the period when levels of violence were high, one saw stories which told the viewer that there was a suicide bombing here and one there, an IED attack here and two there, and this many bodies found dumped in various cities. While typically one act of violence will receive the primary focus, many will at least be mentioned, and so will other types of activities—for example, political developments. It is a sign of success for a terrorist (or an insurgent using terrorist methods) when a story focuses on no other event which took place in Iraq that day. (This is particularly important for television coverage. When a newspaper runs multiple stories out of Iraq the secondary stories will run deeper in the paper, past the front page, thus being read by fewer people, but those secondary stories will still almost always be there, at least in the major national papers. It is unlikely a network news broadcast will run more than one story out of Iraq on a given night unless circumstances are exceptional.)

But again, this is not merely a question of violence in a purely quantifiable sense. On April 12, 2007, a suicide bomber was able to penetrate the security perimeter of the Green Zone and attack Iraq's Parliament. Despite the relatively low body count (with fewer than 10 people dying) the attack was treated as a stand-alone story by ABC, CBS, and NBC. There it was a question of a presumably safe zone being penetrated, so that the point of the stories was the question: how can this have happened inside what is supposed to be the safest point in the country? The message the terrorists hoped to communicate with the bombing was being received loud and clear and passed on exactly as they must have hoped: we can get to *anyone, anywhere*, and nothing you have done has stopped us or (apparently) can stop us. CNN's reporter went ahead and made the message explicit, saying, "The insurgency message is clear: it can infiltrate and strike anywhere."[6]

It didn't hurt, of course, that an Arab network was interviewing one of the Parliament members at the exact instant the bomb went off, making available extremely dramatic footage which was then prominently featured in all three reports,[7] and in cable news stories as well.[8]

The networks do not necessarily move in lockstep with one another, however, nor are there clear-cut numerical standards that are simply applied without interpretation on the part of particular reporters and producers on a given night. On January 16, 2007, an attack on a major university in Baghdad, covered by all three networks, was *not* treated as a stand-alone attack by NBC[9] or by ABC,[10] even though it was of equal magnitude to the Shorja market bombing of February 12, 2007, which was treated as a stand-alone story on NBC[11] and CBS.[12] (CBS, however, did treat the university attack as a stand-alone story.[13])

Another attack seemed to attract ABC's attention as a stand-alone story because of its "cruelty," again a subjective measure having nothing to do with any quantitative figure. Day laborers were targeted, after having gathered around a van that appeared to be stopping to hire workers before detonating.[14] While CBS's report certainly focused on that bombing, they also mentioned a bomb which detonated with minor damage at the entrance of the Golden Domed Mosque in Samarra.[15] It appears NBC didn't cover the bombing per se at all, but merely mentioned it (without the details that explained what made the bombing so "cruel" in ABC's judgment) in the context of a story about political developments on the war.[16]

It should also be remembered that simple pragmatics—what else has happened that day? Were the networks physically able to cover those stories?—are going to have some influence on these judgments as well. Those factors, however, are going to remain opaque to the viewer and to the analyst.

A Hit: Half-Hourly Cable News Headlines

All three of the cable networks interrupt their programming on a regular basis for a news reader to update viewers on what are ostensibly the most important news headlines of the moment. This is typically (although not always) done on the half-hour, always done at least twice an hour, and done on a 24-hour-a-day basis, even when the programming that is being interrupted is not itself live. Despite protestations from throughout the news industry that journalism in a post-9/11 world could not and would not return to "business as usual,"[17] which stories are selected for these news updates can range from the ridiculous to the sublime. Sometimes they are obviously chosen to add a bit of levity or human interest, but at other times all three news networks seem to be channeling Court TV, the E! Entertainment network, or some surreal combination of the two in their determination of which stories are most important that half hour. These networks, after all, devoted more than 50 percent of their "newshole" for a period of days to the death of a former Playboy bunny,[18] and hours more to the jailing of a woman most famous for being famous.

Given that the newsreaders are being given approximately 90 seconds to deal with domestic political stories, foreign affairs, late-breaking weather news—another perennial cable news favorite—along with any news pertaining to the wars in Iraq and Afghanistan, a terrorist has a hard row to hoe if he wants an attack to stand out among the day's events to the point where it is actually mentioned during one of these newsbreaks, much less several in a row. For an attack to be mentioned *and* footage to be shown (as opposed to a graphic, such as a map of Iraq, a file photo of a burning vehicle, or an iconic still picture of an American soldier superimposed over a map of Iraq or an Iraqi flag) is quite an accomplishment.

The Blockbuster Attack: Cable News'
Full Attention for Several Hours

The next rung of the ladder occurs when the three cable news networks—CNN, MSNBC, (cable partner of NBC), and Fox News—focus exclusively on the coverage of a given attack for a sustained period of time, ignoring all other stories and taking no commercial breaks for several hours. While it is possible to imagine this rung being partially met in a situation where one or two networks made this choice while the others do not it is highly unlikely, as when it comes to this type of decision the three tend to move in a pack. (The three tend to move together any time it's a question of moving to the coverage of a live event, even when they are abandoning one live event for another, as when they left a speech on February 22, 2003, in which the secretary of Homeland Security was rolling out the department's major new—and long awaited—public information campaign to instead cover the rescue of a puppy.[19])

This can produce some very odd juxtapositions. On June 29, 2007, two cars rigged with propane tanks were discovered in London before they exploded. Because the threat had been averted, all three networks did begin to take commercial breaks at some point during the morning, although less frequently than usual. After several hours all three were mentioning other stories, although only briefly. But early in the morning, for all three, the sole focus was the story of the two cars in London, which was being reported with great intensity as breaking news of great significance.

Meanwhile, on NBC, Matt Lauer, the co-host of NBC's morning "news" program, *The Today Show*, was actually in London, in preparation for the upcoming concert to celebrate Princess Diana's memory. Thus their anchor was in perfect position, and they could capitalize on this coincidence to jump on the story and make it their own. Instead, after reporting the story about the cars as part of their usual rapid-fire dispensing with the hard news of the day, they used the fact that he was in London and the other co-host still in New York to make a light-hearted attempt to test the iPhone, on the market for the first time that day, laughing and mugging for the camera.

The Epic: Networks' Full Attention for Several Hours

To get the traditional broadcast networks in the United States (ABC, CBS, and NBC) to join the cable news networks in shifting away from their regular programming, also with no commercial interruption—as they did after the attacks on the London subways on July 7, 2005—is a higher rung on the ladder, simply because it is a more difficult accomplishment for a terrorist. For the cable networks to shift involves ignoring other news stories. Certainly there is financial loss for them when they skip commercial breaks, just as there is financial loss when the broadcast networks skip commercials. But it is still a less painful choice for the news networks for two reasons.

First, it is when there is a major, breaking story that the news networks' ratings spike.[20] This has been the case since CNN first invented the format in the late 1980s. There may be short-term financial loss, but it is offset by the fact that it is in those moments that they have the opportunity to win over viewers for the long term, since inevitably some of the viewers who turn to these networks for coverage of these short-term stories "discover" the networks and return to them afterward.[21] It is in these moments that they have the opportunity to establish their brand. Second, it is other news stories that they are pushing aside, so that there is little chance the viewers they had at the moment they switched to the major, breaking story will be disappointed and turn away.

In contrast, broadcast networks covering a major event have turned away from their regular programming, which during the day involves game shows, soap operas, and so forth—entertainment programming which has nothing to do with news. (In the evenings, obviously, their programming is also generally entertainment of some sort, whether that's sports, regular programming, movies, or what have you. Frankly, even the evening shows produced by the network news divisions tend to be closer to entertainment than hard news: true crime stories, for example.) Shifting to a news story involves greater financial loss (since their ratings tend to be far higher than those of the news networks) with less promise of long-term gain stemming from the choice, more chance that the viewers they have at the moment they make the shift will turn away—now that we live in a world where the viewer is not limited to three networks, but can turn to any one of dozens of entertainment networks on cable—or select their own programming using videos or DVDs or even turn to the Internet. It's a higher risk move for them. Thus it signals an attack that was judged somehow more significant. For an attack to reach this level of coverage means that the terrorists who staged it were, ultimately, more successful.

The Spectacular: The Pinnacle of Success for Media-Driven Terrorists

The final two rungs would encompass the Spectaculars. What, then, defines a Terrorist Spectacular? Establishing those parameters precisely is far from easy. First and foremost, successfully creating a Terrorist Spectacular is not entirely in the terrorist's hands—the media has to cooperate, has to agree that a particular attack is, indeed, a Spectacular, that it deserves to be treated as such, and then has to treat it that way. *Whatever the characteristics that in the end make the attack itself a Spectacular, the final determination depends on the quality and particularly the quantity of the coverage.* The point here is that the final determination is not under the terrorists' control. No matter how elaborate a terrorist attack may have been, or how "spectacular" it may seem to be looking only at quantitative measures, what ultimately defines a Terrorist Spectacular is the amount of media attention a terrorist attack receives. And the media's standards for when an attack crosses that line and becomes a Spectacular, unfortunately for the modern terrorist, are unclear—or at the very least, inconsistent.

Except for the most obvious (and therefore most unusual) cases such as 9/11, where there will be no doubt and no debate that a particular attack is, in fact, a Spectacular, what makes an attack Spectacular has nothing to do with the attack itself and everything to do with the way it is covered.

There is no question the London subway attacks, for example, were a Spectacular. In the United States, not only the three cable news networks but all three broadcast networks focused exclusively on the subway attacks for hour after hour. This makes perfect sense: Britain is not only an ally but arguably the United States' closest ally. There was, of course, the shock of an attack in the heart of Europe, the West, the developed world, where terrorism of this magnitude is never expected and is always treated as more of a shock and more serious. (There is empirical support for this: two economists from Zurich—Bruno Frey and Dominik Rohner—compared press coverage of terrorist attacks in Western Europe and North America with those in the Third World, and they discovered that it took so many more casualties for terrorists operating in the Third World to get an equivalent amount of press coverage to those launching attacks in Europe and North America that "increasing the number of fatalities and injuries is their only possibility of obtaining the desired coverage."[22])

But if it makes sense for all these reasons for London to have been treated as a Spectacular, why not the Madrid train bombings of March 11, 2004? (Obviously each would have been treated as Spectaculars by the media in the countries in which they occurred; we are interested here in the behavior of the American press.) Every element present in the London bombings was present in Madrid (Spain at the time of the bombing was not the closest ally of the United States but was arguably its closest ally next to Britain.) In addition there were three times as many deaths in Spain, as a result of four times as many bombs (although admittedly in Spain only one train station was bombed, while in London the bombers spread out across the transit system, creating a far more powerful initial impression of an entire *system* under assault).

Yet not only did the broadcast networks not take any particular notice until their regularly scheduled news programs, the cable news networks treated it as merely another news story that day, to be sure one worth mentioning each hour, but not one worthy of their sustained and sole focus.

It is reasonable to ask how useful a metric this actually is if the suggestion here is that Madrid was a failure—when it was probably the Madrid train attack that led to the collapse of the Aznar government. If the point of terrorism is for groups to use public opinion as a lever to impact government policy, then Madrid would seem to be a textbook example of a successful terrorist attack. Unable to force the Spanish government to withdraw its support for the war in Iraq, the terrorists used the attack as a means to indirectly produce a government more willing to go along with their preferred policy.[23]

Yet it is worth asking why it was so important to get Spain to withdraw its forces. While their presence was no doubt of great symbolic importance, they hardly had a large enough force to make a difference on the battlefield. But there is evidence to suggest that Islamist analysts believed that (electorally) the Spanish government was the "low-hanging fruit" of the Western democracies participating in the Iraq war coalition. Spanish public opinion could be brought to bear to force the government to change policy and withdraw (by changing the government)—which might then help convince other countries to do so. Yet those other countries had even smaller contingents of forces (except for the British, who would presumably be the last to go.) Why did they matter? Because as each nation dropped out of the coalition, it would contribute to the perception that the United States was isolated.[24] In other words, it is at least possible that the Madrid attack, while designed to pressure the Spanish, was actually a bank shot aimed ultimately at U.S. public opinion. But for that strategy to work, it would have to receive attention *in the United States*.

To be sure, this argument is highly speculative. It remains the case, however, that there is a body of evidence that the "global jihad" is always interested in how their actions play in the United States. So even if the Madrid attack was a success for the terrorists, it can still be counted a failure for them in terms of this particular metric, which evaluates the way it played out in front of the American audience. This choice made by the television networks, both broadcast and cable, was in any event noteworthy because there was no competing news story that day which could explain their neglect of Madrid.

Similarly, when Istanbul suffered two large bombings on November 20, 2003, one might have thought that, too, had all the necessary criteria to be treated as a Spectacular by the American networks. Turkey is not only an American ally, it is arguably our only truly democratic Muslim ally, and therefore a country of unique and special interest. The targets were both British, therefore involving the interests and citizens of our closest ally, and the attacks were timed for a day when President Bush was visiting London (not particularly subtle). Furthermore, all the signatures of an al-Qaida attack were there—multiple, simultaneous, suicide car bombings—and based on purely quantitative measures the attacks were, indeed, relatively spectacular, with 30 killed and approximately 400 wounded.

But in that case the U.S. networks were too focused on a competing (and in comparison, an obviously irrelevant) story to stay with Istanbul for any length of time. That just happened to be the day that a plane in a hangar in California was rumored to have Michael Jackson on board, and it was further rumored that if he deplaned he might be indicted for child molestation. So rather than covering the immediate aftermath of a massive double bombing in the capital of a critical NATO ally, hours were spent in random speculation based on essentially no information regarding a question of no consequence.[25] Even if one were to concede that there was some importance to the Michael Jackson question, or that the networks wanted to cover it because doing so might spike their ratings, it is unclear why they didn't cover Istanbul, going to Los Angeles when something worth covering actually happened.

At around 8 PM local time on August 14, 2007, four coordinated suicide bomb attacks detonated in the northern Iraqi towns of Qahtaniya and Jazeera, targeting members of the Yazidi communities (a Kurdish religious minority). An Iraqi Interior Ministry spokesman said that two tons of explosives were used in the blasts, which crumbled buildings, trapping entire families beneath wreckage as entire neighborhoods were flattened. Initial reports suggested that over 500 were killed and thousands injured.[26] (It is the initial reports that matter, even if they later turn out to be wrong, because it is those reports that shape the first coverage decisions.) These attacks were universally framed as "the worst since the American invasion of Iraq," and the coverage was commensurate with a particularly bad attack in that context: the attack led network newscasts, and it received a great deal of attention on cable news, without either treating the attacks as a story that should swamp every other event of the day, much less one that should alter the norms and conventions of regular programming.[27] When the death toll stood at 260 (although it was clear it would go much higher) CNN called the attacks "the bloodiest coordinated attack of the war,"[28] while on NBC they were "the worst attacks of this war so far."[29] Yet the attacks, if those figures held—and certainly if there had been

500 killed—could just as easily have been framed as the worst attacks on civilians any-where in the world after 9/11, and had they been framed that way, the frame itself would have demanded a very different style and degree of coverage.

Why did the networks, both broadcast and cable, all make the choice that arguably underplayed the importance of these attacks? In this case, the choice may have been dictated by simple pragmatics: the scene of the attack, far in the rural north of the coun-try, was just too hard to get to. As a result, the coverage was severely truncated. The last CNN story was on August 18, three days after the attack, and it is a report on comments made about the attack by the American military, not a report from the scene.[30] Fox's last report was on August 16, and although the story was on the attack itself, their reporter was not on the scene either.[31] NBC's last report was on August 16, and they made a point of mentioning how difficult it was to get their reporter to the scene.[32] For all intents and purposes this massive attack—larger than London, larger than Madrid, larger than Bali, larger than any of the attacks which received enough news coverage for their names to immediately evoke a specific memory—was gone from the media within 72 hours.

If the fact that control is ultimately in the hands of the media, and not the terrorists, is the first element in understanding Terrorist Spectaculars, the second is that these attacks are literally *spectacles*, which is to say events the viewer finds it almost impossible to look away from. Spectacles may be defined by their sheer magnitude, in every dimen-sion (e.g., the size of the attack, the casualties caused, etc.), or any single dimension—the attack may be a symbolic or visual spectacle because of the nature of the target or the quality of the footage. There is no hard-and-fast threshold in terms of a particular level of violence that will trigger the media's categorization of an attack as a Spectacular, but the quality of the visuals makes an enormous difference.

In his discussion of Spectaculars, 30 years ago, J. Bowyer Bell wrote:

> These new transnational gunmen are, in fact, television producers constructing a package so spectacular, so violent, so compelling that the networks, acting as execu-tives, supplying the cameramen and the audience, cannot refuse the offer. Given the script with an uncertain ending, live actors—the terrorists, the victims, the security forces, the innocent bystanders—and a skilled director who choreographs the unfold-ing incident for maximum impact, television is helpless.[33]

When Bell was writing, the type of incident he was envisioning was something akin to the attack on the Israeli Olympic team at Munich, a situation where terrorists were holding hostages, so that while fewer lives may have been at stake, the outcome remained uncer-tain for a period of time, during which the terrorists held the media's attention in a very literal sense. The press—and through them, the audience—were held hostage as much as those physically under the control of the men with the guns. This is very different from the type of terrorist attack dominant today, where a bomb is detonated. The event is over as soon as it has begun. Michele L. Malvesti has developed a quite elegant distinction:

> . . . *faits accomplis* [are] already accomplished and irreversible in nature; they were not on-going incidents [instead they were] incidents that had come to fruition and were, in

effect, over the moment the explosives detonated. There would be no on-going crisis to manage, only consequences with which to contend.[34]

Thus over time control has shifted *toward* the press and *away* from the terrorists.

A spectacle may also be a purely visual spectacle, as is the case whenever an attack—no matter how small or ultimately unsuccessful—is captured on film, as was the case with the attack on the Iraqi Parliament. That case was serendipity, but of course terrorists and insurgents try whenever possible to ensure that attacks are captured on film, hence the use of the "staggered bomb."

Reporters often note the tactic of planting a second bomb, delayed enough after the first one to catch either first responders or survivors trying to escape. What the press does not tell its audience is that the other benefit of the staggered bomb from the terrorist or insurgent point of view is that the later bomb will go off after the cameras have arrived, guaranteeing that an explosion will be captured on film. And if an explosion is on film, it is hard to imagine that film will not actually air, a point that has been raised with me by several military officers. Regarding groups in Iraq, particularly al-Qaida, Colonel Tovo noted:

> A lot of times they'll do the dual attack. The first bomb goes off [and] part of it's to get subsequent casualties among the first responders but . . . a second bomb goes off, a lot of that's to make sure the cameras catch the second bomb, which heightens the chance that it makes the [news]. It's part of their TTPs [tactics, techniques, and procedures].[35]

It makes sense to refer to this as a "staggered" bomb rather than a "second" bomb since it sometimes might involve multiple bombs, as was the case in Madrid. There the staggered bomb footage wasn't actually released until some time after the attack itself, when security camera footage was released of crowds fleeing the station after the attack, ducking in reflex, and screaming as the last explosion goes off. The delay in that case may not even have been intentional—the bombers apparently meant for all their bombs to detonate simultaneously—but because that last bomb went off late, and the explosion was captured on film, it provides a clear example of how powerful such footage can be, even when, as in this case, it is only low-quality footage from a security camera.[36]

The low quality may have actually magnified its power, creating a "cinema verité" effect. And the long delay between the event and the release of the footage also magnified the power of the images, since they served to bring to life again an event the memory of which may well have faded for many who were not directly involved.

Notice that despite the fact that the footage was of an event now months old and added no new substantive information, it was aired on every network, with or without a contextualizing story to explain why the images were suddenly being released now.[37] There was no question it would be aired—the news value rested not in whether there was any actual information of a substantive nature embedded in the footage. It was spectacular, and so, by definition, assumed to be newsworthy.

September 11, 2001, was, of course, the most spectacular "staggered bomb" of all time, the first plane hitting the first Tower, ensuring that all news networks were there and covering the moment live (not to mention the countless still photographers present) when the second plane hit the second Tower. This meant that the attack on the second tower was the most photographed historic event in history—since prior to the advent of cell-phone cameras as ubiquitous accessory, the chance that cameras would just happen to be present when history happened was low, meaning that, the Zapruder film excepted, we tend to have images of the aftermath of historic events, rather than images capturing the exact instant history happened. It also meant that millions if not billions were watching live when the Towers fell, which is the instant when the bulk of the deaths occurred.[38]

Which leads us to the third problem in determining when a particular attack crosses the line and becomes treated as a Spectacular by the media: the basis for making the determination is left opaque. Obviously the criteria are subjective, and there is some element of inconsistency here. The size of the attack (in quantitative, measurable terms) clearly matters to the extent that, while attacks that are small in quantitative terms will only make the cut if there is some specific circumstance setting the attack apart (for example, footage of a bomb detonating), attacks that are particularly large in quantitative terms may well make the cut for that reason only. The target itself clearly matters, too. The blunt truth is that Western targets matter more when these determinations are being made, and the threshold for what counts as spectacular is lower when dealing with targets in the West. Consider the relative treatment of the London subway attacks and the bombings which took place at almost the same time in Sharm-el-Sheikh, Egypt. In quantitative terms, the two attacks were roughly similar (more were killed in Egypt—88—while fewer were wounded, only 150, while in London fewer were killed—52—while many, many more were wounded, approximately 700). The Egyptian attacks did receive a great deal of cover-age initially, particularly on cable, but nothing close to what London received, and the comparison on the broadcast networks isn't even close, given that the broadcast networks actually went "wall-to-wall," interrupting regular programming without commercial inter-ruption the entire morning of the London bombings. (In this case, the difference becomes particularly stark when we look past the first day, the day of the attacks themselves.[39])

CUES AND GRADATIONS

If the characteristics of a Terrorist Spectacular are in the media's hands, are subjective, and are only partially clear, what does that leave us of any use? What we can say is that television more than any other medium provides clear if subtle cues as to the gradations between stories.[40] The medium itself provides ways to signal viewers how important the people behind the camera believe any particular attack to be. These cues are easily avail-able, because all that has to be done is for the basic norms American viewers have come to expect to be violated or broken in some way. If the story is very important, and the people behind the camera wish to signal a strong, or large, gradation between the norm and what is happening on the screen, they can make an explicit announcement, which is what happens when they break into regular programming.

For other stories the cues may be more subtle, but just as real. Everyone knows the cable news networks are serious when, like a new entertainment series, a story gets its own theme song and title. When the cable news networks go wall-to-wall, focusing exclusively on a single story, they don't typically announce that they are doing so. The average American viewer may take a few moments to realize that there are no longer commercial breaks, but over a lifetime of television viewing, one becomes conditioned to expect a break within a certain amount of time, and eventually even someone paying only minimal attention will realize that something is different—and stop to wonder why the network isn't pausing, as they normally do.

And of course, although we refer to the "24-hour news networks," in truth the cable news networks are generally no such thing. All three of them—CNN, MSNBC, and Fox News—begin their prime time programming at 8 PM Eastern, and on all three networks (to varying degrees) prime time programming relies on talk and opinion shows, which are shows *about* the news, not news shows per se. And all three networks for years began rerunning that programming at 11 PM throughout the night. (CNN now runs an additional hour of original programming from 11 PM to midnight Eastern.) The single most important signal that the cable news networks can send that a story is important is to begin airing original news programming during the night,[41] as all three networks did, for example, when Chechens took over a Moscow theater in October 2002.

Networks also cue viewers simply by staying with a story over a period of days, particularly if the story leads their programming on several days in a row. And of course there is the ultimate cue as to a story's importance—the anchors themselves travel to the scene, rather than continuing to report from New York. The shooting at Virginia Tech University in the spring of 2007 was not actually a terrorist attack, but it functioned in much the same way, and so it's a particularly informative case study, as the choices made by the news outlets parallel those they face after terrorist attacks. In that case, by the time of the evening news broadcasts on the evening of the day the shooting took place, two of the three broadcast anchors, several of the cable news anchors, and a large number of the anchors for both sets of morning news shows[42] had arrived on the scene.

It is also clear that the assumption made by those working in television is that the audience will notice these cues and understand their significance—indeed, even come to anticipate them in certain circumstances. Thus, for example, the night of the Virginia Tech shootings, the host of NBC's morning show was already on campus and was interviewed on the air during a late-night special on the shootings. Consider the implications of this comment:

> And across from the dormitory about 40 yards is one of the main cafeterias on campus. And I walked in there this afternoon and there were maybe 40 or 50 students stopping and eating. What struck me, Brian, as odd was some of them were surprised to see me. *And what it tells you is* this hasn't sunk in yet, the magnitude of what's happened on their campus has not sunk in. They think it's still a Virginia Tech story, not realizing this is something, this is historic.[43]

Lauer assumes, in other words, that the students will, as soon as they absorb the magnitude of what's happened, immediately understand the implications of that for the way the story will be covered: that it will not only be covered by the networks' morning shows but that it will be covered by them live, on location. The one follows the other as the night the day. He assumes, in other words, that the basic routines, codes, and templates used by the networks to cover stories that trip a certain threshold, entailing certain coverage patterns, have simply been *absorbed* by the average American to the point where, being caught up in such a story, people would expect to see the hosts of the morning news shows appear. What surprises him, therefore, is that *they* are surprised by his appearance. Caught up in tragedy, whether man-made or natural, assuming that tragedy is spectacular enough, shouldn't one anticipate the presence of the networks' franchise players in person?

IRAQ: RAISING THE BAR AND CHANGING THE STANDARDS

In Iraq, because of the sheer regularity of terrorist violence, the bar was to some extent raised over time. Thus violence of a degree and magnitude that, had it occurred anywhere else in the world, would surely be treated as a Terrorist Spectacular, merited merely a stand-alone story, if that.

Many commentators noted at the time—although again, it was not terrorism per se, in that it was surely not politically motivated violence but the act of a lone madman—the shootings at Virginia Tech initially received nearly around-the-clock coverage, not only from the American networks but from outlets from around the world. Bombings at Iraqi universities, some of the oldest in the world, should have been just as shocking, since they too were attacks on locations that should have been, as President Bush said at the time of the Virginia Tech shootings, "a sanctuary." But the tragic truth was that the Iraqi bombings weren't, because they were viewed not merely as attacks on universities but as universities *in Iraq*, where apparently there is no longer any such thing as a sanctuary. Thus while it can plausibly be argued either that Virginia Tech was overcovered or that the university bombings in Iraq were undercovered, the rungs as described here were being applied differently to attacks in Iraq than they were being applied to terrorist attacks elsewhere.

It hardly needs to be pointed out that if an attack anywhere else in the world— probably to include Afghanistan—was initially thought to have cost 500 lives, it surely would have been framed as the largest attack on civilians since 9/11. Only in Iraq is there an alternate frame available that can even suggest that the 2007 attack on the Yazidis might not be a Terrorist Spectacular, deserving of massive amounts of coverage.

As mentioned earlier, a study by Frey and Rohner comparing press coverage of terrorist incidents in Europe and Northern America versus coverage of incidents in the Third World found that as a general rule terrorism outside the developed world would be bloodier:

> . . . to make it into the news, terrorists operating in Western countries can commit some minor terror incident, with few fatalities, whereas terrorists in developing countries need to "produce" a lot of blood to attract the attention of the Western media. The terrorists' main goal is to obtain media attention to espouse their ideology . . . attacks in

developing countries should tend to be bloodier. [Our research] shows this to be the case.[44]

This would explain, for example, why the attacks in London and in Egypt, roughly comparable in size, received nothing like comparable coverage. But something more than that is going on in Iraq, no doubt in part because these attacks occur in the context of a deep American involvement. The study by Frey and Rohner did not distinguish between terrorism that merely took place in the Third World geographically and terrorism that took place in the Third World but was targeted against citizens of Western countries, for example, the Bali nightclub bombing in Indonesia in October 2002. Not only were the majority of victims Australian in that case, it was fairly clear that was the intent.

Yet the second Bali bombing is also worth mentioning, despite the fact that far fewer people were killed. (Estimates ranged as high as 26, which would have put the casualty figures from the second bombing an order of magnitude lower than the first.) The reason, even though it received far less coverage in quantitative terms, speaks to a major weakness in the Frey and Rohner study—a tourist had his camera on immediately before and after the detonation. Ostensibly the footage was being aired because the bomber was apparently caught on film, but all the networks let the footage run past the point where the bomber appears, to show the aftermath of the blast. The visuals were of terrible quality, but that added to their power, since what they were being used to convey was, of course, the chaos and fear in the seconds immediately after the blast. The study doesn't account for this kind of disparity. Some attacks will function as outliers because for whatever reason—particularly, as in this case, when the quality of the available visuals is unique—they may simply make a better story. Any time there is footage of a bomb going off, whether that is by design, as is the case with staggered bombs, or by serendipity, as was the case in Bali, or when the Iraqi Parliament was bombed or when UN headquarters in Baghdad was bombed, those attacks will get a great deal of attention from the press, whether the other elements of the story would seem to warrant it or not.

But in Iraq, the ground rules seem to be different. While the majority of victims for most attacks may be Iraqi, they are killed in the context of an American war, and their deaths always at least implicitly raise the question of whether American policies are succeeding or failing. The level of violence increased over time, and the amount of violence required for the media to pay attention also rose, but this seems to be due to something other than the factors studied by Frey and Rohner. This is apparent in the fact that the threshold for what level of attack merited, for example, a stand-alone story, rose over time in Iraq (before proceeding to then fall again.)

When well over 100 were killed in a single car bombing on April 18, 2007, rather than focus on that one act, both CBS and ABC lumped together every car bomb in Baghdad that day in order to ratchet up the body count in their stories to 175—that way they were able to make the story about "the deadliest day" since the troop surge had begun.[45] By contrast, several years earlier, the bombing of the Jordanian embassy, which killed far fewer people (only 17), received much greater press attention. Simply compare the relative arcs of the two stories—in other words, the amount of attention the story received *after* the day of the event itself, how well the press covered the aftermath of the event.

Looking at the 10 days after the bombing of the embassy on August 7, 2003, all the networks but one had at least one follow-up story.[46] By contrast, news of the massive bombing of April 18, 2007, was almost immediately forgotten in the rush of subsequent events. On ABC on April 19, Iraq news was the visit of Defense Secretary Gates; on CBS, no Iraq news was reported until a bomb killed 13 on April 22; on NBC, by April 19 they were merely listing subsequent attacks; and news of this massive series of bombs appears to be absent on CNN after April 20.[47] But it is also the case that on CNN as other acts of violence occur in Iraq they simply displace discussion of the bombings, despite the fact that they are far *smaller* in scale. They describe how U.S. troops are in a firefight with insurgents, a Shia politician's convoy is ambushed, and bomb-making materials—including chlorine—are discovered in a mosque. The so-called "police blotter" marches on, and the events of the day before or two days before are simply lost to history.[48]

The change in the amount of attention given to violence in Iraq can be seen even with more "message-driven" attacks. Consider, for example, the attack on the Parliament that was treated as a stand-alone story despite the fact that few people died, because the perpetrators were able to make a larger point ("we can even reach inside the Green Zone"). An earlier somewhat parallel attack was that on UN headquarters on August 20, 2003. This was an enormously symbolic target, demonstrating that no one would be considered neutral, as even humanitarian aid organizations would be targeted. But like the attack on the Green Zone, an important subtext of the attack on UN headquarters was the question of how what should have been a secure compound was in fact vulnerable. The attacks are also similar in that simply by serendipity, cameras were rolling inside at the time (for a press conference that would otherwise have probably gone unnoticed) and as a result there was spectacular footage from the inside of a building as it was being bombed, available to be replayed over and over on television.

So what are the comparative arcs for the two stories, how do the two play out over the days following the actual event? The UN story was followed for at least several days even by the networks which moved on the most quickly. On CNN, 100 pieces dealt with the bombing between August 20 and 30.[49]

Compare that to the way the coverage played out after the Iraqi Parliament was attacked by a bomber wearing a suicide vest on April 12, 2007. On the networks the story was basically gone after another day. On CNN, 44 pieces kept the story alive through April 15.[50]

These examples would seem to prove what anyone would already know from casual observation: as time went by it became more difficult to get the press's attention with individual acts of violence in Iraq. And it's harder to get coverage for violence in Iraq than it is for violence in the West. (The cable news networks did devote hour after hour to two failed attacks in the United Kingdom, the first on June 29, 2007, when police discovered and disarmed two car bombs, the second the following day, when a car bomb was driven into the Glasgow International Airport and exploded. There were no deaths, and only minor injuries reported—other than to one of the attackers. Had these events occurred in Iraq, they would barely have merited mention. Actually, they happen all the time—one of the complaints made against the press by the military is that their successes—for example in increasing the rates of IEDs discovered and successfully disarmed—are not given adequate attention. In other words, what counts as "good news" in Iraq, and therefore is not considered newsworthy, is a major terrorist threat when it occurs in London, and is worth hour after hour of coverage.)

RECOMMENDATIONS FOR COVERAGE OF TERRORISM AND INSURGENCIES

To be fair, of course, there is a fundamental paradox at work here. What is it that we want from the news media? If coverage defines success for terrorists, then we certainly want the press to truncate its coverage of attacks. On the other hand, when we see the media decide to devote its time to the burning question of whether or not Michael Jackson is about to be arrested, rather than focusing on a major attack, we know that isn't right either. What we should ask of the media is not that they artificially restrict the amount of time an attack receives, based on some sense that this will deny terrorists the "oxygen" they need. What we should ask, instead, is that determinations about the amount of coverage be driven by considerations of the relative importance of attacks and nothing more, and that what the terrorists have or have not accomplished be kept in perspective.

What are the implications of these findings for the meaning of responsible journalism? First and foremost, this is not a call for reporters to avoid, in any sense, reporting the "bad news." If anything, the problem today is that the bad news—meaning the coverage of violence, successful attacks, particularly of American casualties—is reported too cryptically, with too little context and detail.

Second, every "bad news story" does not necessarily need to be balanced by a "good news story" of roughly comparable length. I have spoken with many military officers who have criticized the press because despite the fact that in Iraq the American military has assisted in innumerable school, hospital, and clinic openings, these events are almost never covered by the media. But this is too simplistic an understanding of what it is the military should hope for—or be able to expect from—the press. For while it is certainly true that, for example in Iraq, the press failed to report good news that was necessary to contextualize and fully understand the bad—they were far behind the curve in reporting the changes in the situation in Anbar Province, for example, almost universally[51]—what we should ask for is reportage on the good news that helps us understand how to weigh the bad, how important it is, and what it means, rather than good news for the sake of good news. What we can and should ask for is that the bad news that is reported be reported not only accurately but responsibly. In this context "responsible journalism" involves certain constraints and standards that might not be necessary in other reportage. Just as the business or sports beats involve their own specific standards and constraints, so should there be basic parameters for reporting on acts of political violence, and these parameters should take into account some understanding of how terrorists and other violent groups are trying to use media coverage to advance their strategic objectives. In other words, the answer to poor coverage of terrorist attacks is better coverage of terrorist attacks, not the coverage of school openings.

Accounting for the Metrics of Success in Reportage

How was it that just as there were real signs of progress on the ground in Iraq, most especially in Anbar Province, once written off as a "lost cause," just as there were reports that al-Qaida was in retreat and on the run, that the American public in larger numbers than ever before believed that the war was going badly and might even itself be a lost cause?[52] The reason is that the metric for success that was being used to evaluate the war (in terms of the rhetoric of news reports) was not one that was related to any military criteria. The metric for success that was being used belonged to the terrorists and insurgents. Their attacks, whether they mattered to the ultimate military outcome on the ground or not, were what was driving press coverage. Often this coverage provided not just no context but no explanation whatsoever—merely the police blotter, the day's rundown of attacks and casualties. Neil Munro, writing in the *National Journal*, offered a metric that might be more finely tuned to the high rate of attacks seen in Iraq. He pointed to the measure public relations professionals routinely use: simply calculate how much they would have had to pay for a comparable amount of column inches and air time if they were buying it in the form of ad time. Using that measure, he points out, insurgents more than got their investment's worth for many attacks (given how little they cost to mount). He further pointed out that the military appeared incapable of getting any return on investment.[53]

In that context, it is not enough for the military to say that things are going well or that progress is being made. The first counternarrative that is needed is one that clearly articulates *how success should be measured* and seizes that rhetorical ground back from the insurgents.

Why did a subsequent poll conducted by the Pew Charitable Trusts show a near reversal of the numbers of Americans feeling optimistic regarding the outcome of the Iraq war?[54] Because repeated reports focused on massive reductions in both American and Iraqi casualties and the complete reversal in the status of Anbar Province itself, beginning to give the American public some metric that might counter that preferred by the terrorists—an obsessive focus only on the anecdotal instances of violence. Even so, press stories on continued violence tend to be structured as "we are told violence is down—yet today there was a bombing!" as if the anecdotal single instance were somehow disproof of the overall statistics.[55]

At the end of the day we do have a right to expect our media outlets will give at least as much thought to how their coverage will benefit whatever group has staged a particular act of violence (and what that group was hoping to get out of the coverage) as they give to what their competition is doing. This is not an entirely new way of proceeding: outlets now cover stories while carefully balancing the newsworthiness of individual images against various questions regarding the appropriateness of using particularly graphic images.[56] This type of thought process in the newsroom, therefore, would not change *what* events are covered, but it might change *how* they are covered, or it might change the transparency of the coverage, so that reporters might tell audiences what they believe to underlie particular attacks, what might be truly motivating them (as in the case of staggered bombs.)

Transparency in coverage would make a great deal of difference to an audience's understanding of events. Consider the case of the staggered bomb. This is particularly interesting because the dual bomb technique is often mentioned by the press, but it's always mentioned as a way simply—meaning exclusively—of creating casualties among first responders. Yet the way this technique also benefits the terrorists and insurgents, insofar as it provides the media with better visuals, is never explicitly discussed by the press.

Partially this is consistent with the media's general dislike of ever discussing the way they themselves are part of anyone's strategies or planning (with the glaring exception, of course, of American domestic politics, where the element of campaign strategies for "spinning" the press is discussed obsessively by the press, right on camera and on the printed page or posted Web site). But perhaps part of their reticence here is that doing so would require their discussing the fact that in reality, "better" visuals of terrorist attacks from their perspective means more dramatic visuals, that the terrorists know that and plan accordingly. That planning involves additional bombs which kill or harm more people. It cannot be a comfortable subject for the press: these people were killed in order to make the story more attractive for us— *and it worked, exactly as the terrorists knew it would.* Even if saying that on the air would mean being more transparent about their own coverage and better educating their viewers about terrorist tactics, it is easy to imagine why they would want to avoid the conversation.

The press is in a no-win situation here. They cannot *not* cover these secondary attacks: they are, after all, news. Yet their own standards for what constitutes news, which are hardly a secret, have left them as vulnerable to manipulation by terrorists as they are by presidential candidates. The only difference is that the stakes are somewhat higher here, and they aren't quite as willing to discuss the details with their audience, whereas the tactics and strategies presidential campaigns employ for manipulating the press are dissected explicitly and in excruciating detail. To be sure, this might mean discussing terrorist intentions and motives before they are fully known—in other words, introducing an element of speculation into reportage—and this makes some reporters, who are careful to tell their audiences what they know and only what they know as a point of pride, enormously uncomfortable.[57]

This discomfort grows out of the professional integrity of individual reporters; however, the idea that discussing motivations would be inappropriate because it might demand reporters speculate seems a somewhat disingenuous concern for the profession as a whole given how freely reporters speculate in every other imaginable scenario. Why was the young movie star found dead with a rolled up bill next to his body? Who killed the young mother? Are the white athletes guilty of raping the black stripper? Pointing out that terrorists engage in terrorism for propaganda purposes hardly seems a stretch of professional ethics as they are practiced across the board.

Again, this is not an argument against covering newsworthy events; it is an argument for covering those events more responsibly and completely. How much and what type of coverage should a particular attack get? Most critically, what visuals should be aired, repeated how many times?

How should a particular event be framed? How transparent should the press be about the choices they are making about coverage and about what they know (or believe) to be the case about the way these events reflect the strategic choices made by terrorists and insurgents? Many outlets shy away from the use of the words "terrorist" or "terrorism" for several reasons, including the fact that the motivation of a given actor may be unclear before a reporter has to file his or her story.[58] Rather than simply deploy euphemisms, however, why can't reporters simply tell their audiences what they know and what they don't know? Of course, doing so would mean rupturing the voice of omniscience used by reporters in most stories. Outlets have often used the passive voice when reporting on suicide bombings (as in, "a car bomb went off today"). The rationale here, too, is that stories must be filed before it can be known if it really was a suicide bombing,[59] but as we all know, car bombs don't kill people, the drivers of car bombs do. There's no question that it's too much to ask that reporters simply wait until they have all the information, but if they don't then they ought to tell their audiences that rather than disguise the fact. When they do it creates the impression that these acts are not the product of human agency.

News networks appear to have concluded on their own that the activities of terrorists which are newsworthy and must be covered must also be covered responsibly, and that their own practices can and should be reviewed, and in some cases altered, in at least one case already, ending the practice of airing terrorist-produced videos on which hostages were seen begging for their lives.

There was hardly a better example of an instance where networks allowed themselves to be used by terrorists, not merely reporting a newsworthy event but showing precisely the footage produced *by the terrorists* in precisely the manner they had produced it, if in truncated form.

It is when hostage videos are released by kidnappers that it becomes most obvious that the media has the potential to serve—on occasion has served—as conduit for the terrorist or insurgent message. Not, critically, for the simple substance of the information they wish to have conveyed, but for the actual message itself, as they constructed it, designed it, and staged it. There is as wide a difference as can be imagined in seeing or hearing the words, "today the kidnappers released a video in which the victim can clearly be seen and heard begging for his life," coming from a reporter who is attempting to accurately distill, describe, and explain what is on a tape, and actually seeing some poor man or woman doing just that. And there is little question that it benefits the terrorist or insurgent group more to have the public view the emotional spectacle than to merely read or hear about it second hand.

To be sure, there seems little question that these videos are newsworthy material, and that there is a basis for the choice the news networks made, early on, to air at least a few seconds of these videos. That does not mean, however, that the choice to do so was an inevitable or self-evident one, or that it was the choice that best served their viewers or that other considerations should not have outweighed whatever led them to use cuts from these videos. Certainly choices regarding how much to use from some of these videos were hotly debated, both before and after they were aired.[60]

Is it necessary that any of these tapes be aired for an audience to be informed? This seems to be the question networks were revisiting, as of the end of the spate of brutal executions of hostages in 2004. When Jack Hensley was killed, the video was mentioned by NBC, but no clips were aired. The question is, was the viewer ill served by simply hearing NBC's reporter say: "The report tonight on an Islamic Web site claiming Jack Hensley, a contractor from Georgia, has been executed, the second American hostage killed in as many days."[61] One must ask if the difference in what CBS's viewers learned on two nights, one when a clip was shown from a terrorist video of a hostage and one when it wasn't, was so profound as to justify the fact that on the first night CBS exposed their audience to the powerful manipulative effects of enemy propaganda. Did they do so purposefully? Hardly. But they did do so without explaining that the material they were airing was designed and intended to manipulate, in part precisely by drawing powerfully on the viewer's emotions.

Gradually the networks began replacing their use of terrorist footage with reporters reporting that such footage existed, even describing it, with no apparent loss to their audiences. They still knew what happened, but without the networks complicity with the terrorists in the most grotesque manipulation of emotions imaginable. And if there is no market for these videos, there is no need for the hostages needed to make the videos. The practice will perhaps not end but slow to a crawl—and indeed Westerners do seem to be taken in nothing like the numbers they were at the peak of the practice.

CONCLUSIONS

Brigitte L. Nacos wrote in 1994, "In spite of suggestions that media organizations should exercise self-restraint and critique one another as to the volume and quality of terrorism reporting, there is no realistic prospect for disrupting terrorism's exploitation of the media."[62] There has been no evidence, unfortunately, in the years since to suggest that she was wrong.

There is such a thing as too little coverage of a terrorist attack. When the coverage of the Iraq war is in one of its regular valleys on the network nightly news, attacks may be dealt with in as little as a sentence or two. This kind of coverage, if it can even be called that, does a profound disservice to the public, leaving out entirely any background and context that might be used by them in understanding what had happened or interpretation of its meaning.

This should not be about measuring the ratio of casualties to words and keeping that ratio as high as possible. The truth is that sometimes the interests of the terrorists and the public will in fact intersect and overlap. The goal should be to balance what the terrorists and the public are both getting out of the story and ensuring that the terrorists never get more out of a story than the public does.

ACKNOWLEDGMENTS

This chapter draws from a major research project focused on the impact of terrorist and insurgent media strategies on Western press coverage of the Long War, which will appear in book form as *True Lies: The Impact of Terrorist and Insurgent Media Strategies on the Western Press*. Portions of this work have been presented to the John F. Kennedy School for Special Warfare, the Canadian

Forces College, to NATO Public Affairs Officers, and for the Special Operations Command. The author would like to thank Carol K. Winkler, Georgia State University; Edward Rankus, UNC-Chapel Hill; Julie Dumont-Rabinowitz; and Colonel Steve Boylan, Public Affairs Officer for General David Petraeus, Multinational Forces–Iraq 2007–2008, for their comments on earlier drafts.

NOTES

1. Interview with the author, Ft. Carson, Colorado, September 21, 2006.

2. See Mia Bloom, *Dying to Kill: The Allure of Suicide Terror* (New York: Columbia University Press, 2005), p. 60.

3. All the major Canadian and Australian papers provided regular and thorough coverage of the Tamil Tigers, for example, between 2000 and 2002, the period when they were moving from continued fighting to tentative peace negotiations with the Sri Lankan government. During that same period the two American papers with the most extensive foreign coverage, the *New York Times* and the *Washington Post*, carried two and seven pieces, respectively (between January 1, 2000, and December 31, 2002, using the search terms "LTTE" or "Tamil Tiggers," the Tigers official name, using Lexis Nexis Academic.)

4. There was one wave of coordinated attacks on Baghdad so large the networks had no choice but to report it. But NBC reported at the time, "A senior U.S. commander told NBC News the attacks were timed to embarrass the Iraqi government while its leaders are in the United States, *and to put Zarqawi back in the media spotlight after almost nonstop coverage of Hurricane Katrina.*" Richard Engel, September 14, 2005, *NBC Nightly News with Brian Williams*, emphasis added, Lexis Nexis Academic, downloaded March 13, 2008.

5. In the language of the well-known mass communication researcher Shanto Iyengar, in other words, terrorism-related stories are consistently presented according to an "episodic" as opposed to a "thematic" frame. See Iyengar, *Is Anyone Responsible? How Television Frames Political Issues* (Chicago: University of Chicago Press, 1991).

6. Arwa Damon, "The Situation Room," CNN April 12, 2007, Lexis Nexis Academic, downloaded January 14, 2008.

7. Hilary Brown, "Bomb Blasts Iraq Parliament," *ABC World News Tonight with Charles Gibson*, at http://abcnews.go.com/Video/videoEmbed?id=3035887&challenge=&authenticated= true&start=Y2RhdWJlckBlbWFpbC51bmMuZWR1A&end=bGF1ZHB1cw%3D%3D&save=O N&save=OFF, via the *Tyndall Report* (tyndallreport.com), downloaded May 24, 2007; Martin Seemungal, "Eight Killed in Baghdad Blast," *CBS Evening News*, April 12, 2007, at http://www .cbsnews.com/sections/i_video/main500251.shtml?id=2679179n, via the *Tyndall Report* (tyndallreport.com), downloaded May 24, 2007; and Richard Engle, "Suicide Bomber Hits Iraq Parliament," *NBC Nightly News with Brian Williams*, April 12, 2007, http://video.msn.com/v/us/v .htm?g=13e30694-1048-4798-8a8e-8c975ccfeeb8&f=34&fg=rss, via the *Tyndall Report* (tyndallreport.com), downloaded May 24, 2007.

8. See, for example, Anderson Cooper, *Anderson Cooper 360 Degrees,*"CNN (10 pm), April 12, 2007, Lexis Nexis Academic, downloaded January 14, 2008. Fox News, which barely mentioned the story on its premiere evening newscast, nonetheless still aired the footage. See Brit Hume, *Fox Special Report with Brit Hume*, Fox News Channel, April 12, 2007, Lexis Nexis Academic, downloaded January 14, 2008.

9. See Ned Colt, "Scores Killed in Baghdad Blasts," *NBC Nightly News with Brian Williams*, January 16, 2007, http://video.msn.com/v/us/v.htm?g=c2aede03-a06a-4b3e-a7b2-8438480b7470 &f=34&fg=rss, via the *Tyndall Report* (tyndallreport.com), downloaded May 24, 2007.

10. "Grim Year in Baghdad," *ABC World News Tonight with Charles Gibson*, January 16, 2007, http://abcnews.go.com/Video/playerIndex?id=2799836, via the *Tyndall Report* (tyndallreport.com), downloaded May 25, 2007.

11. Jane Arraf, "Scores Dead in Baghdad Blasts," *NBC Nightly News with Brian Williams*, via the *Tyndall Report* (tyndallreport.com) at http://video.msn.com/v/us/v.htm?g=df2c93c4-0426 -44f5-ab21-d58e3d8e0961&f=34&fg=rssFebruary 12, 2007, downloaded May 25, 2007.

12. Lara Logan, "Bombings Mark Anniversary," *CBS Evening News*, via the *Tyndall Report* (tyndallreport.com) at http://www.cbsnews.com/sections/i_video/main500251.shtml?id=24663 25n, downloaded May 25, 2007.

13. Lara Logan, "Brutal Violence in Baghdad," *CBS Evening News*, January 16, 2007, http://www.cbsnews.com/sections/i_video/main500251.shtml?id=2365080n, via the *Tyndall Report* (tyndallreport.com), downloaded May 25, 2007.

14. Dan Harris, "Deadly Suicide Attack in Iraq," *ABC World News Tonight*, December 12, 2006, http://abcnews.go.com/Video/videoEmbed?id=2721297&challenge=&authenticated=true &start=Y2RhdWJlckBlbWFpbC51bmMuZWR1A&end=bGF1ZHB1cw%3D%3D&save=ON& save=OFF, via the *Tyndall Report* (tyndallreport.com), downloaded May 25, 2006.

15. Randall Pinkston, *CBS Evening News*, December 12, 2006, Lexis Nexis Academic, downloaded January 14, 2006.

16. David Gregory, *NBC Nightly News with Brian Williams*, December 12, 2006, Lexis Nexis Academic, downloaded January 14, 2008.

17. See, for example, Ken Auletta, "Battle Stations: How Long Will the Networks Stick With the News?" *New Yorker*, December 10, 2001, http://www.kenauletta.com/battlestations.html, downloaded January 30, 2008.

18. In the first days after Anna Nicole Smith's death, the cable news networks devoted 50 percent of their time to the story. Other mediums did better, but not by much. See Project for Excellence in Journalism, "Anna Nicole Smith: Anatomy of a Feeding Frenzy, The Feverish First Days," April 4, 2007, http://www.journalism.org/node/4874, downloaded January 14, 2007.

19. Barry Saunders, "For Security, Ice the Fido-on-a-Floe Show," *Raleigh News and Observer*, February 22, 2003, p. A-17, Lexis Nexis Academic, downloaded February 2, 2008.

20. Scott Collins, *Crazy Like a Fox: The Inside Story of How Fox News Beat CNN* (New York: Penguin Group Ltd., 2004), p. 2.

21. While viewers who turn to the news networks for hard news stories will return subsequently, those who turn to them for the more "tabloid" stories, such as the death of a movie star or celebrity, will not return, so that those ratings spikes tend to be completely temporary. Brit Hume, interview with the author, March 12, 2007, Washington, DC.

22. Bruno S. Frey and Dominik Rohner, *Blood and Ink! The Common-Interest-Game Between Terrorists and the Media*, Institute for Empirical Research in Economics, University of Zurich Working Paper Series, April 2006, p. 20.

23. An extensive investigation into the group who carried out the Madrid bombing conducted by the *New York Times* noted that "The plot seems to have gained momentum in December 2003, when a 42-page document became available on a well-trafficked jihadi Web site. Fakhet got hold of the document, which was produced by a militant Islamic think tank of sorts. It analyzed the political situation in Spain and argued that 'painful blows' were needed to force the Spanish government to withdraw its troops from Iraq. It also suggested making 'the utmost use' of the approaching elections." Andrea Elliott, "Where Boys Grow up to Be Jihadis," *New York Times Magazine*, November 26, 2007, p. 6, http://www.nytimes.com/2007/11/25/magazine/25tetouan-t.html, downloaded December 20, 2007.

24. See the analysis by Reuven Paz, "Qa-idat al-Jihad, Iraq, and Madrid: The First Tile in the Domino Effect?" PRISM Series of Special Dispatches on the Global Jihad, 2 (2004), http://www.e-prism.org/images/PRISM_Special_dispatch_no_1-2.pdf downloaded July 4, 2007.

25. This is what was happening, for example, on CNN:

KYRA PHILLIPS, CNN ANCHOR: All right. We're going to take you back live out to the Santa Barbara County Airport now. You are seeing the arrival of a Gulfstream now at the airport. We had been reporting earlier that we were told through our sources, various sources within the airports via Las Vegas and Santa Barbara, that Michael Jackson and—now, it's saying here Michael Jackson's plane lands at Santa Barbara Airport. Are we confirming this? Is this indeed Michael Jackson's airplane?

MILES O'BRIEN, CNN ANCHOR: I've just been told . . .

PHILLIPS: What have you been told?

O'BRIEN: I've been told this: that the tail number on this one, which I'm still having some difficulty making out, but some of our people have. And if you could let me know in my ear what it is, I'd appreciate it. But it matches the tail number of the Gulfstream which left Nevada presumably with Michael Jackson on board. Now, where that plane has been in the interim, anybody's guess. Once again, if the art of deception is what you're after, perhaps there was an interim stop at which point Michael Jackson could have exited and moved on to his ultimate destination another way. Nevertheless, this tail number does in fact match an aircraft, Gulfstream, same aircraft, which left Las Vegas earlier today. Charles Feldman, do you see the Gulfstream where you are?

CHARLES FELDMAN, CNN CORRESPONDENT: Yes, Miles, hi. We saw the Gulfstream, and we are told that it is matching, the tail number is matching the number that we have been told is the Gulfstream that is carrying Michael Jackson. It's pulling up now right in front of me. I'm standing outside, again, Signature Aviation here in Santa Barbara Airport. . . . I can see that there's a lot more activity on the field than there was before. So this is either Michael Jackson or it's one hell of a false alarm. Now, the plane I'm looking at, it's now—it's pulling up by a hangar in a fenced-off area where there seems to be a lot of people gathered. I can't tell from my distance if these are people in the press or if they're Michael Jackson fans. . . .

O'BRIEN: I've got to tell you, I half expect to see a white Bronco drive into view here given what we've been covering this morning. [laughter]

PHILLIPS: And hopefully, it won't drive fast. We'll have flashbacks of O. J. Simpson.

O'BRIEN: That's at least an Explorer, anyhow. But nevertheless, it is reminiscent of a scene we all witnessed several years ago now.

This type of discussion went on for some time. "Jackson's Plane Arrives at Airport," CNN Breaking News, November 20, 2003, Lexis Nexis Academic, downloaded May 27, 2007.

26. Damien Cave and James Glanz, "Toll in Iraq Truck Bombings Is Raised to More Than 500," New York Times, August 21, 2007, http://www.nytimes.com/2007/08/22/world/middleeast/22iraq-top.html; Paul Tait, Baghdad, "Al-Qaeda blamed for Yazidi carnage," Scotsman, August 16, 2007, http://thescotsman.scotsman.com/international.cfm?id=1294152007; and "Truck Bombings Kill at least 500," CNN, August 15 2007, http://edition.cnn.com/2007/WORLD/meast/08/15/iraq.main/index.html. In another report, the Iraqi Red Crescent estimated the bombs killed 796 and wounded 1,562 people. See also Leila Fadel and Yasseen Taha, "Death Toll from Iraq Bombings Likely to Be Worst of War," McClatchy Papers, August 15, 2007, http://www.mcclatchydc.com/homepage/story/18959.html, downloaded January 18, 2008.

27. That same frame dominated the print press. See for example, Carol J. Williams, "Attack Aftermath; Beleaguered Sect; Militia's Strength; Death Toll in Bombing of Sect Rises; Death Toll in Bombing of Yazidi Refugees in the North are Put at More Than 250. No Single Attack in the

War Has Been Deadlier," *Los Angeles Times*, August 16, 2007, p. A-6, Lexis Nexis Academic, downloaded January 18, 2007; or James Glanz et al., "Iraq Toll Reaches 250 in the Deadliest Attack in the War," *New York Times*, p. A-6, Lexis Nexis Academic, downloaded January 18, 2008; or the editorial, "21st Century Barbarism; The Deadliest Attack to Date in the Iraq War Is Aimed at Civilians," *Washington Post*, August 16, 2007, p. A14, Lexis Nexis Academic, downloaded January 18, 2008.

28. Miles O'Brien, "The Situation Room," CNN 4 PM, August 15, 2007, Lexis Nexis Academic, downloaded January 18, 2008.

29. Brian Williams, *NBC Nightly News with Brian Williams*, August 16, 2007, Lexis-Nexis Academic, downloaded January 18, 2008.

30. Barbara Starr, *Lou Dobbs This Week*, CNN 6 PM, August 18, 2007, Lexis Nexis Academic, downloaded January 18, 2008.

31. Jennifer Griffin, *Special Report with Brit Hume*, Fox News Channel, August 16, 2007, Lexis Nexis Academic, downloaded January 18, 2008.

32. Jane Arraf, August 16, 2007, *NBC Nightly News with Brian Williams*, Lexis Nexis Academic, downloaded January 18, 2008.

33. J. Bowyer Bell, "Terrorist Scripts and Live-Action Spectaculars: As Skilled Producers of Irresistible News, Terrorists Can Control the Media," *Columbia Journalism Review* (May/June 1978): 50.

34. Michele L. Malvesti, "Explaining the United States' Decision to Strike Back at Terrorists," *Terrorism and Political Violence*, 13 (Summer 2001), reprinted at http://fletcher.tufts.edu/news/2002/january/terrorism.htm, downloaded March 13, 2008.

35. Interview with the author, Ft. Carson, Colorado, September 21, 2006.

36. See the timeline at "Madrid Train Attacks," BBC News, n.d., http://news.bbc.co.uk/2/shared/spl/hi/guides/457000/457031/html/nn2page1.stm, downloaded February 13, 2008.

37. See, for example, Bob Woodruff, *Good Morning America*, ABC 7 AM, October 20, 2004, Lexis Nexis Academic, downloaded January 20, 2007; Carol Costello, *CNN Daybreak*, 5 AM, October 20, 2004, Lexis Nexis Academic, downloaded January 20, 2008; Ann Curry, *The Today Show*, NBC, 7 AM, October 20, 2004, Lexis Nexis Academic, downloaded January 18, 2008; on none of which was there any explanation given for the sudden appearance of the footage—it was simply there. The same was true the night before when the story was first presented. See Jim Sciutto, *ABC World News Tonight with Peter Jennings*, October 19, 2004, Lexis Nexis Academic, downloaded January 18, 2008. CNN made reference to the tapes having just been released by Spanish police—they also relentlessly teased the footage, interestingly enough. See Al Goodman, *CNN Wolf Blitzer Reports*, 5 PM, October 19, 2004, Lexis Nexis Academic, downloaded January 18, 2008.

38. I develop this argument in greater detail in "YouTube War: Fighting in a World of Camera in Every Cell Phone, Photoshop on Every Computer," (Strategic Studies Institute monograph, U.S. Army War College, forthcoming.)

39. Doing Nexis searches for the four networks for the 10 days following both attacks, the difference in the way the two arcs progress rapidly becomes apparent.

40. While this is not precisely the same argument that they make, central to my thinking here is the work of Daniel Dayan and Elihu Katz, *Media Events: The Live Broadcasting of History* (Cambridge, MA: Harvard University Press, 1992).

41. CNN will sometimes simply begin showing their American viewers CNN International, which is obviously broadcasting during what are nighttime hours here in the United States. They did that for a number of years, before instead offering American viewers reruns of *Larry King Live*—now it is a signal that a major international story is under way.

42. ABC's Charles Gibson remained in New York, and Fox News's Brit Hume, anchor of their 6 PM broadcast, which is the closest parallel to the broadcast networks' 6:30 broadcast remained in Washington, DC—although Shepard Smith, anchor of their 7 PM broadcast, was in Blacksburg by that night.

43. Matt Lauer, "Massacre at Virginia Tech," *Dateline NBC*, April 16, 2007, emphasis added, Lexis Nexis Academic, downloaded June 13, 2007.

44. Frey and Rohner, *Blood and Ink*, p. 18.

45. Hilary Brown, April 18, 2007, *World News Tonight with Charles Gibson* (140 in worst of single bombings) via *Tyndall Report* (tyndallreport.com) at http://abcnews.go.com/Video/videoE mbed?id=3054891&challenge=&authenticated=true&start=Y2RhdWJlckBlbWFpbC51bmMuZ WR1A&end=bGF1ZHB1cw%3D%3D&save=ON&save=OFF, downloaded May 24, 2007, and Martin Seemungal, "Has the Troop Increase Helped?" *CBS Evening News* (only says over 100 in worst of single bombing) via *Tyndall Report* (tyndallreport.com) at http://www.cbsnews.com/sections/i_video/main500251.shtml?id=2702559n, downloaded May 24, 2007.

46. These numbers were determined by using the search terms "Jordanian," "embassy," and "bomb" for the dates August 7, 2003, through August 17, 2003, for the relevant networks in Lexis Nexis Academic. Downloaded June 6, 2007. I excluded Fox from these counts, as Lexis Nexis Academic apparently doesn't index their regular daily coverage, which is what is relevant here (as opposed to the prime time shows).

47. These dates were determined by using the search terms "car," "Iraq," and "bomb," for the dates April 18 through April 28, 2007, for the relevant networks on the Lexis Nexis Academic database. Downloaded June 6, 2007.

48. "Baghdad, Shi'ite Convoy Ambushed," CNN 8:55 AM April 20, 2007, via Lexis Nexis Academic, downloaded June 7, 2007.

49. These numbers were determined by using the terms "bomb," "UN," and "headquarters," for the dates August 20, 2003, through August 30, 2003, for the relevant networks, in the Lexis Nexis Academic database. Downloaded June 6, 2007. Although after August 28 on CNN those were mostly a comparison with a bombing of a holy Shia shrine in Najaf. Still, there were fewer than 10 of those stories, so that's an extraordinary amount of coverage devoted to the UN bombing, stretching out over quite a few days after the event itself.

50. This is established by entering the search terms "green," "zone," and "bomb," for the dates April 12, 2007, through April 22, 2007, into the Lexis Nexis Academic database. This search actually pulled up 63 hits on CNN through April 22; the later stories were not about the bombing of the Green Zone, but merely mentioned it in passing, and so I did not count them for my purposes here.

51. One exception was Pamela Hess, in part because she was one of the few reporters who bothered to travel there. See, for example, "Analysis: Al Qaim Is Island of Stability," UPI , March 7, 2007, Lexis Nexis Academic, downloaded March 12, 2008, or "Analysis: Loudspeaker Diplomacy," UPI, February 15, 2007, Lexis Nexis Academic, downloaded March 12, 2008.

52. Relevant polling results available at Pollingreport.com include the following: NBC/ *Wall Street Journal:* Do you think the goal of achieving victory is still possible? 37 percent, Is not still possible? 56 percent. December 14–17 *USA Today*/Gallup November 30 -December 2, 2007: U.S. can win but won't: 20 percent, Cannot win: 37 percent. Downloaded March 13, 2008, http://pollingreport.com/iraq.htm, which archives data. On February 15, 2007, Pew reported: "Confidence in a successful outcome in Iraq, which remained fairly high last year even as perceptions of the situation grew negative, also has eroded. The public is now evenly divided over whether the U.S. is likely to achieve its goals in Iraq—47% believe it will definitely or probably succeed, while 46% disagree. Three months ago, 53% saw success as at least probable and 41% disagreed." "War

Support Slips; Fewer Expect Successful Outcome." http://people-press.org/reports/display .php3?Report ID=304, downloaded March 13, 2008.

53. Neil Munro, "Issues and Ideas: The Dollar Value of Murder," *National Journal*, February 17, 2007, Academic Search Premier, http://search.ebscohost.com/login.aspx?direct=true&db=ap h&AN=24290900&site=ehost-live, downloaded February 11, 2007.

54. Pew Research Center for the People and the Press, "Increasing Optimism About Iraq; Obama Has the Lead, But Potential Problems Too," February 28, 2008, p. 19, http://people-press. org/reports/pdf/398.pdfhttp://people-press.org/reports/pdf/398.pdf downloaded March 13, 2008. "The number of Americans who say the military effort is going very or fairly well is much higher now than a year ago (48% vs. 30% in February 2007). There has been a smaller positive change in the number who believe that the U.S. will ultimately succeed in achieving its goals (now 53%, up from 47% in February 2007)."

55. For examples of this form of argument, see James Glanz and Eric Schmitt, "Iraq Attacks Lower, but Steady, New Figures Show," *New York Times*, March 12, 2008, http://www.nytimes .com/2008/03/12/world/middleeast/12iraq.html?ex=1205985600&en=54adad339d0a5511&ei=5 070&emc=eta1, downloaded March 13, 2008, and particularly (although it is an opinion piece), Eugene Robinson, "Iraq's Surging Violence," *Washington Post*, March 11, 2008, p. A-19, http:// www.washingtonpost.com/wp-dyn/content/article/2008/03/10/AR2008031002245.html? referrer=emailarticle, downloaded March 11, 2008.

56. For example, as many scholars and commentators have noted, there is tremendous reluc- tance on the part of the American media to display images of dead bodies, particularly the bodies of Americans. For this reluctance to be trumped, a particular image must be judged to be extraor- dinarily newsworthy, and even then there is tremendous sensitivity in the way a particular image is displayed. This sensitivity is present in both broadcast and print news outlets. So, for example, the images of American soldiers being dragged through the streets of Mogadishu were judged so newsworthy that they were widely used by American newspapers, but almost never on the front page. A reporter surveyed metro dailies and found that the photograph of the corpse (he does not specify which of the series) ran on the front page of only 11 out of 34 (including the *New York Times* and *USA Today*). Fifteen put the photograph inside the front section, while another eight, including the *Baltimore Sun* and the *Dallas Morning News*, declined to use the image at all. Lou Gelfand, "If You Ran the Newspaper," *Minneapolis Star Tribune*, October 19, 1993, Lexis Nexis Academic. Some have argued that this is some kind of ideological choice, made to "sanitize" war and make it more acceptable. But in fact the American news system sanitizes every type of story that involves bodies. (That included the coverage of September 11, particularly compared to that seen in other countries, so that, for example, almost no images were shown of those jumping from the Towers, and essentially none at all of those burned or killed in the Pentagon.) Car crashes are a staple of local television news, but the images that accompany such stories, in every media market in the country, on every network's affiliates, are images of proxies of death rather than images of death itself. A Boston paper was judged by its readers to have used an image of a woman shot during a riot on its front page that was too graphic and received so much criticism from them that it had to offer an apology to them and to the woman's family. "Herald Editor Apologizes for Publishing Shooting Photos," *Boston Herald*, October 23, 2004, p. 2, Lexis Nexis Academic. When a California paper published a photograph of a sheep that had been badly burned in a wildlife fire, it received complaints precisely paralleling those papers receive when they pub- lish graphic war images, and their public editor wrote a column describing the decision to publish the image which precisely paralleled the columns which are published when papers are criticized for publishing combat images readers find to be too graphic. See Armando Acuna, "Bee Went Too Far with Burned-Sheep Photo, Some Say," *Sacramento Bee*, October 1, 2003, p. E-3, Lexis Nexis

Academic. The news sanitizes war in the United States, in other words, because the news sanitizes *everything.*

57. This question of intent can even go to the issue of whether a particular act is considered terrorism, because without knowing intent there is no way to know whether the motive might have been, for example, criminal intimidation or assassination for criminal purposes. This is the reasoning that leads some journalists to avoid the term "terrorism," at least in some cases, in favor of terms that can be considered euphemism. This point was raised in an interview with the author by Pamela Hess, then the Pentagon correspondent for UPI, March 9, 2007, Washington, DC.

58. I discuss this in more detail in *True Lies.*

59. Author interview with Pamela Hess, March 9, 2007, Washington, DC. The result, according to Hess (now with Associated Press) is that this becomes a war with "victims, but no heroes."

60. After all, in the cases where the tapes included the filmed execution of a hostage, no responsible outlet was going to air what was in essence a terrorist snuff film.

61. Ned Colt, "Another American Hostage Beheaded by Insurgents in Iraq," *NBC Nightly News with Tom Brokaw,*September 21, 2004, Lexis Nexis Academic, downloaded June 24, 2007.

62. Brigitte L. Nacos, *Terrorism and the Media, from the Iran Hostage Crisis to the Oklahoma City Bombing* (New York: Columbia University Press, 1994), p. 15.

PART II

IMPLICATIONS
FOR
COMBATING TERRORISM

6

The Strategic Dimensions of Terrorism

Concepts, Countermeasures, and Conditions in the Search for Security

Frank L. Jones

" 'HE HAS BEEN THREATENING SOCIETY with all sorts of horrors,' continued the lady, whose enunciation was caressing and slow, 'apropos of this explosion in Greenwich Park. It appears we all ought to quake in our shoes at what's coming if those people are not suppressed all over the world.' "[1] The unnamed woman utters these words in *The Secret Agent*, Joseph Conrad's novel of anarchistic terrorists who attempt to blow up Great Britain's Greenwich Observatory. The theme that ignited Conrad's imagination came straight from the day's news. He wrote this work, literary critic Morton Dauwen Zabel observes, as a citizen of Europe exposed to international disturbance and revolutionary danger, a man of his age apprehensive about the fate of a continent, and as an analyst of political-historical studies concerning "the destiny of man as determined by forces of power and anarchy," their sinister influence on the future.[2] Today, the subject of Conrad's novel would be equally popular as a thrilling tale of mystery, intrigue, and desperate characters. But it has also become the topic of serious deliberation and debate by government officials, scholars, and citizens alike because of the ability and implied intent of terrorists to wreck mass destruction beyond that of destroying a single structure.

Nonetheless, despite volumes of books, articles, and studies of terrorism, there has been scant investment made in developing a theory of terrorism. Instead, scholars and practitioners devote their efforts to writing about the history of terrorism, examining a variety of terrorist movements, discussing the influence of political ideologies and religious belief on terrorists' motives, dissecting their operational environments, or analyzing the psychological makeup of terrorists. This has resulted in a broken looking glass approach to understanding terrorism whereby each shard casts a portion of the image but not a complete likeness. As Richard Schultz points out, there has been intense study of terrorism, but the literature has been "primarily descriptive, prescriptive and very emotive in form."[3] This is still the case three decades after Schultz made that assertion, and such an approach continues to suggest why terrorism is often simply understood as a tactic.

This is an unfortunate state of affairs with serious repercussions, perhaps even disastrous results. It leads government officials to fixate on tactics, which, in turn, leads to the belief that there is a political, social, or economic antidote or vaccine—some combinatory "drug cocktail"—that, if used, can eliminate terrorism. Tactics, as Carl von Clausewitz observed, are fighting techniques that can be addressed with prescriptive doctrine— that is, at a level where method and routine are useful and even essential. Strategy involves questions of broad purpose in which complexity, contingency, and difficulty rule; doctrine is not only useless, it is unattainable.[4]

Therefore, this chapter seeks to advance a strategic theory of terrorism as it relates to all orders of nonstate actors by using an interdisciplinary approach that integrates social science and the theory of war and strategy. In essence, the proposed theory argues that terrorists make choices to attain a future state or condition. Those choices concern how (concept or way) they will use the coercive or persuasive power (resources or means) available to exercise control over circumstances or a population to achieve objectives (ends) in accordance with their policy. This calculated relationship among ends, ways, and means—which is a rational construct for strategy—forms the basis for this theoretical approach. Any theory or theoretical approach should specify essential terminology and definitions, explicate underlying assumptions and premises, present substantive propositions that can be translated into usable hypotheses, and last, provide or identify methods that can be used to test the hypotheses and modify the theory as appropriate. Ideally, it should also meet certain standards such as economy of language, applicability to the largest possible range of cases, and conformance to the facts.[5]

Further, in posing such a theoretical framework for the study of terrorism, the inevitable question is, "What can a state, particularly a democratic state, offer as a counterstrategy?" The answer is more difficult to construct because of the dilemmas the state confronts in terms of political judgment, institutional response, and policy prescriptions. It must balance policy concerns with a number of other factors, including values, beliefs, the rule of law, and legitimacy, to name a few. Nonetheless, in responding to terrorism, countermeasures have both strategic and operational contexts and rely on the use of strategic appraisal, the relationship of political identity and discourse in a war of perceptions, and the integration of the instruments of power, with some taking precedence. There is no foolproof counterstrategy, however, and because of this, its guiding principles require a realistic understanding of the conditions of security.

DEFINING TERRORISM

One of the reasons for a lack of focus on theoretical and conceptual issues, it is argued, stems from the definitional problems associated with the term "terrorism." Some scholars have become so discouraged by the lack of an accepted definition that they have abandoned any attempt to devise it. Walter Laqueur, a noted scholar of terrorism, contends, "A comprehensive definition of terrorism . . . does not exist nor will it be found in the foreseeable future."[6] However, sociologist Jack Gibbs suggested that it is impossible to pretend to study terrorism without some form of definition, otherwise, discussion lapses into obscurantism. He also argues that one of the problems is definitional parsimony to the degree that oversimplification occurs: "it is inconsistent to grant that human behavior is complex and then demand simple definitions of behavioral types."[7] As Martha Crenshaw remarked, clarity is often sacrificed for brevity.[8] In attempting to meet these challenges, Gibbs defines terrorism as "illegal violence or threatened violence directed against human or nonhuman objects" that has five characteristics: (1) the violence is undertaken to alter or maintain at least one putative norm in at least one population; (2) it has secret, furtive, and/or clandestine features so the participants can conceal their identity and location; (3) it is not undertaken to further the permanent defense of territory; (4) it is not conventional warfare and because of the participants' concealed personal identity and concealment of their location, their threats, and/or their spatial mobility, the participants perceive themselves as less vulnerable to conventional military action; and (5) this violence is perceived by the participants as contributing to the normative goal previously described by inducing fear of violence in persons (perhaps an indefinite category of them) other than the immediate target of the actual or threatened violence and/or by publicizing some cause.[9] This definition lacks one essential aspect, which one of the earliest definitions of terrorism found in the 1948 edition of the *Encyclopedia of Social Sciences*, provides. This text defines terrorism as a "method or a theory behind the method whereby an organized group or party seeks to achieve its avowed aims chiefly through the systematic use of violence."[10]

The value of joining these two definitions is not only that it seeks to explain a complex subject in the manner it deserves. That is, it addresses the complexity associated with human motivation, where the mixture of political motives, as an example, cannot be readily distinct from personal motives. It also has another valuable feature: it recognizes terrorism as a theory with violence as the essential feature. Violence—collective violence to be precise—is the strategic concept, the way, used to advance a strategy consisting of a putative norm that the terrorists are attempting to alter and maintain using various tactics (e.g., bombing, assassination) in a strategic environment.

PREMISES

For the purposes of this chapter, "strategy" is defined as what Harry Yarger calls a "synergy and symmetry of objectives, concepts and resources to increase the probability of policy success and the favorable consequences that follow from that success. . . . Strategy accomplishes this by expressing its logic in rational, linear terms—ends, ways and means."[11] In adopting such an approach, several premises are critical to framing a strategic theory of terrorism.

The first premise is that "political purpose dominates all strategy."[12] "Political" as defined herein is an enunciation of policy, an expression of the preferred end state, whether it is attainable or not. Ideally, this policy is clearly articulated by the terrorist leaders as it represents guidance for the employment of means (the instruments of coercive or persuasive power) toward the achievement of aims. Nevertheless, policy can change as the strategic environment or circumstances change, creating limitations imposed by others on the means available to the terrorists.

A second premise is the primacy of the strategic environment, which has a number of dimensions.[13] Terrorist leaders strive to attain a thorough understanding of the strategic situation and knowledge of the strategic environment. The strategic environment is physical and metaphysical, domestic and international, requiring an understanding of cultures, beliefs, and worldviews of adversaries, allies (actual or potential), and neutralists. In implementing his strategy, the terrorist creates a security dilemma for other actors; he introduces change, and change upsets the status quo, the equilibrium of the strategic environment. The other actors are forced to do something.[14]

It is in the strategic environment that signaling occurs in order to have a psychological influence on political behavior and attitudes.[15] The terrorist sends a signal that a target is vulnerable, that the perpetrators of violence exist, and that these perpetrators have the capability to strike numerous times. The signals are usually directed at three different audiences: the target or victims themselves, who may be killed and therefore can no longer be influenced; the group that identifies with the victim and therefore are affected by the implicit message that they are vulnerable as well; and all others, a "resonant mass." This group is composed of those who may react emotionally in a positive or negative manner, depending on which side they sympathize with in the conflict, as well as the government, the legitimate power, responsible for protecting the victims.[16]

The strategic environment should also be understood in terms of social geometry, which permits conspiratorial theories to flourish. Donald Black stresses, "Although a longstanding grievance usually underlies terrorism [and therefore justifies the resort to violence], the grievance alone does not explain the violence. It must have the right geometry—a particular location and direction in social space."[17] In other words, a condition of "social polarization" exists between society and the aggrieved. For the terrorist, society must be understood as having certain characteristics: it is sick and the illness cannot be cured, the state is violence itself and can be opposed only with violence, and the truth of the terrorist's espoused cause justifies any action that supports this stated objective.[18]

A third premise is that adaptation—that is, learning from experience—is required by all involved, and the key is who is adapting quicker, the terrorists or the government and its security forces. The terrorists and the governments with which they contend must recognize the magnitude of change required and strive for an improved fit between the organization and its external environment. The rate of change internal to the states, its leaders, institutions, and organizations must keep pace with the rate of change in the environment in order to cope with unfolding events and the terrorists' countermoves.[19] Thus, strategy is a "process, a constant adaptation to shifting conditions and circumstances in a world where chance, uncertainty, and ambiguity dominate."[20]

The fourth premise is that "strategy has a symbiotic relationship with time." Deciding when to execute the strategy is crucial to the terrorist leaders. If the historical timing is appropriate, then small actions can have large strategic effects. These effects can be cumulative and thus become part of the interplay between continuity and change.

They also become part of the continuities of the strategic environment. If the timing is not propitious, then the results may be meager, require additional exertion, and cost more in terms of tangible and intangible resources. Even in failure, the strategic effects become part of the framework of change and interaction in the strategic environment and thereby influence future actions.[21]

A fifth premise is that for terrorists, efficiency of action is subordinate to effectiveness. This is not to suggest that efficiency is not valued, but that the purpose of the strategy is to attain strategic effect. If strategic objectives are achieved, they in turn generate or contribute to the generation of the strategic effects that favor the realization of the desired end state.[22] The strategic effect in terrorism is to create a sense of vulnerability and intimidation. It is "intended to create a state of fear that is acute and long-lasting enough to influence behavior."[23]

The sixth premise is that the terrorists' strategy seeks a proper balance among the objectives wanted, the methods used to pursue the objectives, and the resources available for the effects desired. In formulating the strategy, the ends, ways, and means are interconnected, working synergistically to accomplish the strategic effect.[24] Terrorist leaders must be understood as rational calculators.

The seventh and final premise is that terrorists understand the importance of strategic risk; recognize the inherent existence of uncertainty, chance, and nonlinearity in the strategic environment; and attempt to produce a favorable balance in the ends-ways-means calculation to overcome or at least ameliorate the impact. Nonetheless, the risk of failure remains.[25] Since action is imperative, terrorist leaders must take risks in order to maintain the organization. Action also serves to address internal factors such as solidifying shared values and objectives though a sense of belonging and unity, generating excitement, elevating social status, and acquiring interpersonal or material reward. It also promotes external objectives such as recruitment and material and popular support from sympathizers and constituencies. Therefore, the terrorist strategists and leaders must manage the friction between their need to preserve the organization (since action risks destruction by government forces) and the foot soldiers' demand for action. Inaction can breed internal power struggles and major disagreements on any number of subjects.[26]

To paraphrase Carl von Clausewitz, terrorism has a grammar of its own, changing from age to age and place to place, but its logic—the rationale for terrorism—remains durable. The violent act is designed to send a message to a wide audience, not just the immediate victim that will "create, instill or perpetuate a perception of fear within that audience." Further, "no specific ideological, theological, or bases are assumed, since the intent to create or foster a sense of fear beyond the immediate victim remains the principal *raison d'être* for the violent act or threat."[27] Thus, terror is the strategic effect and violence provides the strategic concept, which is why it must be discussed first.

THE STRATEGIC CONCEPT OF TERRORISM AND ITS MEANS

Violence is the principal way or strategic concept by which terrorists will achieve their espoused ends. The terrorist uses collective violence, that is, personal injury by a group, albeit a small one, as a form of protest, a quest for justice, the purposeful expression of concrete and identifiable grievances, which are precipitated by any number of social, economic, cultural, or political issues.[28]

Terrorism is also an organized form of violence that includes the concept of collective liability. Collective liability means that a group or members of the offender's group or social category are held accountable for the offender's conduct. The population of the offending government is answerable for the government's actions, the source of oppression, and impediment to the terrorists' ideal state. Thus, any member of this population, including women, children, and the elderly, may be vulnerable to attack.[29] In the words of French anarchist Emile Henry, "Il n'y a pas d'innocents"[30] (There are no innocents); therefore, the violence is justified since all are complicit.

Moreover, as Martha Crenshaw notes, violence is the "primary method of action," and terrorists are individuals who have a bias for action—and are "impatient for action."[31] This preference for violent action is made explicit to the victim of terror in the hope it will be coercive: "the power to hurt is often communicated by some performance of it. Whether it is sheer terroristic violence to induce an irrational response, or cool premeditated violence to persuade somebody that you mean it and may do it again, it is not the pain and damage itself but its influence on somebody's behavior that matters."[32] This approach bypasses the Clausewitzian formula that resistance is a product of two variables—means and will.[33] The terrorist has no interest in reducing the adversary's means because the terrorist is less powerful and less capable than the adversary is. The way must therefore focus almost exclusively on the will. The terrorist must determine "what an adversary treasures" and "what scares him"; while the adversary must comprehend what the terrorist wants in order to be compliant, to know how to avoid pain or loss. The threat of violence must be personalized so that the adversary's pain or loss is "so anguishing as to be unendurable" and makes surrender a relief.[34] It must also lead to political action on the part of the government.

There appear to be two factors that promote this aim of prompting governmental action. First, there is some evidence that if the terrorist tells the target how to find relief from the stress there is less chance of inaction. Second, sporadic violence, as opposed to sustained relentless violence, appears to be more psychologically and socially effective by creating fear, anxiety, and a feeling of vulnerability as well as undermining society's networks of trust, solidarity, cooperation, and interdependence.[35] If emotional terror and social anomie occur, with each individual only concerned about his or her personal survival, then the state has failed, for this sense of insecurity signals the fact (or at least influences the perception) that the provision of security as a public good—the very purpose for the state—can no longer be guaranteed by the state.[36] The state becomes the locus of frustration, and people blame it for not protecting them. If, however, a certain level of violence can be tolerated psychologically, then the antidote to the violence lies in its management by the government, which should implement prudent countermeasures to meet this objective.

Thus, for the terrorist, the threat of violence must combine with unpredictability in the mind of the potential victims. Violence becomes a form of "costly signaling." Terrorists employ costly signaling to indicate their resolute and credible willingness to resort to violence, a costly action. The terrorists cannot afford to bluff or lie since to do so would only undermine their claims of strength and capability to impose costs on those who oppose them.[37]

By inflicting pain (accomplishing the aim), the feeling of vulnerability is heightened and violence serves a purpose. Strangely, this purpose is not only one of coercion or destruction; for the terrorist it can also be a redemptive act, symbolic in meaning. A terrorist act is a scene in a morality play within the theater of protest. The allusion to drama is strong: labeled by some social scientists as a form of symbolic action in a "complex performative field" and a "dramaturgical framework"[38] or a "bloody drama played out before an audience."[39] As George Sorel notes, violence is a purifying act.[40] The terrorist is a moralist. A moral order must be returned to equilibrium.

The tactics of terrorism are simple. They are the visible and violent acts taken by the means or resources available, which include not only terrorist foot soldiers but also other resources such as finances, weapons, and other matériel. These tactics further the group's ends, as well as provide inducements needed to recruit and maintain a membership. These acts consist of assassination, arson, bombings (including suicide bombings), armed robbery, and kidnapping for the purposes of extortion. They are used to destabilize society in three respects: political instability by killing government leaders and undermining the political process; social instability by disrupting various systems of exchange (e.g., social, economic) and by propagating such fear that distrust becomes normal and disorder results; and moral instability by provoking authorities to respond to these political and social threats with brutal actions that will delegitimate vital institutions in the society.[41]

DEFINING THE ENDS OF TERRORISM

The late Philip Windsor argued that terrorists' objectives are rooted in the "conditions of an historical legacy that have created a cause that can no longer be defined in terms of political compromise but instead must be redefined in terms of a moral claim."[42] "The agenda is dominated by long-standing historical legacies that have created a universe of moral problems." Thus, terrorists understand themselves to be "inheritors dispossessed by history." It is this historical grievance of being cheated of their "rightful" inheritance and their "quest for legitimacy in an as-yet only imagined proper order that lends them moral justification." This is an important distinction, for the tendency among those who seek to counter terrorism is to act as if only two options are available: either terrorism must be wiped out because it hampers civilized political discourse, or a dialogue with the terrorists is critical to coopt them into the political process. Both of these avenues may prove sterile. The extermination of terrorists tends to breed more terrorists and thus confirms the moral claims of the terrorists, while cooptation can prove futile because moral claims cannot always be solved by political resolution.[43]

The objectives of terrorist organizations are often grandiose and visionary, calling for sweeping and uncompromising change in the allocation of power in society or contesting the legitimacy of political and social elites.[44] Yet the commitment of terrorist organizations to a specific ideology is often weak or inconsistent;[45] it certainly is not homogenous. Ideas are often borrowed loosely from a number of theoretical sources to define ends that have ranged from Marxist-Leninism to a variety of religious doctrines. Instead, the ideology should be understood more broadly, "in the sense of being based on beliefs that comprise a systematic, comprehensive rejection of the present political world and the promise of future replacement."[46] In appealing to diverse audiences to support the terrorists or to at least cooperate and support them, the terrorists' ends are syncretist.

More dangerous, the vast majority of terrorists cannot articulate the political stages or tasks necessary to achieve their objectives, but instead offer only an end state. Further, terrorism may be considered, according to Jeffrey Alexander, "postpolitical"—that is, "it reflects the end of political possibility."[47] If that becomes the case, then it is an experience of overwhelming political impotence expressed through "drawing blood." Its tactics "deliver maiming and death; they serve a strategy of inflicting humiliation, chaos, and reciprocal despair."[48] In other words, terror becomes an end unto itself. This has led one scholar to conclude that the "cause is not the cause." The cause, as articulated by the group's ideology, becomes the rationale for the violent acts the terrorists commit.[49]

TERROR AS AN END

In this respect, terrorism is a deliberate political choice by a political actor to use the power to hurt.[50] This power to hurt is not incidental to the use of force, but is an object itself. The power to hurt, as Thomas Schelling argued, is the capacity to "influence somebody's behavior, to coerce his decision or choice."[51] It is a coarse form of behavior modification in which both the afflicter and the victim know that pain can be imposed, even anticipated, and there is equally the understanding that it might be avoided under certain conditions. However, as Windsor suggested, the terrorist has no patience with the complexities involved in political matters. This is not the protracted armed struggle of the people's army in the process of revolutionary war, as an example, where the people's army is built progressively during the course of the war. Where time, patience, or ingenuity is in short supply, the terrorist will slash through this Gordian knot. He reverts to brute force where destruction is the strategic end.[52]

This should not be surprising because as Michel Wieviorka observed, terrorism is an "extreme, degenerate, and highly particularized variety of social antimovement."[53] Terrorist actors exhibit three defining principles of this phenomenon, principles that fuse or "feed on themselves." Terrorism "takes the form of a course of violence, which, possessed of a rationale all its own, propagates itself without its perpetrators having to verify their words or deeds with the people in whose name they claim to be acting."[54] Instead, the actor and the cause become indistinguishable. "In the most extreme of cases, and less often than one may think, he internalizes—sometimes to the point of nihilism and self-destruction—the inability of a social movement to assert itself." The enemy is objectified, a target to be assailed, a person to be eliminated, a system to be destroyed. Last, a radical disengagement occurs, a death struggle ensues and attainment of a utopian state, a new order, or a just society is dismissed. "The ends become confused with their means, with all sense of vision being reduced to plans for the destruction of all that stands in the way of the actor's subjectivity."[55] In other words, the desire for annihilation—self, opponent, and the state—comes to fore. In some cases, the oppressor's values are such an abomination that annihilation is the only course if the enemy will not convert to the terrorists' view. This is not the destruction of the politico-military power of the bourgeoisie or oligarchic state as part of the armed struggle of Marxist-Leninist theory. Terrorists are not interested in the eradication of their adversaries' military power. Instead, they are interested in radical change to structures or conditions through violent means or the threat of violence. The terrorist is committed to planning and strategy. These plans and strategies presume a situation of total war that advocates unlimited violence and a standard of action that, carried to its furthest extremes, can result in martyrdom and self-destruction. However, terrorism as an end unto itself is an anomaly and is not the usual manner in which terrorist organizations end.

Ultimately, terrorism is an exceedingly rational strategy, calculated in terms of costs and benefits with the terrorist relying on the accuracy of those calculations.[56] For the vast majority of terrorists, the strategic environment is reduced to a power struggle between opposing forces wherein the terrorist assumes an ethic of total resistance. In the system in which the terrorist lives and moves, as Wievorka notes, "this ethic can only take a martial—and thereby planned and strategic—form."[57]

TERRORISM AND WAR

Terrorism operates in two dimensions simultaneously—as a theory of violence and as a strategy of violence perpetrated to achieve a supposed end. Tying these two concepts together, which is the thrust of this chapter, the strategic theory of terrorism is a theory of action (to paraphrase Bernard Brodie), with violence as the critical and defining element in both of these dimensions.[58] Thus, how should we understand the violence that terrorism uses, its "martial form?" The answer to this question is again hindered by the definitional debate highlighted previously, since scholars hold a legion of differing views describing what it is not rather than what it is, but largely distinguishing it from other forms of collective violence (e.g., lynching, rioting, and vigilantism).[59]

There are some problems with this categorization, simply characterizing it as solely another variety of collective violence. These other types of collective violence are not modes of political behavior, nor do the people involved seek to challenge the authority of the state and to acquire political influence. Further, terrorist groups are not mobs, but organizations with "internally consistent values, beliefs, and images of the environment." They seek a logical means to advance a particular (though not always clearly articulated) ends using rational decision-making calculations to attain short-term and long-term objectives.[60] Colin Gray, however, offers a way out of the definitional wilderness by questioning whether terrorism is war.

Gray answers the question by referring to two theorists: Clausewitz and Hedley Bull. Clausewitz defined war as "an act of force to compel our enemy to do our will."[61] Political scientist Hedley Bull followed Clausewitz's line of reasoning and wrote, "war is organized violence carried on by political units against each other."[62] Thus, terrorism meets this definition since terrorists apply this force, violence, for a political end. If it is not for this end, then it "may be sport, or crime, or banditry of a kind integral to local culture, but it is not war. War, its threat and actuality, is an instrument of policy."[63] As Colin Gray notes, "war has many dimensions beyond the political, but its eternal essence is captured by Clausewitz and Bull." From his perspective, the political context is principal, though he admits that it is far from the "sole, driver of the incidence and character of war."[64] In other words, Gray is willing to concede that terrorists use force to achieve ends that are political, social, or religious in nature.

Some thinkers suggest that terrorism is a form of "new war," and that Clausewitz overlooks unconventional and so-called nontrinitarian war, thereby arguing that Clausewitz and his remarkable trinity is not relevant.[65] These critics define the concept of the trinity as the commander and his army, the people, and the government. In Gray's view, this is a serious misreading of Clausewitz and neglectful of the primary trinity, which still pertains. That primary trinity consists of passion (violence, hatred, and enmity), chance and probability, and subordination to reason or policy.[66] In this context, policy can be understood as the decision to take an action and perform this act in a particular way, or it can be described as the activities and relationships that influence the formulation of policy. For Clausewitz, the formulation of policy was a matter of judgment and other qualities, and could be undertaken by both states and nonstates (he uses the example of the Tartar tribes). Thus, Clausewitz thought not only in terms of the nation-state model.[67]

Nonetheless, terrorism contains all three elements of both trinities, with the primary trinity's relationship to terrorism being self-evident. In the secondary trinity, the titles are changed, but the functions remain the same: the strategist; the operational commander of terrorist groups consisting of foot soldiers and members of the support network who execute the missions or provide the financial and logistical support; and the broader populace, which as Borum describes, "provides expressive and instrumental support for the terrorists or sympathy to their cause."[68]

Thus, terrorism fully meets the definitions set out by Clausewitz and Bull. It is a form of war, irregular war, similar to insurgency but having its own characteristics. Nonetheless, it shares with insurgency and other forms of violent military conduct the capacity to generate a strategic effect. That effect can be produced on the mind, the military or security forces of the opponent, or both, but all have in common that they must have political consequences.[69] In truth, it matters not whether the character of the war has a regular or irregular feature—the qualifying adjectives are of no import. Clausewitz's general theory of war and strategy are equally valid to both. A general theory of war and strategy explains both regular and irregular (terrorism) warfare. While they are different forms of warfare, they are not different strategically.[70]

STRATEGIC APPRAISAL FOR COMBATING TERRORISM

Governments react immediately to a terrorist attack to create for their public a perception of order, to exert control over a potentially destabilizing event, and to communicate a message to both the populace and the perpetrators that all instruments of the government will be used to hunt down the malefactors and "bring them to justice." While such a response is necessary to mitigate fear and the sense of vulnerability that weighs upon the victims, governments sometimes fail to recognize that this type of response is merely palliative. Policy makers throw existing organizations into the breach or immediately create new organizations, thereby elevating organizational response to an end. Ironically, the further bureaucratization of the state by establishing additional agencies yields marginal benefits and introduces new organizational pathologies or weakens accountability and regulation because of a dispersion of political control. Further, what is often described as a counterterrorism strategy is actually a combination of policies, legal measures, and organizational activities. While these aspects are important components in a response to terrorism, a more expansive outlook is required. It necessitates a strategic view as opposed to an institutional one.

A strategic view defines problems by conducting a focused appraisal of the strategic environment to select key strategic factors that must be addressed to advance or protect state interests successfully. From the synthesis and evaluation of these factors, the strategist produces a rational statement of the ends, ways, and means that create effects leading to the desired future.[71] Institutions are part of the calculus, but they are the framework through which the ways and means are defined and executed—that is, through their roles and responsibilities (diplomacy, law enforcement) and their resources (financial and human).

In addressing the state's interests, the strategist must recognize that the execution of the strategy does not occur in a vacuum and that there are factors in the environment that impose constraints on the strategy. One of the most powerful and potentially limiting strategic constraints is the ethical and legal dimensions of combating terrorism and their major expression in the just war tradition and other conventions codified in international law and domestic statutes. While the terrorists may not be constrained by such precepts, most governments adhere to a moral norm for the treatment of combatants and noncombatants, as well as the protection of civil liberties. The existence of these norms does not ensure observance, but adherence confers on the state legitimacy for its actions in combating the terrorists. Combating terrorism is a political act and therefore, the state and the activities it undertakes must be sensitive to the political environment, both domestic and international. As one scholar has noted, this is especially true in democracies—and arguably more intently since the advent of mass communications—where strategic policy is the subject of intense scrutiny and debate.[72]

Another factor is strategic culture, the way in which a state wages war. There is also a correlation between strategic culture and national values as these values, political and moral judgments, represent the core beliefs of the government, the military (or security forces in general) and the people. The strategic culture defines how the government and the security forces perform and the way in which they need to behave in order to succeed in warfare against an irregular enemy. There is, however, as Colin Gray suggests, no algebraic formula that can produce such an outcome.[73] It relies on recognition of the situation and an understanding of the relationship between policy and performance— that is, it demands the ability to perform strategically by adapting the tools of national power to the circumstances. It also requires humility by taking the enemy seriously as a strategic entity. As Sun Tzu, the ancient Chinese theorist of war, advises:

> Thus it is said that one who knows the enemy and knows himself will not be endangered in a hundred engagements. One who does not know the enemy but knows himself will sometimes be victorious, sometimes meet with defeat. One who knows neither the enemy nor himself will invariably be defeated in every engagement.[74]

To paraphrase one specialist, anyone having any responsibility for dealing with terrorists must know his enemy and what the enemy is trying to do, and respond not by being reactive, like countering the moves of an adversary in chess, but taking the initiative.[75] To win, or to "get the big things right,"[76] means taking the initiative and recognizing that the strictures of culture must be understood and mitigated through flexibility and adaptability. Moreover, it means that the problem of terrorism can only be resolved by fashioning a "true community of political values."[77] Such a notion has far-reaching consequences when dealing with transnational terrorists, for it makes common cause more difficult when values must be shared across geographic boundaries and cultures.

Thus, the strategist must contend with these coordinates: strategic/institutional, interest/ethics, culture/values. It requires a tailoring of these elements to the character of the warfare at hand, recognizing that the Clausewitzian conditions of uncertainty, fog, and friction are involved. Nonetheless, as terrorism is a form of irregular warfare, then principles derived from fighting irregular warfare are of use.

ESSENTIAL QUESTIONS AND PRINCIPLES

Renowned counterinsurgency expert Sir Robert Thompson stressed that any government should attempt to defeat a subversive movement at the first sign of violence. The problem for governments is that they do not always recognize the signs of its existence or they may ignore or deny it for shortsighted political reasons. Further, it is not easy to alert the public to the danger and if it overreacts, the government may be accused of repression.[78] While prevention is better than having to discover the cure, the cure is neglected because the strategic problems from which the violence was generated are either unidentified or they were not present in a form that allowed them to be distinguished. As Raymond Aron wrote, "strategic thought draws its inspiration each century, or rather at each moment of history, from the problem which events themselves pose."[79] It is not until the problem becomes distinguishable that the strategist can act. To do so prematurely, the strategist would be more a soothsayer than a rational calculator of ends, ways, and means.

While terrorism provides the purpose that alone is not sufficient to lay the foundation on which to formulate countermeasures, the strategist who intends on defeating terrorists must ask some fundamental questions in order to conduct the strategic appraisal mentioned earlier. These questions are threefold:

- What is the nature of the war we face?
- What is our political objective?
- What is the adversary's strategy?

The answers to these three questions form the basis for how the government should pursue its strategy, recognizing that it is gambling that its perseverance in pursuing the answers will yield success at an acceptable cost. The answers to these questions also form the critical concepts for the strategy.

Confusion and misjudgment about this first principle undermines all other efforts. Here again, Clausewitz serves as the guide: "The first, the supreme, the most far-reaching act of judgment that the statesman and commander have to make is to establish . . . the kind of war on which they are embarking: neither mistaking it for, nor trying to turn it into, something alien to its nature. This is the first of all strategic questions and the most comprehensive."[80] As indicated previously, terrorism is a form of irregular warfare and therefore, for most states, it requires not only a recognition that the situation and the enemy are different, as they are in any war, but also a willingness to recognize that atypical nature is paramount to how it counters the terrorists. Combating terrorism requires a total response—political foremost, but legal, social, police, financial, and military activity are important as well. Thus, it demands a balanced response, with attention to its attendant political dimensions. Two factors weigh heavily in understanding the nature of the war: perception and communication.

Robert Komer's study of bureaucratic response to unconventional threats is instructive regarding the first factor. While many in government may perceive the political nature of the conflict, it is common for government leaders to miscalculate both its full implications and what coping with it requires. Governments may underestimate the strengths of the terrorists and overestimate their own capacities. Politically, governments must give due weight to the dynamic nature of the situation, the popular appeal of the terrorists, the vulnerabilities of the government and the society it seeks to protect, and in the case of transnational terrorists, the weaknesses of its allies and partners in prosecuting the counterterrorism strategy. Additionally, the depth of factionalism and bureaucratic turf wars that exist within the institutions of government may blur perceptions. Thus, there can be serious perceptual delays in recognizing the extent of the threat which only hampers the proper function of the most critical element of countering the terrorist threat—intelligence collection and analysis. Further, the government may underestimate the terror potential, the terrorists' ability to escalate and to frustrate the much larger and better-equipped apparatus of the state through hit-and-run tactics that rely on unpredictability, elusiveness, and evasion.[81] These features may make a military response not only ineffective but also perhaps counterproductive.

The issue of communication is of equal importance in defining the nature of the conflict and recognizing terrorism for what it is and not for what the government would like it to be. As suggested earlier, terrorism is an "extreme form of political dialogue," and terrorist acts are narratives of political violence communicated among the terrorists, its perceived sympathetic audience, and the target state and its supporters. Therefore, the government's response is a form of communication as mediated overtly through its words and actions. These actions, if repressive, only serve to undermine the state's legitimacy and lend credibility to the terrorists' claims. However, legitimacy is a double-edged sword. Eroding the perception of the terrorist legitimacy is also possible and may contribute to disintegration of group cohesion or a decision to abandon the armed struggle. It may also contribute to the concept of a backlash, whereby the populace that supported the terrorists perceives that the terrorists are engaged in a private war with the state and not concerned about addressing the supporters' grievances.[82]

Clausewitz is again our Virgil regarding a response to the second question. "War is simply a continuation of political intercourse, with the addition of other means," he writes.[83] It is an instrument of policy. It asks the question: What political ends is the war meant to achieve? Wars "must vary in the nature of their motives and of the situations which give rise to them."[84] The "political object" determines the subordinate objectives and the amount of effort that the government, in its various functions, must take. Therefore, political aims must be clearly understood so that the instruments of power may be applied judiciously and with effect. Clausewitz puts forward the concept of two types of war, "either to totally destroy the enemy . . . or else to prescribe peace terms to him"—in other words, total or limited war.[85] Is the political aim defined as decisive victory or something less? While the latter is anathema as a matter of declared policy, with all its associated practical and psychological drawbacks, if the first is chosen, what is the chance of succeeding and how will such success be measured?

The answer, Colin Gray reminds us, relies on an appreciation of the merit in limitations on the use of force. The strategist "must cope with the uncertain exchange rate between military [or any security force's] effort and political effect."[86] If the elimination of the adversary is not the policy goal, then "the strength and durability under pressure of his political will must be a crucial determinant of whether or not a decisive victory is achievable at tolerable cost."[87] There is every reason to believe that realistic attainment of decisive victory may be unrealized if the enemy chooses not to be coerced into acquiescence by the amount and kinds of pressure that is applied. In opting for limited war, which is a reasonable course of action, it must be understood that there can be no decisive victory unless the adversary is willing to cooperate, although under duress. Only then can a government claim some variation of decisive success. If that is not the case, then the terrorist can choose to continue to fight, calculating that the political decision the government seeks will be judged to be not worth the human, economic, and political costs of a protracted conflict.[88] Governments, Gray rightfully declares, would be better off recognizing and articulating a concept of decisive victory as a range of possibilities, rather than characterizing it as a proposition in which failure is understood as the only alternative.[89] This is a realization that Clausewitz first articulated when he stated, "each age had its own kind of war, its own limiting conditions, and its own peculiar preconceptions."[90]

We are again in the infernal realm of perceptions. More precisely, the perceptions of policy makers are central to understanding how choices are made and the strategies executed. The cognitive frames of the policy makers and of the society itself shape the decisions, as well as the reaction to government efforts. These frames are the product of experience, culture, belief systems, fears, expectations, and the demands of domestic politics.[91] All of these variables influence and control the nature and course of warfare in important ways, and are (as mentioned previously) central to understanding strategic constraints on war, as are legal and moral norms and legitimacy. Ultimately, however, the strategist's performance must be judged in political terms: how effectively did he use the means available to meet his desired end?[92]

In his classic work, *The Art of War*, Sun Tzu writes, "what is of supreme importance in war is to attack the enemy's strategy."[93] This principle appears in the chapter titled "Offensive Strategy" and answers in part a fundamental question for the strategist: How should the war be fought? It would be a misinterpretation to understand Sun Tzu's axiom as referring solely to military action. Sun Tzu was a theorist who advocated advancing the state's interests through several means, and in countering terrorism, such an approach is imperative. Countering terrorists, as is true with insurgents, "is first and foremost an intellectual exercise," as one military historian has noted. It requires a "deep and thorough understanding of the nature of the war. . . . Single-track strategies, especially those emphasizing the military element of power, seldom prove effective."[94] Instead, they require strategies that utilize all elements of power to varying degrees. Nonetheless, as Sun Tzu suggests, an offensive strategy is necessary. Constant adaptation is critical; the government must at least keep pace with the rate of change in which the terrorists act, sensitive to the shifting conditions and situation in an environment where chance, uncertainty, and ambiguity dominate. "What is of the greatest importance in war is extraordinary speed; one cannot afford to neglect opportunity," the ancient master advises.[95]

However, there are moments when the state will not be able to adapt as quickly as the terrorists will and cannot conceivably protect all citizens and key assets, and where chance and uncertainty upset the state's attempt to maintain pace. In those instances, the state assumes the defense. Although Sun Tzu characterizes the defensive posture as invincible, he also states, "One defends when his strength is inadequate."[96] This point raises the issue of maintaining effective deterrence, a concept derided by some scholars and practitioners as obsolete, unreliable, and without value in counterterrorism. The arguments against deterrence often rest on the outdated and misinformed belief that terrorists are irrational adversaries, which has been coupled with the conviction that they are incapable of being deterred because they lack fixed assets, and further, as to their motivations, they cannot be weakened by the usual forms of menace. While there are elements of truth in terms of the theory's reliability, the heart of the argument is based on the faulty assumption that mistakes rationality for reasonableness, which was addressed previously.[97] Terrorist organizations contain rational, calculating strategists, who are prone to error like all human beings and must grapple with the possibility of strategic failure through the miscalculation of the adversary's capability and perseverance. As Colin Gray contends, "There is no adequate substitute for understanding the minds and the values they [terrorists] seek to maximize, that are targets for influence." Therefore, deterrence—which seeks to influence behavior—remains a pragmatic part of a counterterrorism strategy, but it must be understood anew. In short, deterrence must also be part of a broad strategy of influence, designed to influence others.[98]

Deterrence must be understood from the view of the enemy and their worldview; the deterrence threat must influence them and those who would cooperate with them.

It doing so, it consists of two aspects: "deterrence by punishment" and "deterrence by denial."[99] The second is the most commonly used formula by which targets are hardened and other measures are taken to make an attack too costly for the adversary to attempt, or to create the impression in the mind of the adversary that such an attempt would be fruitless.

Deterrence by punishment also seeks to exact a cost, but the cost is measured in terms of harming something the adversary values if it takes an undesired action, and making credible to the adversary the deterrer's promise to harm. The likelihood of deterrence by punishment working relies on the intensity of motivation on the part of the adversary. If the adversary values life over political goals, then this form of deterrence is likely to succeed. However, if the adversary values political goals over life, then the punishment may be only temporarily effective. Given this high intensity of motivation, the deterrer must take a systemic approach, focusing on the weak points in the terrorist network, and the weakest links are the financiers and the logisticians. Finding and punishing these participants, often the least fanatical, provide the best opportunity to disrupt the network's ability to function. Another group that is most vulnerable to deterrence is a state sponsor; they are readily identifiable for punishment.[100] A third group that may be deterred is the terrorist group that interacts with and supports the primary target. There is considerable overlap and cooperation between some terrorist groups, especially in terms of financing and logistics. Thus, the deterrer seeks to punish the cooperating group for aiding the primary target. The best method is again an attack on terrorist financing, such as the activities of front companies and charities, which has a ripple effect, disrupting several organizations at once by cutting off a key node.[101]

In responding to the three questions posed earlier, the countermeasures have three primary ends. First, it is an active offense that seeks to eliminate or render ineffective the terrorist organization both in terms of its ability to undertake violent acts and the support provided to it. It is important, however, to be realistic as to this goal. Terrorism can be contained, diminished, or defeated in some instances, but not prevented or stamped out comprehensively once it appears. It is not, as some have suggested, like piracy.[102] Second, it is a strategy of influence that serves to build and maintain effective deterrence through punishment and denial. Third, it sets realistic expectations of success and protection in the minds of the populace, taking heed to guard against the fallacy of total security. The populace should also fully understand the state's aims in the fight against the terrorists. The war against terrorism is often characterized as a war of ideas. It is more correctly a war of perceptions.

THE WAR OF PERCEPTIONS: DISCOURSE AND IDENTITY

The concept that combating terrorism involves the state and the terrorists in a battle of ideas is flawed. Like so many slogans, the "battle of ideas" is reductive to the point that it oversimplifies the issues involved. What is at stake is the communication of contending ideas through language. This is not to dismiss ideas as part of the ongoing political dialogue between the state and terrorists. The deficiency in this approach is that it makes ideas the center of gravity when it should be the terrorists' use of violence as a justifiable and legitimate manner to articulate grievances. Terrorists use ideas expressed through language to legitimize their actions by making common cause with those who have grievances. Ronald Munck points out, "For discourse theory, language can no longer be viewed as a simple instrument of communication." Words and the ideas they convey assume meaning in conflicting discourses. "More specifically, language takes on meaning and discourses are constructed through struggle." In short, all discourses are ideologically positioned, not neutral. Further, they are related to systems or modalities of power. In the context of Michel Foucault's conception of power, discourse and language are central to the social processes of modern society and the controlled management of populations.[103]

Thus, if ideas are to be accepted by the receiver, there must be common language and understanding, a similarity of discourse, and ultimately, agreement to a common set of values. However, in communicating its position, the state may resort to binary oppositional and abstract concepts, such as terrorism versus democracy/freedom. This approach presupposes not only a level of understanding of meaning, but places the receiver of that message into a position of having to choose between two options, both of which may be untenable, unknown, or unacceptable. These concepts are not value-free, but conduct a heavy political charge. They are also highly related to political identity, as are the acts of violence—the so-called propaganda of the deed.

Identity is no longer understood today as a fixed, predefined social role, but is viewed as more unstable or fluid, relative, ambiguous, and incomplete. As alluded to earlier, the motivation of terrorists are not homogenous but are open to multiple interpretations and shift not only in various historical periods but based on the dynamics derived from the forces influencing it. These forces can create antagonisms and in a world of change, frightening change, some cannot face that ambiguity and want the certainties of the old myths or some other solid foundation on which to base their identity. Thus, the terrorists' language, their narrative, appeals to different audiences and offers comforting words and symbols with culturally situated meanings.[104] What is needed is a counternarrative.

This counternarrative should not be an attempt to win others to the government's cause, a conversion experience. Such an approach turns the "secular quest for security" into a religious foray for redemption and atonement, reducing all discourse to the Manichean dyad of good and evil.[105] This turn to theistic language and imagery may be particularly self-defeating when the political and cultural distance between the state and the terrorist is vast. The message must speak to the audience's values, not to the values of the foreign government that is communicating the message. It is also naive to believe that all who hear the message will be dissuaded. There are always sufficient martyrs for the cause among the foot soldiers. Instead, the message must demonstrate that terrorism fails and historically, the data bear it out—90 percent of emerging terrorist groups last less than a year. Most fail to achieve their ultimate objectives. This approach takes time and patience for it operates on the belief that such a narrative can create doubts in the minds of adherents and sympathizers that ultimately, their aims are futile.[106] Other scholars have pointed out the fragile nature of terrorist groups that promotes their decline, including factionalism and internal rivalry, and that terrorist leaders struggle to maintain organizational viability.[107] Martha Crenshaw stresses that the government's message must serve to not only reduce the probability of violence but influence the terrorist organization's incentive structure, offer nonviolent incentives, increase the opportunities to exit the terrorist group, or promote internal dissension; in essence, a government's policy should "aim to make the organization less destructive and less cohesive rather than to defeat it militarily."[108]

THE PRIMACY OF POLICING

Although terrorism may be a matter of political and moral judgment and therefore, a strategic problem reliant on effective communication, a balanced approach is required, using the full array of policy instruments. The military instrument should not have primacy; it should be used selectively (and more usefully) for overseas operations against transnational terrorists. Characterizing terrorism in military terms such as a "war on terrorism" can blind governments to the limits of their society's political tolerance (especially true in a democratic state), and it can frame a problem inaccurately. Consequently, what is needed is a finely tailored military instrument, able to function with substantial flexibility and precision for well-defined political ends. These facets make special operations forces the preferred military tool for direct military action, especially overseas, because of the small footprint and familiarity with irregular warfare.[109] David Ignatius notes that the combined use of "hard-nosed" special operations forces and the "soft power tactics" of personnel involved in social, political, and economic development are proving increasingly effective against the Taliban insurgents in Afghanistan.[110] Conventional forces are best suited for deterrence, defense, and if necessary, to punish, particularly states that harbor or support terrorist groups by allowing their territory for training or as a logistical base.[111]

Another argument for not giving primacy to the military is that the reaction to terrorist attacks both internationally and domestically should conform to the same principles of the rule of law. Terrorists should be treated as criminals, as opposed to adversaries to be defeated militarily, since terrorism is prohibited by both national and international law. This approach has a moral dimension as well, in that it is faithful to established international norms involving just war, and it lessens the likelihood of causing civilian casualties through combat operations. This approach serves to legitimize the combating terrorism activities by strengthening institutions and promoting international cooperation.[112] It also reduces the likelihood of a global backlash that will assist the terrorists in recruiting or in gaining supporters. A policing approach has other advantages domestically. It is a form of "soft power" and therefore, it is an essential tool for combating terrorism.[113] To understand the validity of this claim, it is necessary to examine the nature of terrorist attacks.

Sufficient evidence exists to make the case that the most influential factors in the success or failure of a terrorist attack are those that occur in the preexecution phase. Thus, the focus should be on detecting the plot in the planning stages, relying on exploiting a failure in the terrorists' operational security, an observant public that notices suspicious behavior and international cooperation in cases where the threat crosses geographic borders. However, the primary tool is law enforcement or police, vigilant and trained security services that have the needed information and intelligence on which to conduct investigations or to detect and interdict the terrorists. This approach also places emphasis on community policing, where the public will come to trust the police and be willing to provide information about suspicious behavior.[114]

Sociologist Martin Innes proposes that counterterrorism activity has prospective and retrospective aspects. The prospective "precrime" aspects, also known as the "offender search" strategy of counterterrorism, are performed on a continuing basis and are intended to prevent, deter, and disrupt the activities of those thought to be involved in terrorism, primarily through surveillance and direct interventions. The second dimension is the reactive "postcrime" activities associated with incident response. This is the investigative component, which seeks to identify the perpetrators and prosecute them, as well as locating a support network to target it for prevention and deterrence efforts. To this element have been added community protection measures such as hardening targets before an event occurs and conducting "reassurance patrols" after an incident to provide the perception of security and in some cases, ameliorate community tensions, particularly those flashpoints where interethnic and interfaith volatility could be ignited. This typology divides police work between high- and low-policing agencies, those involved in intelligence gathering and investigation and those involved in community policing. Not only is there a connection between these levels, but greater attention, according to Innes, needs to be placed on local policing because of the uncertainty of the threat, the need to manage public anxieties and reduce the adverse social, economic, and political effects of terrorism, and the possibility that terrorist incidents can enflame community tensions and destroy community cohesion.[115]

Innes's proposal is consistent with the substantial literature in irregular warfare that emphasizes the importance of policing as both a method of combating terrorism and insurgency, and a means of making certain the prominence of civil control. Success is built on interpersonal trust and the recognition by community leaders that they can influence the style of policing in their community. The advantages of such a mutual arrangement for the police are twofold. First, police can establish a network of intelligence relationships that provide a reasonably useful means of maintaining surveillance over groups and communities that are difficult for the police to penetrate overtly or covertly. Second, police develop and manage relationships that are termed "strategic contacts." This term refers to the overt establishment of deliberate relationships with community leaders and opinion makers from groups the police believe are strategically important to the policing environment. These leaders provide intelligence about individuals and groups of interest and serve as a communication channel into these communities to counteract misinformation or to disseminate information useful to the police.[116]

Community policing encourages social trust between the authorities and communities of interest and in doing so, fosters legitimacy and forms the basis on which to collect and exploit intelligence essential to the welfare of the larger society. It is but another method for dealing with the uncertainty generated by the unpredictability of terrorist acts. It must be closely monitored in order to ensure that it does not become a method of oppression or undermine civil liberties. Moreover, it cannot guarantee uncovering accurate and timely intelligence; it is not foolproof or a panacea.

THREE CONDITIONS UNDERLYING INSECURITY

The political dilemmas that governments confront when dealing with terrorism relate to both policy and practice. The former concerns issues such as use of force, legitimacy, relations between states, and the domestic agenda. The latter emphasizes the institutional and technical aspects, such as intelligence collection and analysis. Both facets are intertwined with political judgment.[117] Yet no matter how astute the political judgment or how well coordinated the activities of organizations or how harmonious the relations between states that have a common cause, there are some issues that cannot be swept aside. The state must labor under these underlying conditions.

Strategic Surprise

Colin Gray has observed that the "the problem is not surprise . . . Rather the problem is the effects of surprise." No nation can make itself "surprise-proof."[118] It is also true that strategic surprise rarely results in decisive victory. Instead, the objective is to take as a many measures as possible to mitigate the harmful effects of surprise. Of course, alertness and flexibility are essential—that is, the ability to adapt to surprise, quickly and decisively, should be the primary characteristic of contemporary security planning and not bureaucratic reform. Resilience and the ability to control the consequences of surprise through effective response and recovery are critical to the well being of the state. The state can control these facets, for the element of surprise is controlled by the adversary. The obligation of the state is to be prepared and not "exaggerate the dangers of surprise."[119]

Severe damage can result from surprise, but it must be recognized as a momentary tactical success. The guiding principle that Gray offers is that of minimizing regrets. By this, he means that the goal for policy makers, strategists, and planners "is to make only minor errors." The challenge is to design and execute a surprise effect–tolerant security posture. Success is measured not in terms of guarantees or a risk-free environment, but "as getting the big things right enough."[120]

Too often, political leaders assume that when an attack occurs the public is not only politically unforgiving but also subject to panic. However, like the exaggeration of the potency of surprise, the media's portrayal of such a response is misleading. The media and policy makers have contributed to the perception of a public prone to panic and a descent into lawlessness. In truth, the public's behavioral responses appear to be highly tuned to risk perceptions, adopting responses proportionate to the risk. In other words, society is reasonably resilient and with the use of effective risk communications that includes targeted information and opening up channels of "two-way" communication to make the public a partner in managing risk, a nation can be prepared psychologically for terrorist attacks.[121]

Partners: The Flawed Instrument

In his classic study of bureaucracy and irregular warfare, Robert Komer underscores that in irregular war, a government's allies or partners are critical components in the effort, as is recognizing the flawed nature of multinational collaboration. This is especially true in dealing with a transnational threat. The quality of the other governments' leadership, administration, intelligence capabilities, and security forces must be adequate to the task. If those regimes are inept, corrupt, and faction-ridden or lack the capacity to govern—to administer the machinery of government—then the probability of success diminishes. There must be a careful assessment of the capabilities and limitations of the partner for it must be ready politically, economically, militarily, and administratively to meet the demands associated with combating terrorism. If it cannot meet these demands, then it is critical that it receive the support to do so, while recognizing that there are limitations here as well. The partner may choose to disregard advice (assuming it is wise in the first place) or to refuse material support. If leverage is attempted by putting conditions on the provision of support, then the partner can pledge to meet the conditions, but not actually do so. This reluctance may spiral into either additional ultimatums or stronger commitment on the part of the supplier of material goods and services to demonstrate good faith. However, if the partner is politically weak or unstable, then there is a concern that too much pressure on it may result in its collapse.[122]

Shunting the partner aside and assuming responsibility for its role can be counterproductive. This approach not only undermines the sovereignty of the partner but places a sizable burden on the government that assumes responsibility, extending well beyond advice and support. In short, massive intervention actually reduces leverage. As long as the supporting government is willing to use its resources (financial and human) as a substitute for the partner, then there is little incentive for the partner to assume the burden or share the responsibility. The partner may also be perceived by its people and other external audiences as the puppet of the supporting government.[123] Although there are instruments that can be used to influence the partner, they must be tested for feasibility, suitability, and acceptability.

Obstacles to Institutional Learning

Bureaucracies inherently resort to their institutional repertoires in executing their responsibilities, and while this may be appropriate for meeting their established roles and missions, it is often unproductive or irrelevant when confronted with a new situation. These patterns of organizational behavior and the underlying culture have a strong influence on how the organization reacts. Modifying or adjusting the repertoires when a dynamic, adaptive response is needed is difficult, but it can be made more difficult in instances where there are obstacles to organizational learning. As Robert W. Komer

notes, overcoming these impediments necessitates focusing on the "bureaucratic properties of organizations—insensitivities, blindnesses and distorted incentives—which
slow up the learning process."[124]

Institutional inertia is one of the obstacles. Bureaucrats prefer to deal with issues in
a familiar way. They are more comfortable and find it more convenient to follow standard procedures and to operate in the time-honored fashion, moving slowly and incrementally in response to the changing environment. Further, the more highly hierarchical
and disciplined the bureaucracy is, the slower the change. Once change is recognized,
these large-scale organizations are ponderous in their movement, for there are procedures and processes to follow as well as programs, budgets, and personnel that have
been committed and now have to be directed elsewhere. More of the same is usually the
answer. This inertia—when coupled with a lack of institutional memory, a tendency to
neglect lessons available because they lie outside institutional experience, and inadequate analysis of performance because of concerns about internal or external criticism—
only exacerbate the problem of adaptability.[125]

CONCLUSION

Some scholars point to the apocalyptic cast of contemporary terrorism, particularly its
religious variant, suggesting that this form of terrorism is unlike its predecessors in that
the actors are irrational, self-destructive, and are marching willingly to martyrdom; or
that religious terrorism represents a new "wave"; or it is a "cosmic war," significantly
different from political terrorism.[126] Nonetheless, the continuities terrorism manifests
over the past centuries make one skeptical of any explanation that puts the emphasis on
uniqueness.[127] Further, in classifying and giving prominence to terrorism in this form
and with this ideology, they propagate a new stereotype of terrorism that is not conducive to thinking about terrorism as a rational, calculated strategic mode of thinking. This
perspective perhaps underscores a strategy deficit, a failure to perceive war and politics
as a unity in which war is fused with political considerations that include social and
religious dimensions.[128] For how else should we interpret the notion of a caliphate but as
a theocratic understanding of the notion of the state?

While terrorists' ideology, regardless of its stripe, offers a criticism of the existing political system and a prophecy of a perfectly just and harmonious society that will last the ages,
it is imperative as well to understand the strategic challenge that terrorism represents.[129] If the
fight against terrorist adversaries is a "long war," then the Cold War—as David Jablonsky
suggests—has a lot to teach us about the "importance of patience, perseverance and
endurance in the face of protracted conflict without prospects of clear victory."[130]

ACKNOWLEDGMENTS

The views expressed in the chapter are those of the author and do not necessarily reflect
the official policy or position of the U.S. Army, Department of Defense, or the U.S. government.

The author thanks Boone Bartholomees and H. R. Yarger for their insights and comments. An earlier version of this chapter appeared in the *U.S. Army War College Guide to National Security Policy and Strategy*, third edition.

NOTES

1. Joseph Conrad, *Tales of the East and West*, edited and with an introduction by Morton Dauwen Zabel (Garden City, NY: Hanover House, 1958), 490.

2. Ibid., xxviii–xxix.

3. Richard Schultz, "Conceptualizing Political Terrorism: A Typology," *Journal of International Affairs* 32, no. 1: 7.

4. Jon Tetsuro Sumida, "The Relationship of History and Theory in *On War:* The Clausewitzian Ideal and Its Implications," *Journal of Military History* 65 (April 2001): 336.

5. Gregory D. Foster, "A Conceptual Foundation for a Theory of Strategy," *Washington Quarterly* 13, no. 1 (Winter 1990): 47; Roberta Senechal de la Roche, "Toward a Scientific Theory of Terrorism," *Sociological Theory* 22, no. 1 (March 2004): 3.

6. Walter Laqueur, *Terrorism* (London: Weidenfeld and Nicolson, 1977), 5.

7. Jack P. Gibbs, "Conceptualization of Terrorism," *American Sociological Review* 54, no. 3 (June 1989): 329.

8. Martha Crenshaw Hutchinson, "The Concept of Revolutionary Terrorism," *Journal of Conflict Resolution* 16, no. 3 (September 1972): 384.

9. Gibbs, "Conceptualization of Terrorism," 330.

10. Quoted in Hutchinson, "The Concept of Revolutionary Terrorism," 383.

11. Harry R. Yarger, *Strategic Theory for the 21st Century: The Little Book on Big Strategy* (Carlisle, PA: Strategic Studies Institute, U.S. Army War College, 2006), 1.

12. Ibid., 6–7; Martha Crenshaw, "An Organizational Approach to the Analysis of Political Terrorism," *Orbis* (Fall 1985): 472.

13. Yarger, *Strategic Theory for the 21st Century*, 7.

14. Ibid., 7–8.

15. Hutchinson, "The Concept of Revolutionary Terrorism," 385.

16. Charles Tilly, "Terror, Terrorism, Terrorists," *Sociological Theory* 22, no. 1 (March 2004): 9; H. Edward Price Jr., "The Strategy and Tactics of Revolutionary Terrorism," *Comparative Studies on Society and History* 19, no. 1 (January 1977): 52; and T. P. Thornton, "Terror as a Weapon of Political Agitation," in H. Eckstein, ed., *Internal War* (New York: Free Press, 1964), 78–79.

17. Donald Black, "The Geometry of Terrorism," *Sociological Theory* 22, no. 1 (March 2004): 18.

18. Arthur H. Garrison, "Defining Terrorism: Philosophy of the Bomb, Propaganda by Deed and Change Through Fear and Violence," *Criminal Justice Studies* 17, no. 3 (September 2004): 260.

19. Amy Zegart, "An Empirical Analysis of Failed Intelligence Reforms Before September 11," *Political Science Quarterly* 121, no. 1 (Spring 2006): 35–36, 39.

20. Williamson Murray and Mark Grimsley, "Introduction: On Strategy," in *The Making of Strategy, Rulers, States, and War* (Cambridge: Cambridge University Press, 1994; 1997), 1.

21. Yarger, *Strategic Theory for the 21st Century*, 13–14.

22. Ibid., 14.

23. Alison M. Jagger, "What Is Terrorism, Why Is It Wrong, and Could It Ever Be Morally Permissible?" *Journal of Social Philosophy* 26, No. 2 (Summer 2005): 208.

24. Yarger, *Strategic Theory for the 21st Century*, 14.

25. Ibid., 15–16.

26. Crenshaw, "An Organizational Approach to the Analysis of Political Terrorism," 472–482; Randy Borum, *Psychology of Terrorism* (Tampa: University of South Florida, 2004), 24, 52–56. Also see *Harmony and Disharmony: Exploiting Al-Qaida's Organizational Vulnerabilities* (West Point, NY: Combating Terrorism Center, 2006).

27. Daniel S. Gressang IV, "Terrorism in the 21st Century: Reassessing the Emerging Threat," in *Deterrence in the 21st Century*, ed. Max Manwaring (Portland, OR: Frank Cass, 2001), 73.

28. Roberta Senechal de la Roche, "Collective Violence as Social Control," *Sociological Forum* 11, no. 1 (March 1996): 97–98; Martha Crenshaw, "The Causes of Terrorism," *Comparative Politics* 13, no. 4 (July 1981): 381–384.

29. Senechal de la Roche, "Collective Violence as Social Control," 103.

30. Quoted in Garrison, "Defining Terrorism: Philosophy of the Bomb, Propaganda by Deed and Change Through Fear and Violence," 268.

31. Crenshaw, "An Organizational Approach to the Analysis of Political Terrorism," 466.

32. Thomas C. Schelling, *Arms and Influence* (New Haven, CT: Yale University Press, 1966), 3.

33. Carl von Clausewitz, *On War*, ed. and trans. by Michael Howard and Peter Paret (Princeton, NJ: Princeton University Press, 1984), 77.

34. Schelling, *Arms and Influence*, 3–4.

35. Hutchinson, "The Concept of Revolutionary Terrorism," 387–389.

36. Philip G. Cerny, "Terrorism and the New Security Dilemma," *Naval War College Review* 58, no. 1 (Winter 2005): 16.

37. Andrew H. Kydd and Barbara F. Walter, "The Strategies of Terrorism," *International Security* 31, no. 1 (Summer 2006): 58, 78.

38. Jeffrey C. Alexander, "From the Depths of Despair: Performance, Counterperformance, and 'September 11,'" *Sociological Theory* 22, no. 1 (March 2004): 88, 90.

39. Anthony Oberschall, "Explaining Terrorism: The Contribution of Collective Action Theory," *Sociological Theory* 22, no. 1 (March 2004): 27.

40. H. Stuart Hughes, *Consciousness and Society: The Reorientation of Social Thought, 1890–1930* (New York: Vintage Books, 1958), 165.

41. Alexander, "From the Depths of Despair," 89.

42. Philip Windsor, "Terrorism and International Order," in *Studies in International Relations: Essays by Philip Windsor*, ed. Mats Berdal (Portland, OR: Sussex Academic Press, 2002), p. x, 195.

43. Ibid., 195.

44. Crenshaw, "An Organizational Approach to the Analysis of Political Terrorism," 466; Alexander, "From the Depths of Despair," 89.

45. Crenshaw, "An Organizational Approach to the Analysis of Political Terrorism," 471.

46. Ibid., 481.

47. Alexander, "From the Depths of Despair," 89.

48. Ibid.

49. Borum, *Psychology of Terrorism*, 24.

50. Martha Crenshaw, "Theories of Terrorism: Instrumental and Organizational Approaches," in *Inside Terrorist Organizations*, ed. David C. Rapoport (Portland, OR: Frank Cass, 2001), 13.

51. Schelling, *Arms and Influence*, 4.

52. Windsor, "Terrorism and International Order," 193.

53. Michel Wieviorka, *The Making of Terrorism*, trans. by David Gordon White (Chicago: University of Chicago Press, 1993), 9.

54. Ibid., 7–8.

55. Ibid., 8.

56. Hutchinson, "The Concept of Revolutionary Terrorism," 394.

57. Wieviorka, *The Making of Terrorism*, 11–12.

58. Brodie's exact words are: "strategy is nothing if not pragmatic. . . . Above, all, strategic theory is a theory for action." Quoted in Colin Gray, "What Is War? A View from Strategic Studies," in *Strategy and History: Essays on Theory and Practice* (New York: Routledge, 2006), 185.

59. Senechal de la Roche, "Collective Violence as Social Control," 102.

60. Crenshaw, *The Causes of Terrorism*, 379–386.

61. Carl von Clausewitz, *On War*, 75.

62. Quoted in Gray, "What Is War?", 185.

63. Ibid.

64. Ibid., 187.

65. Ibid., 186.

66. Ibid., 187, and Colin S. Gray, *Irregular Enemies and the Essence of Strategy: Can the American Way of War Adapt?* (Carlisle, PA: Strategic Studies Institute, U.S. Army War College, 2006).

67. Antulio J. Echevarria II, "Clausewitz and the Nature of the War on Terror," in *Clausewitz in the Twenty-First Century*, eds. Hew Strachan and Andreas Herberg-Rothe (Oxford: Oxford University Press, 2007), 196–230.

68. Borum, *Psychology of Terrorism*, 54.

69. Gray, *Modern Strategy*, 295–296.

70. Gray, *Irregular Enemies and the Essence of Strategy: Can the American Way of War Adapt?*, vi, 4–5.

71. H. Richard Yarger, private correspondence with the author, January 9, 2008.

72. J. Boone Bartholomees, ed., "Theory of War and Strategy," Course Directive, Academic Year 2008, Department of National Security and Strategy, U.S. Army War College, Carlisle, PA, pp. 33, 37. The concepts in this paragraph derive from Bartholomees's writings for the lessons on strategic constraints.

73. Gray, *Irregular Enemies and the Essence of Strategy*, 2; Antoine Henri de Jomini, *The Art of War* (Novato, CA: Presidio Press, 1992), 325.

74. Sun Tzu, *The Art of War*, trans. Ralph D. Sawyer, (Boulder CO: Westview Press 1994), 179.

75. Robert Thompson, *Defeating Communist Insurgency* (New York: Frederick A. Praeger, 1966), 50.

76. Colin S. Gray, *Transformation and Strategic Surprise* (Carlisle, PA: Strategic Studies Institute, U.S. Army War College, 2005), 29.

77. Colin S. Gray, "Combatting Terrorism," *Parameters* 23, no. 3 (Autumn 1993): 20.

78. Thompson, *Defeating Communist Insurgency*, 50.

79. Raymond Aron, "The Evolution of Modern Strategic Thought," in *Problems of Modern Strategy*, ed. Alastair Buchan (London: Chatto and Windus, 1970), 25. Quoted in Colin S. Gray, *Maintaining Effective Deterrence* (Carlisle, PA: Strategic Studies Institute, U.S. Army War College, 2003), 3.

80. Clausewitz, *On War*, 88.

81. Robert W. Komer, *Bureaucracy at War: U.S. Performance in the Vietnam Conflict* (Boulder, CO: Westview Press, 1986), 5.

82. Tom Parker, "Fighting an Antaean Enemy: How Democratic States Unintentionally Sustain the Terrorist Movements They Oppose," *Terrorism and Political Violence* 19, 158, 172–173;

Ronaldo Munck, "Deconstructing Terror: Insurgency, Repression and Peace," in *Postmodern Insurgencies: Political Violence, Identity Formation and Peacemaking in Comparative Perspective*, Ronald Munck and Purnaka L. de Silva, eds. (New York: St. Martin's Press, 2000), 1.

83. Clausewitz, *On War*, 605.

84. Ibid., 88.

85. Michael Howard, *Clausewitz* (Oxford: University of Oxford Press, 1983), 35.

86. Colin Gray, *Defining and Achieving Decisive Victory* (Carlisle, PA: Strategic Studies Institute, U.S. Army War College, 2002), 17.

87. Ibid.

88. Ibid.

89. Ibid., 19.

90. Quoted in Howard, *Clausewitz*, 49.

91. Tami Biddle, Strategic Constraints: Limited War," in J. Boone Bartholomees, ed., "Theory of War and Strategy," Course Directive, Academic Year 2008, Department of National Security and Strategy, U.S. Army War College, Carlisle, PA, p. 41.

92. Howard, *Clausewitz*, 37.

93. Sun Tzu, *The Art of War*, translated and with an introduction by Samuel B. Griffith (New York: Oxford University Press, 1963), 77.

94. J. Boone Bartholomees, ed., "Theory of War and Strategy," Course Directive, Academic Year 2008, Department of National Security and Strategy, U.S. Army War College, Carlisle, PA, p. 77.

95. Sun Tzu, *The Art of War*, translated and with an introduction by Samuel B. Griffith (New York: Oxford University Press, 1963), 69–70.

96. Ibid., 85.

97. Gray, *Maintaining Effective Deterrence*, vi–viii.

98. Ibid., ix.

99. Glenn H. Snyder, *Deterrence and Defense: Toward a Theory of National Security* (Princeton, NJ: Princeton University Press, 1961), 14–16.

100. Robert F. Trager and Dessislava P. Zagorcheva, "Deterring Terrorism: It Can Be Done," *International Security* 30, no. 3 (Winter 2005/06): 96–98.

101. Matthew Levitt, "Untangling the Terror Web: Identifying and Counteracting the Phenomenon of Crossover Between Terrorist groups," *SAIS Review* 24, no. 1 (Winter 2004): 33–35.

102. Gray, "Combatting Terrorism," 18.

103. Munck, "Deconstructing Terror: Insurgency, Repression and Peace," 2–4.

104. Ibid., 4–6, 9.

105. Robert L. Ivie, "Fighting Terror by Rite of Redemption and Reconciliation," *Rhetoric and Public Affairs* 10, no. 2 (2007): 221–223.

106. Gray, *Maintaining Effective Deterrence*, 33–34; Borum, *Psychology of Terrorism*, 62–63; Gray, "Combatting Terrorism, 22.

107. Crenshaw, "An Organizational Approach to the Analysis of Political Terrorism," 482–487; Borum, *Psychology of Terrorism*, 63. Also, see Combating Terrorism Center at West Point, *Harmony and Disharmony*, 2006.

108. Crenshaw, "An Organizational Approach to the Analysis of Political Terrorism," 487–488.

109. Gray, "Combatting Terrorism," 21–22.

110. David Ignatius, "Learning to Fight a War," *Washington Post*, February 10, 2008, p. B7.

111. Gray, "Combatting Terrorism," 21–22.

112. Alison Jagger, "Responding to the Evil of Terrorism," *Hypatia* 18, no. 1 (Winter 2003): 175, 177; Daniele Archibugi and Iris Young, "Toward a Global Rule of War," *Dissent* 49, no. 2 (Spring 2002): 28–29.

113. Martin Innes, "Policing Uncertainty: Countering Terror through Community Intelligence and Democratic Policing," *Annals of the American Academy of Political and Social Science* 605 (May 2006): 233.

114. Edward McCleskey, Diana McCord, and Jennifer Leetz, *Underlying Reasons for Success and Failure of Terrorist Attacks: Selected Case Studies, Final Report* (Arlington, VA: Homeland Security Institute, 2007), 1–3.

115. Innes, "Policing Uncertainty: Countering Terror through Community Intelligence and Democratic Policing," 222–228.

116. Ibid., 232–233.

117. Christopher Hill, "The Political Dilemmas for Western Governments," in Lawrence Freedman et al., *Terrorism and International Order* (London: Royal Institute of International Affairs, 1987), 77.

118. Gray, *Transformation and Strategic Surprise,* vi.

119. Ibid., 2–16.

120. Ibid., 27–29.

121. Ben Sheppard, G. James Rubin, Jamie K. Wardman, and Simon Wessley, "Terrorism and Dispelling the Myth of a Panic Prone Public," *Journal of Public Health Policy* 27, no. 3 (2006): 219–226, 232, 238–241.

122. Komer, *Bureaucracy at War,* 21–29.

123. Ibid., 30–38.

124. Ibid., 15–16, 70.

125. Ibid., 70–76.

126. See Mark Juergensmeyer, *Terror in the Mind of God: The Global Rise of Religious Violence* (Berkeley: University of California Press, 2000) and David C. Rapoport, "The Four Waves of Modern Terrorism," in *Attacking Terrorism: Elements of a Grand Strategy*, eds. Audrey Kurth Cronin and James Ludes (Washington, DC: Georgetown University Press, 2004), 46–73.

127. Oberschall, "Explaining Terrorism: The Contribution of Collective Action Theory," 27.

128. Gray, *Irregular Enemies and the Essence of Strategy,* vi.

129. Bernard Crick, *In Defence of Politics*, 4th ed. (Chicago: University of Chicago Press, 1992), 34–35.

130. David Jablonsky, "Introduction," in David Jablonsky, Ronald Steel, Lawrence Korb, Morton H. Halperin, and Robert Ellsworth, *U.S. National Security: Beyond the Cold War* (Carlisle, PA: Strategic Studies Institute, U.S. Army War College, 1997), 31.

7

The Strategic Influence Deficit of Terrorism

Max Abrahms

WHAT DISTINGUISHES TERRORISM FROM OTHER types of crime or combat is its political communication strategy. The victims of a terrorist attack and the intended audience are never the same. The terrorist's ultimate goal is not to punish or even terrorize civilian populations per se; rather, it is to communicate the costs to their governments of refusing to appease the terrorist's policy demands.[1] But historically, terrorist attacks against civilians have failed to coerce their governments into making policy concessions. Terrorism is an extremely ineffective coercive instrument precisely because terrorism is an extremely ineffective communication strategy. In this chapter, I show that terrorist organizations seldom achieve their political objectives because terrorist acts miscommunicate them to the target country.

ASSESSING THE POLITICAL OUTCOMES OF TERRORISM

There is surprisingly little empirical research on whether terrorism is an effective coercive strategy—that is, on whether substate actors tend to exact policy concessions from governments by attacking their civilian populations. Over two decades ago, Martha Crenshaw observed that "the outcomes of campaigns of terrorism have been largely ignored" as "most analyses have emphasized the causes and forms rather than the consequences of terrorism."[2] Ted Robert Gurr added that terrorism's policy effectiveness is "a subject on which little national-level research has been done, systematically or otherwise."[3] And yet despite extensive research on terrorism and insurgencies throughout the 1980s and 1990s, there remains an acute lack of data and analysis on the political outcomes of terrorist campaigns.

In recent years, several scholars have claimed that terrorism works, but this body of research suffers from five methodological problems.[4] First, it is sometimes said that terrorism is effective because it attracts a lot of media attention.[5] Brigitte Nacos, for example, has shown that the media serve a vital role in spreading the terrorist's propaganda, enabling terrorist organizations to gain attention and sympathizers.[6] Similarly, Cindy Combs has demonstrated that the media have become a tool of modern terrorists by offering a "showcase" for them to threaten the target country, recruit and train new members, and support and coordinate an emerging network of followers. She notes that a symbiotic relationship exists between news organizations, which seek dramatic stories to increase their ratings, and terrorists, who seek attention and supporters.[7] Walter Laqueur points out, however, that there is a big difference between exploiting the media and achieving one's political goals because "unless the publicity is translated into something tangible, it is no more than entertainment."[8]

Second, scholars have argued that terrorism is politically effective because it occasionally leads to tactical victories, such as prisoner releases and the derailment of peace processes.[9] The utility of these studies is marginal; they tend to focus on what Thomas Schelling calls the "intermediate" objectives of terrorists rather than their ultimate goals.[10] Such research suffers from what Roger Peterson refers to as "the bias of [focusing on] tactical victories amid strategic losses."[11]

Third, scholars often suggest that terrorism is an effective coercive strategy because they mistakenly focus on the political outcomes of guerrilla warfare campaigns, which are directed against military targets, not civilian ones.[12] The evidence that terrorism is politically effective typically centers on guerrilla campaigns such as Hizballah's success in ousting the multinational peacekeepers and the Israeli Defense Forces from Lebanon.[13] In Robert Pape's research, for example, nearly half of the "terrorist" campaigns analyzed were actually waged by guerrilla groups, which account for all of the asymmetric victories in his sample.[14]

Fourth, it is even alleged that terrorism is politically effective regardless of its effect on the target country. Andrew Kydd and Barbara Walter, for example, say that terrorist organizations should be deemed politically successful not only when they compel policy concessions, but also when terrorism elicits the exact opposite response by provoking the target country to annihilate the terrorist organization and its ideological supporters.[15] According to philosopher of science Imre Lakato, the use of contradictory evidence to sustain a thesis is evidence of an empirically dubious or "degenerative" argument.[16]

Finally, several scholars have concluded that terrorism is policy effective based on their analysis of a tiny, unrepresentative sample of terrorist organizations.[17] According to the Rand Corporation, there are over 860 known terrorist organizations in the world.[18] Yet Alan Dershowitz concludes that "terrorism works" based on a single case study.[19] Similarly, Pape claims that terrorism pays based on his analysis of 11 selective asymmetric campaigns from 1980 to 2003. These campaigns were directed against only a handful of countries: 10 of the 11 campaigns analyzed were directed against three countries (Israel, Sri Lanka, and Turkey), and 6 of those 10 were directed against a single country (Israel). The inclusion of six terrorist campaigns against Israel biases the results because Palestinian terrorism has been described as "the paradigmatic example of terrorism that has worked."[20] The emerging body of research on terrorism's political effectiveness generally contains several of these methodological shortcomings.

A noteworthy exception is a recent study in *International Security*, which avoids these shortcomings by assessing the political effectiveness of every foreign terrorist organization (FTO) designated by the U.S. Department of State since 2001.[21] The analysis demonstrated that the terrorist groups achieved their policy demands only 3 out of 42 times—a 7 percent success rate. Within the international relations literature, this rate of success is considered extremely low.[22] Furthermore, the 7 percent success rate actually overstates terrorism's political effectiveness. The Department of State's list of FTOs does not distinguish between (1) groups that focus their attacks primarily on civilian targets and (2) those that mostly attack military targets but occasionally attack civilians. In other words, the list does not distinguish between guerrilla groups and pure terrorist groups. When the FTOs were reclassified by target selection, a clear trend emerged: the guerrilla groups were responsible for all of the successful cases of coercion, and thus, no group accomplished its main political objectives when its attacks were primarily directed against civilians.[23]

This chapter builds on these findings by developing a theory and then applying it to three case studies in order to demonstrate the inherent limitations of terrorism as a political tactic. Together, the two approaches suggest that terrorists are unable to translate their political violence into concrete political gains because terrorism is an inherently flawed communication strategy.

THE LIMITATIONS OF TERRORISM AS A COMMUNICATION STRATEGY

Terrorism is a coercive strategy intended to communicate to target countries the costs of noncompliance. This notion is key for understanding the poor track record of terrorist groups. The following analysis develops a theory for why terrorist groups—especially ones that primarily target civilians—do not achieve their policy demands. The basic contention of this chapter is that terrorist groups fail to coerce because they miscommunicate their policy objectives to the target country by attacking its civilian population.

Within the field of international relations, it is firmly established that countries are more inclined to compromise over limited policy objectives than maximalist policy objectives.[24] Limited objectives refer to demands over territory and other natural resources, whereas maximalist objectives refer to demands over beliefs, values, and ideology, which are more difficult to divide and relinquish.[25] The problem for terrorist groups is that target countries infer from attacks on their civilians that the terrorists want to destroy these countries' values, society, or both. Because countries are reluctant to appease groups that are believed to harbor these maximalist objectives, terrorist groups are unable to win political concessions by attacking civilians.[26]

This model is grounded in two ways. First, it is consistent with attributional research in the social psychology literature; correspondent inference theory offers a framework to show that target countries infer that terrorist organizations—regardless of their policy demands—have maximalist objectives when their violence is directed against civilians. Second, correspondent inference theory is applied to three case studies: the responses of Russia to the September 1999 apartment bombings, the United States to the September 11 attacks, and Israel to Palestinian terrorism in the First Intifada. The three cases offer empirical evidence that (1) target countries infer that groups have maximalist objectives when they target civilians, and (2) the resultant belief that terrorist groups have maximalist objectives dissuades target countries from making political concessions. The two methodological approaches combine to offer an externally valid theory for why terrorist

Figure 7.1   Contingency Model of Civilian Centric Terrorist Groups

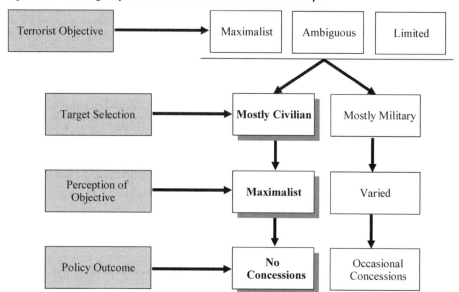

groups, when their attacks are directed against civilians, do not achieve their policy goals.

Objectives Encoded in Outcomes

Correspondent inference theory provides a framework for understanding why target countries infer that terrorist groups have maximalist objectives, even when their policy demands suggest otherwise. The theory was developed in the 1960s and 1970s by social psychologist Edward Jones to explain the cognitive process by which an observer infers the motives of an actor. Jones showed that observers tend to interpret an actor's objective in terms of the consequence of the action.[27] He offered the following simple example to illustrate the observer's assumption of similarity between the effect and objective of an actor: a boy notices his mother close the door, and the room becomes less noisy; the correspondent inference is that she wanted quiet.[28] The essential point is what Jones called the "attribute-effect linkage," whereby the objectives of the actor are presumed to be encoded in the outcome of the behavior.[29] Levels of correspondence describe the extent to which the objectives of the actor are believed to be reflected in the effects of the action.[30] When an action has high correspondence, the observer infers the objectives of the actor directly from the consequences of the action. With low correspondence, the observer either does not perceive the behavior as intentional or attributes it to external factors, rather than to the actor's disposition.[31]

The theory posited here is that terrorist groups that target civilians are unable to coerce policy change because terrorism has extremely high correspondence. Countries believe that their civilian populations are attacked not because the terrorist group is protesting unfavorable external conditions such as territorial occupation or poverty. Rather, target countries infer from the short-term consequences of terrorism—the deaths of innocent citizens, mass fear, loss of confidence in the government to offer protection, economic contraction, and inevitable erosion of civil liberties—the objectives of the terrorist group.[32] In short, target countries view the negative consequences of terrorist attacks on their societies and political systems as evidence that the terrorists want them destroyed. Target countries are understandably skeptical that making concessions will placate terrorist groups believed to be motivated by these maximalist objectives. As a consequence, terrorist attacks on civilians do not coerce target countries into entering a political compromise, even when the political rationale is not maximalist.

The three case studies that follow show that terrorism is a flawed method of coercion because (1) terrorism has high correspondence, and (2) inferences derived from its effects militate against political compromise. To highlight the effect of the independent variable—terrorist attacks—on the proclivity of target states to bargain, a supporting case must conform to five empirical criteria: (1) the coercing party is not motivated by a maximalist objective, that is, the desire to destroy the target state's values or society; (2) the coercing party either uses terrorism or is suspected of doing so to further its limited policy objectives; (3) the target country fixates on the short-term effects of the terrorist acts, rather than the coercing party's policy demands; (4) the target country infers from the effects of the terrorist acts that the coercing party has maximalist objectives; (5) the target country's inference that the coercing party wants to destroy its society or values impedes it from making political concessions.[33]

CASE STUDY 1: RUSSIA'S RESPONSE TO THE APARTMENT BOMBINGS

Russia's response to the three apartment bombings that killed 229 Russian civilians in September 1999 illustrates why terrorist groups do not achieve their policy goals by targeting civilians. Before the bombings erupted throughout Russia, there was widespread agreement among Russians that Chechen objectives were limited to establishing an independent Chechen state. During this period, most Russians favored territorial compromise. After the apartment bombings, however, large segments of Russian society fixated on their short-term consequences and inferred from them that the presumed perpetrators (the Chechens) surreptitiously wanted to destroy Russia. This view that the Chechens are irredeemably committed to destroying Russia has eroded support for granting Chechen independence. The attitudinal shift after the bombings offers preliminary evidence that (1) terrorism has high correspondence, and (2) inferences of Chechen objectives resulting from the terrorist attacks militated against making concessions. I detail this attitudinal shift by tracing the evolution of Russian opinion on Chechnya between the two Chechen wars.

The First Chechen War, 1994–1996

With the collapse of the Soviet Union in the late 1980s, several North Caucasian republics declared sovereignty. In 1991 Chechnya's first president, Dzhokar Dudaev, took the additional step of declaring independence. Federal forces invaded Chechnya in December 1994 to reestablish control in the breakaway republic. For the next 20 months Russian federal forces battled Chechen guerrillas in an asymmetric war based in Chechnya. During this period of guerrilla warfare, Russians recognized that Chechen objectives were limited to self-determination. John Russell has noted that in the first Chechen war "the Russian public [believed] that Chechens perceived their struggle as one of national liberation."[34] Michael McFaul has similarly observed that "the Russian military and the Russian people believed that the [Chechen] rationale for this war was self-defense."[35] The Russian military shared the view that Chechen objectives were territorial, calling the first Chechen war the war for the restoration of territorial integrity.[36]

During this period, most Russians were prepared to make significant concessions over the status of Chechnya. When the war broke out, the Russian public and even the secret police perceived it as precipitate, believing diplomatic solutions had not been exhausted.[37] Boris Yeltsin's position on the war did not gain popularity as it unfolded. Top military commanders openly resigned and condemned the president for not pursuing negotiations.[38] From the onset of military operations until the cease-fire in August 1996, some 70 percent of Russians opposed the war.[39] Disdain for the war manifested itself most clearly in public attitudes toward Defense Minister Pavel Grachev. Opinion polls rated his approval at only 3 percent, just a few points lower than the Russian public's support for Yeltsin's handling of the Chechen problem in general.[40] By early 1996, domestic opposition to fighting the guerrillas imperiled Yeltsin's electoral prospects. The *Economist* predicted in February that "Mr. Yeltsin can scarcely afford to let the conflict drift violently on if he hopes to win a second term of office in June's presidential election."[41] Yeltsin folded to domestic pressure, calling for an end to all troop operations in Chechnya and the immediate commencement of negotiations with Dudayev over its future status. Yeltsin's approval rating climbed from 21 percent in February 1996 to 52 percent three months later.[42] In May Yeltsin admitted in an interview that he would lose the upcoming election if he did not proceed with granting Chechnya de facto sovereignty.[43] The Khasavyurt agreement of August 1996 committed the Russian Federation to relinquish Chechnya by December 2001.[44] In the interim period, Chechnya would have a de facto state with free elections, a parliament, a president, and autonomy over its finances and resources.[45] Noting the generous terms of the accord, the BBC remarked that the status reserved for Chechnya "essentially signified its independence."[46] In Khasavyurt, Yeltsin formally acknowledged that Russians preferred territorial compromise to fighting the guerrillas.

The Second Chechen War, September 1999–Present

On September 8, 1999, Russia experienced its "first taste of modern-day international terrorism."[47] A large bomb was detonated on the ground floor of an apartment building in southeast Moscow, killing 94 civilians. On September 13, another large bomb blew up an apartment building on the Kashmirskoye Highway, killing 118 civilians. On September 16, a truck bomb exploded outside a nine-story apartment complex in the southern Russian city of Volgodonsk, killing 17 civilians. The Kremlin quickly fingered the Chechens as the perpetrators.[48]

Russians responded to the terrorist attacks by fixating on their effects, while ignoring the Chechens' persistent policy demands. Russia watchers noted during the bombing campaign that "attention is being directed more at the actual perpetration of terrorist acts, their visible, external and horrific effects with perhaps not so much emphasis on the [stated] cause."[49] Indeed, polls showed that following the terrorist acts only 15 percent of Russians believed the Chechens were still fighting for independence.[50] The Public Opinion Foundation reported that "this motive is mentioned less frequently now. . . . It is gradually dying out."[51] As Timothy Thomas observed after the bombings, "The Chechens were no longer regarded as a small separatist people struggling to defend their territory."[52] Yeltsin's successor, Vladimir Putin, contributed to the view that the Chechens ceased to be motivated by the desire for national self-determination, declaring that "the question of Chechnya's dependence on, or independence from, Russia is of absolutely no fundamental importance anymore." Following the terrorist attacks, he stopped referring to Chechens altogether, instead labeling them as "terrorists." The campaign for the "restoration of territorial integrity" became "the campaign against terrorism." Russian counterattacks became "counter-terrorist operations."[53] Putin's focus on the effects of Chechen violence was most evident after September 11, 2001, when he told Western countries that "we have a common foe," given that the World Trade Center attacks and the apartment bombings appear to "bear the same signature."[54]

After the bombings Russians concluded that Chechen objectives had suddenly become maximalist. Polls conducted after the terrorist attacks showed that Russians were almost twice as likely to believe that Chechen motives were now to "kill Russians," "bring Russia to its knees," "destabilize the situation in Russia," "destroy and frighten Russian society," and "bring chaos to Russian society" than to achieve "the independence of Chechnya."[55] Putin's public statements suggest that he, too, inferred Chechen objectives from the effects of the terrorism, asserting that the presumed perpetrators are attacking Russia so it "goes up in flames."[56] This postbombing belief that Chechen objectives had become maximalist was accompanied by an abrupt loss of interest in making concessions and unprecedented support for waging war. The Public Opinion Forum found that a strong majority of Russians (71 percent) supported the idea of trading land for peace but had come to believe that "the Chechens are not trustworthy."[57] When Russians were asked to explain why they no longer trusted the Chechens to abide by a land-for-peace deal, the most common explanation given was "because of the terrorist acts."[58] Whereas Russians had demanded Yeltsin's impeachment over the first Chechen conflict, after the apartment bombings they were "baying for blood."[59] In the first Chechen war, Russians favored, by a two-to-one margin, an independent Chechen state over battling the guerrillas in the breakaway republic; after the bombings, these numbers were reversed, even when respondents were told that federal forces would "suffer heavy losses."[60] Popular support for war remained remarkably stable after the bombings; six months after they occurred, 73 percent of Russians favored "the advance of federal forces into Chechnya" compared with only 19 percent of Russians who wanted "peaceful negotiations with the Chechen leadership."[61] Since 2000, support for President Putin's Chechnya policy has not dropped below 67 percent.[62]

Apartment Bombings' High Correspondence

In the mid-1990s, foreign jihadists began using Chechen territory as a safe haven, but links between the two groups have been exaggerated. Russia scholars widely agree that since the Soviet Union unraveled in the late 1980s, Chechen objectives have remained constant—to establish an independent Chechen state.[63] Russian perceptions of Chechen objectives changed profoundly, however, as a result of the apartment bombings. The barrage of attacks on Russian civilians in September 1999 had high correspondence. Russians fixated on the short-term consequences of the bombings and suddenly concluded that the suspected attackers evidently want Russia destroyed. Once Russians believed that Chechen objectives were no longer confined to achieving national self-determination, enthusiasm for compromise abruptly declined while support for a military solution increased.

CASE STUDY 2: THE U.S. RESPONSE TO THE SEPTEMBER 11 TERRORIST ATTACKS

The response of the United States to the September 11, 2001, attacks further illustrates why groups that target civilians are unable to coerce policy change. The U.S. response provides supporting evidence that (1) terrorism has high correspondence, and (2) inferences derived from the effects of the attacks have not been conducive to offering concessions. The following case study shows that Americans—especially in the immediate aftermath of the terrorist attacks—have tended to ignore al-Qaida's political rationale for violence. Instead of focusing on al-Qaida's policy demands, Americans fixated on the immediate effects of the terrorist attacks and inferred from them that the terrorists are targeting the United States to destroy its society and values. These inferences have hampered al-Qaida from translating its violence into policy successes in the Muslim world.

Al-Qaida's Stated Objectives

Al-Qaida describes its use of terrorism as a communication strategy to demonstrate to the United States the costs of maintaining its unpopular foreign policies in the Muslim world.[64] Osama bin Laden has implored Americans to rid themselves of their "spiritless materialistic life," but a comprehensive perusal of al-Qaida's public statements reveals scant references to American popular culture. Bin Laden has threatened that "freedom and human rights in America are doomed," but American political values are also not a recurrent theme in al-Qaida communiqués. The relative silence on these issues suggests that American values are not a principal grievance.[65] In fact, bin Laden has explicitly rejected the claim that al-Qaida's goal is to change these values. On multiple occasions, he has warned American audiences that those who repeat this "lie" either suffer from "confusion" or are intentionally "misleading you."[66]

Since bin Laden declared war on the United States in February 1998, his policy demands have remained notably consistent. First, his most well-known ultimatum is for the United States to withdraw its troops from Saudi Arabia, "Land of the two holy places." His statements indicate that he objects not only to the U.S. stationing of troops in "the holiest of places," but also to U.S. bases serving as a "spearhead through which to fight the neighboring Muslim peoples." In al-Qaida communiqués, criticisms of U.S. military interference in Saudi Arabia have invariably been coupled with complaints about the treatment of its "neighbors," especially Iraq. For the al-Qaida leadership, deploying U.S. troops to Saudi Arabia during the lead-up to the 1991 Persian Gulf War was not only an egregious provocation in itself; the bases represented and facilitated the occupation of "its most powerful neighboring Arab state." Bin Laden and his lieutenants have thus threatened that the United States will remain a target until its military forces withdraw from the entire Persian Gulf.[67] Second, al-Qaida spokesmen say that its terrorist acts are intended to dissuade the United States from supporting military interventions that kill Muslims around the world. In the 1990s these interventions included "crusader" wars in Chechnya, Bosnia, and East Timor. Bloodshed in Israel and Iraq during this period generated the most intense opposition. Since the September 11 attacks, al-Qaida's condemnation of the United States has focused on events in these two countries.[68] Third, al-Qaida communiqués emphasize the goal of ending U.S. support for pro-Western Muslim rulers who suppress the will of their people. Al-Qaida leaders routinely denounce the House of Saud and President Pervez Musharraf's Pakistan in particular as the most "oppressive, corrupt, and tyrannical regimes" whose very existence depends on the "supervision of America."[69] A prominent al-Qaida Web site has equated U.S. financial and political support of Saudi Arabia and Pakistan to colonization.[70] Fourth, al-Qaida leaders describe Israel in similar terms, as a colonial outpost. Based on its communiqués, al-Qaida's final objective is thus to destroy the "Zionist-Crusader alliance," which enables Israel to maintain its "occupation of Jerusalem" and "murder Muslims there."[71]

Effects Trump Rationale

Americans have focused on the effects of al-Qaida violence, not its stated purpose. Ronald Steel noted in the *New Republic* after the June 1996 attack on the Khobar Towers in Saudi Arabia that American journalists fixated on "who or what bin Laden attacked" and "the method of attack." By contrast, "what bin Laden had been saying about why he and his al-Qaida forces were attacking was given short shrift."[72] British journalist Robert Fisk similarly observed that after the August 1998 attacks on the U.S. embassies in Kenya and Tanzania, U.S. leaders emphasized the carnage and devastation, but "not in a single press statement, press conference, or interview did a U.S. leader or diplomat explain why the enemies of America hate America."[73] The terrorist acts on September 11 likewise overshadowed their political rationale. According to Leonard Weinberg and William Eubank, "the media repeatedly communicated vivid descriptions and pictures of terrorism's victims," but "there was also an increasing tendency to depict their acts as ones of senseless bestiality devoid of serious political content."[74] These observations are consistent with Christopher Hewitt's conclusion that "media coverage of Islamic terrorism both before and after September 11 has generally ignored the motives of those responsible."[75]

High Correspondence of September 11

President George W. Bush's public pronouncements indicate that he deduces al-Qaida's motives directly from the short-term consequences of the September 11 terrorist attacks. According to Bush, "We have seen the true nature of these terrorists in the nature of their attacks," rather than in their professed political agenda.[76] For Bush, September 11 demonstrated that the enemy "hates not our policies, but our existence."[77] In the resulting panic weeks after the attacks, he concluded, "These acts of mass murder were intended to frighten our nation into chaos." With Americans hesitant to fly after the four planes were hijacked, he asserted, "they [the terrorists] want us to stop flying."[78] The toppling of the World Trade Center towers and the economic contraction that followed revealed that "the terrorists wanted our economy to stop" and that "they want us to stop buying." With American civil liberties inevitably restricted in the wake of the attacks, he proclaimed that al-Qaida's goals, inter alia, were to curtail "our freedom of religion, our freedom of speech, our freedom to vote and assemble and disagree with each other."[79] Given that al-Qaida and its affiliates are mute on these topics, it is difficult to imagine Bush ascribing them to the terrorists had Americans not been greatly frightened for their safety, hesitant to fly, and worried about their political and economic future in the wake of the terrorist attacks.

For President Bush, any group that deliberately attacks American civilians is evidently motivated by the desire to destroy American society and its democratic values. When asked by a reporter in October 2001 if there was any direct connection between the September 11 attacks and the spate of anthrax attacks that followed, he replied: "I have no direct evidence but there are some links . . . both series of actions are motivated to disrupt Americans' way of life."[80] This interpretation of the motives of the unknown terrorist perpetrator(s) is revealing: the identity of the person(s) who sent the anthrax is irrelevant because all terrorists who disrupt the American way of life must be motivated by this maximalist objective.[81]

The American public has tended to share President Bush's interpretation of the terrorists' motives. Polls conducted after September 11 show that most Americans believed that al-Qaida was not responding to unpopular U.S. foreign policies. After the attacks, only one in five respondents agreed with the statement that "there is any way that the United States has been unfair in its dealings with other countries that might have motivated the terrorist attacks."[82] In a separate question, only 15 percent of Americans agreed that "American foreign policies are partly the reason" for al-Qaida terrorism.[83] Instead of attributing al-Qaida terrorism to U.S. foreign policies, large segments of American society apparently shared Bush's belief that the goal of the terrorists was to destroy American society and values. Since September 11, more Americans have polled that the terrorists are targeting the United States because of its "democracy," "freedom," "values," and "way of life" than because of its interference in the Muslim world.[84]

Al-Qaida's Miscommunication Strategy

Bin Laden and his lieutenants frequently complain that the United States has failed to "understand" the "true reason" for the September 11 attacks. Instead of attacking because "we hate freedom," the attacks are a response to the fact that "you spoil our security" and "attack us."[85] Attributional research provides a framework to explain why al-Qaida's communication strategy has failed. As correspondent inference theory predicts, President Bush and large segments of American society focused on the disastrous effects of al-Qaida's behavior and inferred from them that the terrorists must want to destroy American society and its values—despite al-Qaida's relative silence on these issues.[86]

To be sure, even if terrorism had not delegitimized al-Qaida's policy demands, it is inconceivable the United States would have ever fully complied with them. Paul Wilkinson has observed that in deciding whether to negotiate with terrorists, the target government must first decide whether their demands are "corrigible" or "incorrigible." When demands are perceived as corrigible, the target government engages in a "roots debate"—an assessment of the pros and cons of conciliating the terrorists. When terrorists are perceived as incorrigible, concessions are rejected outright because the demands are deemed so extreme that they fall outside of the realm of consideration. In Wilkinson's model incorrigible terrorists are not categorically implacable, but placating them would exact a prohibitive cost.[87] In the discourse of international relations theory, realists would support the view that the United States has not entered a post–September 11 roots debate because it is strategically wedded to the Middle East.

Realists are on strong ground in their prediction that the world's most powerful country would not willingly concede a geographically vital region of the world to terrorists. But it is doubtful that had Americans viewed al-Qaida's stated grievances as credible they would have embraced a counterterrorism strategy after September 11 that systematically aggravated them. In response to the September 11 attacks, the United States: (1) increased troop levels by 15 times in the Persian Gulf; (2) strengthened military relations with pro-U.S. Muslim rulers, especially in Pakistan and Saudi Arabia; (3) supported counterterrorism operations—either directly or indirectly—that have killed tens of thousands of Muslims around the world; and (4) strengthened relations with Israel.[88] Although the September 11 attacks achieved al-Qaida's intermediate objectives of gaining supporters and attention, most Islamists believe that 9/11 was a major setback for achieving their policy goals.[89] Al-Qaida's post–September 11 policy failures are a testament, at least in part, to its flawed communication strategy.

CASE STUDY 3: ISRAEL'S RESPONSE TO THE FIRST INTIFADA

The First Intifada may seem like an unlikely case study to illustrate the limitations of terrorism as a coercive strategy. The mass uprising in the Gaza Strip and West Bank was an exceptionally moderate period in the history of Palestinian terrorism. The revolt from December 1987 to January 1991 killed only 20 Israeli civilians. Compared to the "Revolutionary Violence" campaign of the 1970s and the outbreak of the Second Intifada in September 2000, the First Intifada was a peaceful interlude.[90] Furthermore, the spontaneous insurrection was a bottom-up initiative. It circumvented Palestinian terrorist groups, which were ideologically opposed to a two-state solution. These groups were momentarily sidelined for three reasons. First, the Marxist groups (e.g., the Popular Front for the Liberation of Palestine and the PFLP-General Command) were reeling from the recent loss of their Soviet patron with the end of the Cold War. Second, the Islamist groups (e.g., Hamas and Islamic Jihad) did not yet pose a significant challenge to the Palestine Liberation Organization (PLO). Third, the PLO was based in Tunis during this period, largely detached from Palestinian life in the territories.[91] Facing relatively little competition from other Palestinian groups, the PLO coopted the mass uprising in the late 1980s by recognizing the Israeli state within its pre-1967 borders and formally renouncing terrorism. Despite the unusually moderate tactics and objectives of the Intifada, the Israeli response to it underscores that (1) the limited use of Palestinian terrorism had high correspondence, and (2) Israeli inferences of Palestinian objectives undermined support for making concessions.

High Correspondence of Palestinian Terrorism

Edy Kaufman has noted that "the primary purpose of the First Intifada was to communicate to Israelis the need to end the occupation of the territories."[92] Terrorist acts, even in small numbers, interfered with the message. Throughout the Intifada, only 15 percent of Palestinian demonstrations were violent.[93] Yet an absolute majority of Israelis (80 percent) believed that the means employed by the Palestinians to protest Israeli rule were "mainly violent." Of the violent Palestinian acts, the vast majority consisted of rock throwing against the Israel Defense Forces in the territories, with few incidences of terrorism inside the Green Line. An even broader consensus of Israelis (93 percent) felt the Intifada was directed "both towards civilians and towards the army."[94] Notwithstanding the Intifada's restrained use of violence, Israelis appear to have fixated on the intermittent attacks against Israeli civilians.

The Louis Guttman Israel Institute of Applied Social Research conducted a series of polls in December 1990 to assess the Israeli public's views of Palestinian objectives in the First Intifada. As correspondent inference theory predicts, a strong majority of the respondents surveyed (85 percent) believed its purpose was to "cause damage and injury"—as it surely did—while only a fraction (15 percent) believed the goal was to "express protest." Similarly, the majority (66 percent) believed that the Intifada was directed against "the existence of the state of Israel," while a minority (34 percent) believed the purpose was to liberate the West Bank and Gaza Strip.[95] The disconnect between the PLO's policy demands and Israeli perceptions of Palestinian objectives has been explained by (1) inconsistent rhetoric on the part of Palestinian leaders about the aims of the Intifada and (2) Jewish apprehension that contemporary violence against

Israel is akin to previous traumatic experiences in which Jewish survival in the diaspora was threatened.

The evidence suggests, however, that terrorism informed the Israeli view of Palestinian objectives. In a fascinating study based on the polling data contained in the Guttman report, Kaufman observed that the respondents who perceived Palestinian tactics as "mainly violent" were more likely to believe that the Palestinian goal was to "destroy Israel." Conversely, the more Israelis perceived Palestinian tactics as nonviolent, the more they believed the goal was to liberate the territories. The positive correlation between perceived Palestinian terrorism and maximalist objectives existed independent of the respondents' political affiliation, suggesting that the association was not a function of their preexisting political attitudes.[96] Not surprisingly, Israelis were twice as likely to believe "less in the idea of peace" than before the Intifada.[97] Because the majority of Israelis regarded the intifada as a protracted terrorist campaign, and Israelis inferred from Palestinian terrorism their intentions of wanting to destroy Israel, the Intifada undermined Israeli confidence in the Palestinians as a credible partner for peace.

In the early 1990s, Israeli Prime Ministers Yitzhak Shamir and Yitzhak Rabin came under increased pressure to trade "land for peace" with the Palestinians. The sources of pressure were twofold. First, President George H. W. Bush, determined to improve U.S.–Arab relations after Israel had lost its strategic utility as a Cold War satellite, "forced the Israelis to the negotiating table" by linking U.S. financial assistance to Shamir's participation in the Madrid peace conference in October 1991. Second, Israeli military strategists recognized that the Jewish state faced a long-term demographic problem in occupying a growing and restive Palestinian population.[98] In September 1993 Israel consented to the land-for-peace formula outlined in the Declaration of Principles known as the Oslo Accords, but the pattern remained: although Palestinian terrorism demonstrated to Israel the costs of the occupation, it undercut Israeli confidence in the Palestinians as a credible partner for peace, reducing support for making territorial concessions.[99] Throughout the 1990s, the Jaffee Center for Strategic Studies periodically polled Israeli respondents on their perceptions of Palestinian aspirations. The "dominant" response was that the Palestinians wanted to "conquer Israel" and "destroy a large portion of the Jewish population," a position that peaked during heightened levels of terrorist activity.[100] The perception that the Palestinians hold maximalist aspirations has been the principal impediment to Israel's willingness to make significant territorial concessions. Since 1994 the Tami Steinmetz Center for Peace Research has polled a representative sample of Israelis on two questions: Do you believe the Palestinians are viable partners for peace? And do you support the peace process? Instances of Palestinian terrorism systematically incline Israelis to answer "no" to both questions.[101]

In sum, since the First Intifada, Palestinian violence has created pressure on Israel to change the status quo. Paradoxically, terrorism has simultaneously convinced Israelis that the Palestinians are not committed to a two-state solution, which has eroded support for making the territorial concessions necessary to achieving it.

CONCLUSION

Terrorism, by definition, is a communication strategy; the attacks on civilians are designed to convey to their government the costs of maintaining the political status quo. The problem for terrorists is that their violence miscommunicates their political objectives to the target country. Ironically, instead of amplifying their policy demands, terrorism marginalizes them for two reasons. First, target governments tend to focus on the terrorist acts themselves rather than their political rationale. Content analysis of the media's coverage of the IRA, Red Brigades, and Puerto Rican FALN has shown that the reporting fixated on the fallout of the terrorism, while its political purpose was "largely ignored."[102] Second, Peter Neumann and Mike Smith point out that terrorist acts "will focus public attention on the purely negative aspects of a campaign to the exclusion of the presumably 'positive' political message that the terrorists will hope to project."[103]

Correspondent inference offers a theoretical framework for why target countries tend to (1) ignore the terrorists' policy demands and (2) presume that the terrorists are motivated simply to destroy. The responses of Russia to the September 1999 apartment bombings, the United States to the attacks of 9/11, and Israel to Palestinian terrorism in the First Intifada suggest that target governments infer terrorists' motives not from their stated objectives but from the consequences of their violent behavior. Target countries view the deaths of their citizens and the resulting turmoil as proof that the perpetrators want to destroy their societies, their publics, or both. It is therefore not surprising that terrorist organizations seldom achieve their policy demands by attacking civilians.[104] As Ariel Merari observes,

> If the government considers the struggle as a matter of life and death, it will not succumb to terrorist harassment, however protracted and unpleasant it may be. Moreover, when the government fights for its life or for the existence of the state, it is likely to take off its gloves and employ all means necessary . . . [in which case the terrorists have] a very slim chance of winning.[105]

Terrorists themselves are keenly aware of their strategic influence deficit. Bin Laden has repeatedly complained that Americans misinterpreted al-Qaida's political objectives from the 9/11 attacks. Similarly, Ayman al-Zawahiri's letter in July 2005 to Abu Musab al-Zarqawi urges him to desist with grisly terrorist attacks that may rally militant Islamists, but will obfuscate al-Qaida's political message in the media and international community, undermining the political cause.[106] In the long-term, the self-defeating policy consequences of terrorism will ultimately dissuade potential jihadists from supporting it. Polling data from Muslim countries suggest that the terrorism backlash is already under way. The Pew Research Center reported in its July 2005 Global Attitudes Project that compared with its polls conducted in 2002, "In most majority-Muslim countries surveyed support for suicide bombings and other acts of violence in defense of Islam has declined significantly," as has "confidence in Osama bin Laden to do the right thing in world affairs."[107] Similarly, major Islamist groups and leaders are increasingly denouncing terrorist attacks as counterproductive, even as they encourage guerrilla warfare against the Iraqi occupation.[108]

This is sage advice for al-Qaida to achieve its political objectives. The jihadists stand to gain from restricting their violence to military targets. Whereas countries infer from attacks on their civilians that the terrorists are motivated by maximalist objectives, countries infer from attacks on their militaries that the terrorists are merely protesting unpopular policies, making coercion possible. Mounting U.S. casualties in Iraq and the absence of a post–September 11 attack on the homeland have convinced many Americans that the terrorists aim to evict them from the Middle East rather than to destroy their way of life. Predictably, American support for maintaining its troop presence in Iraq has plummeted as al-Qaida's target selection has shifted away from the American public. The sooner al-Qaida realizes that its political fortunes are served by refraining from attacking civilian targets, the sooner it will avoid precipitating politically counterproductive counterterrorism reprisals.

NOTES

1. For a couple of works exploring the notion that terrorism is a communication strategy, see Ronald D. Crelinsten, "Terrorism as Political Communication: The Relationship between the Controller and the Controlled," in Paul Wilkinson and A. M. Stewart, eds., *Contemporary Research on Terrorism* (Aberdeen, Scotland: Aberdeen University Press, 1987), pp. 3–31; Bruce Hoffman and Gordon H. McCormick, "Terrorism, Signaling, and Suicide Attack," *Studies in Conflict and Terrorism,* Vol. 27, No. 4 (July/August 2004), pp. 243–281.

2. Martha Crenshaw, ed., *Terrorism, Legitimacy, and Power: The Consequences of Political Violence* (Middletown, Conn.: Wesleyan University Press, 1983), p. 5.

3. Ted Robert Gurr, "Empirical Research on Political Terrorism," in Robert O. Slater and Michael Stohl, eds., *Current Perspectives on International Terrorism* (New York: St. Martin's Press, 1988), p. 125.

4. For a critique of this literature, see Max Abrahms, "Why Terrorism Does Not Work," *International Security*, Vol. 31, No. 2 (fall 2006), pp. 45–46.

5. See, for example, Alan Dershowitz, *Why Terrorism Works: Understanding the Threat, Responding to the Challenge* (New Haven, Conn.: Yale University Press, 2002).

6. Brigitte L. Nacos, "Mediated Terrorism: Teaching Terror through Propaganda and Publicity," in James J. F. Forest, ed., *The Making of a Terrorist,* Vol. 2: *Training* (Westport, CT: Praeger Security International, 2005).

7. Cindy R. Combs, "The Media as a Showcase for Terrorism," in James J. F. Forest, ed., *Teaching Terror: Strategic and Tactical Learning in the Terrorist World* (Lanham, Md.: Rowman & Littlefield, 2006).

8. Walter Laqueur, *Terrorism* (Boston: Little, Brown and Company, 1977), p. 216.

9. See, for example, Robert A. Pape, "The Strategic Logic of Suicide Terrorism," *American Political Science Review*, Vol. 97, No. 3 (August 2003), pp. 39–40; Andrew Kydd and Barbara Walter, "Sabotaging the Peace: The Politics of Extremist Violence," *International Organization*, Vol. 56, No. 2 (spring 2002), pp. 263–296.

10. Thomas C. Schelling, "What Purposes Can 'International Terrorism' Serve?" in R.G. Frey and Christopher W. Morris, eds., *Violence, Terrorism and Justice* (Cambridge University Press, 1991) p. 20.

11. Roger Dale Petersen, *Resistance and Rebellion: Lessons from Eastern Europe* (New York: Cambridge University Press, 2001).

12. See, for example, Andrew Kydd and Barbara Walter, "The Strategies of Terrorism," *International Security*, Vol. 31, No. 1 (Summer 2006), p. 49; Robert A. Pape, *Dying to Win: The Strategic Logic of Suicide Terrorism* (New York: Random House, 2005), p. 39.

13. See, for example, Ehud Sprinzak, "Rational Fanatics," *Foreign Policy*, No. 120 (Sept. –Oct., 2000), pp. 66–73.

14. Pape, *Dying to Win*, pp. 39–40.

15. Kydd and Walter, "Strategies of Terrorism," p. 59.

16. See Colin Elman and Miriam Fendius Elman, "How Not to Be Lakatos Intolerant: Appraising Progress in IR Research," *International Studies Quarterly*, Vol. 46, No. 2 (June 2002), pp. 231–262.

17. Pape, "The Strategic Logic of Suicide Terrorism," p. 343.

18. MIPT Terrorism Knowledge Base, RAND, http://www.tkb.org/Home.jsp.

19. Dershowitz, *Why Terrorism Works*, p. 88.

20. Dershowitz, *Why Terrorism Works*, p. 88.

21. See Max Abrahms, "Why Terrorism Does Not Work," *International Security*, Vol. 31, No. 2 (fall 2006), pp. 45–46.

22. Robert A. Pape, "Why Economic Sanctions Do Not Work," *International Security*, Vol. 22, No. 2 (Fall 1997), p. 99.

23. Abrahms, "Why Terrorism Does Not Work," pp. 45–46.

24. Robert A. Dahl, *Who Governs? Democracy and Power in an American City* (New Haven, Conn.: Yale University Press, 1961); Theodore J. Lowi, "American Business, Public Policy, Case Studies, and Political Theory," *World Politics*, Vol. 16, No. 3 (July 1964), pp. 677–715; and Marvin Ott, "Mediation as a Method of Conflict Resolution, Two Cases," *International Organization*, Vol. 26, No. 4 (Autumn 1972), p. 613. The distinction between limited and maximalist issues is also expressed in terms of tangible versus intangible issues, respectively. See John A. Vaquez, "The Tangibility of Issues and Global Conflict: A Test of Rosenau's Issue Area Typology," *Journal of Peace Research*, Vol. 20, No. 2 (Summer 1983), p. 179; William Zartman, *Elusive Peace: Negotiating an End to Civil Conflicts* (Washington, D.C.: Brookings, 1995).

25. See, for example, Kalevi J. Holsti, "Resolving International Conflicts: A Taxonomy of Behavior and Some Figures on Procedure," *Journal of Conflict Resolution*, Vol. 10, No. 3 (September 1966), p. 272; Robert Jervis, *Perception and Misperception in International Politics* (Princeton, N.J.: Princeton University Press, 1976), p. 101; and Daniel Druckman and Benjamin J. Broome, "Value Differences and Conflict Resolution: Facilitation or Delinking?" *Journal of Conflict Resolution*, Vol. 32, No. 3 (September 1988), p. 491.

26. Thomas Schelling makes a related point that coercion stands to work only when the coerced party understands the coercer's demands. See Schelling, *Arms and Influence* (New Haven, Conn.: Yale University Press, 1966), p. 3. Several studies analyze how groups use terrorism to signal their capabilities and resolve. These studies tend to ignore the question of whether terrorism effectively conveys to the target government the terrorist group's policy objectives. See Harvey E. Lapan and Todd Sandler, "Terrorism and Signaling," *European Journal of Political Economy*, Vol. 9, No. 3 (August 1993), pp. 383–397; Per Batlzer Overgaard, "The Scale of Terrorist Attacks as a Signal of Resources," *Journal of Conflict Resolution*, Vol. 38, No. 3 (September 1994), pp. 452–478; and Hoffman and McCormick, "Terrorism, Signaling, and Suicide Attack," pp. 243–281.

27. Edward E. Jones and Daniel McGillis, "Correspondence Inferences and the Attribution Cube: A Comparative Reappraisal," in John H. Harvey, William J. Ickes, and Robert F. Kidd., eds., *New Directions in Attribution Research*, Vol. 1 (Hillsdale, N.J.: Erlbaum, 1976), pp. 389–420; Edward E. Jones and Richard E. Nisbett, "The Actor and the Observer," in Edward E. Jones, David E.

Kanouse, Harold H. Kelley, Richard E. Nisbett, Stuart Valins, and Bernard Weiner, eds., *Attribution: Perceiving the Causes of Behavior* (Morristown, N.J.: General Learning Press, 1972), p. 87.

28. See "A Conversation with Edward E. Jones and Harold H. Kelley," in Harvey et al., *New Directions in Attribution Research*, p. 378; Edward E. Jones and Keith E. Davis, "From Acts to Dispositions: The Attribution Process in Person Perception," in Leonard Berkowitz, ed., *Advances in Experimental Social Psychology*, Vol. 2 (New York: Academic Press, 1965), p. 225.

29. Jones and Davis, "From Acts to Dispositions," p. 227.

30. Crittenden, "Sociological Aspects of Attribution," p. 427; and Jones and Davis, "From Acts to Dispositions," p. 263.

31. Jones and Davis, "From Acts to Dispositions," p. 264.

32. These common consequences of terrorist attacks are carefully explored in Ami Pedahzur, *Suicide Terrorism* (New York: Polity, 2005).

33. A potential objection to this framework is that it lacks a time dimension: terrorist groups, even if not initially motivated by maximalist intentions, may adopt them upon achieving more limited objectives. Violent means are often self-sustaining and can distort the ultimate goals of perpetrators, rendering ends and means conceptually indistinct. With this proviso in mind, the framework is not meant to imply that the publics of target countries are necessarily in a state of "false consciousness." Rather, the point is simply that the short-term consequences of terrorist acts inform target countries' understanding of the perpetrators' objectives and that this inference undercuts the terrorists' ability to win political concessions.

34. John Russell, "Mujahedeen, Mafia, Madmen: Russian Perceptions of Chechens during the Wars in Chechnya, 1994–1996 and 1999–2001," *Journal of Post-Communist Studies and Transition Politics*, Vol. 18, No. 1 (March 2002), p. 80.

35. Michael McFaul, "Russia under Putin: One Step Forward, Two Steps Back," *Journal of Democracy*, Vol. 11, No. 3 (July 2000), p. 21.

36. Russell, "Mujahedeen, Mafia, Madmen," p. 77.

37. Mike Bowker, "Russia and Chechnya: The Issue of Succession," *Nations and Nationalism*, Vol. 10, No. 4 (Winter 2004), pp. 469, 473.

38. Liliia Federovna Shevtsova, *Yeltsin's Russia: Myths and Reality* (Washington, D.C.: Carnegie Endowment for International Peace, 1999), p. 117.

39. John Russell, "Terrorists, Bandits, Spooks, and Thieves: Russian Demonization of the Chechens before and since 9/11," *Third World Quarterly*, Vol. 26, No. 1 (July 2005), p. 105.

40. Shevtsova, *Yeltsin's Russia,* p. 117.

41. "Russia and Chechnya: Yeltsin's Vietnam," *Economist*, February 10, 1996, p. 51.

42. "Mid-month Polls," VCIOM, posted by Russian Independent Institute of Social and National Problems, http://www.cs.indiana.edu/~dmiguse/Russian/polls.html.

43. "Hope for Chechnya," *Economist*, June 1, 1996, p. 16.

44. Mark A. Smith, "The Second Chechen War: The All-Russian Context," *Strategic and Combat Studies Institute Occasional Papers*, No. 40 (September 2000), p. 5.

45. "Chechnya's Truce," *Maclean Hunter*, June 10, 1996.

46. "Kremlin Deputy Chief of Staff Elaborates on Putin's Political Reform Proposals," BBC Monitor, October 4, 2004, http://www.russiaprofile.org/cdi/article.wbp?article-id=5FEB1101-585F-4CDB-841B-7D467FF7F83B, accessed September 3, 2005.

47. Russell, "Mujahedeen, Mafia, Madmen," p. 77. The September 1999 apartment bombings were not the first terrorist attacks against Russian civilians, but there is general agreement that the bombings represented a watershed. Henceforth, Russian civilians became a primary target. See Mia Bloom, *Dying to Kill: The Allure of Suicide Terror* (New York: Columbia University Press, 2005), p. 127.

48. Since the bombings a conspiracy theory has continued to circulate that the Federal Security Services framed the Chechens to build support for a counteroffensive. Less than 10 percent of Russians accept this theory as credible. Even though the identity of the perpetrators has never been definitely established, the essential point is that the Russian public believed the Chechens were responsible for the terrorist attacks. See A. Petrova, "The Bombing of Houses in Russian Towns: One Year Later," Public Opinion Foundation, poll conducted September 14, 2000, http://bd.english.form.ru/report/cat/az/A/explosion_house/eof003701.

49. Quoted in Charles W. Blandy, "Military Aspects of the Two Russo-Chechen Conflicts in Recent Times," *Central Asian Survey,* Vol. 22, No. 4 (December 2003), p. 422.

50. Russell, "Mujahedeen, Mafia, Madmen," p. 88.

51. "Chechen Labyrinth," Public Opinion Foundation, June 6, 2002, http://bd.english.form.ru/report/cat/02/Chechnya/A/ed022239/html.

52. Timothy Thomas, "Manipulating the Mass Consciousness: Russian and Chechen 'Information War' Tactics in the Second Chechen-Russian Conflict," in A.C. Aldis, ed., *The Second Chechen War* (Washington, D.C.: Conflict Studies Research Center, 2000), p. 116.

53. Quoted in Roman Khalilov, "The Russian-Chechen Conflict," *Central Asia Survey*, Vol. 21, No. 4 (January/February 2002), p. 411.

54. Quoted in John O'Loughlin, Gearoid O. Tuathail, and Vladimir Kolossov, "A 'Risky Western Turn'? Putin's 9/11 Script and Ordinary Russians," *Europe-Asia Studies*, Vol. 56, No. 1 (January 2004), p. 9. There is a tendency to dismiss Putin's comparison of September 11 to the apartment bombings as instrumental rhetoric designed to artificially shore up Russian relations with the West. This assertion, though true, misses an important point: even Russians who opposed stronger relations with the West after September 11, 2001, believed the attacks were analogous to the apartment bombings, despite their belief that the Chechens were the perpetrators. See John O'Loughlin, Gearoid O. Tuathail, and Vladimir Kolossov, "Russian Geopolitical Storylines and Public Opinion in the Wake of 9-11," p. 13, http://www.colorado.edu/IBS/PEC/johno/pub/Russianstorylines.pdf.

55. "The Bombing of Houses in Russian Towns," Public Opinion Foundation, poll conducted September 14, 2000.

56. Quoted in Yana Dlugy, "Putin Calls on Religious Leaders to Aid in Anti-terror Fight," Agence France-Presse, September 29, 2004.

57. S. Klimova, "Negotiating with Maskhadov," Public Opinion Foundation, conducted November 21, 2002, http://bd.english.form.ru/report/map/klimova/ed024629.

58. S. Klimova, "Attitude to Chechens: Pity and Fear," Public Opinion Foundation, January 30, 2003, http://bd.english.form.ru/report/cat/az/A/Chechenian/ed030429.

59. Graeme P. Herd, "Information Warfare and the Second Chechen Campaign," in Sally Cummings, ed., *War and Peace in Post-Soviet Eastern Europe* (Washington, D.C.: Conflict Studies Research Center, 2000), p.32.

60. "Chechnya—Trends, 2000–2005," Levada Center (formerly VCIOM), September 30, 2000, http://www.russiavotes.org/Mood_int_tre.htm.

61. Smith, "The Second Chechen War," p. 6.

62. O'Loughlin et al., "Russian Geopolitical Storylines," p. 22.

63. See Gail W. Lapidus, "Putin's War on Terrorism: Lessons from Chechnya," *Post-Soviet Affairs*, Vol. 18, No. 3 (January/March 2002), p. 45; Roman Khalilov, "The Russian-Chechen Conflict," *Central Asia Survey*, Vol. 21, No. 4 (January–February 2002), p. 411; Richard Pipes, "Give the Chechens a Homeland of Their Own," *New York Times*, September 9, 2004; and Pedahzur, *Suicide Terrorism*, p. 113.

64. In his May 1997 interview with CNN, bin Laden described terrorism as a "message with no words." Four years later he characterized the coordinated strikes on Washington and New York

as "speeches that overshadowed all other speeches." In his treatise for waging jihad, bin Laden's ideological counterpart, Ayman al-Zawahiri, asserted that terrorism is "the only language understood by the West." An al-Qaida spokesman referred to the 2002 attack on a French tanker off the coast of Yemen as a "political message" to Washington. See "Interview with Osama bin Laden," CNN, interview broadcast May 10, 1997, http://fl1.findlaw.com/news.findlaw.com/cnn/docs/binladenintvw-cnn.pdf; videotape from Afghanistan made in November 2001, quoted in Brigitte L. Nacos, "The Terrorist Calculus behind 9/11: A Model for Future Terrorism?" *Studies in Conflict and Terrorism*, Vol. 26, No. 8 (January/February 2003), p. 1; and Ayman al-Zawahiri, *Knights under the Prophet's Banner—Meditations on the Jihadist Movement* (London: Al-Sharq al-Awsat, 2001), quoted in *Oxford Analytica*, No. 14, May 2002, at *Oxford Analytica, "*Middle East/Afghanistan: Al Qaida Threat," http://www.ciaonet.org/pbei/oxan/oxa05142002.html, accessed on May 4, 2005. For an almost identical statement, see "Al-Qaida Urges More Attacks, Al-Zawahiri Tape," May 21, 2003, Aljazeerah.com, http://www.aljazeerah.info/News%20archives/2003.html.

65. Osama bin Laden's two-minute audio broadcast October 6, 2002, on al-Jazeera, quoted in Rohan Gunaratna, "Defeating Al Qaeda—The Pioneering Vanguard of the Islamic Movements," in Russel D. Howard and Reid L. Sawyer, eds., *Defeating Terrorism: Shaping the New Security Environment* (New York: McGraw-Hill, 2003), p. 26; see also Clark McCauley, "Psychological Issues in Understanding Terrorism and the Response to Terrorism," in Chris E. Stout, ed., *Psychology of Terrorism: Coping with the Continuing Threat* (Westport, Conn.: Praeger, 2004), p. 51. Several experts have remarked that al-Qaida leaders almost always emphasize their hatred of U.S. foreign policies, not American values. See, for example, Peter L. Bergen, *Holy War, Inc.: Inside the Secret World of Osama Bin Laden* (New York: Free Press, 2001), p. 223; and Rohan Gunaratna, *Inside Al Qaeda: Global Network of Terror* (New York: Columbia University Press, 2002), p. 45. For a detailed analysis of al-Qaida's objectives, see Max Abrahms, "Al-Qaeda's Scorecard: A Progress Report on Al-Qaeda's Objectives," *Studies in Conflict and Terrorism*, Vol. 29, No. 4 (July–August, 2006), pp. 509–529.

66. Al-Jazeera, "Bin Laden: 'Your Security Is in Your Own Hands,'" October 30, 2004, http://edition.cnn.com/2004/WORLD/meast/10/29/bin.laden.transcript.

67. World Islamic Front, "Jihad against Jews and Crusaders," February 22, 1998, http://www.fas.org/irp/world/para/docs/980223-fatwa.htm; Osama bin Laden, "Declaration of War against the Americans Occupying the Land of the Two Holy Places," August 1996, http://www.pbs.org/newshour/terrorism/international/fatwa_1996.html; Middle East Media Research Institute, "Osama Bin Laden Speech Offers Peace Treaty with Europe, Says Al-Qa'ida 'Will Persist in Fighting' the U.S.," Special Dispatch, No. 695, posted April 15, 2004, http://memri.org/bin/articles.cgi?Page=arch ives&Area=sd&ID=SP69504. Interview first broadcast on al-Jazeera April 15, 2004; and "Al-Qaeda Urges More Attacks, Al-Zawahiri Tape," Agence France Presse, May 21, 2003.

68. See, for example, "Bin Laden Rails against Crusaders and UN," November 3, 2002, BBC.com, http://news.bbc.co.uk/1/hi/world/monitoring/media_reports/1636782.stm. Statement first broadcast on November 3, 2002, on Aljazeera.com. See also "Bin Laden's Warning: Full Text," October 7, 2001, BBC.com, http://news.bbc.co.uk/1/hi/world/south_asia/1585636.stm. Statement first broadcast on July 7, 2001, on Aljazeera.com.

69. ABC News, "Interview: Osama Bin Laden," May 1998, http://www.pbs.org/wgbh/pages/frontline/shows/binladen/who/interview.html; and Ayman Zawahiri, quoted in Bergen, *Holy War*, p. 208; see also *Observer*, "Full Text: bin Laden's 'Letter to America,'" http://observer.guardian.co.uk/worldview/story/0,11581,845725,00html. The letter first appeared on the Internet and was then circulated by supporters in Britain.

70. This statement is based on conclusions reported by the Center for Islamic Studies and Research in The Operation of 11 Rabi al-Awwal: *The East Riyadh Operation and Our War with*

the United States and Its Agents, published in 2003. The book was translated by the Foreign Broadcast Information Service. For excerpts, see http://www.why-war.com/files/2004/01/qaeda_east_riyadh.html.

71. Middle East Media Research Institute, "Osama Bin Laden Speech Offers Peace Treaty with Europe"; and World Islamic Front, "Jihad Against the Jews and the Crusaders," February 23, 1998.

72. Ronald Steel, "Blowback: Terrorism and the U.S. Role in the Middle East," *New Republic*, July 28, 1996, pp. 7–11.

73. Robert Fisk, "As My Grocer Said: Thank You Mr. Clinton for the Fine Words . . . ," *Independent*, August 22, 1998, p. 3.

74. Weinberg and Eubank, p. 138. Found in Hewitt, *Consequences of Political Violence*, 48.

75. Christopher Hewitt, *Understanding Terrorism in America* (London: Routledge, 2003), p. 113.

76. George, W. Bush, presidential speech to the Warsaw Conference, Warsaw, Poland, November 6, 2001.

77. George, W. Bush, remarks by the president to the UN General Assembly, New York, November 10, 2001, at http://www.usunnewyork.usmission.gov/01_162.htm.

78. Richard A. Clarke, *Against All Enemies: Inside America's War on Terror* (New York: Free Press, 2004), p. 17; and George W. Bush, presidential speech to the California Business Association, Sacramento, November 17, 2001.

79. Quoted in Clarke, *Against All Enemies*, p. 17; George W. Bush, presidential address to a Joint Session of Congress, Washington, D.C., September 23, 2001.

80. George W. Bush, remarks by the president to the Dixie Printing Company, Glen Burnie, Maryland, October 24, 2001, http://www.globalsecurity.org/military/library/news/2001/10/mil-011024-usa03c.htm.

81. President Bush is not the only U.S. president to infer these objectives from terrorist attacks. The claim that al-Qaida attacked the United States to destroy its society and values were also espoused by President Bill Clinton after the terrorist attack on the World Trade Center in 1993. See Clarke, *Against All Enemies*, pp. 129–130.

82. Pew Research Center, Roper Center, September 21, 2001. Seventy percent of Americans rejected the idea that "unfair" U.S. foreign policies contributed to the terrorist attacks.

83. IPSOS-REID, Roper Center, September 21, 2001.

84. Harris Poll, Roper Center, September 19–24, 2001, http://www.pollingreport.com/terror9.htm, accessed October 20, 2005.

85. Quoted in Anonymous, *Imperial Hubris*, p. 153; and Aljazeera.com, "Bin Laden: 'Your security is in your own hands.'"

86. Ronald Spiers, "Try Clearer Thinking about Terrorists," *International Herald Tribune*, January 14, 2003; Bergen, *Holy War, Inc.*, p. 223; and Gunaratna, *Inside Al Qaeda*, p. 45. See also Anonymous, *Imperial Hubris*, p. x.

87. Paul Wilkinson, "Security Challenges in the New Reality," lecture, Tufts University, Boston, Mass., October 16, 2002.

88. For a detailed analysis of al-Qaida's effect on U.S. policies in the Muslim world, see Max Abrahms, "Al-Qaeda's Scorecard." In this study, al-Qaida is tagged with failures in three of the core policy objectives outlined in its 1998 declaration of war: the inability to reduce U.S. support for Muslim "apostate" regimes; Israel; and what it derides as "crusader wars," such as Operation Iraqi Freedom. Al-Qaida's policy effectiveness in the Persian Gulf is designated as a "limited success." Overall, the September 11, 2001, attacks did not reduce U.S. interference in the Gulf. On the contrary, the attacks served as the critical impetus for the American public's decision to support the

operation, which has led to the long-term occupation of Iraq and unprecedented U.S. military coop-eration with the Gulf monarchy countries. The one modest success was the American decision to draw down its troop presence in the Saudi Arabian Peninsula after September 11, 2001. Al-Qaida does not regard this policy outcome as noteworthy for two reasons. First, the decision to withdraw hundreds of American troops from the Saudi desert after September 11 palls in comparison to the roughly 150,000 additional U.S. troops that were deployed to the same theater during this period. Second, U.S. interference in the political affairs of the Saudi kingdom increased markedly after the September 11 attacks owing to the joint U.S.-Saudi interest in fighting the jihadists. I thank Michael Knights of *Jane's Intelligence Review* for offering his expertise in this area. For support-ing analysis, see Chaim Kaufman, "Threat Inflation and the Failure of the Marketplace of Ideas: The Selling of the Iraq War," *International Security*, Vol. 29, No.1 (Summer 2004), p. 31; Pape, *Dying to Win,* pp. 46, 84.

89. Khalid Hasan, "Postcard USA: Osama bin Laden Unveiled," *Daily Times* (Pakistan), February 26, 2006.

90. B'Tselem, "Fatalities in the First Intifada," http://www.btselem.org/english/statistics/first_Intifada_Tables.asp.

91. See Bloom, *Dying to Win*, p. 24; and Council on Foreign Relations, "Terrorism: Ques-tions and Answers," http://cfrterrorism.org/groups/pflp.html, October 31, 2005.

92. Edy Kaufman, "Israeli Perceptions of the Palestinians' 'Limited Violence' in the Inti-fada," *Terrorism and Political Violence*, Vol. 3, No. 4 (Winter 1991), p. 4.

93. Gene Sharp, "The Intifada and Nonviolent Struggle," *Journal of Palestine Studies*, Vol. 19, No. 1 (Autumn 1989), p. 7.

94. Kaufman, "Israeli Perceptions," p. 4.

95. Louis Guttman Israel Institute of Applied Social Research, Jerusalem, "Public Assess-ment of the Activities and Violence of the Intifada," No. (s)IK1124/E&H (December 1990).

96. Kaufman, "Israeli Perceptions," p. 13.

97. *Jerusalem Post International Edition*, No. 1 (weekend edition August 27, 1988), p. 451.

98. Avi Shlaim, "When Bush Comes to Shove: America and the Arab-Israeli Peace Process," *Oxford International Review*, Vol. 3, No. 2 (spring 1992), p. 4.

99. The limited objectives of the First Intifada should not be confused with the maximalist objectives of the Palestinian terrorist organizations. The six Palestinian terrorist organizations in this study have been largely ineffective in accomplishing their policy objectives. Hamas is typi-cally regarded as the greatest beneficiary of Palestinian terrorism. Even for Hamas, however, the gulf between its policy aims and their outcome is vast. Its Covenant of the Islamic Resistance Movement stresses two goals. First, Israel "or any part of it should not be squandered; it or any part of it should not be given up." According to Hamas, all of historic Palestine is an Islamic *waqf*, which translates as "prohibition from surrendering or sharing." Hamas's only territorial acquisi-tion is in the Gaza Strip, which represents less than 2 percent of the total land area Hamas claims as its own. Even if one assumes that Hamas may ultimately accept a Palestinian state in the West Bank and Gaza Strip, its territorial achievements to date have been minor. The Gaza Strip – one-nineteenth the size of the West Bank – represents less than 6 percent of the disputed land outside the Green Line. Even the most moderate Palestinian nationalist would be categorically opposed to establishing a Palestinian state in this small a territory. Furthermore, according to international law Gaza remains under occupation because Israel still controls the airspace and Palestinian movement on land and by sea. Palestinians share the view that Gaza remains under occupation, commonly referring to Gaza as "the prison." The second major policy objective is to destroy Israeli society. Despite Palestinian violence, Israel's gross domestic product per capita (U.S.$18,000) is higher than those of New Zealand, Spain, Portugal, and Greece. Far from destroying Israel,

Palestinians consistently rate Israel as the country to which the goal of Palestinian statehood should most aspire. See Central Intelligence Agency, "Gaza Strip," *World Fact Book*, http://www.cia.gov/cia/publications/factbook/index.html; "Covenant of the Islamic Resistance Movement," August 18, 1988, http://www.yale.edu/lawweb/avalon/mideast/hamas.htm; Palestinian Center for Policy and Survey Research, "Palestinians Expect It to Grow," June 6, 2005, http://www.pcpsr.org/survey/polls/2005/p16ejoint.html.

100. Asher Arian, *Israel Public Opinion on National Security 2000* (Tel Aviv: Jaffee Center for Strategic Studies, 2000), p. 14.

101. Tami Steinmetz Center for Peace Research, "Peace Index," Tel Aviv University, http://spirit.tau.ac.il/socant/peace. See also David Fielding and Madeline Penny, "What Causes Changes in Opinion about the Israeli-Palestinian Peace Process?" Economics Discussion Paper, Dunedin, New Zealand, School of Business, No. 0601 (March 2006), p. 8.

102. Hewitt, *Consequences of Political Violence*, pp. 46–47.

103. Peter R. Neumann and Mike Smith, "Strategic Terrorism: The Framework and its Fallacies," *Journal of Strategic Studies*, Vol. 28, No. 4 (Aug 2005), p. 587.

104. See also Abrahms, "Why Terrorism Does Not Work."

105. Ariel Merari, "Terrorism as a Strategy of Insurgency," *Terrorism and Political Violence*, Vol. 5, No.4 (Winter 1993), p. 229.

106. English Translation of Ayman al-Zawahiri's Letter to Abu Musab al-Zarqawi, *Weekly Standard*, October 12, 2005, http://www.weeklystandard.com/Content/Public/Articles/000/000/006/203gpuul.asp.

107. Since 2002, public support for terrorism has dropped by 64 percent in Pakistan, 80 percent in Indonesia, 87 percent in Lebanon, and 200 percent in Morocco. Pew Global Attitudes Project, "Support for Terror Wanes among Muslim Publics," July 14, 2005, http://www.pewglobal.org.reports/pdf/248.pdf, pp. 2, 6.

108. Fareed Zakaria, "How We Can Prevail," *Newsweek*, July 18, 2005.

Challenges to Shaping Civilian Attitudes and Behaviors in a Theater of Operations

Christopher Paul, Todd C. Helmus, and Russell W. Glenn

THIS CHAPTER LAYS OUT THE challenges and barriers faced by the U.S. government (USG) generally and the Department of Defense (DoD) specifically as they engage in the war of ideas. The chapter offers only challenges. Understanding the difficult context in which the USG and DoD operate helps frame suggestions and solutions and may serve to focus the lines of inquiry of others looking to contribute solutions. This chapter is drawn from a larger report that does offer suggestions in response to these challenges (*Enlisting Madison Avenue: The Marketing Approach to Earning Popular Support in Theaters of Operation*),[1] as do many of the other chapters in this volume. Our research for that larger effort (and for this chapter) is based on a wide range of interview and written sources. For this project we conducted more than 30 in-person interviews with active duty military, retired military, and defense civilian personnel from public affairs (PA), civil affairs (CA), psychological operations (PSYOP), and information operations (IO). Written resources include thousands of pages of lessons learned, formal analyses, briefings, scholarly articles, and news articles.

In this discussion, we isolate part of the war of ideas and focus on USG and DoD efforts to "shape" the perceptions and behaviors of noncombatant populations in areas in which the military conducts operations. The traditional military use of shaping is with reference to activities designed to constrain "red" (adversary) force options or increase "blue" (friendly) force options. For example, capturing a bridge both prevents red from using it and makes it available to blue; using aerial bombardment to prevent reinforcements from reaching an enemy position limits red options. In 2002, new joint doctrine for urban operations broadened and updated the shaping concept: "shaping includes all actions that the JFC [Joint Force Commander] takes to seize the initiative and set the conditions for decisive operations to begin. The JFC shapes the battlespace to best suit operational objectives by exerting appropriate influence on adversary forces, friendly forces, the information environment, and particularly the elements of the urban triad."[2] Our use of shaping follows from this construction.

We assert that U.S. forces can and should attempt to shape more than just an "adversary," or "the battlespace," in pursuit of goals that go beyond "operational objectives." Efforts to influence a much broader range of persons and activities in pursuit of a wider array of objectives and policy goals should be considered part of shaping. Here, we focus on challenges associated with shaping noncombatant perceptions and behaviors in pursuit of military objectives or other policy goals. We use "shaping" as shorthand for this pursuit throughout.

GENERAL CHALLENGES TO SHAPING

The U.S. military and other executers of U.S. shaping efforts face at least four broad challenges: (1) anti-American sentiment, (2) adversary shaping efforts, (3) news and news media, and (4) context, including global media, local information environments, culture, and technology.

Anti-American Sentiment and Its Challenge to U.S. Policy and Military Operations

Public opinion polls indicate increasing worldwide anti-American sentiment.[3] While ensuring that citizens of other nations are fond of the United States is not a policy goal in and of itself, unfavorable baseline attitudes held by the international community decrease the likelihood of support for or tolerance of U.S. operations and policies. At its most extreme, hostility toward the United States helps terrorists gain recruits and support. At lesser levels of animosity, anti-Americanism impedes U.S. efforts to promote political and social reforms and commercial and cultural relationships in Muslim countries.[4]

Public opinion polls suggest that much of the anti-Americanism observed in the Muslim world today is attributable to U.S. policies rather than to American culture, values, or people. In a 2004 poll, for example, Zogby International found that residents of most Arab countries had positive opinions about "American services and technology," "American freedom and democracy," "American people," "American products," and the like. But many of those same respondents held negative opinions about U.S. policies toward the Palestinian conflict and Iraq.[5]

If existing U.S. policies are hated, new U.S. policies are likely to be met with suspicion and may already have at least two strikes against them. Popular resentment and distrust pose immediate shaping hurdles to expeditionary U.S. forces.[6] The association of messages and messengers with the United States poses at least three additional challenges to effective shaping:

- *U.S. involvement "taints" messages.* Because of widespread distrust and dislike for the U.S. government, any message perceived to originate from the United States is received with suspicion. While the exact same content from a neutral source might be evaluated on its own merit, U.S. messages are met with negative presumptions.
- *Past and present actions damage U.S. credibility.* U.S. credibility is damaged when the United States fails to do what it says it will do and when actions contradict stated intentions. For example, in June 2005 DoD news releases asserted that U.S. forces were "conducting operations side by side with our Iraqi brethren." This was not the

case in all areas of operation and indigenous civilians aware of this discrepancy likely lost some trust in U.S. force pronouncements.[7]

- *Contradictory messages increase confusion.* U.S. credibility is impaired when different speakers give different accounts or explanations of the same thing or when the same speaker explains something differently to different audiences. After the U.S. invasion of Iraq, Department of State (DoS) talking points highlighted different rationales for the invasion. To a U.S. audience they would assert, "We're fighting them there so we do not have to fight them here," with the secondary implication that the United States intends to make the world a safer place. This emphasis was reversed for foreign audiences. Unfortunately, globalized media makes separate messages impossible.[8]

Adversary Shaping Efforts

The United States is not alone in the information environment. Today's adversaries use a variety of approaches to shape attitudes and behaviors of noncombatants and opinions of foreign observers.

Many terrorist organizations recognize shaping (under different terms, of course) as a primary operational objective, and they integrate operations with related media requirements as a matter of course. For example, Hizballah innovatively subjected "virtually all its military action to its propaganda and mass media requirements."[9] Adversaries employ a wide range of general approaches to shaping, including the following:

Threats, intimidation, and coercion are readily available tools to shape noncombatants' behavior. While they are unlikely to encourage favorable attitudes, such approaches can prevent unfavorable attitudes from being turned into actions (consider insurgent efforts in Iraq to assassinate "collaborators"). Physical threats and intimidation discourage locals from "defecting" in favor of even a well-meaning outsider.

By intimidating journalists and controlling their access or by influencing what they are allowed to witness (or influencing what they safely feel they can report on), an adversary can shape the content of the news. In Iraq, journalists face an ongoing barrage of threats of violence, kidnapping threats, and outright attacks.[10] Following a 2004 attack on Al Arabiya's Baghdad bureau, the group claiming responsibility called the attack a "warning" and protested the station's coverage, "demanding that the station support the 'jihad' against the U.S occupation and Iraqi government."[11]

Filming and distributing records of operations. Many insurgent or terrorist groups have adopted this tactic. Regarding Hizballah, Ron Schliefer observes, "Stills, video, and film became so central to the organization's military activities that it might reasonably be claimed that they dictated both its overall strategy and daily operations. Indeed, the organization's motto could be summed up in the words: 'If you haven't captured it on film you haven't fought.'"[12] The effect of distributing video recordings of operations to friendly media multiplies when the original recipients make them available to a broader range of media outlets.[13]

Forging "special" or exclusive relationships with certain media. Adversaries often tip off reporters from sympathetic media outlets about operations, allowing them to record the events, "scoop" other news agencies, and report operations in a manner favorable to the insurgents. The government of Iraq barred Al-Jazeera and Al-Arabiya from reporting there for two weeks in September 2005 because they were "tipped to attacks on convoys and filmed the events without warning authorities."[14]

Engaging in disinformation. Adversaries sometimes fabricate events or, more effectively, lay down a fabrication atop a base of fact. Case in point: On March 12, 2006, attacks in the Sadr City neighborhood of Baghdad killed 48 people (fact). However, radical Iraqi cleric Moqtada al-Sadr accused both terrorists (plausible accusation) and the U.S. military (false accusation) of responsibility for the attacks. "We consider the attack was carried out by groups of Takfir [a derogatory term used to describe terrorists literally meaning 'those who have put themselves outside Islam'] thanks to the cover of American spy aircraft."[15] Today's operating environment facilitates disinformation. In Iraq, adversary forces do not wear uniforms, so after any engagement, there are casualties in "civilian clothes."[16]

Providing basic services or doing good works is a classic approach to winning friends and influencing people. Both insurgent and terrorist networks have adopted this strategy. In Iraq, Moqtada al-Sadr boosts his popularity by building schools, improving the welfare of the poor, and providing food and clothing to coreligionist refugees.[17]

Adversaries also draw on *approaches that are unique to their culture, region, religion, or nation.* These are particularly challenging to U.S. shaping efforts, as there is little opportunity to reply in kind. Fatwas—Islamic religious/legal proclamations—are growing in frequency and are often directed in support of adversary shaping goals.[18] Adversaries employ such shaping approaches through a variety of media platforms. This diversity makes countering adversary shaping difficult for friendly forces. Each of these media platforms holds its own challenges for U.S. shaping efforts:

- *Internet:* As one interviewee noted, "The enemy is Web-dominant. We have to work on that."[19] Internet posting is inexpensive, easy, and relatively safe for an adversary. Further, the technology has reached a critical mass in accessibility, with high-speed Internet access available worldwide, if not at home, then in many communities through Internet cafés or other publicly available resources.
- *Adversary-owned television stations:* Adversary groups have set up their own television stations, either locally broadcast or via satellite.
- *Pulpits and fatwas:* Many adversary groups, especially Islamist groups, make extensive use of religious media platforms. Sermons and fatwas have been used to justify terror attacks, call people to arms against "infidels," and encourage demonstrations against policies or perceived slights.
- *CDs and DVDs:* Adversary groups distribute shaping messages via CDs or DVDs. This allows messages to be distributed in areas otherwise isolated from traditional media such as radio or TV. CD or DVD sales allow adversaries to recoup some of their costs.
- *Word of mouth:* Adversaries spread shaping messages via rumor, word of mouth, and "the grapevine." A 2006 international study found that people indicated that they got their most reliable information from acquaintances or others "just like them."[20] Adversaries take advantage of this phenomenon.

News and News Media Issues

Longtime media scholar Michael Schudson notes with regard to the U.S. press that "[a] comparison of any leading metropolitan paper of 1995 with one of 1895 demonstrates instantly that today's news is shaped much more by a professional ethic and reflects fewer partisan hopes or fears than a truly political press."[21] Journalistic standards guide much of today's free press. These standards are not codified, but there is a U.S. media way of doing business, and the vast majority of U.S. journalists adhere to those standards or at least to their own interpretations of those standards.[22] Nevertheless, there are at least five emerging trends that color today's news and complicate U.S. shaping efforts:

- *Emergence of the 24-hour news cycle:* Historically, news was deadline-driven and had a daily news cycle. It appeared in daily papers or was presented on the evening news. However, with the dawn of continuous 24-hour cable and satellite news networks and continuous live-feed Internet news, the concept of news cycles has changed. Adversaries can time actions to result in leading stories on U.S. television during daytime or evening news hours.[23] The continuous and live nature of television news puts pressure on journalists to report stories first and to fill the news void with content, sometimes to the advantage of U.S. adversaries.
- *Importance of framing:* How a story is structured and the attitude presented regarding an event constitutes the frame of the story. Frames are the perspective of the story.[24] News simplifies the complex, exemplified by the ever-prominent role of sound bytes.
- *Bias:* Accusations of bias are increasingly leveled against "non-Western" media and Arabic media in particular. President Bush complained that Arabic television often gives a false impression of the United States.[25] Iraqi civil leaders have also referred to Al-Jazeera as a "channel of terrorism."[26] Given Al-Jazeera's dominance in the Arabic language market, such accusations have particular resonance with respect to shaping.[27]
- *Too few reporters:* Financial pressures force many news outlets to make do with fewer reporters than in the past. Having too few reporters on the scene is tantamount to having an insufficient number of credible witnesses, which creates an environment rich for adversary disinformation.
- *Control of journalists' access:* With reporter safety a very real concern, insurgents in Iraq control journalistic access in parts of the country where they have influence. Lack of access impacts the depth of reporting; selective access contributes to biased reporting. As U.S. Army Lieutenant Colonel Tim Ryan observes,

> Because terrorists and other thugs wisely target western media members and others for kidnappings or attacks, the westerners stay close to their quarters. This has the effect of holding the media captive in cities and keeps them away from the broader truth that lies outside their view. With the press thus cornered, the terrorists easily feed their unwitting captives a thin gruel of anarchy, one spoonful each day.[28]

Context: Global Media, Local Information Environments, and Culture

Shaping occurs in the context of global media, the local information environment, and culture. These contextual issues influence the execution and success of shaping. With globalized media, every message has the potential to be seen anywhere. Even locally targeted messages—a single flyer or poster stuck to a wall—can be transposed to another medium (e.g., a camera phone) and retransmitted anywhere. It is consequently impossible to qualify a message's audience with the word "only" (for example, "only Americans" or "only Baghdad residents").

This affects USG shaping efforts in two significant ways. First, as Pascale Combelles-Siegel observed, "Catering principally to the national audience may create inadvertent messages worldwide, as comments 'targeted' at US citizens are seen around the world."[29] For example, presidential rhetoric for domestic audiences has included phrases like "crusade against evil," which has increased perceptions in the Arab world that the United States intended a war against Islam.[30] Second, it is impossible to prevent information spread abroad from returning for domestic consumption. This is particularly relevant for military PSYOP messages, which are restricted to "foreign audiences" by policy.

The local information environment is another relevant part of the context. We use the term *information environment* to denote the scheme of media and modes of information exchange within a region or area. What media are in use in an area? How are they used? Which population groups use predominantly which media?

Information environments vary; there is variation at the regional level ("tabloids" appear in Europe, but not so much in Africa), at the national level (Americans watch CNN or Fox News; Saudis watch Al-Jazeera), and within different parts of a country (Los Angeles has 20 FM radio stations; Pittsburgh has 15). There can be variation in the information habits among groups at any of those levels. Further, there may be regional differences in how those media are displayed and what they are used for, even where a particular medium is fairly ubiquitous (newspapers, posters or flyers). Europe, for example, more so than the United States, tends to have kiosks on which to post notices. The information environment in an area is a crucial part of the context for shaping. Effective shaping of a desired audience occurs only through media used by that target audience. Understanding a given information environment and casting shaping messages in forms that are appropriate to that environment pose significant challenges to shaping.

Culture constitutes another piece of the context in which shaping takes place. We use *culture* as a shorthand way of referring to a group or people's "way of life" or "way of doing things" that can vary across contexts or locales and can cause confusion, misunderstanding, or other "losses in translation" when different cultural assumptions come into contact. Certain things do not translate well, and certain actions (or inactions) in the wrong cultural context can be confusing, funny, or highly offensive. What one should or should not do varies across cultural contexts. Danger lies behind assumptions of similarity.

WHAT MAKES SHAPING SO DIFFICULT FOR DoD?

The previous section identified general challenges inherent in conducting shaping activities. This section narrows the focus and explores challenges specific to DoD shaping activities. The discussion considers several factors that make shaping challenging for DoD and its representatives, including (1) the traditional "kinetic" focus of military operations; (2) interactions between U.S. forces and indigenous personnel; (3) information fratricide; (4) the reputation of PSYOP and IO; (5) the lack of shaping resources; (6) legal/policy barriers to shaping; (7) matching message, medium, and audience; (8) the difficulty of measuring shaping effectiveness; (9) intelligence requirements for shaping; (10) dealing with mistakes; (11) fallout and second-order consequences of expedient choices; (12) "damned if you do, damned if you don't" situations; (13) command use of communication assets; and (14) balancing short-, medium-, and long-term goals.

The Traditional Kinetic Focus of Military Operations

U.S. forces may win every combat engagement but fail to garner the support of the noncombatant population. A focus on kinetic operations to the exclusion of shaping activities increases the likelihood of this kind of outcome.[31] U.S. military doctrine and training has traditionally focused on actions against an adversary and force projection. Operations in which the operational focus is on noncombatants and with methods of engagement that do not involve "putting steel on a target" are a step—often, too lengthy a step—away from tradition.

At the tactical and operational levels of war, U.S. forces have been trained to fight, not shape. British Brigadier Nigel Aylwin-Foster, in a seminal *Military Review* article, contends that an overemphasis on killing and capturing insurgents, combined with liberalized rules of engagement and an overemphasis on force protection, has resulted in unacceptably high numbers of civilian casualties in Iraq. These casualties have necessarily angered the population. Combined with a culture that requires the vengeful righting of perceived wrongs, the casualties have, in part, swelled insurgent ranks and their well of support.[32] Violence, destruction, and death can have a positive shaping effect when they hit their targets without undue collateral loss.[33] Kinetic operations are unavoidable in most conflict situations. The challenge is to minimize the adverse shaping consequences of these actions.

Interactions Between U.S. Forces and Indigenes Have Shaping Consequences

The behavior of every soldier, sailor, airman, and marine in a theater of operations shapes the indigenous population. This section discusses the shaping challenges inherent in the "strategic corporal" phenomenon, the danger of differing cultural perspectives in personal interactions, and the importance of personal relationships in shaping.

Strategic Corporal: Because of the globalization of media, how a single soldier handles a tactical situation in an out-of-the-way location still has the potential to make global headlines and have strategic impact. The "strategic corporal" phenomenon has shaping implications that go beyond mass media; indigenous individuals with whom troops interact form favorable or unfavorable impressions from those interactions and spread those impressions by word of mouth throughout surprisingly large networks.

Prior to September 11, 2001, U.S. forces received no significant training for their future interactions with noncombatants.[34] Maintaining proper civilian–soldier interactions is extraordinarily difficult in dangerous operating environments. However, overzealous efforts to maintain proper force protection make U.S. troops their "own worst enemy."[35] Preparing personnel to be the first line in U.S. shaping efforts remains a critical challenge.

Dangers in Different Cultural Perspectives: Cultural assumptions pose a significant threat to shaping operations. Coalition forces have learned the hard way that many cultural assumptions are repeatedly proven wrong. Observes Colonel Steven Boltz:

> Using a stick to separate people during a search. They use a stick to guide animals. . . .
> We use dogs. They are considered very low. To hold somebody down with your boot,
> that's the lowest of the low. . . . If you separate men from women, it's a mistake. If you
> didn't have an enemy when you went in, you've got one now.[36]

Dramatic efforts have since been taken to learn Iraqi and Afghan do's and don'ts and to educate troops accordingly. It is a daunting task, given the young soldiers who bear the brunt of learning and implementing the infinite array of cultural decorum. While coalition forces have learned much during their time in the Afghan and Iraqi theaters, future contingencies in other locations will bring similar challenges again.

Power of Personal Relationships: Great things have been accomplished through the personal relationships formed between U.S. servicepeople and indigenous noncombatants. Even when other shaping efforts have failed or when credibility has been damaged, the sincerity and personal warmth of a U.S. soldier has won over many a reticent sheik or tribal elder.

Several features of military life make shaping through personal connections more difficult. First, there is the tendency in the military to seek technological solutions to problems. As Dave Champagne, head of the 4th PSYOP Group Strategic Studies Directorate noted, "They are trying to come up with a computer solution to a human problem."[37] This emphasis results in constrained resources being focused on technological solutions rather than on better shaping preparation for troops who will have direct personal contact with foreign noncombatants.[38] Second, rotations constantly disrupt relationships between U.S. troops and members of the indigenous population. Scott Leifker, in a report concerning U.S. Marine tactics, techniques, and procedures, observes that "civilian authorities are tired of meeting new people every few weeks/months."[39] When new troops rotate in, personal relationships that have been cultivated over the course of a year restart from square one. As U.S. Army Lieutenant Colonel Gary Martel notes, "It's a new game every time we have a TOA [transfer of authority]."[40] Rotations also result in the loss of institutional knowledge as incoming units must become familiar with cultural decorum, local influencers, population characteristics, and overarching shaping strategies.

Information Fratricide at All Levels

Several barriers confront coordination and deconfliction within DoD and between DoD and the rest of the USG. According to Army Field Manual 3-13, "*Information fratricide* is the result of employing information operations elements in a way that causes effects in the information environment that impede the conduct of friendly operations or adversely affect friendly forces."[41] All too often, information fratricide results in credibility loss, contrary messaging, or other damage to shaping efforts.

Our analysis and interviews regarding recent operations in Iraq and Afghanistan suggest that information fratricide has been seen both in the lack of coordination or synchronization of strategic communication between DoD and other USG agencies and in the lack of coordination between military shaping entities.

Lack of Coordination or Synchronization of Strategic Communication Between DoD and other USG Agencies: To avoid information fratricide at the highest levels, shaping activities must be coordinated across the government. This is often not the case for several reasons. First, even if we consider only the U.S. DoS and DoD, combatant commands' geographical boundaries do not directly correspond with DoS regions.[42] This poses a coordination obstacle between these two organizations that becomes compounded when other USG entities are also participants.

Further, no single federal executive agency currently has the authority to dictate and enforce other agencies' compliance with shaping objectives. DoS has the "lead" in proposed strategic communication-coordinating structures. However, it is unclear whether DoS has been given sufficient authority to actually coordinate high-level shaping or whether it has the personnel to do so. DoS has a very small workforce in comparison to DoD. Those numbers are smaller yet when only DoS's deployable workforce is taken into account. As U.S. Army Lieutenant Colonel George McDonald noted, if you need to have an "American face" on your information efforts, "State Department just doesn't have the footprint."[43]

Third, there is a lack of guidance regarding the objectives of strategic communication themes. "A lack of national-level themes to guide message formulation" is a consistent observation in shaping-related lessons-learned studies.[44] Even if national level themes and guidance becomes available, unless the president and other officials avoid messages that conflict with existing themes, their words will cause inconsistency, confusion, and are likely to compel rapid changes to those themes. An interview respondent called this "policy by transcript" and indicated it is a serious challenge to efforts to integrate and coordinate shaping activities and messages.[45]

Lack of Coordination Between Military Shaping Entities: Coordinating shaping efforts within DoD is also a challenge. Several organizations have shaping-specific responsibilities: PA, IO, PSYOP, defense support to public diplomacy (DSPD), and civil-military operations (CMO). Then there is also the shaping influence of all other U.S. force elements.

IO is the umbrella entity most clearly charged with coordinating shaping. According to joint doctrine, IO has five pillars: electronic warfare, computer network operations, PSYOP, operations security, and military deception (MILDEC).[46]

PA, CMO, and DSPD are considered *related capabilities* and are charged with "work[ing] in close coordination with the IO planning staff."[47] As is sometimes the case, things do not work as smoothly in practice as is laid out in doctrine.

Doctrinal Issue: IO PSYOP Overlap: PSYOP and MILDEC are the only IO pillars that involve content development. The other pillars concern *information systems* rather than information content. While this creates a bit of a split personality in IO doctrine, it does not carry over too heavily in IO practice: in ongoing operations in Afghanistan and Iraq, according to Lieutenant Colonel Jayson Spade, "PSYOP is the biggest tool."[48] During stability and support operations, four of the five IO pillars are given less priority. This leads to a situation in which IO efforts are almost exclusively PSYOP. The redundant layers of command can create challenges.

RAND conducted interviews with both PSYOP and other IO personnel as part of the research for this study. We were struck by the startling similarity in the concerns and frustrations expressed by PSYOP and IO representatives. Responses to interview questions were nearly identical. This suggests that, in current operational practice, PSYOP and IO have highly overlapped portfolios. This creates at least three challenges:

• There is overlapping authority between IO and PSYOP responsibilities (and a potential for consequential animosity).[49]
• There is confusion between respective roles. IO is a staff function and, doctrinally, has strictly a coordinating role. Yet RAND heard anecdotal accounts of IO staffs releasing "IO products," and releasing them without passing them through the rigorous approval process demanded of PSYOP products.[50] Such was the case when Lieutenant Colonel Bradley Bloom of the 4th PSYOP Group encountered an IO cell in Iraq giving product information to an interpreter for vetting. The product went to the newspapers the next day.[51]
• PSYOP's lack of a "seat at the table."[52] With PSYOP subordinate to IO, an IO representative gets direct access to the commander, while PSYOP representatives report to the IO chief. Unless the IO chief is also an expert in PSYOP, this means that relevant shaping expertise is one step removed from the commander. This may contribute to the challenge of integrating shaping activities with other military operations during both the planning and operating phases.

Doctrinal Issue: PA Is Hesitant to Coordinate with Representatives of Other Shaping Functions: PA personnel are often hesitant to coordinate with IO and PSYOP for a variety of reasons. First, the traditional PA culture holds that PA missions are to "inform, not influence" and to communicate PA messages on behalf of the commander. More contemporarily, several of the public affairs officers (PAOs) we interviewed freely admitted that there is no such thing as *value-free information* and that they do indeed influence, though they were very clear that it was always with 100 percent true information. Current joint doctrine, while requiring PA and IO coordination, prohibits PAOs from "planning or executing" PSYOP:

> PA capabilities are related to IO, but PA is not an IO discipline or PSYOP tool. PA activities contribute to IO by providing truthful, accurate and timely information,

using approved DOD PAG [public affairs guidance] to keep the public informed about the military's missions and operations, countering adversary propaganda, deterring adversary actions, and maintain trust and confidence of the U.S. population, and our friends and allies. PA activities affect, and are affected by, PSYOP, and are planned and executed in coordination with PSYOP planning and operations. PA must be aware of the practice of PSYOP, but should have no role in planning or executing these operations.[53]

A second reason for PA hesitation to coordinate with IO is the constraint that it use only the truth.[54] PSYOP and IO are not similarly bound.[55] Third, many PAOs are cautious in establishing closer relationships because they misunderstand PSYOP. A significant number of PAOs we interviewed were under the impression that most of what PSYOP do is based on falsehood, so-called black PSYOP, and that PSYOP are exclusively tactical. In fact, the vast majority of PSYOP activities are not based on deception.[56] PA hesitancy to engage in shaping coordination means that PAOs do not provide input on the possible shaping consequences of planned operations from the perspective of their audiences.[57] Moreover, when PA and IO are not coordinated, the two could release contradictory messages about the same event, undermining the credibility of both sources.

Doctrinal Issue: Coordination with CMO/CA on Shaping Issues: CMO and civil affairs (CA) forces aim to deliver goods and services to noncombatants. Since these are actions, and actions speak louder than words, the potential positive shaping benefit is enormous, yet it often goes unrealized. CA forces are not trained to publicize or leverage their activities for shaping purposes, much less coordinate them with PSYOP, PA, or IO representatives.[58] As one of our interview respondents noted, "CA guys are great, but they do not 'get' that what they do has to be exploited."[59] Also, many CA personnel are hesitant to work with PSYOP (if not PA) personnel, for many of the same reasons that PA is hesitant. One anonymous CA officer observed, "CA wears the white hat; PSYOP can wear the black hat. We should not switch hit."[60] Another officer we spoke to did not mince words: "PSYOP is the evil tool. It's the black art."[61]

Doctrinal Issue: Informing Line Troops About Shaping Themes: Even though DoD has centralized shaping themes and coordinated shaping professionals, shaping is difficult, given that it can involve virtually every solider, sailor, airman, and marine in a theater of operations. Themes must be effectively disseminated to the troops who are in daily contact with noncombatants in such a way that they can understand and adhere to them. Merely giving troops do's and don'ts is insufficient. Soldiers at the tactical level may not understand the overall goals of the shaping campaign and hence may not understand why specific tactics, techniques, and procedures that serve the shaping campaign are necessary. For example, troops may express frustration at rules requiring them to knock before entering a dwelling, believing that it gives potential adversaries time to flee or otherwise prepare. However, if those troops come to understand that apprehending insurgents is subordinate to gaining the support of the local populace, troops will not only be more likely to adhere to knocking rules, but they will find their own additional ways to earn local support.

Doctrinal Issue: Reactive Rather than Proactive Information Approach: The final information fratricide challenge stems from DoD's reactive approach. Virtually no military commanders would dispute the value of having "initiative" in battle. However, the current system presents several obstacles to proactive shaping. First, it is difficult to get the lead time necessary to conduct proactive shaping because shaping is rarely a high priority. Generating shaping messages takes time, and it takes time for shaping to take effect. Second, because they are out of the planning loop, many with shaping-specific responsibilities do not have the opportunity to propose proactive shaping as part of an operation. They instead end up reacting to the (likely negative) fallout. As one PSYOP representative mentioned, "the command tended to fall back on public affairs–type stuff and only when a crisis would occur, they would go, 'Oh my God! Where are the PSYOP guys?'"[62] Third, many aspects of existing processes are not sufficiently agile to "get out in front" of a breaking crisis or opportunity.

The Reputation of PSYOP and IO

Currently, many shaping activities are under the auspices of PSYOP and IO. Unfortunately, the terms *psychological operations* and *information operations* have come to have a negative connotation that smacks of propaganda, deception, and illicit human influence in ways that are contrary to American values. As IO officer Lieutenant Colonel Jayson Spade explained, "PSYOP has negative connotations. The problem? It seems to be the notion that we are trying to influence people."[63]

Lack of Resources for Shaping

In today's environment, DoD information resources are underfunded by a factor of 10, according to one observer.[64] Here are some of the most critical shortfall areas:

- *Personnel:* The force structure of the three main DoD communication entities—PA, PSYOP, and IO—is limited. PSYOP, for example, has only one active-component PSYOP group—the 4th PSYOP Group, out of Ft. Bragg, N.C., totaling around 1,300 personnel—and two reserve-component psychological operations groups (2nd Psychological Operations Group and 7th Psychological Operations Group, comprising another 2,600 personnel). The only other element is the 193rd Special Operations Wing, with six aircraft and associated crews. According to some senior officers, there are not enough PSYOP personnel to do their assigned missions, let alone conduct joint training exercises with other units so that those units are comfortable working with PSYOP.[65] The PA force structure is even thinner.
- *Training and preparation:* PSYOP are significantly limited by training shortfalls. One anonymous interviewee observed, "It is assumed that the officer corps, sergeants, [privates], know PSYOP, that they are graphic experts, can do target analysis, have cultural knowledge . . . which is ridiculous. The average individual is out of high school, they have some cultural training as part of the MOS [military occupation specialty] and no PSYOP background."[66] There are similar training inadequacies in PA. While some PAOs participate in a valuable industry training program, the program's expanse

is too limited. PAO interviewees indicated that the training they receive is not always well focused with respect to pending deployments.

• *Equipment:* Shaping operations and equipment for communicating outside of the military have not traditionally been DoD priorities. Budget allocations for communication entities reflect that. If resources are allocated for increased end strength and more extensive training, money will still be needed for equipment.

Legal/Policy Barriers to Shaping

Shaping efforts are not excused from adhering to the law. Legal issues can create significant barriers to executing effective shaping. Two areas are particularly challenging:

• *Prohibitions on targeting U.S. citizens with PSYOP:* Public Law 402, the U.S. Information and Educational Exchange Act of 1948 (the Smith-Mundt Act), prohibits the now defunct U.S. Information Agency from targeting U.S. audiences. DoD has received legal opinions that indicate it is subject to the same prohibition. With the reach of the Internet and 24-hour news, however, many of the Pentagon's information efforts risk appearing in the U.S. media.[67] PSYOP forces need to obtain the direct permission of the secretary of Defense before distributing material on the Internet, even in a foreign language.[68] The result, according to one interviewee: "We're hamstrung in a lot of ways."[69]
• *PSYOP approval process:* Less a "legal" barrier than a procedural one, this involves product development and approval. A rigorous process makes sense. However, product approval needs should be balanced with timeliness. Finding a process that leads to the right balance is the challenge. As Christopher Lamb notes,

> A dilatory PSYOP product approval process is detrimental to the execution of an effective PSYOP campaign. Before operations begin, a delayed process inhibits PSYOP planning and rehearsal time, while slow approval during an actual campaign can render some military and political products useless, since they may be overcome by events.[70]

Matching Message, Medium, and Audience

Every member of a given population is different—and different in ways that can affect perceptions of a message. Communications that treat everyone in a large population as a homogenous target audience risk missing the mark or, in the extreme, prove deleterious to shaping objectives. Yet identifying target audiences is a difficult task in military operational venues. The intermingling of adversaries and noncombatants and the possibility of an individual's role as friendly, neutral, or enemy changing from day to day compounds the challenges of audience segmentation.[71]

Another challenge is anticipating how messages will impact the target and other groups that are part of the "inadvertent" audience. Culture, language, and other features of the receiving audience (whether targeted or not) impact how messages are perceived.

Both doctrine and industry best practice suggest that focus groups and other forms of product pretesting are important in message development. However, in this case, product pretesting is hindered on several levels. First, the pace of operations and the corresponding need to move products quickly limit time available for pretesting. U.S. shaping forces may also lack adequate access to target audiences. In some cases, such access is simply not available; in others, there may be missed opportunities to pretest, as was the case in at least one instance noted by an interviewee speaking of Afghanistan: "They are doing products for Taliban and using civilians to pretest. We had Taliban as prisoners and defectors; they should have used them."[72]

Identifying the appropriate media to convey a message to a given target audience requires care. Different locales have different information environments and different cultural preferences for the form and style of the media they consume. For example, residents of Kabul, Afghanistan, likely vary considerably from their rural counterparts in terms of media consumption habits.

How Do You Know What You Are Doing Is Working?

Measuring the effectiveness of shaping is particularly challenging. The biggest problem is connecting the shaping action or message with some measurable quantity or quality that is not confounded by other possible causes. For example, many Iraqi soldiers surrendered at the outset of Operation Iraqi Freedom (OIF). Was this due to the PSYOP leaflets dropped instructing them to do so? Was it instead due to the impact of the coalition's massive military might? Were there other causes? What was the most likely combination of causes that resulted in the desirable end? In this case, the possible causes are highly conflated, even though the objective being measured—surrender—is an observable behavior. It would be even more difficult to assess the multiple possible causes underlying other objectives, such as creating positive public attitudes toward the coalition.

One observer notes, "It is possible to establish qualitative performance standards for PSYOP effects that can then be assessed with the use of direct observation, polling, surveys, interviews, and other methods."[73] Yet challenges remain even when measurement is possible. These techniques are difficult to get right and are expensive to implement. Additionally, they are subject to various forms of bias—including response bias (i.e., when the respondent tells you what you want to hear), selection bias (i.e., when the sample is not chosen in a representative fashion), and self-selection bias (i.e., when only people who want to participate in a poll do so, and the responses of these individuals differ substantially from the hypothetical responses of those who did not participate).

Intelligence Requirements for Shaping

Audience segmentation, target-audience analysis, and measures of effectiveness all require intelligence support. Further, many of these intelligence requirements specifically demand human intelligence (HUMINT), while traditionally, U.S. forces have focused on technological means of intelligence gathering.[74] This proved to be the case in OIF, in which intelligence support for IO was excellent with regard to technical sources but struggled with human and cultural intelligence.[75] One observer suggests that part of the problem is that "key IO intelligence requirements are not identified anywhere outside of IO doctrine."[76] To the extent that this is the case, shaping personnel are under an increased burden to make their needs clear to intelligence personnel.

Another factor is that gathering good cultural intelligence and other forms of HUMINT is a difficult and time-consuming task. It also differs in character from more traditional collection efforts. "Our intelligence is still geared to [maneuver warfare]," one interviewee noted. "Human analysis and human influence is a secondary skill in our sector."[77] Given the need to support shaping requirements, such as understanding the motives, relationships, and likely reactions of key members of the public, there is a need for change in this preparedness for maneuver, PSYOP, and other operations.

Mistakes and Errors

Shaping is much less challenging when everything goes as planned. Unfortunately, sometimes U.S. personnel make mistakes or judgment errors, or ordnance goes astray and hits an unintended target. Mistakes can have considerable negative shaping consequences. In such situations, DoD's shaping responses have habitually been poor. As Colonel George Rhynedance notes, "That's the immediate response capability, and we traditionally have not done that well."[78]

Ongoing operations in Iraq and Afghanistan have included several situations in which U.S. forces have made some kind of substantial error with potentially negative shaping consequences. The burning of Taliban corpses; the reputed mass murder in Haditha, Iraq; and the abuse of prisoners at Abu Ghraib are examples of mistakes with adverse shaping consequences.[79]

Fallout and Second-Order Consequences of Expedient Choices

Implicit in the recognition that every action has shaping consequences is the challenge of thinking through the possible consequences. Expedient choices often have negative shaping consequences. Sometimes these are obvious: using threat of force to disperse a crowd will not make members of that crowd any more well disposed toward U.S. forces. More subtly, failure to disperse the crowd by certain means may embolden it to further action, thereby leaving an impression of U.S. inability to control the situation.

This is a situation that is often generically called *the dilemma of force*. Using force can injure the very noncombatants U.S. forces want to protect (and shape), but failure to use force in some circumstances may allow adversary forces to escape or prevail, leading to lack of belief in friendly force capabilities to overcome the foe. Threat of force results in the same kinds of credibility issues faced by other shaping efforts. If threat of force is no longer credible, a valuable shaping tool is lost.

Sometimes, the consequences of expedient choices are less obvious: choosing to work with a specific tribe may appear as inappropriate favoritism in the tangled web of political, religious, and tribal disputes in an area.[80] Similarly, while existing indigenous militias might be attractive partners in the short term, their favored status may grant them undue legitimacy in the eyes of locals and—depending on the motivations of the militia leaders—later inhibit political reform.[81]

Events with Both Potentially Positive and Negative Shaping Consequences

Another shaping challenge is choosing the lesser of two evils, or managing shaping efforts that have both positive and negative consequences: "damned if you do, damned if you don't."

First, there is the dilemma of force, mentioned previously. Another example is the use of adversary body counts. Body counts earned a bad name in Vietnam, as they were neither a reliable measure nor an appropriate metric with which to gauge success. In Afghanistan and Iraq, U.S. forces initially resisted estimates of enemy killed or wounded. However, detailed information has always been made available about U.S. force fatalities. Said one interviewee, "The problem we ran into by not reporting enemy killed/captured/wounded was our press was reporting our casualties very accurately, which gave the impression we were losing, since there [were] no enemy figures to counterbalance."[82]

Command Use of Communication Assets

Like all military assets, control over the drafting and dissemination of PSYOP and other messages is a command responsibility. Unfortunately, there are some commanders—or staff officers acting on behalf of commanders—who do not fully appreciate the subtleties involved in developing and distributing such materials. For example, PA, PSYOP, and IO personnel interviewed during this research effort lamented the missteps made when individuals untrained in the nuances of creating messages took the responsibility upon themselves. Part of the problem is the default assumption that developing such communications is easy. Said one interviewee,

> In the 18th Airborne, it is the artillery guy. He's a hell of an artillery officer. He's making great decisions. Are they great officers? Absolutely . . . but they make beginner mistakes [with communications] and lack background, credibility or confidence to argue for what is required.[83]

Balancing Short-, Medium-, and Long-Term Goals

The final challenge facing U.S. forces with regard to shaping is the need to balance short-, medium-, and long-term goals. A major challenge of short- versus longer-term objectives involves shaping issues that differ from one phase of operations to the next. Consider a sampling of four phases of an operation: a preoperational phase (phase 0); a combat phase (phase 1); a postcombat support, stability, and reconstruction phase (phase 4); and a final transition to indigenous authority (end phase).[84] The most significant challenge is to shape toward the end phase from phase 0 forward, but each phase contains its own shaping challenges beyond keeping the ultimate policy goal in mind.

In phase 0, access to the theater of operations may be the primary, though not insurmountable, challenge. Shaping capabilities generally lack sufficient predeployment access to target audiences for either analysis or message transmission. Since phase 0 is furthest from the end state, the end state may not be well articulated, or the path to the end state may not be clear, making shaping toward that path challenging.

The dilemma of force is prominent during phase 1. Shaping efforts in phase 1 struggle to balance short-term tactical objectives with longer-term postcombat goals. For example, during the investment of Um Qasar during OIF 1, marines encountered regular Iraqi army and fedayeen units. They responded with tank and missile fire to destroy buildings of tactical value to the enemy. Lieutenant Colonel F. H. R. Howes of the Royal Marines commented on the aftermath, noting, "When I moved through the town with my ops officer, there was an incredibly tense feeling about it. . . . The people were extraordinarily scared of the Americans."[85]

At the beginning of phase 4, there is the potential for an even greater shaping challenge: the "gap" in authority between the regime replaced by the U.S. operation and the new order that phase 4 will introduce. Bridging that gap is a considerable challenge, one that was not fully successful during OIF. It is in phase 4 that shaping shortcomings in phases 0 and 1 become apparent. The possible presence of an insurgency or of intragroup conflict is an additional shaping challenge, one that makes the dilemma of force more acute and, perhaps, changes the balance point for use of force.

Transitioning to the end phase also has unique challenges. Several interview respondents were in Iraq during the formal "transfer of sovereignty" and noted that it raised a number of issues. One PAO lamented the near media blackout associated with the "put an Iraqi face on it" campaign. "Information flow stopped dead, and that created a large vacuum. No one trained or otherwise prepared the Iraqis to take over their own PA," leaving the shaping "battlefield" to adversaries.[86] Moving to the end phase requires careful management of noncombatant expectations, expectations of U.S. forces in theater, and others in the region. Failure can seriously undermine support for the new government and coalition.

CONCLUSIONS

In this chapter we have laid out the challenges faced by USG and DoD shaping efforts. While the most general conclusion we can draw is that "shaping is hard," we see several sources for optimism. First, progress is being made. Anecdotally, we have heard many reports of success from forces in theater. Both in our work and in the work of others practical solutions to many of these challenges have emerged and are being recorded and disseminated. Second, shaping activities are an area of renewed emphasis in the DoD and in the USG more broadly, and continue to receive attention and new resources. Third, there are ongoing efforts to coordinate and develop strategic communication and public diplomacy.

Shaping remains difficult, and there is a great deal of ground to be covered. This clear enumeration of the wide range of challenges faced by shaping activities should help put things in perspective. These are not an easy set of challenges. The sheer number and complexity of these challenges makes clear that there is no silver bullet for shaping. A solution to a single shaping challenge, even one of the more significant challenges, will not wholly solve the shaping problem. However, solving or resolving any of these challenges will remove barriers to successful shaping and make future shaping efforts more likely to succeed. Incremental improvement is both possible and desirable.

NOTES

1. Todd C. Helmus, Christopher Paul, Russell W. Glenn, *Enlisting Madison Avenue: The Marketing Approach to Earning Popular Support in Theaters of Operation* (Santa Monica: RAND Corporation, 2007).

2. Joint Joint Chiefs of Staff, *Doctrine for Joint Urban Operations*, Joint Publication 3-06 (September 16, 2002), II-10.

3. See, for example, the Pew Global Attitudes Project, *America's Image Slips, but Allies Share U.S. Concerns Over Iran, Hamas; No Global Warming Alarm in the U.S., China* (Washington, D.C.: Pew Research Center, June 13, 2006), 1.

4. Craig Charney and Nicole Yakatan, *A New Beginning: Strategies for a More Fruitful Dialogue With the Muslim World* (Washington, D.C.: Council on Foreign Relations, May 2005), iii.

5. Zogby International, *Impressions of America 2004: How Arabs View America, How Arabs Learn About America*, a six-nation survey commissioned by the Arab American Institute, 2004, 1.

6. Even seemingly attractive U.S. policy goals and shaping messages can be perceived as unattractive. This was the reason behind the suspension of the publication *Hi*, the U.S. Department of State's Arab youth magazine at the end of 2005 (Middle East Online, "US Suspends Publication of Arab Youth Magazine," last updated December 23, 2005).

7. Joshua Kucera, "Military and the Media-Weaponising the Truth?," *Jane's Defence Weekly* (June 8, 2005).

8. Farah Stockman, "US Image a Tough Sell in Mideast," *Boston Globe* (October 23, 2005), A5.

9. Ron Schleifer, "Psychological Operations: A New Variation on an Age Old Art: Hezbollah Versus Israel," *Studies in Conflict and Terrorism* 29, No. 1 (January 2006), 1–19 [5]. Also, please see the chapter by Guemantes Lailari in this volume.

10. Faraydoon Jalal, "Iraqi Journalists Risking Their Lives," *Kurdish Media* (June 16, 2005).

11. Committee to Protect Journalists, "Attacks on the Press 2004: Documented Cases from Middle East and North Africa: Iraq," (undated Web page), http://www.cpj.org/attacks04/mideast04/iraq.html.

12. Schleifer, "Psychological Operations," 6.

13. Ibrahim Al-Marashi, "Iraq's Hostage Crisis: Kidnappings, Mass Media and the Iraqi Insurgency," *Middle East Review of International Affairs* 8, No. 4 (December 2004), 1–11 [8].

14. Bing West, *No True Glory: A Frontline Account of the Battle for Fallujah* (New York: Bantam Books, 2005), 91.

15. Adnkronosinternational, "Iraq: Al-Sadr Accuses Al-Qaeda and U.S. of Sunday's Carnage" (March 13, 2006), http://www.adnki.com/index_2Level_English.php?cat=Terrorism&loid=8.0.274742248&par.

16. LTC Steve Boylan, U.S. Army, Public Affairs Chief, Strategic Communication, Combined Arms Center, telephone interview with Christopher Paul, May 24, 2006.

17. Salih Al-Qaisi and Oliver Poole, "Sadr Shows How to Win Hearts and Minds," *Daily Telegraph* (London, August 29, 2005), 12.

18. These tactics are likely employed to achieve ends that range from recruitment and radicalization to appeasing and pacifying largely uninvolved publics.

19. LTC Gary Tallman, U.S. Army, Public Affairs Officer, interview with Christopher Paul, Pentagon, Arlington, Va., April 24, 2006.

20. Edelman, "'A Person Like Me' Now Most Credible Spokesperson for Companies; Trust in Employees Significantly Higher Than in CEOs, Edelman Trust Barometer Finds" (New York, January 23, 2006), http://www.edelman.com/news/ShowOne.asp?ID=102.

21. Michael Schudson, *The Sociology of News* (New York: W. W. Norton, 2003), 48.

22. With these ethical principles in mind, U.S. media outlets do tend to cater to audience's political perspectives to a greater or lesser degree (Dirk Blum, Lincoln Group, written comments provided to the authors, February 1, 2007).

23. LTC Tim Ryan, "Media's Coverage Has Distorted World's View of Iraqi Reality," *World Tribune.com* (January 18, 2005), http://www.worldtribune.com/worldtribune/05/breaking245 3389.0680555557.html.

24. David L. Paletz, *The Media in American Politics: Contents and Consequences* (New York: Longman, 2002), 66.

25. "Bush: Arabic TV Gives False Impression of U.S.," Reuters (January 5, 2006).

26. "Al-Jazeera a 'Terror Channel,'" Agence France-Presse (November 24, 2004).

27. West, "No True Glory," 90–91.

28. Ryan, "Media's Coverage has Distorted World's View."

29. Pascale Combelles-Siegel, "Perception Management: IO's Stepchild?," *Low Intensity Conflict & Law Enforcement* 13, no. 2 (Autumn 2005), 131.

30. Peter Ford, "Europe Cringes at Bush 'Crusade' Against Terrorists," *Christian Science Monitor* (September 19, 2001).

31. Please see the chapter by Joshua Geltzer in this volume.

32. Nigel Aylwin-Foster, "Changing the Army for Counterinsurgency Operations," *Military Review* (November–December 2005), 2–15.

33. During ongoing operations in Iraq, U.S. forces used a 2,000-pound bomb on an insurgent stronghold. So impressed by this display of resolve were locales that intelligence tips immediately poured forth.

34. "Another U.S. General did assert that it was unreasonable and impractical to expect front-line soldiers, given their training and pre-eminent warfighting role, to develop the levels of subtlety or master the wider range of skills predicated by the hearts and minds campaign. He implied that their employment must perforce be restricted to combat tasks, leaving post conflict engagement with the populace largely to other organisations, such as the Army's reservist dominated CIMIC [civil-military cooperation] units, and NGOs [nongovernmental organizations]," Aylwin-Foster, "Changing the Army," 5.

35. James Rainey, "Aiming for a More Subtle Fighting Force," *Los Angeles Times* (May 9, 2006), A6.

36. COL Steven Boltz, U.S. Army, G-2, V Corps, interview with Russell W. Glenn and Todd C. Helmus, Heidelburg, Germany, February 26, 2004.

37. Dave Champagne, Head of Strategic Studies Directorate, 4th Psychological Operations Group, interview with Todd C. Helmus and Christopher Paul, Ft. Bragg, N.C., December 14, 2005.

38. Combelles-Siegel, "Perception Management," 117.

39. Scott Leifker, 7th Marines, Tactics, Techniques, and Procedures, "Trip Report Draft—040413," email to Russell W. Glenn, June 7, 2004.

40. LTC Gary Martel, Joint Information Operations Center, interview with Christopher Paul, Lackland Air Force Base, San Antonio, Tex., February 16, 2006.

41. Headquarters, U.S. Department of the Army, *Information Operations: Doctrine, Tactics, Techniques, and Procedures*, Washington, D.C., Army Field Manual 3-13, (November 28, 2003), 1–5. Emphasis in original.

42. Martel, interview.

43. LTC George McDonald, Joint Information Operations Center, and MAJ George Brown, Joint PSYOP Planner, Joint Information Operations Center, interview with Christopher Paul and Todd C. Helmus, Lackland Air Force Base, Tex., February 17, 2006.

44. Christopher Lamb, *Review of Psychological Operations Lessons Learned from Recent Operational Experience* (Washington, D.C.: National Defense University Press, September 2005), 2.

45. Anonymous interview.

46. Joint Chiefs of Staff, *Joint Doctrine for Information Operations*, Joint Publication 3-13 (February, 13, 2006), iii.

47. Joint Chiefs of Staff, *Joint Doctrine for Information Operations*, x.

48. LTC Jayson Spade, J-31 Team Chief, Combatant Command Support Team for U.S. Pacific Command, and MAJ John Hill, J-24 Intelligence Support to Special Operations Team Leader, interview with Christopher Paul and Todd C. Helmus, Joint Information Operations Center, Lackland Air Force Base, Tex., February 16, 2006.

49. CDR Ed Burns, U.S. Navy, Joint Information Operations Center, interview with Christopher Paul and Todd C. Helmus, Lackland Air Force Base, Tex., February 16, 2006.

50. One PSYOP interview respondent, upset with this apparent usurpation, asserted that, according to doctrine, there is no such thing as an "IO product" other than a synchronization matrix for a staff meeting, and further remarked that there is no "IO product" that an Iraqi ever sees (LTC Bradley Bloom, U.S. Army, Commanding Officer, 3rd PSYOP Battalion, 4th Psychological Operations Group, interview with Todd C. Helmus and Christopher Paul, Ft. Bragg, N.C., December 15, 2005). An IO respondent agreed, and indicated that he gave his IO team members these instructions: "IO can develop the theme, let the PSYOPers develop the message" (Burns, interview).

51. Bloom, interview.

52. COL Kenneth A. Turner, U.S. Army, Commanding Officer, 4th Psychological Operations Group, interview with Todd C. Helmus and Christopher Paul, Ft. Bragg, N.C., December 14, 2005.

53. Joint Chiefs of Staff, *Doctrine for Public Affairs in Joint Operations*, Joint Publication 3-61 (May 9, 2005), III-21.

54. LTC Ryan Yantis, Director, U.S. Army Public Affairs—Midwest, telephone interview with Christopher Paul and Todd C. Helmus, May 15, 2006.

55. "In theory, the idea of merging PA, IO, and PSYOP appears to make sense; in practice, however, the goals of these three functions are quite different. Public affairs is charged with informing the public with factual, truthful information, while IO and PSYOP seek to influence their audiences to change perceptions or behavior" (Pamela Keeton and Mark McCann, "Information Operations, STRATCOM, and Public Affairs," *Military Review* [November–December 2005], 83–86 [84]).

56. One respondent was not surprised by the misunderstanding. He examined the PA Defense Information School training curriculum and found that students receive only 30 minutes of IO training, all of it focused on MILDEC, which *is* all about lying (Bob Giesler, Director, Information Operations and Strategic Studies, ODUSD [IWS], Interview with Christopher Paul, Pentagon, Washington, D.C., April 26, 2006).

57. "Public affairs officers do not typically provide input about potential media fallout of specific targeting—in no small part because they frequently are not involved in strike planning.

They often are far enough out of the loop so as not to have knowledge of specific situations or the context of operations" (Combelles-Siegel, "Perception Management," 130).

58. "The problem is that we think of CMO as something that [the Civil Affairs Group] does. We are all more comfortable with kinetic operations so that's what we focus on, and then [we] leave the detailed planning for Phase IV operations to the CA guys on the [operational planning team] who often lack the background and expertise to make it work. We do this even though we all say the Phase IV is the most important phase" (Unidentified Marine Expeditionary Force Planner, U.S. Marine Corps, "Perspectives on HA/CMO in Iraq," briefing, Security Cooperation Education and Training Center, undated, slide 2).

59. Anonymous interview.

60. Anonymous interview.

61. Anonymous interview.

62. Nicholas Novosel, Balkan Area Analyst, U.S. European Command, Strategic Studies Detachment, 4th Psychological Operations Group, interview with Todd C. Helmus and Christopher Paul, Ft. Bragg, N.C., December 14, 2005.

63. Spade, interview.

64. Jeffrey B. Jones, "Strategic Communication: A Mandate for the United States," *Joint Force Quarterly* 39 (October 2005), 108–114.

65. Bloom, interview.

66. Anonymous interview.

67. Mark Mazzetti, "Planted Articles May Be Violation: A 2003 Pentagon Directive Appears to Bar a Military Program That Pays Iraqi Media to Print Favorable Stories," *Los Angeles Times* (January 27, 2006), A3.

68. COL Jack Summe, J-39, PSYOP Division Chief, interview with Todd C. Helmus, McDill Airbase, Tampa, Fla., January 19, 2006.

69. Bloom, interview.

70. Lamb, *Review of Psychological Operations*, 14.

71. Jamison Jo Medby and Russell W. Glenn, *Street Smart: Intelligence Preparation of the Battlefield for Urban Operations* (Santa Monica, Calif.: RAND Corporation, 2002).

72. Spade, interview.

73. Lamb, *Review of Psychological Operations*, 29.

74. Aylwin-Foster, "Changing the Army."

75. MAJ John J. Strycula, "Intelligence Support to Information Operations," unpublished briefing (Santa Monica, Calif.: RAND Corporation, undated).

76. Strycula (undated).

77. Bloom, interview.

78. COL George Rhynedance, Director, Army Public Affairs Center, telephone interview with Christopher Paul, May 23, 2006.

79. Tom Allard, "Film Roles as Troops Burn Dead," *Sydney Morning Herald* (October 19, 2005).

80. Joshua Kucera, "Djibouti: US Foothold in Africa—African Foothold," *Jane's Defence Weekly* (October 26, 2005).

81. The possible second-order consequences of U.S. actions, even well-reasoned ones, can be quite severe. One observer suggests that U.S. policy in Iraq places United States precariously in the divide between Sunni and Shia Islam:

> Many Sunni Muslims are convinced that the Bush administration is subverting their faith by favouring the Shia cause in Iraq and hence promoting Iranian influence. In the

slums of eastern Amman, for example, people hardly knew what Shia Islam was until recently. Now the word has spread that neighbouring Iraq is about to get a Shia-dominated government—and, moreover, that it is all America's fault. ("Political Islam, Forty Shades of Green," *Economist*, [February 4, 2006], 23)

82. COL Glen Collins, U.S. Army (retired), "WP: Enemy Body Counts Revived," e-mail to Russell W. Glenn, October 25, 2005.

83. Anonymous interview.

84. Of course, a different number of phases with different names can be envisioned; these four are cited for illustrative purposes only.

85. Lieutenant Colonel F. H. R. Howes, Commander, 42nd Commando Royal Marines during Operation Telic, interview with Russell W. Glenn and Todd C. Helmus, Upavon, U.K., December 12, 2003.

86. Boylan (2006).

9

The Nonkinetic Aspects of Kinetic Efforts

Joshua Alexander Geltzer

IT HAS BECOME A TRUISM of evaluations of American counterterrorist strategy that a particular dimension of this strategy is sorely lacking. Alternatively labeled "strategic influence," "strategic communication," "public diplomacy," "information operations," "information warfare," "psychological warfare," and a host of other rather fuzzy names, this lacuna is generally understood to mean the absence of a nonkinetic element to counterterrorism—bluntly put, a part of counterterrorism concerned with winning people over rather than blowing people away, so to speak. Such criticism, while by all means well grounded, nonetheless tends to overlook the nonkinetic aspects of American counterterrorist strategy that *have* emerged: namely, the nonkinetic aspects of America's kinetic efforts. In other words, even as the United States has emphasized *doing* things rather than *saying* things, actions themselves convey messages, meaning that kinetic (i.e., active, generally violent) counterterrorist measures have crucial nonkinetic (i.e., persuasive, demonstrative) elements and implications. Strategic influence comes through word as well as through deed—and an analytical focus on just how the latter functions as a form of strategic influence toward America's target audiences is vital, though presently insufficient. As Paul K. Davis and Brian Michael Jenkins, two RAND scholars, aptly note, "The distinction between direct actions and influencing actions is often blurred in practice because a given action may have both direct and indirect effects."[1] In other words, "direct actions" are also "influencing actions."

In this relatively short space, it would be impossible to examine all of the many kinetic efforts that have defined American counterterrorist strategy toward al-Qaida in the wake of the attacks of September 11, 2001, and that have significant nonkinetic components and implications. Instead, the aim here is twofold: first, to reveal a number of ways in which key American counterterrorist policies are predicated, in significant part, on their potential to exercise strategic influence beyond their direct practical effects; and second, to suggest the difficulty—but also the importance—of assessing what influence those policies have had, are having, and will and can have on their intended audiences, whose members are characterized by rather distinct—and in some respects unusual—worldviews. This discussion is intended to open up a crucial and relatively unexplored line of research for those studying terrorism and counterterrorism, rather than to suggest any last word on the subject.

Like so many buzzwords, "kinetic" has come to possess a number of related but slightly different meanings; in turn, the distinction between the "kinetic" and the "non-kinetic" has been described in different ways. Some use the terms to distinguish between the violent and the nonviolent aspects of military action; others use them to delineate between actions designed to have direct and indirect effects; still others employ the terms to differentiate between efforts to attack, as opposed to influence, the enemy; and, finally, a former commander of the U.S. Joint Forces Command described nonkinetic technologies as "weapons that hinder the enemy, but don't go boom."[2] Here, "kinetic" will be used to refer to active, usually violent measures designed primarily for practical, direct effects; "nonkinetic" will be used to describe the aspects or consequences of those measures intended to have demonstrative, persuasive effects—in other words, to exercise strategic influence. To be sure, the line between the kinetic and the nonkinetic often is blurred, but the basic distinction will prove useful in the discussion that follows.

STRATEGIC INFLUENCE THROUGH KINETIC EFFORTS

A number of America's most significant post-9/11 counterterrorist policies toward al-Qaida have been justified by the Bush administration on the grounds that those policies' kinetic components, in addition to providing practical benefits, would exert a beneficial strategic influence on some set of target audiences, ranging from the terrorist leadership itself to the would-be or potential terrorist to the existing and potential state sponsors of terrorism. Examining a few of those policies will reveal the ways in which America's kinetic counterterrorist efforts have been heavily grounded in nonkinetic aims and expectations for exercising strategic influence.

America's campaign in Afghanistan, launched in October 2001, clearly had direct, practical intentions—namely, to rout al-Qaida and its Taliban hosts. At the same time, the American leadership explicitly hoped that the war would also exert a distinctly nonkinetic strategic influence. Hence, consider President George W. Bush's words to his team just days after 9/11: "Let's hit them hard. We want to signal this is a change from the past."[3] Even before the campaign in Afghanistan had commenced, President Bush demonstrated his concern with the message that America's exceedingly kinetic actions would convey; he soon added, "What we do in Afghanistan [will] be a signal to other countries about how serious we are on terror."[4] In particular, and as President Bush's words suggest, the notion of signaling a *change* played a central role in the Bush administration's thinking. Drawing on a critique of the Clinton administration's reactions to al-Qaida's attacks in 1998 and 2000, the Bush team sought to use military force not only to disrupt and eliminate al-Qaida's membership, but also to demonstrate that America, in the wake of 9/11 and under President Bush's more aggressive leadership, was a transformed actor. Victory in Afghanistan thus hinged not only on what the United States did, but also on what perception of the United States the campaign cultivated in the minds of America's audiences. Hence, Harvard University Professor Graham Allison notes that America's campaign in Afghanistan "heralded a new assertiveness in U.S. foreign policy and demonstrated America's unparalleled military dominance. The speed and efficiency with which U.S. forces dispatched the Taliban drove home both points."[5] Those points were essentially nonkinetic ones, and they were intended to demonstrate to a variety of audiences that America was a changed, fiercer international actor, especially when it came to counterterrorism.

Yet in a somewhat ironic manner, Afghanistan proved an inhospitable place for the United States to demonstrate its newfound commitment to waging an aggressive counterterrorist campaign. The Taliban was simply too weak to allow a full demonstration of American power or a true indication of America's unwillingness, in light of 9/11, to tolerate potential state sponsors of terrorism, especially those states who might offer weapons of mass destruction to terrorists. Hence, while the rationale for the war in Iraq was clearly complex and replete with very practical objectives, at the same time the notion that bold kinetic actions could have beneficial nonkinetic effects was evidently part of the Bush administration's thinking. Former National Security Council Counterterrorism Coordinator Richard Clarke has argued from firsthand experience that the Bush administration viewed "dealing with Iraq as a way of demonstrating America's power" to al-Qaida and to America's other potential enemies.[6] Clarke adds that President Bush, in particular, "felt a need to 'do something big' to respond to the events of September 11"—and invading Iraq provided a "big, fast, bold, simple move that would send a signal at home and abroad, a signal that said 'don't mess with Texas, or America.'"[7] Similarly, Christopher Meyer, who was serving as Britain's ambassador in Washington during the build-up to war in Iraq, later explained, "The time had come . . . to show that no one attacked America with impunity," and the place was to be Iraq.[8]

Comments such as these underscore the heavy influence of nonkinetic aspirations on Washington's part in its decision to undertake a very (indeed, violently) kinetic campaign in Iraq. Similarly, Daniel Benjamin and Steven Simon, former Clinton counterterrorist officials monitoring the Bush administration's reactions to 9/11, concurred that this nonkinetic element was significant in the decision to invade Iraq, "as if the terrorists' spectacular demonstration of their power demanded a similar demonstration from the American side. . . . [D]ecisive military action in the Middle East would not only restore fear of the United States but would lead to the kind of radical reform the region needed."[9] And one particularly well-informed journalist, Ron Suskind, reported that "the primary impetus for invading Iraq, according to those attending NSC briefings on the Gulf in this period, was to make an example of [Saddam] Hussein, to create a demonstration model."[10] In other words, based on this account, the element of strategic influence that Bush administration officials hoped would emerge from a campaign in Iraq may even have been foremost in the administration's thinking. Nonkinetic aspirations were very much at the heart of Washington's kinetic plans.

In addition to serving the rather broad strategic objective of providing a "demonstration model" of American power, the campaign in Iraq had the more focused objective of warning existing and potential state sponsors of terrorism that America would no longer tolerate any support for terrorists. Hence, while overthrowing Saddam Hussein's regime in Iraq was very much a direct, kinetic action, the deterrent message designed for a wider audience and intended to flow from such efforts was an exercise in strategic influence—a major factor in the Bush administration's thinking.

"The link between terrorist organizations and state sponsors became the 'principal strategic thought underlying our strategy in the war on terrorism,' according to Douglas Feith, the third-ranking official in the Pentagon" from 2001 to 2005.[11] Hence, in the Bush administration's view, "the key to defeating terrorism is to modify the behavior of the states that sponsor terror," in the words of Benjamin and Simon.[12] In order to exercise the strategic influence necessary to bring about such a modification of other states' behavior, the Bush administration felt that it had to send a signal of its seriousness and of its capacity—and that signal would be sent most effectively and unmistakeably by bold military action in Iraq. Columbia University Professor Robert Jervis writes that "many American leaders believed that overthrowing Saddam would establish a reputation for taking bold moves, and that this would have a favorable impact on the behavior of many other countries"—including those potentially inclined to harbor terrorists: "Before the war Bush declared that when Saddam was overthrown, 'other regimes will be given a clear warning that support for terror will not be tolerated.'"[13] That intended warning—in other words, that element of desired strategic influence—was a decidedly nonkinetic aspiration of the American campaign in Iraq.

With the initial campaign in Afghanistan intended to signal America's transformation as a counterterrorist actor and the invasion of Iraq designed to demonstrate American power and deter potential state sponsors of terrorism, America hoped to exercise a strategic influence that would counter al-Qaida's claims about the United States. More was believed needed, however; in particular, the Bush administration explicitly was concerned about countering al-Qaida's assertion that America lacked the resolve necessary to prosecute a successful, long-lasting counterterrorist campaign. President Bush's second statement on 9/11 immediately invoked the centrality of the notion of resolve: "The resolve of our great nation is being tested," Bush declared; he continued, "But make no mistake: We will show the world that we will pass this test."[14] Continuing in a similar vein, in his 2003 State of the Union address President Bush explained, "Our war against terror is a contest of will in which perseverance is power."[15] Even more revealing are the words of the 2006 *National Security Strategy*, which claims that "the terrorists are emboldened more by perceptions of weakness than by demonstrations of resolve. Terrorists lure recruits by telling them that we are decadent and easily intimidated and will retreat if attacked."[16] By employing such language, the *National Security Strategy* explicitly embraced the importance of the nonkinetic role played by kinetic actions such as American retreats. In particular, such a view of American strategy suggested that by America's continuing kinetic engagement in Afghanistan and in Iraq, the United States might demonstrate a resolve denied by its enemies and, in so doing, counter those enemies' claims by exerting a contrary strategic influence.

In turn, and again with a certain grim irony, the longer the United States was forced to remain in Afghanistan and in Iraq, and the more the situations in those places deteriorated, the greater the opportunity that arose for America to redefine its image from a country that could not sustain casualties and long engagements to one that could and would endure losses and remain patient and steadfast in pursuit of victory. Vice President Dick Cheney publicly explained his belief that in the past, "weakness, vacillation, and unwillingness of the United States to stand with our friends [had been] provocative" and had encouraged America's adversaries to challenge America.[17] Iraq would be different: America would "stay the course," in President Bush's words.[18]

"We will not run in the face of thugs and assassins," Bush proclaimed, adding, "If we were to leave Iraq before the job is done, the enemy would follow us here," to American shores.[19] President Bush was often explicit in his understanding of how al-Qaida would interpret an American withdrawal from Iraq: "You see, the enemy has made it clear that they expect us to lose our nerve. They have made it clear that they don't believe America has what it takes to defend ourselves."[20] America's continuing presence in Iraq—and, it should not be forgotten, in Afghanistan as well—is thus intended to have a strategic influence that goes beyond the practical objectives being pursued in both places. In particular, projecting American resolve constitutes a distinctly nonkinetic intention of America's continuing actions on the ground. Indeed, as Osama bin Laden recognized in one of his own statements, Bush is quite concerned that "the withdrawal of troops would send a wrong message to the enemy"—a message that could only be countered with continued kinetic engagements in Iraq and in Afghanistan.[21]

In the midst of the unfolding of the campaigns in Afghanistan and in Iraq, and as America's efforts at counterterrorism, counterinsurgency, and nation-building continued in both places, America periodically engaged in another type of dramatically kinetic counterterrorist action, namely, targeted strikes. Perhaps most notably, the United States used an unmanned Predator drone in November 2002 to kill al-Qaida's alleged chief in Yemen. Among other strikes, America also sent F-16 fighter jets in June 2006 to kill al-Qaida's leader in Iraq, and worked with the Pakistani military to target (though unsuccessfully) al-Qaida's "number two," Ayman al-Zawahiri, in an air strike in northwest Pakistan in October 2006.

An anecdote describing President Bush's reaction to the first of these strikes underscores the strategic influence, beyond obvious practical effects, that American officials hope to exercise through the use of targeted strikes. As Ron Suskind recounts in his recent book, *The One Percent Doctrine*, on receiving word of the success in Yemen, President Bush apparently was decidedly pleased: "'We're talking to them in a way they can understand,' Bush said to a senior adviser, a line he often repeated. 'Capability like this changes the game.'"[22] The notion that a targeted strike constitutes a form of *talking*, in addition and beyond its role in *doing*, is precisely at issue here. In particular, targeted strikes appear to have been intended to demonstrate the relentlessness of America's pursuit of al-Qaida, by showing continuing, unflagging actions to target the group's leadership. Such a perspective is reflected in the assertion by the *National Strategy for Combating Terrorism* that "relentless action" is the key to "*defeat*[*ing*] terrorist organizations of global reach."[23] With each targeted strike, America hoped not only to profit off the kinetic elimination of al-Qaida's ranks, but also to benefit from the nonkinetic strategic influence promoted by America's visibly relentless pursuit of the group's leaders.

One more element of American efforts at strategic influence through kinetic actions merits mention here so as to provide a sense of the spectrum covered by such activity. Measures designed to improve homeland security defy obvious classification as directly kinetic or nonkinetic endeavors. Clearly, such measures are not violent, a characteristic of most policies defined as kinetic. Yet on their surface at least, they might well be labeled kinetic in that they are actions taken with primarily practical intentions in mind, such as providing tangible buffers and barriers designed to minimize the damage that a terrorist attack would cause. At the same time, and like the other primarily kinetic measures already explored, homeland defenses have also been justified by their nonkinetic potential, whose logic deserves exploration.

The *National Strategy for Combating Terrorism* asserts that terrorists are "emboldened by success," implicitly suggesting that potential failure or disappointment—the objectives of homeland security—can play a vital role in influencing such terrorists.[24] Indicating the Bush administration's underlying logic in this regard, David Frum and Richard Perle—former speechwriter and former chairman of the Defense Policy Board Advisory Committee, respectively—note that, "Nobody wants to die on a fool's errand," meaning that making "terrorism marginally more difficult" might be all that is necessary "to push the terrorists past that tipping point to paralysis."[25] Homeland Security thus was seen as a form of "deterrence by denial" in which "hardening targets . . . can lessen terrorists' motivation by reducing the benefits of terror tactics," as two scholars phrase it.[26] By suggesting that terrorist attacks might fail or fizzle, Homeland Security was intended to send a message of its own, thus exerting a strategic influence on those eager to strike America yet less inclined to do so should their attempts prove wasted or unimpressive.

From Afghanistan to Iraq to America's own shores, America responded to 9/11 more through taking action than through tailoring the type of message or narrative typically characteristic of strategic influence. Yet as this discussion illustrates, even as the United States focused on kinetic counterterrorist measures, the nonkinetic aspects and implications of those measures played major roles in the thinking underlying such measures. Signaling America's transformation as a counterterrorist actor, demonstrating American power and relentlessness, intimidating state sponsors of terrorism, exhibiting American resolve, and visibly hardening America's defenses are just a few of the kinetic counterterrorist policies adopted by Washington in the wake of 9/11 with nonkinetic aspirations in mind.

AMERICA'S AUDIENCES

The preceding discussion demonstrated that nonkinetic aspirations and intentions are inextricably bound up with key American counterterrorist policies enacted in the wake of the 9/11 attacks. Strategic influence, however, does not exist in a vacuum; rather, an actor such as the United States only influences other actors successfully if policies are designed with a detailed understanding of the relevant audiences. In the case of the policies just discussed, a great deal of uncertainty persists regarding precisely who constitutes the target audiences and, perhaps more important, whether America's actions convey the types of signals that register as intended with those audiences, given their distinct worldview. The following discussion examines a number of attributes of the audiences relevant to America's counterterrorist campaign against al-Qaida, and suggests that far more research must be done to understand whether America's attempts at strategic influence are, in fact, having the desired effects.

Perhaps most basically, the United States has demonstrated an ambivalence about whether its nonkinetic efforts are designed to influence the existing terrorist leadership, potential terrorists, or both. At times, the dedicated core of al-Qaida appears to be included as the crucial audience, with the presumption being that deterrence still has some role to play in counterterrorism; hence, the insistence of the 2006 *National Security Strategy* that terrorists "must in turn be deterred."[27] Yet, the Bush administration also repeatedly expressed the view that terrorists "cannot be deterred," suggesting that the would-be terrorist was the crucial audience for Washington.[28] At times, that audience was dismissed as well; instead, broader communities—the Arab world, or the Muslim world— appeared to constitute the crucial audience, as far as Washington was concerned. State sponsors have also been a consistent emphasis in America's attempts at strategic influence, yet it remains unclear what meaningful and direct relationship al-Qaida actually and presently maintains with any governments or regimes. It is, of course, exceedingly difficult to design effective policies for strategic influence without knowing whom one is trying to influence.

Moreover, the target audiences for American counterterrorist policies are known to possess a number of characteristics that affect precisely what influence American actions have on them. For example, most of those drawn to al-Qaida exhibit an intense religious faith. In turn, many are characterized by an intense confidence in the eventual triumph of al-Qaida, thanks to divine intervention and assistance. According to Professor Paul Wilkinson of the University of St. Andrews, "Al Qaeda members firmly believe that they will ultimately succeed because they are certain Allah is on their side."[29] Harvard University Professor Louise Richardson, writing about an even wider audience, adds that "for radical Islamists their faith that Allah is on their side best explains their optimism" in eventually securing their objectives despite America's overwhelming conventional capabilities.[30] Indeed, Osama bin Laden himself has remarked: "We remind you that victory comes only with God. All we need to do is prepare and motivate for jihad."[31] Is strategic influence even capable of deterring such divinely confident warriors? Can the demonstration of American power dissuade or deter those for whom faith trumps capacity? Considerations of nonkinetic influence must be filtered through considerations of this disposition to be effective, yet such vital analyses have not yet begun.

Emerging in large part from the religious faith characteristic of those drawn to al-Qaeda is a sense of historical time that also affects the ways in which American policies influence their target audiences. Wilkinson explains that those associated with al-Qaeda "have a very different historical calendar from that of secularized western societies. . . . Hence they are psychologically prepared to wage a long-term struggle."[32] Clarke also emphasizes that they take "the long view, believing that their struggle [will] take decades, perhaps generations."[33] What constitutes a true setback for an audience with so vast a historical perspective? Can America even deal a blow recognizable as such to a group so utterly patient—and so confident that patience will eventually be rewarded, thanks to faith and to divine intervention? Again, the answers provide the grounds on which America's efforts at strategic influence must be evaluated, yet those answers remain wanting.

Also linked to the religious fervor characterizing those drawn to al-Qaida is the pursuit of martyrdom which al-Qaida has put to such deadly use. For example, according to Terry McDermott's account, the 9/11 hijackers, "before they left Afghanistan, . . . made videotaped declarations of their willingness—no, eagerness—to become martyrs."[34] In a similar vein, one journalist who secretly penetrated a cell of al-Qaida reports being told by one member that "his dream was to die 'a martyr for Allah's cause'"; on another occasion, the same member explained, "Paradise is my goal. You know, killing people like them brings you closer to God."[35] Professor Gilles Kepel of Paris's Institute for Political Studies has also vividly described those who share al-Qaida's perspective in similar terms: "Convinced that their death will trigger a cataclysm which can save the community of believers and that they will be transported immediately to Paradise, they eagerly volunteer for suicide operations."[36] What impact does a demonstration of force have on those actually pursuing their own death—or their own martyrdom, at least as they see it? Does improving homeland security dissuade from violence those whose priority, on an individual level, may be to die in the process rather than to cause destruction of a certain magnitude? These aspects of America's target audiences must be analyzed and understood if the United States is to know whether its actions are, indeed, having a productive strategic influence on those audiences.

In addition to certain characteristics of those drawn to al-Qaida, the group's unconventional (or asymmetric) strategy also affects the actual strategic influence achieved—or not achieved—by America's counterterrorist efforts. In other words, whether America is, in fact, demonstrating its power in an effective way, or exhibiting resolve in a beneficial manner, depends on the particular strategy being pursued by America's terrorist adversaries. Terrorist strategy is unconventional in a number of ways that complicate the potential for America to exert strategic influence; just a few of those ways can be discussed here.

First, unlike most strategies designed by states, the strategy of terrorists, and of al-Qaida in particular, relies on *inducing,* rather than avoiding, retaliation. While traditional deterrence is based on the notion that states want to avoid the use of force against their territory, al-Qaida's asymmetric strategy is designed to provoke America into using its potent military force, thus arousing the wrath of Muslims worldwide, leaving American troops vulnerable and sapping America's resources and energy. As one expert cites from the Internet posting of a prominent al-Qaida strategist, the 9/11 attacks' "primary goal [was] enticing the United States into direct interventions in the Arab region. Only America's entrance into the region in force—especially the occupation of Iraq—would allow al-Qaida to achieve its goal: to awaken the Islamic umma and 'create a direct confrontation between Americans and Arabs/Muslims at the popular level.'"[37] Eliciting American retaliation was central to al-Qaida's designs, as bin Laden's own words make clear: "This is what everyone was hoping for. Thank Allah America came out of its caves."[38] In turn, the strategic value of the United States demonstrating itself to be a transformed—and thus more active, forceful, potent, and resolved—counterterrorist actor is less than clear. For a group whose strategy is predicated on provoking American retaliation, do such kinetic efforts grounded in nonkinetic considerations serve a useful purpose?

Similarly, the role played by demonstrable American resolve is uncertain in the context of prosecuting a campaign against an adversary employing an asymmetric strategy.

In many traditional conflicts, exhibiting a willingness to absorb casualties and expend resources may well provide useful indications of the commitment of an actor to achieving its objectives. For al-Qaida, however, America's continued deployments in Afghanistan and in Iraq appear to have become central to the group's strategy and, in turn, rather welcome developments. Bin Laden has explicitly embraced America's presence abroad as indications of al-Qaida's success, citing "the fact that the mujahidin forced Bush to resort to an emergency budget in order to continue fighting in Afghanistan and Iraq. This shows the success of our plan to bleed America to the point of bankruptcy, with God's will."[39] While American forces have remained for a number of years in harm's way, especially in Iraq, al-Qaida "has used the war for its own ends: Iraq has become its training ground," comments journalist Abdel Atwan.[40] Given al-Qaida's apparent ability to profit off America's continued deployments abroad, is America's presence actually demonstrating the type of resolve that might counter al-Qaida's claims about the United States? Or are such deployments in fact fulfilling aspects of al-Qaida's unconventional strategy, by leaving American forces "spread out, close at hand, and easy to target," as one al-Qaida statement phrases it?[41]

A third aspect of al-Qaida's asymmetric strategy is linked to both of the previously discussed elements. By retaliating for acts of terrorism and by remaining in conflict zones, America—al-Qaida hopes—will inevitably cause the type of civilian casualties that will enrage Muslims worldwide and validate al-Qaida's own claims about its view of a pernicious, anti-Muslim America. As Kepel explains, "The terrorism of September 11 was above all a provocation. . . . Its purpose was to provoke a similarly gigantic repression of the Afghan civilian population and to build universal solidarity among Muslims in reaction to the victimization of their Afghan brothers."[42] While al-Qaida initially hoped to profit off the inevitable civilian casualties of America's campaign in Afghanistan, the group soon expanded what it viewed as its area of opportunity, calling attention—through statements as well as through slickly produced slide shows and videos—to the civilian casualties mounting in Iraq. With respect to America's attempts at strategic influence, the question then becomes whether the demonstration of American power and American resolve are the points picked up and understood by the relevant audiences, as opposed to the inevitable civilian casualties which al-Qaida goes to great lengths to emphasize and on which the group's very strategy is predicated. A very different type of strategic influence emerges depending on what, in fact, is viewed as the central signal sent by America's kinetic efforts.

A fourth element of al-Qaida's unconventional strategy against America is that the group's strategy relies far less on any type of victory on the battlefield than on provoking America into overspending and overextending its own resources. In turn, attacks such as those executed on 9/11 not only cause damage in their own right, they also encourage America to spend heavily on Homeland Security; and America's retaliations and deployments abroad not only serve the aforementioned purposes, but also have the insidious effect of gradually draining America's resources. Ohio State University's Professor John Mueller notes that "the direct economic costs of September 11 amounted to tens of billions of dollars, but the economic costs in the United States of the much-enhanced security runs several times that," with the Homeland Security Department alone spending almost $50 billion per year; he also quotes a risk analyst who comments: "If terrorists force us to redirect resources away from sensible programs and future growth, in order to pursue unachievable but politically popular levels of domestic security, then they have won an important victory that mortgages the future."[43] Such expenditures on domestic security, while enormous, nonetheless pale in comparison to what the United States has spent and continues to spend in Afghanistan and in Iraq. What all of this amounts to is the potential for America's actual strategic influence on its target audiences to emerge more from the apparent success of al-Qaida's attempts to coax away precious resources from American coffers than from the effects intended and sought by American officials. It all depends on the nature of the audiences in question—a nature that remains insufficiently investigated and analyzed.

Hence, both in the worldview of America's audiences and in the strategy of al-Qaida, the United States faces characteristics and attributes unlike those common to many traditional actors on which America has, in the past, attempted and often succeeded in exercising productive strategic influence. Whether the types of nonkinetic effects produced by the kinetic efforts described in the first half of this discussion actually have exerted the strategic influence sought by American officials depends on precisely these features of the relevant audiences for counterterrorism and the relevant strategy on the part of America's terrorist adversaries. Have we understood yet what deters, dissuades, or otherwise helpfully influences those exhibiting religious fervor, a long-term sense of historical time, and an eagerness for martyrdom? Have we understood what American measures project a helpful impression of the United States when America's adversaries rely on an unconventional and asymmetric strategy designed to elicit retaliation, to take advantage of vulnerable American troops stationed abroad, to call attention to inevitable civilian casualties caused by the American military (despite its best efforts to avoid them), and to provoke American expenditures? Despite all that has been invested in America's campaign against al-Qaida, it appears that we have not—yet we must.

Indeed, decades of research into signaling and perception leave us with some general tendencies that have been found to apply to many audiences and that might well prove useful in evaluating the relevant audiences for America's attempts at strategic influence in counterterrorism. For example, we know that audiences overwhelmingly "fit incoming information into pre-existing beliefs and . . . perceive what they expect to be there," as Jervis explains.[44] Similarly, research points to a strong bias toward what Lee Ross and Craig Anderson term "belief perseverance," in which existing beliefs prove "remarkably resilient in the face of empirical challenges that seem logically devastating."[45] Also well established is the finding that actors tend to see almost any feedback, no matter how ambiguous or even contradictory, as confirmation that their strategy of choice is proving effective for achieving their objectives. As Ross and Anderson note, "Once people have decided that a policy will be a success in the future, is currently a success, or was a success, they are disinclined to admit any significant negative aspects."[46] Another widespread phenomenon characterizing many audiences is an egocentric bias, in which events are interpreted as relating to oneself and "perceptions are biased in a self-serving manner called *egocentrism*," according to Harvard University Professor Max Bazerman.[47]

These examples are just a few of the significant number of tendencies that have been identified through the combined study of history, politics, and psychology to apply to many audiences in many contexts. But do they apply to America's target audiences for its current counterterrorist efforts? If so, what form do they take, and how are these general tendencies filtered through the lenses of *these* specifics audiences, given the types of audience characteristics and strategic attributes elucidated above? Attempting to answer such questions is vital to a proper and thorough analysis and evaluation of the strategic influence exerted by America's kinetic counterterrorist actions.

CONCLUDING THOUGHTS

Strategic influence takes many forms, as the diverse subjects covered in this volume demonstrate. In the midst of well-deserved calls for America to devote greater attention to purely nonkinetic forms of strategic influence, an analysis of the persuasive aspects of existing kinetic measures has, unfortunately, been neglected. With America's leaders justifying so many of America's responses to 9/11—from the wars in Afghanistan and Iraq and the continued deployments in both places to targeted strikes and Homeland Security measures—on the grounds that, beyond their practical effects, such measures also offer nonkinetic benefits, the urgency of assessing those justifications becomes clear. Moreover, given the complicated nature of America's target audiences for strategic influence in counterterrorism—in particular, audience characteristics such as religious fervor, a long-term historical perspective, and a thirst for martyrdom, as well as an unconventional strategy predicated on retaliation, America's deployments abroad, civilian casualties, and American expenditures—such an analysis of those target audiences becomes all the trickier, yet is all the more vital. Kinetic efforts have nonkinetic implications and consequences, but determining what they are constitutes the crux of the matter—and, perhaps, a way ahead for exercising productive strategic influence as part of a unified and coordinated counterterrorist campaign.

ACKNOWLEDGMENTS

Sincerest thanks to James J. F. Forest for helpful and insightful discussion that gave shape to this chapter. Thanks as well to Air Commodore M. J. Harwood, Daniel Morris, and my father for their input and assistance.

NOTES

1. Paul K. Davis and Brian Michael Jenkins, *Deterrence and Influence in Counterterrorism: A Component of the War on al Qaeda* (Santa Monica: RAND, 2002), p. 35.

2. William F. Kernan, quoted in David S. Yost, "The US Nuclear Posture Review and the NATO Allies," *International Affairs*, Vol. 80, No. 4, p. 716.

3. Bob Woodward, *Bush at War* (London: Pocket Books, 2003), p. 98.

4. George W. Bush, quoted in ibid., p. 167.

5. Graham Allison, *Nuclear Terrorism: The Risks and Consequences of the Ultimate Disaster* (London: Constable, 2006), p. 127.

6. Richard Clarke, *Against All Enemies: Inside America's War on Terror*, updated ed. (London: Free Press, 2004), p. 244.

7. Ibid., pp. 265, 266.

8. Christopher Meyer, *DC Confidential* (London: Weidenfeld & Nicolson, 2005), p. 237.

9. Daniel Benjamin and Steven Simon, *The Next Attack: The Globalization of Jihad* (London: Hodder & Stoughton, 2005), pp. 264–265.

10. Ron Suskind, *The One Percent Doctrine: Deep Inside America's Pursuits of Its Enemies Since 9/11* (London: Simon & Schuster, 2006), p. 123.

11. Douglas Feith, quoted in Ivo Daalder and James Lindsay, *America Unbound: The Bush Revolution in Foreign Policy* (Washington, DC: Brookings Institution Press, 2003), p. 85.

12. Daniel Benjamin and Steven Simon, *The Age of Sacred Terror: Radical Islam's War Against America* (New York: Random House, 2003), p. 476.

13. Robert Jervis, *American Foreign Policy in a New Era* (New York: Routledge, 2005), pp. 72, 83.

14. George W. Bush, quoted in David Frum, *The Right Man: An Inside Account of the Bush White House*, updated ed. (New York: Random House, 2005), p. 119.

15. George W. Bush, "President Delivers 'State of the Union,'" http://www.whitehouse.gov/news/releases/2003/01/20030128-19.html.

16. George W. Bush, "The National Security Strategy of the United States of America," http://www.whitehouse.gov/nsc/nss/2006/nss2006.pdf.

17. Dick Cheney, "Interview with Vice-President Dick Cheney, NBC, 'Meet the Press,'" http://www.mtholyoke.edu/acad/intrel/bush/cheneymeetthepress.htm.

18. George W. Bush, "Press Conference by the President," http://www.whitehouse.gov/news/releases/2006/11/20061108-2.html.

19. George W. Bush, "Remarks by the President at Missouri Victory 2006 Rally," http://www.whitehouse.gov/news/releases/2006/11/20061103–1.html.

20. Ibid.

21. Osama bin Laden, quoted in Mohammad-Mahmoud Ould Mohamedou, *Understanding Al Qaeda: The Transformation of War* (London: Pluto Press, 2007), p. 108.

22. Suskind, p. 182.

23. George W. Bush, "National Strategy for Combating Terrorism," http://www.whitehouse.gov/news/releases/2003/02/counter_terrorism/counter_terrorism_strategy.pdf.

24. Ibid.

25. David Frum and Richard Perle, *An End to Evil: How to Win the War on Terror* (New York: Ballantine Books, 2004), p. 201, 198.

26. Robert Trager and Dessislava Zagorcheva, "Deterring Terrorism: It Can Be Done," *International Security*, Vol. 30, No. 3, p. 106.

27. Bush, "The National Security Strategy of the United States of America."

28. George W. Bush, "President Delivers Commencement Address at the United States Military Academy at West Point," http://www.whitehouse.gov/news/releases/2006/05/20060527–1.html.

29. Paul Wilkinson, *Terrorism versus Democracy: The Liberal State Response*, 2nd ed. (London: Routledge, 2006), p. 40.

30. Louise Richardson, *What Terrorists Want: Understanding the Enemy, Containing the Threat* (New York: Random House, 2006), p. 99.

31. Osama bin Laden, quoted in Bruce Lawrence, ed., *Messages to the World: The Statements of Osama bin Laden* (London: Verso, 2005), p. 181.

32. Wilkinson, p. 207.

33. Clarke, p. 227.

34. Terry McDermott, *Perfect Soldiers: The Hijackers: Who They Were, Why They Did It* (New York: HarperCollins, 2005), p. 220.

35. Mohamed Sifaoui, *Inside Al Qaeda: How I Infiltrated the World's Deadliest Terrorist Organization*, George Miller, trans. (New York: Thunder's Mouth Press, 2003), pp. 30, 92.

36. Gilles Kepel, *The War for Muslim Minds*, Pascale Ghazaleh, trans. (Cambridge, MA: Belknap Press of Harvard University Press, 2004), p. 290.

37. Marc Lynch, "Al-Qaeda's Constructivist Turn," *Praeger Security International*, http://lanfiles.williams.edu/~mlynch/mlynch/QaedaConstructivistTurn.pdf, p. 2.

38. Osama bin Laden, quoted in Vaughn Shannon and Michael Dennis, "Militant Islam and the Futile Fight for Reputation," *Security Studies*, Vol. 16, No. 2, p. 315.

39. Osama bin Laden, quoted in Lawrence, p. 242.

40. Abdel Atwan, *The Secret History of al Qaeda* (Berkeley: University of California Press, 2006), p. 10.

41. Quoted in Michael Scheuer, *Through Our Enemies' Eyes: Osama bin Laden, Radical Islam, and the Future of America*, rev. ed. (Washington, DC: Potomac Books, 2006), p. 221.

42. Gilles Kepel, *Jihad: The Trail of Political Islam*, Anthony Roberts, trans. (Cambridge, MA: Belknap Press of Harvard University Press, 2002), p. 4.

43. John Mueller, "Six Rather Unusual Propositions about Terrorism," *Terrorism and Political Violence*, Vol. 17, p. 491; David Banks, quoted in Mueller, p. 492.

44. Robert Jervis, *Perception and Misperception in International Politics*, Morningside ed. (Princeton: Princeton University Press, 1976), p. 143.

45. Lee Ross and Craig Anderson, "Shortcomings in the Attribution Process: On the Origins and Maintenance of Erroneous Social Assessments," in Daniel Kahneman et al., eds., *Judgment Under Uncertainty: Heuristics and Biases* (Cambridge: Cambridge University Press, 1982), p. 144.

46. Dominic Johnson and Dominic Tierney, *Failing to Win: Perceptions of Victory and Defeat in International Politics* (Cambridge, MA: Harvard University Press, 2006), p. 46.

47. Max Bazerman, *Judgment in Managerial Decision Making,* 5th ed. (Hoboken: John Wiley & Sons, 2002), p. 70.

10

Online Recruitment, Radicalization, and Reconnaissance

Challenges for Law Enforcement

Simon O'Rourke

THERE IS AN EXPECTATION BY the wider community that the police and law enforcement agencies will provide protection for life and property, in accordance with their primary mandate.[1] This now includes the prevention of terrorist attacks and the mitigation of the fear that is associated with the specter of terrorism. In order to be successful, police need to capture, analyze, and act on information pertaining to terrorist activities, while the terrorists are still in the preparatory stages.[2] Much of the information needed to accomplish this now resides in the cyber realm, an environment that poses significant challenges for police and law enforcement agencies.

A Homeland Security survey commissioned by the International Association of Chiefs of Police in 2003 indicated that there was a significant expectation by the government and public that local policing agencies would provide protection from a terrorist act. While this enhancement of the traditional role of the police as guardians of the community was acknowledged, a significant number of those surveyed believed that they could not meet these expectations with their current resources. Most believed that their responsibility has increased without any corresponding escalation in funding, training, or resources. Further, according to the study, most felt they were in a better position to meet the challenge of responding to an incident rather than the complex task of preventing one.[3]

The attacks on New York City by al-Qaida on September 11, 2001, and the subsequent media coverage brought the threat of radical Islamist (salafi-jihadist) terrorism to the attention of a global audience. The attacks significantly altered the political and legislative landscape, resulting in substantial increases in the resources provided to police and law enforcement agencies. Terrorism had moved beyond its traditional geographic boundaries, as extremists sought to strike their perceived enemies in places like New York, London, Madrid, and Bali. Henry identifies the effect the attacks have had on the manner in which "police, law enforcement and other public safety agencies do business, ultimately requiring that these agencies substantially alter their traditional policies, training, operations and interactions with other agencies as well as the communities they serve."[4]

In a statement to the U.S. Senate Committee for Homeland Security and Government Affairs, Lieutenant Colonel Joseph Felter—the director of the Combating Terrorism Center at West Point—identified the ideology of radical jihadism as being "the real center of gravity of the violent movement that sustains al-Qa'ida."[5] He also noted how this ideology is promulgated via the Internet and results in networks being formed by those who share similar views, and that the dissemination of extremist material to a self-selecting audience further complicates the mission for the law enforcement, because for the first time extremists across the globe can unite online.[6] This chapter examines the implications of this globally dispersed, Internet-connected terror threat for local law enforcement agencies and identifies some components of a successful counterterrorism response.

THE EVOLVING POLICE COUNTERTERRORIST PARADIGM

The structure and operational mindset in many countries' policing agencies has been predominately aligned with a siege/hostage type of scenario. This mindset dates back to the 1970s when groups like the Popular Front for the Liberation of Palestine (PFLP) took hostages and made demands, using the subsequent media coverage to generate publicity for their cause. This required governments to develop a tactical capability designed to rescue hostages deemed to be in imminent jeopardy should negotiations fail. The counterterrorist methodology in these countries has previously centered on this framework, as reflected in their investments in certain types of training and equipment. With the possible exception of the Russian Federation and the Chechen conflict, the current terrorist methodology has evolved from a siege situation—where hostages are taken and demands made—to direct attacks.

Police officers are taught during basic training to cordon-contain-isolate-negotiate whenever possible in all incidents from domestic violence to suburban sieges. However, this model does not develop the skill set needed to match the observed trend in terrorist incidents. Terrorist trends indicate that the use of direct attacks, like suicide bombing or the placement of explosive devices, will continue. These attacks deny the police and other agencies the ability to cordon and negotiate at an incident scene. Suicide bombers, improvised explosive devices (IEDs), and vehicle-borne IEDs—among other contemporary terrorist tactics—pose a significant challenge to law enforcement agencies charged with protecting the community and require new models of training.

Policing agencies also need to adapt to new communications technologies in order to proactively collect intelligence from cyberspace. Traditional sources, including informants, may be able to provide crucial information regarding the online activities of persons of interest, including the addresses of Web sites, bulletin boards, and chat rooms. The Internet is serving as a communications conduit for terrorist groups and traditional investigative methodologies should be expanded and adapted to meet evolving trends.

Some Internet messages or strategic documents compiled by known terrorist entities can provide insight into future activities. It is these documents that need to be identified and prioritized for analysis. Once such document was posted online in December 2003 and according to Brynjar Lia of the Norwegian Defence Research Establishment (FFI), the document was of strategic value to the ongoing insurgency in Iraq, but was only reviewed after the March 11, 2004, attacks in Madrid.[7] The FFI analysis of the document clearly identifies economic cost as a key weakness in the sustainability of the U.S.-led operation in Iraq, and argues that if coalition partners were forced to withdraw from Iraq, then the United States would not be able to fund the operation either economically or politically on its own. Spain was identified as the most vulnerable coalition member because of the significant public opposition to the war.[8] The subsequent attack on the rail infrastructure at peak hour in Madrid just prior to the Spanish general elections resulted in the loss of office by the reigning political party and the subsequent withdrawal of Spanish troops from Iraq. This was interpreted by some as a significant victory for the terrorists, who target particular communities in order to generate public demands for change to a nation's foreign or domestic policies. It could also be seen as vindicating their use of force to achieve a political objective.[9]

In a speech at Queen Mary's College in London on November 9, 2006, Dame Manningham-Buller—the director general of the U.K. Security Service, better known as MI5—spoke of the global threat fueled by an ideology developed and marketed by groups like al-Qaida via the Internet, an ideology that links the approach taken by Western countries to regional issues in the Muslim world and is interpreted by extremists "as evidence of an across-the-board determination to undermine and humiliate Islam worldwide."[10] Previous methods of identifying persons of interest as a result of their attendance at training camps and jihad operations in Afghanistan, Chechnya, and Iraq are of limited effect as they don't include the current evolution of extremists. Terrorist ranks now include disenfranchised members of many communities, who while outwardly maintaining the veneer of normality elect to take action at a local level in support of an overarching global ideology. Terrorist activity by nationals was graphically demonstrated by the suicide bombings in London in which those involved became radicalized, while outwardly maintaining the veneer of being part of the U.K. culture.

Felter has also described the capability that the Internet provides for exerting influence on the worldviews of disenchanted individuals.[11] These home-grown extremists know little of the homeland of their parents or grandparents, yet they feel aggrieved by the foreign policies of their country of birth or by the perceived injustice being experienced by groups overseas.[12] This emotional attachment to a group with whom they share little in common other than a religious belief is being fed by images of jihad warriors fighting in conflicts in places like Afghanistan, Chechnya, and Iraq. The importance of propaganda is clearly understood by terrorist groups who videorecord their attacks, and then upload them onto the Internet for editing and hosting by various Web sites. These videos serve as a powerful tool for recruitment.[13] In addition to being shown on the Internet, the videos cause controversy and generate debate when they are shown on mainstream Western media like CNN.[14]

Dame Manningham-Buller also highlighted the difficulties facing the Security Service and police given the sheer numbers involved and the volume of information requiring analysis. She referred in her speech to the existence of over 1,600 individuals who formed part of 200 known networks,[15] and according to Evans the number of individuals of concern has now increased to approximately 2,000.[16] Some of these individuals have been (or are still being) radicalized in the online world of Web sites and forums.[17] The possibility exists for an individual or group to become completely radicalized via the Internet, while remaining virtually unknown to police and intelligence agencies.

The numbers identified by the U.K. Security Service provide an overview of the difficulties that lie ahead. The pervasiveness of the Internet combined with our increasingly networked societies present significant challenges when attempting to monitor users' access to Web sites and extremist material. Parents, teachers, and librarians would have genuine difficulty in monitoring the online activities of those using their facilities. Education programs regarding cyberpredators and explicit material have clearly shown how difficult a task it is to control and successfully monitor an individual's use of the Internet.

TERRORIST USE OF THE WORLD WIDE WEB

The use of the Internet by terrorists appears to diverge into two distinct modes, neither of which is mutually exclusive. The first is focused on how terrorists can use the Internet as a platform to launch cyberattacks against critical infrastructure nodes and key government and private sector networks. Other focus on the use of the Internet by terrorists for recruitment, covert communications, financial activities, and information gathering.[18] For example, Weimann recently described how the Internet was used for organizing and planning the terror attacks in New York, Madrid, and London.[19]

Recent legal proceedings involving those accused of terrorist related offenses also illuminate the role of the Internet. For example, in 2004 Babar Ahmad was indicted in the U.S. District Court in Connecticut on a variety of terrorist offenses relating to his online activities. The indictment alleged that Ahmad "helped create, operate and maintain and caused to operate and maintain"[20] Web sites that were intended to facilitate communications, fund-raising, recruitment, and the hosting of extremist materials. At the time of the alleged offenses, Ahmad was living in London and using the Internet to provide support to Taliban forces engaged in armed conflict with members of the U.S. armed forces.

In Australia, the Commonwealth Director of Public Prosecutions (DPP) in the material facts regarding *R v. Lodhi* alleges that the accused used the Internet to access and download photographs of selected establishments that he wished to attack. The Commonwealth DPP also alleges in the material facts regarding *R v. Khazall* that the accused in this case compiled and partly authored an electronic document titled, "Provision in the Rules of Jihad—Short Wise Rules and Organizational Structures that Concern every Fighter and Mujahid Fighting against the Infidels." It is further alleged that this document was then uploaded onto a Web site with unrestricted access where it remained for a period of eight months.[21] These cases demonstrate the use of various modern communications technologies, most notably the Internet, as an aid to planning and intelligence gathering rather than as a mode of attack. In this case the Internet can be seen as an enabler to assist in achieving the desired outcome.

Recent advances in information and communications technology are providing a medium for individuals or groups who subscribe to extremist worldviews to form networks, access training, and obtain information. The Internet is facilitating global virtual communities through social networking services like Second Life, MySpace, and Facebook. The 2006 Nielsen Net Ratings highlights the exponential growth of these social networking sites over a 12-month period, noting how (for example) membership in MySpace grew by 367 percent over the survey period.[22] These services are also providing an anonymous meeting place for disenfranchised individuals to gather, share ideas, and post and exchange information regarding their particular ideology. Like-minded individuals can find each other in cyberspace, via online blogs and chat rooms. As Adam notes, "The arrival of the Internet has provided the first forum in history for all the disaffected to gather in one place to exchange views and reinforce prejudices."[23] Such growth is being readily exploited by terrorist groups as they seek to increase recruitment and support. According to Custer, "Without a doubt, the Internet is the single most important venue for radicalization of Islamic youth."[24]

The destruction of terrorist training camps in Afghanistan by U.S. and coalition forces has necessitated the transition from physical training locations to online training environments. Terrorist groups are forming electronic networks, thereby retaining the ability to market themselves and indoctrinate new recruits, while simultaneously developing strategies for future attacks.[25] Participation in the resultant extremist sites provides for those involved a sense of belonging to a global cause where the actions of an individual can be aligned with and be seen to contribute toward something which they see as more significant than their own lives. This transition will significantly complicate the task of identifying and locating these extremists.[26]

Police and law enforcement agencies will need to enhance their intelligence gathering capabilities in order to successfully identify individuals or groups in cyberspace who warrant further investigation and the subsequent allocation of finite resources. When utilized correctly, these resources can identify potential targets of attack, as well as gather the necessary evidence to support a prosecution. Reports of a group who recently planned to flood lower Manhattan by breaching walls on the New York train system with explosives have focused on the monitoring of electronic communications and chat rooms by the FBI.[27]

The operational structures and communications methodologies adopted by contemporary terrorists could result in the individuals involved and their tactics not being identified by law enforcement or intelligence agencies.[28] These online communities present complex problems for police in their efforts to identify those individuals or groups undergoing virtual radicalization and training. This identification needs to occur before the transition from virtual radicalization to physical acts of terrorism. As Mitchell Waldrop states, "it's time to take intelligence gathering and interpretation into the network age."[29]

The increasing availability of comparatively cheap, reliable, and high-bandwidth communications have aided the increasing globalization of businesses and commercial services. Many of these same inputs can be seen as aiding the globalization of terror networks. The trend that was clearly seen for the first time in the 1970s when organizations such as the PFLP began to use the global media network in order to publicize their agenda has continued. In the specific case of Islamist terrorism, the dispersed nature of recruiting and communications has caused a fundamental shift in how to define and approach the threat posed by this utilization of leading-edge communications technology.

Leaders of these groups are placing material on the Internet in order to survive and maintain the ability to instruct new members in case their physical infrastructure is destroyed. This has made the information more readily available to a wider audience. It has, however, also made the information more vulnerable to interception by police and law enforcement agencies, who will study it in order to discern the modus operandi of the groups involved.[30]

MONITORING EXTREMISM IN CYBERSPACE

The manner in which terrorist cells communicate and distribute propaganda and training materials and other pertinent information via the Internet makes it problematic for state and national law enforcement agencies to track and curtail their activities. The ability to log on anonymously in Internet cafés around the globe makes it problematic for conventional law enforcement strategies to be effective. Anonymous Web browsing and routing capabilities combined with software- and hardware-based encryption systems are creating significant technical challenges for investigators. These dual-use technologies are evolving faster than the tools required to lawfully intercept them and forensically recover digital evidence.

Terrorist cells are exploiting this technology and communicating covertly via the Internet, thereby minimizing discernible links to known parent terrorist organizations. In place of a centralized command-and-control structure, there exists a flatter, more diversified loose cluster of senior cells offering spiritual and operational guidance via the Web.[31] This diversified structure allows them to be tactically autonomous,[32] while ensuring that the individual cells still adhere to an overarching strategic effort. This view is supported by Whine, who also identifies the resilient nature of such a structure due to the increased stability provided by the physical and electronic diffusion of those involved.[33] This presents a challenge to law enforcement agencies in identifying these cells prior to an incident. "The radicalization process is occurring more quickly, more widely, and more anonymously in the Internet age."[34]

The openness of the Internet also presents difficulties for police and law enforcement agencies to track seemingly innocuous message traffic between cell members, unless they have already been identified as being of interest. The nature of the challenge posed by attempting to track down and identify amorphous terrorist networks can be resource-intensive.[35] However, while Clarke and Newman advocate that these resources may be better utilized in preventive actions, they acknowledge the use of the Internet by terrorist groups for recruitment and the transmission of messages from charismatic leaders.[36] The last message sent by Mohammed Atta to the other members of the 9/11 terrorist cell read as follows: "We've obtained 19 confirmations for studies in the faculty of law, the faculty of urban planning, the faculty of fine arts, and the faculty of engineering."[37]

This message would clearly have not triggered any warnings on monitoring systems hardwired into Internet service providers like the FBI's Carnivore system (otherwise known as DCS100).[38] In hindsight, authorities now recognize that the message referred to the targets to be attacked by the hijacked aircraft as well as the number of terrorists who would be taking part.

In addition to using the Internet for coordination and exchange of information prior to an attack, terrorists can also conduct research on potential targets and obtain detailed photos and plans electronically, thereby minimizing the actual time they are exposing themselves during a physical reconnaissance of a target.[39] The recent attacks on mass transit systems have highlighted the volume of publicly available information regarding schedules, routes, and timetable changes that is available for download from various government and private Web sites. This can be combined with imagery from sites like Google Earth when planning a terrorist attack as it provides additional detail about the potential target and its surroundings. Current insurgent operations in Iraq are exploiting this technology in planning operations against U.S. forces. They are also accessing technical information regarding U.S. vehicles directly from the supplier's Web sites.[40]

The lessons learned from the London bombings on July 7, 2005, clearly show that the timeframe in which to identify a person in the process of becoming radicalized is extremely short.[41] Recent arrests in Australia as a result of Operation Pendennis demonstrate the wide spread nature of the threat of home-grown extremism for many nations. Indeed, the Australian government recently acknowledged that "the terrorist threat to Australia does not only come from external sources. It can also come from people living and working in Australia."[42] Potential terrorists may be second- or third-generation Australians, and may not have traveled to countries of interest or conducted themselves in such a manner as to draw attention from the Australian Security Intelligence Organization or other national agencies like the Australian Federal Police. According to Downer, "It is terrorism of a previously unknown scale. It is a different kind of conflict, perpetrated in the name of a Muslim extremist cause. We must understand it if we are to defeat it."[43]

Terrorist groups operate as amorphous, fluid networks providing them significant advantages over rigidly structured state and nation based law enforcement agencies. As Jeff Jonas notes, "We are currently losing the war on terrorism due to Web 2.0," and the reasons cited for this are the capabilities for "these folks to communicate, share tradecraft, recruit and synchronize at a velocity and resiliency that is unprecedented."[44] In addition, terrorist groups are exploiting the combination of rapidly evolving technology and incommodious legislation to prevent detection. Kirby acknowledges that while the occurrence of self-radicalization had its roots in social issues, Islamist ideology permeates it.[45] Its promotion via the Internet however, makes Western countries who do not limit access vulnerable. As Richardson explains, "It's a different type of warfare. It's a battle of perceptions. And al-Qaida understands it. And America needs to understand it."[46] The Internet allows terrorist groups like al-Qaida to direct a global movement at the strategic level without any requirement to interact with local groups.[47]

Weimann identifies the widespread use of the Internet by various extremist groups to market their causes, keep in touch with their support base, and "teach and train" their operatives.[48] It is this use of the Internet that poses the greatest challenge for police in identifying persons of interest from the billions of packets of data traveling across the Web. This view is supported by Ronczkowski, who identifies the sheer volume of electronic communications used by terrorists as disturbing.[49] Terrorists have identified the inherent risks and limitations imposed by traditional structures, and in line with recent changes to corporate business structures they are now evolving toward electronically networked transnational groups.[50] These groups provide greater resilience in the event of a successful police operation. Their loose, widely dispersed structure ensures that not all operatives and resources are vulnerable to interception from a single law enforcement operation. In addition, this model provides increased flexibility and the devolution of authority, resulting in decisions being made and action taken at a local level. Weimann illuminates al-Qaida's evolving structure following the U.S.-led operations in Afghanistan, identifying the evolution toward multiple networked groups providing worldwide coverage and capable of adapting to meet operational requirements.[51] This has created a new cadre of terrorists, whom Kirby classifies as self-starters who have attained a level of operational autonomy unmatched by any comparable terrorist or government entity.[52] This autonomy allows individuals and groups to identify, select, and carry out attacks against targets without any further authority or approval from groups with whom they see themselves as being aligned.

Kirby details the crucial role that technology plays in this new evolution of terrorism. Unlike previous candidates for jihad, individuals can now nominate themselves and become involved, while still living in their country of residence or birth.[53] There is no longer a sense of compulsion to travel to places like Afghanistan, Chechnya, or Iraq unless that is what the individual desires in order to become a mujahid (holy warrior). Previous logistical and in some cases financial impediments to undertaking jihad have being largely negated by advances in technology, thereby making such activity available to a much wider group than at any time previously. This stance is supported by Weimann, who cites the online magazine *Al Battar* (Arabic for "training camp") as an example of what is provided in cyberspace by al-Qaida for those unable to travel, yet who still wish to undertake training. This provides an online learning environment whereby individuals can attain the requisite skill set necessary to carry out their own attacks.[54]

Whine identifies two extremist groups as being pivotal in the use of the Internet by terrorists—the Islamist extremists and members of the far right or white supremacist movement.[55] While the Islamists seek a return to the caliphate, the far right seek a utopia where they can live untroubled by other races, politicians, or the rule of law.[56] Given the very nature of the ideology of these groups, it is of concern that they appear to be forming virtual alliances against what they perceive as a common enemy, even if it is an alliance of convenience. This common enemy is seen as the state of Israel and the disproportionate influence on global activities they perceive exerted by members of the Jewish faith.[57]

One of the better known far right organizations is Aryan Nations.[58] On their Web site, posted next to Nazi SS symbols, are links to Web sites about mujahideen and militant Islam and to forums about Islamist-related topics. Another far right site is Stormfront's White Pride World Wide, and while this site as yet has no links to Islamist Web sites, it shares many of the characteristics of other extremist sites.[59] These include multimedia, ideology, training, physical fitness, and merchandise to promote the group.

The Islamist sites act as a conduit for information to those who are ideologically close but geographically distant. These sites provide material with a narrow puritanical interpretation of Islam from well-known extremist authors, thereby creating the opportunity for someone to become virtually radicalized without ever having contact with a member of a terrorist group in person. These sites are also useful in recruiting new members.[60] The former leader of the Finsbury Park Mosque, Abu Hamza, used to promote his sermons and worldview by recording them on cassette tapes for sale across the United Kingdom.[61] Among those attracted to Hamza's particular interpretation of Islam were university-educated young men who understood the potential of the Internet. They began converting the sermons and writings of Hamza into digital format and uploaded them onto various Web sites, making them freely accessible to anyone. Since the arrest of Hamza on terrorism-related offenses in the United Kingdom, some of these sites have been shut down while others continue to relocate.[62]

RECRUITMENT AND RADICALIZATION

Terrorist entities are amplifying their capabilities via the Internet in order to present themselves as a greater tactical threat than they can physically achieve. As Custer explains, "It's a war of perceptions. They understand the power of the Internet. They don't have to win in the tactical battlefield. They never will. No platoon has ever been defeated in Afghanistan or Iraq. But, it doesn't matter. It's irrelevant."[63] The Web is being used to facilitate the active recruitment of individuals who have grown up in Western societies and are comfortable meeting new people and discussing issues in cyberspace. Weimann details how the full suite of multimedia capabilities facilitated by the Internet are being used to generate support for their cause and to motivate individuals to participate on a variety of levels.[64] A variety of terrorist groups, including radical Islamists, are marketing themselves in such a manner as to generate support for their causes and identify and radicalize those they identify as potential converts to their interpretation of Islam. This approach is particularly effective given what is now known about the recruitment of potential terrorists. Sageman conducted extensive research into terrorist networks and recruitment methods and discovered an absence of "brainwashing" or "top-down recruitment."[65] Instead candidates were self-recruiting and searching for ways to join either via the Internet or by introductions from members of their current social network who may already be members. The only recent deviation from this recruitment methodology was uncovered by the SITE Institute and details the 2003 recruitment drive by al-Qaida, seeking fighters who would undertake jihad in Iraq against U.S. and coalition forces operating there.[66]

Madeleine Gruen identifies the need for Islamist groups to recruit and radicalize their intended audience while minimizing any detectable contact.[67] This would allow them to avoid physical police surveillance operations of persons or places of interest. Instead they reach their targets via the Internet where they can broadcast their ideology anonymously from international servers. The Web sites used to attract potential candidates need to be visually appealing with excellent multimedia and in the native language of the target group. Terrorist entities also have to ensure that these sites do not promote extremism to a degree that would warrant additional attention from police and law enforcement agencies. However, these groups do monitor those who browse their sites and retain information about them including IP and e-mail addresses if acquired. Should these individuals then be of interest to such groups by virtue of their geographical location or other criteria, they are often contacted.[68]

Once contact is established, then the candidate can then be drawn further into the extremist world and granted access to far more radical sites hidden from public view and inconspicuous enough not to warrant further investigation by police if located by commercial search engines. Katz and Devon describe several password-protected sites including forums and message boards as the most utilized communications medium.[69] These candidates are likely to be individuals susceptible to indoctrination who are dissatisfied with their current status and position in life regardless of any outward veneer of normality or success. Terrorists then seek to segregate these individuals by supplementing their social structure with a new network of like-minded individuals in cyberspace.[70] This ensures that the indoctrination process can proceed unimpeded by contrasting views or arguments from family and former friends and colleagues. Individuals are made to feel highly valued and special by their new friends. This virtual world provides camaraderie and a sense of belonging regardless of their physical location or cultural identity.[71] They are often assigned a mentor who keeps in personal contact and advises and guides them on their journey. While this entire process can occur in cyberspace, Weimann is of the opinion that the Internet may only be used to select suitable individuals for further indoctrination and possible recruitment.[72] This is due to the potential by police and intelligence agencies to introduce cyberoperatives to the network in a methodology not dissimilar to that employed against online pedophile groups.

The potential exists for an individual or group to actively seek out extremist sites, become radicalized, undergo training, and prepare for an attack while remaining undetected by conventional policing techniques. Following the July 7 attacks in London the British police and intelligence agencies were confronted with the need to review their operational policies regarding extremism even though their structures were well attuned to terrorism from their previous IRA experience. This is due to the paradigm shift required to deal with the new threat posed by groups whose actions were sanctioned by Islamist teachings posted in cyberspace.[73] Therefore, new methodologies need to be introduced and where necessary legislation amended to allow police to keep pace with the terrorist groups who are fast surpassing them in terms of expertise and resources.[74] This will also require a change in mindset for police agencies as they come to terms with the realization that individuals or very small groups may radicalize in cyberspace and then fund their own attacks, all without any contact or discernible instruction from an existing terrorist entity. Accordingly, these new terrorists may be home-grown and have had no previous dealings with police. This presents the possibility that there are currently individuals in Australia who are in the process of evolving from cyber-radicals to active terrorists. Therefore, as Kirby notes, "new paradigms are needed to understand the process by which individuals are driven to embrace terrorism and execute attacks."[75]

Terrorist groups are now providing online training that would rival the offerings of most established universities. The training can encompass a wide variety of topics, all designed to slowly indoctrinate and alter the worldview of students while simultaneously equipping them with the skill set necessary to carry out attacks. In addition to the techniques learned online, Hamm has identified a variety of skills that individuals from diverse socioeconomic backgrounds contribute when forming terrorist cells.[76] These range from academic expertise in fields as diverse as chemistry and computer security to knowledge of police methodologies and criminal contacts gained from the streets. This combination is being well utilized by the terrorists, who understand the modern asymmetric battlefield better than those charged with stopping them. Terrorist groups will actively target their enemies on a variety of levels, blurring the traditional distinctions between the battlefield and civilian environments, resulting in a new form of conflict, which some have referred to as fourth-generation warfare.[77]

INHERENT CHALLENGES

While the evolving terrorist threat of self-starters comes from within a nation's own borders, comprising mostly of individuals lacking in operational experience from theaters like Iraq and Afghanistan, they are no less of a threat.[78] In the case of Jam'iyyat Ul-Islam Is-Saheeh in California, the manifesto of the group's leader, Kevin James, was posted on the Internet following his indictment on terrorism charges. In addition, a target list and letter to be left at the scene of attacks was also posted on the Investigative Project on Terrorism's Web site.[79]

Ronczkowski has examined the technical capabilities of many terrorist groups and their ability to learn from previous encounters with police and law enforcement agencies.[80] Full-disclosure legislation in Australia and elsewhere can potentially provide these groups with insights into the methodologies used by police to intercept and track electronic communications, thereby ensuring that terrorist groups learn how to better secure and hide their electronic signature. The vastness of the Internet and the volume of data transmitted would challenge even the resources of specialist interception agencies like the U.S. National Security Agency or the Australian Defence Signals Directorate. Post-9/11 the United States began evaluating new forms of data mining as a means to uncover terrorist plots prior to them being executed.[81] After legislation was identified that could prevent data mining from being utilized to its full potential, the situation was in part rectified by the introduction of section 215 of the USA PATRIOT Act, which allows broad requests for information holdings from the private sector without specifying any individual or group, as was previously required. This facilitates the cross-matching of large data sets to identify individuals, patterns, or themes of concern.

This is causing understandable concern among civil liberties groups due to the volume of data that is required and the number of people with no active involvement in criminal behavior whose private information ends up on government databases as a result. However, this effort can propel police and intelligence agencies into the digital age as they try to identify themes and relationships using various computer-based applications in an effort to successfully undertake large-scale data mining.[82] These types of data analysis operations are resource-intensive. They can also be limited due to the lack of an accepted common protocol that would enable the rapid transfer of data between servers, as well as searches of proprietary systems and information held by a variety of public and private organizations.[83] It is not just the flow of data between servers that is crucial to this effort; there needs to be a synthesis between analysts and investigators, with both parties actively contributing and sharing information and concepts.[84] Analysts need to understand and where possible preempt the needs of investigators. Jeff Jonas, a leading software developer, identifies the crucial aim of data analysis as producing actionable intelligence, not just more information or data. He defines this as "information that puts the analyst in a position to act appropriately in a given context."[85]

IBM recently acquired a company in Nevada called Systems Research and Development, and Jonas, the former head of the company, is now a distinguished engineer with IBM. His original software, called Nonobvious Relationship Awareness, was designed to provide a solution to the identity matching problems being faced by the casinos in Las Vegas. It has now being further enhanced and is marketed by IBM as Identity Resolution and Relationship Resolution. Jonas has generated interest with his view that the potential for conventional data mining as a tool to identify and predict terrorist activity is very limited, and his agreement with Harper that data mining would not be of any significant value. Their rationale is that unlike the private sector or established crime types, terrorism has very few events by which to develop a framework against which to benchmark analysis.[86] This is in stark contrast to other crimes like fraud or the commercial applications of data mining, where private entities use data mining to profile their customers and identify market trends and shifting consumer demand and spending patterns. What Jonas proposes in its place is a system whereby data pertaining to key individuals is able to be tracked down and utilized,[87] requiring the shared access by agencies of various databases both public and private.

While software continues to be developed and refined, the legal and moral arguments regarding data mining by police and intelligence agencies will continue. Jonas and IBM are currently developing new technology that will allow all the analysis to be done while the data sets are still in encrypted form, thereby ensuring that privacy is retained unless a particular piece of data is identified as of concern and warrants further investigation.[88] The two approaches to data mining relevant to counterterrorism are subject- and pattern-based.[89] Once a person of interest is identified, then data including electronic communications, bookings, and transactions can be scanned to identify linkages with places, individuals, or groups. These individuals can then be further investigated, allowing the analyst to build up a picture of the network or group and attempt to discern their activities and possible objectives. As previously identified, for such an endeavor to be successful the analyst requires the ability to interrogate and retrieve data from numerous databases. In order to use pattern-based data mining successfully, the statistical framework needs to be able to recognize critical yet innocuous pieces of information.

There are however, opposing views to Jonas regarding the potential of data mining to successfully provide police and intelligence agencies with another capability to add to their investigative portfolio. Some programs, like Total Information Awareness, undertaken by the U.S. Defense Advanced Research Projects Agency, are attempting to provide a digital solution to the problem. Such capability is critical given the data that is being transmitted and the difficulties in providing real-time monitoring of sites of interest and those accessing them. It is estimated that over 80 percent of the data held on individuals are in the hands of the private sector, and much of this is available on a commercial basis. Databases such as ChoicePoint, LexisNexis, and Axion provide search capacity and electronic profiles beyond that held by police databases. Accordingly, terrorist groups operating in the United Kingdom actively recruited members with computer expertise to assist with camouflaging their electronic traffic and availed themselves of services provided by a variety of Internet cafés and pay-as-you-go ISPs.[90]

Former Australian Federal Communications Minister Helen Coonan tabled a bill in Parliament proposing to give the commissioner of the Australian Federal Police the power to order ISPs to block access to terrorism and cybercrime Web sites.[91] Restricting access to extremist sites poses technical challenges and is indicative of the frustrations faced by lawmakers regarding some of the ideology that is being actively promoted via the Internet. Placing the responsibility directly at the ISP level would prove extremely difficult to enforce. Many of the service providers that host extremist Web sites have no knowledge of their activities and remove them once advised. However, many of these sites are located offshore in countries that actively support such extremist views and their promulgation. Other difficulties exist as once these sites are removed or taken down they can still be accessed via applications like the Internet Archive.[92] This means that while they aren't being updated with the latest propaganda, they can still be accessed by anyone with even limited technical knowledge. Rather than drive such sites underground, another approach may involve the use of electronic surveillance to monitor those who access their content and subsequently interact with them. This would allow police to build up a profile of persons of interest and their online activities and identify the electronic address of those they come in contact with. It would also provide insight into the more extremist sites including their hosts, users, content, and most critically their future intentions.

CHALLENGING THE INFLUENCE OF MAINSTREAM MEDIA

The Internet is being used by extremists to articulate a particular view often contrasting with mainstream media, thereby allowing them to generate the desired publicity for their cause as well as justifying violent acts.[93] General John Custer recently noted that on some of these sites terrorists could "download scripted talking points that validate you have religious justification for mass murder."[94]

The media themselves are being seen as legitimate targets in locations like Iraq. Journalists are no longer viewed as impartial in their role as the fourth estate, and they can be kidnapped and become part of the story rather than reporting on it.[95] The Internet is proving to be crucial to terrorist campaigns because it facilitates the promotion of a particular ideology and allows groups to present events from their perspective. This is crucial to their efforts because, as Walker notes, "publicity is the oxygen of terrorism."[96] This technology is facilitating a medium for extremists and their political supporters to promote their ideology and activities on the world stage with minimal infrastructure and costs. Digital video cameras, laptops, and editing software can all be utilized to advocate the cause of the particular terrorist group involved.

Terrorism expert Walter Laqueur once noted that "the media are the terrorist's best friend. The terrorist's act by itself is nothing, publicity is all."[97] However, the availability of modern digital technologies and the ubiquity of communications channels such as the Internet can be seen as making these groups their own media entity. They no longer need to rely on the presence of third-party media organizations to record and distribute their message, at least to a sympathetic audience. Once the video and accompanying imagery are prepared, they can then be uploaded onto the Internet and accessed from almost anywhere, providing the contemporary terrorist with the ability to potentially influence activities at the national and international level.[98] It also provides for anonymity when accessing and viewing the material for those who may share the same ideological views as the terrorist organization.[99] Against this background of widely available communications and digital media technology it is hardly surprising that terrorist groups are utilizing it to maximum effect. For example, at the 2005 World Summit on the Information Society in Tunis, Israeli Foreign Minister Silvan Shalom delivered an address clearly identifying the dangers posed by Hamas and its use of the Internet, stating that it "is one of the most active terrorist groups on the Net. It runs no less than eight Internet sites in seven languages."[100]

A prime example of a media organization that is highly supportive of terrorist acts is the Al-Manar Satellite Television network. This network demonstrates the understanding that groups like Hizballah have regarding the impact and reach of mass media. The ability for subscribers across the globe to access the network provides a medium, which can be used to communicate and influence a wide audience. The potential exists for some subscribers to use this as a primary source of news and information, instead of commercial networks in countries where they now reside. This could influence their judgment on key issues and alter their opinions regarding foreign policies of the governments in their new homes. It can also limit assimilation and lead to a sense of self-imposed isolation from the remainder of the community.

The linkage between Al-Manar and Hizballah is such that cameramen are often in position to get footage that no other news agency has access to. This level of cooperation clearly indicates a high degree of trust with the inference that Al-Manar journalists and camera crews may have prior knowledge of Hizballah and Palestinian operations.[101] The ability to disseminate material favorable for their cause has enhanced Hizballah's standing and esteem in the Arab world. The medium by which to exert influence is normally accompanied by the responsibility that it entails. These guiding ethics of journalism have led to it being cited as the fourth estate where truth and integrity in reporting pertinent and newsworthy information are seen as key principles. Al-Manar has by definition always admitted its journalistic bias in reporting, and it was one of the first Arabic media outlets to perpetrate the conspiracy theory regarding the events on 9/11.[102] This has resulted in many in the Arab world believing that the attacks were carried out by

Mossad with some U.S. assistance, thereby removing any sympathy that would be normally generated by such a large loss of civilian life.

One way in which governments have reacted to the identified threat posed by Al-Manar is to legislate and prevent its provider service from broadcasting it in their respective countries. However the current broadcast technology makes it difficult to actually achieve this without the cooperation of the service provider. In France, this was achieved by political pressure on Eutelsat, which is a French-owned company that was carrying the Al-Manar signal. However, Nilesat, which is Egyptian-owned, and Arabsat, which is Saudi-owned, are still capable of broadcasting to an audience in France.[103]

While not in the same ideological frame as Al-Manar, the Doha-based Arabic news network Al-Jazeera has frequently being the first media organization to air controversial videos from conflicts in places like Iraq. While the ability of this network to reach Arabic-speaking viewers globally is understood there is some debate regarding its new English-language news channel and the manner in which it will frame issues like "terrorism and resistance."[104] This is pertinent when considering the dramatic expansion in viewer audience that is likely.

Clearly, the challenge is how to present an alternative viewpoint. The United States has invested heavily in its own Arabic-language satellite network, which is not being well received by its intended audience in the Middle East, who view it as a propaganda tool.[105] It is, however, a step in the right direction and acknowledges the need to communicate a different viewpoint in a foreign language, to an audience who if receptive could alter the perception of the United States in that region.

CONCLUSION

It is intriguing that terrorist groups with such a puritanical worldview would avail themselves of one of the freedoms to which they are so vehemently opposed when communicating or spreading their ideology.[106] The use of the Internet by terrorists will need to be continually monitored and the material they circulate examined in an effort to both understand their motivations and prevent further incidents. As technology progresses, both terrorists and those charged with preventing them from committing atrocities will have to remain abreast of innovative developments. The phrase, "the Internet interprets censorship as damage and routes around it" —attributed to John Gilmore, one of the co-founders of the Electronic Frontier Foundation[107]—clearly identifies the potential challenges of attempting to prevent the use of cyberspace by terrorist entities. While there are technical means to attack such Web sites, the legal challenges posed by the transnational nature of these activities place them beyond the legislative capabilities of nation-states.[108] Clearly, more work is required at the international level to enact legislation that can successfully meet this exploitation of the Internet by terrorist entities.

The difficulty is ensuring cooperation between the governments and law enforcement agencies of those nation-states involved. Existing information sharing infrastructure and procedures could be enhanced so organizations like Interpol can take a lead role in prosecuting offenders regardless of where they reside. It is not only police and law enforcement agencies that are seeking to learn from the Internet; the terrorists are also watching and learning. They review failed operations to see what prompted intervention by the police, they look at material presented in open court which reveals capabilities, and they also examine media reports, particularly those that might include leaks regarding sensitive investigations.[109] As identified by Hoffman, there is a need for terrorists to continually take action, and in order to do so effectively they need to be able to evade those measures put in place by policing agencies.[110] Terrorist groups and innovative individuals are continually identifying and exploiting potential weakness to achieve their objective.

Policing agencies need to ensure that future investments in equipment and personnel for counterterrorism are not limited to a tactical resolution or postincident response capability. Highly skilled intelligence analysts and the supporting IT framework should receive equal priority for funding in order to prevent the loss of life and reduced sense of security in the event of an attack. Actionable intelligence is critical to any law enforcement counterterrorism program. Agencies need to be willing to recruit specialists and invest in the training and retention of their staff. Given the long-term nature of the threat and the time necessary to develop the necessary competencies in this area, some current management practices may need to be revised. Policies like tenure (regular rotation of staff every two to three years) will need to be altered and career pathways developed within the counterterrorism intelligence portfolio. Remuneration and working conditions should provide the opportunity for specialists to remain within the analytical field where their skills can be best utilized. As Katz and Devon observed, "While authorities play catch up on the Internet, the online terrorist network continues to expand, recruiting others to jihad and growing stronger each day."[111] Lessons learned from cyberpedophile investigations and the methodologies developed could be adapted to meet the requirements of counter terrorist teams. The combination of federal resources and information provided to local police by the community may be successful in preventing future terrorist attacks.

NOTES

1. Vincent E. Henry, "The Need for a Coordinated and Strategic Local Police Approach to Terrorism: A Practitioner's Perspective." *Police Practice and Research*, 3(4) (2002), p. 319–336.

2. Ibid.

3. International Association of Chiefs of Police, *Homeland Security Preparedness Survey* (Alexandria, VA: 2003).

4. Henry (2002), p. 319.

5. Joseph Felter, "The Internet: A Portal to Violent Islamist Extremism" (2007), Testimony prepared for the U.S. Senate Committee for Homeland Security and Government Affairs. Retrieved May 10, 2008, from http://ctc.usma.edu/profiles/felter/050307Felter.pdf.

6. Ibid.

7. Lia Brynjar and Thomas Hegghammer, 2004, cited in Gabriel Weimann, *Terror on the Internet: The New Arena, the New Challenges* (Washington, DC: U.S. Institute of Peace, 2006), p. 133.

8. Ibid., p. 134.

9. Lorenzo Vidino, *Al-Qaida in Europe: The New Battleground of International Jihad* (New York: Prometheus Books, 2006), p. 292.

10. Dame E. Manningham-Buller, *The International Terrorist Threat to the UK* (2006). Retrieved November 12, 2006, from http://www.mi5.gov.uk/output/Page568.html.

11. Felter, 2007.

12. Dame Manningham-Buller, 2006.

13. Ibid.

14. CNN, 2006. Also, please see the chapters by Karen Walker and Cori Dauber in this volume.

15. Dame Manningham-Buller, 2006.

16. Jonathan Evans, *Intelligence, Counter-Terrorism and Trust* (2007). Retrieved from http://www.mi5.gov.uk/output/Page562.html.

17. Dame Manningham-Buller, 2006.

18. Michael Whine, "Cyberspace—A New Medium for Communication, Command and Control by Extremists," *Studies in Conflict and Terrorism* 22 (1999), p. 234.

19. Ibid.

20. United States of America (2004), Indictment: *USA v. Babar Ahmad*. Retrieved from http://www.investigativeproject.org/documents/case_docs/96.pdf.

21. Commonwealth Director of Public Prosecutions (2006), Submission To The Security Legislation Review Committee, 31 January 2006. Retrieved November 12, 2006, from http://www.ema.gov.au/.../$file/Edited+Submission+from+DPP+-+31+January+2006+-+PUBLIC+VERS.PDF.

22. Nielsen (2007), "NetRatings: A global leader in Internet media and market research." Retrieved October 10, 2007, from http://www.nielsen-netratings.com.

23. Adam, 1997, cited in Michael Whine 1999.

24. Custer cited in Scott Pelley (2007), *Terrorists Take Recruitment Efforts Online*. Retrieved September 30, 2007, from http://www.cbsnews.com/stories/2007/03/02/60minutes/printable2531546.shtml.

25. Rita Katz and Josh Devon (2007), "Web Of Terror." *Forbes* [electronic version]. Retrieved October 15, 2007, from http://members.forbes.com/forbes/2007/0507/184a_print.html.

26. Gabriel Weimann, "Virtual Training Camps," in *Teaching Terror: Strategic and Tactical Learning in the Terrorist World*, ed. James J. F. Forest (Lanham: Rowan & Littlefield, 2006), p. 110–111.

27. Fox News (2006), "FBI Busts 'Real Deal' Terror Plot Aimed at NYC-NJ Underground Transit Link." Retrieved May 10, 2008, from http://www.foxnews.com/story/0,2933,202518,00.html.

28. Mark Hamm, *Terrorism as Crime: From Oklahoma City to Al-Qaeda and Beyond* (New York: New York University Press, 2007), p. 209.

29. Mitchell Waldrop, "Can Sense-Making Keep Us Safe?" *Technology Review* (2003), pp. 43–48. Retrieved October 12, 2007 from http://www.technologyreview.com.

30. Jarret M. Brachman and William F. McCants, "Stealing Al Qaeda's Playbook," *Studies in Conflict and Terrorism* (29) (2006).

31. Weimann, 2006, p. 115.

32. Ibid., p. 116.

33. Michal Whine, 1999, p. 238.

34. U.S. Government (2006), *Declassified Key Judgments of the National Intelligence Estimate, Trends in Global Terrorism: Implications for the United States*. Retrieved September 29, 2006, from http://www.dni.gov.

35. Ronald V. Clarke and Graeme R. Newman, *Outsmarting The Terrorists* (Westport, CT: Praeger Security International, 2006), p. 80.

36. Ibid.

37. According to Melman, 2002, cited in Weimann, 2006, p. 132.

38. Weimann, 2006, p. 11.

39. U.S. Government, 2006.

40. Felter, 2007.

41. U.K. House of Commons (2006), *Report of the Official Account of the Bombings in London on 7th July 2005*. London: Stationery Office.

42. Commonwealth of Australia (2004), *Transnational Terrorism: The Threat To Australia*. Retrieved June 12, 2006, from http://www.dfat.gov.au/publications/terrorism, p. 73.

43. Downer, cited in Commonwealth of Australia (2004), p. v.

44. Jeff Jonas (2007), *Web 2.0—Al Qaeda's Most Effective Force Multiplier*. Retrieved October 14, 2007, from http://jeffjonas.typepad.com/jeff_jonas/2007/05web_20_al_qaeda.html.

45. Aidan Kirby, "The London Bombers as 'Self-Starters': A Case Study in Indigenous Radicalization and the Emergence of Autonomous Cliques," *Studies in Conflict and Terrorism*, 30(5) (2007), pp. 415–428, p. 415.

46. Custer, cited in Pelley, 2007, p. 3.

47. Richardson, cited in Ruth Walker, "Terror Online, and How to Counteract It," *Harvard University Gazette* (2005), p. 2. Retrieved October 14, 2007, from http://www.hno.harvard.edu/gazette/2005/03.03/01-cyberterror.html.

48. Weimann, 2006, p. 111.

49. Michael R. Ronczkowski, *Terrorism and Organised Hate Crime: Intelligence Gathering, Analysis, and Investigations* (2nd ed.) (Boca Raton: CRC Press, Taylor & Francis Group, 2007), p. 226.

50. John Arquilla et al., cited in Weimann, 2006, p. 117.

51. Weimann, 2006, p. 116.

52. Kirby, 2007, p. 416.

53. Ibid.

54. Weimann, 2006, p. 111.

55. Whine, 1999.

56. Ibid.

57. Ibid.

58. Aryan-Nations (2006). http://www.aryan-nations.org. Retrieved November 15, 2006.

59. Stormfront (2006), "White Pride World Wide." Retrieved November 15, 2006, from http://www.stormfront.org.

60. For example, see "The Ignored Puzzle Pieces of Knowledge" (2006). Retrieved September 10, 2006, from http://inshallahshaheed.wordpress.com/books/

61. Sean O'Neill and Daniel McGrory, *The Suicide Factory: Abu Hamza and the Finsbury Park Mosque* (London: Harper Collins, 2006).

62. Supporters of Shariah (2006). Retrieved October 14, 2006, from http://www.angelfire.com/bc3/johnsonuk/eng/index.html.

63. Custer cited in Scott Pelley (2007), "Terrorists Take Recruitment Efforts Online." Retrieved September 30, 2007, from http://www.cbsnews.com/stories/2007/03/02/60minutes/printable2531546.shtml.

64. Weimann, 2006, p. 118.

65. Marc Sageman, *Understanding Terror Networks* (Philadelphia: University of Pennsylvania Press, 2004), p. 108.

66. Gabriel Weiman, "Virtual Training Camps," in *The Making of a Terrorist*, ed. James J. F. Forest (Westport, CT: Praeger, 2005), p. 61.

67. Madeleine Gruen, "Innovative Recruitment and Indoctrination Tactics by Extremists: Video Games, Hip-Hop, and the World Wide Web," in *The Making of a Terrorist*, ed. James J. F. Forest (Westport, CT: Praeger, 2005), p. 12.

68. Weimann, 2005, p. 60.

69. Rita Katz and Josh Devon (2007), "Web of Terror" [electronic version], Forbes.com. Retrieved October 15, 2007, from http://members.forbes.com/forbes/2007/0507/184a_print.html.

70. Gruen, 2005, p. 14.

71. Katz and Devon, 2007, p. 1.

72. Weimann, 2005, p. 60.

73. Kirby, 2007, p. 426

74. Ronczkowski, 2007, p. 227.

75. Kirby, 2007, p. 423.

76. Hamm, 2007, p. 208.

77. Lindt et al., cited in Colleen McCue, *Data Mining and Predictive Analysis: Intelligence Gathering and Crime Analysis* (Burlington: Butterworth-Heinemann, (2007).

78. Hamm, 2007, p. 208.

79. See http://www.investigativeproject.org/cases.php.

80. Ronczkowski, 2007, p. 227.

81. Jeff Jonas and Jim Harper (2006). *Effective Counterterrorism and the Limited Role of Predictive Data Mining*. No. 584. Retrieved October 10, 2007, from http://www.cato.org/pub_display.php?pub_id=6784.

82. John Markoff and Scott Shane, "Agencies Look for More Ways to Mine Data," *New York Times* (February 25, 2006).

83. Waldrop, 2003, p. 45.

84. McCue, 2007, p. xix.

85. Jonas and Harper, 2006, p. 5.

86. Ibid., p. 2.

87. Ibid., p. 4.

88. Florence Olsen (2006), "FlipSide: A few minutes with Jeff Jonas" [electronic version]. *Federal Computer Weekly*. Retrieved October 13, 2007, from http://www.fcw.com/print/12-2/news/92036-1.html.

89. Jonas and Harper, 2006.

90. O'Neill and McGrory, 2006, p. 115.

91. Karen Dearne (2007), "Coonan Seeks to Censor the Web," *Australian IT.*

92. See http://www.archive.org/index.php.

93. Ruth Walker (2005), "Terror Online, and How to Counteract It," *Harvard University Gazette*. Retrieved October 14, 2007, from http://www.hno.harvard.edu/gazette/2005/03.03/01-cyberterror.html, p. 3.

94. Custer, cited in Pelley, 2007, p. 1.

95. Custer, cited in Pelley, 2007, p. 2.

96. Walker, 2005, p. 3.

97. Walter Laqueur, 1976, p. 104, cited in Y. Tsfati and G. Weimann (2002), "www.terrorism.com: Terror on the Internet," *Studies in Conflict and Terrorism* (25), p. 318.

98. Whine, 1999.

99. Ibid.

100. Intelligence and Terrorism Information Center at the Center for Special Studies (2005). "Using the Internet to market terrorism" [electronic version].

101. Avi Jorisch, *Beacon of Hatred: Inside Hizballah's Al-Manar Television* (Washington DC: Washington Institute for Near East Policy, 2004), p. 23.

102. Ibid., p. 39.

103. Intelligence and Terrorism Information Center at the Center for Special Studies (May 18, 2005), "French Culture Minister calls upon members of the European Union to join France in banning Al-Manar broadcasts" [electronic version].

104. BBC News, http://news.bbc.co.uk/2/hi/middle_east/6105952.stm.

105. Jorisch, 2004.

106. Weimann, 2006, p. 7.

107. Michael Geist (2006), "Tough Choice for CRTC in Hate Blocking Case." Retrieved November 30, 2006, from http://www.michaelgeist.ca/content/view/1392/159.

108. D. K.Matai, "Cyberland Security: Organised Crime, Terrorism and the Internet." Paper presented at the Oxford Internet Institute (University of Oxford, February 10, 2005).

109. Dame Manningham-Buller, 2006.

110. Bruce Hoffman, *Inside Terrorism*, revised and expanded ed. (New York: Columbia University Press, 2006), p. 252.

111. Katz and Devon, 2007, p. 2.

11

Who's Winning the Battle for Narrative?

Al-Qaida versus the United States and Its Allies

Sebastian Gorka and David Kilcullen

> *The confrontation that we are calling for with the apostate regimes does not know Socratic debates, Platonic ideals, nor Aristotelian diplomacy. But it knows the dialogue of bullets, the ideals of assassination, bombing, and destruction, and the diplomacy of the canon and machine-gun.*
>
> —Al-Qaida Training Manual[1]

THE MODERN MASTER OF STRATEGY, Carl von Clausewitz, is a notoriously difficult author to read and understand. The fact that his most famous work, *On War*, remained unfinished on his death and was published posthumously by his widow, only adds to the problems of interpretation. Even his most famous dictum, which sees war as the continuation of politics by others means, can be understood in several ways. Nevertheless, whatever the final interpretation, the saying clearly underscores the function of will within conflict. For von Clausewitz, politics was but one method for a nation to realize its will. He understood that at times one can only reach such goals through the use of force. In such cases, a government employs violence to impose its will on the enemy after other tools have proven inadequate. In the endeavor to force our will and our version of future reality on our foe, communication plays an absolutely vital role. On the one hand it helps our population and our forces maintain the will to fight and to win. Strategic communications can also be very effective in undermining the will to fight of our adversary.[2] Unfortunately, in the seven-year global conflict between the United States and al-Qaida, it is the enemy that is winning the war of strategic communications.

This chapter examines the message that al-Qaida has been broadcasting, what the message from the United States and its allies has been, and the contextual reality behind both. We also explore why al-Qaida has been much more successful in communicating its ideology and the justifications for its actions than the United States and its allies have been. And finally, based on this analysis we will recommend a simple format and preliminary content for a doctrine of strategic communication to undermine the current enemy and strengthen U.S. national interests.

AL-QAIDA'S MESSAGE

Although al-Qaida operates in secret and is very unlike the nation-state foes the United States and its allies have faced in the past, Osama bin Laden and his ideological adviser Ayman al-Zawahiri are not shy individuals who shun the limelight. Long before the attacks of September 11, 2001 (9/11), the leaders of this salafist terrorist organization openly telegraphed the justifications for the violence perpetrated by their operatives to the whole world and broadcast in detail what end-state they envisaged as a result of their global campaign of terror. In fact, three years before the attacks which killed nearly 3,000 innocent civilians in New York, Washington, and Pennsylvania, bin Laden openly declared war against the United States and the West in his 1996 fatwa.[3] Today, numerous official and commercial publications are available which collect all similar al-Qaida pronouncements, interviews, and video and audio transcripts, and therefore it is relatively simple to summarize the content of bin Laden's strategic communications.

The Al-Qaida Narrative
The nations of the Arab and Muslim world have all fallen from the path of True Islam. They exist in a state of pagan heresy or ignorance similar to that which existed on the Arabian Peninsula at the time of Islam's birth, a state of jahalia. The leaders of these nations either behave in ways that are not true to the example of Mohammad and the Khoran and/or maintain relations with the West that contravene the core tenets of the Muslim faith. As a result, just as the Salafi and Wahabi schools of Islam decree, true fidelity is to be found in following the example of the first generations of leaders that followed the Prophet, the age of the Four Righteous Caliphs. The true believer must return to a lifestyle that emulates the values and behavior of 7th century Islam. All those who do not do so are our enemies. Our enemies include therefore not only the apostate leaders of the Arab and Muslim world and all Christians and Jews but even all those who call themselves Muslims but who do not follow the fundamentalist ways of the Salafi and Wahabi creed. Following the doctrine of takfir, these people are not in fact Muslims but kafir and should be treated as enemies just as much as the Crusaders. Our goal is to return the ummah, the global community of true Islam, to its former glory and reinstate the Caliphate that was unjustly dissolved by Kemal Ataturk after World War I. We are not fighting for self-determination or national independence, for the nation-state is itself a heretical construct of the Christian Crusaders. In this global war True Islam is under attack by the West and subsequently we must all live the life of defensive Jihad. The current situation of American and Western dominance can only be reversed if Holy War is raised to be the sixth pillar of Islam. It is now the duty of all Muslims to fight the Near Enemy—the leaders of the apostate regimes in the Middle East—and the Far Enemy—America and its allies. In fact, it is the duty of all who seek the global establishment of Dar al-Islam to acquire Weapons of Mass Destruction and to deploy them against the infidel. The West is decadent and fundamentally weak morally. Its citizens love life as much as we love death, therefore we will win.

Note that bin Laden's narrative is coherent and comprehensive: join our jihad ("live the life of defensive Jihad . . . fight the Near Enemy"), for we are certain to win, and when we do justice will prevail.

AMERICA'S MESSAGE

As we finalized this chapter, the conflict is in its seventh year and the campaign globally dispersed from Central Asia to the Middle East, Southeast Asia, Africa, and beyond. And yet, the strategic communications aspect of the Global War on Terror (GWOT), or Long War as it has now been dubbed, has developed in a haphazard fashion without unitary direction or meaningful substance. The mere fact that several years into the conflict, the Department of Defense felt it was necessary to change the name of the campaign from GWOT to the Long War, speaks to a level of confusion at the very highest level.

As a nation America is not even clear as to whom it is at war with. At various times the U.S. government has stated that we are at war with the organization al-Qaida; other times, officials have stated that we are war with all terrorist groups with global reach; and then on still other occasions government leaders have stated that we are at war with terrorism and not with a distinct group that employs terrorism as a tactic.

On the other side of the communication effort, the government has stated that its post-9/11 campaign is about global liberty and democracy, that all the peoples of the world would rather live with political choice and that the creation of a democratic Iraq is the first step in the spread of representative government in the Middle East and across the Arab and Muslim world. Throughout all this, without much effect, the official communications strategy has attempted to stress that the United States (and the West) is not at war with the Muslim world and that the likes of bin Laden only represent a tiny fraction of extremists.

On the very first page of the *U.S. National Strategy for Public Diplomacy and Strategic Communication* (NSPDSC),[4] President Bush is quoted: "We will lead the cause of freedom, justice, and hope, because both our values and our interests demand it." The quote continues: "We also know that nations with free, healthy, prosperous people will be sources of stability, not breeding grounds for extremists and hate and terror. By making the world more hopeful, we make the world more peaceful." According to the document, released in 2007, the national communications strategy must flow from the eight objectives articulated in the overarching *U.S. National Security Strategy:*

- Championing human dignity,
- Strengthening alliances against terrorism,
- Defusing regional conflicts,
- Preventing the threat of weapons of mass destruction,
- Encouraging global economic growth,
- Expanding the "circle of development,"
- Cooperating with other centers of global power,
- Transforming America's national security institutions to meet the challenges and opportunities of the twenty-first century.

Specifically, the NSPDSC states that all communications and public diplomacy activities should:

- Underscore America's commitment to freedom, human rights, and the dignity and equality of every human being;

- Reach out to those who share our ideals;
- Support those who struggle for freedom and democracy; and
- Counter those who espouse ideologies of hate and oppression.

Just as with bin Laden and al-Qaida, the U.S. government has also stated the justifications for its actions and the vision of the future its policies are there to serve. The NSPDSC calls these "core messages." These represent the U.S. narrative.

The U.S.-GWOT Narrative
As a diverse, multicultural nation founded by immigrants, America includes and respects peoples of different nations, cultures and faiths. America seeks to be a partner for progress, prosperity and peace. The American government wants to work in partnership with others nations and peoples of the world in ways that effect a better life "for all the world's citizens." We believe that all people wish to live in societies that are just, governed by the rule-of-law, and not corrupt. We do not expect every country to shape its government like that of the United States, but we believe that citizens should be able to participate in choosing their governments and that these governments should be accountable to their citizens. With its exclusive ideology of hatred and violence, al-Qaida represents the greatest current threat to global peace and prosperity. The likes of bin Laden cannot be reasoned with and must be stopped before there acquire Weapons of Mass Destruction. It is in the interest of all reasonable peoples and legitimate governments of the world to cooperate in the fight against global terrorism.

Note that this is the narrative as best depicted by the NSPDSC and other official statements, but the message is far less coherent across the departments of government than is al-Qaida's.

WHAT IS STRATEGIC COMMUNICATIONS
AND WHY CAN'T WE DO IT?

According to the editor of the journal *Military Review*, Colonel William M. Darley—who happens to be the director of Strategic Communications at the Combined Arms Center, Fort Leavenworth—although we may now have the NSPDSC, that does not mean that it works. According to Darley,

Shockingly, almost 6 years after the attacks against the Twin Towers and Pentagon, a national-level process for organizing and conducting an effective, synchronized program aimed at countering enemy ideas is still not in place. Therefore, many observers both in and out of government are now expressing deep concern that the United States is losing both the global war of ideas against Islamic extremists and the war on terror itself.[5]

While we have become accustomed to members of the community of talking heads lambasting the administration for failing in its communications strategy, it is now clear that even inside the U.S. government and the armed forces there is open recognition of the lack of both substance and effective process in communicating the whys and wherefores of the Long War. There are therefore two obvious questions which follow: what is strategic communications, and why does the United States seem incapable of doing it in the current threat environment?

From our perspective, "strategic communications" is a catch-all phrase that has been overused, is little understood, and has lost essential meaning. In this regard it is closely related to public diplomacy, information operations, and psychological warfare.[6] All of the above, to a lesser or greater extent, are phrases that were invented to circumvent the opprobrium that became associated with the word propaganda in twentieth century, especially after World War I. Today, it is hard to identify exactly what each term refers to, which agency has the lead responsibly to execute particularly functions, how they differ from one another and how these concepts all differ from the classic, nonpejorative sense of propaganda and the related Cold War concept of political warfare.

According to U.S. Army officer Melanie Reeder, "communication is the link between what an organization intends to do and the understanding and support needed from particular groups and the general public to ensure the ultimate achievement of its program goals."[7] Additionally, she notes, "A strategic communication plan is a long term comprehensive plan to successfully communicate themes, messages, goals, and objectives of an overarching vision. *It is the means by which the strategy is articulated.*"[8]

This would seem to be a reasonable definition. If a strategy is the plan by which a nation's goals are related to the means at its disposal to achieve those goals, then strategic communications are the tools we use to garner support for that plan and the vision behind it, and the tools used to undermine an enemy's ability to obstruct us in achieving that vision. Subsequently, in order for the United States to have a workable strategic communications plan, it must be able to:

1. Define the end-state it wishes to achieve,
2. Define the enemy it wishes to defeat,
3. Identify the audiences for its strategic communication,
4. Identify realistic tools to communicate its goals to those audiences, and
5. Undermine the enemy's own strategic communications.

Let us take these first two requirements in turn. What is the end-state which the United States wishes to achieve? The first question is the easiest one to answer. Clearly, America wishes to destroy al-Qaida, or at the very least make it irrelevant, no longer a threat to its national security. But the second is seemingly more problematic.

The U.S. government has yet to clearly tell the world who it is fighting. Initially, with post-9/11 operations being launched against al-Qaida in Afghanistan and the fundamentalist Taliban regime, the enemy was understood as being the organization that had perpetrated the 9/11 attacks and the government that had provided it with safe haven. But then came the Iraqi invasion and the removal of Saddam Hussein. With this step, America communicated that the enemy included not just al-Qaida and those that harbored it but also any nations inimical to the United States which possessed (or were suspected of possessing) weapons of mass destruction (WMDs), and which could conceivably pass those weapons on to groups such as al-Qaida. Additionally, after the invasion resulted in sectarian violence within Iraq, America has identified Iraqi insurgents and foreign fighters as also part of the enemy kaleidoscope. On top of that, the administration has made it clear that any group which shares al-Qaida's extremist religiously fueled ideology is also to be counted with the enemy, as is any terrorist groups with global capabilities. Last, with its more recent joint activities in Africa, especially in the southern Sahel region, the government has targeted ungoverned areas which can be exploited by terrorist or insurgent groups.

Subsequently, through its actions and what it has said, the United States has defined its enemy as:

- al-Qaida,
- Groups that share al-Qaida's ideology,
- Insurgent groups and foreign fighters in Iraq,
- States that aid al-Qaida,
- States that could provide WMD capabilities to al-Qaida,
- Any terrorist group with a global network and capabilities,
- Ungoverned areas.

Sun Tzu, the ancient Asian strategist, advises that one must know one's enemy if one is to have a chance of defeating him. In this case the United States has described for itself a rather heterogeneous set of actors and conditions under the moniker of enemy. More problematic than the breadth of definition are the actors it omits, yet which by rights should be included given the original parameters.

It is now a matter of public record that Iran has been assisting insurgent fighters in Iraq. Saudi Arabia, founded as it was on the Wahhabi school of Islam, has been internationally propagating ideological materiel, especially in the form of the so-called Noble Qur'an that is used by fundamentalist imams the world over.[9] Similarly, the role of Pakistan in the further survival of al-Qaida, in particular with reference to the federally administered tribal areas bordering Afghanistan, cannot be dismissed. If the potential supply of WMD capability to al-Qaida and similar terror groups is part of the definition of the enemy, one cannot discount Pakistan, given the sentiments of certain members of its armed forces, intelligence services, and WMD scientists, nor can one exclude North Korea. Last, if extremist groups of global reach are all to be considered enemies, then one can reasonably ask when the United States will begin operations against Hizballah, Jemaah Islamiya, or even Hizb ut Tahrir, to name just three.

Even if one ignores all these secondary targets and stays purely with the top of the list, al-Qaida, then there remain definitional problems. Official guidance is confusing and often unclear. Is al-Qaida just an organization? Is it a network of like-minded groups? It is a franchise of unconnected but similar extremist organizations? Or has it become a global ideology, or even an insurgency on a global scale?[10]

It is clear that al-Qaida has been evolving over time. Started under another name, the Arab Service Bureau, a coordinating body and clearinghouse for Arab mujahideen fighting in Soviet-occupied Afghanistan, only after the first Gulf War did it become the globally dispersed terror group that would be responsible for the first Twin Towers attack of 1993, the East African embassy bombings, the USS *Cole* attack, and eventually 9/11. Nevertheless, we must be able to understand more deeply how al-Qaida has developed and changed over time—especially after the U.S. invasion of Afghanistan forced it into a new form of existence—if we are to stand a case of defeating it and in the process communicating to all observers why we are at war and what we wish to achieve.

It is not the purpose of this chapter to discuss at length what exactly post-9/11 al-Qaida is,[11] but it is important in relationship to the question of counter-strategies to know what al-Qaida is not. Al-Qaida is no longer a unitary organization; it is not—despite what the media would have us believe—a simple global network; and it is not an ideology in the sense of ideology that we are used to, since it is largely informed by religion; and last, it is misleading to portray it (as some commentators have) as some sort of franchise organization akin to a McDonalds (to truly be such a franchise it would need a functioning headquarters, a universally accepted end-state for all its members, and each unit would have to have exactly the same skill sets).

Al-Qaida proper is a tiny minority of a minority which has connected to it several groups around the world who self-associate with the image and rhetoric of al-Qaida but do so most often as a result of some local and far more limited goal they wish to achieve. This heterogeneous aspect of what we today misleadingly term al-Qaida is important.

The multifaceted nature of al-Qaida and its popularity can be illustrated with an anecdote. Several years into the GWOT, a colonel from Pakistani military counterintelligence commented to one of us that the most popular boys' name in his country in the previous 12 months was Osama. To this astonishing fact the author responded by asking, "Does this mean that bin Laden enjoys the popular support of most Pakistanis?" The colonel replied of course not, there is hardly anyone in his country who would in their right mind wish to live in a caliphate under the leadership of Osama bin Laden. Yet while the strategic aims that he espouses and the tools he uses are anathema to them, when bin Laden refers to issues such as the freedom of Palestine or the sanctity of Mecca and Medina, the colonel went on to say that many, many Pakistanis find these sentiments to be sympathetic. This is by far not an unusual attitude outside of Pakistan in other Muslim nations and communities. It is this form of cognitive dissonance that makes our understanding of al-Qaida so difficult and which differentiates it in a distinct fashion from the unified and centralized ideologies of the past such as Nazism, fascism, and communism.

What then is the model which will help us understand and then defeat al-Qaida? Fred Kagan of the American Enterprise Institute advises us to compare the al-Qaida of today with the Bolsheviks of the early 1900s prior to the Russian Revolution of 1917.[12] The analogy is a useful one given the fact that we can reasonably portray communism as a secular religion instigated by a tiny minority without the support of the millions of people the Bolsheviks said they were acting on behalf of. But instead of comparing al-Qaida with the prerevolutionary Bolsheviks, it may be more informative to understand our enemy as the equivalent of that tiny group of Bolshevik extremists at a point after 1917, after a failed attempt at revolution. In this way we can understand the original

Table 11.1   A Comparison of Messages and Reality

The Message of Osama bin Laden and al-Qaida	The Reality Behind the Message
Only the Islam we follow is true	There are numerous schools of Islam
The caliphate must be reestablished under Shari'a law	The vast majority of Muslims/Arabs do not wish to live in a fundamentalist caliphate modeled on
Islam is under attack	the Taliban regime
The West must be destroyed. There are no innocents.	There is no concerted effort by the nations of the developed Judeo-Christian world to destroy
Those who profess to be Muslim but disagree with us are kafir	Islam
	Al-Qaida cannot match the United States let alone destroy the West. There are no international norms or laws that permit the killing of unarmed civilians
	Bin Laden has no political or clerical credentials to make fatwas or exercise takfir

The Message of the United States and its Allies	The Reality Behind the Message
Al-Qaida is the threat to global peace and stability	Very few nations agree with the U.S. threat assessments, even within NATO
We wish to cooperate will all nations that denounce terrorism	Following 9/11 and to this day, the United States has taken a deciding unilateral approach to its
We stand for democracy and liberty	national security agenda
Regime change in Central Asia and Iraq will bring broader peace and stability	Several policy decisions and specific GWOT tactics have undermined rule of law, due process and international human rights norms
	It is at least unclear at the moment whether Afghanistan and Iraq can survive as functioning democracies, let alone whether this model will spread further in the respective regions

members of al-Qaida as totalitarian merchants of political violence who are now in hiding, who enjoy the permissive yet uninformed support of many, and whose significance or apparent size seems to increase as more and more local actors and groups self-associate with some of their ideas or beliefs.

At this point it may be useful to summarize the strategic communications of both sides in this conflict and compare what is being communicated with actual reality (see Table 11.1).

In both cases there are discrepancies. We cannot allow the discrepancies to persist on our side of this confrontation. Every instance in which we communicate a stance that is not reflected in reality represents a small victory for the enemy. Therefore we must rethink how our strategic communications are done and what their content should be.

HOW TO COMMUNICATE STRATEGICALLY (OR, IT'S HARD TO STRATEGICALLY COMMUNICATE WITHOUT A STRATEGY)

One of the more important reasons for the lack of an effective communications strategy on behalf of the United States is the lack of a clear and overarching strategy for the post-9/11 era. While we have been given first the GWOT and now the Long War, we are still looking for our generation's George Kennan who will write the new version of the Long Telegram, a document which can be used to formulate a doctrine on the strategic level of the Cold War's containment policy.[13] Without a strategic level doctrine it is very difficult to execute effective strategic communications.

At the same time we can learn much about how not to formulate a strategic communications plan by examining what has been provided already in the official documents despite the doctrinal vacuum. If we return to NSDPSC, we can see that a communications plan citing "America's commitment to freedom, human rights and the dignity and equality of every human being" is at odds with suspension of habeas corpus, extraordinary renditions, and the use of special detention facilities and interrogation techniques. Likewise stressing the fundamental need to "reach out to those who share our ideals" remains a useless core statement of communications policy if we cannot say what this means in real life. The same is true when we express our commitment to "counter those who espouse ideologies of hate and oppression." Do we mean this sincerely to apply to all people, even heads of state? And then, what does our intent to "support those who struggle for freedom and democracy" actually mean? Are we prepared to do this everywhere, from North Korea to Belarussia? If not, then we must either rephrase our strategic communications plan or risk it losing credibility immediately.

After World War II, our ability to effectively communicate what the stakes of the confrontation were, why America had to act and what we wished to achieve were much easier. This was due to several reasons. Communication is best when it clearly demonstrates values. After four years of engagement in a global war against a totalitarian enemy, America's values were clear. Likewise after 30 years of the Soviet Union, the values of the enemy were not obtuse or difficult to grasp. With the Berlin Blockade, the launch of *Sputnik*, and the first Soviet atomic test, it was clear that the game was one of survival, of Them or Us. The enemy was clearly an enemy; the United States knew what the enemy was capable of and what they wanted and, most important of all, the previous four years had shown the United States who we were. September 11 was different.

In the hazy days of post–Cold War peace dividends, since our enemy had been vanquished (or rather had become our "friend"), it was hard to remember what America and the West stood for. The attack itself came as a huge surprise. Despite the 1993 World Trade Center bombing, the USS *Cole*, attack and the embassy bombings, we did not appreciate the scale of the threat, the intention of the enemy or his true capabilities. Even after 9/11 we have been obstructed in our understanding of our foe by the fact that his motivation is not simply political or rational but is religiously informed and has nothing to do with the logic of nation-state behavior. It is thanks to this confusion that today when you ask someone anywhere in the world whom they associate with the word *caliphate* they will more often as not give the name of Osama bin Laden. If you ask the same person which person or country they associate with the words *democracy* or *liberty*, it is unlikely to be the United States. Not so long ago, neither statement would have been true.

How then to proceed? According to the aforementioned study by Lieutenant Colonel Reeder, a strategic communication plan must be designed to:

- Define the threat,
- Inform and educate,
- Promote support for policies, programs, and actions,
- Counter myths, misconceptions, rumors, and misinformation,
- Persuade or call to action,
- Serve as a tool to identify and allocate resources,
- Provide personnel within the organization a reference guide of coherent and consistent messages.[14]

Above all, it must do this in a way that clearly demonstrates to the audience the positive values that are the foundation for our system of government and which inform and guide our actions both domestically and abroad. Our policies cannot contravene these core values.

To simplify matters, and given the urgency of the task, we can boil the above down into three fundamental questions the United States and its allies must answer if they are to have any chance of building a coherent strategic communications platform which can delegitimize al-Qaida. These are:

1. Who is the enemy? The answer to this question should be short and simple.
2. Who are we? What do we believe in and what do we stand for as a nation and what we require of others nations that hold themselves to be part of the community of peace-loving and freedom-loving countries?
3. What are the core values which inform our behavior and our policies and which are not negotiable?

Given the weakness of communications to date, we would suggest one additional twist. At the moment it would be a waste to spend significantly more money on trying to make the United States or the "West" look good in the eyes of non-Western audiences. This will most likely come when we are judged by our actions. Instead we should focus on making the enemy look bad. For example, how is it that a man without any clerical qualifications issues fatwas and why is it that since 9/11 al-Qaida has been responsible for the death of far more Muslims than Westerners? This is how one can delegitimize and marginalize bin Laden.

There is, however, one last point which all the discussion of strategic communications in the past seven years has omitted. While it is true that we were much better at strategic communications (or rather propaganda and political warfare) during the Cold War, there is a very important reason for his. When America established tools such as Voice of America, Radio Liberty, and Radio Free Europe, it was targeting a completely different audience. For the most part, the citizens of the captive nations behind the Iron Curtain were not staunch communists who had to be converted through these broadcasts. The people of Hungary, Poland, East Germany, the Baltic states, and so on believed in democracy and longed to be free. They did not tune into our federally funded stations because they wanted to be converted to our value system. They were already on our side and simply wanted access to information denied them by their illegitimate masters. This is not the case today. Yesterday the audience was with us but captive. Today the audience may be suffering under a less than democratic regime or an authoritarian government, but that does not mean they are necessarily on our side. In the Cold War it may have been about winning "hearts and minds" but today we are in the era of having to win "hearts and souls."

ACKNOWLEDGMENTS

The views expressed in the chapter are those of the authors and do not purpose to reflect the official policy or position of any department or agency of the U.S. government.

NOTES

1. *Military Studies in the Jihad Against the Tyrants/The Al-Qaeda Training Manual*, edited by Jerrold M. Post with a preface by Amb. Paul Bremer, USAF Counterproliferation Center, Maxwell Air Force Base, Alabama, 2004, p. 13.

2. The early land campaign of the first Gulf War provides a perfect example of U.S. will exerted successfully on the enemy, as tens of thousands of Iraqi troops deserted and surrendered to Coalition Forces in the first 100 hours of battle.

3. Declaration of War against the American Occupying the Land of the Two Holy Places.

4. *U.S. National Strategy for Public Diplomacy and Strategic Communication, Strategic Communication and Public Diplomacy*, Policy Coordinating Committee (PCC), June 2007, p. 1.

5. W. M. Darley, "The Missing Component of U.S. Strategic Communications," *Joint Forces Quarterly*, Issue 47, 4th quarter, 2007, National Defense University Press.

6. Please see the introduction to this volume for definitions of these and other related terms.

7. Lt. Col. Melanie Reeder, *The Strategic Communications Plan: Effective Communication for Strategic Leaders*, Strategy Research Project, U.S. Army War College, Carlisle, PA, 1998, p. iii.

8. Ibid, p. 3; emphasis added. Compare this definition to definitions for "public diplomacy" and "psychological warfare." A phrase supposedly first coined by U.S. diplomat Edmund Gullion, according to the State Department, "Public Diplomacy seeks to promote the national interest of the United States through understanding, informing and influencing foreign audiences." While psychological warfare consists of "activities, other than physical combat, which communicate ideas and information intended to affect the mind, emotions, and actions of the enemy, for the purpose of disrupting his morale and his will to fight." Both quoted in N. J. Cull et al,. *Propaganda and Mass Persuasion, a Historical Encyclopedia, 1500 to the Present*, ABC-CLIO, Santa Barbara, 2003.

9. Officially distributed during the annual Hajj to English-speaking pilgrims visiting Mecca. The Noble Qur'an, aka the Hilali-Khan translation, King Fahd Publishers, Saudi Arabia.

10. For a discussion of the question of what al-Qaida is, see S. L. v. Gorka, "Al Qaeda and von Clausewitz—Rediscovering the Art of War," presentation to the First Annual Symposium: Countering Global Insurgency, US Joint Special Operations University, Hurlburt Field, Florida, May 5, 2006, available at http://www.itdis.org. For a discussion of al-Qaida as global insurgency, see David Kilcullen, "Countering Global Insurgency," *Journal of Strategic Studies*, 28, no. 4, August 2005, and "Three Pillars of Counterinsurgency," remarks delivered at the U.S. Government Counterinsurgency Conference, September 28, 2006, Washington, http://www.usgcoin.org/docs1/3PillarsOfCounterinsurgency.pdf.

11. For more details, see S. L. v. Gorka, "Al Qaeda's Next Generation," Jamestown Foundation, *Terrorism Monitor*, Vol. 2, Issue 15, June 29, 2004, http://chechnya.jamestown.org/images/pdf/ter_002_015.pdf.

12. See Fred Kagan, *The New Bolsheviks: Understanding Al Qaeda, National Security Outlook*, American Enterprise Institute, November 16, 2005, www.aei.org/publications/pubID.23460/pub_detail.asp.

13. The Council for Emerging National Security Affairs recently compiled a survey of national security practitioners and academics judging the various potential doctrines that have already been penned but have not yet won universal adoption by the administration. For details see "The Search for Mr. X" at http://www.censa.net.

14. Reeder, *The Strategic Communications Plan*, pp. 5–6.

Uncover
uses

uctive hypermedia"[1] for terrorists, with official and
chat rooms that appeal to their extremist supporters
tended to advance a group's propaganda in order to
while some have operational missions.

It is not only terrorists who benefit from cyberspace. The widespread use of the Internet by terrorist groups and their supporters also offers myriad opportunities for the counterterrorism community to monitor and track their activities, pronouncements, and discussions in cyberspace, so as to gather intelligence information about their motivations, agendas, and ongoing and future warfare activities. Although it falls below the threshold of terrorist warfare per se, such monitoring also provides an opportunity to understand the root causes driving terrorist warfare.

Thus, the counterterrorism community can track terrorists' use of the Internet to uncover insights about their mindset, communications, information gathering, training and education, fund-raising, operational planning, command and control, publicity and propaganda, and the messages and methods they employ to radicalize and recruit potential operatives. In addition, "official" postings on their Web sites—as well as discussions in their forums and chat rooms—also provide information about some of the root causes driving their grievances, ambitions, and other factors that motivate them to conduct terrorist activities.

This chapter's objective is to provide a methodology to enable counterterrorism analysts to hierarchically decompose the underlying factors driving a terrorist insurgency. Such an analysis would focus on the content of official terrorist Web sites and their accompanying forums and chat rooms, in order to formulate appropriate responses—whether coercive or conciliatory—that will be capable of resolving such conflicts.

ROOT CAUSES OF INSURGENCIES

Terrorism is a type of insurgent warfare by subnational groups against the state. Groups are driven to commit acts of terrorism, in which they target innocent civilians or armed military, by a spectrum of motivations.[3] These include real or perceived grievances, psychological dispositions, ambitions, and other factors. Terrorism does not emerge in a vacuum, but is the product of a confluence or coalescence of factors, whether in the societies where terrorist groups originate or in those of their targeted adversaries. Terrorism is not necessarily the product of a single causal factor, but is often rather a convergence of many interrelated factors and causes. These causes vary from one conflict to another and change dynamically over time.

One must also consider how new sets of underlying causes that emerge over time sustain a terrorist insurgency. It is important to analyze all of these underlying factors, because, at least in theory, addressing such factors or drivers would solve problems that have identifiable root causes. Uproot the cause and the problem is solved. By contrast, leave the roots intact and the terrorism problem will persist.

Nevertheless, it must be recognized that due to a variety of factors,[4] some root causes may be resolvable through conciliatory measures, such as a negotiated settlement, while others may only be resolvable through continued military means.

As mentioned, root causes are not static but are dynamic and constantly changing. In fact, even when a government begins to address what it considers to be the primary root cause underlying a conflict, it is always possible for the terrorist group to claim that another (yet unresolved) root cause needs to be attended to. Thus, to attain a complete picture of the underlying causes driving an insurgency, it is crucial to examine them at levels that are both general and specific. These levels include the individual, group, societal, and governmental levels.

At the individual level, moreover, different root causes influence different types of operatives within a terrorist group, including their supporters. Thus, different drivers may influence members of a group's combat unit and its supporting "civilian" infrastructure. Such key members include those responsible for funding and logistical arrangements, as well as individuals who sympathize with a group's cause, and whose views can be gleaned from their Internet discussions.

Root causes also need to be examined and synthesized from the divergent points of view of the insurgents, the targeted governments, and academic researchers, the latter of whom may offer a more objective and independent assessment of such underlying drivers.

Any conceptual framework designed to explain the causes underlying a terrorist insurgency needs to overcome what Marc Sageman calls the "problem of specificity."[5] While it may be possible to identify some of the necessary conditions for such outbreaks, Sageman argues that "such an approach is overly broad and leads to the fundamental problem of specificity. Many people share the identified characteristics of such an analysis, but very few become terrorists. What accounts for this vast difference?"[6]

Thus, the first step is to resolve these theoretical and empirical issues regarding the correlation of factors characteristic of aggrieved populations (or populations that perceive themselves to be aggrieved) and factors characteristic of those who ultimately become terrorists. Thereafter, a conceptual framework can be applied to investigate how terrorist-related Web sites can reveal the underlying conditions of specific conflicts. Such an examination should take into account the factors driving terrorists to attack particular adversaries, and their choice or use of particular weapons in such warfare.

The framework proposed here for understanding the root causes of terrorist insurgencies is based on seven interrelated steps, presented in successive order.

TOWARD A CONCEPTUAL FRAMEWORK

First, one needs to identify a terrorist insurgency's "physical" and "virtual" manifestations. These take the form of a spectrum of activities on the ground, ranging from the type of terrorist warfare being waged against a targeted country (or community) to political warfare (e.g., increasing a group's supporting constituency). Types of physical warfare include, for example, the use of tactics involving conventional low impact, conventional high impact, or chemical, biological, radiological, and nuclear (CBRN) weapons and devices.[7] Political warfare includes radicalization and recruitment of operatives from supporting communities, including mosques, schools, community centers, prisons, and other facilities.

In the Internet's virtual space, evidence of political warfare can be found in terrorist-related Web sites, forums, and chat rooms, where a group's propaganda is intended to radicalize supporters, recruit new members, and maintain a high level of mobilization. Interestingly, cyberspace provides terrorist groups with unlimited geographical reach, unconstrained by national borders, enabling them to reach audiences around the world instantaneously. This is particularly important for terrorists—like al-Qaida—whose ideology transcends nation-state boundaries, as well as for groups whose ideology appeals to a broadly dispersed diaspora community.

Within this virtual space, as explained by Gabriel Weimann, terrorists "narrow-cast" their messages to "trap" selected audiences of adherents.[8] Taking this further, according to Boaz Ganor, the "captured" adherents are then indoctrinated and radicalized by emphasizing a problem, such as threats posed by a common enemy or humiliation suffered by Muslims at the hands of their adversaries.[9] Among Islamist extremists, emphasizing the religious obligation of Muslims to confront their enemies and the challenge to their faith is a common denominator that binds the audience into their new virtual community. Similar aspects of duty and obligation are prominent among Tamils, Chechens, and other nonreligiously oriented terrorists as well. The official Web site of the Sri Lankan Liberation Tigers of Tamil Eelam (at http://www.ltteps.org), for example, highlights what they consider to be "the long history of deception by the chauvinistic Sinhala State" and the duty of "the global Tamil community to support the Tamil Eelam freedom struggle."[10] Segments of the sympathetic community are then activated into a variety of activities on behalf of the terrorist group, such as fund-raising, recruitment, training, and warfare.

For each of these physical and virtual manifestations, a root cause would then be identified. For example, in terms of an insurgency's physical manifestations, one would attempt to identify the root causes that would justify the rationale for a group to embark on conventional low impact, conventional high impact, or CBRN warfare, or "conventional" versus suicide martyrdom tactics in order to achieve its strategic objectives.

Second, a terrorist insurgency's ideological drivers need to be identified. Ideas— and in the contemporary period, especially radical religious ideologies—are among the major drivers that mobilize individuals and groups into committing acts of terrorism and provide them with a cultural and religious underpinning and guide for action.

The problems facing individuals whose societies are transitioning from traditional to modern ways of life are an important determinant of terrorist insurgencies. This is a particular concern with terrorist groups that espouse fundamentalist religious ideologies. The drive toward modernization produces socioeconomic and political dislocations in society, and individuals are left to cope with the challenges ushered in by modernization. This change fosters the rise of new elites, who represent democratization, secularization, industrialization, and technocracy. These elite individuals emerge into positions of influence, replacing their more traditional counterparts. This changeover results in a series of conflicts between the advocates and opponents of modernity.

According to Arie Kruglanski, radical ideologies appeal to individuals experiencing psychological uncertainty because such ideologies are "formulated in clear-cut, definitive terms" and provide "cognitive closure."[11] Thus, among those who cling to traditional religious values and ways of life, some will respond by espousing revivalist ideologies that promote resentment and even xenophobia toward those who believe in the benefits of modernity. Often, this perceived opponent includes foreigners, especially as represented by Western Europe and the United States. Such revivalist ideologies—which affect not only Muslim societies but Christian and Jewish ones as well—promote a vision that advocates restoration of their own societies to a state of religious "purity," which supposedly existed in previous centuries. These kinds of revivalist movements provide fertile ground for the support of and recruitment into terrorist organizations.

Internet Web sites can be monitored to learn about such radical mindsets, motives, persuasive buzzwords, audiences, operational plans, and potential targets for attack. Monitoring also reveals their inner debates and disputes, as demonstrated by Gabriel Weimann's chapter in this volume.

Thus, in examining terrorist Web sites and accompanying chat rooms, it is important to identify the ideologies, whether political or religious, that motivate their adherents to embark on terrorism. For example, the Palestinian Hamas is driven by a combination of Palestinian nationalism and Muslim Brotherhood ideologies; al-Qaida and its affiliated groups are influenced by salafi-jihadi ideologies; the Provisional IRA, during its prime, was motivated by a blend of Irish Catholic nationalism and certain socioeconomic beliefs; and Kahane (an ultra-right-wing Jewish extremist group) is influenced by the racist, anti-Arab ideology of its founder, the late Rabbi Meir Kahane, as articulated on the group's Web site, http://kahane.org. On these groups' Web sites, their ideologies are represented by what the groups consider to be their traditional religious, historical, or secular nationalistic symbols.

Third, it is crucial to examine the structural preconditions underlying a terrorist insurgency. According to Gus Martin, structural preconditions "focus on social conditions ('structures') that affect group access to services, equal rights, civil protections, freedom, or other quality-of-life measures."[12] Examples of structural preconditions include government policies, actions by security forces, access (or lack thereof) by a local population to social institutions, and so on.[13] The state or government is the key focus in structural theories of terrorism, because of its role in serving as the precipitating factor for a terrorist uprising. According to this theory, societal injustice, popular discontent, the alienation of elites, and a sense of societal crisis are key ingredients for a terrorist eruption in society.[14]

In addition to such structural preconditions which depend on the central role of the state and its instruments of power in causing terrorist rebellions, other preconditions depend on the confluence of factors below the state level. Relative deprivation theory, which was developed by Ted Robert Gurr, focuses on the relationship between frustration and aggression.[15] As applied to the terrorism milieu, according to Gurr, feelings of frustration and anger underlie individual decisions to engage in collective action against the perceived source of their frustration and constitute one of the necessary conditions for joining a terrorist group. The motive for such individuals to engage in political violence is a perception that they are *relatively* deprived, vis-à-vis other groups, in an unjust social order. When rising expectations are met by governmental resistance in the form of sustained political repression, low-ranking socioeconomic or political status, or lack of educational opportunities, a group is likely to turn to political violence.

As a corollary to relative deprivation, absolute deprivation theory holds that when a group has been deprived of the basic necessities for survival by a government or social order (which includes being subjected to physical abuse, poverty, or starvation), it turns to political violence.[16] Thus, the difference between relative and absolute deprivation is based on the degree of discrepancy experienced by an individual or group. Absolute deprivation is the discrepancy between what people have and what they need for daily sustenance, while relative deprivation refers to what they have versus what they believe they deserve vis-à-vis others in society. Both types of deprivation are capable of driving those believing themselves to be aggrieved into carrying out acts of political violence.

Moving from these general theories to more specific indicators of terrorist outbreaks, there are underlying structural factors that need to be examined at the societal, group, and individual levels. At the societal level, countries that are vulnerable to terrorism are those which experience economic and social inequality, poverty, low levels of social services, a lack of political or civil rights, low literacy rates and a lack of education, and ethnic conflict. These factors are likely to serve as springboards for terrorism, or at least some manifestation of active discontent that may fall below the threshold of violence.

The group level of analysis intervenes between the societal and individual levels. Thus, at the group level, agents of mobilization—such as charismatic leaders or radical movements and their political and religious ideologies—serve as causal factors for terrorist outbreaks. At the individual level, susceptibility to radicalization and actual recruitment into terrorist organizations are additional causal factors. The ecological framework for examining terrorist insurgencies therefore comprises at least three levels—individual, group, and societal, with additional explanatory value provided by theories at more general levels.

As demonstrated by these approaches, no single theory or structural (or substructural) factor provides a sufficient explanation for terrorism. Links between poverty, lack of education, and other socioeconomic variables—including the clash between tradition and modernity—and terrorism, are complex, as are the links between state repression, lack of political opportunities, and terrorism. Other political factors may also contribute to terrorism, such as the ability of terrorist groups to exploit political disorder or a lack of political order in weak or failed states. At other times, however, groups may actually receive political support from governments, such as support by the Iranian and Syrian governments to the Lebanese Hizballah.

Theories or models for understanding terrorism therefore need to focus on the causal mechanisms or processes in which multiple factors, working together in specific social and other contexts, influence and drive terrorist insurgencies. Causal mechanisms alone are insufficient to bring about a terrorist insurgency; another intervening variable is crucial to initiating such an outbreak.

In this fourth interrelated step, certain types of enablers—in the form of leaders, radical subcultures, and susceptible individuals—are necessary to mobilize and empower a disaffected population to embark on a terrorist insurgency.

While effective leadership traits may be contextually dependent,[17] certain management traits are necessary for an effective terrorist leader. Leaders with charismatic personalities are able to transform grievances and frustrations into a political agenda for violent action, radicalize supporters, and recruit and mobilize operatives to sacrifice their lives for the cause. They also attract a coterie of dedicated and capable associates to help manage and sustain the group, as well as imposing strict discipline over the rest of the group.

An extremist group's Web sites can be used to identify and locate their political and religious authorities, propagandists, chat room discussion moderators, and active participants, as well as moderate religious clerics and other figures they regard as particularly threatening.

Radical subcultures are another crucial enabler in driving a terrorist insurgency, through the provision of new operatives. The relationship between terrorist groups and their sympathizer and support communities can be viewed as a pyramid, with the terrorist groups at the apex and the sympathizers and supporters at the base. The higher levels of the pyramid are characterized by increasing levels of mobilization, commitment, and engagement in terrorist activities. For a terrorist group to grow and sustain itself over time, it requires a continuous and ever-expanding connection to the larger pyramid for support, and a pool of recruits to replace operatives who are arrested or killed in action. Terrorist groups could not survive without community support, which is often based on ethnic or religious ties.

In addition, radical subcultures, whether they exist in immigrant communities or prisons, can be termed "susceptible" or "feeder communities," because of the ease with which they can be infiltrated by terrorist movements for potential recruits and supporters.

Susceptible individuals constitute another type of enabler. For example, using social network analysis, Marc Sageman found that a significant proportion of terrorists who join the global salafi-jihadist movement are drawn into such groups by social bonds. Some are linked through marriage and family connections, and others through friendships acquired at a local mosque. He argues that such social interactions are a crucial factor in explaining why, for example, upwardly mobile, middle-class, and yet lonely and disaffected men turn to certain mosques, where they become radicalized and recruited into terrorism. For other individuals, such as Muhammad Atta (one of the 9/11 operatives), after leaving their home country in the Middle East to be educated in West, religion provides them with a means to find friends, gain a sense of spiritual fulfillment, and restore their sense of self.[18]

The fifth interrelated step in causing a terrorist insurgency or influencing the decision to carry out major attacks are precipitants in the form of triggering events. Such events might include outrageous acts committed by a group's adversary; political failure (e.g., the breakdown of the June 2000 Camp David negotiations was used as a pretext for instigating violence); certain provocative events (e.g., Ariel Sharon's visit to the Temple Mount in Jerusalem on September 28, 2000); the publication of controversial cartoons, or an Internet site, such as the controversial Dutch politician's Geert Wilders's http://www.fitnathemovie.com that features strong criticism of the Qur'an. There are other types of events which can act as precipitants, too, and they inevitably receive extensive coverage in terrorist-related Web sites.

Terrorist insurgencies also persist over time. In the sixth step, it is crucial to examine the factors that sustain such outbreaks over time.[19] These factors include unresolved root causes that continue to drive the insurgency—new and different factors that have little or nothing to do with the initial root causes. These include cycles of revenge, the need for a group to provide for its members or for the survival of the group itself, profitable criminal activities, and a feeling by a group's operatives that they have no choice but to continue with their armed struggle because it offers the only alternative to imprisonment or death at the hands of the authorities.

In the seventh step, in ideal cases, it is hoped that the previous six steps of mapping a conflict's root causes will produce the knowledge and insight on the part of governments to formulate appropriate responses to terrorism. Decisions must be made regarding which response would be most effective in terminating a terrorist insurgency, whether peacefully, militarily, or through a combination of such measures. By incorporating an understanding of a conflict's underlying causes into a government's "combating terrorism" campaign,[20] such response strategies and tactics can be effectively calibrated to address the specific challenges and threats.

CONCLUSION

Addressing a conflict's root causes may not necessarily or automatically lead to conflict termination. First, there may not always be a direct correlation between a specific root cause and a terrorist rebellion, because of the myriad alternative forms of action, ranging from nonviolent to violent, that may be available to a group to express its underlying grievances and demands. In fact, a terrorist movement is likely to occur only when certain significant propitious circumstances—in the form of political, economic, social, military, and other underlying trends—coincide and coalesce. But even these trends may not be sufficient to launch such rebellions, unless they are buttressed by the availability of effective leaders, organizational formations (including a willing cadre), access to particular types of weaponry, and the logistical and other covert capabilities necessary to carry out an operation against an adversary.

Second, root causes should not be viewed as necessarily static. Some of the root causes that might play a significant role in the initial phase of a conflict may later on become peripheral, whereas other root causes may emerge as paramount at a later phase in a conflict.

Once the spectrum of a conflict's underlying root causes are mapped and identified—initially, in most cases, at the academic level, and then at the governmental level—it will be up to governments and their security and military organizations to formulate the appropriate response measures to resolve these underlying problems and combat terrorism.

To counteract the strategic influence efforts of jihadi Web sites, for example, a government's actions must ceaselessly anticipate and respond to the reactions of the targeted terrorist Web sites. For instance, when a site is brought down, it usually reemerges in a different configuration elsewhere. Moreover, we need to prioritize the audiences to be targeted by such influence campaigns. For example, devoted activists may be considered a lost cause, while potential recruits who have not yet been activated into terrorism represent new opportunities for influence operations.

Such influence campaigns must be led by moderate political and religious leaders from Islamic communities who can formulate alternative messages and narratives to the radical Islamic ideologies. Here, further differentiation is required because, for example, mainstream Islam in the Middle East will be different than its counterparts in Southeast Asia or Europe. It is crucial that whatever is being communicated must be as authentically Islamic and as close to the "ground" truth as possible. It is here that the root causes underlying the problems that the radical Islamists are exploiting for their own purposes must be resolved.

For the underlying factors to be resolved, however, it is also up to the insurgents to incorporate into their demands grievances and other objectives that are amenable to the give and take of compromise and negotiations. Otherwise, even addressing a conflict's root causes may not succeed in terminating the insurgency.

Hopefully, the seven-step framework offered in this chapter provides a methodology for counterterrorism analysts to derive insight from the content and discussions on terrorist Web sites and their accompanying chat rooms. This insight would focus on the underlying factors driving the terrorist insurgencies that are being promoted by the relevant sponsoring groups. With terrorist groups and their supporters increasingly resorting to cyberspace to establish their "virtual" communities (while continuing to operate in "physical" space), the Internet provides an important medium to glean valuable information. This information pertains to both the underlying causes driving terrorist insurgencies, as well as the measures that are necessary to terminate them.

NOTES

1. The term "seductive hypermedia" is drawn from Boaz Ganor et al., editors, *Hypermedia Seduction for Terrorist Recruiting* (Lancaster, U.K.: IOS Press, 2007). This chapter is a revised and updated version of the author's chapter in Ganor's edited volume.

2. For a comprehensive discussion of terrorists' use of the Internet, see Gabriel Weimann, *Terrorism and the Internet* (Washington, DC: U.S. Institute of Peace, 2006).

3. In my definition of terrorism, groups that engage in such tactics target both noncombatant civilians and the armed military as part of their insurgency to strike terror at their adversary in order to achieve their political objectives. One can make the claim that a definition of terrorism should be restricted to cover attacks only against noncombatant civilians, while attacks against the armed military should constitute guerrilla warfare, but such clear-cut distinctions tend to obscure the full spectrum of operations that terrorist groups conduct. On the other hand, perhaps a comprehensive definition of terrorism should include a guerrilla component, since many of today's terrorist groups also engage in various types of guerrilla operations.

4. For initial examinations of root causes, see Walter Reich, editor, *Origins of Terrorism: Psychologies, Ideologies, Theologies, States of Mind* (Washington, DC: Woodrow Wilson Center Press, 1998); and Tore Bjorgo, editor, *Root Causes of Terrorism* (New York: Routledge, 2005).

5. Marc Sageman, "Threat Convergence: The Future of Terrorism Research" unpublished paper prepared for the workshop on "Threat Convergence: Possible New Pathways to Proliferation— Terrorism, Weapons of Mass Destruction, and Weak and Failing States," April 7, 2006, Washington, DC; cited by permission.

6. Ibid.

7. In this framework, *conventional low impact* refers to the use of conventional means to cause relatively few casualties; *conventional high impact* to the use of conventional means to cause catastrophic damages, such as crashing airliners into the World Trade Center towers; and *chemical, biological, radiological or nuclear* (CBRN) warfare to the use of "unconventional" means to inflict mass casualties (although chemical and radiological devices may also cause a relatively low number of casualties). This is not intended to be a rigid trichotomy, and it is possible for groups to use a combination of these types of weapons and devices in their warfare.

8. Weimann had elaborated on his notion of "narrowcasting" at a NATO Advanced Research Workshop that was held in Eilat, Israel, in mid-September 2006, which led to the publication of the Ganor et al. edited volume on *Hypermedia Seduction*. Weimann had kindly permitted me to cite his notion in Joshua Sinai, "Defeating Internet Terrorists," *Washington Times*, October 8, 2006.

9. Ganor's notion was elaborated on at the NATO Advanced Research Workshop.

10. Ibid.

11. Arie Kruglianski, "Inside the Terrorist Mind," paper presented to the National Academy of Science annual meeting, Washington, DC, April 29, 2002.

12. Gus Martin, *Understanding Terrorism: Challenges, Perspectives, and Issues* (Thousand Oaks, CA: SAGE, 2003), p. 67. Martin based his analysis on the works of Steven E. Barkan and Lynne L. Snowden, *Collective Violence* (Boston: Allyn & Bacon, 2001) and Jack A. Goldstone, "Introduction: The Comparative and Historical Study of Revolutions," in Jack A. Goldstone, editor, *Revolutions: Theoretical, Comparative, and Historical Studies* (San Diego, CA: Harcourt Brace Jovanovich, 1986).

13. Ibid.

14. Ibid., p. 68.

15. Ted Robert Gurr, *Why Men Rebel* (Princeton, NJ: Princeton University Press, 1970).

16. See Charles Y. Glock, "The Role of Deprivation in the Origin and Evolution of Religious Groups," in R. Lee and M. E. Marty, editors, *Religion and Social Conflict*, (New York: Oxford University Press, 1964), pp. 24–36.

17. John Horgan, "The Search for the Terrorist Personality," in Andrew Silke, editor, *Terrorists, Victims and Society: Psychological Perspectives on Terrorism and its Consequences* (New York: John Wiley & Sons, 2003), pp. 3–27.

18. Marc Sageman, *Understanding Terror Networks* (Philadelphia: University of Pennsylvania Press, 2004).

19. The discussion of factors responsible for sustaining a terrorist insurgency is based on Tore Bjorgo, "Introduction," in Tore Bjorgo, editor, *Root Causes of Terrorism* (New York: Routledge, 2005).

20. *Combating terrorism* is an umbrella concept incorporating antiterrorism, which is defensively oriented, and counterterrorism, which is offensively oriented.

PART III

CASE STUDIES
OF
STRATEGIC INFLUENCE

13

U.S. Strategic Communication Efforts during the Cold War

Daniel Baracskay

THE COLD WAR REFERS TO the period in international relations when two antagonistic superpowers, the United States and the former Soviet Union, dominated politics in the global arena. Characterized by tension and distrust, an ideological divide emerged at the close of the Second World War and lasted until 1990. It symbolized decades of an enduring rivalry for global power and dominance, affecting the politics and affairs of industrialized and developing states on every continent.[1] The policies, communication modes, and strategies of the two superpowers became components of a contest between the geopolitical territories distinguished as the East and West.

This chapter explores the chronology of American and Soviet communication strategies during the Cold War era, with particular emphasis on their effects on the developing world. Traditionally, strategic communication efforts have been intimately linked to foreign policies. With technological advancements in the twentieth century, communication modes became distinctly institutionalized in the United States and former Soviet Union, as well as in other industrialized states. In democratically governed nations, communication strategies consisted of a combination of public and private sector organizations. For instance, the Voice of America (VOA) and United States Information Agency (USIA) were both created from congressional mandates in the mid-twentieth century to oversee communication strategies and to collaborate with private sector media outlets in the transmission of American broadcasts. In communist states, media outlets were collectively controlled by authoritarian regimes that utilized communications to globally expand Marxist-Leninist doctrines and to counteract the prodemocracy movement. Both blocs competed for influence over the policies of developing states on every continent. This chapter explores these developments in greater detail and concludes by examining several implications of this analysis.

THE IDEOLOGICAL PATH TOWARD THE COLD WAR: THE SUBSTANCE OF STRATEGIC COMMUNICATIONS

The second half of the twentieth century was classified as a bipolar system where the United States and Union of Soviet Socialist Republics (USSR) dominated world politics.[2] The Soviet government promoted communist imperialism worldwide, while the United States used communication modes to weaken Marxist-Leninist doctrines and support a prodemocracy movement. This Cold War occurred after World War II, transforming the United States into what some have called a "national security state."[3]

The Cold War signified an end to the toleration that had typified U.S.–Soviet relations from 1918 until 1945.[4] World War I had left Russia in a state of disarray, draining valuable natural and economic resources. Social upheaval tore at the core of the country as Russian citizens protested the absolutist regime which had dominated for three centuries. Tsar Nicholas II was forced to abdicate his post and a provisional government was established. The Bolsheviks, a radical socialist faction led by Vladimir Ilyich Lenin, emerged to lead the efforts of Russian revolutionaries.[5] Lenin was a follower of Karl Marx's theories, and had used them in his own writings as a guide for Russia's development. In a coup d'état, Lenin's Bolshevik supporters took control of the Winter Palace in October 1917,[6] installing communism as Russia's new guiding order and political ideology.

The Bolshevik regime under Lenin held socialism to be the answer to the pressing social, economic, and political problems that existed under the old tsarist system. The Bolsheviks also envisioned their doctrines as a countermovement that would eventually collapse what was considered the shaky capitalist system of the West and advance a worldwide revolution.[7] The inevitability of this global revolution would occur gradually by spreading communist doctrine from continent to continent, state to state via communication channels, with a particular focus on developing countries. The imperialism of procommunist doctrines by the former Soviet Union in the East contrasted with the procapitalist doctrines of the United States in the West.[8]

While formal communication strategies in the Soviet Union were developed and implemented before World War II, they were relatively unsophisticated. Further, the Soviet government was in a state of flux despite the Bolsheviks' efforts to propagate Marxist doctrines throughout Russian society. The stability of the new republic was uncertain and particularly challenged when a series of strokes led to Lenin's death in 1924, causing an internal power struggle among the Bolsheviks for control of the country. From this struggle, Josef Stalin[9] succeeded Lenin. Despite this leadership change, as Daniel Papp observes, Lenin's "theories of imperialism and colonialism remained the basis for Soviet discussions of Western-colonial and Western-developing world relations."[10] Stalin was the Commissar for Nationality Affairs and a leading Bolshevik theoretician in Russia. He applied his scholarship to issues related to nationalism and revolution, and further developed Lenin's ideas of spreading communism through numerous communication outlets across the globe.[11]

While Lenin was considered a vibrant theorist and strategist whose writings closely paralleled the traditions of Marx, Stalin was perceived as a shrewd, strong-willed pragmatist with stellar administrative skills.[12] Stalin bolstered the development of the Soviet state through a series of plans designed to transform the rural economy.[13] However, his strategies to spread communism worldwide were hindered by the growing tensions of Adolph Hitler's Nazi regime in Germany, which drove the international arena toward conflict and World War II.[14] With Nazi Germany being staunchly anticommunist and hostile to the USSR, the Soviet government rationally joined the Allied Forces after the German invasion of Russian territory. The Potsdam Conference, convened at the conclusion of World War II, left a perceptible East–West divide as procommunist forces rivaled the prodemocracy movement, signaling the continuation of ideological conflict and the start of the Cold War. A speech by Stalin in February 1946 concerned American foreign policy experts in Washington, D.C. The State Department cabled the U.S. embassy in Moscow for information on Stalin's intentions. George Kennan received the cable, and drafted an 8,000-word response which he then cabled back to the State Department. That notorious cable, known as the Long Telegram, became the catalyst for a shift in American perceptions on the Soviet Union and the evolution toward what became a policy of "containment" during the Cold War around which communication strategies revolved.[15] The Long Telegram foreshadowed the imminent rivalry between democracy and communism and stressed the zeal that Stalin and other communist leaders had in spreading Marxist-Leninist doctrines.

This ideological contrast created an intense U.S.–Soviet rivalry and became the basis for Cold War communication strategies between the two superpowers. In the aftermath of World War II, the Soviet Union was in ruins. Twenty-seven million Soviet citizens had lost their lives, and thousands of cities and villages were destroyed. Yet the Red Army remained strong and became the largest military force in the world.[16] Stalin's attention after the war shifted toward establishing a buffer around Russian borders so that the invasion of Soviet territory which had occurred during World War II could not be repeated in the future. His attention also shifted toward suppressing internal opposition and promoting the spread of communism nationally. These strategies paved the way for his vision of a worldwide revolution. The internal resistance movement that opposed communist doctrines was eradicated by the actions of the secret police, as millions were forced into labor camps or killed. Stalin had perceived capitalism and pro-Western ideologies as the driving forces behind the war, even though he was forced to side with the Allies to prevent Nazi Germany from being victorious in Russian territories. The United States had suffered casualties from the Japanese raid on Pearl Harbor, but was otherwise left intact as a great industrial power. Its economy had grown substantially from wartime production, and research and development during the war led to the introduction of new communication technologies that could be used during the Cold War.

The contrast in political ideologies between the United States and Soviet Union caused an escalation of tensions between the two superpowers. With the advancement of technology, this tension was exacerbated as the strategic communication policies of the two antagonists were channeled into an intense scenario where "information warfare" became as volatile and unstable as traditional modes of armed physical combat. The polarization of world politics divided the international arena into procommunist and prodemocracy camps, with other nondesignated states also existing, most of which were developing nations that were consequently influenced by both superpowers. External communication strategies were designed by the United States and Soviet Union to build and consolidate a bloc of nations that would maximize their respective power capabilities and minimize any vulnerability to outside threats. These strategies also focused on devising policies to counteract the rival bloc's tactics, and to neutralize international threats.[17] Multifaceted communication channels were used by both sides and became integrated with Soviet and American foreign policies.

ADVANCEMENTS IN U.S. STRATEGIC COMMUNICATIONS BEFORE THE COLD WAR

Before World War II

The American communication channels and processes of the Cold War reflected a progression and refinement of technologies used earlier in the nation's history, during both war and peace times. Prior to the creation of formal organizations like the VOA and the USIA, which functioned both domestically and abroad, the United States had implemented several initiatives to communicate overseas. For instance, early in the twentieth century, the Signal Corps of the U.S. Army was in the experimental stages of using "wireless" communication. This was particularly effective in promoting ship-to-shore communications. The first field radios were introduced in 1906 to foster communications on the battlefield. The first Radio Bulletin was sent by the Department of State through Morse code transmissions. Radio stations were subsequently installed, which allowed for limited communications between participants. Cable communications had been in use for years, but presented challenges from weather and environmental conditions.[18]

The Committee on Public Information was created during World War I by President Woodrow Wilson to facilitate communications and serve as the worldwide propaganda organization on behalf of the United States.[19] It spent approximately $6.9 million on propaganda initiatives over an 18-month period, and despite the committee's dissolution at the end of the war, its functions were maintained by other agencies during World War II. These committees and organizations designed campaigns to communicate with foreign audiences, particularly in developing countries, and to sway their viewpoints toward the interests of American policy.[20] In addition, the *Wireless File* was created in 1935 to disseminate official texts, speeches, and policy statements throughout the government.[21]

Cultural exchange programs were designed to share information and learn about foreign nations. These types of programs began in the 1920s on a lesser scale in the developing states of Latin America, and were more formally instituted by 1938 with the Buenos Aires Convention, when the Interdepartmental Committee for Scientific and Cultural Cooperation and the Division of Cultural Cooperation advanced cultural and educational exchanges with Latin America and China.

During World War II

During World War II, President Franklin Roosevelt founded several federal agencies to strategize against Axis propaganda. The Office of the Coordinator of Inter-American Affairs, created in 1940, was designed to thwart German and Italian propaganda in Latin America. Other information agencies like the Office of Facts and Figures, the Office of Government Reports, and the Coordinator of Information were established to deflect enemy propaganda.[22] The U.S. Central Intelligence Agency (CIA) was also extensively involved in the politics of U.S.–Soviet communications, resulting in widespread criticism from the Soviet government.[23]

In addition, Roosevelt established the U.S. Foreign Information Service (FIS) in 1941 and appointed his speechwriter Robert Sherwood as the service's first director. From the FIS headquarters in New York City, broadcasts were transmitted to Europe through private sector shortwave radio stations. With the Japanese attack on Pearl Harbor in December 1941, American broadcasting efforts intensified internationally to counteract the effects of German propaganda. In June 1942, Roosevelt established the Office of War Information (OWI), which shortly thereafter became the International Information Administration.[24] Along with the creation of the OWI, the VOA was established in 1942 as the radio and television broadcasting service of the federal government. The VOA was intimately linked with the USIA throughout the Cold War. A majority of the VOA's daily broadcasts involved news programs, with more than 800 hours of programming over shortwave, medium wave, and satellites each week in English and numerous other languages. On average, these broadcasts reached approximately 83 million people worldwide each week.[25] Audiences for VOA transmissions were broad, including Scandinavia, Egypt, Syria, the Persian Gulf, and Central and South Africa.[26] In its first broadcast on February 24, the VOA summarized its platform as "The news may be good. The news may be bad. We shall tell you the truth."[27] Broadcasts were transmitted in French, Italian, and English.[28] In 1943, the OWI established the American Broadcasting Station in Europe, which was designed to communicate the Allies' plans for an invasion in the region.

Both the United States and former Soviet Union grounded their communication strategies in propaganda techniques and in many instances spread misinformation about their opponent. This trend began long before the start of the Cold War and lasted throughout the Cold War era. According to Davison and George, international political communication can be defined as "the use by [nation-states] of communications to influence the politically relevant behavior of people in other [nation-states]. . . . [This includes] the propaganda and information activities of most government agencies."[29] This communication process can be formulized as "*Who* says *what* to *whom* through what *medium* for what *purpose* under what *circumstances* and with what *effects*."[30]

Political propaganda has traditionally been employed by states with an intent to mobilize hostile feelings against an enemy, and to demoralize the opposition, while also preserving friendship with one's allies and other neutral parties.[31] Correspondingly, after World War II, Soviet and American communication strategies were focused on influencing developing countries that had relatively unstable governments. The use of propaganda through media outlets became a persuasive force in nondesignated states. For instance, from the end of World War II until 1980, the Soviet Union devoted approximately 31 percent of its economic aid, and 62 percent of its total military aid to "socialist path states," particularly through assistance agreements with nations like Afghanistan, Angola, Ethiopia, and Syria, along with others like India and Iraq. In terms of regional aid, from 1952 to 1980, 73 percent of all Soviet economic assistance went to developing world states specifically in the Middle East and South Asia.[32] The United

States likewise devoted considerable resources to influencing the citizens and governments of developing nations.

From these early beginnings, U.S. strategic communication efforts were institutionalized during the Cold War era through the VOA and the USIA, along with other public sector media channels that worked domestically and abroad to deter the spread of communism. In many instances, public organizations worked jointly with companies in the private sector. Surprisingly, the assumption that propaganda efforts in foreign countries were primarily a public sector activity is inaccurate. At the beginning of the Cold War, American advertisers in the private sector spent $280 million in other countries, a trend that was continued throughout the era.[33] These trends are explored later in this chapter.

INFORMATION WARFARE: A CHRONOLOGY OF COLD WAR STRATEGIC COMMUNICATION POLICIES BETWEEN THE UNITED STATES AND SOVIET UNION

This section provides a decade-by-decade chronology of Cold War strategic communication policies of the United States and Soviet Union.

The Late 1940s

The communication strategies of the United States and Soviet Union during the Cold War became integrated with the public diplomacy efforts and foreign policies of both superpowers. Their strategies revolved around influencing developing states. Also, as described later in this section, the concepts of information warfare and public diplomacy evolved considerably throughout the Cold War.

In the United States, the National Security Act of 1947 was instrumental in constructing a military infrastructure, with a plethora of departments and agencies for use during the Cold War. From this infrastructure, a complex communications network was institutionalized to provide information to American citizens, and also to converse with and influence the people of other nations, particularly in developing countries. The U.S. Information and Educational Exchange Act (Public Law 402) became the charter for U.S. overseas information and cultural programs in January 1948.[34] It also brought the VOA under the Office of International Information at the Department of State.[35] The Hoover Commission (1947–1949) recommended the creation of an independent agency to coordinate U.S. information programs. The modeling of the new agency was based on the President's Committee on International Information Activities and the U.S. Senate's Special Subcommittee on Overseas Information programs.

Also in 1948, the Smith-Mundt Act (Public Law 402) was passed by Congress and signed by President Harry S. Truman. Also referred to as the U.S. Information and Educational Exchange Act, it stipulated the terms by which the U.S. government could engage in public diplomacy and use propaganda and communication strategies to influence other countries, particularly in the developing world. Table 13.1 summarizes these milestones.

Table 13.1   1940s Communication Milestones

1947	• Cold War begins
1948	• The U.S. Information and Educational Exchange Act passed
	• Smith-Mundt Act passed

The 1950s

Misunderstandings and miscommunication abounded on both sides. The Soviet perceptions of Western foreign policies presented a more negative image of "Amerika" than
what Americans wanted to portray to the world. Yet the challenges of understanding
Russian culture were also vast. Soviet society, inclusive of government and party members, media outlets, journals, and so on, were the product of Marxist-Leninist ideology,
Russian nationalism, and other bureaucratic forces, as mentioned earlier. This made it difficult to isolate "real" perceptions of Soviet society from the "propaganda" which became
so common throughout the Cold War.[36]

Both superpowers had their own lenses through which they viewed global events.
The procommunist governments of the Soviet Union and East Asia, particularly North
Vietnam, consistently persuaded their citizens not to listen to VOA broadcasts. In many
instances, VOA broadcasts and reports were outright refuted by central European newspapers and radio stations.[37] This was actually a common theme through much of the
Cold War. Despite this, the success of VOA transmissions in Europe and worldwide was
well documented. Studies revealed extensive numbers of references by communist officials in foreign countries regarding the impact of VOA messages on their societies. For
instance, about 900 references to the VOA were found in material from April 1, 1951, to
June 30, 1952.[38] Communist Party propaganda worked to counteract the effects of these
transmissions. The Soviet mass media covered current events in the news but within "the
context of Marxist-Leninist outlooks" and with an angle that reinforced the position of
the party.[39]

One of the principal incidents that influenced communication policies in the United
States occurred early in the 1950s. Senator Joseph McCarthy, chairman of the Senate
Committee on Government Operations, alleged that an investigation by the Permanent
Subcommittee on Investigations found evidence of the infiltration of communism in
U.S. overseas information programs. This became the catalyst for the period known as
McCarthyism, when paranoia of an expanding communist movement raised tension lev-
els in the United States. The journal *Problems of Communism*, launched in 1952, became
an outlet for Western countries to research communism in nations where the ideology
was practiced.[40]

President Dwight Eisenhower's creation of the USIA in August 1953 under the
Reorganization Plan no. 8 (authorized by the Smith-Mundt Act of 1948)[41] broadly
encompassed information programs that were previously functions of the Department of
State. The inspiration for the USIA was rooted in the aforementioned Committee on
Public Information (the Creel Committee), convened during World War I.[42] The USIA

was placed in the executive branch and charged with promoting the national interest, overseeing diplomatic processes, and functioning as a medium between American foreign policy institutions and their equivalents in other countries. Throughout its existence, the USIA was instrumental in collaborating with nongovernmental organizations worldwide to cultivate diplomacy.[43] The mandate which created the USIA emphasized a research component as part of the agency's ongoing agenda. Research was performed by the Office of Research and Media Reaction, which was designed to inform executive branch appointees and personnel from various federal departments and agencies of changes in U.S. policies and programs. The agency also measured the perceptions of foreign governments and citizens through public opinion surveys.[44] The Office of Citizen Exchanges within the USIA was charged with coordinating the growing number of partnership programs between the United States and other countries.[45] During the Eisenhower administration, the head of the USIA became a member of the Operations Coordinating Board, which included members from the Department of State, Department of Defense, the head of the Foreign Aid Agency, and the head of the CIA along with members from other complementary departments. This group of high-ranking government officials discussed Soviet policies and containment strategies weekly.[46]

Tensions over communist doctrines also inspired other initiatives, including the creation of the National Committee for an Adequate U.S. Overseas Information Program in 1953. Headed by Edward Bernays, the committee consisted of 28 leaders from various communications and international affairs fields, who convened to strategize against antidemocracy messages. Shortly after the USIA's creation, the VOA headquarters were relocated from New York City to Washington, D.C., in 1954. The U.S. Information Service (USIS) (as mentioned previously) was gaining influence in Japan with the post–World War II reconstruction process. Despite anti-American attitudes, the USIS worked with educators, the media, and labor to influence the policies of the Japanese government and the country's postwar economy. This continued the theme in American foreign policy where the United States counteracted Soviet propaganda and the spread of communism by establishing a presence in Asia and by building a prodemocratic regime in Japan. For instance, the Regional Service Center (RSC) printing facilities in the Philippines, established early in the 1950s by the International Information Administration, printed materials that were dispersed throughout portions of East and South Asia. The RSC's role expanded during the Korean and Vietnam Wars. With the invasion of South Korean territory, the Smith-Mundt Act was adapted into the Campaign of Truth program to prevent the spread of communism across the world.[47] This involved the dissemination of leaflets and other printed materials in villages. Similarly, in later years, millions of leaflets were printed by the RSC and air-dropped by the Department of Defense to counter the spread of communism and support democratization efforts during the Vietnam War.

Despite initial Cold War tensions between the United States and the Soviet Union, there were documented cultural exchanges between the two superpowers. For instance, in July 1956, the magazine *America Illustrated* (*Amerika*) was published and later distributed uncensored in the Soviet Union. It contained information and cultural insights on American society which were communicated directly to the Soviet people. In turn, the Russian magazine *Soviet Life* was distributed in the United States. Neither magazine was designed to be exclusively a source of political propaganda, but rather a cultural exchange that illuminated and clarified the perceptions of each side.

A revolt against the communist government of Hungary in 1956 fueled a significant increase in VOA broadcasts in 14 different languages across Europe. Footage assembled by the USIA on the Hungarian demonstrations was broadcast to the free world, and film excerpts, along with printed transcripts of correspondence, were also widely disseminated. New motion pictures and television transmissions were produced with prodemocracy themes. Books like George Shuster's *In Silence I Speak* were published and translated into numerous foreign languages and stocked in foreign libraries.[48] The USIA's Book Translation Program translated and reprinted books on government, society, history, economics, and literature for foreign readers. About 70 percent of the programs beamed to orbital satellites and transmitted overseas were broadcasted despite efforts by the former Soviet Union and other communist regimes to censor and jam these transmissions.[49]

The signing of the Cultural Exchange Agreement between the United States and Soviet Union in 1958 facilitated the exchange of scientific, technological, athletic, cultural, artistic, and other research achievements.[50] The American Cultural Specialist program exchanged literary, film, and performing artists between the United States and the Soviet Union, as well as other developing states. While exchanges like these occurred between the two superpowers and developing countries, there was still a predominant mood of competition. This was particularly exemplified in the Brussels Universal Exposition from April to October 1958. The United States and Soviet Union both displayed booths on opposite sides of the site. This tone of competitiveness persisted at a number of American-Soviet expositions worldwide and was exacerbated by the precedent set by the famous Nixon-Khrushchev "kitchen debate" which was held at the American National Exhibition in Moscow's Sokolniki Park on July 24, 1959. This debate between then-Vice President Richard Nixon and Soviet Premier Nikita Khrushchev relayed a restrained and collected Nixon conversing calmly with his more aggressive and volatile counterpart Khrushchev to the world through various media outlets. These milestones are summarized in Table 13.2.

Table 13.2   1950s Communication Milestones

1952	• The journal *Problems of Communism* launched
1953	• The U.S. Information Agency (USIA) created
	• National Committee for an Adequate U.S. Overseas Information Program created
1954	• VOA headquarters relocated from New York City to Washington, D.C.
1956	• The magazine *America Illustrated* (Amerika) published uncensored in the Soviet Union, and the Russian magazine *Soviet Life* published in the United States
1958	• Cultural Exchange Agreement between the United States and Soviet Union
1959	• Nixon-Khrushchev "kitchen debate" at the American National Exhibition in Moscow's Sokolniki Park

The 1960s

The VOA charter was signed into law in 1960 (Public Law 94-350). It defined the agency's mission and reinforced its mandate. The core principles outlined in the charter were designed to (1) serve as a reliable source of news that would be accurate and objective; (2) represent America and present a balanced and comprehensive view of American thought and institutions; and (3) present the policies of the United States clearly and effectively, and stimulate discussion and opinion on these policies.[51] In tandem, the USIA's communication strategies advanced democratic principles by promoting a free market economy, an independent judiciary, an open and fair electoral system, and a free and independent media system with information delivered through multiple sources.[52] Its information programs were managed by the Bureau of Information and involved a variety of communication outlets as the *Washington File*, academic journals, propaganda pamphlets, and other miscellaneous electronic and library data sources.[53] Based on the content presented via these outlets, a 1961 *Newsweek* article summarized the agency's approach as "to portray this country as it really is. The truth must be our guide. . . . We offer no panaceas. Basically, the overriding job of USIA is to make this country understood."[54]

The Bureau of Educational and Cultural Affairs was established in the Department of State late in 1961.[55] The presidential administration of John F. Kennedy established the New York Foreign Press Center to serve as an interface with foreign correspondents that covered American news events. About this time, the VOA began transmitting messages on nuclear tests conducted by the communist government to listeners in the Soviet Union. Previously, Eisenhower had opposed Soviet imperialism by using a defense strategy that centered on the use of atomic weapons. In contrast, Kennedy focused on preventing communist threats in developing countries through Special Forces trained in guerrilla warfare. Also early in the Kennedy administration, the Agency for International Development was established to coordinate foreign aid, and the Peace Corps (Public Law 87-293) was created in 1961 to organize the activities of American volunteers sent abroad to assist developing countries.[56]

The USIA's role was significant in communication strategies during the Bay of Pigs Invasion and the Cuban Missile Crisis, both of which occurred early in the Cold War era. Eisenhower's new CIA training programs were continued by the Kennedy administration. Kennedy used CIA operatives to help build a small army of anti-Castro Cuban exiles in Central America. However, the outcome was ultimately disastrous, as the Bay of Pigs invasion on April 17, 1961, did not produce the expected uprising among Cuban citizens, and Castro's forces easily ended the mission in the beginning stages. After this foreign policy debacle, Kennedy met with Khrushchev in June 1961. In general, Khrushchev was considered to be more pragmatic than his predecessor, and his perceptions of the developing world reinforced his foreign policies.[57] Tension was high between the two superpowers, and Khrushchev threatened war against the United States for supporting the prodemocratic movement in West Berlin of East Germany. The East German government, at the prompting of the Soviet government, constructed a wall between East and West Berlin later that year.[58] The U.S.–Soviet relationship intensified as intelligence reports indicated that the Soviet Union had been installing military equipment and missiles in Cuba as a counterstrategy to American missile sites in Turkey. Communication exchanges were strained between both superpowers, but on October 26, 1962, the Kennedy administration received a message from the Soviet Union indicating that it would remove its Cuban missile bases if the United States would pledge not to invade Cuba. The crisis ended with Kennedy's consent. Throughout these series of events, the USIA communicated to Cuban audiences through radio stations located in the Southeastern shores of the United States. Three shortwave stations also provided a link to Cuban citizens. The radio stations agreed to carry VOA Spanish-language broadcasts after Kennedy's Press Secretary Pierre Salinger requested their assistance.[59]

Leonid Brezhnev succeeded Khrushchev as the Russian leader, reigning from 1964 to 1982. Under Brezhnev's leadership, Soviet foreign policy toward the United States emphasized a strategy of détente, or deescalation and diplomacy. Khrushchev had been a staunch Stalinist, and viewed "international affairs as a gladiators' arena where capitalism and socialism would fight to the death."[60] Brezhnev's foreign policies were not a significant departure from his predecessor's, although he was credited with signing the strategic arms limitation treaties, SALT I and SALT II, during his tenure. The focus of the strategic communications and foreign policies of both superpowers was concentrated on the Vietnam War throughout much of the 1960s and early 1970s. The Kennedy administration backed a faction of South Vietnamese generals in an effort to destabilize and topple the leader of South Vietnam, Ngo Dinh Diem, after his relationship with the United States was undermined by a 1963 South Vietnamese political demonstration in which several Buddhist monks protested the faltering Diem government. The post-Diem regime was unstable, and a series of new governments in South Vietnam failed to maintain stability in the nation. To prevent the spread of Soviet communism in Vietnam, President Lyndon Johnson sent military advisors to the region and convinced Congress to pass the Gulf of Tonkin Resolution after unconfirmed reports had blamed the sinking of American destroyers in the Gulf of Tonkin on a North Vietnamese torpedo boat. The war escalated on land with the deployment of over 500,000 troops in Vietnam by the late 1960s and in the air as well with substantial commitments of planes through the auspices of the Military Air Command, Vietnam.[61]

In 1965, the Joint United States Public Affairs office (JUSPAO) was established in Saigon to coordinate the exchange of information with troops in Vietnam.[62] JUSPAO Director Barry Zorthian organized a country-wide propaganda effort in Vietnam in 1966 which became a source of entertainment for citizens in rural communities. It was based on the Chinese traveling opera company's model, which had implemented a similar approach used by the Viet Minh against the colonial French and the Viet Cong against the government of South Vietnam a few years earlier. The JUSPAO campaign gathered together a group of men and women called the Van Tac Vu, who communicated to rural citizens by distributing magazines and giving performances in villages.[63] These activities persisted until a series of internal reorganizations weakened the JUSPAO, and it began to lose touch with the USIA by the end of 1966. Within the USIA, the roles of its members became more formalized in 1968, when President Johnson signed the Pell-Hays Bill (Public Law 90-494) to create a Foreign Service Information Officer Corps in

Table 13.3   1960s Communication Milestones

1960	• VOA charter signed into law
1961	• The Bureau of Educational and Cultural Affairs established
	• Peace Corps established
1965	• The Joint United States Public Affairs office (JUSPAO) created in Saigon
1968	• President Lyndon B. Johnson signed the Pell-Hays Bill to create a Foreign Service Information Officer Corps within the USIA

the agency.[64] This legislation elevated the status of agency officers, particularly at the upper echelons of the organization, and improved their abilities to respond to foreign policy challenges. The corps program created key cultural, public affairs, and information officer positions at U.S. embassies overseas. These personnel were supported by foreign service nationals, or citizens of the foreign host countries who provided assistance and information to the communication efforts abroad throughout the Cold War. A summary of communications milestones during the decade of the 1960s is shown in Table 13.3.

The 1970s

JUSPAO was eventually deactivated when American troops withdrew from South Vietnam in 1972, and its functions were assimilated by the USIS and other agencies. However, the USIA continued. The USIA's mission was generally consistent throughout the Cold War era. The intensity by which the agency pursued its mandate varied based upon the intensity of events that occurred in the global arena. It also reflected the influence of presidential directives and the agendas of its managing directors. For instance, Frank Shakespeare, the USIA's director from 1969 to 1973, made the agency's top priority an anticommunist campaign to thwart Soviet imperialism.[65] The agency was sustained through periods of intense organizational change and reorganization. The reorganization that occurred in 1978 with the approval of President Jimmy Carter was significant, with the USIA joining with the Bureau of Educational and Cultural Affairs at the Department of State to become the United States International Communication Agency (USICA). The new agency became instrumental in promoting President Carter's human rights program abroad. Functionally, there was a greater focus on reducing misinformation between the United States and other states.[66]

Also during the 1970s, advancements in technology had allowed the VOA to transmit its broadcasts through international satellites rather than traditional shortwave broadcasts. The Arab *Wireless File* was established in 1977 in English, Spanish, and French to transmit to nations in the Middle East. These milestones are shown in Table 13.4.

The 1980s

By the early 1980s, the VOA began modernizing its programmatic and technical capabilities. Television had become the primary mode for global communications, particularly

Table 13.4   1970s Communication Milestones

1970s	• VOA broadcasts began transmitting through international satellites rather than traditional
1972	• JUSPAO deactivated when American troops withdraw from South Vietnam
1977	• The Arab *Wireless File* established
1978	• President Jimmy Carter approved reorganization of the USIA, which joined it with the Bureau of Educational and Cultural Affairs at the Department of State to become the U.S. International Communication Agency (USICA)

since the unit price for TV sets had dropped as economies of scale made them more affordable and accessible. For example, the USIA aired its TV production *Let Poland Be Poland* in January 1982. The program was shown worldwide and on American stations to support the Polish struggle against communism.[67] The Polish labor union, Solidarity, had been distributing the proceedings from their meetings to international news agencies and broadcasters like the VOA, the British Broadcasting Corporation (BBC), and Radio Free Europe. The movement grew to approximately 10 million members in a relatively brief period of time. Poland's communist government unsuccessfully opposed Solidarity's efforts, ultimately leading to the collapse of the Warsaw Pact. This considerably impacted the former Soviet Union, which also later collapsed.[68]

USICA's name reverted back to the U.S. Information Agency with Public Law 97-241, signed by President Ronald Reagan in 1982. Under the Reagan administration, the USIA's strategy in the 1980s promoted the principle of reciprocity, where a series of television exchanges were aired in the United States and Soviet Union between President Reagan and the Russian leader, Mikhail Gorbachev.[69] Gorbachev was more amenable to creating an open Soviet society with greater access to information than his predecessors had been. Through his policies,[70] the Soviet government consented to discontinue jamming USIA, VOA, and other international broadcasts.

Soon after the passage of Public Law 97-241, the WORLDNET Film and Television Service was established in 1983 and became the USIA's principal mode for facilitating public diplomacy via television broadcasts. It replaced the Television Service that had been previously established in 1952. Other TV outlets were also surfacing globally. For instance, Radio Marti was established by the Cuba Act of 1983 (Public Law 98-111). This legislation gave Radio Marti a programming mandate consistent with the VOA standards of objectivity, accuracy, and balance, focusing primarily on domestic and international news that was not reported by the Cuban media controlled by Fidel Castro. By the mid-1980s, WORLDNET was transmitting programs 24 hours a day in numerous languages. The VOA charter was applied to WORLDNET Film and Television Service in December 1988 with the passage of congressional legislation.

The prodemocracy demonstration in Tiananmen Square in the spring of 1989 by young Chinese citizens showed that communism was dangling by a thread. VOA coverage of the uprisings in Tiananmen Square were received by Chinese citizens and worldwide. It provided an alternate source of information to the Chinese government's media

Table 13.5   1980s Communication Milestones

1980s	• The VOA began modernizing its programmatic and technical capabilities
1982	• The USIA aired TV production *Let Poland Be Poland*
	• USICA's name reverted back to the U.S. Information Agency
1983	• WORLDNET Film and Television Service established
	• Radio Marti established by the Cuba Act

outlet, which had denied the strength of the uprising.[71] Communication milestones for the decade of the 1980s are displayed in Table 13.5.

The 1990s and Forward

TV Marti, another surrogate station of the Cuban broadcasting system, was created and first transmitted in March 1990. Its focus was on news and events, along with culture and entertainment. Transmissions for TV Marti programming came from Cudjoe Key in Florida.[72] Also in 1990, the Bureau of Broadcasting was established, and included VOA and WORLDNET. The following year, the Office of Affiliate Relations was created within the bureau to sustain a network of 1,100 radio and television stations which today broadcast VOA and WORLDNET programs around the world.[73] One example of their joint programmatic initiatives was a 1993 television program titled "Window on America," which was broadcast in the Ukraine by the VOA and WORLDNET. This program was viewed by one-fourth of the country's citizens.[74]

Besides the increasingly popular television broadcasts, the USIA continued to transmit through various radio and news services, and published a vast number of magazines, book translations, outreach libraries, academic sources, and exhibitions, many of which targeted developing countries throughout the Cold War era.[75] Print publications included the Russian monthly magazine *America Illustrated,* the *Topic* (which was published in Africa), the Arabic publication *Al-Hayat* (Life in America), and the academic journal *Problems of Communism.*[76] The USIA discontinued its magazine publications in 1994. Television broadcasts and other publications were circulated with the assistance of 202 USIA offices in 124 countries. These offices were supported by staff in Washington, D.C., as well as officers at overseas posts.[77] President Bill Clinton signed the International Broadcasting Act of 1994 (Public Law 103-236), which created the International Broadcasting Bureau within the USIA. This consolidated civilian-government broadcasting— including the VOA, WORLDNET, and Radio and TV Marti—all under the authority of the nine-member bipartisan Broadcasting Board of Governors. WORLDNET sustained its influence with the 1994 documentary *Crimes Against Humanity,* a program that focused on human rights violations in the former Yugoslavia. The Yugoslavian leader Slobodan Milosevic prohibited citizens from viewing programs from overseas sources like the BBC and VOA.

The Cold War may have ended, but the aftereffects of strategic communication strategies from the era continue to exist in the new era of international politics. Despite

Table 13.6   1990s and Forward Communication Milestones

1990	• TV Marti created
	• U.S. Bureau of Broadcasting established
1991	• Cold War ends
1993	• Television program "Window on America" broadcasted in the Ukraine by the VOA and WORLDNET
1994	• President Bill Clinton signed the International Broadcasting Act which created the International Broadcasting Bureau within the USIA
	• WORLDNET aired its documentary *Crimes Against Humanity*, which focused on human rights violations in the former country of Yugoslavia
1998	• President Clinton signs the Foreign Affairs Reform and Restructuring Act
1999	• The USIA abolished

its accomplishments, the USIA was abolished on October 1, 1999, after President Clinton signed the Foreign Affairs Reform and Restructuring Act of 1998. All of the USIA's components except the International Broadcasting Bureau were integrated into the Department of State.[78] Yet the influence of the VOA continues through broadcasts by 1,200 local affiliate stations in 45 languages via FM and AM radio waves and satellite, as well as the Internet. With a fiscal year 2006 budget of $166 million, and more than 1,100 employees, the VOA reached an audience of approximately 115 million people each week through more than 1,000 hours of programming.[79] These communication milestones are shown in Table 13.6.

IMPLICATIONS AND LESSONS FROM THE COLD WAR THAT ARE APPLICABLE TO TODAY'S MODERN INFORMATION AGE

While the tensions of the Cold War are relegated to American history, the twenty-first century has presented new challenges in public diplomacy. The Cold War and the War on Terrorism share innate similarities, including the central role of a hostile ideology and the necessity of effective communication strategies.[80] New departments and bureaucratic restructuring has occurred in recent times, particularly after the attacks of 9/11, which parallels trends from a half century ago. The passage of the USA PATRIOT Act (Public Law 107-56) signed in October 2001 and the formation of the Department of Homeland Security in November 2002 represent components of the War on Terror. Yet these expansions of executive branch authority also encompass the need to integrate communication strategies into a changing bureaucratic infrastructure and policy environment. America's Cold War strategy seemed lucid with its concentration on one primary and distinct rival—the Soviet Union. Today, as noted in a recent Defense Science Board report, the contemporary security environment is a "strategically awkward—and potentially dangerous—situation," where "in stark contrast to the Cold War, the United States today is not seeking to contain a threatening state/empire, but rather seeking to convert a broad movement within Islamic civilization to accept the value structure of Western modernity."[81]

Public diplomacy from a prodemocratic standpoint preserves the commitment to free market economies and the expression of democratic ideals. The collapse of socialist ideology in Eastern European countries and the Soviet Union was in part attributed to the efforts of several sets of military and economic institutions, particularly NATO, the European Community, the Warsaw Treaty Organization, and the Council for Mutual Economic Assistance.[82] This value system guides the contemporary setting of strategic communications, although the modes employed to realize this vision have evolved considerably in the past 15 years, primarily through the maturity and ease of access afforded by Internet technology. The incorporation into the Department of State of several Cold War agencies during the Clinton administration has not obviated essential tasks that are performed within diplomatic channels. Rather, it makes them more imperative in a highly fragmented world where rogue states and radical fundamentalists use modern technology to oppose pro-Western societies, sometimes by violent means.

Essentially, one primary distinction between the Cold War era and the contemporary War on Terror is that some Muslim societies are much less receptive to alternative viewpoints and sources of information than citizens of the former Soviet Union and other communist regimes were during the Cold War.[83] Pockets of citizens in the rural villages of Eastern Europe and East and South Asia were receptive to foreign propaganda and media broadcasts which promised that the communist movement would one day collapse from the strain of prodemocracy resistance forces, leaving inhabitants free of authoritarian rule. While they may have feelings of oppression, Muslims in developing countries today do not consider themselves enslaved by their governments, like Soviet citizens did during the Cold War. An American and pro-Western presence in Middle Eastern politics is considered meddlesome by many in the region.

Further analysis of Cold War communication strategies reveals a relatively steady propaganda style, where the former Soviet Union's policies safeguarded the status quo and worked toward the spread of communism in the developing world. It was based on the notion that once a stable communist movement was established through Marxist-Leninist doctrines, a global revolution would be inevitable. This is in contrast to the Islamist militarism of today. The War on Terror is dynamic and constantly changing. New terrorist groups and rogue states persistently challenge the existing world order, and the push by countries like Iran and Syria to become nuclear capable signifies fragmentation and disorder. During the Cold War, U.S. foreign policies were generally accepting of regimes that were authoritarian as long as they rejected communist doctrines and were at least receptive to the concepts of freedom and democracy. This concentrated the attention of pro-Western states and other friendly nations on the policies of the former Soviet Union and the movement to suppress the spread of communist imperialism. It also allowed for a consistent communication strategy that evolved incrementally over the course of the Cold War, adjusting to Russian foreign policies in steps. Today, the multiplicity of thought that pervades across societies and cultures worldwide makes the focus on one rival impossible. Post-9/11 national security policy in the United States has shifted from its Cold War mentality toward a broader stance which acknowledges the existence of multiple aggressors all acting simultaneously, but on the basis of diverse ideological positions in different regions of the world. Despite these ideological and geographical distinctions, these participants are soldiers of an information war from multiple fronts who use various communication modes like the Internet, computer technology, and other modern communication networks to spread their cause.[84]

Cold War communication strategies revolved around an East–West rivalry between the forces of communism and democracy. Contemporary strategies have a different focus that sorts through information relating to the activities of terrorist networks and autocratic regimes that are guilty of human rights violations, as was seen in Kosovo and the former Yugoslavia. The postmodern information-driven economies of industrialized countries have forced governments to use diplomacy for conflict resolution in the social, economic, and political policies of states more so than for physical engagements. While the Iraq War and ongoing battle in Afghanistan are physical conflicts abroad, economic sanctions are used more robustly in the twenty-first century and modern technology has created a sophisticated form of information warfare where troops and equipment are mobilized and deployed quickly via communication channels, and powerful computer systems have been integrated into virtually every aspect of battle to reduce casualties.

In particular, Internet access has spread worldwide, and many societies that functioned in relatively closed environments now have opportunities to consult alternative information sources from across the globe that authoritarian regimes are unable to easily monitor. While the former Soviet Union and procommunist regimes of the Cold War prevented information from spreading by jamming transmissions, satellite technologies and instantaneous access of transmissions that originate from a seemingly infinite number of sources can reach citizens abroad without difficulty. The Internet has become part of the new economic infrastructure in numerous regions of the world. Broadcasts and news stories that were once transmitted by public organizations like the USIA, USIS, and VOA are now shared and relayed through major news media outlets like CNN, MSNBC and Fox News, as well as Internet Web sites, e-mail networks, and other virtual modes that allow for faster and more efficient delivery. Modern information dynamics are characterized by both the speed at which information becomes available, and the convergence of means by which various forms of information are used (visual, audio, print) in a digital world.[85]

Old communication channels still exist, but in modernized forms. Before the USIA's termination in 1999, it continued to serve as a vital diplomatic agency in the post–Cold War era when human rights violations presented new challenges in the international community. Remnants of the USIA's influence are still perceptible today. For instance, USIA communications and efforts to help displaced refugees were instrumental during the Serbian government's ethnic cleansing in Kosovo. The scenario in Kosovo was the focus of a paper titled "Erasing History," which was distributed and posted on Web sites. Cybertechnology benefited Kosovo refugees by a mode that was not available during the Cold War. Virtual Web programs like the Refugee Internet Assistance Initiative provided a link between government agencies, private sector companies, and international relief organizations to help refugees rebuild their communities.[86] Today, the Refugee Internet Assistance Initiative used in Kosovo during the 1990s has provided a model for other initiatives like the Global Technology Corps—a private-public partnership that uses information technology to help developing nations build sustainable infrastructures.[87] The Information Bureau, which spearheaded these and other Internet initiatives, uses Web technology to enhance public diplomacy. It executes many of the tasks once performed by the USIA, mainly the collection of policy documents and papers that are available on Web sites. These Internet libraries provide instant access to data and information.[88]

The *Wireless File* created in 1935, later renamed the *Washington File*, also continues to function under the auspices of the State Department. Roosevelt had intended to use these files to disseminate U.S. policy statements, and the successor of the early *Wireless File* produced correspondence in English, Spanish, Russian, and other languages to disseminate speeches, policies, and other information during World War II and the Cold War. Today, five editions of the *Washington File* are geographically broadcasted—Africa, the American Republics, East Asia, Europe and the former Soviet Union, and the Near East and South Asia. Governments abroad have come to rely on these transmissions for news that is broadcast through foreign media outlets, local newspapers, radio broadcasts, and television stations.[89] The *Washington File*, prepared daily by the International Information Programs office of the Department of State, also provides agencies within the U.S. government with official statements, features, and articles that are useful for policy making.

CONCLUSION

Global security challenges reflect the complexity of modern technology. The world economy allows for information to cross borders easily, and the information age has made it very difficult to control what citizens read and perceive. The shift from industrial to information economies has affected more than market performance. Technological progress has affected government institutions, the methods through which public diplomacy is conducted, and how military systems evolve. Today, a multipolar world exists with many industrialized states. The violent actions of groups like al-Qaida occur without the authority of a legitimate governmental regime. Developing states, particularly ones in the Middle East like Iran and Syria, continue to work toward nuclear capability, making global security more complex and diffused than the dichotomy of the Cold War. While the Cold War was waged on ideological platforms—communism versus democracy, socialism versus capitalism—the modern international arena is one where other forces like ethnicity and religion play as much a role in motivating the behaviors of rogue states and groups as communist imperialism did in the latter half of the twentieth century. An extremist mentality is apparent in the actions of militant groups that attack targets worldwide, and who use communication outlets to bolster their causes. Yet the international community has responded—examples include the adoption of the Inter-American Democratic Charter by the 34 countries of the Organization of American States in 2001 in the aftermath of 9/11, the formation of the Community of Democracies, and the creation of the Democracy Practitioners Network. All three of these initiatives basically link government officials, academics, nongovernmental organizations, and citizens together to discuss democratic ideals.[90]

The future of communications strategies in the United States will depend on studying and understanding international public opinion further, and coordinating the communication process more effectively with other industrialized states through the use of public diplomacy, public affairs, and international broadcasting. It will also depend on the efforts of Congress to plan, coordinate, and fund communication strategies, as well as the executive branch to implement them in this postmodern world of information warfare. In sum, America's strategic communication policies will rely on both presidential direction and bipartisan support from Congress in terms of funding and cooperation, direction and coordination by relevant national security departments and agencies, and support through private-public sector relationships, which have jointly provided for national security in this advanced age of technocracy.[91] The Cold War may be ended, but challenges persist in new forms.

NOTES

1. Jeremy Isaacs and Taylor Downing, *Cold War: An Illustrated History, 1945–1991* (Boston: Little Brown, 1998).

2. John T. Rourke, *International Politics on the World Stage,* 12th ed. (Boston: McGraw-Hill, 2008).

3. The Defense Science Board Task Force, Office of the Under Secretary of Defense, *Report of the Defense Science Board Task Force on Strategic Communication* (Washington, D.C.: Office of the Under Secretary of Defense, September 2004).

4. The Soviet Union had fought as an Allied Power with the United States and Great Britain during World War I. The Allies opposed the ideology of Hitler's Nazi regime in Germany. Shaken by the war effort and the social upheaval associated with the dissolution of Nicholas II's regime, the Bolsheviks signed a peace treaty with Germany in March 1918. Lenin founded the Russian Communist Party with the support of his Bolshevik revolutionaries, and the new Union of Soviet Socialist Republics was established to provide Russian citizens with education, health care, and common ownership of land. See Isaacs and Downing, *Cold War.*

5. See Paul Kecskemeti, "The Soviet Approach to International Political Communication," *Public Opinion Quarterly,* Vol. 20, No. 1 (Spring 1956), pp. 299–308.

6. The Bolshevik's seizure of Winter Palace during the October Revolution occurred on October 24, 1917, by the old style calendar, but actually occurred on the night of November 6, 1917, under the new calendar; see Isaacs and Downing, *Cold War.*

7. Isaacs and Downing, *Cold War.*

8. The Western powers perceived the Bolshevik revolution with anxiety. The antagonistic ideology of socialist radicals was considered a threat that would destabilize international politics in Europe, and plausibly on other continents as Soviet communication channels spread communism globally. See Isaacs and Downing, *Cold War.*

9. Stalin, known as the "man of steel," assumed this name later in life after being born with the name Josef Vissarionovich Dzhugashvili.

10. Daniel S. Papp, *Soviet Perceptions of the Developing World in the 1980s: The Ideological Basis* (Massachusetts: D.C. Heath, 1985), p. 77.

11. Papp, *Soviet Perceptions of the Developing World in the 1980s.*

12. Isaacs and Downing, *Cold War.*

13. See Isaacs and Downing, *Cold War,* and Papp, *Soviet Perceptions of the Developing World in the 1980s.*

14. See Isaacs and Downing, *Cold War*; Walter LaFeber, ed., *The Origins of the Cold War, 1941–1947* (New York: John Wiley & Sons, 1971); and Alan Brinkley, *The Unfinished Nation: A Concise History of the American People* (Boston: McGraw-Hill, 2004).

15. Isaacs and Downing, *Cold War.*

16. Ibid.

17. W. Phillips Davison, and Alexander L. George, "An Outline for the Study of International Political Communications," *Public Opinion Quarterly,* Vol. 16, No. 4 (Winter 1953), pp. 501–511.

18. For instance, the submarine cable that formed the Alaskan Telegraph System was severely damaged by an ice break-up around 1900 when temperatures rose. See William R. Blair, "Army Radio in Peace and War," *Annals of the American Academy of Political and Social Science,* Vol. 142 (March 1929), pp. 86–89.

19. W. Phillips Davison, "Some Trends in International Propaganda," *Annals of the American Academy of Political Science and Social Science,* Vol. 398 (November 1971), pp. 1–13.

20. W. Phillips Davison, "Political Communication as an Instrument of Foreign Policy," *Public Opinion Quarterly,* Vol. 27, No. 1 (Spring 1963), pp. 28–36.

21. The United States Information Agency, "A Commemoration: 1953–1999" (Washington, D.C., 1999).

22. Ibid.

23. For instance, over time the CIA was rebuked for its activities in Central America and the Caribbean, for coup d'états and assassinations in Africa and other developing countries, and its involvement in the separatist activities of the Sikhs in India, Eritreans in Ethiopia, and Ovimbundu in Angola. See Papp, *Soviet Perceptions of the Developing World in the 1980s.*

24. Overseas, the OWI functioned as the U.S. Information Service (USIS).

25. U.S. Information Agency, Office of Public Liaison, "The United States Information Agency" (Washington, D.C.: USIA's Regional Service Center, October 1998); http://www.usia.gov.

26. Leonard Carlton, "Voice of America: The Overseas Radio Bureau," *Public Opinion Quarterly,* Vol. 7, No. 1 (Spring 1943), pp. 46–54.

27. U.S. Information Agency, "A Commemoration: 1953–1999" (Washington, D.C.: USIA's Regional Service Center), p. 52.

28. Ibid.

29. Davison and George, "An Outline for the Study of International Political Communications," p. 501.

30. Ibid., p. 502.

31. Harold D. Lasswell, *Propaganda Technique in World War I,* new ed. (Cambridge: Mass.: MIT Press, 1971).

32. Papp, *Soviet Perceptions of the Developing World in the 1980s,* pp. 130, 132.

33. Davison, "Political Communication as an Instrument of Foreign Policy," pp. 28–36.

34. From this initiative, the United States and Soviet Union later agreed to a reciprocal exchange program which facilitated the trade of over 50,000 citizens who shared ideas in subject areas like education, culture, science, and technology. This exchange program occurred from 1958 to 1988. See U.S. Information Agency, "A Commemoration: 1953–1999."

35. Ibid.

36. Papp, *Soviet Perceptions of the Developing World in the 1980s.*

37. Carlton, "Voice of America: The Overseas Radio Bureau."

38. Paul W. Massing, "Communist References to the Voice of America," *Public Opinion Quarterly*, Vol. 16, No. 4 (Winter 1952–53), pp. 618–622.

39. Papp, *Soviet Perceptions of the Developing World in the 1980s*, p. 23.

40. The journal *Problems of Communism* was widely read and published until the break-up of the Soviet Union, with its last issue in May/June 1992. See U.S. Information Agency, "A Commemoration: 1953–1999."

41. The Smith-Mundt Act advocated an approach to information use "to promote a better understanding of the United States in other countries, and to increase mutual understanding." See Davison, "Political Communication as an Instrument of Foreign Policy," pp. 28–36.

42. U.S. Information Agency, Office of Public Liaison, "The United States Information Agency."

43. Ibid.

44. U.S. Information Agency, "A Commemoration: 1953–1999."

45. U.S. Information Agency, Office of Public Liaison, "The United States Information Agency."

46. U.S. Information Agency, "A Commemoration: 1953–1999."

47. See Edward W. Barrett, *Truth Is Our Weapon* (New York: Funk & Wagnalls, 1953) and Foy D. Kohler, "The Voice of America: Spokesman of the Free World," *Proceedings of the Academy of Political Science*, Vol. 24, No. 2 (January 1951), pp. 92–100.

48. U.S. Information Agency, "A Commemoration: 1953–1999."

49. Ibid.

50. Ibid.

51. U.S. Information Agency, Office of Public Liaison, "The United States Information Agency."

52. Ibid.

53. Ibid.

54. U.S. Information Agency, "A Commemoration: 1953–1999," p. 30.

55. Ibid.

56. Brinkley, *The Unfinished Nation*.

57. Papp, *Soviet Perceptions of the Developing World in the 1980s*.

58. Brinkley, *The Unfinished Nation*.

59. U.S. Information Agency, "A Commemoration: 1953–1999."

60. Aleksei Novikov in Suzanne P. Ogden, ed., *World Politics*, 11th ed. (Connecticut: Dushkin Publishing Group, 1990).

61. Brinkley, *The Unfinished Nation*.

62. U.S. Information Agency, "A Commemoration: 1953–1999."

63. Ibid.

64. Ibid.

65. Ibid.

66. Ibid.

67. Ibid.

68. Ibid.

69. Ibid.

70. Glasnost (democratizing) and perestroika (a restructuring of Soviet society inclusive of foreign and defense policies) promised to create a more open Soviet society with greater availability of information to the citizens and less manipulation of the public indicated a new way of Soviet thinking. The Soviets' "new thinking" came in the 1980s with Mikhail Gorbachev, who came to power in March 1985 with greater toleration for ideas than his predecessors, particularly

Brezhnev. Gorbachev's policies saw unprecedented changes and political reforms like elections to the Congress of People's Deputies and televised broadcasts and speeches that even included criticisms of Gorbachev himself and the Communist Party. He was able to persuade 99 percent of the Communist Party leaders in the Soviet Union to surrender their hold over the country. Gorbachev's foreign policy accomplishments were also extensive, with the disarmament of numerous warheads in the mid- to late 1980s, the withdrawal of 50,000 troops and 500 nuclear weapons from Eastern Europe, and the withdrawal of thousands of troops from the Sino-Soviet border. He also allowed for the withdrawal of intermediate-range nuclear forces stationed in Europe. See Ogden, *World Politics.*

71. U.S. Information Agency, "A Commemoration: 1953–1999."

72. U.S. Information Agency, Office of Public Liaison, "The United States Information Agency."

73. U.S. Information Agency, "A Commemoration: 1953–1999."

74. Ibid.

75. Richard E. Bissell, "Foreign Speakers Projects of the USIA's American Participant Program," *Political Science,* Vol. 16, No. 1 (Winter 1983), pp. 53–55.

76. U.S. Information Agency, "A Commemoration: 1953–1999."

77. Bissell, "Foreign Speakers Projects of the USIA's American Participant Program," pp. 53–55.

78. U.S. Information Agency, "A Commemoration: 1953–1999."

79. Voice of America, http://www.voanews.com/english, 2007.

80. Defense Science Board Task Force, Office of the Under Secretary of Defense, *Report of the Defense Science Board Task Force on Strategic Communication* (Washington, D.C.: Office of the Under Secretary of Defense, September 2004).

81. Ibid., pp. 35, 36.

82. Celeste Wallander and Jane Prokop in Robert O. Keohane, Joseph S. Nye, and Stanley Hoffman, eds., *After the Cold War: International Institutions and State Strategies in Europe, 1989–1991* (Cambridge, Mass.A: Harvard University Press, 1993).

83. Defense Science Board Task Force, *Report of the Defense Science Board Task Force on Strategic Communication.*

84. Ibid.

85. Ibid.

86. U.S. Information Agency, "A Commemoration: 1953–1999."

87. Ibid.

88. Ibid.

89. U.S. Information Agency, Office of Public Liaison, "The United States Information Agency."

90. International Information Programs, Bureau of International Information Programs, U.S. Department of State, "Democracy Network Created for the Americas" (November 29, 2007), http://usinfo.state.gov.

91. Defense Science Board Task Force, *Report of the Defense Science Board Task Force on Strategic Communication.*

14

The *Cook Report* and Perceptions of Loyalists in Northern Ireland

Lessons for Counterterrorism

James Dingley

PROPAGANDA IS A SERIOUS WEAPON for all terrorists; to succeed they need to acquire legitimacy within their own client population and to an outside world. In this sense they need to be able to promote a relatively "pure" image of themselves, both to enhance their own reputation and, by implication, to lessen that of their opponents, usually the state. Above all they must produce an image of themselves as true and incorruptible servants of their cause and the people they claim to be fighting for, which is not always easy since by their nature they are law breakers. However, the power and force of the law lies primarily in its moral power to legitimate, hence if law breaking can be seen as legitimate it will be seen as acceptable and the law breaker will in turn be morally absolved, at least by the client audience. To do this, such law breaking must be seen as specifically enhancing the terrorist cause and not simply furthering individuals' own pecuniary interests.

In Northern Ireland, with a deeply divided (along ethnoreligious lines) population, this has never been such a problem for the antistate terrorists (republicans) whose own (minority) client population already views the state, and hence its laws, as nonlegitimate. For the pro-state terrorists this is always a more problematic proposition, since the state itself and its laws are accepted by the majority population and so breaking the law on its behalf becomes more difficult to justify. Hence for pro-state law breakers it is probably even more vital that they can legitimate their acts, and when they are found to be simply working for their own pecuniary interests it can have much more serious implications for the organization.

Such personal pecuniary interests were startlingly revealed to be behind the criminal acts of pro-state terrorists (loyalists) in 1987, when they were caught on camera in a TV current affairs program (the *Cook Report*), which highlighted the many "rackets" they ran, whose proceeds appeared to be going straight into private pockets and not to the organization (they had sticky fingers, in the local vernacular). Many believe it had a major adverse affect on them in terms of military and political impact, however, others have doubted the extent to which it caused them real long-term harm, suggesting that the result was merely temporary embarrassment. The aim of this chapter is to examine the effect of this particular case in the light of subsequent perceptions of the loyalists both within and without Northern Ireland.

PLAYERS AND BACKGROUND

"Players" is local vernacular for those involved in Northern Ireland's long ongoing "troubles" (1969–2007). Briefly, serious rioting broke out between the Protestant and Catholic working-class communities in 1968–1969; both communities had long led deeply segregated lives, and sporadic violence between them was almost endemic.[1] What precisely caused the troubles is still open to debate, but various claims by the minority Catholic community of discrimination against them certainly helped to set it off (but this must also be seen against a long history of large elements—i.e., nationalists—of that community being antistate in the first instance). In turn the majority Protestant community, with some justification, felt that there were other revolutionary forces behind the Catholics. At the same time, the local devolved government (Stormont) was implementing a series of reforms aimed at tackling many of the Catholic grievances.[2] However, the situation was also muddied by major structural changes occurring in the local economy that were deeply unsettling to local social, political, and economic reward systems of status, jobs, and patronage.[3]

In addition there was a general whiff of revolution in the air,[4] and Northern Ireland had 200 years of sectarian violence to inform its discourses about revolution, which to many Protestants simply meant a Catholic/nationalist revolt against them.[5] It was a confused time and the Protestant majority felt increasingly insecure. Several ill-judged marches by Catholic organizations and inflammatory Protestant reactions helped stir the pot. And serious rioting between them broke out in 1968–1969. This in turn led to a sustained terrorist campaign by the Irish Republican Army (IRA) and was followed by various Protestant counterorganizations, and the violence has continued ever since, even after the Belfast Agreement (1998) and acts of decommissioning of some terrorist weapons after that.

The players are legion, but the main protagonists necessary to follow events are as follows: the IRA (of which Sinn Fein is an wholly owned and directed subsidiary) is a terrorist organization dedicated to overthrowing the state in Northern Ireland for an all-Ireland republic. In 1970–1971 it split between its Marxist wing (Official IRA) who wanted to call off the terrorist campaign—as sectarian and against working-class unity—and the Provisional IRA (PIRA), dedicated to a pure ethnoreligious ideal and rooted solely in the Catholic community. It is PIRA who were and are the effective terrorist threat the state had to combat since 1971; the Official IRA almost faded from view as a serious force.[6] Next to this, one has the SDLP (Social Democratic and Labour Party) who represented the nonviolent and constitutional wing of Catholic/nationalism (also committed to a united Ireland) and politically represented the bulk of their community until the rise of Sinn Fein (who now form the largest nationalist party in Stormont) in the 1990s.[7] "Nationalism" is a generic term to refer to all who wish to achieve an all-Ireland state; republican generally refers to the militant wing of nationalism, proviolence such as the IRA, while nationalists more generally refers to the constitutional wing, such as the SDLP.

On the Protestant/Unionist side there was the Ulster Unionist Party (UUP), the established unionist party that had ruled Northern Ireland since its inception in 1920–1921. It was an awkward cross-class and cross-religion entity (Ulster Protestants being divided among many competing and disputatious sects, even including an element of middle-class Catholics), whose main purpose of rule was to maintain the Union and resist nationalism. However, as change affected the province in the 1960s there was increased criticism of Unionist rule from within unionism, which finally manifested itself around Reverend Ian Paisley, who finally led a split from the UUP to form his own Democratic Unionist Party (DUP) in the 1970s. Ever since there has been a slow erosion of confidence in the UUP until in recent years the DUP has easily surpassed the UUP in terms of unionist support and is now the largest party in Stormont.[8] The DUP stands for a very hard-line approach to defence of the Union and has been associated with a very fundamentalist Protestantism and strong security policy, while the UUP is associated with a softer and more inclusive approach to the Union. However, both have to be distinguished from loyalism, which refers to the militant wing of unionism, with Protestant terror groups at their extreme.

The other major player is the U.K. state, which until the troubles broke out had virtually ignored Northern Ireland and simply let Stormont run its own devolved government. Only when the troubles became so bad with the PIRA's terrorist campaign in full swing did they formally take over direct rule of the province (1972).[9] When they finally did assume direct rule they immediately found themselves running a province of which they had little knowledge or experience, yet they were taking over from a devolved government that for all its knowledge and experience could not cope with the extensive terrorism of PIRA.

However, the U.K. central government (London) now assumed control at a time when PIRA appeared to be winning, traditional unionism could not cope, and London was even prepared to enter into negotiations with PIRA.[10] All of this was very unsettling for Unionists and helps explain the appeal of Paisley's DUP, but it also led to the formation of the UDA (the subject of the *Cook Report*) and other loyalist groups.

The Ulster Defence Association (UDA) had its first meeting in 1971 and was formed out of a rag-tag ensemble of local working-class Protestant groups, many genuine in their concerns, others anti-Catholic, others opportunistic. But what they most represented was a fear of PIRA's terrorism getting out of hand; the state's security forces could not cope, traditional unionism had let them down, and the United Kingdom was likely to "sell them out" in a deal with PIRA. Genuine fear for their own safety and their future to remain in the state of their choice was the motivation, whatever followed later. There were some very dubious characters involved from the start, but the majority were probably sincere in their fears and worries that their own state could not protect them at a time when PIRA had virtually brought the province to a standstill.

At first the UDA simply organized marches as shows of force, but then they began to organize into local battalions or brigades in order to police local neighborhoods, participate in riots, and then to go on the offensive against Catholic-nationalist-republican enemies—that is, carry out their own terrorism. However, they never acquired the expertise or sophistication that PIRA had and they were always a fairly loose and ill-disciplined organization, where local "brigadiers" often wielded more clout than headquarters and were inclined to do their own thing. Central command and control was more of a public relations myth, but while the troubles of the 1970s raged and PIRA strength and perceived state weakness seemed a serious threat, they could be relatively focused on the "enemy" and their communities saw them as providing an essential role.[11]

However, from the mid- to late 1970s the state began to get a better handle on Northern Ireland and the security forces began to come to terms with PIRA and make serious inroads into tackling them. This was a process of trial and error and better experience, resources, training, and material and a realization by the state that PIRA's politics were fantasy and they could not, politically, realistically be dealt with. Also, the Catholic population itself was deeply divided, not just in its attitude to PIRA but even whether it really wanted a united Ireland.[12] The upshot was a growing state success against PIRA, which in turn led to the question of the UDA's future role and purpose amongst their supporters.

UDA AND THE PURPOSE OF PRO-STATE TERROR

Most terrorist groups are antistate and so their relationship to it can be quite simple, but for pro-state groups it is quite difficult (excluding Central and South American examples, where they were actually sponsored by the state).[13] The UDA came into existence because the state was perceived to be unable to carry out its proper security and law and order functions in the face of the PIRA, and so it was at first accepted relatively uncritically within its communities and had popular support. It was also tolerated by the state, at first, since it operated openly and posed as a political organization; even though it spawned its own terrorist wing—the Ulster Freedom Fighters (UFF), who carried out attacks on republicans/Catholics—it always managed to maintain a technical legal distinction (much like PIRA and Sinn Fein). However, when the state began to get to grips with PIRA, the UDA's raison d'être began to erode, but even before that it had serious question marks hanging over it.

Given that the state was being criticized for a failure to maintain law and security, the justification for the UDA embarking on their own illegal campaigns and further undermining security was always problematic at the moral and legitimacy level in a way it was not for republicans. The UDA could be on relatively safe ground when it simply stuck to defense of Protestants from attack, but when it went on the offensive and murdered republicans it was denying the very principles it claimed to uphold—that is, anti-terrorism. In addition, in carrying out its own illegal acts of violence it was undermining the role of the state to which it claimed allegiance. For republicans to claim they only attacked legitimate targets was easy given their ideological position that denied state legitimacy and so gave a moral gloss to their acts, but precisely the opposite was true for the UDA who claimed to uphold the state—there were no legitimate targets for them.

In addition, whom were they to attack? Police and soldiers? State servants? Targets for revenge or defense attacks were always difficult, even if restricted to PIRA activists and supporters, since by their terrorist nature they were difficult to identify even for the security forces. And mounting assassinations of PIRA members in alien, closed, Catholic communities—even if targets were correctly identified—would have been extremely hazardous. Consequently their attacks often ended up targeting ordinary Catholics in a quite random manner, on the pretext that since republicans gained support from the Catholic community all Catholics were fair game.[14]

Further, the state's own security forces regarded the UDA with deep disdain, as murderous thugs and "hoods" (gangsters) who not only got in the way of their own operations and attempts to combat the main threat (PIRA) but also helped give some legitimacy to the PIRA.[15] In addition, the state did not like to have other players muscling in on its domains, since it undermined their own authority and rights. A major consequence of this was that good quality recruits tended to join the security forces not the UDA (for PIRA it worked the other way around) where they received proper training, good pay, status, and a career and also came under a very disciplined formal chain of command and control.[16]

One upshot of this was that once the main threat appeared to recede, so did the relevance of the UDA; once the security forces seemed to have the better of PIRA, bombings and murders decreased,[17] and there was less need for UDA counterviolence. Under these conditions even within the UDA they began to lose what focus they had and the practical implications of their lack of discipline, command, and control, together with their low level of recruits, began to assert themselves in a downward drift to simple crime and personal aggrandizement.

ORGANIZED CRIME AND TERRORISM

Terrorism is very expensive for all groups, and funding is a continual problem. The buying of arms and ammunition, maintaining a functioning structure and logistics—with full-time operatives, safe houses, training, and intelligence—and developing political wings rapidly ate up finances. This led both PIRA and the UDA into organized crime to gain funds, and as the crime became better organized and extensive it sometimes even led to collusion and cooperation between PIRA, the Official IRA, and the UDA (and Ulster Volunteer Force), such as carving up territory, exchanging goods and information on how to run fraudulent operations, sharing profits, and even arranging for unwanted members of their own side to be assassinated by the other.[18]

Organized crime began for both sides with running illegal clubs and pubs (drinking dens) and then to the supply of alcohol and cigarettes (sometimes hijacked, sometimes not) for them. From this it expanded on to black taxis (old London cabs bought secondhand and running bus-like shuttle services to and from their own communities) run and operated by the terrorists, whose own actions had led to the suspension of normal busing in many areas. These in turn were often aided and abetted by the legitimate banks and breweries unable to sustain the losses otherwise incurred by the troubles, as ordinary pubs and clubs were bombed out and normal public services ceased to operate in the worst affected areas. From this, both sides branched out into rackets such as protection and "security companies" for legitimate businesses operating in the province. Small businesses were particularly vulnerable, especially building contractors working in the more trouble-prone districts. Not to contract meant going out of business, so paying protection often became the only means to stay in business (something covertly recognized by the state, which accepted protection payments as legitimate tax expenses), apart from which the very business they were contracting for was often the result of replacing buildings actually blown up by the terrorists. This in turn was added to by a large number of armed robberies of banks, building societies, and post offices, all of which began to bring in large sums of money.[19]

However, here a distinct difference emerges between loyalist and republican crime. Loyalist crime tended to stay at this relatively low level and overt form of criminality, which often evolved around overt physical violence and threats, as well as directed primarily at members of their own community and against their own state. This could be tolerated as a necessity while the state seemed unable to effectively counter PIRA terrorism, but became less so when the state appeared to effectively respond to their challenge.[20] Meanwhile, republicans never had to worry about perceptions of legitimacy from their own community, since the state was seen as illegitimate anyway. Further, the major targets of armed robberies were also associated with the state and republicans perception of a capitalist/imperial occupation. Even so, republicans moved on to much more sophisticated levels of crime that was far less prone to target Catholics (the core of Northern Ireland's economy had always been largely Protestant-owned anyway) and could even be regarded as benefiting the Catholic community and hence displayed the better quality of recruit to the PIRA who were able to think more effectively in these terms, and specifically not to act in ways that directly had an adverse affect on their own community.

Today republicans run everything from cross-border smuggling operations, counterfeit goods manufacturing (often located abroad), and pirating of tapes, videos, DVDs, and video game consoles, to the distilling and distribution of their own illicit vodka (for sale in their own pubs), manufacturing their own unlicensed cigarettes (again, sold in their own pubs and clubs), and many other scams. In doing so, they help provide a service of cheap (if not good-quality) goods within their own community and so help subsidize low-income working-class Catholic families. In addition, they have a range of front organizations ("legitimate" businesses) that were originally set up to launder proceeds from robberies, but now generate so much income in their own right that the laundering is almost secondary. In turn, these help provide jobs and careers within their communities and semi-legitimate employment, that is, they can be seen to provide a service to the community, something the limited minds and opportunities for loyalists cannot provide.[21]

Further, as republican coffers began to swell, they moved into legitimate business in their own right, based on illegal proceeds, developing extensive property portfolios of houses, hotels, pubs, and clubs that generate more and safer income than ordinary crime. In this, both wittingly and unwittingly, banks and other financial institutions have been drawn and tied in. Republicans still engage in robberies, but only very large-scale ones where specific funds are required for specific purposes, such as the Northern Bank raid

(2004) where the £26 million stolen was reported as being to finance the purchase of a bank in Bulgaria,[22] which should give some indication of the scale and sophistication that republicans have developed in their financial activity. (PIRA members were still carrying out hijackings of alcohol and cigarette trucks until quite recently, when the companies involved simply refused to drive their trucks through certain areas anymore.) Current finance is mostly designed to support their politics (Sinn Fein) and is tightly controlled via PIRA's own finance department,[23] and all proceeds strictly accounted for and going to the organization. In this way personal rewards are distributed through the organization in the form of jobs and career opportunities, so loyalty to the central command and organization are ensured in the same way that they can "purchase" the community loyalty of nonmembers.

PIRA have never involved themselves directly in drugs, although they have licensed dealers to operate in the areas they control. Equally, they have not engaged directly in prostitution and people trafficking, although they are known to license and franchise criminal activities in their areas on quite a wide scale, so the exact extent of their involvement in such activities may be open to some debate. As several senior members of the security forces observed in 2006,[24] PIRA economic control in their communities is now so extensive they don't need to use violence any more, except to maintain a certain level of internal discipline as a last resort.

This represents a remarkable growth in criminal thought on behalf of republicans that continues to evolve up to this day (2007). Further, and more important, it can be seen as legitimate within their communities and among their supporters not just as part of the cause but also as a community service that only adversely affects their enemies. The same cannot be said for loyalists, beyond protection rackets (the subject of the *Cook Report*) and armed robberies they have only evolved into drugs and prostitution. Their criminality is overt and crude and riddled with sticky fingers (money sticks to the fingers of individual operatives, not the organization).

The very undisciplined nature of the UDA and its lack of unified command and control leave its operations wide open for internal abuse. The kind of low-quality recruit they get also implies a more criminally minded and less pure terrorist, one unable to think long term and the good of the organization leading to the good of the individuals involved. Further, their operations increasingly became pointless as the state got the measure of PIRA, so what were the proceeds of criminal activity for? Further, the UDA was always more of a defensive reaction, not an ideologically thought out political program with clear aims and objectives other than to save the Union. It was thus also widely open for many a nonpure political element to move in as merely a cover for their own purposes and as the UDA lost purpose, this became a bigger problem.

Bruce (1992) makes it quite clear that these kinds of problems were already affecting the UDA long before the *Cook Report* (1987); the organization was already in a downward spiral and internal dissensions were on the increase, with splits between areas/brigades and the emergence of strong personal battles for local hegemony and autonomy as strong men took over and imposed their will in lieu of any political ideology—greed easily replaced any ideals. Also, being of a lesser character than PIRA recruits, they were less skillful at masking their activities either from the police or behind a political screen and had more difficulty in selling themselves as a legitimate force within their own communities, against whom the bulk of their activities were directed (since there were few other opportunities open for them to act on). The UDA thus lived off their own community in a way the PIRA did not. Consequently, they were a much easier target for investigative journalists to penetrate.

THE *COOK REPORT* AND ITS AFTERMATH

The *Cook Report* was a series of current affairs programs very popular on British television during the 1980s and was named after its chief investigative reporter Roger Cook. The style of the program was always combative, with Cook seeming to delight in confronting ne'er-do-wells who frequently not only abused him but also physically attacked him. It was sensationalist, excellent television, entertaining and often even quite informative and obviously well researched. The program was not based in Northern Ireland but mainland Britain, and so was regularly networked throughout the United Kingdom, although focusing on incidents or events in different regions each week. Consequently, it was wide-reaching and authoritative and very difficult for anyone in London to ignore, which often happens to regional issues.

In August 1987, the *Cook Report* ran a program in which Cook disguised himself as a building contractor seeking to bid for a lucrative contract in Portadown, County Down (about 30 miles southwest of Belfast). As a result of this ruse he was contacted by senior UDA men who made extortion demands on him, and he arranged to meet the mid-Ulster UDA brigadier in a rigged car to discuss the terms. The result is best put in Steve Bruce's words:

> The program team laid one trap that made dynamiting fish out of the water look sophisticated. . . . He [Cook] was approached by the UDA and arranged a meeting to discuss "security." Concealed cameras filmed Eddie Sayers, the brigadier of mid-Ulster UDA, making unambiguous extortion demands.[25]

Sayers and prominent Belfast UDA man Jimmy Craig were revealed as deeply involved in rackets that seemed to be the sole raison d'être of large parts of the UDA, whose tentacles seemed to cover the province.

For the police the program was "a propaganda godsend"[26] in their own long-running campaign to tackle the UDA. And this is an important point to bear in mind—the police had long known all about the UDA's activities and had been after them for many years. Their problem was not in getting evidence or witnesses, but evidence that would stand up in court and witnesses who were not afraid to testify in open court. Both the UDA and PIRA were expert in intimidation of witnesses, and even anonymous informants risked easy detection and punishment from the terrorists in small communities who knew everyone and could easily deduce who could have known what and informed. The *Cook Report* thus openly blew the lid on UDA activity and helped the police garner public awareness and cooperation to crack down on them, although it did not lead to convictions.

However, and more important, it had major ramifications within the UDA, where the embarrassment of such overtly criminal activity—which most of their own community strongly suspected, if not knew, was going straight into private pockets and not to Protestant defense—produced a serious loss of prestige. But the timing was also important, since internal splits and divisions were already emerging as to the direction and purpose of the UDA. Added to this, the aforementioned Jimmy Craig had been arrested and brought to trial in 1985, although the case collapsed when the trial judge denied witnesses anonymity and they refused to testify. Now, Craig had been a senior UDA man responsible for many of their rackets in Belfast, and when he was absent "at Her Majesty's pleasure" pending trial, the rest of the UDA senior staff got their first look at the books and were astounded at the discrepancy between amounts earned from rackets and the sums received by the UDA.

There was thus already disquiet even within the UDA. In addition, many in the Protestant community either knew or suspected that funds from rackets were increasingly attached to sticky fingers, while the security forces' credibility was rising, and so the need for groups like the UDA was increasingly open for debate, especially since they had engaged in few acts of war against republicans since the early 1980s. Finally, the incredibly heavy handed extortion techniques used against members of their own community increasingly alienated fellow Protestants. As already suggested, UDA sophistication was low and techniques were crude (if actually no less lethal or nasty than the more sophisticated PIRA), thus they had already alienated part of their own community and also provided the basis for deep internal schisms[27] in ways PIRA carefully avoided.

What the *Cook Report* appears to have done is to act as a kind of catalyst or conjunction for a series of events and underlying currents. The seriousness of Cook's exposure was that it brought things out into the open that were already there but had not come together.

The UDA's image and credibility took a serious blow and led to the ousting of Craig and Sayers as well as an internal investigation by another up-and-coming senior UDA man John McMichael (whose own finances did not stand too much scrutiny), previously a friend and confidant. This in turn seems to have set off much internal feuding and infighting, with recriminations and greed playing an equal part. Both McMichael and Craig were subsequently murdered—strongly rumoured to be internal jobs, although with McMichael, there was a suggestion of possible PIRA collusion (Northern Ireland is a strange and murky world).[28] McMichael was killed only four months after the *Cook Report*, while Craig continued to operate informally and at a lower level until his demise in 1989.[29]

Other casualties continued to fall in the wake of the *Cook Report*, both from internal pressure and from security force operations. Two senior UDA men (Jackie MacDonald and Artie Fee) were arrested and charged with racketeering by the police less than two years after McMichael's murder, and in a significant shift of attitudes not only were the police able to obtain incriminating recordings of the two attempting to extort but were also able to get witnesses prepared to come forward in court.[30] In addition, only two weeks after the *Cook Report* was broadcast the police intercepted a large cache of loyalist weapons in transit, thus forming another blow to the UDA leadership, and its leader (Andy Tyrie) was forced to resign.

In addition to the embarrassment caused by the exposures, the subsequent internal dissension and feuding it created had a serious affect on UDA morale and operations, such as they were. Meanwhile, the UDA also had to be wary of the rise of another loyalist organization, the Ulster Volunteer Force (UVF), which—although more rooted in the rural areas of Northern Ireland, as opposed to the UDA's predominantly urban base—was able to pose a threat to the UDA, a group that was increasingly seen by many as a cynical and crony-ridden organization for self-enrichment (again, something few could accuse PIRA of).

The UDA was now faced with having to renew not only its leaders but also its organization, structures, and political appeal if it was to reestablish any sense of legitimacy even among its own client population. A series of internal murders and the ousting of others from the organization was part of the process. However, so was the reorganization into a cellular structure with a tighter central command that was more difficult for the security forces to penetrate. Further, it embarked on a new killing spree of republicans/Catholics (loyalist murders went up from 2 in 1985, to 17 in 1987, and then 47 in 1993),[31] presumably to reassert its pure credentials in taking the "war" to republicans. One upshot of this was that the UDA was finally outlawed in 1992.

Paradoxically, the *Cook Report* may have helped in reforming the UDA into a more focused and efficient terrorist organization precisely by exposing its corruption and forcing it underground. Up to this stage, the UDA had just held on to its legal status (in a similar way to Sinn Fein), and thus men like Craig or McMichael could pose as officers of a lawful political organization (and some prominent members like Glen Barr did engage in serious political thinking). What being so overtly and crudely caught out as racketeers did was to expose the UDA as a thinly disguised front for criminal activity, even if technically just confined to individual members. Up to this stage as well, the role of the UFF could also be technically regarded as not UDA. However, after serious exposure such figments became increasingly difficult to maintain, and once the UFF murder campaign reemerged in earnest, the banning of the UDA became almost inevitable. This also displayed the difference from their republican counterparts, who never allowed themselves to be so easily tarnished and, anyway, by this time were moving on to more sophisticated criminal activity.

The security forces were delighted to be able to tackle the UDA and no doubt strongly recommended their banning. However, whether this also led to a loss of control over the organization as it went underground and cleaned up its act is a mute point; one of the reasons often given for not banning political fronts is precisely to keep them out in the open so that they can be better monitored.

THE UDA, 1992–2007

They didn't go away; in some ways they even got stronger as they went underground and reorganized. The UFF continued to murder, and interviews with members of the security forces during the 1990s revealed that their intelligence on targets was increasingly good, with far fewer random victims and more genuine republican players. After 1992, it also reemerged politically as the "associated" Ulster Democratic Party (UDP) and played a significant role in the talks leading to the Belfast Agreement (1998), with relatively articulate spokesmen such as the late John McMichael's son Gary, John White, and David Adams. Indeed, the government deliberately arranged voting procedures so that they and their competitor loyalists the Popular Unionist Party (PUP), "associated" with the UVF, could be represented despite their minority status in relation to all the other parties.[32]

However, the whiff of corruption and racketeering never totally went away, and reemerged in stark form in the guise of Johnny "Mad Dog" Adair in the years following the Belfast Agreement (1998). He had long been associated with the UDA and had been a target for PIRA in the 1990s, but after 1998 he began to emerge as an overtly serious hood, running his own fiefdom on Shankill Road, West Belfast. He had few brains, but masses of brawn—developed by muscle-pumping exercises in prison—and was streetwise. From this he developed not just rackets but lucrative drug dealings and reigned supreme in his fiefdom through a mixture of fear and admiration.[33] A school teacher interviewed on Shankill Road once told how the most popular career move for his primary school pupils (age 5–11) was to join the UDA and work for Johnny Adair.

But the apparent paradox in all this is that UDA (UDP) political support is still low and always has been. There seems to be a contradictory attitude toward the UDA; that whatever its criminal activities, the embarrassment is only temporary and the longer term community sympathy more permanent, yet this has never translated into votes. Both the UDA's and UDP's electoral record is dismal (as are all the other loyalist parties like the UVF/PUP). Before the 1990s they did not bother to contest elections, usually tending to lend their support to the more strident unionism of Paisley's DUP. However, they became political in the sense of contesting elections in the 1990s, and their first real test was the 1996 Forum election, in which the PUP polled 3.47 percent and the UDP 2.22 percent of the popular vote. For both, this was their finest performance.[34]

Later election results make even more dismal reading for loyalists: in the 1998 Assembly (Stormont, devolved government) elections, the PUP received 2.55 percent and the UDP 1.07 percent of the total vote. By the 2001 general election (Westminster, U.K. national government), the UDP did not stand at all and the PUP received only 0.6 percent of the vote, although in local government elections that year (where they could expect to do better) they received 2 percent of the vote and in 2005 the PUP received 1 percent; once again, there were no UDP candidates.[35]

Yet while electoral wipe-out was occurring for loyalists (and Sinn Fein was becoming the party of choice for Catholic/nationalism, in place of the SDLP), Johnny Adair was almost achieving cult status as a hero of loyalism, and the UDA was universally popular among inner-city, working-class Protestants.[36] Along with Adair other hoods—such as the Shoukri brothers—were also making names for themselves as ruthless racketeers and extortionists in North Belfast (they were finally expelled from the UDA in June 2006[37] and are currently on remand awaiting trial), and loyalists were moving into such unsavory areas as vice and prostitution to go along with drugs. Yet by and large, the UDA are still accepted in their communities, their criminality not simply tolerated but even admired by many, even though they appear to have lapsed back to the ways of 1987 and the *Cook Report*.

This is where one must be careful about claiming too much credit for investigative journalism or one particular program and their ability to undermine organizations. First, the *Cook Report* revealed nothing that most members of the Protestant/Unionist community and the police did not already know or suspect. The overt publicity and extent of the corruption may have surprised many, especially those outside of Northern Ireland, and caused acute embarrassment to the UDA, but it was not really such big news to most on the ground. Indeed, one can actually argue that it kept the UDA away from even worse crimes, such as political murders, and so could have been tolerable in that context.

Second, part of the impact of the *Cook Report* lay in its (presumably fortuitous) timing, just when other things were also coming to a head for the UDA. One must look at a confluence of events and a police force delighted with the opportunity it has been offered. The entire episode seems to have provided the UDA with an opportunity for internal reform and, it is suggested by many, an opportunity to settle internal personal scores. But one must also recall that this did not lead to the demise of the UDA, nor appear to lessen its popular support. Popular support is hard to assess, since the UDA were not contesting elections, but by the time of the Forum elections (1996) the government certainly felt that they represented an important enough section of popular opinion or sentiment to devise an electoral system to enable them to be represented in the Forum, although their electoral support was miserable.[38] This in turn tells us something else, that elections don't always reflect true popular opinion, which is frequently far too complex for psephologists to pick up.

So what is the true attitude of working-class Protestant opinion toward the UDA, and how was it affected by the *Cook Report*? Here, the best data comes from personal experience of talking to and interviewing ordinary working-class Protestants, police, community representatives, and politicians and of generally living and researching in Northern Ireland for 27 years. First, attitudes toward the UDA are ambivalent: they are seen as something to be tolerated by even the more respectable elements of the community as a fall-back, a final resort when all else has failed. In particular, this refers to two things: first, they do not trust their own politicians; second, they do not trust their own state. They fear betrayal, sell-out, and disloyalty everywhere, especially from their own Protestant middle classes (who form the backbone of the UUP and a large section of the DUP), who they think will do any deal (with the United Kingdom and the Republic of Ireland) to preserve their middle-class privileges and protect their economic position. This class antagonism and division is one that has long existed within unionism,[39] although is little reported. Further, such suspicions were reinforced by the UUP's negotiating the much-reviled Belfast Agreement, support for which was almost exclusively confined to nationalists and middle-class unionists.[40]

There was some brief hope that the rise of the DUP may help allay fears over political leaders, but Paisley was never really trusted by inner-city working-class Protestants, who were more secularized than his evangelical revivalism. And in 2007, this suspicion of Paisley was confirmed by his decision to go into devolved government with Sinn Fein and Martin McGuinness (former commanding officer of the Londonderry PIRA), despite having campaigned against the Belfast Agreement and overtaken the UUP as the prime party of unionism because of the DUP's constant opposition to any form of government power sharing with Sinn Fein/PIRA.[41]

Constitutional politics is viewed with deep suspicion by many working-class Protestants, hence the UDA. While its current and past activities may be viewed with reservations, it acts as an important fall-back for them and reflects an un-thought-out sentiment of fear and insecurity. They are constantly looking over their shoulders at the time when they may have to fight for their own survival, in which case the already existing UDA (and UVF) could be important structures to mobilize, having maintained certain organizational, offensive, training, and logistical capabilities. The UDA thus also acts as a kind of zeitgeist—it reminds, recalls, and reflects deep emotion and sentiments not always translatable into conventional politics.

This then fits in with attitudes toward the U.K. state, to which they profess a loyalty. They know they are not wanted by their own state, who find them an embarrassment, inconvenience, and expense. In particular, they see the state regarding them as a nuisance to important relations with the Republic of Ireland, a source of bad international press, and a constant drain on the exchequer. A constant refrain from working-class Protestants is their sense of rejection by their own state, which makes them feel very insecure. The UDA thus reflect their own community's deep sense of insecurity and of being unwanted and unloved, even by their own state. Currently they may not be called on to act, but they may well be in the future, in which case the UDA can be taken out and cleaned up and made fit for purpose. This has been the prevailing attitude most recently found toward the UDA and it has been fairly constant over the last 20 years or so, despite the *Cook Report*.

Another factor to affect attitudes to the UDA has been its image not only as a source of economic opportunity (not unlike PIRA, but less sophisticated) for the otherwise unemployed in a deindustrialized wasteland with high unemployment, but also as a way of cocking a snook at the state that despised them. Johnny Adair especially became a role model for assertiveness, wealth, local status, and being someone in communities denied legitimate ways of doing the same.[42] Unloved and unwanted, they found new expression and purpose via UDA-controlled crime and looked up to Adair as defying not just republicans but mainland and middle-class politicians. At the same time, it also was a way of defying the Belfast Agreement, almost wholly despised by inner-city working-class Protestants. Looked at in this longer term perspective, the *Cook Report* has had little affect.

CONCLUSION

While some authors (such as John Horgan[43]) have seen the *Cook Report* on the UDA as affecting a major change of attitude, those on the ground are a little more sanguine about its effects. Certainly at the time it was embarrassing for the UDA and triggered some extensive internal reorganization, but its longer term affects are rather more dubious. The UDA lost credibility for a time but it also reemerged stronger, purer and more deadly, and its long-term role within its communities remained intact. In addition, it has continued to retain its role and function as a rather nasty criminal route to riches and infamy for many individuals.

This sustenance of its position may be due to three factors, the first of which is the already mentioned role of fall-back as an ultimate response to republicanism. The second is the fact, often expressed by police,[44] that it was not really a prime threat to the state. The reason for this was that it was pro-state and thus competed in an area where the state was always much stronger and more effective and so its purpose less threatening. Further, the quality of its members and hence its organization and operations were also much lower than republicans, which—combined with the fact that it operated in pro-state areas amongst a pro-state population, whose quality recruits would join the security forces anyway—meant that the security forces found they could easily penetrate it and gain intelligence on it. As several policemen commented, "it leaked like a sieve."[45] Finally, by the early 1990s the government was trying to woo loyalist sentiment to engage in the talks leading up to the Belfast Agreement, and since then has been very keen to keep them on board, which may have involved a certain turning of blind eyes to what the terrorist groups were actually up to—again, something several senior police have observed.[46]

Hence the UDA were easy to penetrate for police and investigative reporters in a way that the PIRA is not, and it is the PIRA who have really established extensive economic control over entire communities and have been able to transfer this economic clout into effective politics. Consequently, when looked at over the 20 years following the *Cook Report*, the true affects may be less dramatic than some commentators at the time believed. As was stated in the introduction, to succeed terrorists need a degree of legitimacy, at least from their client population, and it is the situation that loyalists feel themselves in that primarily gives legitimacy to the UDA. That has not changed, something tacitly acknowledged by the government including them into political talks.

However, this is not to deny that the report had any affect, rather that it was more limited than believed. Had there been more follow up reports, and had the PIRA been similarly exposed,[47] things may have been different. As it was, the report was too much of a one-off affair to have a lasting effect. Equally, had there been an alternative "purer" loyalist group then loyalty might have been transferred to them and the UDA might have gone into terminal decline, but as it was there wasn't. This should remind us that organizations alone do not ultimately make a cause or terrorist campaign; it is the issues they represent that sustain terrorism, and for loyalists the issues have not gone away just because the only group that appears to represent it is found to be wanting.

NOTES

1. Jonathan Tonge (1998), *Northern Ireland, Conflict and Change,* Hemel Hempstead: Prentice Hall, provides a very thorough and accurate description of the segregated nature of Northern Ireland in all walks of life.

2. Thomas Hennessey (2005), *The Origins of the Troubles,* Dublin: Gill & Macmillan, provides an exhaustive and authoritative account of all the events leading up to the introduction of the army on to the streets to control the rioting that led up to the start of PIRA's campaign.

3. Paul Bew, Peter Gibbon, and Henry Patterson (1979), *The State in Northern Ireland* Manchester: Manchester University Press, provides a good analysis of these structural changes.

4. The rise of Marxist analysis in the universities, the Paris Spring, the Cold War, anti–Vietnam War movements, and the influence of black power movements and civil rights in the United States are important backdrops to this period.

5. Hennessey, *Origins of the Troubles*, chapters 3 and 4.

6. M. L. R. Smith (1997), *Fighting for Ireland*, London: Routledge, chapter 3.

7. See http://cain.ulst.ac.uk/issues/politics/election/elect.htm.

8. Ibid.

9. Thomas Hennessey (1997), *A History of Northern Ireland, 1920–1996*, Dublin: Gill & Macmillan, chapter 4.

10. Richard English (2004), *Armed Struggle, the History of the IRA*, London: Macmillan, chapter 4, section 1.

11. Steve Bruce (1992), *The Red Hand*, Oxford: Oxford University Press, provides a thorough history and analysis of loyalist terrorist/paramilitary groups in Northern Ireland.

12. Even today, around 50 percent of Catholics wish to remain within the United Kingdom, http://cain.ulst.ac.uk/ni/religion.htm.

13. Walter Laqueur (1987), *The Age of Terrorism*, London: Weidenfeld & Nicolson, chapter 7.

14. Bruce, *The Red Hand*, p. 173.

15. Author's own interviews with security force personnel.

16. Bruce, *The Red Hand*, chapter 11.

17. Steve Bruce (1994), *The Edge of the Union*, Oxford: Oxford University Press, chapter 1.

18. Bruce, *The Red Hand*, p. 180, p. 194, p. 195, p. 247. Jack Holland and Henry McDonald (1994), *INLA, Deadly Divisions*, Dublin: TORC, chapter 9.

19. Bruce, *The Red Hand*, chapter 7.

20. Ibid., chapter 1.

21. Author's own interviews with senior members of the security forces and local investigative journalists Henry McDonald and Chris Ryder.

22. Author's own interviews with senior members of the security forces.

23. John Horgan and Max Taylor (1999), "Playing the Green Card—Financing the Provisional IRA," *Terrorism and Political Violence*, vol 11, no. 1.

24. Author's own interviews with senior members of the security forces.

25. Bruce, *The Red Hand*, p. 248.

26. Ibid., p. 247.

27. Ibid., chapter 10.

28. Ibid., p. 249.

29. Bruce, *Edge of the Union*, p. 16.

30. Bruce, *The Red Hand*, chapter 10.

31. Bruce, *Edge of the Union*, Appendix 1, p. 54.

32. Thomas Hennessey (2000), *The Northern Ireland Peace Process*, Dublin: Gill & Macmillan, p. 102–103.

33. David Lister and Hugh Jordan (2004), *Mad Dog: The Rise and Fall of Johnny Adair and 'C' Company*, Edinburgh: Mainstream Publishing.

34. See http://cain.ulst.ac.uk/issues/politics/election/elect.htm.

35. Hennessey, *Northern Ireland Peace Process*.

36. Bruce, *Edge of the Union*.

37. See http://news.bbc.co.uk/2/ni/uk_news/northern_ireland/5099082.stm.

38. Lister and Jordan, *Mad Dog*.

39. Bew, Gibbon, and Patterson, *State in Northern Ireland*. Austen Morgan (1991), *Labour and Partition*, London: Pluto.

40. Peter Shirlow and Brendan Murtagh (2006), *Belfast, Segregation, Violence and the City*, London: Pluto, chapter 2.

41. Bruce, *Edge of the Union*.

42. Bruce, *Edge of the Union*. James Dingley (2002), "Peace in Our Time: The Stresses and Strains on the Northern Ireland Peace Process," *Studies in Conflict and Terrorism*, vol. 25, no. 6.

43. John Horgan (2006), "Disengaging from Terrorism," *Jane's Intelligence Review*, December.

44. Personal interviews, including those already cited.

45. Ibid.

46. Ibid.

47. A lack of criticism of PIRA's criminality has also been frequently alluded to in the interviews I have conducted.

Al-Qaida's Strategy for Influencing Perceptions in the Muslim World

Sammy Salama and Joe-Ryan Bergoch

THE ABILITY TO INFLUENCE THE masses is vital to the success of an Islamist revolution. The case of the Egyptian al-Jihad al-Islami in 1981 illustrates this point. The plot to assassinate Egyptian President Anwar Sadat, while successful, was meant to constitute only the first stage of a larger multipronged strategy for seizing power. The entire operation, planned by al-Jihad's military strategist Col. Abbud Abd al-Latif al-Zumur, involved seizing control of numerous facilities in Cairo, including the Egyptian Army's operation room and the Central Security headquarters, as well as the Radio and Television and Telephone Exchange buildings, where al-Jihad members would broadcast a communiqué announcing the beginning of the "Islamic Revolution."[1]

According to the plan set by al-Zumur, on the same day of the operations in Cairo the Upper Egyptian branch of the group would take over the city of Asyut in central Egypt, from where they would advance north.[2] Yet the uprising in Asyut did not occur for another two days and was swiftly suppressed by Egyptian security forces. While al-Jihad members were able to kill Sadat in a spectacular fashion, the rest of their plan failed to materialize. Al-Jihad underestimated the hardiness of the Egyptian government and overestimated their support among the Egyptian populace. In fact, with the exception of their cohorts—primarily the Asyut branch of al-Jama'a al-Islamiya—few other Egyptians believed in the mission of the Egyptian al-Jihad or opted to join their Islamic revolution.

The plan to assassinate Sadat was initially proposed to Muhammad 'Abd al-Salam Farraj, the leader of al-Jihad al-Islami, by the would-be assassin Khalid al-Islambouli in late September 1981. Lieutenant Islambouli was put in command of an armored transport vehicle that was to take part in a military parade, and he saw this as a unique opportunity to reach Sadat.[3] Ironically, when the particulars of the operation and its viability were discussed by the leaders of the group during a meeting on September 26, al-Zumur opposed the timing of the Sadat assassination for practical considerations.[4] He argued that they were not yet ready to launch a revolt against the government and that more time was necessary to recruit additional members. His objections were overruled by the leading ideologues, and as a result, the group's overall revolt failed to materialize. Farraj, Islambuli, and the other assassins were consequently hanged, while most remaining members of al-Jihad were swiftly rounded up and imprisoned—including a young Ayman al-Zawahiri.

Al-Qaida has learned a great deal from the failures of al-Jihad al-Islami and other domestic jihadi organizations in the Muslim world—namely, their inability to muster the support of significant segments of Muslim populations to facilitate popular support to their causes and assist in the overthrow of secular regimes. As a global revolutionary salafi-jihadi movement, al-Qaida and its affiliates aim not only to carry out military operations on Western and Muslim soils but also to enhance and facilitate their revolutionary activities by instilling their vision, religious ideology, and political doctrine in the minds of the Muslim masses. Unfortunately, recent advances in communication technology have greatly facilitated this endeavor. Unlike the early 1980s, when governments in the Muslim world exercised a virtual monopoly on media outlets that routinely broadcasted their message and orientation, the advent and global expansion of the Internet in recent decades has provided terrorist organizations like al-Qaida with a sophisticated and robust public relations capability, enabling them to influence perceptions in ways previously unheard of. This chapter discusses the various aspects of al-Qaida's strategy for influencing perceptions in the Muslim world by (1) using the Internet to export its revolution; (2) borrowing historical terminology to evoke collective memory; (3) demonizing and attacking Westerners to divide the Muslim community; (4) portraying its activities as part of a popular revolution; and (5) redefining the conflict with the West and its allies as a long-term war of attrition in order to minimize the importance of tactical setbacks.

EXPORTING THE REVOLUTION: AL-QAIDA AND THE USE OF THE INTERNET

The use of the Internet as the primary means for transmitting and dispersing a wide array of written and audiovisual jihadi media has come to characterize the modus operandi of every level of the al-Qaida network. Al-Qaida's central leadership apparatus, transnational network of operational and logistical support cells, and affiliated Islamist terrorist groups—in addition to the vast (and largely unknown) number of like-minded jihadi individuals and groups whose connections to the al-Qaida "core" are either distant or nonexistent—all utilize the Web as an easy-access, low-cost medium for propagating their ideology and facilitating the jihad. The importance of the Internet to al-Qaida and its affiliates, moreover, has rapidly increased in the past eight years. While al-Qaida's use of the Internet is by no means a new phenomenon, the years since the attacks of September 11, 2001, have witnessed a meteoric rise in both the number and breadth of jihadi Web sites and Web forums.[5] While the precise rate of this increase has yet to be calculated, the number of jihadi sites and forums is conservatively estimated to have grown from 150 sites to 4,000 sites during the 2000–2005 period.[6]

Web sites erected by al-Qaida's leadership apparatus, global cells, and affiliated groups (such as al-Qaida in Iraq and al-Qaida in the Arab Maghreb) are central to al-Qaida's efforts to influence perceptions in the Muslim world. However, Web-based jihadi media is produced and distributed by a variety of actors including lone sympathizers, virtual media "studios" that are associated, by varying degrees, with the al-Qaida network, as well as al-Qaida and its affiliates themselves.[7] Moreover, the number of official Web sites directly maintained by al-Qaida and its affiliates is dwarfed by a rising sea of sympathetic Web sites, online jihadi forums, and blogs. It has been observed that online forums are "the most popular and widespread means of delivering" jihadi media.[8] These sites contain or display links to textual, audio, and video materials that convey religious doctrines and justifications for activities, propagandistic diatribes against the West and friendly Arab governments, morale-boosting pieces that describe or applaud particular terrorist attacks or idealize specific "martyrs," and instructive materials dealing with operational methodology, tactics, and weapons production. Regardless of the strength of the bonds that connect the al-Qaida core to the individuals or groups who create and maintain jihadi Web pages, one central fact remains: the online activities of nearly all of these actors have the capacity to further the strategic aims of al-Qaida.

A survey of Jihadi websites that primarily address the movement's present *cause célèbre*, the conflict in Iraq, demonstrates the startling effectiveness of the Internet as a propaganda tool in the hands of al-Qaida. While the majority of Iraqi insurgents ascribe to an ideology that is primarily one of Sunni nationalism, the language and symbolism of Salafi Jihadism has dominated insurgent media from the outset of the war. Now, as Daniel Kimmage and Kathleen Ridolfo recently observed, the "explicitly religious framing of the conflict in Iraq renders insurgent rhetoric virtually indistinguishable from the rhetoric of the global Jihadist movement."[9] Even websites of insurgent groups that have clashed with al-Qaida over political matters employ similar religious motifs and jihadist rhetoric. The propagation of al-Qaida's ideology thus occurs explicitly and implicitly, both increasing the direct exposure of Muslims to al-Qaida-affiliated media, and indirectly saturating the Web sites of other (often inimical) groups with salafi jihadism.

Moreover, Web sites and online forums maintained by al-Qaida members, affiliates, and sympathizers host or link to practically the entire corpus of al-Qaida-related media products. This includes statements of leaders like bin Laden, books and pamphlets written by al-Qaida members, texts outlining historical or doctrinal matters, and perhaps most alarming, scores of official al-Qaida magazines, leaflets, and operational manuals. Al-Qaida operatives, affiliates, and aspiring "fellow travelers" are thus provided with a veritable virtual classroom with which to communicate and learn from compatriots thousands of miles away. Indeed, the potential for this learning process to enhance the operational capabilities of jihadis worldwide should not be underestimated.[10]

Of the media materials posted to jihadi sites and forums, it is important to note that only a small minority—less than 10 percent—address topics of *operational* significance. The vast majority of jihadist material is primarily propagandistic or religious in nature, directed toward shaping Muslims' worldview according to al-Qaida's ideology. These materials include operational statements by al-Qaida and its affiliates, inspirational poetry or biographies of "martyrs," official statements outlining political or doctrinal stances, web periodicals like al-Qaida's *Sawt al-Jihad*, recorded statements of prominent leaders, videotaped attacks, downloadable books, and even films.[11] In spite of their relatively small number, it is those operational Web sites that concentrate specifically on target selection, preparations, and training for existing or aspiring jihadi terrorists, however, that arguably pose the greatest immediate threat to international security.[12]

Assessing the size and scope of the jihadi operational Web sites' viewership is of central importance. It is also extremely difficult to do so with precision. One must take into account the fact that the same users frequent multiple sites, and that a single individual may posses memberships to multiple sites. Moreover, in terms of the usage patterns of operational jihadi Web sites, precise data is difficult to come by due to the fact that the majority of these sites do not make this information readily available. There are some exceptions, however. For example, back in 2006 one relatively new site, al-Nusra, listed an average of 30 members logged in simultaneously and a total of 1,171 members (regular users) as of April 16, 2006.[13] Al-Muhajirun, an extremely popular site at the time, reported a total of 8,378 members as of April 25, 2006.[14] The older site al-Sakifah, however, claimed a much larger total of 13,708 members and an average of 200 members logged in at the same time as of April 16, 2006.[15] It may be reasonable to conclude that the usage patterns of most operationally oriented sites fall somewhere within this range. A rough approximation of the online jihadi community viewing operationally oriented Web sites could comprise 40,000–60,000 regular users. That this number has grown is presently not a subject of debate. The rate of this growth, however, is.

Jihadi Web sites that provide operationally applicable information have evolved considerably over the past years. The primary al-Qaida site directly following September 11 was al-Neda, which posted theological justifications for transnational jihad, celebrations of al-Qaida's attacks, and statements and pictures of Osama bin Laden.[16] A handful of new operational Web sites maintained by al-Qaida, its affiliates, and its sympathizers, however, had arisen by November 2004. One of the more prominent was al-Ma'asada al-Jihadiyya ("The Jihadi Lion's Den"), which contained a section tailored specifically to jihadi cells.[17] Al-Ma'asada linked to a second operational site, the most notorious and extensive to date. Mawsu'at al-I'idad ("Preparation Encyclopedia") displays links to dozens of portals that disseminate the tactical knowledge of jihadis worldwide. Hundreds (if not thousands) of pages provide detailed information on topics ranging from marksmanship to biological weapons, frequently linking to Western sites treating similar issues. Since late 2004, however, the number of jihadi operational Web sites has grown an estimated 1,500 percent. Combined with the attendant rise in these sites' viewership and the increasing quality (and lethality) of the information being provided, the threat of Web-based jihadi activities is clear.

In addition to spreading its militant Islamist ideology and transforming perceptions within the Muslim world, al-Qaida is increasingly able to establish, indoctrinate, train, and coordinate terrorist cells via the Internet. Al-Qaida's training facilities are now, by and large, located in the safety of cyberspace. Moreover, while the materials provided by jihadi Web sites are often second-rate in production quality, they in many cases constitute first-class terrorist training. Indeed, Saif al-Adel, al-Qaida's military chief who personally trained Mohammed Atta and the other 9/11 hijackers, is a regular contributor to online operational magazines. Michael Scheuer, former head of the CIA Bin Laden unit, has remarked that "it used to be they had to go to Sudan, they had to go to Yemen, they had to go to Afghanistan to train."[18] At present, the Internet provides a would-be cell member with the necessary materials and information, so that he "no longer has to carry anything that's incriminating. He doesn't need his schematics, he doesn't need his blueprints, he doesn't need his formulations."[19] The material "can be sent ahead by encrypted Internet, and it gets lost in the billions of messages that are out there."[20]

Attempting to counter the proliferation of Web sites that increase the number and operational capability of transnational jihadis is both necessary and extremely challenging. Jihadi Web site administrators are highly redundant in disseminating operational information, routinely posting the same content on numerous URLs (mirrors), and almost immediately reposting nearly identical information when a Web site is neutralized. The example of the document "A Course in Popular Poisons and Deadly Gases" is a case in point. This manual, which contains directions for the manufacture of numerous crude chemical weapons and biological toxins, was originally posted on the Mawsu'a al-I'adad (The Preparation Encyclopedia) Web site.[21] It has subsequently been posted to dozens of jihadi sites. On April 16, 2006, the manual was located on the jihadi Web site al-Nusra, which had posted a link to the manual only the day before. Unfortunately, the sheer number and ease of replicability of jihadi operational Web sites presently poses a challenge to the counterterrorism community.

Quality of Operational Materials on Jihadi Web Sites

As indicated previously, it is important not to underestimate the quality of instruction in operational training manuals circulated on jihadi Web sites—in many cases, these provide first-class terrorist training. Some analysts may not have a clear understanding of the value of these sites and mistakenly assume that they contain information of poor quality, yet many of the operational training manuals have in fact been prepared by seasoned al-Qaida veterans and leading operational planners. In fact, some operational manuals are authored by the leading al-Qaida operatives and trainers, including Saif al-Adel, head of al-Qaida's military committee; Yousef bin Saleh al-'Ayeeri (also known as Sheikh al-Battar), a former trainer in Afghanistan and former commander of al-Qaida in Saudi Arabia; and his successor, Abu Hajir Abd al-Aziz al-Muqrin. Other manuals are written by obscure authors and are likely less valuable. In addition, operational manuals posted on jihadi Web sites also vary greatly in size; the largest is the colossal 1,081-page "Encyclopedia of Jihad," while some are no longer than 2 pages. Overall, though, a large number of operational manuals often empower would-be jihadis with deadly skills, precious insights, and a detailed level of instruction.

Why Proliferate Operational Materials?

That al-Qaida regularly proliferates training manuals and materials on the Internet for public viewing is likely meant to serve a dual purpose. Not only do they equip prospective al-Qaida cell members with deadly skills taught to them by terrorist masterminds that are applicable for carrying out attacks, but they are also likely meant to provide a sense of empowerment among its supporters within the global Muslim community, as well as the impetus for joining the global jihadi revolution and taking up arms against "apostate" governments. In most Arab states, the regime's security services are often dreaded and feared by the masses, and popular perceptions prevail of the invulnerability of these agencies and their total control over all aspects of security in a country. In many cases, these popular perceptions have been intentionally nurtured by various regimes, through repeated brutal practices intended to dissuade the masses from contemplating taking up arms against them. Given that most ruling regimes in the Muslim world appear to exercise a monopoly over power and strictly limit military training and the possession of firearms, a secondary objective of al-Qaida is likely to provide sympathetic Muslims with the impression of military empowerment by providing first-rate training via its Web sites along with specific instructions for the manufacture of numerous weapons systems. This also exaggerates the capabilities of the global jihadi movement and portrays it as capable of learning and disseminating traditionally restricted knowledge. Successful message dissemination and stunning attacks on Muslim lands combine to chip away at a regime's fear-inspiring and all-powerful image.

BORROWING HISTORICAL TERMINOLOGY TO EVOKE COLLECTIVE MEMORY AND DEMONIZE ITS ENEMIES

In an effort to influence perception in the Muslim world, al-Qaida often utilizes specific provocative terminology from Islamic history to evoke the collective memory of the Muslim masses and demonize its enemies. Among the most common terms used by al-Qaida and its affiliates are:

- *Salibiyin*—Crusaders: Used to refer to the United States and other Western nations
- *Tatar*—Mongols: Used to refer to Arab governments
- *Rafida*—Rejectionists: Used to refer to Shi'a Muslims
- *'Alaqima*—Decedents of Ibn al-'Alqami: Used to refer to Shi'a Muslims

The use of the term Salibiyin (Crusaders) is meant to draw a parallel to the Christian Crusades to the Holy Land that occurred from the eleventh through the thirteenth centuries A.D. While viewed differently in Western accounts, in Muslim eyes the Crusades are seen as a brutal and systemic effort by the Church and Western Christian powers to extend their influence over and dominate the Middle East, including Jerusalem, the third holiest site in Islam. The Crusaders were initially very successful. They claimed Jerusalem in 1099, and thereafter established the Kingdom of Jerusalem which extended over the eastern shores of the Mediterranean and included Gaza, Ascalon, Jaffa, Caesarea, Haifa, Acre, Tyre, Tiberia, Nablus, and Hebron. The excessive brutality of the Crusaders against the residents of Jerusalem and the surrounding territories cultivated a collective sense of anger and enmity among the greater Muslim community. As a result, the Kurdish general Salah al-Din al-Ayubi (Saladin) was able to capitalize on this collective anger and assemble a massive Muslim army that overwhelmed the Crusader forces and regained Jerusalem in 1187. Al-Qaida, which wishes to replicate the success of Salah al-Din, labels the United States and its Western allies "Crusaders" and claims that contemporary American policies in the Middle East are a mere continuation of the Crusades of old.[22] As stated in *al-Battar* magazine, a preeminent al-Qaida operational publication:

> The crusader church with all its sects protestant, catholic and orthodox is not absent from the [current] events. As it was the church that launched and supported the crusades against the Muslims, today it is still doing so only from behind the scenes in order to hold on to its (missionary) appearance that claims to oppose wars and destruction regardless of justification.
>
> No matter how much time passes we will not forget how the church of old launched the crusades against Islam, and we will not forget the inquisition campaign in Andalusia, and we will not forget the position of the Orthodox Church in supporting the Soviet war on Afghanistan. Although the soviets at the time did not even recognize religion, the church played a role in getting close to them at the expense of Muslim blood. Then came the Serbian ethnic cleansing of the Bosnian Muslims and the Orthodox Church in Greece played a big role in this ugly crime. It recruited 70,000 volunteers to take part in the ethnic cleansing of Muslims; it did the same in the first Chechen war and is doing so in the second Chechen war.
>
> And the Protestant Church is no less evil than the Orthodox, it pushed the gang of the Black House to launch a crusade against Islam from 1973 until today. The Catholic Church in the Vatican has helped it in launching these wars and in fanning the flames of war around the world that make way for Christian missionary campaigns. We do not forget that the day the Pope heard Bush declaring a crusade that starts in Afghanistan, that old man opted to travel to all the neighboring countries of Afghanistan to gather support for this crusade.[23]

By using this terminology, al-Qaida seeks to evoke the collective memory of Muslims to boost Muslim opposition to American policies in the region. It also strives to draw on an increasing sense of discontent toward contemporary Western actions in the Middle East, and to inspire the Muslim masses to rise up and eventually overwhelm and remove Western presence from the region. By drawing this parallel al-Qaida, at the very least, hopes to swell its ranks with Muslim volunteers who will continue its campaign against the West and its allies in the region.

Another popular term in jihadi literature is Tatar, an Arabic term for Mongols that is often used to depict the Saudis and other Arab governments who al-Qaida considers apostates. Decades after the Mongols sacked Baghdad and destroyed the caliphate in 1258, they converted to Islam in 1295. However, Ghazan, the leader of the Mongols, did not rule by Shari'a law and continued to adhere to the Yasa, the code of Genghis Khan. This prompted the noted Hanbali cleric Ahmed Ibn Taymiyya to denounce the Mongols as "Muslims by name only" who are no better than apostates. In 1300, Ahmed Ibn Taymiyya issued his famous fatwas calling on Muslims to wage armed jihad against the Mongol rulers. He decreed that jihad is the sixth pillar of Islam and is more important than pilgrimage. Al-Qaida routinely borrows from the sayings and writing of Ahmed Ibn Taymiyya, and draws a parallel between their contemporary opposition against moderate or secular Muslim governments and Taymiyya's opposition to the Mongols. The government of Saudi Arabia is often labeled as Tatar and Murtaddin (apostates) in al-Qaida's publications.[24] As stated in *Sawt al-Jihad*, the official publication of al-Qaida in the Saudi kingdom:

> No one is exempt from religious law regardless of their ethnicity, nationality, flag, slogan or association. As the foreign Tatars committed unbelief so did the al-Saud and other Arabs. If they were from the land of the two holy places, then the land does not make anyone holy. Religious law is uniform and does not vary according to time, location, policies and regimes.[25]

Al-Qaida and its outlets regularly refer to Shi'a Muslims as Rafida (rejectionists or defectors).[26] The term *Rafida* was originally used against the Shi'a in the nineteenth and early twentieth centuries by Sunni ulama (religious scholars) at a time when many Shi'a tribes who feared increasing Wahhabi influence in the Arabian peninsula migrated to Mesopotamia. A large number of Sunni tribes in Mesopotamia subsequently converted to Shi'ism, both out of fear of the Wahhabis and in an attempt to avoid conscription into the Ottoman army.[27] These trends in migration and conversion resulted in Shi'a Muslims becoming a majority in Mesopotamia, which became modern Iraq in 1920.[28] Salafi-jihadis claim that due to their practice of *Ijtihad* (learned interpretation of the Qur'an), and their veneration of saints, the Shi'a have rejected the true calling of Islam and are in essence no better than infidels and must be fought. Salafi-jihadi literature and Web sites are full of blatant anti-Shi'a treatises and diatribes.[29] Another point of contention against the Iraqi Shi'a in particular is their alliance with the United States. For that, the salafi-jihadis continuously preach that the Rafida are a "fifth column" of heretics who routinely act as agents of foreign forces in the Arab and Muslim world. They accuse the Shi'a of always taking sides with the foreign enemies of Islam, from the alleged Shi'a alliance with Hulagu in 1258 A.D., up to current Shi'a assistance to the United States in Iraq. A message posted in 2004 on al-Tawhid wal-Jihad's (al-Qaida in Iraq) official Web site illustrates this: "As stated by Sheik Ibn Taymiyya . . . the Rafida . . . always align with and aid the infidel Christian and Jews, in fighting the Muslims."[30] In addition, many pro al-Qaida Web sites have entire pages filled with substantial anti-Shi'a literature dedicated to questioning the validity of the Shi'a Muslim faith and besmirching the memory of prominent Shi'a leaders and organizations.

Another term often used by Al-Qaida in Iraq to describe the Iraqi Shi'a is *'Alaqima*, in reference to Mu'ayid al-Din Muhammed Ibn al-'Alqami, a thirteenth-century Shi'i *Wazir* (minister) in the government of the last Abbasid caliph al-Musta'sim. It is reported that in the lead up to the Mongol invasions Ibn al-'Alqami betrayed al-Musta'sim and played a significant role in weakening the Abbasid government and later assisted the Mongols in their occupation of Baghdad and their sacking of the caliphate in 1258. Of note is his urging of the Abbasid caliph to forgo the safety of the walls of Baghdad and go out to meet with Hulagu the Mongol leader. Upon their approach, the Abbasid caliph and his companions were brutally killed by the Mongols. Current jihadis use the term

'Alaqima to draw a parallel between the acts of al-'Alqami in the thirteenth century and the Shi'a alliance with the United States in postwar Iraq. As noted previously, al-Qaida, its affiliates, and supporters claim that the Shi'a minority are a fifth column among Muslims who align themselves with foreign occupiers to weaken the Sunni majority. As stated in the magazine of *Ansar al-Sunna*, an al-Qaida affiliate in Iraq:

> All through history the leaders of the Rafida committed sabotage within the Muslim state and carried out their conniving plans and were always in the service of the enemy . . . be it crusader or Jewish or Mongol . . . for that, it is not surprising that today we see their grand children in the service of the occupying crusader . . . so we draw on the role of the Rafida in bringing down the Muslim state as personified in the role of Ibn al-'Alqami for example to show their grudge and conniving actions against the Muslim nation.[31]

The considerable animosity between the United States and the Shi'i Islamic Republic of Iran since the late 1970s seems to be lost on al-Qaida, as is Hizballah's bloody conflicts with Israel since 1982.

This tactic is not exclusive to jihadis. Borrowing historical terminology to evoke collective memory is also used by secular leaders in the Middle East. Prior to the onset of Operation Iraqi Freedom, Iraqi President Saddam Hussein equated the United States with the Mongol invaders who occupied Baghdad in 1258 and brought down the Abbasid caliphate. He called U.S. troops "new Mongols" and stated, "Baghdad, its people and leadership, is determined to force the Mongols of our age to commit suicide at its gates."[32] Hussein meant to rally the Arab masses and claim that despite their various stated justification for initiating the conflict, in reality the American-led coalition forces were no different than the invading Mongols of the thirteenth century who wished to dominate the region.

Since Saddam's speech in January 2003, this term has gained considerable acceptance among Arab pundits who oppose American policies in the Middle East, and repeat Hussein's argument that American forces in Iraq are no different than the old Mongols who ravaged the Abbasid caliphate. Many Arab pundits currently use the term *al-Maghul al-Judud* (new Mongols) to describe the United States and its forces in Iraq. Using the term "new Mongols" with reference to the American occupation of Iraq is deliberately meant to strike a chord with the Arab masses by evoking the memories of the fall of Baghdad in 1258 and the destruction of the Abbasid caliphate. This is viewed as the most traumatic event in Muslim history, the time when Islam fell from grace and Muslims became dominated. This is meant to create a unique sense of urgency among the masses by invoking a collective memory of humiliation and occupation.

The use of provocative historical terminology by al-Qaida is meant to strike a chord with the Muslim masses and to shape their perceptions of the West and its allies in the region as well as their perceptions of al-Qaida itself. As such terminology gains acceptance among the Muslim masses, it is meant to gradually demonize the United States and its allies in the Muslim world and by default render al-Qaida and its activities legitimate in the eyes of an increasing number of Muslims.

DEMONIZE AND ATTACK

Persistently Claiming a Western Conspiracy to Subjugate Islam and Rob Muslims

An integral part of al-Qaida's overall communication strategy in the Muslim world is repeatedly claiming a long-term and inherent Western conspiracy to subjugate and humiliate Islam, and to steal Muslim treasure and resources. Such theories and flawed interpretations of political dynamics are not new to Middle Eastern political milieus. Since the early twentieth century, numerous nationalist and Islamist political thinkers and leaders in the region have pointed to the historical role of European colonial powers in the division of the Middle East and the creation of modern nation-states in the aftermath of World War I. In addition to this role, regional critics of the West point to numerous cases of occupation of Muslim lands by Western powers, beginning with Napoleon's invasion of Egypt in 1798, along with the occupation of numerous other Muslim territories in the early twentieth century and the dreaded mandate scheme which most in the region view as quasi-colonialist.

Due to this blemished history of Western power involvement in the region, many in the Middle East inherently view Western influence and actions in the region with a modicum of suspicion. Previous anti-Western revolutionary movements in the region including the Nasserites, Baathists, Khomeinists, and others have opted to play up these inherent fears among the regional populace to validate their policies and promote adherence to their ideologies. While anti-Western secular nationalists view Western interference in the Middle East as a means to further the Western powers' economic and political interests in the region, the Islamists differ in that they allege that the cause of flawed Western policies toward Muslims is their "inherent" dislike and animosity toward the religion of Islam and Muslims in general.

Similarly, al-Qaida opts to capitalize on these inherent suspicious within the Muslim populace to validate its own message and worldview by claiming that current American actions in the Middle East are a direct continuation of early twentieth-century Western injustice against Muslims. The fact that unlike its European counterparts, the United States did not have a history of colonial involvement in the Middle East prior to World War II, or that it actually labored to support Muslims during numerous conflicts—specifically the 1956 Suez War, the liberation of Kuwait, or the defense of Bosnian Muslims—is routinely ignored by al-Qaida and its supporters. They simply ignore these facts altogether and play up America's historical support to Israel, its alliance with authoritarian Muslim regimes, and its recent occupation of Iraq as more revealing indications of American interests and allegedly sinister intentions.

Al-Qaida regularly invokes in their speeches and publications an alleged long-term Western animosity toward Islam, arguing that the West intends to rob Muslim treasures as it supposedly always has. As stated in the following message issued by Osama bin Laden in 2005:

> One of the foremost motivations of our enemies is the desire to subjugate our lands and to steal our oil, for that, you should spare no effort is stopping the greatest theft in history from current and future generations through the work of collaborators.

They take if for cheap knowing that the price of every other commodity has multiplied many times except for oil which is the base of industry. Its price has been reduced numerous times, while it was sold for $40 two decades ago; it was sold for $9 in last decade. Its price today should be at least $100 per barrel. Be vigilant to put a distance between them and oil, and concentrate your operations on it especially in Iraq and the gulf. This would be their end.[33]

Doing so is not only meant to generate sympathy and support for al-Qaida's actions among Muslims but it is also meant to cast al-Qaida's activities in a "defensive" light. By arguing that the West is intrinsically hostile to Islam and that it seeks to rob Muslim treasure, al-Qaida justifies its own murderous terrorist attacks as simple acts of defense and resistance on behalf of Islam and Muslims, acts that are necessary to halt the Western juggernaut. This strategy is further enforced by al-Qaida's attacks on Westerners in the West and on Muslim lands.

Attacking Western Targets to Divide Muslims Into "Two Camps"

Attacks on Western targets constitute a fundamental pillar of al-Qaida's overall strategy for influencing perceptions in the Muslim world. The intention to carry out such attacks is not erratic nor spontaneous, but is meant to draw a distinct line in the sand and divide Muslim societies into two camps. Al-Qaida thus hopes to create a dualistic, "you are either with us or with them," political climate. In this polarized environment, Muslim leaders and populations will be forced to choose sides in this epic battle, standing either within the camp of the "true" Muslims who reject humiliation and defeat or among the ranks of the "infidels" and their alleged agents in the Muslim world. This dovetails with al-Qaida's systematic effort to demonize Westerners and their policies toward the Muslim world.

Coincidental to the ongoing and methodical campaign of demonization pursued on all al-Qaida-related Web portals, as well as through the videos and communiqués they provide to Muslim media outlets, al-Qaida carries out attacks on targets in the West to "draw the line and divide the people into two camps." Through these attacks, al-Qaida wishes to distinguish themselves from other, more moderate trends in the Middle East who are quick to renounce such actions. Indeed, al-Qaida members, supporters, and sympathizers routinely accuse their detractors of waffling and downright sedition against the Muslim cause and of adhering to "a curriculum of humiliation." Such libels of sedition and treason to Islam are also routinely leveled against Muslim regimes—namely, the Gulf Cooperation Council states, Jordan, and Pakistan—that provide Western powers with territory for military bases that are used to support operations within Muslim lands. Carrying out attacks against the West also influences perceptions in the Muslim world by undermining a popularly preconceived notion of American invulnerability and by raising average Muslims' awareness of all matters articulated by the network, such as the alleged treason of Arab regimes and the righteous quest to reinstate the caliphate. As articulated in a July 2004 al-Qaida communiqué:

The New York and Manhattan operation [September 11] was the onset of an Islamic intifada against the crimes of the crusaders toward the Muslim nation. Yes, Islam is a religion of peace toward those at peace with Islam; but toward those who are hostile to Islam, it is an unrelenting religion of war.

The Benefits of This Operation:

- Exposing the new world order and revealing its true face.
- Exposing the lie of democracy, individual rights and human rights. Guantanamo, Abu Ghraib and the prisons of thousands of Muslims without trials in the United States, Britain and Europe are the biggest proof. Look at Kuwait which the United States entered in the name of freedom and democracy; it is still ruled by a tyrant and is a dictatorship that is protected by America. Who defends these bloody rulers except for America and Europe? As is also the case in Saudi Arabia, Tunisia, Algeria, Morocco, and Iraq when the tyrant Saddam was on their side.
- Exposing the Arab and Muslim rulers.
- Destroying the American economy. Up until this day, America is still suffering economically from trade deficits and inflation.
- Destroying the image of an invulnerable America.
- Revival of the spirit of Jihad and rise of the victorious sect [members of al-Qaida].
- Drawing the line and dividing the people into two camps.
- Collapsing the secular and national forces that are represented in the government and artificial opposition.
- Exposing and bankrupting the loyalist Islamic movements that are aligned with the apostate governments who adhere to a curriculum of humiliation.

. . .

- Raising the general awareness, when even common people discuss matters such as the Caliphate, treason of leaders, and loyalty, which in the past they did not know of.[34]

Moreover, perpetrating attacks against Western persons or institutions in the Muslim world provides al-Qaida with an even greater public relations opportunity. Not only do they portray themselves as the true champions of Islam and the only ones who reject humiliation and dare to attack the "infidel" Westerners, they also draw attention to the "apostate" regimes' willingness to defend Western instillations and persons in their countries, sacrificing their soldiers and policemen who die in clashes with the jihadis or in the bombings carried out by al-Qaida members. Al-Qaida argues that, by such actions, it is exposing the true nature of apostate regimes as simple lackeys and servants of Western powers who will fiercely protect their "masters," even to the point of jeopardizing their own people. As stated by former al-Qaida commander in Saudi Arabia, Abu Hajir Abd al-Aziz al-Muqrin, in an urban warfare training manual that instructs cell members to attack Westerners residing in Muslim cities, the benefits of such attacks are:

- Improving the morale of the nation, improving the morale of the mujahideen. Degrading if not destroying the morale of the enemies.
- Validating the group's truthfulness among members of society. The fact that these operation occur in the cities, makes the people watch us and watch the intended targets, so the media will not be able distort the picture.
- Deterring and containing the regime.

. . .

- Loses of influential members and symbols of these countries and regimes.

- Affecting the economies of these countries.
. . .
- Preparing the nation and its members to the prophesized blood shed.
- Gaining new supporters with every successful operation and increasing the popularity of the Mujahideen.
- Pushing the regime to change its policies.
- Shaking the confidence among members of the regime, and as we previously mentioned increasing the possibility of a clash among the military and the political wing or a clash among the political parties. So if the strikes increased—with god's permission— symbols of the state will find no confidence among themselves.[35]

POPULAR REVOLUTION: CALLING ON MUSLIM MASSES
TO AID AND PARTICIPATE IN JIHAD

As discussed previously, the planned October 1981 revolt by al-Jihad al-Islami failed largely due to their inability to overcome the military might of the Egyptian government and to their exclusivist conception of jihad as the duty of a righteous vanguard. The manifesto of al-Jihad was provided by the group's founder, Mohammed Abd al-Salam Farraj, in his treatise, "al-Faridah al-Gha'ibah" (The Neglected Duty). Farraj begins his manuscript by stating that "Jihad for God's cause . . . has been neglected by the ulema of this age," and he portrays violent jihad as the sixth pillar of Islam, drawing on the precedent set by Ibn Tamiyya.[36] The primary goal of Farraj and his cohorts was to establish an Islamic state in Egypt, through revolution brought about by a righteous vanguard of believers. Farraj contends that jihad is *not* a popular struggle, for "Islam does not triumph by (attracting the support of) the majority."[37]

In contrast to their jihadi predecessors, al-Qaida does not view its mission as the responsibility of a righteous vanguard of believers. Rather, it perceives itself as spearheading a popular global jihadi movement. Al-Qaida has learned from the mistakes of al-Jihad and conversely opts to portray their struggle as a popular revolution in which they repeatedly call on the Muslim masses to aid and participate in jihad. As stated in an al-Qaida communiqué issued in July 2004:

> *What is Required of the Brothers, Members of the Victorious Sect:*
> - Devotion to God almighty and patience knowing that victory is around the corner and god protects those who serve him.
> - Establishing small groups under various different names such as al-Tawhid wal-Jihad and Abu Hafez al-Masri Brigades . . . etc. This makes it difficult for the enemy to expose and track down these groups. In addition, this thins out the pressure of the security services.
> - Jihadi education including doctrinal teaching, loyalty, purity and work according to these teachings.
> - Military and physical training and spreading this among sons and members of the clans (for the battle may be protracted).

- Learning modern skills like computers and the Internet and all that can be beneficial to the Mujahideen and Muslims.
- Igniting a psychological war against the enemy.

What is Required of the Muslim Nation:
- Learning the doctrine . . . especially loyalty and purity.
- Sincere repentance for neglecting Jihad.
- Wishing for the Mujahideen and providing them with financial and moral support.
- Setting up small cells inside and outside the cities.
- Sheltering and protecting the Mujahideen.
- Defending their honor.
- Joining their ranks.
- Advising them.[38]

To further inspire popular support for its actions and operations, al-Qaida routinely calls on the Muslim masses to join the jihad. One of the most prolific manuals distributed on al-Qaida Web sites since 2003 is titled "39 Ways to Serve the Jihad and the Mujahideen in the Path of God." This 49-page manual, authored by Muhammad Bin Ahmed al-Salem, is specifically geared toward the Muslim public. As its title implies, it advocates 39 ways that cell members and, more significantly, the surrounding community can serve the global jihadi movement both directly and indirectly. It asks its readers, depending on their circumstances and abilities, to ask God for martyrdom and prepare for jihad; volunteer and pursue jihad; support the jihad financially; help the families of martyred, injured, or imprisoned mujahideen both financially and by other means; collect contributions for the mujahideen and give them *Zakat* (charity); assist the wounded mujahideen; champion their causes; encourage them; defend them; call on the masses to join them; keep their secrets; and expose government collaborators. This popular manual also instructs its readers to stay informed of news of the global jihad; proliferate jihadi books and literature; boycott the goods of the enemy (Western products); and issue fatwas in support of the mujahideen. As for individuals who wish to take a more active part in the jihad against the West and "apostates," the manual instructs them to become skilled in physical fitness, weapons training and marksmanship, first aid, swimming and horse riding, and computer hacking; and to learn jihadi doctrine by reading the literature of Abdallah Azzam, Abu Muhammad al-Maqdisi, Yousef al-'Ayeeri, Abu Qatada, and Abd al-Qadr Abd al-Aziz.[39]

These efforts have so far enjoyed a level of success, as al-Qaida has been able to inspire the formation of numerous independent jihadi cells worldwide. In many cases, these cells are formed and staffed by young Islamists who have no direct connection to al-Qaida and its leadership and who have not been recruited by its members or trained in its camps. The cells are often made up of groups of friends or relatives who, being enamored of al-Qaida's ideology and inspired by its activities, take it upon themselves to self-organize, self-train, and act independently in service of the global jihad. They often learn about the global jihadi movement by frequenting jihadi Web sites where they receive religious indoctrination and operational training. Equally important, since 2003 al-Qaida has been successful in inspiring and mobilizing hundreds of young Muslim volunteers to journey from their home countries to join its branch in Iraq as volunteer fighters and suicide bombers. The actions of al-Qaida in Iraq under the previous leadership of Abu Musab al-Zarqawi, however, have also demonstrated the diminished ability of al-Qaida "central" to direct its affiliates' target selection and the messages transmitted to Muslim audiences by these actions. Al-Zarqawi's assassinations of Sunni tribal leaders, indiscriminate bombings of Sunni civilians, and his prosecution of a sectarian war with the Shi'a not only directly contravened directives from al-Qaida's highest leaders but directly undermined public support for al-Qaida in the Muslim world. For its successes in inspiring others to join the jihad, al-Qaida must pay the price of decreased message control.

REDEFINING THE NATURE OF THE CONFLICT: A LONG-TERM WAR OF ATTRITION

Perhaps the most important aspect of al-Qaida's strategy for influencing perceptions in the Muslim world is its ability to redefine the nature of its conflict with the West as a long-term "war of attrition" where tactical defeats are irrelevant. The network is thus able to avoid the appearance of defeat regardless of high casualties within its ranks and any setbacks it might encounter. With every loss it inflicts on the West it is able to claim victory. This is in contrast to previous secular Arab leaders like Gamal Abdel Nasser in Egypt and Saddam Hussein in Iraq who also attempted to portray their battles as part of a wider struggle against Western imperialism waged on the behalf of the Arab and Muslim masses. In their case, following the decisive defeat of the combined Arab armies in the Six-Day War in June 1967, Nasser and other Arab nationalists lost a great deal of credibility and political momentum among the Arab masses. The same is true of Saddam Hussein, who promised the Arabs "the mother of all battles" in his confrontation with United States and coalition forces in January 1991. The decisive defeat of his so-called 1 million man army by the American-led coalition in mere weeks shattered Hussein's image and support among the same Arabs who during the 1980s largely viewed him favorably for his role in containing increasing Iranian influence.

The short yet decisive military campaigns in June 1967 and January 1991 were largely able to discredit Nasser and Hussein, two nationalist leaders who had previously enjoyed great popularity among Arab and Muslim masses. The Islamists, by comparison to their nationalist counterparts in the Middle East, have purposely adopted a gradualist, long-term strategy to deflect and minimize the effects of any short-term losses that are inevitable due to military superiority of the West and its allies in the Muslim world. As long as the jihad continues, al-Qaida members are able to carry out attacks on Western targets in the West or in Muslim lands, and al-Qaida leaders issue threatening videos and speeches ridiculing the West and calling on Muslims to join the global jihad, al-Qaida is able to claim victory by framing the battle against the West as a long-term war of attrition that may take "decades or centuries." Indeed, in his book *Knights Under the Banner of the Prophet*, Ayman Zawahiri states that one of al-Qaida's goals is "maintaining a state of fear among the enemy by continuing to issue threats."[40] Regardless of how many jihadis are killed, how many cells are disrupted, and how many senior al-Qaida leaders are captured, the al-Qaida network portrays the battle as raging on and maintains the ability to cause fear among its enemies by constantly issuing threatening videos, audio messages, and communiqués. Actually, the fact that Osama bin Laden and Ayman al-Zawahiri have evaded capture or death for six years since the 9/11 attacks is by itself often touted as a victory by al-Qaida and its supporters.

Al-Qaida presently places principal emphasis on its prosecution of *Harb Istinzaf*, the war of attrition against the United States and its Western allies. Al-Qaida's foremost strategic objective presently is to "bleed" and overextend the financial and military resources of the United States by forcing it to spend enormous amounts of money to guard its domestic and international interests from terrorist attacks, and by dragging it into prolonged military deployments overseas. The hypothesized U.S. withdrawal from the Muslim world will be the result of *financial* considerations, first and foremost. Thus, al-Qaida sees its present struggle as one of economic warfare. In an audio recording released on December 26, 2001, bin Laden remarked that "America has been set back . . . and the economic bleeding still goes on today. Yet we still need more strikes."[41] More recently, Abu Mus'ab al-Najadi, a Saudi member/supporter of the network, stated in October 2005 that "this period is based on economic war due to the peculiar nature of the adversary. . . . Usually wars are based on military strength. . . . But our war with America is fundamentally different, for the first priority is defeating it economically."[42] Another al-Qaida member has remarked that targeting the economies of the West is "the most dangerous and effective arena of Jihad, because we live in a materialistic world."[43] Likewise, Abu Bakr Naji in his "Management of Barbarism" treatise advises jihadi cells to not underestimate the value of "small" attacks against Western targets in favor of the more grandiose, "qualitative, medium" operations like the bombings in Bali and Iraq. The smaller scale attacks, according to Naji, play the important role of exhausting and overextending the enemies' financial and military resources. He also encourages cells to both diversify their targets and to conduct multiple operations against similar targets in order to maximize the enemies' perception of vulnerability, and thus, their security expenditures.[44]

That al-Qaida pursues a long-term war of attrition against the United States is not only a sound military strategy due to the network's inability to compete with the military prowess of its enemy, it also constitutes the cornerstone of its communication strategy in the Muslim world, aimed at motivating the Muslim masses to rise up in a "global intifada" against the West, and at deflecting short-term tactical military defeats as effectively irrelevant by emphasizing that this conflict is destined to extend into the distant future. As stated bluntly in an al-Qaida communiqué in July 2004, "The enemy may be patient, but it cannot endure. As for us with our doctrine, belief and love for meeting god, we can endure until the enemy crumbles. If this takes decades or centuries, we are charged with fighting them come victory or martyrdom."[45]

CONCLUSION

While al-Jihad's failure to instigate an Islamist revolution in Egypt in October 1981 continues to inform al-Qaida's efforts to shape perceptions in the Muslim world, another incident, one that arguably led to the demise of al-Jihad as a viable terrorist organization, has wrought a particular influence on al-Qaida's second in command, Ayman al-Zawahiri. The "unintended"[46] killing of a schoolgirl named Shayma during the attempted assassination of a former Egyptian prime minister in December 1993 galvanized the Egyptian public's condemnation of al-Jihad.[47] Less than two years after the death of the "innocent child,"[48] al-Zawahiri was forced to issue an internal memo instructing his operatives to suspend armed operations in Egypt, due in large part to the virtual absence of any sympathetic base.[49] Al-Zawahiri later argued, predictably, that the global jihad will succeed only through effective mobilization of the Muslim masses, and that "the jihad movement must be in the middle of the nation." Under his ideological direction, al-Qaida maintains that the establishment of the caliphate will no longer be the work of an enlightened Islamic vanguard, and that victory will only come if "the slogans of the mujahideen are understood by the masses."[50]

In an audio recording broadcast on April 23, 2006, bin Laden referred to Iraq as the "fulcrum" of al-Qaida's jihad against the West.[51] The fact that Iraq presently constitutes the prime focal point of the Muslim public's attention is unlikely a coincidence. However, the ability of al-Qaida's central leadership to dictate the progression of the global jihad is not what it once was, as recent events in Iraq demonstrate. Forced to relinquish direct operational control to its regional affiliate al-Qaida in Iraq, the al-Qaida "central" also lost its ability to ensure ideological homogeneity within the movement. Al-Zawahiri's 2005 letter to al-Qaida in Iraq commander Abu Musab al-Zarqawi is revealing in this regard. Al-Zawahiri criticizes al-Zarqawi's conduct of the jihad and expresses concern over al-Zarqawi's understanding (or lack thereof) of al-Qaida's long-term strategy in Iraq. Stating that "we are in media battle in a race for the hearts and minds of the Umma," al-Zawahiri therefore argues that "the mujahed movement must avoid any action that the masses do not understand or approve."[52] Al-Zawahiri singles out al-Zarqawi's tendency to target Sunni leaders, publicly criticize prominent Iraqi ulama, and air footage of beheadings as particularly counterproductive.[53] Furthermore, al-Zarqawi was later ordered by a high-ranking al-Qaida member to follow orders from bin Laden and al-Zawahiri on major strategic issues, such as initiating a war against the Shi'a, undertaking large-scale operations, or operating outside of Iraq.[54] Evidence abounds that al-Zarqawi's gruesome conduct of the jihad in Iraq has significantly damaged the reputation and standing of al-Qaida among the Muslim masses.[55] Unsurprisingly, al-Qaida in Iraq's name was officially changed to the Islamic State of Iraq following al-Zarqawi's death in June 2006.

Al-Qaida in Iraq continually deviated from the strategic vision of its namesake, while resisting the attempts of al-Qaida's leaders to exert control over target selection or message management in Iraq. For a network forced to rely on its regional affiliates for operational momentum and effectively operating as a media organization, al-Qaida remains primarily focused on its efforts to shape perceptions in the Muslim world.

ACKNOWLEDGMENT

In memory of Sgt. Joshua C. Brennan of the 2nd Battalion, 503rd Airborne Infantry Regiment, 173rd Airborne Brigade Combat Team, who was killed in action in Afghanistan on October 26, 2007.

NOTES

1. Nemat Guenena, "The Jihad: An Islamic Alternative in Egypt," *Cairo Papers in Social Science* 9, no. 2 (Summer 1986): 73–74.

2. Ibid.

3. Gilles Kepel, *Muslim Extremism in Egypt: The Prophet and the Pharaoh* (Berkley: University of California Press, 1984), 210.

4. Ibid., 210–212.

5. The number of postings at a specific URL.

6. Estimates of the rate of jihadi Web site proliferation vary, from roughly 20 in 2000 to about 4,000 in 2005, and about 150 sites in February 2000 to 4,000 sites in October 2005, to 12 sites in 1998 to more than 4,800 sites in April 2006. See, respectively, "Suicide Bombers Turning to Websites," Agence France Presse, September 29, 2005; B. Raman, "From Internet to Islamnet: Net-Centric Counter-Terrorism," South Asia Analysis Group, Paper no. 1584 (October 22, 2005); and "Terrorism on the Internet," *Voice of America*, April 11, 2006.

7. Among the more notable "studios" are the al-Sahab Institute for Media Production, the al-Furqan Institute, the al-Fajr Media Center, and the Global Islamic Media Front.

8. Daniel Kimmage and Kathleen Ridolfo, *Iraqi Insurgent Media: The War of Images and Ideas* (Washington: Radio Free Europe Radio Liberty, 2007), 53.

9. Ibid., 10.

10. The manufacture of the explosive hexamethylene triperoxide diamine (HMDT) by the perpetrators of the attempted bombing in London on July 21, 2005, is a possible case in point. See "NYPD Officials Reveal London Bombing Details," Associated Press, August 4, 2005. Instructions for the production of HMDT had previously been made available on the notorious jihadi Web site the Aqsa Jihadi Encyclopedia (Mawsu'at al-Aqsa al-Jihadiya). See "Military Preparation—Acetone Peroxide," Mausu'at al-Aqsa al-Jihadiya; and Stephen Ulph, "For Mujahideen, Bomb-Making Information Readily Accessible Online," *Terrorism Focus* 2, no. 15 (August 5, 2005), http://www.jamestown.org/terrorism/news/article.php?articleid=2369759 (accessed September 1, 2007).

11. See Kimmage and Ridolfo for a useful classification of jihadi Web-based media products.

12. For more on this, see James Forest, ed., *Teaching Terror: Strategic and Tactical Learning in the Terrorism World* (Lanham, MD: Rowman & Littlefield, 2006), especially chapters 1 through 6.

13. "Rules and Guidelines of al-Nusra Jihadi network," al-Nusra Web site (accessed on April 16, 2006).

14. "al-Muhajirun Islamic Network Front Page," al-Muhajirun Web site (accessed on April 25, 2006).

15. "The Website—Our Goal Is Rebuilding and Correcting the Path for this Awakening," al-Sakifah Web site (accessed on April 16, 2006).

16. Al-Neda was shut down in 2003, following the death of its Webmaster, Yusef al-'Ayeeri, a Saudi sheikh and former al-Qaida instructor in Afghanistan. In addition to commanding al-Qaida cells in Saudi Arabia, Al-'Ayeeri was also a prolific contributor to al-Qaida's *Sawt al-Jihad* and *Muaskar al-Battar* online magazines.

17. "Main page," Al-Ma'asada al-Jihadiya Web site.

18. Steve Coll and Susan B. Glasser, "Terrorists Turn to the Web as Base of Operations," *Washington Post*, August 7, 2005, A1.

19. Ibid.

20. Ibid.

21. Abu Hadhifa al-Shami, "A Course in Popular Poisons and Deadly Gases," Islamic Media Center.

22. "Questions concerning the Jihad against the Crusaders in the Arabian Peninsula," *Sawt al-Jihad* 11, pp. 43–44.

23. Yousif al-'Ayeeri, "The Future of Iraq and the Arabian Peninsula Following the Crusader Invasion," *Mu'askar al-Battar (al-Battar Camp) Magazine*, 21, pp. 16–17.

24. Abdullah Bin Muhammed al-Rashud, "A Reading of the Writings of Sheik al-Islam Ahmed Ibn Taymiyya, Chapter One: The Tatar and al-Saud," *Sawt al-Jihad* 11, pp. 36–38.

25. Ibid., 38.

26. Sa'ed al-'Ameri, "Dangers to the Mujahid: Rafida," *Mu'askar al-Battar (al-Battar Camp) Magazine*, 6, pp. 22–24; "Zarqawi Letter: February 2004 Coalition Provisional Authority English Translation of Terrorist Musab al Zarqawi Letter Obtained by United States Government in Iraq," U.S. Department of State, http://www.state.gov/p/nea/rls/31694.htm.

27. Yitzhak Nakash, *The Shi'is of Iraq* (Princeton: Princeton University Press, 1994), 25–44.

28. Ibid.

29. "Shi'a," al-Tawhid Web site (accessed on November 3, 2004); "Al-Rafida," Defense of Sunna Network Web site (accessed on February 10, 2005).

30. "Shi'a," al-Tawhid.

31. "The Rafida: Always Collaborators Upon Request," *Ansar al-Sunna Magazine* 12p, p. 6–7.

32. "Saddam: 'New Mongols' Face Defeat," *CNN.com*, January 17, 2003, http://www.cnn.com/2003/WORLD/meast/01/17/sproject.irq.saddam/index.html (accessed January 18, 2003).

33. "The Complete Text of Sheikh Usama Bin Ladin Especially to the Muslims of Saudi Arabia and General Muslims Elsewhere," *al-Tawhid wal-Jihad* Web site (accessed on December 15, 2005).

34. Abu Hafez al-Masri Brigades—al-Qaida in Europe, "A Communiqué," July 1, 2004.

35. Abi Hajer Abd al-Aziz al-Muqrin, "Military Sciences—Targets in the Cities," *Mu'askar al-Battar (al-Battar Camp) Magazine* 7, pp. 23–27.

36. Johannes J. G. Jansen, *The Neglected Duty: The Creed of Sadat's Assassins and Islamic Resurgence in the Middle East* (New York: Macmillan, 1986), 160–161, 200.

37. Ibid., 186.

38. Abu Hafez al-Masri Brigades [al-Qaida in Europe].

39. Muhammad Bin Ahmed al-Salem, "39 Ways to Serve the Jihad and the Mujahideen in the Path of God," 2003.

40. "Directions for Destruction of Buildings and Bombings of Embassies: Points in the Combat Curriculum," *al-Firdaws* Web site (accessed on October 2005).

41. Bruce Lawrence, ed., *Messages to the World: The Statements of Usama bin Ladin* (London: Verso, 2005), 155.

42. Abu Musab al-Najadi, "Al-Qaeda's Battle is Economic Not Military" (October 3, 2005).

43. Nur al-Din al-Kurdi, "The Arenas of Jihad," *Dharwat al-Sunam* ("Peak of the Camel's Hump) 3, pp. 27–28.

44. Abu Bakr Naji, "*Idarat al-Tawahush* [The Management of Savagery]: The Most Critical Stage through Which the Umma Will Pass," trans. William McCants (Cambridge, MA: John M. Oline Institute for Strategic Studies at Harvard University, 2006), 9–10, 19.

45. Abu Hafez al-Masri Brigades [al-Qaida in Europe].

46. Ayman al-Zawahiri, *Knights Under the Prophet's Banner*, in Laura Mansfield, trans., *His Own Words: A Translation of the Writings of Dr. Ayman al-Zawahiri* (TLG Publications, 2006), 103.

47. Muntasir al-Zayyat and Ibrahim M Abu-Rabi', *The Road to al-Qaeda: The Story of Bin Laden's Right-Hand Man* (London: Pluto Press, 2004), 20.

48. Mansfield, *His Own Words*, 102–105.

49. Fawaz A. Gerges, *The Far Enemy: Why Jihad Went Global* (New York: Cambridge University Press, 2005), 100.

50. Mansfield, *His Own Words,* 205.

51. "Al-Qaeda Leadership Issues New Statements," *Jane's Terrorism and Security Monitor* (May 17, 2006).

52. "Letter from al-Zawahiri to al-Zarqawi, October 11, 2005," in Mansfield, *His Own Words*, 250–279.

53. Ibid.

54. Harmony Project, *Cracks in the Foundation: Leadership Schisms in al-Qa'ida from 1989–2006* (West Point, NY: Combating Terrorism Center, 2007), 68–69.

55. Pew Global Attitudes Project, *Islamic Extremism: Common Concern for Muslim and Western Publics* (Washington, D.C.: Pew Research Center, 2005), http://pewglobal.org/reports/display.php?ReportID=248 (accessed September 1, 2007).

16

The Information Operations War Between Israel and Hizballah during the Summer of 2006

Guermantes E. Lailari

THE U.S. GOVERNMENT IS BECOMING more interested in information operations (IO) especially as a result of its involvement in the Middle East. As a reflection of this, the Department of Defense (DoD) and the military services have developed a range of IO doctrines. Nonstate actors, on the other hand, such as terrorist groups, have been using IO adeptly for decades based on the necessity to strengthen their support base and counter their enemies' military advantages. In essence, IO is very useful for a terrorist group since it is often a cheap and powerful asymmetric tool against states, especially against regional or superpowers.

Hizballah has been skillful in conducting IO since its inception in the early 1980s, while Israel's efforts in the IO realm have been mixed. Most recently, both actors demonstrated their capabilities during the Israeli-Hizballah Summer 2006 War—referred to by the Israelis as the Second Lebanon War and by the Lebanese as the Tammuz War or July War. This chapter briefly examines the IO war between the two and extrapolates some implications for state policies against violent nonstate actors (and in some cases their state supporters).

This chapter uses the most recent DoD definition of IO: "The integrated employment of the core capabilities of electronic warfare (EW), computer network operations (CNO), psychological operations (PSYOPS), military deception (MILDEC), and operations security (OPSEC), in concert with specified supporting and related capabilities, to influence, disrupt, corrupt or usurp adversarial human and automated decision making while protecting our own."[1] The five core IO capabilities described in this definition provide a useful framework for examining the IO dimension of the Israeli-Hizballah War. Finally, this chapter concludes with some recommendations for the future and some concerns if these recommendations are not heeded.

A BRIEF OVERVIEW OF HIZBALLAH AND ISRAEL

Most readers are familiar with the history of Israel, which was created in 1948 by the Zionist movement that argued and fought for a Jewish state as a result of anti-Semitism in the nineteenth and twentieth centuries, especially driven home by the Holocaust. During the establishment of Israel, over 800,000 Jews were expelled from or left Arab countries and many resettled in Israel. A slightly less number of Palestinians left or were strongly encouraged to leave both by Israeli and Arab leaders for different reasons, and now they mainly reside in the countries surrounding Israel. Currently, around 400,000 Palestinian refugees from various Israeli-Arab wars reside in Lebanon.[2] These refugees were prevented from becoming Lebanese citizens or having any other citizenship, due to the belief that these refugees should return to Palestine where they had lived before. As a result, the 12 official refugee camps in Lebanon became breeding grounds for terrorist activities from 1948 through today.[3] The Palestinian Liberation Organization's (PLO) main base of operations moved from Egypt to Jordan, and then to Lebanon as a result of King Hussein's expulsion of the PLO in September 1970 (also known to some as Black September).

Due to the attempted assassination of the Israeli ambassador to the United Kingdom and as a result of constant raids from Lebanon, Israeli Prime Minister Begin ordered the invasion of Lebanon on June 6, 1982. The primary goal of Operation Peace for Galilee was to expel the PLO from Lebanon, especially from southern Lebanon (which some have called "Fatahland," as Fatah is the Arabic reverse acronym for the PLO). The Israelis successfully expelled the PLO from Lebanon by September 1, 1982, but shortly after the departure of the PLO, atrocities were committed against the Palestinians in the Sabra and Shatilla refugee camps by Lebanese Christian Phalang Militia with the apparent complicity of the Israel Defense Forces (IDF). The Phalang militia went on a rampage as a result of the assassination of their leader, President Bashir Gemayel (on September 14, 1982) and killed several hundred Palestinians.

After leaving Lebanon, the PLO went to Tunis, Tunisia. Some of the Lebanese Shia who fought against Israel and were supported by Iran, created a new group called Hizballah (drawing on the Qur'anic phrase Hezb Allah, from Surah 58:22, which means the Party of God) in 1982. Hizballah's main goals are to (1) establish a Shia theocracy in Lebanon, (2) eradicate Israel and liberate the area for Palestinians, and (3) remove the influence of the West (especially the United States) from the Middle East.[4] As its base of support, Hizballah looked to the Shia population of Lebanon, estimated to be 28–35 percent of the population or approximately 1.1–1.3 million,[5] as well as state sponsorship from Iran and Syria. Hizballah gained more control of the country when it took over a large portion of southern Lebanon (much of which is not Shia) after the vacuum created when Israel left that region in May 2000. They have also continued to maintain and increase their control in other Shia areas of Lebanon, such as Baalbek in the northeast and parts of Beirut.

Since Hizballah's inception, its fight with Israel has been continuous in a variety of arenas, including IO. The evolution of the IO struggle between these two foes has reflected the ebb and flow of the overall conflict. For Hizballah, the IO campaign has consistently been an area of high interest and priority because it provides an asymmetric strength; however, in contrast Israel has shown varied levels of interest and commitment toward IO. Indeed, most Israelis have acknowledged that their public relations efforts have been abysmal.

Differences in Commitment to IO

Like most of the West, Israel's approach to countering terrorist groups involves spending significant resources on tactical weapon systems to go after the terrorists (such as smart bombs, jets, helicopters, sophisticated electronic surveillance, etc.) or to protect against terrorist attacks —for example, in the United States creating the Joint Improvised Explosive Device Defeat Organization (JIEDDO) as well as building up security at airports and ports, and so on. Comparatively fewer resources are spent on operational planning, and the least amount is spent on strategy. Barely any attention is given to the IO or strategic communications aspect of a comprehensive counterterrorism strategy.

In contrast, contemporary terrorist groups tend to put considerable effort into their strategy (as well as the asymmetric IO and strategic communications dimension of that strategy), less on operational planning, and the least amount of effort in their tactics. For example, the cost of a suicide bomber and all the expenses associated with that kind of attack is a few hundred dollars. The United States spends the majority of its resources (billions of dollars) on tactical dimensions of counterterrorism. For example, the JIEDDO costs U.S. taxpayers over $3.3 billion in FY 2006, $4.6 billion in FY 2007, and $4.1 billion planned for FY 2008.[6] In comparison, the cost of the 9/11 attack for al-Qaida is estimated to be between $400,000 and $500,000, and the economic impact of that attack has been estimated by some to reach $1 trillion nationwide.[7] A similar but less dramatic example of the return on investment of asymmetric warfare is seen in the impact of Hizballah's rocket attacks against northern Israel. Here again, the costs to the victim, to the economy, and to the society's morale are much higher than the costs to the attacker.

The conflict between Israel and Hizballah has a long history which cannot be adequately revisited in this chapter. However, a brief historical overview of how computer network operations (CNO) have been used during during this period is useful for understanding the differing levels of commitment to IO prior to 2006. In late 1999 and 2000, Israel, the Palestinians, Hizballah, and other groups participated in what is known as from various sources as e-Intifada, cyber-Jihad, e-Jihad, cyber Holy War,[8] and "Interfada"—a play on words combining the English word "Internet" and the Arabic word "Intifada" (uprising, rebellion, or pushing off referring to resisting the Israeli occupation of Palestine).[9] The Interfada was a cyberwar component of the Second Intifada, which took place from 2000 to 2002 (the First Intifada occurred from 1987 to 1990 and predated the World Wide Web, which started in 1991).[10] The 2000–2002 cyberwar is best summed up by Markku Jokisipilä, who wrote:

> High-intensity conflict raged for months and accurately mirrored events in the real world. There were bouts of frantic cyber activity immediately following suicide bombings, car bombs and IDF artillery barrages. Over the course of next two years, hundreds of websites on both sides were subjected to different types of cyber attacks, including distributed denial of service attacks, website defacements, misinformation campaigns, system penetrations, Trojan horses and viruses. The computer programs used in attacks, so-called "exploit scripts," were actively, widely and rapidly disseminated and thus even people with little or no experience in programming were able to participate

in attacks. The electronic infrastructure in the region was under a great strain as the attacks and counterattacks shut down popular information and financial sites for days at a time or otherwise disrupted the normal functioning of Internet Service Providers. All of this contributed to a significant decline in the public's confidence in online security. In some cases, real world costs were considerable, especially where repeated website defacements made commercial transactions over the Internet virtually impossible.[11]

Through these attacks, according to Patrick Allen, "over 548 Israeli domain (.il) websites were defaced out of 1,295 defacements in the Middle East."[12] Considering the 2000–2002 cyberwar was the precursor to the Israeli-Hizballah 2006 summer war, advances in cyberwar capabilities became one of the main stories of the 2006 conflict. The key point here is that the cyberworld can presage the kinetic world and vice versa, and the cyberworld has become another key battlefield.

COMPARING HIZBALLAH'S AND ISRAEL'S 2006 WAR GOALS

During the 2006 war, Hizballah's war strategy can be extracted from Secretary General Nasrallah's speeches[13] and observations of a Hizballah think tank[14] both during and after the war. The Iranian press published the best summary of Hizballah's war strategy in the form of commentary by a Hizballah think tank, which describes their principles of operations, challenges, possibilities, and executive principles. A select list of IO-relevant items is provided here (italics added for emphasis).[15]

Principles of Operations
- The *liberation of Lebanese, Palestinian, and Iranian prisoners detained by Israel.*
- To *neutralize the policy of America and Israel* regarding the theory that, whenever the war is to their interest, it should continue, but, whenever it is not, a cease-fire must be implemented.
- To *attract extensive and popular support for Hizballah*, in order to boost and reconstruct the national pride of the Lebanese nation in encountering the Israeli and American invaders.
- To *endanger the security of East and West Mediterranean region, in order to disturb the situation in Europe*, which is a strong ally of America.
- To *establish greater solidarity and more continuous resistance inside the Islamic world*, especially in Lebanon, until the annihilation of Israel.

Challenges
- The *political and media support of Arab governments*, like those of Saudi Arabia, Jordan, and so on, for the Israeli regime, because of the fear of the increasing power of Hizballah.

Possibilities
- The *support of the excited public opinion*, the awareness of the entire Muslim and Shia world, and even the global non-Muslim combatants.

- The *inability to accuse Hizballah of terrorism* because of their operational jihad to defend the soil and security of their own country.

Executive Principles
- The principle of the *expansion of Hizballah's line of fire* deep into the land of Israel.
- The principle of *preparing the necessary technology* for missile attacks against Western and Arab countries from Lebanon.
- The principle of starting a *psychological war* by questioning the reasons behind the silence of international organizations and countries regarding the arrest of more than half of the members of the Palestinian government and parliament.

Prime Minister Ehud Olmert's speeches[16] and statements from Israel's Political Security Committee[17] help illuminate their country's strategy and goals in the 2006 war. For example, two speeches by Prime Minister Olmert to the Israeli Knesset (Parliament) on July 17 and August 14, 2006, and a statement by the Israeli Political Security Committee on July 19, 2006, all note the same four Israeli goals during and after the war:

- The return of the hostages, Ehud (Udi) Goldwasser and Eldad Regev.
- A complete cease-fire.
- Deployment of the Lebanese army in all of southern Lebanon.
- Expulsion of Hizballah from the area, and fulfillment of UN Resolution 1559.[18]

Although Israel's aims seem clear and concise, Hizballah's goals are more comprehensive and closely reflect their overall strategy. Furthermore, they are trying to appeal to sympathetic audiences not only in Lebanon but also in the Arab and Muslim worlds, as well as some in the Western world. The Israeli goals are very narrow and focus mainly on their immediate concerns in Lebanon. The only item that is international is the UN resolution, which does not help the average person in the West or the Middle East understand what Israel wants. Finally, in the IO realm, Israel's use of IO in its goals appeared to lose traction when Lebanese civilian casualties began to rise at the end of July whereas Hizballah's position was strengthened.

COMPARING INFORMATION OPERATIONS BETWEEN ISRAEL AND HIZBALLAH

This section provides highlights of the IO war between Israel and Hizballah. The 2006 IO war described here is limited by open sources and could be compared to a tip of an iceberg of what actually happened. The Israeli government completed the Winograd Commission in April 2007, which was tasked to critique Israeli actions and inactions and was harshly critical of the Israeli leadership. Although not all information will be released to the public, the author believes that the information that is available and interviews conducted immediately following the war are sufficient enough to provide insight into the IO war and draw conclusions that will affect the future of warfare, especially between democracies and violent nonstate actors.

As discussed earlier in this chapter, the West focuses much of its efforts toward achieving victory on the traditional battlefield. However, the "mediafield" is a larger arena than the battlefield, according to James P. Pinkerton, especially when dealing with nonstate actors like Hizballah. When referring to the Qana incident—where the IDF was accused of killing several dozens of innocent civilians in an apartment building in Qana, Lebanon, on July 30, 2006—Pinkerton notes:

> Many will denounce this script as dishonest propaganda [by Hizballah]. Furthermore, it's possible to write a completely different script for Lebanon, placing all the blame for the recent violence on Hizballah, along with Syria and Iran. But that's the point: The real struggle has to be waged on the mediafield, and waged just as effectively as on the battlefield. That's the true key to victory. . . . That's the power of the mediafield. Strategic victory is far more important than tactical success on the battlefield.[19]

An example of how the Qana incident is viewed by the Arab world after July 30 is shown in a cartoon published on the www.omayya.com Web site on July 31: an Israeli tank is rolling over a U.S. flag which is on top of a bloodied pile of bodies leading to the city of Qana. A cartoon from Iran's Al-Wifaq news service on July 31 shows a child sitting dressed in a Lebanese flag crying because someone is pouring gasoline on him while he burns; the gasoline container has the Israeli flag on it. The West has not demonstrated an understanding of how to change the Middle East Muslim narrative in a more positive direction. The Middle East narrative often depicts the West as evil; the United States is the great Satan and Israel is the little Satan. The West has yet to find ways of effectively dealing with such reflections of hate against us.

The cartoons in the Western press show the paradox of the situation. A cartoon published on www.drybonesblog.com (an Israeli Web site) on August 4, 2006, shows Hizballah's leader Nasrallah declaring: "When our missiles kill their civilians, we rejoice. When they kill our civilians, we get world support; that's what's so great about Hizballah—no matter who dies . . . we're happy." In the United States, several Web sites depict the conflicting narratives in several cartoons. At the beginning of the war (on July 23, 2006), the site www.coxandforkum.com showed an illustration with people in the United States demonstrating with signs in favor of Hizballah, with two U.S. Marines looking on. The signs say: "Victory to Hizballah," "Islam will dominate," "We support Hizballah," and "I heart Nasrallah." One Marine looking at the demonstration says to the other: "I seem to recall Hizballah murdering 241 of us in '83." The other replies: "This IS America, right?"

Toward the end of the war, the Middle Eastern press showed a defeated Israel. On August 10, 2006, the prominent *Al-Quds* Arabic newspaper published an illustration of a black bull with a Jewish star branded on it and with rockets stuck on its back like swords, much like which happens during bull fights in Spain. Another cartoon, published in Gaza's *Al-Risalah* on August 7, depicts Nasrallah in a military uniform as a Lebanese hero with dead Israeli soldiers hanging down from his uniform as campaign ribbons. On August 2, Saudi Arabia's *Al Hayat* published a drawing of Prime Minister

Ehud Olmert shooting a Lebanese child, visually reminiscent of a famous photo from the Vietnam War (published on February 1, 1968) in which a South Vietnam police chief shoots a man who he suspects of being a Viet Cong soldier. On August 13, 2006, an image published on www.coxandforkum.com depicted Nasrallah and a Lebanese soldier in a discussion about disarmament. Nasrallah is shown as saying: "So, you think you'll disarm Hizballah? I guess we'll have to change our flag." Then they both break out in hysterical laughter, since the Hizballah flag has an AK-47 prominently shown on top.

Operational security (OPSEC) for Hizballah has been a continuous—and at times a difficult—Darwinian lesson. Much like other terrorist groups who had to fight against a Western high-technology adversary, Hizballah learned the hard way that they had to keep a high degree of OPSEC to avoid detection by Israeli technology or human intelligence. Several senior leaders in Hizballah have been killed by Israel, so there is a strong motivation to maintain a high degree of OPSEC.[20] Israel, on the other hand, did not keep a high degree of vigilance in this dimension and was surprised by the sophistication of Hizballah's capabilities. For example, when the IDF went into Jubail, Lebanon, on July 25, 2006, they found a treasure trove of sophisticated communications intelligence (COMINT) equipment able to collect voice from both cell phones and land lines along with lists of phone numbers in Israel;[21] overall, they were surprised by Hizballah's ability to conduct COMINT against the IDF and civilian population.

Israel did attempt to promulgate sound OPSEC policies, however. For example, the IDF military censor's office distributed a policy memo among reporters in Israel describing what information should and should not be reported due to OPSEC considerations (in other words, preventing the public dissemination of information that could prove operationally useful to Hizballah). A document leaked by international journalists, issued by the Israeli military censor's office on July 16 reads as follows.

CENSORSHIP POLICY REGARDING FIGHTING IN THE NORTH

1. As of now, over 1,200 rockets have been fired at Israel; it is expected that this will continue.
2. Therefore, following are the Military Censor's relevant guidelines:
    a. The Military Censor will not approve reports regarding visits of Israeli Government and IDF officials in the north of Israel until the visits are over due to the clear connection between officials' visits and missile attacks on the area in question.
    b. The Military Censor will not approve reports on missile hits at IDF bases and/or strategic facilities.
    c. The Military Censor will not approve reports on missiles that fall in the Mediterranean Sea.
    d. The Military Censor will not approve reports on time periods when citizens are permitted to leave their shelters. Warnings of such times are utilized by the enemy for timing attacks.
    e. Reporting on locations in which there are public defense and organizational difficulties should be avoided as much as possible.

3. Real-time reporting on the exact location of rocket hits must be strictly avoided!

> . . . If a news outlet reports immediately that a missile splashed into the sea, for example, any guerrilla with an internet connection knows to aim left. Report that an oil refinery in Haifa went in flames, and Hizballah will surely celebrate and reload. Report that a senior official is headed north, and rockets will be raining down in no time.[22]

Computer network operations activities on both sides have grown significantly and were developing at a much greater rate than kinetic options, since CNO appears to be an area where deterrence is less likely to affect either participant's activities. As was previously mentioned, during the so-called Interfada from 2000 to 2002, both sides conducted CNO against each other and against other world participants based on their political loyalties.[23] The summer 2006 war can be seen as a natural progression of these activities, using newer tools available from various hacker sites. The Israeli Web sites attacked included several government agencies (including the prime minister's office, police, Mossad, and the Israeli Security Agency)[24] and industry (including Bank HaPoalim, Rambam Hospital, Subaru Israel, McDonald's Israel, and Netvision, the largest Israeli Internet service provider).[25] Pro-Israeli hackers responded by countering the various anti-Israel hacker groups in countries such as Turkey, Morocco, Iran, Jordan, Kuwait, and Lebanon.[26]

PSYCHOLOGICAL OPERATIONS (PSYOPs)

PSYOPs was another key area that both sides spent a lot of effort applying their energies to. Hizballah used local and foreign media (TV, newspapers, Internet, and radio) to transmit their messages. Israel did the same, but with less success in the Arab and European media, especially toward the end of the war. At the beginning of the summer war, several Arab papers appeared to have a sympathetic tone toward Israel, a first for Israel—in an emergency Arab meeting in Cairo on July 16, 2006, the Saudi representative took the lead in criticizing Hizballah, and was joined by Egypt, Jordan, Kuwait, United Arab Emirates, Bahrain, and even the Palestinian Authority.[27] This occurred when it was apparent at the beginning of the conflict that Hizballah had initiated the conflict by their attack on the Israel–Lebanon border and abducting two Israeli soldiers. However, as the war progressed and more Arab civilians were killed by Israeli actions, this opinion changed, especially after the July 30 Qana incident.

Within Lebanon, Israel used leaflets, cell phone messaging, and other PSYOPs methods in its overall strategic communications effort, but did not conduct a strong public relations campaign beyond its own borders. On the other hand, Hizballah conducted a much more comprehensive, broad-based PSYOP and public relations campaign than the Israelis did, due to their connectivity with the Muslim world as well as years of conducting PSYOPs in Europe and the rest of the world. At an Israeli workshop on communications in September 2006, Tzvi Yehezqeli—an Arab affairs reporter for Israel's Channel 10—noted that "Hizballah leader Hasan Nasrallah spends four hours per day reading Israeli media, including polls and research reports, catching even the smallest details in Israeli newspapers."[28] Jonathan Davis, Vice President for External Relations for the Interdisciplinary Center in Herzliya, suggests we might consider relating to the media as a "weapon system." He also quotes Gissin (media advisor to Prime Minister Ariel Sharon), who said Hizballah is "10 years ahead" of Israel in using the media. And he cites professor Gabriel Weimann's research indicating that Hizballah's Al-Manar television station has a budget of $15 million, which is more than the budget of the entire IDF Spokesman's Office, the Foreign Ministry, and "everything to do with" public diplomacy in Israel.[29]

In the 2006 war, typical psychological operations products such as radio and TV broadcasts, cartoons, photographs, and leaflets were used by both sides in their strategic communications efforts. Additionally, Hizballah used other advanced methods such as high-technology weapons (C-802 antiship missile, unmanned aerial vehicles [UAVs], signals intelligence, etc.) and a new fighting spirit which increased the fear (PSYOPS) among the IDF and civilian population. Israelis used advanced methods to get their messages out via e-mails, text messages, and phone calls.[30] Dr. Jerrold Post, a U.S. psychology expert and a critic of Israeli PSYOPs, notes that Israel should not be trying to change supporters of Hizballah, rather, it should dissuade new recruits and delegitimize Hizballah.[31]

Both sides used image defacements in their war. Israel was able to manipulate Hizballah FM radio broadcasts and Al Manar, several times by changing words, video, and photographs. For example, on July 31, 2006, Nasrallah's face was defaced for several minutes on Al Manar's broadcast. The following phrases also appeared on viewers' screens: "Your days are numbered" and "Nasrallah, your time is up. Soon you won't be with us anymore."[32] According to Preatoni, three methods are possible for hacker attacks on TV broadcasts:

- by social engineering: being able to substitute the tapes before the airing;
- by hacker means: hacking into the postproduction/digital storage unit networks;
- by hijacking the aired satellite signal: this can be performed at the signal originating point as well as the uplink station.[33]

As reported in the August 10, 2006, broadcast of the BBC Monitoring World Media:

> [Levi] Alongside the war on the ground there is also a war over the minds of the people. Ehud, is Israel once again interfering with Al-Manar broadcasts?
>
> [Ya'ari] Yes, it is doing so to the terrestrial broadcasts in Lebanon. We showed one example two weeks ago. Here is another. This is what is seen in Beirut, not what is seen by those watching Al-Manar via satellite. Nasrallah is seen here saying the battle on the ground is what will decide the situation. Then we see Israel taking over the broadcast and what is seen in Tyre, Sidon and Beirut is bodies of Hizballah fighters in the field with a caption saying: Nasrallah is lying. He promised not to hide Hizballah losses, but he does so all the time. Another broadcast shows Nasrallah kissing the foreheads and hands of Hizballah fighters and this is also superimposed with pictures of Hizballah dead in the field. We won't say how this is done, but Israel takes over Hizballah broadcasts inside Lebanon.[34]

In contrast to Israel's success at infiltrating and altering Al Manar broadcasts, Hizballah and its allies were only able to deface and cause denial of service to Web sites.

Israel, in typical Western fashion, has a free press which showed the good and the bad of the war and was especially critical of the indecisiveness of the Israeli government and its poor response to the Israelis living in northern Israel who suffered from the Hizballah rocket attacks.[35] The Arab/Muslim press used familiar anti-Israel, anti-U.S., anti-Semitic, and Muslim suffering motifs to reinforce common stereotypes held by the Arab masses.

Some photographs used in the print media were shown to be fabricated or manipulated to exaggerate their anti-Israel message; this process is called "fauxtography."[36] For example, 920 photos by Adnan Hajj—a Lebanese Reuters photographer—were eventually removed from Reuters files since many of them were questionable.[37] This revelation was first noted by a Web site called Little Green Footballs (www.littlegreen-footballs.com) which had previously discovered that Dan Rather's *60 Minutes* special on President George W. Bush had used faked documents to disparage his military service.[38]

Examples of PSYOP products are T-shirts, pamphlets/leaflets, and cartoons. On August 10, 2006, the *Bahrain Tribune* showed pictures of T-shirts being sold in Lebanon depicting Hassan Nasrallah as the new hero of Muslims. Some of the Israeli leaflets used during the war were intended to warn the public about an impending military attack, warning the civilians to leave the area and demeaning Hizballah; they were also meant to convince the Lebanese to stop supporting Hizballah. On August 8, Dubai's Al-Arabiyah Television (in Arabic) showed an example of an Israeli leaflet which stated the following:

> To the Lebanese Citizens south of Al-Litani River: Read This Statement Carefully and Comply With the Instructions: The IDF will escalate its operation and will strongly attack the terrorist elements, who use you as human shield and who fires rockets at the State of Israel from inside your houses. Any car of any type will be attacked on suspicion of transporting rockets, military hardware, and terrorists. You should know that anyone moving in any vehicle will endanger his life. [Signed] The State of Israel

ADVANCED WEAPONS AND THEIR PSYCHOLOGICAL EFFECT

As far away as Jakarta, Indonesia, a leaflet handed out during Friday prayers on August 4 in the Grand National Mosque Istiqlal showed pictures of the late Hamas leader Sheikh Ahmad Yasin and Hizballah leader Sayid Hasan Nasrallah; at the bottom are logos or pictures of Fanta, Sprite, Coca-Cola, Johnson & Johnson, Carrefour, Nescafé, Nestlé, Danone, Hugo Boss, L'Oréal, Sara Lee, and Revlon. The front of the leaflet reads in Indonesian: "Oh, followers of Islam, Unite! You will surely be strong and victorious. Buying American and Israeli products means joining in the killing of Palestinian and Lebanese fighters. Boycott American and Israeli products."

The use of advanced weapons (including UAVs carrying explosives,[39] anti-ship C802 missiles, and massive rocket barrages) also had a *psychological effect*; these weapons are not one would expect from a terrorist group. In fact, these are weapons of some of the larger armies of the world. One of Nasrallah's stated goals was to show that his forces had similar capabilities as the IDF.[40]

Nasrallah clearly wanted to project the image to Hizballah members, Lebanese, Israelis, and the rest of the Muslim world that his military had similar capabilities as the IDF. In his August 3 speech on Al Manar TV, he claimed that if Israel struck Beirut, Hizballah would strike Tel Aviv. Had the Israeli Air Force not destroyed Hizballah longer range missiles, his threats could have come true.[41] Overall, Hizballah's rockets did create fear in the Israeli psyche, with over 250,000 civilians leaving the north.[42]

Electronic warfare (EW) provided the biggest tactical surprise to the IDF, especially the Israeli Navy. One would have assumed that Israel would be the lead in this area compared to the Hizballah. However, with the assistance of Iran and Syria, Hizballah seems to be increasing its capabilities at a much quicker rate than the Israelis. During the Israeli occupation of Lebanon through 2000, Hizballah employed a variety of remotely detonated shaped charge improvised explosive devices (IEDs) against the IDF, weapons that have also found their way to Iraq and to Afghanistan against U.S. and coalition forces. These devices continue to expand in capability and lethality. The Israelis tried to employ a variety of kinetic and nonkinetic tools against Al Manar, Hizballah's television station, with minimal effect.

Israel should have assumed that when they were fighting Hizballah, that they were fighting Iran, albeit at a lesser capability. The mistake made by the sailors of the Israeli Navy Ship *Hanit* reflects this judgment error. Although open source information on the Hizballah acquisition of the C-802 cruise missile was clearly available, the crew of the INS *Hanit* apparently chose not to activate their EW measures capabilities against this threat. One retired senior military intelligence source noted that the Israeli Navy should have looked at the coast of Lebanon as the coast of Iran and acted accordingly.[43]

THE FUTURE?

The future will determine how well both sides learned from their 2006 summer experiences. However, lessons learned are not only happening between Hizballah and Israelis but also in the Arab and Muslim world. According to one source interviewed for this chapter, Syria has studied the Hizballah model of fighting the IDF and plans to create their own doctrine based on Hizballah successes.[44] Some observers have also warned that the insurgents in Iraq and Afghanistan will also take lessons and successful tactics from other theaters of conflict and use them against coalition forces.[45] These could include the use of extensive tunnels, short-range rockets, and Russian antitank missiles.[46] All of these new tactics are easily employed and can have a huge IO effect against the U.S. and coalition forces in the following pillars: PSYOPs (morale), MILDEC (surprise), CNO (new capabilities and effects), EW (use of high-tech weapons such as advanced ship-to-air missiles and antiship missiles), OPSEC, and collecting intelligence on coalition forces. In comparison, Western IO efforts might have some effect against a terrorist enemy's IO, but will probably cost many times more than what the insurgents spent on their efforts in this arena.

Other radical Islamic groups were emboldened by the successes of Hizballah against the IDF, including Hamas in the Gaza Strip. Similarly, Hamas's successful coup against the Palestinian Authority in the summer of 2005 in the Gaza Strip and the kidnapping of an Israeli soldier *before* the Israel–Hizballah 2006 summer war also inspired Hizballah to take sympathetic action against Israel in accordance with their January 2005 strategic agreement.[47] Hizballah is giving them a path to success at many levels, and recent trends indicate increasing radicalization in Muslim monarchies (Bahrain, Jordan, Morocco), in autocratic Muslim countries (Egypt, Pakistan), and even nascent democratic Muslim countries (Lebanon, Turkey, Iraq, etc.).

Israel will also be conducting a vigorous process of assessing lessons learned. One senior Israeli observer noted that although in the short term the summer 2006 war was a tactical failure, it accomplished the following positive results for Israel: (1) it provided insights to Israel on some of the advanced Hizballah capabilities; (2) the war reduced the anxiety of Western leaders on what actions Iranian proxies could do to them; (3) the war will allow Israel and especially the IDF to retool and prepare for the next war with Hizballah; and (4) it will force Israeli politicians to rethink their strategy of giving up land for peace as they did in Gaza and parts of the West Bank in the summer of 2005.[48] Another Israeli colleague noted that the history of Israel's wars has always been a cycle of successes and almost failures.[49] For example, 1948 was almost a disaster, but 1967 was a clear decisive success; 1973 was almost a total loss, but 1982 was a clear success in kicking the PLO out of Lebanon. The 2006 summer war was clearly a failure, but there was never a threat of total loss. In the long term, Israel can use the war as a means to apply lessons learned and, as long as it doesn't assume that the next war will be the same as the last one, it could deal better with the next conflict. On the other hand, with all of Israel's neighbors taking note of the outcome, the threat to Israel and pro-Western Muslim countries could be put at risk because the war could embolden the anti-Western Muslim countries and anti-Western nonstate actors to press forward harder with their agenda.

CONCLUSIONS

The main conclusions from this study are that terrorist groups, much like state actors, continue to improve their technology, fighting doctrine, and their IO. Furthermore, a terrorist organization does not have the bureaucratic constraints that state actors have regarding the development and production challenges of new capabilities; their decision cycle is much more flexible and allows for innovation against a Western military. Furthermore, the terrorists have a greater motivation in the fight since to them it is their survival; state actors are not in such dire straits, at least not in the short term.

Second, as terrorists improve their tactics, techniques, and procedures, these are now quickly spread worldwide due to the information revolution, so that the learning cycle is much faster than it used to be. Nations with nascent terrorist groups now become targets of extremist violence and become more vulnerable as they spend more resources to counter the threat. Instead of using their resources for economic development for their people, governments are forced to spend resources defending their populations which could drive a vicious cycle creating more poverty, less freedoms, more violence, more costs to help the injured, and more strain on families that have lost a source of income through injury or death of a family member.

With the end of the Cold War, small groups of radicals are less constrained since they do not have anyone keeping them in check as was the case when superpowers often determined their strategies and operational constraints. During the Cold War, if a group supported by a superpower didn't pander to it, they were often squeezed out and denied resources. Today, we live in a multipolar world with a multitude of regional powers vying for influence, which contributes to proxy wars and surrogates (for example, Iran's long-standing support for Hizballah against Israel). Further, many of the high-tech countries continue to sell advanced weapons to countries through which various terrorist groups around the world eventually find access to them. This was the case of antitank missiles found in Lebanon which came through a circuitous route originally through Russia, Syria, and Italy.[50]

With respect to IO, the fighting in this arena extends beyond borders and normal military engagements. When pro-Hizballah hackers around the world can participate in the fighting by attacking Israeli Web sites, the IO war is no longer contained. It means that any individual can participate from anywhere, potentially making countries around the world liable for anyone who attacks from their borders. For example, Hizballah is considered the "A Team" terrorist organization by the CIA;[51] many other Islamic violent organizations are inspired to replicate its capabilities. These capabilities will migrate to Iraq, Afghanistan, and anywhere that similarly minded Muslims feel empowered to take action. IO provides an asymmetric and indirect way to attack the United States, Israel, and Western nations as well as others. These IO tools could also potentially be used by radical Muslim terrorist groups against any of the 57 Muslim countries in the Organization of Islamic Conference[52] or countries with large Muslim populations to manipulate them into "true believers" of radical Islam.[53]

Terrorists have creativity on their side, for example, because it is simply much easier to destroy parts of a country's infrastructure than is it to maintain the entire system. An unfortunate example of this is Iraq's electrical grid or its oil system; it has been systematically attacked since 2003 and has been effectively neutralized, preventing the Iraqi people from fully benefiting from it, slowing down their country's road to recovery from war and internecine violence. Additionally, as technology improves, terrorists are able to use tools that have greater impacts on greater numbers of people. An example of technology access is the proliferation of radiation sources that a terrorist could use or threaten to use. An example of the potential affects are clearly provided by the 1987 accidental release of cesium-137 powder in Goiania, Brazil, that contaminated 249 people and caused four deaths, with 112,000 Brazilians requiring examinations. Another example was the Chechen rebels' *threatened use* of cesium-137 in September 1995. Luckily, Russian authorities found it in the park exactly where the Chechens told them it was. Cobalt-60, cesium-137, and other medical or industrial radiation sources are not difficult to find and besides their physical effects on people and resources, their IO effects could have equaled or have caused greater devastation.

As the various sides in the conflict go about preparing for the next war, Hizballah continues to innovate on other fronts, for example, in computer gaming. Hizballah released a computer game called *Special Force* in 2003,[54] and a year after the 2006 summer war they produced an upgraded version called *Special Force 2: Tale of the Truthful Pledge*,[55] focused on fighting Israel with the 2006 war as the backdrop. The first mission scenario is to capture Israeli soldiers, as was done in the 2006 war; another scenario is planning the attack on the Israeli Navy Ship *Hanit*, and other scenarios include attacking Israeli tanks and helicopters. With these types of games, they are able to inspire the youth not only in Lebanon but throughout the Arabic speaking world. The games are available only in Arabic at this time but an English version is under development.[56]

As each capability discussed in this chapter becomes refined and continues to be successful against modern armies, more and more violent groups will be encouraged by these successes. These successes will make the art of fighting against terrorists or insurgents more difficult and could put us on a path of greater violence and more collateral damage which is part of the desire of these groups—to show that the government is unable to protect its citizens. Without a clear grand strategy to counter violent nonstate actors and their supporting state actors, coupled with ongoing successes of these actors, we will fail in our current endeavors and possibly change the nature of our current lifestyle. Returning to a "competitive strategy" concept advocated by those who won the Cold War is one way of coherently solving our current and future challenges.[57]

DISCLAIMER

The views expressed in this chapter are those of the author and do not reflect the official policy or position of the U.S. government, the Department of Defense, or the U.S. Air Force.

NOTES

1. *Dictionary of Military Associated Terms*, Joint Publication 1-02, 12 Apr 01 (amended through 16 Oct 06), http://www.dtic.mil/doctrine/jel/new_pubs/jp1_02.pdf, 20 Nov 06, p. 261; and *Information Operations*, Joint Publication 3-13, 13 Feb 06, http://www.fas.org/irp/doddir/dod/jp3_13.pdf, 1 Oct 06 (GL-9).

2. *Amnesty International Annual Report*, "Lebanon," http://web.amnesty.org/report2006/lbn-summary-eng#8, 19 Nov 06; and United Nations Relief and Works Agency for Palestinian Refugees in the Near East, "Lebanon," http://www.un.org/unrwa/refugees/lebanon.html, current as of 31 Dec 2003, 19 Nov 2006.

3. United Nations Relief and Works Agency for Palestinian Refugees in the Near East, "Lebanon."

4. MIPT Terrorism Knowledgebase, "Hizbollah Group Profile." http://www.tkb.org/Group.jsp?groupID=3101, accessed 13 Jan 08.

5. Department of State, "Lebanon," http://www.state.gov/g/drl/rls/irf/2006/71426.htm, 19 Nov 06.

6. "FY 2008 Global War on Terror Request," www.defenselink.mil/comptroller/defbudget/fy2008/2008_Budget_Rollout_Attachment.pdf, accessed 26 Dec 08.

7. Press Briefing by Tony Snow, Office of the Press Secretary, White House, 1 Aug 2007, http://www.whitehouse.gov/news/releases/2007/08/20070801-3.html.

8. Patrick D. Allen, "The Palestinian-Israel: Cyberwar," *Military Review*, March–April 2003, http://www.findaricles.com/p/articles/mi_m0PBZ/is_2_83/ai_106732244/print, 9 Aug 06.

9. Jacqueline-Marie Wilson Wrona, *From Sticks and Stones to Zeros and Ones: The Development of Computer Network Operations as an Element of Warfare a Study of the Palestinian-Israeli Cyberconflict and What the United States Can Learn From the "Interfada,"* Naval Postgraduate School, September 2005, http://stinet.dtic.mil/cgi-bin/GetTRDoc?AD=ADA439507&Location= U2&doc=GetTRDoc.pdf, 15 Aug 06, p. 4.

10. Richard T. Griffiths, *The History of the Internet*, Chapter 2, "From the Internet to the World Wide Web," Leiden University (last updated 15 Oct 2002). http://www.let.leidenuniv.nl/history/ivh/chap2.htm#From%20Internet%20to%20World%20Wide%20Web, 19 Nov 06.

11. Markku Jokisipilä, "Interfada: The Israeli-Palestinian Cyberconflict," 19 Oct 04 pp. 4–5, http://vanha.soc.utu.fi/polhist/vaihtuvat/jokisipila_Interfada.pdf, 29 Aug 2006.

12. Allen, "The Palestinian-Israel: Cyberwar."

13. Hezbollah Secretary General Hasan Nasrallah,, speeches, Beirut Al-Manar Television, 16, 27, 30 July; 3, 6, 12 Aug; 22 Sep 06, http://www.almanar.com.lb, accessed 14 Nov 06.

14. "Need to Define War of Attrition against Israel," *Hezbollah* (Persian), 25 Jul 06, p. 4 (special view column), Tehran, Iran. Commentary by Hezbollah think tank. Accessed 1 Dec 06.

15. Ibid., emphasis added.

16. Speeches by Prime Minister Ehud Olmert on 17 Jul 06 and on 14 Aug 06 to the Israeli Knesset (Parliament), http://www.pmo.gov.il/PMOEng/Communication/PMSpeaks/speechknesset 170706.htm and http://www.pmo.gov.il/PMOEng/Communication/PMSpeaks/speechknes140 806.htm, accessed 1 Dec 06.

17. Statement by the Israeli Political Security Committee on 19 Jul 06, http://www.pmo.gov .il/PMOEng/Communication/Spokesman/2006/07/spokekab190706.htm, accessed 1 Dec 06.

18. Speeches by Prime Minister Ehud Olmert and Statement by the Israeli Political Security Committee.

19. James P. Pinkerton, "Tactical Victory No Match for Media Superiority," *Newsday*,1 Aug 06, http://www.infowar-monitor.net/modules.php?op=modload&name=Newsfile&article&sid=13 40, 3 Aug 06.

20. Helena Cobban, "Hizballah's New Face—In Search of a Muslim Democracy," *Boston Review*, Apr/May 05, http://bostonreview.net/BR30.2/cobban.html, 29 Nov 06.

21. Felix Frisch, "IDF: Hizballah Eavesdropped on Our Cellular Phones," *Ma'ariv*, 30 Jul 06, 16 Aug 06.

22. "Israeli Military Censor Orders All Media in Israel to Comply with Censorship Order," International Middle East Media Center, 25 Jul 06.

23. Wrona, *From Sticks and Stones to Zeros and Ones*.

24. "Israeli Official Comments on Recent Hacker Attacks," *Cyber Threat Media Highlights*, 26 Jul 06, accessed 14 Aug 06.

25. "Islamic Hackers Strike Again at Israel; Israeli Hackers Respond," *Cyber Threat Media Highlights*, 18 Jul 06 (originally from www.israelvalley.com, 14 Jul 06), accessed 14 Aug 06; "Iranian Youths Plan Internel Attack Against Israel," Tehran *Siyasat-e Ruz*, in Persian, 18 Jul 06, p. 2, 14 Aug 06; and Abdellatif El Azizi, "Computer Activism: The Intigada of the Moroccan Hackers," Casablanca *Tel Quel*, 14 Jul 06, 14 Aug 06.

26. "Islamic Hackers Strike Again at Israel; Israeli Hackers Respond."

27. "Correct the Damage," *Jerusalem Post*, 16 July 2006, http://www.jpost.com/servlet/Sate llite?cid=1150886011436&pagename=JPost%2FJPArticle%2FPrinter, accessed 18 Jan 08.

28. "Anonymous and Accessible Communications: A Current Terror Arena," Sixth International Counter Terrorism Conference, Institute for Counter-Terrorism, Herzliya, Israel, 13 Sep 06, 30 Oct 06.

29. Ibid.

30. Ilene R. Prusher, "Wooing Lebanese Hearts, One Leaflet at a Time," *Christian Science Monitor*, 2 Aug 06, http://www.csmonitor.com/2006/0802/p11s01-wome.html, 29 Nov 06.

31. Ibid.

32. Roberto Preatoni, "Defacement Goes Live: Hezbollah's Leader Nasrallah Gets Defaced Live by Israeli TV-Hackers," 2 Aug 2006, http://www.zone-h.org/content/view/13938/30, 13 Aug 06.

33. Ibid.

34. August 10, 2006, broadcast of the BBC Monitoring World Media, p. 37 (Channel 2 TV, Jerusalem, in Hebrew 1700 GMT, 8 Aug 06).

35. Ilan Marciano, "Committee: Government Failed in Dealing with Home Front," Tel Aviv *Ynetnews*, 0543 GMT, in English, 13 Sep 06, accessed 11 Nov 06.

36. For example, see "Charles Foster Johnson," Wikipedia, 25 Nov 06, http://en.wikipedia .org/wiki/Charles_Johnson_(blogger), 30 Nov 06.

37. "Reuters on the Run," Little Green Footballs, 7 Aug 06, http://littlegreenfootballs.com/ weblog/?entry=21976&only, 29 Nov 06.

38. Charles Johnson, "Bush Guard Documents Forged," Little Green Footballs, 9 Sep 04, http://littlegreenfootballs.com/weblog/?entry=12526, 30 Nov 06.

39. Ya'aqov Katz, "Hizballah Drove Shot Down Over Acre Was Carrying Explosives," *Jerusalem Post*, 19 Sep 06, accessed 11 Nov 06.

40. Nasrallah speeches.

41. "Source A" does not want to be identified for security reasons. Met source in Sep 06. Source is a retired senior officer from the Israeli Security Agency. Also, see David A. Fulghum and Robert Wall, "Israel Starts Reexamining Military Missions and Technology," 20 Aug 06, http://www.aviationnow.com/avnow/news/channel_awst_story.jsp?id=news/aw082106p2.xml, 20 Nov 06; and Alon Ben-David, "Israel Develops Comprehensive Defences against Varied Missile, Rocket Threats," *Jane's International Defence Review*, Jan 2006, p. 61.

42. Uzi Rubin, "Hizballah's Rocket Campaign against Northern Israel: A Preliminary Report," 31 Aug 06, Jerusalem Center for Public Affairs, http://www.jcpa.org/brief/brief006-10 .htm, 15 Sep 06.

43. "Source B" does not want to be identified for security reasons. Met source in Sep 06. Source is a retired senior IDF intelligence officer.

44. "Source A" does not want to be identified for security reasons. Met source in Sep 06. Source is a retired senior officer from the Israeli Security Agency.

45. For example, see James J. F. Forest, ed., *Teaching Terror: Strategic and Tactical Learning in the Terrorist World* (Boulder, CO: Rowman & Littlefield, 2006).

46. "Source A" does not want to be identified for security reasons. Met source in Sep 06. Source is a retired senior officer from the Israeli Security Agency.

47. Aaron Klein, "Hamas, Hezbollah Vow to Continue Terror," World Net Daily, 31 January 2005, http://www.worldnetdaily.com/news/article.asp?ARTICLE_ID=42621, accessed 15 Feb 08.

48. "Source B" does not want to be identified for security reasons. Met source in Sep 06. Source is a retired senior IDF intelligence officer.

49. "Source C" does not want to be identified for security reasons. Met source in Sep 06. Source is a retired senior IDF operations officer.

50. Fulghum and Wall, "Israel Starts Reexamining Military Missions and Technology."

51. "Hearing before the Select Committee on Intelligence of The United States Senate," 108th Congress, First Session, Current and Projected National Security Threats to the United States, 11 Feb 2003, http://www.fas.org/irp/congress/2003_hr/021103transcript.pdf, 30 Nov 06, p. 80.

THE INFORMATION OPERATIONS WAR BETWEEN ISRAEL AND HIZBALLAH 327

52. Organization of Islamic Conference, http://www.oic-oci.org, 30 Nov 06.

53. "Muslims in Europe: Country Guide," BBC News, 23 Dec 05, http://news.bbc.uk/2/hi/europe/4385768.stm, accessed 18 Jan 08.

54. For a good description of this game, see *Teaching Terror*, p. 98.

55. "Special Force 2: Tale of the Truthful Pledge," http://www.specialforce2.org/support.htm, accessed 5 Jan 08.

56. Ibid.

57. Michael Cantanzaro, "The 'Revolution in Military Affairs' Has an Enemy: Politics," American Enterprise Institute, Oct 01, http://www.sourcewatch.org/index.php?title=Andrew_Marshall, 30 Nov 06.

17

Strategic Uses of the Internet by Hizbut Tahrir-Indonesia

Frank Hairgrove, Douglas M. McLeod, and Dhavan V. Shah

HIZBUT TAHRIR-INDONESIA (HT-I) IS part of the Hizbut Tahrir (HT) transnational movement, an organization that seeks to mobilize Muslim populations toward the goal of reestablishing the Islamic caliph as the political authority, first over Islamic countries, then worldwide.[1] Though it is nonviolent, HT—along with its branches, such as HT-I—does not rule out violence to accomplish its goals, especially in its final stages.[2] Members of HT have been known to have links with terrorist organizations, though HT itself is not listed as a terrorist organization because of its current nonviolent stance.[3]

Social movement organizers generally have at least two organizational communication goals. The first is to communicate internally with its constituents regarding the organizational mobilization activities. The second objective is to communicate and persuade target populations to accept the movement's objectives.[4] These tasks become more dependent on the Internet as the movement becomes transnational. Mario Diani argues that computer-mediated communication (CMC) in transnational social movements can function as a double-edged sword.[5] It can bring diverse groups together by maintaining ideological tenets of the movement as it crosses national lines, but likewise it can also make the organization less personal as it becomes "virtual." Craig Calhoun references this pattern to Melvin Webber's classic definition of "community without propinquity."[6] To overcome the tendency of the virtual community to become less personal, organizers use CMC both transnationally and locally (within national borders) by employing and benefiting from the strength of small local networks. In a sense, CMC needs to connect networks and networks of networks by providing a constant flow of information between, to, and from organizers. The messages disseminating from the local networks to local target populations must reflect the transnational message in order to "brand" the organizational goals yet feel local.

For a message to have a broad effect in the public discourse, it needs to be diffused through multiple media channels. In an early study of this, Paul Lazarsfeld and colleagues argued that media effects were weak. This notion was countered by scholars who said the Lazarsfeld's conclusion of limited media effects was based on a limited conception of the nature of media effects.[7] When messages are embedded in a social system via trusted networks (media), they can have a measurable effect.[8] The stronger the social bonds and the more embedded the message is in the ethos of the social system, the more significant effects that message will produce.[9]

Some researchers have argued that the Internet is being used by terrorist organizations as a weapon for persuading discontented populations to join jihad and as a central weapon in their arsenal of terror.[10] Though there is some evidence of the Internet being used in this manner, Gabriel Weimann observes that these exaggerated threats have hidden the power of the mundane and yet typical use of the Internet for the exchange of information.[11]

When the Internet was first introduced as a mass communication tool, visions abounded for the potential of this medium. It was fast, cheap, and unmediated by gatekeepers, and would thereby expand civic knowledge by making knowledge more accessible to the masses and encouraging greater debates on issues of democratic importance. However, recent research has found that Internet use actually reduces civic knowledge because it allows purveyors to filter out dissenting opinions by using key word searches for spokespersons whose opinions are like theirs.[12] Additional research has found that Internet users approach the medium with a mix of objectives, such as entertainment, consuming (online shopping), information gathering (news), and researching information.[13] Hedonistic users were less informed than information seekers, and information seekers were less knowledgeable about countering opinions. In other words, the "selective exposure" feature of the Internet made users more myopic in their views.[14]

This selective exposure approach to Internet use means people will be exposed to media that support opinions that they currently hold, are more apt to discuss the material with people whose opinions they share and will not expose themselves to counteropinions.[15] For this reason, the Internet will theoretically be most effective for reinforcing the users' beliefs if the CMC message is consistent with their currently held beliefs, and if the Internet consumer is embedded in a network of people who share those beliefs. On the flip side, the Internet will be weaker in persuading the masses (who do not already embrace the mobilization goals) to accept the mobilization goals of the organization.

BACKGROUND ON HT-I

Sheikh Taqiuddin al-Nabhani founded Hizbut Tahrir in 1952 in Jordan as a splinter group from the Muslim Brotherhood, which he felt was not aggressive enough in reestablishing the caliphate and addressing the Palestinian conflict.[16] After a dialogue with Muslim Brotherhood radical Sayyid Qutb, al-Nabhani rejected violence as proposed by Qutb, but he did incorporate jihad language in his treatise. He also adopted a quasi–Muslim Brotherhood position that incorporated Qutb's thinking regarding a global strategy (as compared to a local strategy) for reestablishing the caliphate.[17] For this reason, Hizbut Tahrir began as a transnational movement with the goal of reestablishing the caliph though nonviolent means, if possible.[18]

To reach its goal, HT follows a definable three-stage vision for an Islamic revolution to reestablish the caliph. Once HT enters a country, it seeks to "educate" that population on its philosophy and the ideology of HT. It will often collaborate with similar organizations in seminars and conferences and then coopt members. It also seeks to raise its profile though mass media events and issues. In the second stage, it will seek to consolidate cadre by encouraging them to become an outreach arm of the movement and recruit new members.[19] It also seeks to infiltrate government infrastructures and gain influence within military apparatuses. In the third stage, they will seek to topple the current regime and replace it with a government that will implement Shari'a and support the caliph.[20]

To accomplish the second and critical stage of developing cadre, HT follows a three-level training program for recruits. In the first level, recruits join gender-specific small groups, called *halaqa*, which meet weekly to study the Qur'an and books written by Hassan al-Banna and Taqiuddin al-Nabhani. Recruits who show promise are asked join a next-level halaqa, where material becomes less religious and more strategy-oriented. Members who display skills needed for the organization are invited to a leadership-level halaqa where, upon completion, they are invited to become full-fledged members of HT as a *naquib* or organizer. Once someone becomes a naquib, he/she is able to start a new HT halaqa, and the cycle is repeated with new recruits.[21]

The Indonesian branch of HT began in Bogor, West Java, in 1982. Because the HT strategy was to overthrow the government and establish a pan-Islamic nation under the caliph, it chose to remain "nameless" and clandestine until 1990 when it felt it had sufficient organizational strength to become an active mobilization organization. Recruits first came from the secular universities in Bogor and Bandung where they met in small groups to study books written by al-Banna, Qutb, and al-Nabhani. Meeting locations varied from week to week, and those attending arrived at varied times and left at staggered times to avoid detection. Membership grew steadily through the 1990s and early 2000s as members proceeded though the recruitment and training process.[22]

HIZBUT TAHRIR'S IMPACT IN INDONESIA

HT-I launched its first Internet site in March 2004 after first publishing pamphlets in early 2000, and subsequently added translated books and then later a magazine.[23] Currently it produces a million weekly flyers called *al Islam*, which are sold for 200 rupiah each (or about $0.025) and distributed by local HT members at their mosques each Friday.[24] The files for the weekly flyers are sent via e-mail to networks that produce them locally via low-cost and low-quality methods. HT-I also produces a monthly 72-page magazine with glossy full color cover called *al-wa'ie,* whose 40,000 copies are distributed through various venues and sell for 5,500 rupiah each ($0.60). Their media strategy also includes a daily updated Web site called Hizbut Tahrir-Indonesia. Hits on the site[25] averaged 1,089 per day in late 2006,[26] but after a change in the site layout in March 2007, hits and Web page views have made it the fourth most popular Indonesian-language Islamic Web site in Indonesia. The communications network is so well organized that Ismail Yusanto, spokesperson for HT, noted he could arrange a nationwide demonstration within two hours by using e-mail and phone text messages.[27]

In terms of evaluating organizational strength, one has to interpolate since HT-I remains a secretive organization. Sidney Jones, an expert on Indonesian radical groups with International Crisis Group Indonesia, estimates that HT-I has about 13,000 committed cadre actively participating in weekly halaqa meetings, and twice that amount in associate status (i.e., not active in halaqa studies) for an organizational strength of nearly 50,000 members.[28] In support of Jones's estimates, the Third International Caliphate Conference sponsored by HT-I and held in Jakarta on August 12, 2007, drew 90,000 participants, most of whom were Indonesians in their twenties.[29]

MEASURING INTERNET EFFECTIVENESS

In any media marketing campaign, decision makers seek to position their message in combination with other messages in a media mix so as capitalize on the synergistic power of messages that reinforce each other across different media.[30] In the media mix, each message and each medium has specialized persuasive functions, and may even be targeted to different audiences in a manner that is coordinated to maximize campaign effectiveness.[31] The confluence of the media mix makes it difficult to isolate the influence of one particular medium without considering its specific role and influence as part of the synergistic persuasive campaign. Without this broader context, as well as the interpersonal and cultural situations in which the messages are received, one is bound to underestimate message influence.[32] For this reason, measurement of the effectiveness of a medium is related to target objectives in its context.

Scholars have shown that Internet messages are extensions of offline messages in both advertising and political discourse.[33] In research on bloggers, the reverse was found; online forums influenced offline discourse.[34] By evaluating online messages and online conversations, one can observe how media decision makers sought to use the medium, and how the users extend the transmission of the message.

Tabulating Internet traffic can be misleading when measuring effectiveness of a Web site's information strategy. Researchers driven by profit motives have developed creative ways of measuring Internet traffic. Some have proposed measuring flow through the routers,[35] and others query the DNS caches,[36] all requiring complex algorithms, software, and access to servers. Other researchers have proposed approaches of measuring networks and networks of networks to determine the spreading effect of influence.[37] These approaches atomize the media mix and fail to capture the gestalt power of the Internet within a media mix. Everett Rogers proposes that to fully understand the effectiveness of a medium, one should observe how the medium is used in intermedia connections, including interpersonal interactions.[38]

To accomplish intermedia synergism, it is necessary to use multiple methods to observe the interaction of a medium with the other media components within its media bundle. A more appropriate approach to measure effectiveness would be to observe how users interact with the Internet; how he/she correlates Internet messages with other media, both mass media and interpersonal. This chapter, therefore, takes a multimethods approach in observing HT's Internet use and impact by looking at quantitative data of Web site activity from various sources, combined with a qualitative analysis of topics posted and discussion on those topics. By correlating these different types of data, one can identify the intentions of Internet site designers and their effectiveness in achieving their objectives.

INFLUENCE OF HIZBUT TAHRIR-INDONESIA'S INTERNET ACTIVITIES

HT-I's Internet site was fairly simple prior to March 2007. The site posted articles by a range of authors; many were full text or abridged versions of articles found in the *al-Islam* newsletter or *al-wa'ie* magazine. At times, content was original, and some were responses to criticisms from editorials or newspaper articles. Links along the left side of the Web page allowed visitors to go to HT Web sites in other languages, or to online versions of the *al-Islam* newsletter and *al-aw'ie* magazine. A visitor counter was placed at the bottom of the Web page. Web site activity was recorded September through December 2006, a time span that included the high Islamic holiday Ramadan. Weekdays were observed as being more active than weekends, with Mondays having the most traffic, and a significant increase in postings and activity was recorded surrounding an incident when the pope made comments about Islam that were offensive to some Muslims, and again following the announcement of a visit to Indonesia by President Bush.[39]

The site change in March provided an opportunity to explore visitors' activity. In the updated design, the visitor counter was removed, and the site was made interactive, with visitors being able to add comments to each of the articles. It was less glitzy compared to the old site, but was easier to navigate. Like the old site, it offered links to the other 19 HT sites in various languages, as well as archived online versions of *al-Islam* and *al-wa'ie*. The new site made those links more prominent.

The greatest advantage to the new site was the added ability for users to post their comments. As illustrated in Figure 17.1, comments from March 2007 through September 2007 were grouped under 12 themes based on article headings, and the average frequency of these comment groupings were calculated. In total, there were 70 articles and 812 comment postings, with an average of 11.6 postings per article. The top four categories of comment postings were *caliphate conference* (held August 12, 2007), *hegemony* (by governments suppressing or oppressing Muslims), topics related to the *establishment of the caliphate*, and issues related to *Israel*. The largest proportion of articles posted (24 percent) addressed the theme of *dakwah* (outreach meeting announcements), followed by *caliphate* (with 14 percent of all articles posted).[40]

To determine whether the postings were from a few enthusiasts or were from diverse users, the diffusion of postings was analyzed. For the month of September there were 96 postings, of which 35 were multiples. One person had 10 postings, one had 5 postings, two had 3 postings each, and seven had 2 postings each. If one excludes the one unique user with 10 postings, then diffusion spread is nearly one post per commenter, or in other words, the data reflect a diverse group of users.

Were visitors who posted comments actually engaging in the dialogue by adding to the intellectual content, or were they merely registering support? Two researchers fluent in Indonesian reviewed the comments to determine into which of two categories the

Figure 17.1   Average Comments per Article Theme

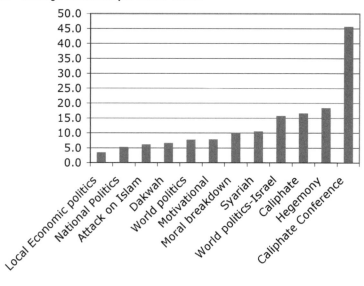

comments fell: engaging in the intellectual argument or only support. Results show that 47 percent of the comments were from people who were engaging in the dialogue, with the rest merely posting words supportive of the article. Of those who engaged in the dialogue, none were critical of HT-I's position, expressing pro-HT-I rhetoric instead. Most of the topics followed this pattern, half engaging in the dialogue and half expressing support.

One interesting feature of the comment posting was the date and time of day of the posting. From this one could determine when visitors posted the comments. Judging from typical office hours (8 AM–5 PM except lunch), lunch (11 AM–1 PM), travel home (5 PM–7 PM), and night (7 PM–5 AM), postings followed this pattern: 70 percent of the postings were during office hours, 14 percent were done during lunch, 8 percent were made at home or on the way home possibly at an Internet kiosk, with 5 percent posting at night, and 3 percent during early morning hours, most likely from home. Clearly, 84 percent of HT-I posters did their postings during office hours (office and lunch), presumably using office computers.[41]

Finally, we examined how the HT-I site was ranked by an independent Internet ranking organization, Alexa Internet,[42] recognized as the leading authority by the advertising industry in Indonesia.[43] By observing Alexa site rankings (see Table 17.1), as of October 2, 2007, HT-I was ranked fifth in Indonesia among Islamic religion Web sites, and ranked 2,006th among all sites in Indonesia. Of those logging on to HT-I, 84 percent were from Indonesia, 10 percent were from Palestine, and the rest were from a variety of places. Average views by each visitor were 3.8 pages, which is below the average of 4.7 among the top five sites.

Table 17.1   Alexa Report as of October 8, 2007

Ranking among Islamic Sites		Ranking among All Indonesian Sites	#1 Views From	#2 Views From	Views per Page
1	Eramuslim.com	151	Indo 87%	Malaysia 4.2%	4.4
2	myquran.com	255	Indo 87%	Malaysia 4.2%	6.1
3	Almanhaj.or.id	883	Indo 87.1%	Malaysia 5%	5.7
4	Pesantrenvirtual. com	1,315	Indo 76.9%	Malaysia 14.9%	3.4
5	Hizbut-tahrir.or.id	2,006	Indo 84%	Palestine 10%	3.8

The HT-I visitor count in the Alexa report appears to have been optimized, and there-fore its accuracy can be questioned. But according to data provided by the Alexa service, the volume has double or tripled since the measurement was taken in 2006. Based on a conservative estimate, the HT-I Web site experiences at least 2,000 hits per day and 3.8 Web page views per visitor.

DISCUSSION

The question this research sought to address was whether the HT-I Web site was effec-tive in reaching one or more of it strategic goals. Effectiveness, therefore, is related to the objectives of general education and/or solidifying its cadre base.

HT-I, being a secretive organization, is reticent to reveal its media objectives. To identify its objectives, this research performed a content analysis of the HT-I Web site from March 2007 through September 2007. Two of the most popular articles posted were related to the caliph, a theme that was preeminent with Taqiuddin al-Nabhani's founding of HT. Hegemony, most often related to U.S. policies, and Israel's oppression of Palestine are in the top four issues. Again, these can be traced to philosophies estab-lished by Taqiuddin al-Nabhani. From observing responses, all posters supported HT-I propositions, with over half extending the discussion by adding supporting material; it is thus safe to assume that the Web site functions to support HT-I ideology for its mem-bers. Unlike Gabriel Weimann's description of terrorist groups' use of the Internet, which posits that the Internet is used mainly for communication, propaganda, marketing, and fund-raising,[44] HT-I appears to use the Internet for reinforcement and to solidify mem-bers' support of HT-I ideology, rather than as a recruitment tool.

From the postings that appeared on the HT-I Web site, most visitors were not regular contributors (a few people posting many responses). Rather, visitors posted supportive comments over the course of a month. Experts deduce that there are about 50,000 HT-I members, both hard-core cadre or committed sympathizers. Other research among radical groups observes that content online is further disseminated to friends in halaqa groups who don't have an Internet connection.[45] With HT-I's site having daily hits of over 2,000 visitors, it is safe to assume that diffusion of HT-I's message occurs among core cadre, associates, and sympathizers. Ismail Yusanto's statement of being able to mobilize cadre nationally within a few hours testifies to the efficiency and density of electronic connections within HT-I.

But with the daily numbers of visitors being so low, is HT-I's reach considered relevant? Merlyna Lim reported that Indonesia's Laskar Jihad group's Internet site likewise had a small reach.[46] At that time, Alexa ranked Laskar Jihad fifth among Islamic religion Web sites, and it also ranked above 2,000 among all Indonesia Web sites. But its reach and effectiveness were demonstrated by mobilizing a jihad against the Christians on the Muluku Islands, a multireligious archipelago located on the eastern side of Indonesia. The sectarian conflict left as many as 10,000 dead and 700,000 refugees.[47]

The combination of Internet use and halaqa participation makes for a potentially powerful ideological force. In research conducted in Indonesia in December 2006 by the Program on International Policy Attitudes (PIPA) for the U.S. Department of Homeland Security, the only significant correlation with attitudes supporting suicide bombings was Internet use and discussing the material with associates. This is consistent with persuasion research looking at small group influence on attitude change.[48]

Judging by the postings on HT-I's core issues—the caliph, hegemony, and Israel—the Internet serves alongside other media to reinforce ideology for what Everett Rogers calls strong media effects, especially among radicals engaged in the HT struggle.[49] According to the Alexa data on HT-I, the second largest visitor population was from Palestine, whereas Malaysia, much closer to Indonesia in language and culture, was the second largest population for all the other Muslim Web sites, which reinforces the nature of the transnational audience that the HT-I site has within the greater HT movement.

A final observation is that those who post do so from their offices. This leads to several additional insights. One is that many of the HT-I population hold white-collar jobs that provide computer access. This is logical since HT-I has recruited from colleges, and it appears these recruits have moved on and now hold influential jobs. This model is consistent with Carrie Wickham's observations of the growth of the Muslim Brotherhood movement in Egypt, where organizational leaders were groomed from college chapters.[50] This also reflects the fact that ownership of personal computers is limited, which raises questions about the use of work resources for non–work-related purposes, such as religious pursuits. Interviews with members of the myquran blog community revealed that nearly all participants acknowledged that they access religious Web sites from work. Many stated (unsolicited) that they made sure their work was done before going online for personal use.

CONCLUSION

This case study investigated how HT-I uses the Internet to accomplish its mobilization goals. Data came from personal interviews, observation of their site during two periods in 2006 and 2007, and independent evaluations from Alexa. The study indicates that HT-I uses the Internet mainly for indoctrinating recruits into HT-I ideology. From extrapolation, it appears HT-I is effective at reaching its target audience both online and offline, with members downloading material for distribution among compatriots who are involved with halaqa study groups.

Since it appears that HT-I is using the Internet not for recruitment, but for grounding cadre in basic ideological propositions of HT, HT-I is solidifying its leadership. This should not come as a surprise since it is consistent with their stated objectives in a phase two strategy. The same pattern was reported by Carrie Wickham on the Muslim Brotherhood in Egypt: "It's like planting seeds on the farm . . . You raise Ikhwani (Brotherhood) students in the University, then five years later you have an electoral base for the professional associations."[51] When we asked Ismail Yusanto, spokesperson for HT-I, what his most effective media tool was, it came as no surprise when he responded that it was the halaqa small group.[52]

All media, including the Internet, are used intentionally in the halaqa to establish its grassroots leadership base. Success of this approach can be observed from the organizational growth in terms of numbers—currently 50,000 members—as well as the amount of visitors to its Web sites and the impact of its outreach efforts. The first caliphate conference in May 2000 had 5,000 participants, whereas the 2007 conference exceeded 90,000, reflective of substantial growth in a few short years.[53] HT-I shows healthy signs in both solidifying its leadership and increasing its influence.

HT-I's intentions to reestablish the caliph should not be dismissed by security officials. Though they are not currently violent, by their own admission they do not rule out violence in the final push in phase three. According to Ismail Yusanto, only the rightly chosen caliph can proclaim a fatwa instituting jihad. The choosing of the caliph in phase three is not out of the realm of possibility as they solidify their following in the current phase.

NOTES

1. Zeyno Baran, "Executive Summary" (paper presented at the the Challenge of Hizb ut Tahrir: Deciphering and Combating Radical Islamist Ideology, Washington, 2004), 10; Zeyno Baran, "Hizbut Tahrir—Islam's Political Insurgency," (Washington: Nixon Center, 2004), 18–20; and Hizbut Tahrir, "Mengenal Hizbut Tahrir: Partai Politik Islam Ideologis (Introducing Hizbut Tahrir: An Ideological Islamic Political Party)" (Bogor, Java, Indonesia: Pustaka Thariqul Izzah, 2003).

2. Frank Schneider, "Hizb Ut-Tahrir: A Threat Behind a Legal Facade?" (Naval Postgraduate School, 2006), 56; and Michael Whine, "Is Hizb Ut-Tahrir Changing Strategy or Tactics?" in *Center for Eurasian Policy Occasional Research Paper*, ed. Huston Institute (2006), 3.

3. Shiv Malik, "The Conveyor Belt of Extremism," *New Statesman* (2005), http://www.newstatesman.com/200507180005; and S. Yunanto, *Militant Islamic Movements in Indonesia and South-East Asia* (Freidrich-Ebert-Stiftung and Ridep Institute, 2003), 54–55, 88–89.

4. D. Della Porta and M. Diani, *Social Movements: An Introduction* (Malden, MA: Blackwell Publishing, 2006), 131–34; and John D. McCarthy and Mayer N. Zald, "Resource Mobilization

and Social Movements: A Partial Theory," *American Journal of Sociology* 82, no. 6 (1977): 1212–17.

5. Mario Diani, "Social Movement Networks Virtual and Real," *Information, Communication & Society* 3, no. 3 (2000): 397.

6. Craig Calhoun, "Community without Propinquity Revisited: Communications Technology and the Transformation of the Urban Public Sphere," *Sociological Inquiry* 68, no. 3 (1998): 374.

7. Paul Felix Lazarsfeld, Bernard Berelson, and Hazel Gaudet, *The People's Choice* (New York: Columbia University Press, 1965), 75–91.

8. Everett M. Rogers, "Intermedia Processes and Powerful Media Effects," *Media effects: Advances in Theory and Research* (2002): 211.

9. Pablo Brinol and Richard Petty, "Individual Differences in Attitude Change," in *The Handbook of Attitudes*, ed. Dolores Albarracin, Blair T. Johnson, and Mark P. Zanna (Mahwah, NJ: Lawrence Erlbaum Associates, 2005), 592.

10. Gary R. Bunt, *Islam in the Digital Age: E-Jihad, Online Fatwas and Cyber Islamic Environments* (Sterling, VA: Pluto Press, 2003), 1–3; Maura Conway, "Terrorism and the Internet: New Media—New Threat?," *Parliamentary Affairs* 59, no. 2 (2006): 7; Gabriel Weimann, "www.Terror .Net: How Modern Terrorism Uses the Internet," in *Special Report* (Washington, DC: U.S. Institute of Peace, 2004), 8–9; and Gabriel Weimann, "Virtual Training Camps," in *The Making of a Terrorist*, ed. J. Forest (Westport, CT: Praeger Security International, 2006), 116–17.

11. Weimann, "www.Terror.Net," 9–10. Also, please see Weimann's chapter in this volume.

12. Dietram A. Scheufele and Matthew C. Nisbet, "Being a Citizen Online: New Opportunities and Dead Ends," *Harvard International Journal of Press/Politics* 7, no. 3 (2002): 63–70.

13. Dhavan V. Shah, "Connecting and Disconnecting with Civic Life: Patterns of Internet Use and the Production of Social Capital," *Political Communication* 18, no. 2 (2001): 144.

14. Jennings Bryant and Dolf Miron, "Entertainment as Media Effect," in *Media Effects: Advances in Theory and Research*, ed. Jennings Bryant and Dolf Zillmann (Mahwah, NJ: Lawrence Erlbaum Associates, 2002), 560–61; and Shah, 154.

15. Ibid.; and Dhavan V. Shah, Jack M. McLeod, and So-Hyang Yoon, "Communication, Context, and Community: An Exploration of Print, Broadcast, and Internet Influences," *Communication Research* 28, no. 4 (2001): 470–71.

16. Tahrir.

17. Schneider, 8.

18. Matthew Crosston, "The Hizb-Tahrir in Central Asia: How America Misleads Islamist Threats," *Meria* 11, no. 3 (2007): 2.

19. William Shaffir, "Witnessing as Identity Consolidation: The Case of the Lubavitcher Chassidim," in *Identity and Religion: International, Cross-Cultural Approaches*, ed. Hans Mol (London: Sage Publications, 1978), 50–51.

20. Baran, "Hizbut Tahrir—Islam's Political Insurgency," 20–23.

21. Greg Fealy, "Hizbut Tahrir in Indonesia: Seeking A 'Total Islamic Identity,'" in *Islam and Political Violence: Muslim Diaspora and Radicalism in the West*, ed. Shahram Akbarzadeh and Fethi Mansouri (New York: Palgrave Macmillan, 2007), 153–55; Evgenii Novikov, "The Recruiting and Organizational Structure of Hizb Ut-Tahrir," *Terrorism Monitor, The Jamestown Foundation* 2, no. 22 (2004), http://www.jamestown.org/publications_details.php?volume_id=400&issue_id=3148&article_id=2368890; and Agus Salim, "The Rise of Hizbut Tahrir-Indonesia (1982–2004): It's Political Opportunity Structure, Resource Mobilization, and Collective Action Frames" (MA thesis, Syarif Hidayatullah State Islamic University, 2005), 145–49.

22. Martin van Bruinessen, "Post-Suharto Muslim Engagements with Civil Society and Democratisation," in *Third International Conference and Workshop "Indonesia in Transition"*

(Universitas Indonesia, Depok: KNAW and Labsosio, Universitas Indonesia, 2003); Elizabeth Collins, "Islam Is the Solution: Dakwah and Democracy in Indonesia" (Athens, Ohio: Department of Classics and World Religions, 2004); and Salim, 145–49.

23. Salim, 162–82.

24. Personal interviews with Ismail Yusanto, spokesperson for Hizbut Tahrir-Indonesia.

25. See http://hizbut-tahrir.or.id.

26. Personally monitoring of the Web site October to December 2006.

27. Personal interviews with Ismail Yusanto, August 1, 2007, in Jakarta.

28. Personal interviews with Sidney Jones and Fajri (last name withheld), former ranking member of Hizbut Tahrir, July 27, 2007, in Jakarta.

29. Personally attending the conference and estimating the numbers by counting the stadium sections. Various media reports had estimates ranging from 90,000 to 100,000.

30. William F. Arens and Courtland L. Bovee, *Contemporary Advertising* (Burr Ridge, IL: Irwin 1994), 383–84; and George E. Belch and Michael A. Belch, *Introduction to Advertising and Promotion: An Integrated Marketing Communications Perspective* (Homewood, IL: Irwin 1995), 319.

31. Richard M. Perloff, *The Dynamics of Persuasion* (Mahwah, NJ: Lawrence Erlbaum, 1993), 311–13.

32. Rogers, 212.

33. Merlyna Lim, "Islamic Radicalism and Anti-Americanism in Indonesia: The Role of the Internet," in *Policy Studies* (Washington DC: East-West Center Washington, 2005), 7; Mary Lou Roberts, *Internet Marketing: Integrating Online and Offline Strategies* (New York: McGraw-Hill School Education Group, 2002), 281–87; Scheufele and Nisbet, 69–71; Shah, "Connecting and Disconnecting with Civic Life," 149–54; and Dhavan V. Shah et al., "Information and Expression in a Digital Age: Modeling Internet Effects on Civic Participation," *Communication Research* 32, no. 5 (2005): 535–53.

34. Daniel Drezner and Henery Farrell, "The Power and Politics of Blogs," *American Political Science Association Annual Conference, Chicago, Illinois* (2004): 21; and Sahar Talaat, "Bloggers or Journalist: New Perspective in Arab Media," in *International Association for Mass Communication Research* (American University in Cairo, Egypt, 2006).

35. Nicolas Hohn and Darryl Veitch, "Inverting Sampled Traffic" (paper presented at the Proc. of the 3rd ACM SIGCOMM Conf. on Internet Measurement, Miami, Florida, 2003).

36. C. E. Wills, M. Mikhailov, and H. Shang, "Inferring Relative Popularity of Internet Applications by Actively Querying DNS Caches" (paper presented at the Proceedings of the 3rd ACM SIGCOMM conference on Internet measurement, 2003).

37. Christian Dewes, Arne Wichmann, and Anja Feldmann, "An Analysis of Internet Chat Systems" (paper presented at the Proceedings of the 2003 ACM SIGCOMM conference on Internet measurement, 2003); Drezner and Farrell, 5; and Kathy E. Gill, "How Can We Measure the Influence of the Blogosphere," in *Workshop on the Weblogging Ecosystem at the 13th International World Wide Web Conference* (New York, 2004).

38. Rogers, 212.

39. The daily average for that period was 1,089 hits, with a weekday average of 1,166 hits, Saturday average of 955 hits, and Sunday average of 838 hits. The heaviest daily average occurred on Mondays with 1,203 hits. The average number of hits per day was concurrent with the incident with the pope's comments—1,398 (a four-day average)—and with the announcement of Bush's upcoming travel to Indonesia, hits averaged 1,308 per day (a five-day average). When Bush did arrive in Indonesia, calls were made for HT-I associates to line the streets from Jakarta to Bogor holding protest banners; the hits per day then dropped to 869.

40. The top four categories were the *caliphate conference* (held August 12, 2007) with an average of 45.7 comments on the 3 articles, *hegemony* (by governments suppressing or oppressing Muslims) with an average of 18.4 comments on 5 articles, topics related to the *establishment of the caliphate* with an average of 16.6 comments on 10 articles, and finally, issues related to *Israel* with an average of 15.8 comments on 4 articles In total, there were 70 articles and 812 postings, with an average of 11.6 postings per article. The theme of *Dakwah* (outreach meeting announcements) had the most article postings with 17 postings or 24 percent of all postings with average comments of 6.1 per posting, followed by caliphate with 10 articles posted or 14 percent of all postings.

41. Though it is possible that the majority of Internet posters are students using campus computers, there are several issues to consider. Campus computers are less frequented during the day based on personal observations, and they charge for access time. More research is needed to determine conclusively where access originates, by using IP addresses.

42. See http://www.alexa.com.

43. This was based on interviews with the CDA Group in Jakarta, August 10, 2007.

44. Weimann, "Virtual Training Camps," 113.

45. Lim, 24–25, 37–38.

46. Ibid., 35–36.

47. ICG, "Indonesia: Overcoming Murder and Violence in Maluku" (Jakarta/Brussels: 2000); and Lim, 18.

48. Brinol and Petty, 592; Frank Hairgrove and Douglas McLeod, "Circles Drawing toward High Risk Activism: The Use of Usroh and Halaqa in Islamist Radical Movements," *Studies in Conflict & Terrorism* (2008); and Clark McCauley and Mary Segal, "Social Psychology of Terrorist Groups," in *Group Processes and Intergroup Relations*, ed. Clyde Hendrick (New York: Sage Publications, 1987), 237–39.

49. Rogers, 212.

50. Carrie Wickham, *Mobilizing Islam: Religion, Activism, and Political Change in Egypt* (New York: Columbia University Press, 2002), 195.

51. Ibid.

52. Personal interviews with Ismail Yusanto, August 1, 2007, in Jakarta.

53. Ibid.

PART IV

CONCLUSION

18

Conclusion

Assessing the Conceptual Battlespace

Joshua Alexander Geltzer and James J. F. Forest

IF THERE IS A SINGLE direction in which all the contributions in this volume point, it is to the mind. The mind—of the terrorist, of the would-be terrorist, of the potential supporter of terrorism, of the targeted population member, of the counterterrorist official—*the mind* is the site of acute concern in the world of terrorism and counterterrorism, and in the present information age this is even more so than ever before. Physical geography remains an important dimension of national security, but it is not in the skies above London, on the beaches of Normandy, or amidst the waves off Midway Island that current and future conflicts between terrorists and governments will be decided; rather, it is on the conceptual battlespace, located in the mind itself.

This concluding chapter draws from the contributions to this volume to identify central themes and concepts. After describing the various internal and external dimensions of strategic communication efforts, the discussion examines how terrorists and governments assess their challenges and successes on the conceptual battlespace. The chapter then analyzes various disadvantages faced by governments—particularly liberal democracies—when competing against terrorists and other violent nonstate actors for strategic influence and concludes with implications for policy and further research.

INFLUENCING INTERNAL AND EXTERNAL AUDIENCES

Terrorists and governments compete vigorously to sway a number of different sets of audiences. Sometimes foremost is the internal audience: terrorists strive to generate, sustain, and enhance support, while with equal fervor governments aim to reassure, manage, and placate their populaces. Lawrence Freedman has written insightfully about what he terms "inner-directed strategies"—strategies "geared to mobilizing support"— which are distinguished from "other-directed strategies . . . that are geared to engaging rivals, competitors and enemies."[1] Inner-directed strategies are by no means unique to conflicts between terrorists and governments, as political leaders in many interstate conflicts also have expended great efforts to mobilize domestic support. But inner-directed strategies are particularly crucial for both terrorism and counterterrorism.

As Sammy Salama and Joe-Ryan Bergoch's contribution to this volume makes clear, for al-Qaida, "instilling their vision, religious ideology and political doctrine in the minds of the Muslim masses" is every bit as vital to the group's strategy as instilling fear in Western populations through acts of terrorism.[2] Awakening, rallying, and maintaining the internal audience is not only essential to a terrorist campaign, but doing so has become far easier and far cheaper due to developments in communication and media—a point driven home by Frank Hairgrove, Douglas M. McLeod, and Dhavan V. Shah's chapter. For terrorist groups such as Hizbut Tahrir-Indonesia, "to communicate internally with its constituents regarding the organizational mobilization activities" has become a task more easily and effectively accomplished than in the past.[3] Indeed, as Aidan Kirby and Vera Zakem point out in this volume, with the widespread availability of Web sites, chat rooms, and video games, the internal audience now can become much more than a passive audience, and instead can actively—even proactively—interact with content designed and intended to galvanize a terrorist group's internal audience by influencing minds worldwide, one by one. These efforts to exercise strategic influence illustrate the crucial importance of today's conceptual battlespace.

Equally engaged in the conceptual battlespace with inner-directed strategies are governments working to thwart terrorism. As Frank L. Jones explains, "Governments react immediately to a terrorist attack to create for their public a perception of order, to exert control over a potentially destabilizing event, and to communicate a message to both the populace and the perpetrators that all instruments of government will be used to hunt down the malefactors and 'bring them to justice.'"[4] Reassuring the populace and restoring trust in the government, the economy, and other foundations of order and pillars of daily life are not mere political postures (though they can be abused as such). Rather, such inner-directed strategies are essential components of counterterrorism, as they demonstrate a state's and a society's capacity to withstand and overcome acts of terrorism. The speed and extent of communication in today's world makes such tasks not only more vital for governments but more difficult and immediate, as well.

Another crucial domain within the conceptual battlespace consists of another audience, the external one toward which Freedman's "other-directed strategies" are oriented. Here, terrorist groups generally must rely on other, independent sources for transmission—in particular, the media. Coverage by the media directly bridges the gap between an act of terrorism and the external minds that the act was intended to influence. The extent of that influence depends in significant part on the degree to which those in the media have, as Cori E. Dauber phrases it, "exposed their audience to the powerful manipulative effects of enemy propaganda."[5] The media can determine, to a significant extent, the potency that terrorist groups can bring to bear on the conceptual battlespace and in the minds of their external audience. Further, as Karen Walker's chapter reveals, new media are particularly powerful in carrying out the "amplification, co-production, and diffusion" of terrorist threats.[6]

Governments also employ other-directed techniques of strategic influence as important aspects of countering terrorism. In particular, as the chapter from Christopher Paul, Todd C. Helmus, and Russell W. Glenn examines, the success of current and future American operations depends heavily on the ability to shape the attitudes and behaviors of civilians located within a given theater of operations. Efforts "to garner the support of the noncombatant population" constitute a contest for the minds of those in the zone of conflict, a contest in which one's adversary, the media, and other sources of influence are active competitors.[7] Moreover, governments engaged in counterterrorism seek to influence another element of their external audience: their adversaries themselves. Jones's emphasis on a message designed "to demonstrate that terrorism fails and historically, the data bear it out" underscores the importance of conveying to terrorist enemies that their method of violence will not lead them to their objectives.[8] Joshua Alexander Geltzer's analysis in this volume similarly points to the ways in which American decision makers already view their counterterrorist actions as conveying certain messages to their terrorist adversaries.

Overall, both terrorist groups and counterterrorist governments possess strategies that rely heavily on exercising effective strategic influence toward a number of audiences, internal as well as external. For each side, inner-directed strategies are not only difficult in themselves; they also hold the potential to undermine the exercise of other-directed strategies.

For terrorists, inner-directed efforts to establish one's own group as the most committed, most able, and most worthy of support can prove counterproductive with respect to the group's external audience. Bruce Hoffman and Gordon H. McCormick have brilliantly characterized terrorism "as a signaling game in which high profile attacks are carried out to communicate a player's ability and determination to use violence to achieve its political objectives."[9] Often, they explain, such attacks are designed to rally support internally.[10] Yet as Max Abrahms points out in this volume, those same attention-grabbing attacks can have an external effect counterproductive to the terrorist's strategy: such attacks often are viewed by members of the wider population "as evidence that the terrorist wants them destroyed," a perception that frequently leads to fierce countermeasures and a government's refusal to negotiate (or even to consider negotiating) with terrorists.[11] Thus, terrorists' inner-directed strategies can undermine their other-directed strategies—providing a crucial opportunity ripe for exploitation by counterterrorist governments, as will be discussed further.

Those same counterterrorist governments must be wary of their own inner-directed efforts proving counterproductive externally. Many commentators have already noted the external problems associated with certain language used by the Bush administration in discussing counterterrorism and chosen presumably for the sake of its appeal to an internal audience. Referring to American counterterrorist efforts as a "crusade" or boasting to "bring them on" may have a certain domestic lure, but the counterproductive effects on audience members external to the United States but vital to the success of American counterterrorism have been underscored elsewhere.[12] In similar vein, Guermantes E. Lailari's discussion in this volume demonstrates the challenges and difficulties faced by the Israeli government, during its summer 2006 operations in Lebanon, to balance its various audiences, both internal and external. Coping with an internal audience through inner-directed strategies without undercutting one's own efforts externally proves to be a delicate balancing act indeed, especially as messages today travel both farther and faster.

Not only is the dynamic between internal and external audiences a crucial element of today's conceptual battlespace, but where the dividing line *between* internal and external audiences falls may well define competition over that battlespace. Salama and Bergoch's analysis highlights this vital point. Whether al-Qaida's strategy for influencing perceptions ultimately succeeds or fails depends to a great extent on the group's efforts to convert a potentially external audience into an internal one—namely, by swaying those potentially hostile, skeptical, or at least undecided into becoming full supporters.

From the counterterrorist perspective, as Paul, Helmus, and Glenn discuss, successfully influencing those who sit on the dividing line between being considered internal and external—namely, the civilians located within a theater of operations—is essential to achieving victory in that theater; they must come to see themselves *not* as an utterly external audience to the government operating there, but, at the very least, as something of a partner. The dividing line is hazy, as the authors note: "the possibility of an individual's role as friendly, neutral, or enemy changing from day to day compounds the challenges of audience segmentation."[13] Likewise, as Geltzer's contribution to this volume explores, successful exercise of strategic influence can transform that most external of audiences—those already involved in, or considering involvement in, terrorist activity—into an audience less inclined to pursue its objectives through the use of terrorist violence. Hence, in both terrorist and counterterrorist strategy, the dividing line *between* internal and external audiences constitutes a core area of competition on the conceptual battlespace.

ASSESSING THE CONCEPTUAL BATTLESPACE

Militaries worldwide have recognized the importance of intelligence preparation of the battlefield, described in a U.S. Army field manual as "a systematic, continuous process of analyzing the threat and environment in a specific geographic area."[14] Such threat analysis is clearly crucial to assessing the physical battlefield. But for competition waged largely *beyond* the boundaries of a specific geographic area, and instead on the conceptual battlespace, how can the government engaged in counterterrorism assess the threat and the progress being made against it? In other words, how might one go about intelligence preparation of the conceptual battlespace?

In particular, the question of metrics or milestones for success is a difficult one when posed with respect to the conceptual battlespace. Before a competitor—either a terrorist group or a counterterrorist government—vying for influence on the conceptual battlespace can establish such metrics, that competitor first must define what would constitute success—a difficult problem in itself.

For the terrorist, achieving a delicate balance in the minds of various audiences provides a significant measure of success. As Dauber explains, capturing a sustained level of media attention in the wake of an attack is the sine qua non for a terrorist group's potent exercise of external strategic influence. Yet as Abrahms aptly notes, going *too* far and instilling a terror so profound as to overstate terrorists' true objectives and reasons for employing violence often proves externally counterproductive. So terrorist success hinges on evoking enough terror to induce some type of desired governmental reaction—whether acquiescence, or negotiation, or the enacting of repressive countermeasures—while also producing a steady escalation in support by defining the nature of the struggle and the identities of the actors involved.[15] For the terrorist, success on the conceptual battlespace consists of shaping external perspectives so as to make certain policy choices more appealing and thus more likely, and shaping internal perspectives so as to make the terrorist group itself appear more appealing and more likely to achieve its objectives.

Counterterrorist governments have struggled to define success on the conceptual battlespace. As Geltzer notes, it is unclear what purpose is served by a government's intended demonstrations of power, relentlessness, resolve, and other attributes without knowing what those attributes actually signify for an often poorly understood external audience. Directing and unifying such external efforts must be an overarching emphasis on demonstrating the precise opposite of what a terrorist group hopes to convey—namely, the counterterrorist government must aim to reveal the unappealing nature of the terrorist group and the impossibility of its achieving its objectives through the use of violence. Encouragingly, this recognition appears to have gained increased prominence in American counterterrorist strategy, which now emphasizes "attacking and undercutting the image and ideology of the enemy," in the words of Juan Zarate, former U.S. Deputy National Security Advisor for Combating Terrorism.[16] At the same time, those external audiences not yet aligned with terrorist groups must be reassured as to the counterterrorist government's benign and positive intentions, as well as its capacity to see those intentions transformed into improved conditions on the ground. Finally, the views of the domestic population must be shaped through education and reassurance so as to understand and in turn withstand the terror that attention-grabbing attacks aim to produce, so that the populace will not, in fact, respond to such attacks by calling for the very policies sought by the terrorist.

If success on the conceptual battlespace is defined in such terms, then the metrics for a terrorist group's or a counterterrorist government's evaluation of progress can be outlined. From the terrorist's perspective, attention, publicity, and prominence provide an initial marker of success. The extent to which widespread support is mobilized in favor of the group's terrorist campaign—rather than the mobilization of outrage at its violence or of opposition to the group's stated objectives—is a crucial further metric, and one that is particularly important with respect to evaluating inner-directed strategies. Externally, the degree to which the target population and its leadership come to favor the types of policies sought by the terrorist group is a major indicator of whether that group is effectively wielding strategic influence in its quest for gains on the conceptual battlespace.

For the counterterrorist government, metrics for success are even fuzzier and harder to pin down. As Paul, Helmus, and Glenn write with regard to shaping the attitudes of civilians, "Measuring the effectiveness of shaping is particularly challenging. The biggest problem is connecting the shaping action or message with some measurable quantity or quality that is not confounded by other possible causes."[17] *Influence* is rarely reducible to a measurable quantity or quality. It is a state of being, a potentially transient inflection of the mind—indeed, of many minds—whose current state is not necessarily reflected in particular outward behavior.

Yet the contributions to this volume suggest that metrics for success must be found not in the behavior on which evaluations of counterterrorism typically focus, namely, terrorist attacks themselves. Rather, it is not what happens *during* terrorist attacks but what happens *between* them that signifies the state of affairs on the conceptual battlespace. Internally, the extent to which attacks succeed in producing *sustained* fear and public pressure to adopt the very policies sought by the terrorist is a far more important measure of a government's management of its domestic audience than the panic almost certain to appear at the actual moment of a terrorist attack. Externally, the sense that a counterterrorist campaign is being prosecuted legally, respectfully, capably, and with due regard to the civilians caught up in the conflict is far more significant to gauging counterterrorist success than the (certainly lamentable) flashes of visceral support for terrorist attacks seen as bloodying the nose of powerful governments that emerge in the direct wake of such attacks (e.g., Palestinians celebrating after the attacks of September 11, 2001). It is during the long stretches between terrorist attacks, rather than in the short flashes during the attacks themselves, that counterterrorist success in exercising salutary strategic influence must be evaluated.

PARTICULAR CHALLENGES ON THE CONCEPTUAL BATTLESPACE FOR COUNTERTERRORISM

As the preceding discussion has emphasized, competition for strategic influence on the conceptual battlespace involves a number of challenges for the terrorist group as well as for the counterterrorist government. From balancing inner- and other-directed strategies to formulating metrics for success, seeking victory in the mind is a task fraught with difficulty. But the degree of that difficulty is not equal on both sides of the dynamic between terrorism and counterterrorism. For a whole host of consequential reasons, the counterterrorist government, especially if it is an open, liberal democracy, finds itself at a distinct disadvantage in the competition for strategic influence. This section elaborates on a number of reasons why this is so.

In formulating, implementing, and assessing a nation's strategic influence efforts, there are several issues and questions that must be considered.[18] For example, as a liberal democracy with the world's most advanced telecommunications and media capabilities, what is the United States not doing effectively? What might be hampering the effectiveness of government agencies responsible for strategic communications? In terms of this latter question, a number of observers have rightly described a need to mitigate the "noise" factor—that is, messages (and messengers) which undermine the integrity and validity of the public diplomacy effort. For example, to paraphrase a recent article by Georgetown University professor Daniel Byman, a few years ago Vice President Cheney condoned Israel's assassination of Palestinian officials in a television interview—a position that obviously plays poorly in the Muslim world. While in years past, few Muslims (even in pro-U.S. countries) would have seen Cheney make such a statement because their state-run media would not have shown it, today satellite television and Internet streaming video allow them to watch and hear the vice president's message, as well as the heated debate it generated on various Web forums and in local news throughout the Muslim world.

Similarly, the statements of U.S. evangelical leaders such as Franklin Graham, who offered the invocation at Bush's first inauguration and later decried Islam as a "wicked" religion, received considerable attention in the Muslim world and sparked controversy. In recent years, too many prominent Americans have spoken publicly about Islam from a position of nearly total ignorance (particularly since the attacks of 9/11), and then are somehow surprised when their words inflame the Muslim world. Instances of Americans desecrating copies of the Qur'an are prime examples of how ignorance and irresponsibility can undermine a democracy's public diplomacy efforts, generating significant discussion on jihadist Web sites and bulletin boards worldwide who cite it as "evidence" of how Americans truly feel about Islam. Anti-Islamic speeches and public statements made by political, religious, or social leaders can give even greater strength to the jihadist propaganda machine, as do the infamous photos of the atrocities committed at Abu Ghraib. All these kinds of "noise" make it difficult for U.S. officials to promote the idea that the United States respects Islam.[19]

In essence, the noise created in an age of globally interconnected information providers and consumers allows members of a liberal democracy to undermine their own security. Ignorance and irresponsibility are potentially dangerous in any society. For a democracy that is engaged in an ambitious public diplomacy effort, seeking to influence the hearts and minds of potential terrorist recruits, ignorance and irresponsibility in the information age are perhaps two of the most worrisome constraints we face in trying to achieve our public diplomacy objectives. From this perspective, surely media correspondents, politicians, talk show hosts, newspaper editors, and virtually anyone else with a public bully pulpit who comments about Islam must be held responsible for educating themselves about Islam.

In a democracy, however, the problem of noise runs far deeper than ignorant public officials, clergy, or others whose words can become featured in mainstream press and television news sound bytes. In an information age, we are all empowered to communicate to the same audiences which our leaders in the Global War on Terror are most concerned with. The Internet enables us all to become publishers of words, images, sounds, and videos—some of which can negatively impact our government's ability to achieve a comprehensive public diplomacy agenda. The education of our own citizenry is thus vital to a successful public diplomacy effort. At a minimum, two kinds of education are needed—education about the public diplomacy mission and its importance to national security, and education about being responsible communicators with the rest of the world.

In comparison to the noise generated by the proliferation of information producers in a liberal democracy, nonstate terrorist groups (and even individual adherents of terrorism) have a distinct advantage over nation-states in the realm of strategic communications, an advantage that stems from the lack of constraints on what, when, and where they publish their motivational and operational information. This problem is particularly acute when examining the role of the Internet in the spread of the global salafi-jihad movement influenced by the leaders of al-Qaida. Here, we find an important and potentially powerful advantage not found in liberal democracies—a single, clear message is being put forth by virtually all members of this network: "join our jihad." Al-Qaida's ideologues and propagandists have sought to connect their vision of the future with historical concepts of jihad as a means for rationalizing their use of violence. Various rationales are offered for joining their jihad, and these are crafted in ways which can appeal to a variety of target audiences. Further, individuals can "join" the jihad from the comfort of their home, by providing money, information, and safe haven to those more actively engaged in the violence.

This simple call to join or support the jihad is repeated in various ways by a growing number of voices, supported by a wide range of strategic and religious texts, videos, music, and even video games—a type of viral marketing strategy that often reflects a sophisticated understanding of who will find different kinds of information resources compelling. The terrorists post at will, with a consistent set of messages and a concerted, complementary effort. They use the Internet to recruit, distribute training materials, collaborate on terror plots, share videos of their attacks, and spread their messages to as wide an audience as possible, while also providing false and inaccurate information to key audiences about U.S. policies, intentions, and actions.

Al-Qaida ideologues wrap their messages in the cloak of religion—the world's fastest growing religion—whereas the U.S. ideology of democratic freedoms necessitates a separation of church and state. Osama bin Laden, Ayman al-Zawahiri, and many others provide interpretations of selections from the Qur'an to support their claim of violent jihad as a duty. And they encourage and praise those who support their cause on the conceptual battlespace. For example, terrorism scholar Jerrold Post recently described a message he found on an al-Qaida Web site urging Muslim professionals to use the Internet to serve the jihad. "If you fail to do this, you may be held into account before Allah on the day of the judgment," the message said.[20] In some cases, incentives are provided for contributing one's voice and talents to the chorus of jihadist Web sites. This online grassroots activity is spreading, indicative of a social movement, the likes of which we have not seen before in scale or common mindedness.

Sophisticated armed groups, at least at the outset, generally excel at staying "on message," in the jargon familiar to discussions of American political campaigns. Initially consisting of a relatively small number of tightly knit individuals sharing a similar worldview, a reasonably well organized terrorist group can execute with precision a crisply framed and unwavering approach to exercising strategic influence, rarely straying from the group's central themes and claims. For the counterterrorist government, exerting such consistent and targeted strategic influence is far more difficult, particularly when its competing ideology is more complex than that of the terrorists. For example, explaining democracy to a community in which it has never existed can be complicated and time-consuming, whereas a simple message that calls adherents to perform a duty proscribed within their own religion is easier to communicate and understand. In the second facet, the jihadists can frame their struggle in a terminology of "doing God's

Figure 18.1   Comparative Disadvantages in the Strategic Communications Battlespace

Simple, clear messages (re: the duty to join or support the jihad) communicated by Internet-enabled grassroots network; virtually no constraints on messengers; lack of "noise" distorting the messages		Complex message; bureaucratic and legal constraints on messages and messengers (including structure, process, policies, agency turf, etc.); competing "noise" produced by media, individuals distorting the messages
↓	Influencing an individual's thoughts, emotions and behavior	↓
The Messages of Global Jihad →	←	**The Messages of a Liberal Democracy**
	↓	
	- Possible terrorist recruit or supporter? - Potential ally in the fight against extremists? - The impact of messages is framed by personal history, environment, existing beliefs, etc.	

Note: An earlier version of this figure appeared in James J. F. Forest, "The Democratic Disadvantage in the Strategic Communications Battlespace." *Democracy and Security* 2(a) (2006): 73–102.

will," while democracies are about "people's will"—governance by the people, for the people. Figure 18.1 provides a visual representation of significant disadvantages faced by democracies in the strategic communications battlespace.

To date, there has been a relative absence of "noise" distorting the jihadists' message, while the same cannot be said about liberal democracies.[21] However, there are also additional challenges that can be considered as further hindrances in conducting effective strategic influence efforts in support of a counterterrorism campaign. First, the government lacks the central direction and unity of a terrorist group's propagandists. Instead, the typical counterterrorist government consists of a number of enormous bureaucracies, each with one or more spokespersons and each prone to emphasizing the elements of counterterrorism in which that bureaucracy specializes. That emphasis may undercut the efforts of other bureaucracies, or at least generate a more muddled set of messages. As Jones explains, "factionalism and bureaucratic 'turf' wars that exist within the institutions of government" can contribute to government efforts at strategic influence being far less unified or even coordinated than the messages promulgated by centrally directed small terrorist groups.[22]

Second, while the media can distort the message of the terrorist group, the media's effect on the attempts at strategic influence by the counterterrorist government tends to be more profound. As Paul, Helmus, and Glenn discuss, the media can seize on small incidents or remarks and elevate them to huge prominence, while neglecting government efforts that actually consume far greater time and resources. Furthermore, the inner workings of liberal democracies are subject to exposition, scrutiny, and criticism in a way that the internal affairs of clandestine terrorist groups clearly are not, allowing the media an opportunity to dissect, question, and even undermine democracies' efforts on the conceptual battlespace in a manner from which terrorist groups generally are more insulated.

Beyond (and in addition to) the distinction between the unity of the terrorist group and the disunity of the counterterrorist government in exercising strategic influence, a number of other factors place the latter at a disadvantage in competing with terrorists on the conceptual battlespace. One is the fact that terrorist groups, through their use of an asymmetric strategy, are able to attack on just one or two carefully selected fronts, while the counterterrorist government is responsible for defending its populace on *all* conceivable fronts. As Lailari discusses, not only is this true in kinetic terms, it is also true on the conceptual battlespace: terrorist propagandists can seize on a single grievance or highlight a single image that allegedly reveals the pernicious nature of the government being opposed, while that government must prosecute its many operations in all arenas with the type of care and diligence that denies such opportunities to terrorist adversaries. Hence, the terrorist attacks the government on the few fronts seen by the terrorist group as particularly vulnerable for the government, while that government scrambles to defend its citizens on all fronts.

Moreover, another factor disadvantaging the counterterrorist government in its competition for strategic influence is its need to consider and cope with a whole set of enemies and potential enemies, while the terrorist group typically has just a few. That is, a typical government must prepare for a wide spectrum of threats: criminals, terrorists, insurgents, other states, natural disasters, diseases, and so on. In contrast, a typical terrorist group will face counterterrorist forces from the government being attacked, and perhaps those of its allies as well—and usually little else. Even rival terrorist groups are hesitant to attack each other outright, instead competing for support by trying to outdo each other's attacks and to undercut each other's platforms. The counterterrorist government not only faces many potential adversaries, but those potential adversaries have the ability to learn and benefit from watching the government's conduct toward others.[23] Lailari notes that "many other Islamic violent organizations" watch closely to learn from Hizballah's experiences against Israel, and, similarly, commentators have begun to point out that the United States must consider the ramifications vis-à-vis third parties such as Iran, China, and others in considering the true effects and consequences of America's continued engagement in Iraq.[24]

The often outspoken private sector that exists in liberal democracies adds yet another element complicating government efforts to exert and to direct strategic influence. In addition to the aforementioned media organizations, large corporations are often seen by crucial audience members to represent the countries in which they are based. Of particular note in this regard are entertainment companies, whose very field is one of communication yet whose offerings frequently reflect neither the actual positions and attitudes of their home governments nor the perceptions that those governments are striving to cultivate.

Hence, for these (and undoubtedly still more) reasons, counterterrorist governments find themselves at a particular disadvantage when they clash with terrorist groups on the conceptual battlespace. What can governments do to maximize the potential for succeeding in that arena?

IMPLICATIONS FOR COUNTERTERRORIST POLICY

A number of implications for counterterrorist policy emerge from the contributions to this volume. These implications all stem from a single energizing principle: that counterterrorism should focus less on *defeating* terrorists and more on helping terrorists *defeat themselves*. The inherent contradictions, hypocrisies, internal divisions, operational security vulnerabilities, and other shortcomings that afflict virtually all terrorist groups hold the seeds to those groups' own downfall, if only those seeds can be cultivated and nurtured by well-designed counterterrorist policies.

The historical contributions to this volume suggest that the conceptual battlespace is a particularly conducive arena in which to succeed through enabling others' own failure. Daniel Baracskay's chapter on the Cold War details the ways in which American strategic communication proved effective in part by underscoring the shortcomings and deficiencies of life under communist regimes. Revealing the conditions produced by communist governments contributed to those governments collapsing underneath their own weight. Similarly, James Dingley's account of the *Cook Report*'s effect on Northern Ireland's Ulster Defence Association (UDA) illustrates how revelations of "overtly criminal activity . . . produced a serious loss of prestige" from which the UDA never fully recovered.[25] The seeds of the group's demise thus lurked within its own extant identity and practices.

To be sure, the terrorist groups engaged in combat on today's conceptual battlespace differ in significant ways from the UDA and, even more so, from communist governments. Yet the contributions to this volume suggest that internal weaknesses and divisions can be exploited in ways that might prove similarly potent for counterterrorist governments. Gabriel Weimann's chapter on terrorist debates on the Internet underscores the significance and magnitude of all sorts of debates occurring in the terrorist world: "debates between terrorist organizations, debates within terrorist organizations, personal debates, debates over actions, and debates among supporters."[26] The very existence of these debates reveals the crucial importance of strategic influence in counterterrorism: it matters immensely because the potential already exists to bring terrorist groups down from within, by exacerbating and aggravating divisive debates and by giving those skeptical of terrorist violence firm foundations for arguing that it is abhorrent, futile, or both. Joshua Sinai's contribution to this volume outlines the type of analytical approach that could inform such vital counterterrorist efforts.

What this volume as a whole brings to light is that possibilities for helping terrorists defeat their *own* causes exist on the conceptual battlespace even as they appear frustratingly rare on the physical battlefield. Finding terrorists to kill, capture, and interrogate or even place under surveillance is undoubtedly an essential component of counterterrorism, but the opportunities for doing so are often few and far between. On the conceptual battlespace, however, many possibilities exist for exploiting terrorist groups' capacity to defeat themselves. Taking al-Qaida as an example, already the brutal killing and maiming of civilians, especially Muslim civilians, have harmed the group's standing in the minds of many once sympathetic to the group's agenda. Particular individuals, such as the late Abu Mus'ab al-Zarqawi, have been criticized heavily and thus hurt the standing of the larger movement. Further, as Weimann notes, religious differences have caused serious ruptures among al-Qaida's supporters. Critical accounts such as Montasser al-Zayyat's biography of Ayman al-Zawahiri have called into question al-Qaida's chosen strategy and tactics, demonstrating a tendency for intra-jihadist criticism which Fawaz Gerges has detailed extensively.[27] This combination of humanitarian, individual, ideological, strategic, tactical, and other grounds provides powerful inroads for counterterrorist governments to accelerate and exacerbate terrorist groups' inherent weaknesses—weaknesses that can, if properly exploited, prove fatal to the groups as well as to their causes.[28]

THE FUTURE OF THE CONCEPTUAL BATTLESPACE

The competition between terrorist groups and counterterrorist governments on the conceptual battlespace—a competition for the power to shape perceptions—is certain to evolve in unpredicted and probably unpredictable ways. The overriding burden for counterterrorist governments will be to develop conceptual strategies at least as potent, and ideally more so, than those being formulated and followed by their terrorist adversaries. As Lailari keenly notes, thus far terrorists have tended to invest their efforts in strategy rather than tactics, while governments have tended to emphasize tactics rather than strategy. Yet exercising effective influence must be elevated by governments to the strategic level. Strategic influence cannot succeed if it is conceived as mere "damage control," a narrative employed to "sell" actions already undertaken. Rather, governments must determine which actions "sell" their broader narrative to diverse audiences and act accordingly.

As Aristotle observed in his *Rhetoric*, "The things that are truer and better are more susceptible to reasoned argument and more persuasive, generally speaking." Clearly, the historical record supports a stronger argument for liberal democracies than can be made for radical interpretations of Islam put forward by the global salafi-jihad movement. However, we must also take measures to ensure that in communicating our message to the Muslim world we reduce, not increase, existing perceptions of arrogance, opportunism, and double standards.

Freedman has aptly noted how "strategic narratives" are of steadily increasing importance in today's world of international affairs.[29] On the conceptual battlespace, narrative warfare subsumes tactical and operational warfare, and must be given strategic coherence and, in broad terms, strategic priority. Only by doing so can governments overcome their disadvantages on the conceptual battlespace, effectively influence both internal and external audiences, and promote ways for terrorists to defeat themselves. That combination can prove essential to achieving victory on the conceptual battlespace.

NOTES

1. Lawrence Freedman, "Terrorism as a Strategy," *Government and Opposition*, Vol. 42, No. 3, p. 321.
2. Please see the chapter by Sammy Salama and Joe-Ryan Bergoch in this volume.
3. Please see the chapter by Frank Hairgrove, Douglas M. McLeod, and Dhavan V. Shah in this volume.

4. Please see the chapter by Frank L. Jones in this volume.

5. Please see the chapter by Cori E. Dauber in this volume.

6. Please see the chapter by M. Karen Walker in this volume.

7. Please see the chapter by Christopher Paul, Todd C. Helmus, and Russell W. Glenn in this volume.

8. Please see the chapter by Frank L. Jones, as well as the chapter by Max Abrahms in this volume.

9. Bruce Hoffman and Gordon McCormick, "Terrorism, Signaling, and Suicide Attack," *Studies in Conflict & Terrorism*, Vol. 27, No. 4, p. 244.

10. Ibid., especially p. 246.

11. Please see the chapter by Max Abrahms in this volume.

12. See, for example, Richard Clarke, *Against All Enemies: Inside America's War on Terror*, updated ed. (London: Free Press, 2004), pp. xvii, 270.

13. Please see the chapter by Paul, Helmus, and Glenn in this volume.

14. "Field Manual 34-130: Intelligence Preparation of the Battlefield," Department of the Army (Washington, D.C.: 1994), http://www.fas.org/irp/doddir/army/fm34-130.pdf, p. 1–1.

15. Please see the chapters by Abrahms and by Salama and Bergoch in this volume.

16. Juan Zarate, "Winning the War on Terror: Marking Success and Confronting Challenges," address to the Washington Institute for Near East Policy, http://www.washingtoninstitute.org/templateC07.php?CID=393.

17. Please see the chapter by Paul, Helmus, and Glenn in this volume.

18. The following discussion draws significantly from James J. F. Forest, "The Democratic Disadvantage in the Strategic Communications Battlespace," *Democracy and Security*, 2(a), 2006, pp. 73–102. Used with permission of the publisher and editor.

19. Daniel Byman, "How to Fight Terrorism," *National Interest* (Spring 2005), p. 1.

20. Michel Moutot, "Radical Islamists Use Internet to Spread Jihad," Agence France Presse, June 2, 2005, http://siteinstitute.org/bin/articles.cgi?ID=inthenews7005&Category=inthenews&Subcategory=0.

21. As described in several publications by the Combating Terrorism Center at West Point, distorting the jihadists' message is an important and all too often overlooked avenue for countering the spread of this violent ideology.

22. Please see the chapter by Jones in this volume.

23. For more on the differences in organizational learning capabilities between terrorist organizations and governments, please see Michael Kenney, "How Terrorists Learn," in *Teaching Terror: Strategic and Tactical Learning in the Terrorist World*, ed. James Forest (Boulder, CO: Rowman & Littlefield, 2006).

24. Please see the chapter by Guermantes E. Lailari in this volume.

25. Please see the chapter by James Dingley in this volume.

26. Please see the chapter by Gabriel Weimann in this volume.

27. See Montasser Al-Zayyat, *The Road to Al-Qaeda: The Story of Bin Lāden's Right-Hand Man*, Ahmed Fekry, trans. (London: Pluto Press, 2004); Fawaz Gerges, *The Far Enemy: Why Jihad Went Global* (Cambridge: Cambridge University Press, 2005).

28. For more on this, please see the Combating Terrorism Center report, "Harmony and Disharmony: Exploiting al-Qaida's Organizational Vulnerabilities" (West Point, NY: CTC, 2006), http://www.ctc.usma.edu.

29. Lawrence Freedman, *The Transformation of Strategic Affairs* (London: Routledge, 2006), p. 22.

Bibliography

Abbas, Hassan. "A Failure to Communicate: American Public Diplomacy in the Islamic World," in *The Making of a Terrorist (Vol. 3: Root Causes)*, edited by James J. F. Forest. Westport, CT: Praeger Security International, 2005.

Abrahms, Max. "Al-Qaeda's Scorecard: A Progress Report on Al-Qaeda's Objectives," *Studies in Conflict and Terrorism* 29:4 (July–August, 2006).

Abrahms, Max. "Why Terrorism Does Not Work," *International Security* 31:2 (Fall 2006).

Aldoory, Linda, and Mark A. Van Dyke. "The Roles of Perceived 'Shared' Involvement and Information Overload in Understanding How Audiences Make Meaning of News About Bioterrorism." *Journalism & Mass Communication Quarterly* 83:2 (Summer 2006): 346–361.

Alexander, Jeffrey C. "From the Depths of Despair: Performance, Counterperformance, and 'September 11,'" *Sociological Theory* 22:1 (March 2004).

Allen, Patrick D. "The Palestinian-Israel: Cyberwar," *Military Review* (March–April 2003).

Allison, Graham. *Nuclear Terrorism: The Risks and Consequences of the Ultimate Disaster.* London: Constable, 2006.

Al-Marashi, Ibrahim. "Iraq's Hostage Crisis: Kidnappings, Mass Media and the Iraqi Insurgency," *Middle East Review of International Affairs* 8:4 (December 2004).

Alonso, Rogelio. "The Madrid Attacks on March 11: An Analysis of the Jihadist Threat in Spain and Main Counterterrorist Measures," in *Countering Terrorism and Insurgency in the 21st Century: International Perspectives (Vol. 3: Root Causes)*, edited by James J. F. Forest. Westport, CT: Praeger Security, 2007.

Al-Zawahiri, Ayman. *Knights under the Prophet's Banner—Meditations on the Jihadist Movement.* London: Al-Sharq al-Awsat, 2001.

Al-Zayyat, Montasser. *The Road to Al-Qaeda: The Story of Bin Laden's Right-Hand Man*, translated by Ahmed Fekry. London: Pluto Press, 2004.

Archibugi, Daniele, and Iris Young. "Toward a Global Rule of War." *Dissent* 49:2 (Spring 2002).

Arens, William F., and Courtland L. Bovee. *Contemporary Advertising.* Burr Ridge, IL: Irwin, 1994.

Aron, Raymond "The Evolution of Modern Strategic Thought," in *Problems of Modern Strategy*, edited by Alastair Buchan. London: Chatto and Windus, 1970.

Atwan, Abdel. *The Secret History of al Qaeda*. Berkeley: University of California Press, 2006.

Aylwin-Foster, Nigel. "Changing the Army for Counterinsurgency Operations," *Military Review* (November–December 2005).

Baran, Zeyno. *Hizbut Tahrir—Islam's Political Insurgency*. Washington: Nixon Center, 2004.

Barducci, R. "Burning the Koran on YouTube: Islamophobia on Video-Sharing Websites (II)," *Inquiry & Analysis*, no. 417 (January 30, 2008).

Barkan, Steven E., and Lynne L. Snowden. *Collective Violence*. Boston: Allyn & Bacon, 2001.

Barrett, W. *Truth is Our Weapon*. New York: Funk & Wagnalls, 1953.

Bazerman, Max. *Judgment in Managerial Decision Making*, 5th ed. Hoboken: John Wiley & Sons, 2002.

Beitler, Ruth Margolies. "The Complex Relationship between Global Terrorism and U.S. Support for Israel," in *The Making of a Terrorist (Vol. 3: Root Causes)*, edited by James J. F. Forest. Westport, CT: Praeger Security International, 2005.

Belch, George E., and Michael A. Belch. *Introduction to Advertising and Promotion: An Integrated Marketing Communications Perspective*. Homewood, IL: Irwin Homewood, 1995.

Bell, J. Bowyer. "Terrorist Scripts and Live-Action Spectaculars: As Skilled Producers of Irresistible News, Terrorists Can Control the Media," *Columbia Journalism Review* (May/June 1978).

Benjamin, Daniel and Steven Simon. *The Age of Sacred Terror: Radical Islam's War Against America*. New York: Random House, 2003.

Benjamin, Daniel and Steven Simon. *The Next Attack: The Failure of the War on Terror and a Strategy for Getting it Right*. New York: Times Books, 2005.

Bergen, Peter L. *Holy War, Inc.: Inside the Secret World of Osama Bin Laden*. New York: Free Press, 2001.

Bew, Paul, Peter Gibbon, and Henry Patterson. *The State in Northern Ireland*. Manchester: Manchester University Press, 1979.

Black, Donald. "The Geometry of Terrorism," *Sociological Theory* 22:1 (March 2004).

Blair, William R. "Army Radio in Peace and War," *Annals of the American Academy of Political and Social Science* 142 (March, 1929).

Blandy, Charles W. "Military Aspects of the Two Russo-Chechen Conflicts in Recent Times," *Central Asian Survey* 22:4 (December 2003).

Bloom, Mia. *Dying to Kill: The Allure of Suicide Terror*. New York: Columbia University Press, 2005.

Borum, Randy. *Psychology of Terrorism*. Tampa: University of South Florida, 2004.

Bowker, Mike. "Russia and Chechnya: The Issue of Succession," *Nations and Nationalism* 10:4 (Winter 2004).

Brachman, Jarret M. "High-Tech Terror: Al-Qaeda's Use of New Technology," *Fletcher Forum of World Affairs* 30:2 (Summer 2006): 149–164.

Brachman, Jarret. "Jihad Doctrine and Radical Islam," in *The Making of a Terrorist (Vol. 1: Recruitment)*, edited by James J. F. Forest. Westport, CT: Praeger Security International, 2005.

Brachman, Jarret, and James J. F. Forest. "Terrorist Sanctuaries in the Age of Information: Exploring the Role of Virtual Training Camps," in *Denial of Sanctuary: Understanding Terrorist Safe Havens*, edited by Michael Innes. London: Praeger Security International, 2007.

Brachman, Jarrett M., and William F. McCants. "Stealing Al Qaeda's Playbook." *Studies in Conflict and Terrorism* 29 (2006).

Brinkley, Alan. *The Unfinished Nation: A Concise History of the American People*, Boston: McGraw-Hill, 2004.

Brinol, Pablo, and Richard Petty. "Individual Differences in Attitude Change," in *The Handbook of Attitudes*, edited by Dolores Albarracin, Blair T. Johnson and Mark P. Zanna. Mahwah, NJ: Lawrence Erlbaum Associates, 2005.

Bruce, Steve. *The Edge of the Union*. Oxford: Oxford University Press, 1994.

Bruce, Steve. *The Red Hand*. Oxford: Oxford University Press, 1992.

Bruinessen, Martin van. "Post-Suharto Muslim Engagements with Civil Society and Democratisation," in *Third International Conference and Workshop "Indonesia in Transition."* Universitas Indonesia, Depok: KNAW and Labsosio, Universitas Indonesia, 2003.

Bryant, Jennings, and Dolf Miron. "Entertainment as Media Effect." In *Media Effects: Advances in Theory and Research*, edited by Jennings Bryant and Dolf Zillmann. Mahwah, NJ: Lawrence Erlbaum Associates, 2002.

Bunt, Gary R. *Islam in the Digital Age: E-Jihad, Online Fatwas and Cyber Islamic Environments*. Sterling, VA.: Pluto Press, 2003.

Byman, Daniel. "How to Fight Terrorism," *National Interest* (Spring 2005).

Calhoun, Craig. "Community without Propinquity Revisited: Communications Technology and the Transformation of the Urban Public Sphere," *Sociological Inquiry* 68:3 (1998).

Carlton, Leonard. "Voice of America: The Overseas Radio Bureau," *Public Opinion Quarterly* 7:1 (Spring, 1943).

Cerny, Philip G. "Terrorism and the New Security Dilemma," *Naval War College Review* 58:1 (Winter 2005).

Charland, Maurice. "Searching for the Rhetorical Sphere," *Review of Communication* 3:2 (April 2003): 105–109.

Charney, Craig, and Nicole Yakatan. *A New Beginning: Strategies for a More Fruitful Dialogue With the Muslim World*. Washington, DC: Council on Foreign Relations, May 2005.

Clark, Robert M. *Intelligence Analysis: A Target-Centric Approach*. Washington, DC: CQ Press, 2004.

Clarke, Richard A. *Against All Enemies: Inside America's War on Terror*. New York: Free Press, 2004.

Clarke, Ronald V., and Graeme R. Newman. *Outsmarting the Terrorists*. Westport, CT: Praeger Security International, 2006.

Cobban, Helena, "Hizballah's New Face—In Search of a Muslim Democracy," *Boston Review* (April/May 2005).

Cohen, Stephen F. "American Policy and Russia's Future," *Nation* 256(14) (April 12, 1993).

Collins, Scott. *Crazy Like a Fox: The Inside Story of How Fox News Beat CNN*. New York:; Penguin, 2005.

Combating Terrorism Center. *Harmony and Disharmony: Exploiting Al-Qaida's Organizational Vulnerabilities*. West Point, NY: Combating Terrorism Center, 2006.

Combelles-Siegel, Pascale. "Perception Management: IO's Stepchild?" *Low Intensity Conflict & Law Enforcement* 13:2 (Autumn 2005).

Combs, Cindy R. "The Media as a Showcase for Terrorism," in *Teaching Terror: Strategic and Tactical Learning in the Terrorist World*, edited by James J. F. Forest. Lanham, MD: Rowman & Littlefield, 2006.

Commonwealth of Australia. *Transnational Terrorism: The Threat to Australia* (2004). www.dfat.gov.au/publications/terrorism.

Conrad, Joseph. *Tales of the East and West*, edited and with an introduction by Morton Dauwen Zabel. Garden City, NY: Hanover House, 1958.

Conway, Maura. "Terrorism and New Media: The Cyber-Battlespace," in *Countering Terrorism and Insurgency in the 21st Century: International Perspectives*, edited by James J. F. Forest, vol. 2, *Combating the Sources and Facilitators*, 363–384. Westport, CT: Praeger Security, 2007.

Conway, Maura. "Terrorism and the Internet: New Media—New Threat?" *Parliamentary Affairs* 59:2 (2006): 283–298.

Cragin, Kim, and Scott Gerwehr. *Dissuading Terror: Strategic Influence and the Struggle Against Terrorism.* Santa Monica, CA: RAND Corporation, 2005.

Crelinsten, Ronald D. "Terrorism as Political Communication: The Relationship between the Controller and the Controlled," in *Contemporary Research on Terrorism*, edited by Paul Wilkinson and A. M. Stewart. Aberdeen, Scotland: Aberdeen University Press, 1987.

Crenshaw, Martha (ed.). *Terrorism, Legitimacy, and Power: The Consequences of Political Violence.* Middletown, CT: Wesleyan University Press, 1983.

Crenshaw, Martha. "An Organizational Approach to the Analysis of Political Terrorism," *Orbis* (Fall 1985).

Crenshaw, Martha. "The Causes of Terrorism," *Comparative Politics* 13:4 (July 1981).

Crenshaw, Martha. "Theories of Terrorism: Instrumental and Organizational Approaches," in *Inside Terrorist Organizations*, edited by David C. Rapoport. Portland, OR: Frank Cass, 2001.

Crick, Bernard. *In Defence of Politics*, 4th ed. Chicago: University of Chicago Press, 1992.

Crosston, Matthew. "The Hizb-Tahrir in Central Asia: How America Misreads Islamist Threats," *Meria* 11(3) (2007).

Daalder, Ivo, and James Lindsay. *America Unbound: The Bush Revolution in Foreign Policy.* Washington, DC: Brookings Institution Press, 2003.

Dahl, Robert A. *Who Governs? Democracy and Power in an American City.* New Haven, CT: Yale University Press, 1961.

Dame Manningham-Buller, Eliza. *The International Terrorist Threat to the UK* (2006). http://www.mi5.gov.uk/output/Page568.html.

Danah, Boyd. "Why Youth (Heart) Social Network Sites: The Role of Networked Publics in Teenage Social Life," in *MacArthur Foundation Series on Digital Learning—Youth, Identity, and Digital Media Volume*, edited by David Buckingham. Cambridge, MA: MIT Press, 2007.

Dartnell, Michael Y. *Insurgency Online: Web Activism and Global Conflict.* Buffalo, NY: University of Toronto, 2006.

Davis, Paul K., and Brian Michael Jenkins. *Deterrence and Influence in Counterterrorism: A Component of the War on al Qaeda.* Santa Monica: RAND, 2002.

Davison, W. Phillips. "Political Communication as an Instrument of Foreign Policy," *Public Opinion Quarterly* 27:1 (Spring, 1963).

Davison, W. Phillips. "Some Trends in International Propaganda," *Annals of the American Academy of Political Science and Social Science* 398 (November, 1971).

Davison, W. Phillips, and Alexander L. George. "An Outline for the Study of International Political Communications," *Public Opinion Quarterly* 16:4 (Winter, 1953).

Dayan, Daniel, and Elihu Katz. *Media Events: The Live Broadcasting of History.* Cambridge, MA: Harvard University Press, 1992.

de Jomini, Antoine Henri. *The Art of War.* Novato, CA: Presidio Press, 1992.

Defense Science Board Task Force, Office of the Under Secretary of Defense. "Report of the Defense Science Board Task Force on Strategic Communication." Washington, DC: Office of the Under Secretary of Defense, September 2004.

Della Porta, Donatella, and M. Diani. *Social Movements: An Introduction.* Malden, MA: Blackwell Publishing, 2006.

Dershowitz, Alan. *Why Terrorism Works: Understanding the Threat, Responding to the Challenge.* New Haven, CT: Yale University Press, 2002.

Diani, Mario. "Social Movement Networks Virtual and Real," *Information, Communication and Society* 3:3 (2000).

Dingley, James. "Peace in Our Time: The Stresses and Strains on the Northern Ireland Peace Process," *Studies in Conflict and Terrorism* 25:6 (2002).

Druckman, Daniel, and Benjamin J. Broome. "Value Differences and Conflict Resolution: Facilitation or Delinking?" *Journal of Conflict Resolution* 32:3 (September 1988).

Dunwoody, Sharon, and Kurt Neuwirth. "Coming to Terms with the Impact of Communication on Scientific and Technological Risk Judgments." In *Risky Business: Communication Issues of Science, Risk, and Public Policy*, edited by Lee Wilkins and Philip Patterson. Westport, CT: Greenwood Press, 1991.

Echevarria, Antulio J. II. "Clausewitz and the Nature of the War on Terror," in *Clausewitz in the Twenty-First Century*, edited by Hew Strachan and Andreas Herberg-Rothe. Oxford: Oxford University Press, 2007.

Elman, Colin, and Miriam Fendius Elman. "How Not to Be Lakatos Intolerant: Appraising Progress in IR Research," *International Studies Quarterly* 46(2) (June 2002).

English, Richard. *Armed Struggle, the History of the IRA.* London: Macmillan, 2004.

Farrell, Thomas B. "Knowledge, Consensus, and Rhetorical Theory," *Quarterly Journal of Speech* 62:1 (February 1976): 1–14.

Farrell, Thomas B., and G. Thomas Goodnight. "Accidental Rhetoric: The Root Metaphors of Three Mile Island," reprinted in *Landmark Essays on Rhetoric and the Environment*, edited by Craig Waddell. Mahwah, NJ: Lawrence Erlbaum, 1998.

Fealy, Greg. "Hizbut Tahrir in Indonesia: Seeking A 'Total Islamic Identity,'" in *Islam and Political Violence: Muslim Diaspora and Radicalism in the West*, edited by Shahram Akbarzadeh and Fethi Mansouri. New York: Palgrave Macmillan, 2007.

Forest, James J. F. (ed.). *Countering Terrorism and Insurgency in the 21st Century* (3 volumes). Westport, CT: Praeger Security International, 2007.

Forest, James J. F. "The Democratic Disadvantage in the Strategic Communications Battlespace," *Democracy and Security* 2:2 (2006): 73–102.

Forest, James J. F. "Introduction," in *Teaching Terror: Strategic and Tactical Learning in the Terrorist World.* Lanham, MD: Rowman & Littlefield, 2006.

Forest, James J. F. "Knowledge Transfer and Shared Learning Among Armed Groups," in *Armed Groups: Studies in National Security, Counterterrorism, and Counterinsurgency*, edited by Jeffrey Norwitz. Newport, RI: Naval War College, 2008.

Forest, James J. F. "Terrorists Use of WMD," in *Know Thy Enemy*, edited by Mike Kindt, Jerrold Post, and Barry Schneider. Maxwell AFB, AL: Air War College, 2008.

Forest, James J. F. "Terrorist Training Centers Around the World: A Brief Review," in *The Making of a Terrorist: Recruitment, Training and Root Causes*, edited by James J. F. Forest. Westport, CT: Praeger, 2005.

Forest, James J. F. "Training Camps and Other Centers of Learning," in *Teaching Terror: Strategic and Tactical Learning in the Terrorist World.* Lanham, MD: Rowman & Littlefield, 2006.

Frank, Russell. "When the Going Gets Tough, the Tough Go Photoshopping: September 11 and the Newslore of Vengeance and Victimization." *New Media & Society* 6:5 (2004): 633–658.

Freedman, Lawrence. "Terrorism as a Strategy," *Government and Opposition* 42(3).

Freedman, Lawrence. *The Transformation of Strategic Affairs.* London: Routledge, 2006.

Frey, Bruno, and Dominik Rohner. *Blood and Ink! The Common-Interest-Game Between Terrorists and Media*. Institute for Empirical Research in Economics, University of Zurich Working Paper Series, April 2006.

Frum, David. *The Right Man: An Inside Account of the Bush White House*. New York: Random House, 2005.

Frum, David, and Richard Perle. *An End to Evil: How to Win the War on Terror*. New York: Ballantine Books, 2004.

Garrison, Arthur H. "Defining Terrorism: Philosophy of the Bomb, Propaganda by Deed and Change Through Fear and Violence," *Criminal Justice Studies* 17:3 (September 2004).

Gerges, Fawaz A. *The Far Enemy: Why Jihad Went Global*. New York: Cambridge University Press, 2005.

Gibbs, Jack P. "Conceptualization of Terrorism," *American Sociological Review* 54:3 (June 1989).

Glass, Andrew J. "The War on Terrorism Goes Online," in *Terrorism, War, and the Press*, edited by Nancy Palmer, 47–80. Hollis, NH: Hollis Publishing, 2003.

Glock, Charles Y. "The Role of Deprivation in the Origin and Evolution of Religious Groups," in *Religion and Social Conflict*, edited by R. Lee and M. E. Marty. New York: Oxford University Press, 1964.

Goffman, Erving. *Frame Analysis: Essays on the Organization of Experience*. New York: Harper and Row, 1974.

Goldstone, Jack A. "Introduction: The Comparative and Historical Study of Revolutions," in *Revolutions: Theoretical, Comparative, and Historical Studies*, edited by Jack A. Goldstone. San Diego, CA: Harcourt Brace Jovanovich, 1986.

Gray, Colin S. "Combating Terrorism," *Parameters* 23:3 (Autumn 1993).

Gray, Colin S. *Defining and Achieving Decisive Victory*. Carlisle, PA: Strategic Studies Institute, U.S. Army War College, 2002.

Gray, Colin S. *Irregular Enemies and the Essence of Strategy: Can the American Way of War Adapt?* Carlisle, PA: Strategic Studies Institute, U.S. Army War College, 2006.

Gray, Colin S. *Maintaining Effective Deterrence*. Carlisle, PA: Strategic Studies Institute, U.S. Army War College, 2003.

Gray, Colin S. *Transformation and Strategic Surprise*. Carlisle, PA: Strategic Studies Institute, U.S. Army War College, 2005.

Gray, Colin S. "What Is War? A View from Strategic Studies," in Colin Gray, *Strategy and History: Essays on Theory and Practice*. New York: Routledge, 2006.

Gregory D. Foster, "A Conceptual Foundation for a Theory of Strategy," *Washington Quarterly* 13:1 (Winter 1990).

Gressang, Daniel S. IV. "Terrorism in the 21st Century: Reassessing the Emerging Threat," in *Deterrence in the 21st Century*, edited by Max Manwaring. Portland, OR: Frank Cass, 2001.

Guenena, Nemat. "The Jihad: An Islamic Alternative in Egypt," *Cairo Papers in Social Science* 9:2 (Summer 1986).

Gunaratna, Rohan. *Inside Al Qaeda: Global Network of Terror*. New York: Columbia University Press, 2002.

Gurr, Ted Robert. "Empirical Research on Political Terrorism," in *Current Perspectives on International Terrorism*, edited by Robert O. Slater and Michael Stohl. New York: St. Martin's Press, 1988.

Gurr, Ted Robert. *Why Men Rebel*. Princeton, NJ: Princeton University Press, 1970.

Hairgrove, Frank, and Douglas McLeod. "Circles Drawing toward High Risk Activism: The Use of Usroh and Halaqa in Islamist Radical Movements," *Studies in Conflict and Terrorism* (2008).

Hamm, Mark. *Terrorism as Crime: From Oklahoma City to Al-Qaeda and Beyond*. New York: New York University Press, 2007.

Hauser, Gerard A. *Vernacular Voices: The Rhetoric of Publics and Public Spheres*. Columbia: University of South Carolina, 1999.

Hazan, D. "Al-Tajdeed Versus Al-Hesbah: Islamist Websites and the Conflict between Rival Arab & Muslim Political Forces," *MEMRI's Special Dispatch* 275 (May 17, 2006), http://www.memri.org/bin/opener_latest.cgi?ID=IA27506.

Helmus, Todd C., Christopher Paul, and Russell W. Glenn. *Enlisting Madison Avenue: The Marketing Approach to Earning Popular Support in Theaters of Operation*. Santa Monica: RAND Corporation, 2007.

Hennessey, Thomas. *A History of Northern Ireland, 1920–1996*. Dublin: Gill & Macmillan, 1997.

Hennessey, Thomas. *The Northern Ireland Peace Process*. Dublin: Gill & Macmillan, 2000.

Hennessey, Thomas. *The Origins of the Troubles*. Dublin: Gill & Macmillan, 2005.

Henry, Vincent E. "The Need for a Coordinated and Strategic Local Police Approach to Terrorism: A Practitioner's Perspective," *Police Practice and Research* 3:4 (2002): 319–336.

Herd, Graeme P. "Information Warfare and the Second Chechen Campaign," in *War and Peace in Post-Soviet Eastern Europe*, edited by Sally Cummings. Washington, DC: Conflict Studies Research Center, 2000.

Hewitt, Christopher. *Understanding Terrorism in America*. London: Routledge, 2003.

Heymann, Phillip. "Dealing with Terrorism: An Overview," *International Security* (Winter 2001–2002): 24–48.

Hill, Christopher. "The Political Dilemmas for Western Governments," in Lawrence Freedman et al., *Terrorism and International Order*. London: Royal Institute of International Affairs, 1987.

Hoffman, Bruce. *Inside Terrorism*, revised and expanded edition. New York: Columbia University Press, 2006.

Hoffman, Bruce. "Using the Web as a Weapon: the Internet as a Tool for Violent Radicalization and Homegrown Terrorism." Statement provided to the U.S. House Committee on Homeland Security (November 6, 2007).

Hoffman, Bruce. *Terrorism and Weapons of Mass Destruction: An Analysis of Trends and Motivations*. Santa Monica, CA: RAND, 1999.

Hoffman, Bruce, and Gordon H. McCormick, "Terrorism, Signaling, and Suicide Attack," *Studies in Conflict and Terrorism* 27:4 (July/August 2004).

Holland, Jack, and Henry McDonald. *INLA, Deadly Divisions*. Dublin: TORC, 1994.

Holsti, Kalevi J. "Resolving International Conflicts: A Taxonomy of Behavior and Some Figures on Procedure," *Journal of Conflict Resolution* 10:3 (September 1966).

Homeland Security Policy Institute. "NETworked Radicalization: A Counter Strategy." George Washington University Homeland Security Policy Institute and University of Virginia Critical Incident Analysis Group, 2007.

Horgan, John. "The Search for the Terrorist Personality," in *Terrorists, Victims and Society: Psychological Perspectives on Terrorism and its Consequences*, edited by Andrew Silke. New York: John Wiley & Sons, 2003.

Horgan, John, and Max Taylor. "Playing the Green Card—Financing the Provisional IRA," *Terrorism and Political Violence* 11:1 (1999).

Horgan, John. "Disengaging from Terrorism," *Jane's Intelligence Review* (December, 2006).

House of Commons, Northern Ireland Affairs Committee. *The Financing of Terrorism in Northern Ireland, Fourth Report, 2001–2, vol 1*. London: Stationery Office, 2002.

Howard, Michael. *Clausewitz*. Oxford: University of Oxford Press, 1983.

Howard, Russell, and James Forest (eds.). *Weapons of Mass Destruction and Terrorism*. New York: McGraw-Hill, 2007.

Hughes, H. Stuart. *Consciousness and Society: The Reorientation of Social Thought, 1890–1930*. New York: Vintage Books, 1958.

Hutchinson, Martha Crenshaw. "The Concept of Revolutionary Terrorism," *Journal of Conflict Resolution* 16:3 (September 1972).

Innes, Martin. "Policing Uncertainty: Countering Terror through Community Intelligence and Democratic Policing," *Annals of the American Academy of Political and Social Science* 605 (May 2006).

Isaacs, Jeremy, and Taylor Downing. *Cold War: An Illustrated History, 1945–1991*. Boston: Little Brown, 1998.

Ivie, Robert L. "Fighting Terror by Rite of Redemption and Reconciliation," *Rhetoric and Public Affairs* 10:2 (2007).

Iyengar, Shanto. *Is Anyone Responsible? How Television Frames Political Issues*, Chicago: University of Chicago Press, 1991.

Jablonsky, David. "Introduction," in David Jablonsky, Ronald Steel, Lawrence Korb, Morton H. Halperin, and Robert Ellsworth, *U.S. National Security: Beyond the Cold War*. Carlisle, PA: Strategic Studies Institute, U.S. Army War College, 1997.

Jagger, Alison. "Responding to the Evil of Terrorism," *Hypatia* 18:1 (Winter 2003).

Jagger, Alison M. "What Is Terrorism, Why Is It Wrong, and Could It Ever Be Morally Permissible?" *Journal of Social Philosophy* 26:2 (Summer 2005).

Jansen, Johannes J. G. *The Neglected Duty: The Creed of Sadat's Assassins and Islamic Resurgence in the Middle East*. New York: Macmillan, 1986.

Jervis, Robert. *American Foreign Policy in a New Era*. New York: Routledge, 2005.

Jervis, Robert. *Perception and Misperception in International Politics*. Princeton, NJ: Princeton University Press, 1976.

Johnson, Dominic, and Dominic Tierney. *Failing to Win: Perceptions of Victory and Defeat in International Politics*. Cambridge, MA: Harvard University Press, 2006.

Jones, Edward E., and Keith E. Davis, "From Acts to Dispositions: The Attribution Process in Person Perception," in *Advances in. Experimental Social Psychology*, *Vol. 2*, edited by Leonard Berkowitz. New York: Academic Press, 1965.

Jones, Edward E., and Daniel McGillis, "Correspondence Inferences and the Attribution Cube: A Comparative Reappraisal," in *New Directions in Attribution Research*, *Vol. 1*, edited by John H. Harvey, William J. Ickes, and Robert F. Kidd. Hillsdale, NJ: Lawrence Erlbaum, 1976.

Jones, Edward E., and Richard E. Nisbett, "The Actor and the Observer," in *Attribution: Perceiving the Causes of Behavior*, edited by Edward E. Jones, David E. Kanouse, Harold H. Kelley, Richard E. Nisbett, Stuart Valins, and Bernard Weiner. Morristown, NJ: General Learning Press, 1972.

Jones, Jeffrey B. "Strategic Communication: A Mandate for the United States," *Joint Force Quarterly* 39 (October 2005): 108–114.

Joosse, Paul. "Leaderless Resistance and Ideological Inclusion: The Case of the Earth Liberation Front," *Terrorism and Political Violence* 19:3 (Fall 2007): 351–368.

Jorisch, Avi. *Beacon of Hatred: Inside Hizballah's Al-Manar Television*. Washington, DC: Washington Institute for Near East Policy, 2004.

Juergensmeyer, Mark. *Terror in the Mind of God: The Global Rise of Religious Violence.* Berkeley: University of California Press, 2000.

Kaufman, Chaim. "Threat Inflation and the Failure of the Marketplace of Ideas: The Selling of the Iraq War," *International Security* 29:1 (Summer 2004).

Kaufman, Edy. "Israeli Perceptions of the Palestinians' 'Limited Violence' in the Intifada," *Terrorism and Political Violence* 3(4) (Winter 1991).

Kecskemeti, Paul. "The Soviet Approach to International Political Communication," *Public Opinion Quarterly* 20:1 (Spring 1956).

Kenney, Michael. "How Terrorists Learn." In *Teaching Terror: Strategic and Tactical Learning in the Terrorist World*, edited by James J. F. Forest. Boulder, CO: Rowman & Littlefield, 2006.

Keohane, Robert O., Joseph S. Nye, and Stanley Hoffman (eds.). *After the Cold War: International Institutions and State Strategies in Europe, 1989–1991.* Cambridge, MA: Harvard University Press, 1993.

Kepel, Gilles. *Jihad: The Trail of Political Islam*, translated by Anthony Roberts. Cambridge, MA: Belknap Press of Harvard University Press, 2002.

Kepel, Gilles. *Muslim Extremism in Egypt: The Prophet and the Pharaoh.* Berkeley: University of California Press, 1984.

Kepel, Gilles. *The War for Muslim Minds*, translated by Pascale Ghazaleh. Cambridge, MA: Belknap Press of Harvard University Press, 2004.

Khalilov, Roman. "The Russian-Chechen Conflict," *Central Asia Survey*, 21:4 (January/February 2002).

Kilcullen, David. "Countering Global Insurgency: A Strategy for the Global War on Terrorism," *Small Wars Journal* (November 30, 2004).

Kimmage, Daniel, and Kathleen Ridolfo. *Iraqi Insurgent Media: The War of Images and Ideas.* Washington: Radio Free Europe Radio Liberty, 2007.

Kirby, Aidan. "The London Bombers as 'Self-Starters': A Case Study in Indigenous Redicalization and the Emergence of Autonomous Cliques," *Studies in Conflict and Terrorism* 30:5 (2007): 415–428.

Klopfenstein, Bruce. "Terrorism and the Exploitation of New Media," in *Media, Terrorism and Theory: A Reader*, edited by Anandam P. Kavoori and Todd Fraley, 107–120. New York: Rowman & Littlefield, 2006.

Kohler, Foy D. "The Voice of America: Spokesman of the Free World," in *Proceedings of the Academy of Political Science* 24:2 (January 1951).

Komer, Robert W. *Bureaucracy at War: U.S. Performance in the Vietnam Conflict.* Boulder, CO: Westview Press, 1986.

Kydd, Andrew, and Barbara Walter, "Sabotaging the Peace: The Politics of Extremist Violence," *International Organization* 56:2 (Spring 2002).

Kydd, Andrew H., and Barbara F. Walter. "The Strategies of Terrorism," *International Security* 31:1 (Summer 2006).

LaFeber, Walter (ed.). *The Origins of the Cold War, 1941–1947.* New York: John Wiley & Sons, 1971.

Lamb, Christopher. *Review of Psychological Operations Lessons Learned from Recent Operational Experience.* Washington, DC: National Defense University Press, September 2005.

Lapan, Harvey E., and Todd Sandler. "Terrorism and Signaling," *European Journal of Political Economy* 9:3 (August 1993).

Lapidus, Gail W. "Putin's War on Terrorism: Lessons from Chechnya," *Post-Soviet Affairs* 18:3 (January/March 2002).

Laqueur, Walter. *The Age of Terrorism*. London: Weidenfeld & Nicolson, 1987.

Laqueur, Walter. *Terrorism*. Boston: Little, Brown, 1977.

Larsson, JP. "The Role of Religious Ideology in Terrorist Recruitment." In *The Making of a Terrorist (Volume 1: Recruitment)*, edited by James J. F. Forest. Westport, CT: Praeger Security International, 2005.

Lasswell, Harold D. *Propaganda Technique in World War I*, new ed. Cambridge: MA: MIT Press 1971.

Lawrence, Bruce (ed.). *Messages to the World: The Statements of Osama bin Laden*. London: Verso, 2005.

Lazarsfeld, Paul Felix, Bernard Berelson, and Hazel Gaudet. *The People's Choice*. New York: Columbia University Press, 1965.

Leonard, Mark, Catherine Stead, and Conrad Smewing. *Public Diplomacy*. London: Foreign Policy Centre, 2002.

Levitt, Matthew. "Untangling the Terror Web: Identifying and Counteracting the Phenomenon of Crossover Between Terrorist groups," *SAIS Review* 24:1 (Winter 2004).

Lia, Brynjar. *Architect of Global Jihad: The Life of Al Qaeda Strategist Abu Mus'ab Al-Suri*. New York: Columbia University Press, 2008.

Lim, Merlyna. "Islamic Radicalism and Anti-Americanism in Indonesia: The Role of the Internet," in *Policy Studies*. Washington, DC: East-West Center Washington, 2005.

Lister, David, and Hugh Jordan. *Mad Dog: The Rise and Fall of Johnny Adair and 'C' Company*. Edinburgh: Mainstream Publishing, 2004.

Lowi, Theodore J. "American Business, Public Policy, Case Studies, and Political Theory," *World Politics* 16:3 (July 1964).

Lule, Jack. "Myth and Terror on the Editorial Page: The *New York Times* Responds to September 11, 2001." *Journalism & Mass Communication Quarterly* 79:2 (Summer 2002): 275–293.

MacInnes, Duncan. "Strategic Communication and Countering Ideological Support for Terrorism." Statement provided for the U.S. House Armed Services Committee, Subcomittee on Terrorism and Unconventional Threats (November 15, 2007).

Malvesti, Michele L. "Explaining the United States' Decision to Strike Back at Terrorists," *Terrorism and Political Violence* 13:2 (Summer 2001): 85–100; reprinted at http://fletcher.tufts.edu/news/2002/january/terrorism.htm.

Mannheimer, Michael J. "The Fighting Words Doctrine," *Columbia Law Review* 93:6 (October 1993): 1527–1571.

Mansfield, Laura. "Cracks in the Wall of Jihad?" *New Media Journal* (May 5, 2007), http://www.newmediajournal.us/guest/l_mansfield/05052007.htm.

Martin, Gus. *Understanding Terrorism: Challenges, Perspectives, and Issues*. Thousand Oaks, CA: Sage Publications, 2003.

Massing, Paul W. "Communist References to the Voice of America," *Public Opinion Quarterly* 16:4 (Winter 1952–1953).

McCarthy, John D., and Mayer N. Zald. "Resource Mobilization and Social Movements: A Partial Theory," *American Journal of Sociology* 82:6 (1977).

McCauley, Clark. "Psychological Issues in Understanding Terrorism and the Response to Terrorism," in *Psychology of Terrorism: Coping with the Continuing Threat*, edited by Chris E. Stout. Westport, CT: Praeger, 2004.

McCauley, Clark, and Mary Segal. "Social Psychology of Terrorist Groups," in *Group Processes and Intergroup Relations*, edited by Clyde Hendrick. New York: Sage Publications, 1987.

McCleskey, Edward, Diana McCord, and Jennifer Leetz. *Underlying Reasons for Success and Failure of Terrorist Attacks: Selected Case Studies, Final Report*. Arlington, VA: Homeland Security Institute, 2007.

McConnell, Mike. Statement of the Director of National Intelligence provided to the Senate Select Committee on Intelligence (February 14, 2008).

McCue, Colleen. *Data Mining and Predictive Analysis: Intelligence Gathering and Crime Analysis.* Burlington: Butterworth-Heinemann, 2007.

McDermott, Terry. *Perfect Soldiers: The Hijackers: Who They Were, Why They Did It.* New York: HarperCollins Publishers, 2005.

McFaul, Michael. "Russia under Putin: One Step Forward, Two Steps Back," *Journal of Democracy* 11:3 (July 2000).

McLeod, Douglas M., Gerald M. Kosicki, and Jack M. McLeod. "Resurveying the Boundaries of Political Communications Effects," in *Media Effects: Advances in Theory and Research*, edited by Jennings Bryant and Dolf Zillmann. Mahweh, NJ: Lawrence Erlbaum, 2002.

McLuhan, Marshall. *Understanding Media: The Extensions of Man.* New York: McGraw-Hill, 1964.

Medby, Jamison Jo, and Russell W. Glenn, *Street Smart: Intelligence Preparation of the Battlefield for Urban Operations.* Santa Monica, CA: RAND Corporation, 2002.

Merari, Ariel. "Terrorism as a Strategy of Insurgency," *Terrorism and Political Violence* 5:4 (Winter 1993).

Meyer, Christopher. *DC Confidential.* London: Weidenfeld & Nicolson, 2005.

Mohamedou, Mohammad-Mahmoud Ould. *Understanding Al Qaeda: The Transformation of War.* London: Pluto Press, 2007.

Morgan, Austen. *Labour and Partition.* London: Pluto, 1991.

Mueller, John. "Six Rather Unusual Propositions about Terrorism." *Terrorism and Political Violence* 17.

Munck, Ronaldo. "Deconstructing Terror: Insurgency, Repression and Peace," in *Postmodern Insurgencies: Political Violence, Identity Formation and Peacemaking in Comparative Perspective*, edited by Ronald Munck and Purnaka L. de Silva. New York: St. Martin's Press, 2000.

Munro, Neil. "Issues and Ideas: The Dollar Value of Murder," *National Journal* (February 17, 2007).

Nacos, Brigitte L. *Mass-Mediated Terrorism: The Central Role of the Media in Terrorism and Counterterrorism.* New York: Rowman & Littlefield, 2002.

Nacos, Brigitte L. "Mediated Terrorism: Teaching Terror through Propaganda and Publicity," in *The Making of a Terrorist (Vol. 2: Training)*, edited by James J. F. Forest. Westport, CT: Praeger Security International, 2005.

Nacos, Brigitte L. *Terrorism and the Media, From the Iran Hostage Crisis to the Oklahoma City Bombing.* New York: Columbia University Press, 1994.

Nacos, Brigitte L. "The Terrorist Calculus behind 9/11: A Model for Future Terrorism?" *Studies in Conflict and Terrorism* 26:8 (January/February 2003).

Naji, Abu Bakr. "Idarat al-Tawahush [The Management of Savagery]: The Most Critical Stage Through Which the Umma Will Pass," translated by William McCants. Cambridge, MA: John M. Oline Institute for Strategic Studies at Harvard University, 2006.

Nemes, Irene. "Regulating Hate Speech in Cyberspace: Issues of Desirability and Efficacy." *Information & Communication Technology Law* 11:3 (2002): 193–220.

Neumann, Peter R., and Mike Smith, "Strategic Terrorism: The Framework and its Fallacies," *Journal of Strategic Studies* 28:4 (August 2005).

Nissen, Thomas Elkjer. "The Taliban's Information Warfare." Copenhagen, Royal Danish Defence College (December 2007).

Novikov, Evgenii. "The Recruiting and Organizational Structure of Hizb Ut-Tahrir," *Terrorism Monitor* 22 (2004).

Nye, Joseph. *The Paradox of American Power: Why the World's Superpower Can't Go it Alone.* New York: Oxford University Press, 2002.

Nye, Joseph Jr. *Soft Power: The Means to Success in World Politics.* New York: Public Affairs, 2004.

Oberschall, Anthony. "Explaining Terrorism: The Contribution of Collective Action Theory," *Sociological Theory* 22:1 (March 2004).

Ogden, Suzanne P. (ed.). *World Politics,* 11th ed. Connecticut: Dushkin Publishing Group, 1990.

O'Loughlin, John, Gearoid O. Tuathail, and Vladimir Kolossov. "A 'Risky Western Turn'? Putin's 9/11 Script and Ordinary Russians," *Europe-Asia Studies* 56(1) (January 2004).

O'Neill, Sean, and Daniel McGrory. *The Suicide Factory: Abu Hamza and the Finsbury Park Mosque.* London: Harper Collins, 2006.

Ott, Marvin. "Mediation as a Method of Conflict Resolution, Two Cases," *International Organization* 26:4 (Autumn 1972).

Overgaard, Per Batlzer "The Scale of Terrorist Attacks as a Signal of Resources," *Journal of Conflict Resolution* 38:3 (September 1994).

Paletz, David L. *The Media in American Politics: Contents and Consequences.* New York: Longman, 2002.

Palmer, Allen W., and Edward L. Carter. "The Smith-Mundt Act's Ban on Domestic Propaganda: An Analysis of the Cold War Statute Limiting Access to Public Diplomacy," *Communication, Law & Policy* 11:1 (Winter 2006): 1–34.

Pan, Zhongdang, and Gerald M. Kosicki. "Framing as a Strategic Action in Public Deliberation," in *Framing Public Life: Perspectives on Media and Our Understanding of the Social World,* edited by Stephen D. Reese, Oscar H. Gandy Jr., and August E. Grant, 35–66. Mahwah, NJ: Lawrence Erlbaum, 2001.

Pape, Robert A. *Dying to Win: The Strategic Logic of Suicide Terrorism.* New York: Random House, 2005.

Pape, Robert A. "The Strategic Logic of Suicide Terrorism," *American Political Science Review* 97:3 (August 2003).

Pape, Robert A. "Why Economic Sanctions Do Not Work," *International Security* 22:2 (Fall 1997).

Papp, Daniel S. *Soviet Perceptions of the Developing World in the 1980s: The Ideological Basis.* Massachusetts: D.C. Heath, 1985.

Parker, Tom. "Fighting an Antaean Enemy: How Democratic States Unintentionally Sustain the Terrorist Movements They Oppose," *Terrorism and Political Violence* 19.

Paz, Reuven. "Catch as Much as You Can: Hasan al-Qaed (Abu Yahya al-Libi) on Jihadi Terrorism against Muslims in Muslim Countries," Occasional Paper 5:2 (2007), PRISM, http://www.e-prism.org.

Paz, Reuven. "Hamas vs. Al-Qaeda: The Condemnation of the Khobar Attack," Special Dispatch 2:3, PRISM, June 2, 2004, http://www.e-prism.org.

Paz, Reuven. "Hizballah or Hizb al-Shaytan? Recent Jihadi-Salafi Attacks Against the Shiite Group," Occasional Paper 2:1 (2004), PRISM, http://www.e-prism.org.

Paz, Reuven. "Islamic Legitimacy for the London Bombings." Report of the Intelligence and Terrorism Information Center at the Center for Special Studies (C.S.S), July 20, 2005, http://www.intelligence.org.il/eng/sib/7_05/img/july25rp_05.pdf.

Paz, Reuven. "Qa-idat al-Jidad, Iraq, and Madrid: The First Tile in the Domino Effect?" *PRISM Series of Special Dispatches on the Global Jihad.* 2 (2004), http://www.e-prism.org/images/PRISM_Special_dispatch_no_1-2. pdf.

Paz, Reuven. "Sawt al-Jihad: New Indoctrination of Qa'idat al-Jihad," Occasional Paper 1:8 (2003), PRISM, http://www.e-prism.org/images/PRISM_no_8.doc.

Perloff, Richard M. *The Dynamics of Persuasion.* Mahwah, NJ: Lawrence Erlbaum, 1993.

Petersen, Roger Dale. *Resistance and Rebellion: Lessons from Eastern Europe.* New York: Cambridge University Press, 2001.

Pew Global Attitudes Project. *Islamic Extremism: Common Concern for Muslim and Western Publics.* Washington, DC: Pew Research Center, 2005, http://pewglobal.org/reports/display.php?ReportID=248.

Pillar, Paul R. *Terrorism and U.S. Foreign Policy.* Washington, DC: Brookings Institution, 2001.

Price, H. Edward Jr. "The Strategy and Tactics of Revolutionary Terrorism," *Comparative Studies on Society and History* 19:1 (January 1977).

Rapoport, David C. "The Four Waves of Modern Terrorism," in *Attacking Terrorism: Elements of a Grand Strategy*, edited by Audrey Kurth Cronin and James Ludes. Washington, DC: Georgetown University Press, 2004.

Reich, Walter (ed.). *Origins of Terrorism: Psychologies, Ideologies, Theologies, States of Mind.* Washington, DC: Woodrow Wilson Center Press, 1998.

Richardson, Louise. *What Terrorists Want: Understanding the Enemy, Containing the Threat.* New York: Random House, 2006.

Roberts, Mary Lou. *Internet Marketing: Integrating Online and Offline Strategies.* New York: McGraw-Hill School Education Group, 2002.

Rogers, Everett M. "Intermedia Processes and Powerful Media Effects," *Media Effects: Advances in Theory and Research* (2002).

Rogers, Everett M. "A Prospective and Retrospective Look at the Diffusion Model." *Journal of Health Communication* 9 (2004): 13–19.

Romanych, Marc J., and Kenneth Krumm. "Tactical Information Operations in Kosovo," *Military Review* (September–October 2004).

Ronczkowski, Michael. R. *Terrorism and Organized Hate Crime: Intelligence Gathering, Analysis, and Investigations*, 2nd ed. Boca Raton: CRC Press, Taylor & Francis Group, 2007.

Ross, Lee, and Craig Anderson. "Shortcomings in the Attribution Process: On the Origins and Maintenance of Erroneous Social Assessments," in *Judgment Under Uncertainty: Heuristics and Biases*, edited by Daniel Kahneman et al. Cambridge: Cambridge University Press, 1982.

Rourke, John T. *International Politics on the World Stage*, 12th ed. Boston: McGraw-Hill, 2008.

Roy, Oliver. *Globalized Islam: The Search for a New Ummah.* New York: Columbia University Press, 2004.

Russell, John. "Mujahedeen, Mafia, Madmen: Russian Perceptions of Chechens during the Wars in Chechnya, 1994–1996 and 1999–2001," *Journal of Post-Communist Studies and Transition Politics* 18:1 (March 2002).

Russell, John. "Terrorists, Bandits, Spooks, and Thieves: Russian Demonization of the Chechens before and since 9/11," *Third World Quarterly* 26:1 (July 2005).

Sageman Marc. *Leaderless Jihad, Terror Networks in the Twenty-First Century.* Philadelphia: University of Pennsylvania Press, 2008.

Sageman, Marc. *Understanding Terror Networks.* Philadelphia: University of Pennsylvania Press, 2004.

Schelling, Thomas C. *Arms and Influence.* New Haven, CT: Yale University Press, 1966.

Scheuer, Michael. *Through Our Enemies' Eyes: Osama bin Laden, Radical Islam, and the Future of America.* Washington, DC: Potomac Books, 2006.

Scheufele, Dietram A., and Matthew C. Nisbet. "Being a Citizen Online: New Opportunities and Dead Ends," *Harvard International Journal of Press/Politics* 7:3 (2002).

Schleifer, Ron. "Psychological Operations: A New Variation on an Age Old Art: Hezbollah Versus Israel," *Studies in Conflict and Terrorism* 29:1 (January 2006).

Schudson, Michael. *The Sociology of News.* New York: W. W. Norton, 2003.

Schultz, Richard. "Conceptualizing Political Terrorism: A Typology," *Journal of International Affairs* 32:1 (Spring/Summer 1978).

Senechal de la Roche, Roberta. "Collective Violence as Social Control," *Sociological Forum* 11:1 (March 1996).

Senechal de la Roche, Roberta. "Toward a Scientific Theory of Terrorism," *Sociological Theory* 22:1 (March 2004).

Shaffir, William. "Witnessing as Identity Consolidation: The Case of the Lubavitcher Chassidim," in *Identity and Religion: International, Cross-Cultural Approaches*, edited by Hans Mol. London: Sage Publications, 1978.

Shah, Dhavan V. "Connecting and Disconnecting with Civic Life: Patterns of Internet Use and the Production of Social Capital." *Political Communication* 18:2 (2001).

Shah, Dhavan V., Jaeho Cho, William P. Eveland, and Nojin Kwak. "Information and Expression in a Digital Age: Modeling Internet Effects on Civic Participation," *Communication Research* 32:5 (2005).

Shah, Dhavan V., Jack M. McLeod, and So-Hyang Yoon. "Communication, Context, and Community: An Exploration of Print, Broadcast, and Internet Influences," *Communication Research* 28:4 (2001).

Shanahan, James, and Erik Nisbet. *The Communication of Anti-Americanism: Media Influence and Anti-American Sentiment.* Ithaca, NY: Cornell University Press, 2007.

Shannon, Vaughn, and Michael Dennis. "Militant Islam and the Futile Fight for Reputation," *Security Studies* 16:2.

Sharp, Gene. "The Intifada and Nonviolent Struggle," *Journal of Palestine Studies* 19:1 (Autumn 1989).

Sharp, Jeremy M. Coordinator, et al. *Lebanon: The Israel-Hamas-Hizballah Conflict.* CRS Report for Congress (September 15, 2006). Washington, DC: Foreign Affairs, Defense, and Trade Division, Congressional Research Service. http://fas.org/sgp/crs/mideast/RL33566.pdf.

Sheppard, Ben, G. James Rubin, Jamie K. Wardman, and Simon Wessley. "Terrorism and Dispelling the Myth of a Panic Prone Public," *Journal of Public Health Policy* 27:3 (2006).

Shevtsova, Liliia Federovna. *Yeltsin's Russia: Myths and Reality* Washington, DC: Carnegie Endowment for International Peace, 1999.

Shirlow, Peter, and Brendan Murtagh. *Belfast, Segregation, Violence and the City.* London: Pluto, 2006.

Shlaim, Avi. "When Bush Comes to Shove: America and the Arab-Israeli Peace Process," *Oxford International Review* 3:2 (Spring 1992).

Sifaoui, Mohamed. *Inside Al Qaeda: How I Infiltrated the World's Deadliest Terrorist Organization*, translated by George Miller. New York: Thunder's Mouth Press, 2003.

Smith, Mark A. "The Second Chechen War: The All-Russian Context," Strategic and Combat Studies Institute Occasional Papers, No. 40 (September 2000).

Smith, M. L. R. *Fighting for Ireland.* London: Routledge, 1997.

Snyder, Glenn H. *Deterrence and Defense: Toward a Theory of National Security.* Princeton, NJ: Princeton University Press, 1961.

Sprinzak, Ehud. "Rational Fanatics," *Foreign Policy* 120 (September–October, 2000).

Stebenne, David L. *Modern Republican: Arthur Larson and the Eisenhower Years.* Bloomington: Indiana University Press, 2006.

Stern, Jessica. *Terror in the Name of God: Why Religious Militants Kill.* New York: HarperCollins, 2003.

Sumida, Jon Tetsuro. "The Relationship of History and Theory in On War: The Clausewitzian Ideal and Its Implications," *Journal of Military History* 65 (April 2001).

Summy, Ralph and Michael E. Salla (eds.). *Why the Cold War Ended: A Range of Interpretations.* Westport, CT: Praeger, 1995.

Sun Tzu. *The Art of War*, translated and with an introduction by Samuel B. Griffith. New York: Oxford University Press, 1963.

Sun, Tao, Seounmi Youn, Guohua Wu, and Mana Kuntaraporn. "Online Word-of-Mouth (or Mouse): An Exploration of Its Antecedents and Consequences," *Journal of Computer-Mediated Communication* 11 (2006): 1104–1127.

Suskind, Ron. *The One Percent Doctrine: Deep Inside America's Pursuits of Its Enemies Since 9/11.* London: Simon & Schuster, 2006.

Thomas, Timothy L. "Al Qaeda and the Internet: The Danger of 'Cyberplanning,'" *Parameters* 33 (2003), http://www.army.mil/usawc/Parameters/03spring/thomas.htm.

Thomas, Timothy. "Manipulating the Mass Consciousness: Russian and Chechen 'Information War' Tactics in the Second Chechen-Russian Conflict," in *The Second Chechen War*, edited by A. C. Aldis. Washington, DC: Conflict Studies Research Center, 2000.

Thompson, Robert. *Defeating Communist Insurgency.* New York: Praeger, 1966.

Thornton, T. P. "Terror as a Weapon of Political Agitation," in *Internal War*, edited by H. Eckstein. New York: Free Press, 1964.

Tilly, Charles. "Terror, Terrorism, Terrorists," *Sociological Theory* 22:1 (March 2004).

Tonge, Jonathan. *Northern Ireland, Conflict and Change.* Hemel Hempstead: Prentice Hall, 1998.

Tore Bjorgo (ed.). *Root Causes of Terrorism.* New York: Routledge, 2005.

Trager, Robert F., and Dessislava P. Zagorcheva. "Deterring Terrorism: It Can Be Done," *International Security* 30:3 (Winter 2005/2006).

Trujillo, Horacio R., and Brian A. Jackson. "Organizational Learning and Terrorist Groups." In *Teaching Terror: Strategic and Tactical Learning in the Terrorist World*, edited by James J. F. Forest. New York: Rowman & Littlefield, 2006.

Tsfati, Yariv, and Gabriel Weimann. "www.Terrorism.com: Terror on the Internet," *Studies in Conflict and Terrorism* 25:5 (2002): 317–332.

Ulph, Stephen. "For Mujahideen, Bomb-Making Information Readily Accessible Online," *Terrorism Focus* 2:15 (August 5, 2005).

U.S. Information Agency, Office of Public Liaison. "The United States Information Agency." Washington, DC: USIA's Regional Service Center, October 1998.

U.S. Information Agency. "A Commemoration: 1953–1999." Washington, DC, 1999.

U.S. Joint Chiefs of Staff. *Joint Publication 1-02, Department of Defense Dictionary of Military and Associated Terms* (April 12, 2001, as amended through October 16, 2006). Washington, DC: Pentagon, http://www.dtic.mil/doctrine/jel/new_pubs/jp1_02.pdf.

Van Gorp, Baldwin. "The Constructionist Approach to Framing: Bringing Culture Back In," *Journal of Communication* 57 (2007): 60–78.

Vaquez, John A. "The Tangibility of Issues and Global Conflict: A Test of Rosenau's Issue Area Typology," *Journal of Peace Research* 20:2 (Summer 1983).

Vidino, Lorenzo. *Al-Qaida in Europe: The New Battleground of International Jihad.* New York: Prometheus Books, 2006.

von Clausewitz, Carl. *On War*, edited and translated by Michael Howard and Peter Paret. Princeton, NJ: Princeton University Press, 1984.

Walker, Ruth. "Terror Online, and How to Counteract It," *Harvard University Gazette* (March 1, 2005).

Ward, Brad M. *Strategic Influence Operations: The Information Connection*. Carlisle: U.S. Army War College, April 7, 2003.

Weimann, Gabriel. "Terrorist Dot Com: Using the Internet for Terrorist Recruitment and Mobilization," in *The Making of a Terrorist (Vol. 1: Recruitment)*, edited by James J. F. Forest. Westport, CT: Praeger Security International, 2005.

Weimann, Gabriel. *Terror on the Internet: The New Arena, the New Challenges*. Washington, DC: U.S. Institute of Peace, 2006.

Weimann, Gabriel. "The Theater of Terror: Effects of Press Coverage," *Journal of Communication* 33:1 (Winter 1983): 38–45.

Weimann, Gabriel. "Virtual Disputes: The Use of the Internet for Terrorist Debates," *Studies in Conflict and Terrorism* 29:7 (2006): 623–639.

Weimann, Gabriel. "Virtual Training Camps: Terrorists' Use of the Internet," in *Teaching Terror: Strategic and Tactical Learning in the Terrorist World*, edited by James J. F. Forest. Lanham, MD: Rowman & Littlefield, 2006.

Weimann, Gabriel. 2004. *www.Terror.Net: How Modern Terrorism Uses the Internet*, Special Report. Washington DC: United States Institute of Peace.

Wesley, Robert. "Al-Qaeda's WMD Strategy after the U.S. Intervention in Afghanistan," *Terrorism Monitor* 3:2 (2005), http://www.jamestown.org/terrorism/news/article.php?issue_id=3502.

West, Bing. *No True Glory: A Frontline Account of the Battle for Fallujah*. New York: Bantam Books, 2005.

Whine, Michael. "Cyberspace—A New Medium for Communication, Command and Control by Extremists." *Studies in Conflict and Terrorism* 22 (1999): 231–245.

Whine, Michael. "Is Hizb Ut-Tahrir Changing Strategy or Tactics?" *Center for Eurasian Policy Occasional Research Paper*. New York: Huston Institute, 2006.

The White House. *The U.S. National Strategy for Public Diplomacy and Strategic Communication* (May 31, 2007).

Wickham, Carrie. *Mobilizing Islam: Religion, Activism, and Political Change in Egypt*. New York: Columbia University Press, 2002.

Wieviorka, Michel. *The Making of Terrorism*, translated by David Gordon White. Chicago: University of Chicago Press, 1993.

Wilkinson, Paul. *Terrorism versus Democracy: The Liberal State Response*, 2nd ed. London: Routledge, 2006.

Williamson, Murray, and Mark Grimsley. "Introduction: On Strategy," in *The Making of Strategy, Rulers, States, and War*. Cambridge: Cambridge University Press, 1994, 1997.

Winch, Samuel P. "Constructing an 'Evil Genius': New Uses of Mythic Archetypes to Make Sense of bin Laden." *Journalism Studies* 6:3 (2005): 285–299.

Windsor, Philip. "Terrorism and International Order," in *Studies in International Relations: Essays by Philip Windsor*, edited by Mats Berdal. Portland, OR: Sussex Academic Press, 2002.

Woods, James. *History of International Broadcasting*. London: IET, 1992.

Woodward, Bob. *Bush at War*. London: Pocket Books, 2003.

Yarger, Harry R. *Strategic Theory for the 21st Century: The Little Book on Big Strategy*. Carlisle, PA: Strategic Studies Institute, U.S. Army War College, 2006.

Yehoshua, Y. "Dispute in Islamist Circles over the Legitimacy of Attacking Muslims, Shiites, and Non-combatant Non-Muslims in Jihad Operations in Iraq: Al-Maqdisi vs. His Disciple

Al-Zarqawi," Special Report no. 985. Middle East Media Research Institute (MEMRI), September 11, 2005.

Yost, David S. "The U.S. Nuclear Posture Review and the NATO Allies," *International Affairs* 80(4).

Yunanto, S. *Militant Islamic Movements in Indonesia and South-East Asia.* Jakarta, Indonesia: Freidrich-Ebert-Stiftung and Ridep Institute, 2003.

Zalman, Amy. "Strategic Communications and the Battle of Ideas: Winning the Hearts and Minds in the Global War Against Terrorists." Statement provided for the U.S. House Armed Service Committee, Subcommittee on Terrorism and Unconventional Threats and Capabilities (July 11, 2007).

Zanini, Michele, and Sean J. A. Edwards. "The Networking of Terrorism in the Information Age," in *Networks and Netwars: The Future of Terror, Crime, and Militancy,* edited by John Arquilla and David Ronfeldt. Santa Monica, CA: RAND Corporation, 2001.

Zartman, William. *Elusive Peace: Negotiating an End to Civil Conflicts.* Washington, DC: Brookings, 1995.

Zegart, Amy. "An Empirical Analysis of Failed Intelligence Reforms Before September 11," *Political Science Quarterly* 121:1 (Spring 2006).

Index

About the Editor and Contributors

EDITOR

JAMES J. F. FOREST is Director of Terrorism Studies and Associate Professor at the Combating Terrorism Center at West Point. He has published over 12 books on a variety of topics, including *Teaching Terror* (2006), *Weapons of Mass Destruction and Terrorism* (2007), and *Countering Terrorism and Insurgency in the 21st Century* (2007). For the past several years, Dr. Forest has been selected by the Center for American Progress and *Foreign Policy* magazine as one of "America's most esteemed terrorism and national security experts," and he is regularly invited to give lectures and participate in research projects in the United States and abroad. Dr. Forest received his graduate degrees from Stanford University and Boston College, and undergraduate degrees from Georgetown University and De Anza College.

CONTRIBUTORS

MAX ABRAHMS is a Social Science Predoctoral Fellow at Stanford University's Center for International Security and Cooperation, and Ph.D. candidate in Political Science at UCLA. He wrote this chapter when he was a Research Associate in terrorism studies at the Belfer Center for Science and International Affairs in the John F. Kennedy School of Government at Harvard University. An earlier version was published as "Why Terrorism Does Not Work," in *International Security* 31:2 (Fall 2006).

DANIEL BARACSKAY is an Associate Professor of Political Science at Valdosta State University, where he also teaches public administration courses. He has also taught at Cleveland State University, the University of Akron and University of Cincinnati. Dr. Baracskay has contributed to several books and academic journals, and published a book titled *The Rise and Destruction of the Warner & Swasey Company* (2003) with coauthor Peter Rebar. He holds five academic degrees, and his research interests include American politics, public administration, international relations, and comparative politics.

JOE-RYAN BERGOCH is a graduate student at the Monterey Institute of International Studies. He currently works as a research assistant for the James Martin Center for Nonproliferation Studies and the Monterey Terrorism Research and Education Program. His primary research interests include the spread of militant Islamism in Western democracies and the relationship between religious ideologies and terrorists' use of weapons of mass destruction.

CORI E. DAUBER is Associate Professor of Communication Studies, and of Peace, War, and Defense, at the University of North Carolina at Chapel Hill, where she is also a Research Fellow at the Triangle Institute for Security Studies. She is also the 2008–09 Visiting Research Professor at the Strategic Studies Institute, U.S. Army War College. Her work on media representations of war, the military, and terrorism has appeared in journals such as *Armed Forces and Society, Comparative Security Policy*, and *Rhetoric and Public Affairs*.

JAMES DINGLEY is a sociologist and currently Head of the Department of Business, Management, Economics and Finance at the University of Kurdistan, Hawler. Previously he lectured on terrorism and political violence at the University of Ulster and ran his own consultancy–Cybernos Associates. He has published two books, *Combating Terrorism in Northern Ireland* and *Nationalism, Social Theory and Durkheim,* as well as articles in major international academic journals.

JOSHUA ALEXANDER GELTZER is in his first year of studies at Yale Law School. He recently completed his Ph.D. in War Studies from King's College London, where he was a Marshall Scholar. His dissertation examined many of the themes raised in his chapters in this volume, analyzing strategic influence through signaling and messaging as part of American counterterrorist strategy. His undergraduate degree is from the Woodrow Wilson School of Public and International Affairs at Princeton University, where he also received the Myron Herrick Prize for the Most Outstanding Senior Thesis in the Wilson School.

RUSSELL W. GLENN is a Senior Defense Analyst. His more than 30 books and reports include analyses of urban operations, counterinsurgency, and both military and police training. He has appeared as a subject matter expert on MSNBC, CNN, the History Channel, and National Public Radio in addition to being cited by the *New York Times, Los Angeles Times, The Economist, Science, Wired*, the Associated Press, and other national and international media organizations.

SEBASTIAN GORKA is the Founding Director of the Institute for Democracy and International Security, Associate Fellow at the Joint Special Operations University (US Special Operations Command), and teaches at the College of International Security Affairs, National Defense University, Washington. Previously he taught on the faculty of the Program on Terrorism and Security Studies of the George C. Marshall Center, Germany. Dr. Gorka has been a Kokkalis Fellow at Harvard University's Kennedy School of Government and a consultant to the RAND Corporation. He is a regular contributor to the JANES Group of the United Kingdom.

FRANK HAIRGROVE is a third-year Ph.D. student in the School of Journalism and Mass Communication at the University of Wisconsin, Madison.

TODD C. HELMUS is a Full Behavioral Scientist with the RAND Corporation. He has written on such topics as counterinsurgency influence strategies, joint urban military operations, and terrorist radicalization. Dr. Helmus is an author of *Enlisting Madison Avenue: The Marketing Approach to Earning Popular Support in Theaters of Operation*, from which his contribution draws.

BRUCE HOFFMAN is a Professor in the Security Studies Program at the Edmund A. Walsh School of Foreign Service at Georgetown University, and is author of the internationally acclaimed book *Inside Terrorism*. He has studied terrorism and insurgency for 30 years, has served as an advisor to many government commissions, and held the first corporate chair in counterterrorism and counterinsurgency at the RAND Corporation. Dr. Hoffman is a Senior Scholar at the Woodrow Wilson International Center for Scholars and a Senior Fellow at the Combating Terrorism Center at West Point. Dr. Hoffman holds undergraduate and graduate degrees from Oxford University.

FRANK HONKUS, III is an independent researcher and security consultant. He received his master's degree in Public and International Affairs, with a major in Security and Intelligence, from the University of Pittsburgh. He has presented to the National Intelligence Council on the concept of feral cities, as well as to the RAND Corporation on the use of gender in analysis. He currently works as an Analyst in Washington, DC.

FRANK L. JONES is Professor of Security Studies at the U.S. Army War College, Carlisle, PA, where he teaches courses on strategy, U.S. national security policy, and homeland security.

DAVID KILCULLEN, a former Australian army lieutenant colonel, recently served as Senior Counterinsurgency Adviser to the commanding general, Multi-National Force, Iraq. He previously served as chief strategist in the U.S. Department of State's Office of the Coordinator for Counterterrorism and as the Pentagon's special adviser for irregular warfare and counterterrorism on the 2006 Quadrennial Defense Review. His work has been published in the *Journal of Strategic Studies, Small Wars Journal, Survival, Military Review*, and many other journals and periodicals.

GUERMANTES E. LAILARI, Lieutenant Colonel U.S. Air Force, has held assignments in Europe, the Middle East and the United States, and is currently assigned to the Air Staff Headquarters at the Pentagon. He has completed master's degrees that focused on Middle Eastern issues, and has written and taught extensively on the Middle East, terrorism, and counterterrorism.

DOUGLAS M. MCLEOD is a Professor in the School of Journalism and Mass Communication, University of Wisconsin, Madison.

SIMON O'ROURKE is a Ph.D. candidate at the Security Research Centre (SECAU) at Edith Cowan University in Western Australia. His research interests include the use of the Internet by terrorists, and his doctoral thesis examines models of counterterrorism intelligence and policing. He is a former soldier (Australian Special Air Service Regiment) and is now an active duty police officer and member of the Research Network for a Secure Australia. He holds a master's of Leadership and Management (Policing) and a bachelor's of Policing from Charles Sturt University in New South Wales.

CHRISTOPHER PAUL is a Full Social Scientist in RAND's Pittsburgh office. In addition to the work from which his contribution is drawn, Dr. Paul has authored several monographs on psychological operations, information operations, and press–military relations, including *Information Operations–Doctrine and Practice* and *Reporters on the Battlefield: The Embedded Press System in Historical Context.*

SAMMY SALAMA is a Fellow at the Combating Terrorism Center at West Point where he designs curricula on jihadi-inspired terrorism for the FBI. Mr. Salama teaches graduate-level courses at the Monterey Institute of International Studies concerning nonproliferation and terrorism in the Middle East. He also works for the James Martin Center for Nonproliferation Studies in Monterey as a Senior Research Associate and Middle East Analyst.

DHAVAN V. SHAH is a Professor in the School of Journalism and Mass Communication, University of Wisconsin, Madison.

JOSHUA SINAI is a Program Manager for counterterrorism studies and education at the Analysis Corporation in McLean, VA. His initiatives include a project to map the worldwide landscape of terrorism and counterterrorism studies, an assessment of tribalism in Iraq, and curriculum development for counterterrorism education. His publications include chapters in edited academic volumes and national security journals, and his column on Terrorism Books appears regularly in the *Washington Times* book review section.

M. KAREN WALKER is pursuing her doctoral degree from the Department of Communication, University of Maryland College Park. Ms. Walker's dissertation project will contribute to theory-building in diplomatic persuasion by elaborating the rhetorical dimension of soft power evinced through public-private partnerships for international development.

GABRIEL WEIMANN is a Professor of Communication at Haifa University, Israel, and a former Senior Fellow at the U.S. Institute of Peace, Washington, DC. His recent book, *Terror on the Internet: The New Arena, the New Challenges*, was published in April 2006. Dr. Weimann wishes to acknowledge the important contribution of Reuven Paz whose material and analysis were so vital to the chapter contributed to this volume.

AIDAN KIRBY WINN is a Project Associate at the RAND Corporation conducting research and analysis for a variety of defense, intelligence and security studies. Her current research interests include terrorism, counterinsurgency, intelligence policy and security assistance and partner capacity-building. Previous positions include Associate Director of National Security Studies and Analysis at Hicks and Associates, Inc (a subsidiary of SAIC), and Research Associate in the International Security Program at the Center for Strategic and International Studies. She holds an MA from the Norman Patterson School of International Affairs at Carleton University and a BA in history and philosophy from McMaster University.

VERA L. ZAKEM is a foreign policy and national security consultant in the Washington, DC area. She specializes in irregular warfare and counterterrorism, U.S. policies towards the Middle East and Eastern Europe, and comprehensive national security strategy. Her work has been featured in various publications and books, including the *CTC Sentinel* and *World Politics Review.* She holds a master's degree in government and international security from the Johns Hopkins University.